Economic and Financial Modeling with Mathematica®

TELOS, The Electronic Library of Science, is an imprint of Springer-Verlag New York with publishing facilities in Santa Clara, California. Its publishing program encompasses the natural and physical sciences, computer science, economics, mathematics, and engineering. All TELOS publications have a computational orientation to them, as TELOS' primary publishing strategy is to wed the traditional print medium with the emerging new electronic media in order to provide the reader with a truly interactive multimedia information environment. To achieve this, every TELOS publication delivered on paper has an associated electronic component. This can take the form of book/diskette combinations, book/CD-ROM packages, books delivered via networks, electronic journals, newsletters, plus a multitude of other exciting possibilities. Since TELOS is not committed to any one technology, any delivery medium can be considered.

The range of TELOS publications extends from research level reference works through textbook materials for the higher education audience, practical handbooks for working professionals, as well as more broadly accessible science, computer science, and high technology trade publications. Many TELOS publications are interdisciplinary in nature, and most are targeted for the individual buyer, which dictates that TELOS publications be priced accordingly.

Of the numerous definitions of the Greek word "telos," the one most representative of our publishing philosophy is "to turn," or "turning point." We perceive the establishment of the TELOS publishing program to be a significant step towards attaining a new plateau of high quality information packaging and dissemination in the interactive learning environment of the future. TELOS welcomes you to join us in the exploration and development of this frontier as a reader and user, an author, editor, consultant, strategic partner, or in whatever other capacity might be appropriate.

TELOS, The Electronic Library of Science
Springer-Verlag Publishers
3600 Pruneridge Avenue, Suite 200
Santa Clara, CA 95051

Hal R. Varian

Editor

Economic and Financial Modeling with Mathematica®

Includes diskette

THE
ELECTRONIC
LIBRARY
OF
SCIENCE

Springer-Verlag

Hal R. Varian
Department of Economics
University of Michigan
Ann Arbor, MI 48109-1220
USA

Published by TELOS, the Electronic Library of Science, Santa Clara, CA
　　Publisher: Allan M. Wylde
　　Publishing Coordinator: Cindy Peterson
　　TELOS Production and Manufacturing Manager: Sue Purdy Pelosi
　　Publishing Assistant: Kate McNally Young
　　Production Editor: Karen Phillips
　　Compositor: Glenn Scholebo
　　Electronic Production Advisor: Karen Phillips
　　Cover Designer: A Good Thing
　　Promotions Manager: Paul Manning
　　Manufacturing Supervisor: Vincent Scelta

Printed on acid-free paper.

Library of Congress Cataloging-in-Publication Data
Varian, Hal R.
　　Economic and financial modeling with mathematica / Hal R. Varian
　　　　p. cm.
　　Includes bibliographical references.
　　ISBN 0-387-97882-8.–ISBN 3-540-97882-8
　　1. Econometric models–Computer progress.　2. Finance–Computer
programs.　3. Mathematica (Computer file).　I. Title
　　HB143.V37　1992　510'.285'536–dc20　　　　　　　　　　　　　　92-37343

Printed and bound in the United States of America by Edwards Brothers, Inc., Ann Arbor, MI.

9 8 7 6 5 4 3 2

ISBN: 0-387-97882-8 Springer-Verlag New York Berlin Heidelberg
ISBN: 3-540-97882-8 Springer-Verlag Berlin Heidelberg New York

Preface

Mathematica is a tool for doing mathematics using computers. It allows you to manipulate symbols, to do numerical calculations, and to graph relationships in a simple and unified manner. Furthermore, Mathematica provides an elegant programming language that allows you to extend existing capabilities and add completely new capabilities to the software.

This is a book describing how economists can use Mathematica in their research and teaching. Each chapter describes tools that we hope will be useful to other economists. Many of these tools are collected on the disk that comes with this book, so they can be used immediately by the readers. More importantly, these tools can be used as a basis for your own explorations of Mathematica.

I have divided the book into three main sections: economic theory, financial economics, and econometrics.

Economic theory

Economic theory starts off with an analysis of symbolic optimization: how to use Mathematica to understand the structure of optimization problems. In this chapter, I show how to do symbolic comparative statics, solve integrability problems, and analyze finite dynamic programming problems using Mathematica.

Todd Kaplan and Arijit Mukherji analyze screening and self-selection problems in their contribution. Their primary example is incentive mechanisms: how can you design a mechanism to induce agents to supply effort in an efficient way? This problem turns out to be closely related to the problem of nonlinear price discrimination, also analyzed by Kaplan and Mukherji. In order to solve such problems, the authors needed to develop a package for solving Kuhn-Tucker problems. This software is provided on the disk and will likely prove useful in several other contexts.

John Eckalbar describes some applications of Mathematica to economic dynamics. For the most part these methods involve visualization of the solution paths of various dynamical systems. However, Eckalbar also describes how the standard tools of Mathematica can be used to do the various calculations associated with dynamical systems: calculating eigenvalues, verifying Lyaponov functions, and so on.

Ken Judd and Sy-Ming Guu describe how they have used Mathematica to calculate stationary solutions to optimal growth problems using Padé and Taylor series approximation methods. These methods can be used for a variety of other intertemporal optimization problems. The basic idea is to use Padé series and Taylor series to find approximate solutions to Bellman's equation. Mathematica can be used to calculate the terms of the approximating series and to examine how well the approximation fits.

Asahi Noguchi describes ways to use Mathematica for general equilibrium analysis. Much of this work was motivated by international trade considerations. He shows how easy it is to use Mathematica to set up and analyze small general equilibrium models with several interacting markets. This work should be very useful in both teaching and research.

Gary Anderson describes how to solve a class of dynamic macroeconomic models with rational expectations. His paper contains a theoretical discussion of his solution technique, along with a complete Mathematica package which carries out the computations.

There are two contributions concerned with calculations involved in game theory. John Dickhaut and Todd Kaplan describe their package for determining Nash equilibrium. This is a very useful package for computing *all* Nash equilibria for any two-person game with a finite number of strategies. This package eliminates a lot of the tedium involved in analyzing simple games.

Michael Carter describes a number of tools for analyzing cooperative games. He shows how to compute the core, the Shapely value, and a number of other solution concepts for cooperative games. This allows the user to explore the implications of a number of different solution concepts quickly and easily.

Financial economics

Turning next to financial economics, we have two contributions that provide tools for stochastic calculus. Robert Stine and Michael Steele show how to implement the calculations involved in Itô's lemma in Mathematica and use the techniques they develop to derive the Black-Scholes option pricing formula (the Black-Scholes formula is examined in detail in Ross Miller's chapter).

Wilfrid Kendall describes a different approach for representing stochastic calculus in Mathematica and illustrates its use in a portfolio optimization problem. It is interesting to see how different researchers have independently implemented stochastic calculus packages in quite distinct ways.

Colin Rose offers some tools for studying bounded stochastic processes, and illustrates their application in models of exchange rate target zones and irreversible investment under uncertainty. These tools allow for easy simulation and analysis of such processes and should prove useful in other sorts of economic modeling.

Ross Miller describes how to use Mathematica for option valuation. The main tool is, of course, the classic option pricing formula of Black and Scholes. Miller's chapter illustrates how one can study a formula graphically, numerically, and symbolically using the tools provided by Mathematica. He also illustrates a novel implementation of object-oriented programming in Mathematica.

Econometrics

We have several chapters on econometrics. Stephen Brown's chapter is a nice transition from financial economics to econometrics. He shows how to use Mathematica in conjunction with the computer package Gauss to do nonlinear estimation of financial models. As Brown demonstrates you can estimate non-linear models much more quickly if you use Mathematica to derive symbolic representations of the gradients and Hessians.

Mathematica comes with a number of statistical packages that are quite handy for quick data analysis. Although one would probably want to use a dedicated package for large-scale production work, Mathematica is very useful for medium size problems, especially when you want to do a lot of custom graphics. David Belsley has implemented a number of econometric tools in his `Econo-metrics.m` package. These can be used "out of the box" for medium sized problems or used to do Monte Carlo studies of one sort or another.

Eduardo Ley and Mark Steel show how Bayesian methods can be implemented in Mathematica. One of the drawbacks of Bayesian techniques is that they are computation-intensive, and every computation is a little different. Since Mathematica is so flexible, it can easily be adapted to solving a number of different Bayesian estimation problems. I suspect that we will see much more work in this area in the future.

Robert Stine describes a number of useful tools for analyzing time series models. Mathematica's built-in functions for Fourier transforms prove very useful, as well as its graphical and symbol manipulation tools. Prediction and forecasting are prominently featured.

Finally, Robert Korsan demonstrates how Mathematica can be used in decision analysis. This is another example of a case where "every problem is different" so standard statistics packages end up being overly rigid. Mathematica's flexibility and extendibility allow you to analyze these problems in ways that are much more convenient than those that have been available in the past.

Learning Mathematica

My university puts out a guidebook for faculty who will be living abroad. The guidebook says that there are three stages to an extended foreign stay. The first few weeks are filled with delight at the new experiences. The second month or so involves some disillusionment as one copes with various discomforts. But after a few months, one develops a deeper appreciation for the local culture, and gains a more realistic perception of its strengths and weaknesses.

This is much like the experience that many people have with Mathematica. The first few weeks, one is constantly amazed at what it can do. As you type in examples from the Mathematica manual (or the book you hold in your hands) you will likely be surprised and excited by Mathematica's power. But then, when you start to work on your own problems, you may hit the disillusionment phase. You will find expressions that you can simplify, but Mathematica can't. You will find simple systems of equations that Mathematica can't solve. What seemed to be a magic wand that you could just wave over your problems, turns out to be only. . .a computer program.

There are several things happening in this second phase. The first is that new users of Mathematica don't understand all the hidden assumptions that they bring to the problems they want to solve. When Mathematica solves a system of equations, it wants to find *all* the solutions, without imposing any assumptions on the variables. You may know that various terms are positive, real numbers—but Mathematica doesn't. Transformations like taking logs only make sense with real positive numbers; even division requires that numbers be non-zero. Simple transformations like this can only be done if you know something about the problem you are solving; it is dangerous to automate the application of this sort of transformation and the designers of Mathematica avoided this temptation.

Another thing that sometimes happens is that you start to run into hardware limitations. Mathematica uses a lot of memory and a lot of computing power. It is pretty easy to run out of processing power on a machine with 4–6 megabytes of memory. Even fairly simple graphs may overload a small system.

A third problem that arises after the first few weeks involves attempting to program Mathematica. Almost everyone knows a little bit of some programming language nowadays. But Mathematica is quite different from most programming languages. You *can* make a Mathematica program look like a BASIC program—but you shouldn't.

There's an old saying among computer scientists: "to iterate is human, to recurse, divine." The golden rule of Mathematica programming is to avoid iteration. There is a whole assortment of list manipulation functions built into Mathematica; in general these functions are much faster than iteration. Furthermore, these list manipulation operations can be threaded together to construct fast, elegant and efficient solutions to programming problems. Every new Mathematica programmer should take a careful look at these functions. (Programmers who have used LISP and APL will find Mathematica's approach very congenial.)

Mathematica is constantly being updated and improved. Many of the limitations of version n will be removed in version $n + 1$. (This statement holds for all $n > 0$.) Wolfram research has also developed some useful protocols to link Mathematica to other programs to perform various specialized computations. Problems that are too large or too complex for the current version of Mathematica may yield to a combination of Mathematica and some special-purpose software.

About the diskette

The Mathematica packages accompanying the chapters are contained on a disk attached to the back cover. (They are also available via email or ftp from Mathsource, WRI's software archives.) This is an MS-DOS disk that can be read by MS-DOS, Unix, or Macintosh (using a file exchange utility).

Mathematica packages and Notebooks are plain ASCII files, so in principle they can be used on any platform that supports Mathematica. However, the convention for end-of-line differs across platforms. MS-DOS expects a CR-LF, while Unix uses just a LF. Occasionally, MS-DOS machines have problems reading ASCII files that just use LFs to terminate the lines. I've included a little utility, **addcr.exe**, that will add CRs to these files. I suggest running this before you load these files into Mathematica on a MS-DOS or Windows machine. See the readme file on the disk for more information.

The standard way to load a Mathematica package into Mathematica is to use the `Get["package_name"]` command, which is often abbreviated by "`<<package_name`". To load `nash.m` for example, use the command "`<<nash.m`". See the various articles for examples.

Where to get help

There are lots of resources for Mathematica users. The users manual, by Stephen Wolfram, et al. is one of the best computer manuals ever written, in my opinion. The index is one of the best around—it will usually lead you to an answer, or at the least, lead you to formulate your question properly (which is sometimes even more useful than an answer.)

There are also lots of programming examples available via MathSource. This is WRI's electronic distribution mechanism for material related to Mathematica. To use it, send electronic mail to `mathsource@wri.com`. The body of your message should contain the single line `help intro`.

There is a very useful mailgroup for Mathematica, called `mathgroup`. You can use this group to share experiences about Mathematica. It is often a useful place to ask questions and get answers. To subscribe send e-mail to `mathgroup-request@yoda.physics.unc.edu` and ask to be added to the Mathematica mailing list.

Finally there are many good books and journals about Mathematica. You can probably find books about Mathematica in the same place that you bought this book. There are so many available now that it would be fruitless to list them all. However, I will mention three non-book resources that might be a littler harder to find without some help.

The *Mathematica Journal* can be contacted at Miller Freeman, Inc., 600 Harrison Street, San Francisco, CA 94107. Subscription information is available at 415-905-2334. There is also a valuable newsletter called *Mathematica in Education* published by TELOS/Springer-Verlag, 44 Hartz Way, Secaucus, NJ 07096, phone 800-777-4643 or 201-348-4033. Finally, Variable Symbols, 2161 Shattuck Avenue, Berkeley, CA 94705-1313 publishes some nice Mathematica aids.

Teaching

I think that Mathematica has the potential to change the way that we teach economics. It is widely recognized that economics students come to graduate school poorly prepared in mathematics. Perhaps the physical capital of computers can substitute for this lack of human capital. By lowering the cost of doing mathematical analysis, Mathematica encourages students to do more of it. Mathematica can help to bring the formulas in the textbooks to life and make them more vivid and compelling to the students.

Anyone who reads this book will be able to come up with many examples of how Mathematica can be used in graduate teaching. But there are also many places that Mathematica can be used in the undergraduate economics curriculum. To take one example, consider the teaching of statistics and econometrics. Here there are a few conceptual stumbling blocks—random variables, sampling distributions, the concept of a statistic—that prove fatal to many beginning students. Mathematica can be used to illustrate these concepts in a concrete way and give the students a clear picture of the behavior that lies behind the concepts. I think that it can improve the understanding of statistical concepts tremendously.

I have prepared a set of Mathematica Notebooks to accompany the third edition of my graduate economics textbook *Microeconomic Analysis*, W.W. Norton and Company. Preliminary versions of these Notebooks are available via MathSource. To retrieve the Notebooks, send an e-mail message to `math-source@wri.com` with the one line of text in the body of the message that says `help intro`. You might follow this message with one that says `find economics` to get a list of all Notebooks in the MathSource archives that pertain to economics. If you develop some useful tools for economic analysis, consider submitting them to MathSource.

Production of this book

This book was produced in a unique way. We decided that the *linqua franca* of the authors was Mathematica, so it seemed natural to submit material in the form of Mathematica Notebooks. This has the additional advantage that the chapters are required to contain workable Mathematica code.

All of the chapters were submitted via e-mail or `ftp`, and most of the chapters were submitted in Notebook form. Glenn Scholebo, an independent TEX consultant, ran these Notebooks through `nb2tex`, a program provided by Wolfram Research, Inc. that converts the Notebooks to TEX form. The TEX code was then cleaned up and prepared for copyediting. After the copyediting, the TEX code was typeset to create the book.

Call for papers

I have been pleased and impressed with the materials developed by the contributors to this book. But there is a lot more that can be done. If the demand for this book, and the supply of new applications are large enough, we may well publish a second volume. If you develop some interesting applications of Mathematica in economics, please let me know about it. You can send me e-mail at `Hal.Varian@umich.edu`.

Acknowledgements

The inspiration for this book was Allan Wylde, of TELOS/Springer-Verlag. He suggested writing something about Mathematica and economics three years ago. The idea intrigued me, but I didn't want to take on the entire task of writing such a book myself. Luckily, I found several economists who had used Mathematica in their own fields of interest. I think that resulting work is a much better book than any single author could have written.

Wolfram Research has been very supportive of this project. In particular, Dave Withoff and Stephen Wolfram provided encouragement and assistance. I designed the cover, but it took a real artist to make it look good.

Finally, I want to thank the authors of the book for being so cooperative. Everything came in pretty much on time, and it arrived in pretty good shape. It has been a pleasure working on this project. I hope that you, the reader, find it equally pleasurable.

Hal Varian
Ann Arbor
October 1992

Contents

Contributors

Gary S. Anderson received his B.S., A.M. and Ph.D. in Applied Mathematic from Harvard University. He has served as a Research Associate for the Urbai Institute and a Research Economist for the Board of Governors of the Federa Reserve System. He is currently a member of the Economics Department facult at the University of Maryland at College Park and a Principal Investigato for CEMAR, an econometrics, computer, and mathematical analysis consultin; firm. He has published on urban simulation modeling, and macro econometri modeling and estimation techniques.

David A. Belsley received a B.A. from Haverford College and Ph.D. in Eco nomics from M.I.T. He taught at Dartmouth College prior to Boston College where he is currently Professor of Economics. He is also Senior Research Asso ciate at the Center for Computational Research in Economics and Managemen Science (CCREMS) at M.I.T. and is a consultant to both industry and govern ment. His publications include numerous articles and monographs, includin; "Regression Diagnostics" and "Conditioning Diagnostics." His research encom passes regression diagnostics, estimation of simultaneous equations, computa tional economics, and applied econometric studies. He is on the editorial board: of *Computational Economics, Computational Statistics and Data Analysis*, anc the *International Journal of Forecasting*.

Stephen J. Brown is Research Professor of Finance at the Leonard N. Stern Schoo: of Business, New York University. He graduated from Monash University in Australia and studied at the University of Chicago, earning an M.B.A. ir 1974 and a Ph.D in 1976. Following successive appointments as a member oi Technical Staff at Bell Laboratories and Associate Professor at Yale University, he joined the faculty of New York University in 1986. He is past President of the Western Finance Association, has served on the Board of Directors oi the American Finance Association, and was a Founding Editor of the Review of Financial Studies, published by Oxford University Press. He has published numerous articles and three books on finance and economics related areas. He is currently retained as an advisor to Yamaichi Securities Company on investment issues both in the United States and Japan, and has served as an expert witness for the US Department of Justice.

Michael Carter studied at the University of Canterbury (M.Com., B.Sc.) and Stanford University (A.M., Ph.D. in economics). He spent five years in the Research School of Social Sciences at the Australian National University before taking up his current position at the University of Canterbury in 1985. While his primary field of interest is game theory and its economic applications, Dr. Carter has published widely in diverse areas of economics.

John Dickhaut received his B.A. from Duke University and his Masters and Ph.D. (Business) at The Ohio State University. He has taught at the University of Chicago, and the University of Minnesota where he is the Honeywell Professor of Accounting. He studies the performance of multiple-person models of behavior in the laboratory, especially those models with an economics foundation. He is currently a member of the editorial board of *The Journal of Accounting Research*, as well as a member of the Economic Science Association Advisory Board.

John Eckalbar received his Ph.D. in Economics in 1975 from the University of Colorado. His primary research interest is in economic dynamics. Publication topics include philosophy of history, economic history, disequilibrium theory, inventory dynamics, monetary theory, profit sharing, and general dynamics. Professor Eckalbar has taught in Canada and is currently Professor of Economics at California State University, Chico.

Sy-Ming Guu received his B.S. degree in Mathematics from the National Taiwan Normal University, an M.S. in Statistics from Stanford University, and is working on his Ph.D. in Operations Research from Stanford University. He has published work on the linear complementarity problem.

Kenneth L. Judd received B.S. degrees in Mathematics and Computer Science, Masters degree in Mathematics and Economics, and a Ph.D. in Economics from the University of Wisconsin at Madison. He was a Post-Doctoral Fellow at the University of Chicago Department of Economics, a Professor of Business Economics at the Kellogg Graduate School of Management at Northwestern University, has visited the Graduate School of Business at the University of Chicago and the Department of Economics at the University of California-Berkeley, and has taught at the Graduate School of Business and the Economics Department of Stanford University. He is currently a Senior Fellow at the Hoover Institution at Stanford University. Dr. Judd has published in the areas of taxation, industrial organization, economic theory, and computational economics. He is currently writing a text on computational methods for economists.

Todd Kaplan received his B.S. in Economics and Engineering and Applied Science from the California Institute of Technology. He is currently pursuing a Ph.D. in economics at the University of Minnesota. He is also working at the University of Minnesota's Social Science Research Facilities Center. His interests include industrial organization, experimental economics, and macroeconomics.

Robert J. Korsan is the Managing Director of *Decisions, Decisions!*, a management consulting firm based in Belmont, California. He received his B.S. in Physics and Mathematics from Manhattan College, New York, an MSEE from Carnegie Institute of Technology, Pittsburgh and an M.A. in Mathematics from the University of Pittsburgh. Mr. Korsan has worked as a Science Writer for NASA, a Programmer for the National Radio Astronomy Observatory, an Engineer for the Westinghouse Research Labs and was the Director of Mathematics Research for STSC. He was a Senior Management Consultant in the International Management and Economics group of SRI, International (formerly Stanford Research, Inc.), and currently serves as the Technical Editor of *The Mathematica Journal.*

Wilfrid Stephen Kendall received his B.A. and D.Phil. in Mathematics from Oxford University. He has worked as Lecturer and Senior Lecturer in Statistics at the Universities of Hull, Strathclyde, and Warwick. He is now Reader in Statistics at the University of Warwick. His research interests lie in the general area of pure and applied probability theory, with particular reference to applications to geometry, to stochastic calculus and analysis, and to computer methods such as computer algebra. He has written about 50 papers in these areas and co-authored one book, *Stochastic Geometry and its Applications.* His spare time is taken up with some church work and (much to the disgust of his wife and to the delight of his three children) home computing.

Eduardo Ley got his *Licenciado* degree in Economics from the Universidad Complutense in Madrid and his M.A. in statistics and Ph.D. in Economics from the University of Michigan. He is currently an Assistant Professor of Economics at the Universidad Carlos III de Madrid.

Ross M. Miller received his B.S. in Mathematics from the California Institute of Technology and his A.M. and Ph.D. in economics from Harvard University. He served on the faculties of Boston University, the California Institute of Technology, and the University of Houston before taking his present position as a Senior Member of the technical staff of the GE Corporate Research and Development Center. Dr. Miller is author of the book *Computer-Aided Financial Analysis* and has published extensively on information transfer in financial markets and on the design of advanced electronic market systems.

Arijit Mukherji received his Ph.D. in Business from the University of Pittsburgh in 1991. He is currently Assistant Professor of Accounting at the Carlson School of Management at the University of Minnesota. His recent work has been on the economics of information and incentives, and experiments on game theory. His current interests include theories of learning in games and models of decentralization.

Asahi Noguchi is an Associate Professor at Department of Economics, Senshu University, Kawasaki, Japan, where he teaches International Economics. He completed his graduate studies at The University of Tokyo, Japan, in 1988. He has published several papers on international trade theories and on economic equilibrium computations.

Colin Rose is presently based at the Economics Department of the University of Sydney, where he lectures Mathematica, amongst other more general activities. He has varied interests and has undertaken extensive research in fields as diverse as irreversible investment under uncertainty, adverse selection equilibrium models, exchange rate target zones, and discontinuous utility analysis. He is currently completing his Ph.D.

Mark F.J. Steel obtained his B.A. in Applied Economics from the State University of Antwerp. His graduate education took place at the London School of Economics and at CORE, Université Catholique de Louvain, from which he received his M.A. and Ph.D. degrees. He held appointments at Duke University and at Tilburg University, where he was a Senior Research Fellow of the Royal Netherlands Academy of Arts and Sciences. Presently, he is a Visiting Professor in the Department of Statistics and Econometrics at the Universidad Carlos III in Madrid. His publications are mainly in the area of Bayesian econometrics and statistics, and address topics such as exogeneity, multi-equation models, elliptical sampling, stochastic frontiers and time series models.

J. Michael Steele is C.F. Koo Professor of Statistics in the Wharton School of the University of Pennsylvania. He was an undergraduate at Cornell University and he obtained his Ph.D. in mathematics from Stanford in 1975. Professor Steele's research interests cover many aspects of applied probability, but he is particularly involved with the interface of probability and computer science. He currently serves as Editor of *The Annals of Applied Probability*, and he has just completed service as chairman of the National Academy of Sciences Panel on Probability and Algorithms. The panel report was published by the National Academy Press in 1992.

Robert A. Stine is a member of the faculty of the Department of Statistics in the Wharton School of the University of Pennsylvania. Dr. Stine graduated in Mathematics from the University of South Carolina and holds a Ph.D. in Statistics from Princeton University. His current research interests include time series analysis, diffusion models, and a variety of topics in computing.

Hal R. Varian received his S.B. from MIT and his M.A. (Mathematics) and Ph.D. (Economics) from Berkeley. He has taught at MIT and the University of Michigan, where he is the Reuben Kempf Professor of Economics and Professor of Finance. He is the author of two widely used undergraduate and graduate textbooks in microeconomics, *Intermediate Microeconomics* and *Microeconomic Analysis*, both published by W.W. Norton and Co. In the 1992 *Mathematica* Programming Competition, he received First Place for Efficiency, and Third Place for Elegance, perhaps demonstrating his priorities as an economist.

E-mail addresses of authors

Gary Anderson	`gary_s_anderson@umail.umd.edu`
David A. Belsley	`belsley@bcvms.bc.edu`
Stephen J. Brown	`sbrown@stern.nyu.edu`
Michael Carter	`m.carter@canterbury.ac.nz`
John Dickhaut	`jdickhaut@csom.umn.edu`
John Eckalbar	`jeckalbar@oavax.csuchico.edu`
Ken Judd	`judd%hoover.bitnet@cornellc.cit.cornell.edu`
Todd Kaplan	`todd@atlas.socsci.umn.edu`
Robert Korsan	`bobk@decide.com`
W S Kendall	`w.s.kendall@warwick.ac.uk`
Eduardo Ley	`edley@eco.uc3m.es`
Ross M. Miller	`millerrm@crd.ge.com`
Arijit Mukherji	`arijit@vx.acs.umn.edu`
Asahi Noguchi	`e01225@sinet.ad.jp`
Colin Rose	`colinr@extro.ucc.su.oz.au`
Mark Steel	`steel@eco.uc3m.es`
Michael Steele	`steele@wilma.wharton.upenn.edu`
Robert Stine	`stine@wharton.upenn.edu`
Hal Varian	`Hal.Varian@umich.edu`

Symbolic Optimization

Hal R. Varian

Economists spend a lot of time analyzing optimization problems. *Mathematica* can make such analysis easier in a number of ways: 1) it can calculate first- and second-order conditions; 2) it can solve first-order conditions for optimal solutions; 3) it can depict optimal solutions graphically; 4) it can perform comparative statics analysis; 5) it can solve simple dynamic programming problems. In this chapter we will describe how to use *Mathematica* to perform such operations. Most of the calculations are standard in microeconomics; Varian (1992) describes the relevant theory.

Several tools for symbolic optimization analysis are collected together in the Package `SymbOpt.m`, available on the disk.

1.1 Notation

Mathematica's notation for derivatives is described in detail in section 3.5 of Wolfram (1991). Here we will briefly review the parts that we need.

1.1.1 Partial Derivatives

You tell *Mathematica* to take the partial derivative of a function `f[x]` with respect to x by writing `D[f[x],x]`. The second-order partial is denoted by `D[f[x],{x,2}]` or `D[f[x],x,x]`.

```
In[1]:= D[x^n,x]
Out[1]:=     -1 + n
          n x

In[2]:= D[x^n,{x,2}]
Out[2]:=              -2 + n
          (-1 + n) n x
```

If there are several variables, the notation extends in a natural way:

```
In[3]:= D[x1^a x2^b,x1]
```
```
Out[3]:=        -1 + a   b
           a x1        x2
```

```
In[4]:= D[x1^a x2^b,x1,x2]
```
```
Out[4]:=          -1 + a    -1 + b
           a b x1         x2
```

Note that the last expression is the second-order mixed partial.

1.1.2   Generic Functions

Mathematica knows how to manipulate derivatives even when you don't use an explicit functional form. It uses the standard prime notation for derivatives when the function has a single argument, such as `f'[x]`. When there are several arguments, *Mathematica* denotes the derivative of `f` with respect to `x` by `f(1,0)[x1,x2]`. This is less ambiguous than the standard notation, but I prefer to use a notation closer to the standard, especially for educational purposes. `SymbOpt.m` contains instructions to have *Mathematica* use a more standard notation for partial derivatives. The only problem is that the partial deriviative signs appear as d's rather than ∂'s.

```
In[1]:= D[f[x1,x2],x1,x2]
```
```
Out[1]:=      2
            d f
          ---------
          dx1 dx2
```

The second-order own partial is

```
In[2]:= D[f[x1,x2],x1,x1]
```
```
Out[2]:=  2
         d f
         -----
          2
        dx1
```

and so on.

1.1.3   Total Differentials

This notation works well for total derivatives. You tell *Mathematica* to take a total derivative by writing `Dt[f[x1,x2]]`.

```
In[1]:= Dt[f[x1,x2]]
```
```
Out[1]:=           df                df
          Dt[x2] -----  + Dt[x1] -----
                   dx2               dx1
```

Note that *Mathematica* uses `Dt[x1]` to denote the differential element dx_1.

1.1.4   Gradients and Hessians

Mathematica doesn't have built-in notation for gradients and Hessians, but it is simple to write programs to calculate these expressions. These programs are available in `SymbOpt.m`.

```
In[1]:= Grad[f[x1,x2],{x1,x2}]
        Grad[x1^a x2^b,{x1,x2}]
```

```
Out[1]:=     df      df
          {------, ------}
           dx1     dx2
```

```
Out[1]:=       -1 + a    b        a   -1 + b
          {a x1       x2 , b x1   x2       }
```

```
In[2]:= Hessian[f[x1,x2],{x1,x2}]
        Hessian[x1^a x2^b,{x1,x2}]
```

```
Out[2]:=      2         2             2         2
            d f       d f           d f       d f
          {{------, ---------}, {---------, ------}}
              2     dx1 dx2      dx1 dx2       2
           dx1                             dx2
```

```
Out[2]:=                    -2 + a    b          -1 + a   -1 + b
          {{((-1 + a) a x1       x2 , a b x1       x2       },

                  -1 + a   -1 + b                  a   -2 + b
           {a b x1       x2       , (-1 + b) b x1   x2       }}
```

The Hessian is stored as a *Mathematica* matrix: a list of lists. It looks nicer to print this out using **MatrixForm**.

```
In[3]:= MatrixForm[Hessian[f[x1,x2],{x1,x2}]]
```

```
Out[3]:=   2
          d f                  2
          ----               d f
             2             ---------
          dx1              dx1 dx2


                             2
              2            d f
            d f            ----
          ---------           2
          dx1 dx2          dx2
```

1.2   Unconstrained Optimization

The first- and second-order conditions for an unconstrained optimization problem are easy to express using the gradient and Hessian.

1.2.1   First-order Conditions

To get the first-order conditions as a list of equations, use the function **FOC** from `SymbOpt.m`.

```
In[1]:= FOC[f[x1,x2],{x1,x2}]
```

```
Out[1]:=    df              df
         {------ == 0,   ------ == 0}
           dx1             dx2
```

If we have a specific functional form, we can use the *Mathematica* function **Solve** to solve these first-order conditions. For example, suppose that f[x1,x2] is a Cobb-Douglas production function and we want to solve for the profit-maximizing choice of inputs. We simply write:

```
In[2]:= profitCD=x1^(1/4) x2^(1/3) -w1 x1 - w2 x2
        Solve[FOC[profitCD,{x1,x2}],{x1,x2}]
```

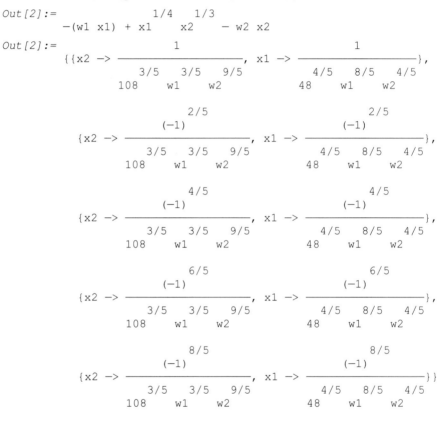

```
Out[2]:=                   1/4    1/3
           -(w1 x1) + x1    x2     - w2 x2
```

Note that *Mathematica* comes up with a whole list of solutions. In general, we are only interested in the real, positive solution, and this is normally (but not always!) the first one in the list. We pick this using [[1]]:

```
In[3]:= solution=Solve[FOC[profitCD,{x1,x2}],{x1,x2}][[1]]
```

```
Out[3]:=                   1                              1
           {x2 ->  --------------------, x1 ->  --------------------}
                    3/5   3/5   9/5              4/5   8/5   4/5
                 108   w1    w2                48   w1    w2
```

1.2.2   Second-order Conditions

We can evaluate the Hessian at the optimum using the following construction:

```
In[1]:= hess1=Simplify[Hessian[profitCD,{x1,x2}]/.solution];
```

I haven't printed the expression as it is rather messy. In any event, all we are interested in is whether this matrix is a negative definite matrix, and I describe a test for this below.

1.2.3   Testing for Definite Matrices

A standard theorem from linear algebra says that a square matrix will be negative definite if the naturally ordered principal minors alternate in sign; it will be positive definite if the naturally ordered principal minors are all positive. *Mathematica* will calculate the minors of a matrix with the function **Minors**. The function **PrincipalMinors[m, ord]** in SymOpt.m extracts the principal minors of a matrix m of order **ord**. The function **NaturalMinors[m]** gives a list of the naturally ordered principal minors of a matrix.
   Here is a matrix:

```
In[1]:= m={{a,b,c},{d,e,f},{h,i,j}};
        MatrixForm[m]

Out[1]:= a    b    c
         d    e    f
         h    i    j
```

Here are the 2 by 2 minors of this matrix:

```
In[2]:= MatrixForm[Minors[m,2]]

Out[2]:= -(b d) + a e    -(c d) + a f    -(c e) + b f
         -(b h) + a i    -(c h) + a j    -(c i) + b j
         -(e h) + d i    -(f h) + d j    -(f i) + e j
```

Here is a list of the 2 by 2 principal minors of the matrix m.

```
In[3]:= PrincipalMinors[m,2]

Out[3]:= {-(b d) + a e, -(c h) + a j, -(f i) + e j}
```

Here are the "naturally ordered principal minors" of orders 1, 2, and 3

```
In[4]:= NaturalMinors[m]

Out[4]:= {a, -(b d) + a e, -(c e h) + b f h + c d i - a f i - b
         d j + a e j}
```

1.2.4   Second-order Conditions and Definite Matrices

The natural minors of the Hessian matrix calculated above are:

$In[1]:=$ **NaturalMinors[hess1]**

$Out[1]:=$

$$\left\{\frac{-3\left(\dfrac{1}{108^{3/5}\,w1^{3/5}\,w2^{9/5}}\right)^{1/3}}{16\left(\dfrac{1}{48^{4/5}\,w1^{8/5}\,w2^{4/5}}\right)^{7/4}},\right.$$

$$\left.5\,72^{8/5}\,w1^{22/5}\left(\dfrac{1}{108^{3/5}\,w1^{3/5}\,w2^{9/5}}\right)^{2/3}\right.$$

$$\left.\mathrm{Sqrt}\left[\dfrac{1}{48^{4/5}\,w1^{8/5}\,w2^{4/5}}\right]\,w2^{26/5}\right\}$$

Inspection shows that the first element of this list is negative and the second is positive. This is a little easier to see if we evaluate the expression at, say, w1=w2=1.

$In[2]:=$ **N[NaturalMinors[hess1]]/.{w1->1,w2->1}**

$Out[2]:=$ {−16.5979, 153.051}

1.2.5 Comparative Statics

The easiest way to do comparative statics using *Mathematica* is to use the total derivative.

1.2.5.1 Single Variable Problem

Consider the general profit-maximization problem for a competitive firm. Define

$In[1]:=$ **profit1 = f[x] - w x**

$Out[1]:=$ −(w x) + f[x]

The first-order condition is

$In[2]:=$ **foc1=FOC[profit1,{x}]**

$Out[2]:=$ $\left\{-w + \dfrac{df}{dx} == 0\right\}$

To see how the optimal choice varies as the parameter w varies, we totally differentiate this first-order condition and solve for Dt[x].

$In[3]:=$ **Solve[Dt[foc1],Dt[x]][[1]]**

$Out[3]:=$
$$\{Dt[x] \rightarrow \frac{Dt[w]}{\dfrac{d^2 f}{dx^2}}\}$$

Since the denominator is negative due to the second-order condition, we see that the optimal choice of the input x is inversely related to changes in w.

1.2.5.2 Multivariate Problems

The same operations work for multivariate optimization problems.

$In[1]:=$ **profit2 = f[x1,x2] - w1 x1 - w2 x2**

$Out[1]:=$ $-(w1\ x1) - w2\ x2 + f[x1,\ x2]$

$In[2]:=$ **foc2=FOC[profit2,{x1,x2}]**

$Out[2]:=$
$$\{-w1 + \frac{df}{dx1} == 0,\ -w2 + \frac{df}{dx2} == 0\}$$

$In[3]:=$ **solution=Solve[Dt[foc2],{Dt[x1],Dt[x2]}][[1]]**

$Out[3]:=$

$$\{Dt[x1] \rightarrow -\left(\frac{Dt[w1]\ \frac{d^2 f}{dx2^2}}{\left(\frac{d^2 f}{dx1\,dx2}\right)^2 - \frac{d^2 f}{dx2^2}\frac{d^2 f}{dx1^2}}\right) + \frac{Dt[w2]\ \frac{d^2 f}{dx1\,dx2}}{\left(\frac{d^2 f}{dx1\,dx2}\right)^2 - \frac{d^2 f}{dx2^2}\frac{d^2 f}{dx1^2}},$$

$$Dt[x2] \rightarrow \frac{Dt[w1]\ \frac{d^2 f}{dx1\,dx2}}{\left(\frac{d^2 f}{dx1\,dx2}\right)^2 - \frac{d^2 f}{dx2^2}\frac{d^2 f}{dx1^2}} - \frac{Dt[w2]\ \frac{d^2 f}{dx1^2}}{\left(\frac{d^2 f}{dx1\,dx2}\right)^2 - \frac{d^2 f}{dx2^2}\frac{d^2 f}{dx1^2}}\}$$

The denominator in this expression is the determinant of the Hessian. We know from the second-order conditions that this determinant will be positive for a maximization problem, so it is convenient to make this substitution. Sometimes *Mathematica* makes the denominator negative, and sometimes it makes it positive; in general we'll have to make the substitution for both cases.

```
In[4]:= solution/.{-Det[Hessian[profit2,{x1,x2}]]->-detHess,
                    Det[Hessian[profit2,{x1,x2}]]-> detHess}
```

```
Out[4]:=
```

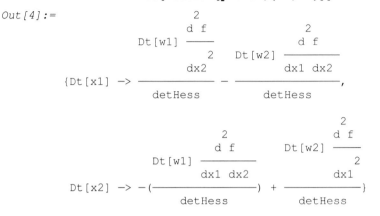

1.2.5.3   Automating Comparative Statics

The package SymOpt.m contains a function **Sensitivity** that automates this process.

```
In[1]:= Sensitivity[profit2,{x1,x2}]
```

```
Out[1]:=
                                              2
                                            d f                          2
                              Dt[w1]  ─────              d f
                                              2    Dt[w2] ───────
                                            dx2              dx1 dx2
          {Dt[x1] ─> -(─────────────) + ──────────────,
                          -detHessian         -detHessian

                                              2
                                            d f              d f
                              Dt[w1]  ─────       Dt[w2] ─────
                                            dx1 dx2              2
                                                                dx1
          Dt[x2] ─> ──────────────── - ──────────────}
                          -detHessian         -detHessian
```

Sensitivity[f,x1,x2] will calculate how the optimal choices x1 and x2 respond to changes in all other variable in the expression f. It totally differentiates the first-order conditions, solves for the comparative statics effects, and substitutes for the determinant of the Hessian.

Sometimes you may want to treat some of the parameters as constants. For example, suppose that you only care about changes in w1. You can set the variation in w2 equal to zero by writing

```
In[2]:= Sensitivity[profit2,{x1,x2}]/.{Dt[w2]->0}
```

```
Out[2]:=
                                      2
                                     d f                                              2
                           Dt[w1]  -----                                             d f
                                      2                                   Dt[w1]  --------
                                    dx2                                            dx1 dx2
          {Dt[x1] -> -(-----------------),  Dt[x2] -> ----------------------}
                          -detHessian                      -detHessian
```

1.2.6   Optimal Value Function

To calculate the optimal value function, substitute the optimal solution back
into the objective function. For example,

```
In[1]:= profitCD=p*x1^(1/2) x2^(1/3) - w1 x1 - w2 x2
Out[1]:=                                 1/3
              -(w1 x1) + p Sqrt[x1] x2      - w2 x2

In[2]:= solution=Solve[FOC[profitCD,
                       {x1,x2}],{x1,x2}][[1]]
Out[2]:=                 6                        6
                        p                        p
          {x2 -> -----------------,  x1 -> ----------------}
                        3   3                    4   2
                   216 w1  w2               144 w1  w2
```

To get the value function, substitute back into the objective function.

```
In[3]:= piCD[p_,w1_,w2_]  := profitCD/.solution
        piCD[p,w1,w2]
Out[3]:=         6                        6
                p     1/3                p
          p (------)      Sqrt[--------]
                3   3              4   2                  6
               w1  w2            w1  w2               5 p
          ----------------------------------- - ----------------
                         72                          3   2
                                                 432 w1  w2
```

According to Hotelling's law, the factor demand function is the derivative of
the profit function. However, if we take the derivative, we get:

```
In[4]:= D[piCD[p,w1,w2],w1]
```

```
Out[4]:=
               7          6                                       7      6     1/3
            -(p   Sqrt[--------])                                p   (--------)
                         4   2                  6                       3   3
                        w1  w2               5 p                       w1  w2
          -------------------------------- + --------------- - --------------------------
                      6                           4   2                      6
                4    p    2/3    3         144 w1  w2                 5      p    2
           72 w1  (------)    w2                              36 w1  Sqrt[--------]  w2
                      3   3                                                  4   2
                     w1  w2                                                 w1  w2
```

It is not obvious that this is correct. The *Mathematica* function **Simplify[]** does not yield anything useful either. In this case, the right function for simplification is **PowerExpand**.

```
In[5]:= PowerExpand[-D[piCD[p,w1,w2],w1]]
```
$$Out[5]:= \frac{p^6}{144 \ w1^4 \ w2^2}$$

1.3   Constrained Optimization

All of the methods described above work for constrained optimization problems as well through the use of Lagrangians. For example, consider the problem of minimizing costs subject to an output constraint. The Lagrangian for this problem has the form

```
In[1]:= L= w1 x1 + w2 x2 - lambda*(f[x1,x2]-y)
```
$$Out[1]:= w1 \ x1 + w2 \ x2 - lambda \ (-y + f[x1, \ x2])$$

The first-order conditions are:

```
In[2]:= FOC[L,{lambda,x1,x2}]
```
$$Out[2]:= \{y - f[x1, \ x2] == 0, \ w1 - lambda \ \frac{df}{dx1} == 0, \ w2 - lambda \ \frac{df}{dx2} == 0\}$$

The second-order conditions involve the bordered Hessian. This is the Hessian matrix of the Lagrangian

```
In[3]:= MatrixForm[Hessian[L,{lambda,x1,x2}]]
```

$$Out[3]:=$$

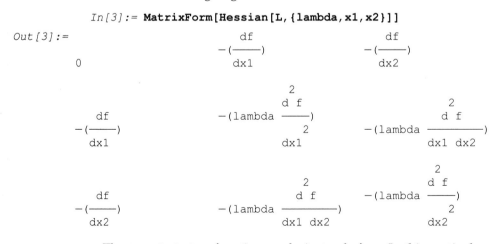

The **Sensitivity** function works just as before. In this particular case, we want to look at the changes holding output fixed

$In[4]:=$ `TableForm[Sensitivity[L,{lambda,x1,x2}]/.{Dt[y]->0}]`

$Out[4]:=$

$$Dt[\text{lambda}] \to -\left(\frac{Dt[w1]\ \left(\text{lambda}\ \dfrac{d\ f}{dx2^2}\ \dfrac{df}{dx1} - \text{lambda}\ \dfrac{df}{dx2}\ \dfrac{d\ f}{dx1\ dx2}\right)}{-\text{detHessian}}\right)$$

$$- \frac{Dt[w2]\ \left(-\left(\text{lambda}\ \dfrac{df}{dx1}\ \dfrac{d\ f}{dx1\ dx2}\right) + \text{lambda}\ \dfrac{df}{dx2}\ \dfrac{d\ f}{dx1^2}\right)}{-\text{detHessian}}$$

$$Dt[x1] \to -\left(\frac{Dt[w1]\ \left(\dfrac{df}{dx2}\right)^2}{-\text{detHessian}}\right) + \frac{Dt[w2]\ \dfrac{df}{dx2}\ \dfrac{df}{dx1}}{-\text{detHessian}}$$

$$Dt[x2] \to \frac{Dt[w1]\ \dfrac{df}{dx2}\ \dfrac{df}{dx1}}{-\text{detHessian}} - \frac{Dt[w2]\ \left(\dfrac{df}{dx1}\right)^2}{-\text{detHessian}}$$

It is easy to see that the own price effect is negative.

1.3.1   Examples

We now have the tools to do almost all the standard microeconomic calculations. We will illustrate this in a series of examples.

1.3.1.1   Cobb-Douglas Utility Function

$In[1]:=$ `L= Log[x1] + Log[x2] - lambda*(m - p1 x1 - p2 x2)`

$Out[1]:=$ $-(\text{lambda}\ (m - p1\ x1 - p2\ x2)) + \text{Log}[x1] + \text{Log}[x2]$

$In[2]:=$ `solution=Solve[FOC[L,{x1,x2,lambda}],{x1,x2,lambda}][[1]]`

$Out[2]:=$ $\{\text{lambda} \to \dfrac{-2}{m},\ x2 \to \dfrac{m}{2\ p2},\ x1 \to \dfrac{m}{2\ p1}\}$

The indirect utility function is given by

$In[3]:=$ `v[p1_,p2_,m_] := L/.solution`

$In[4]:=$ `Simplify[v[p1,p2,m]]`

Out[4]:=
$$\text{Log}\left[\frac{m}{2\ p1}\right] + \text{Log}\left[\frac{m}{2\ p2}\right]$$

Note how nicely Roy's law works:

In[5]:= `Simplify[-D[v[p1,p2,m],p1]/D[v[p1,p2,m],m]]`

Out[5]:=
$$\frac{m}{2\ p1}$$

1.3.1.2   CES Utility Function with rho=-1

Here's the Lagrangian for a utility maximization problem involving a CES utility function with `rho=-1`.

In[1]:= `L=1/(1/x1 + 1/x2) - lambda*(m - p1 x1 - p2 x2)`

Out[1]:=
$$\frac{1}{\frac{1}{x1} + \frac{1}{x2}} - \text{lambda}\ (m - p1\ x1 - p2\ x2)$$

In[2]:= `solution=`
`Simplify[Solve[FOC[L,{x1,x2,lambda}],{lambda,x1,x2}]][[2]]`

Out[2]:=
$$\{\text{lambda} \rightarrow -(\text{Sqrt}[p1] + \text{Sqrt}[p2])^{-2},$$

$$x1 \rightarrow \frac{m}{\text{Sqrt}[p1]\ (\text{Sqrt}[p1] + \text{Sqrt}[p2])},$$

$$x2 \rightarrow \frac{m}{(\text{Sqrt}[p1] + \text{Sqrt}[p2])\ \text{Sqrt}[p2]}\}$$

Note that in this case the positive solution turned out to be *second* in the list of solutions! You can't always count on it being first.

Here's the indirect utility function

In[3]:= `v[p1_,p2_,m_] := 1/(1/x1 + 1/x2)/.solution`

In[4]:= `Simplify[v[p1,p2,m]]`

Out[4]:=
$$\frac{m}{(\text{Sqrt}[p1] + \text{Sqrt}[p2])^2}$$

And here is Roy's law.

In[5]:= `Simplify[-D[v[p1,p2,m],p1]/D[v[p1,p2,m],m]]`

$Out[5]:=$
$$\frac{m}{\mathrm{Sqrt}[p1]\ (\mathrm{Sqrt}[p1]\ +\ \mathrm{Sqrt}[p2])}$$

1.3.1.3   CES Cost Function with rho=-2

$In[1]:=$ **Clear[L,x1,x2,z1,z2,lambda]**

Here's the Lagrangian for a CES cost function with `rho=2`

$In[2]:=$ **L=w1 x1 + w2 x2 - lambda*(1/y^2 - 1/(x1*x1) - 1/(x2*x2))**

$Out[2]:=$
$$\mathrm{w1}\ \mathrm{x1}\ +\ \mathrm{w2}\ \mathrm{x2}\ -\ \mathrm{lambda}\ (-\mathrm{x1}^{-2}\ -\ \mathrm{x2}^{-2}\ +\ \mathrm{y}^{-2})$$

The first-order conditions are

$In[3]:=$ **foc2=FOC[L,{lambda,x1,x2}]**

$Out[3]:=$
$$\{\mathrm{x1}^{-2}\ +\ \mathrm{x2}^{-2}\ -\ \mathrm{y}^{-2}\ ==\ 0,\ \mathrm{w1}\ -\ \frac{2\ \mathrm{lambda}}{\mathrm{x1}^{3}}\ ==\ 0,\ \mathrm{w2}\ -\ \frac{2\ \mathrm{lambda}}{\mathrm{x2}^{3}}\ ==\ 0\}$$

Unfortunately, *Mathematica* finds this system of equations difficult to solve, so we'll have to resort to some tricks. In general, if *Mathematica* finds a system of equations difficult to solve, we should try some transformations to make the system look like a system of polynomials—or, even better, a system of linear equations. In this case, we'll introduce auxiliary variables z1=1/x1 and z2=1/x2. With these additions, the system we want to solve is

$In[4]:=$ **transFOC=foc2/.{x1->1/z1,x2->1/z2}**
    solution=Simplify[
        Solve[Evaluate[transFOC],{z1,z2,lambda}][[1]]]

$Out[4]:=$
$$\{-\mathrm{y}^{-2}\ +\ \mathrm{z1}^{2}\ +\ \mathrm{z2}^{2}\ ==\ 0,\ \mathrm{w1}\ -\ 2\ \mathrm{lambda}\ \mathrm{z1}^{3}\ ==\ 0,$$
$$\mathrm{w2}\ -\ 2\ \mathrm{lambda}\ \mathrm{z2}^{3}\ ==\ 0\}$$

$Out[4]:=\ \{\mathrm{lambda}\ \longrightarrow$

$$\frac{(\mathrm{w1}^{2/3}\ +\ \mathrm{w2}^{2/3})^{2}\ \mathrm{Sqrt}[\mathrm{w1}^{2}\ -\ \mathrm{w1}^{4/3}\ \mathrm{w2}^{2/3}\ +\ \mathrm{w1}^{2/3}\ \mathrm{w2}^{4/3}]\ \mathrm{y}^{3}}{2\ \mathrm{w1}^{1/3}\ \mathrm{Sqrt}[\mathrm{w1}^{2}\ +\ \mathrm{w2}^{2}]},$$

$$\mathrm{z2}\ \longrightarrow\ \frac{\mathrm{w2}^{1/3}\ \mathrm{Sqrt}[\mathrm{w1}^{2}\ -\ \mathrm{w1}^{4/3}\ \mathrm{w2}^{2/3}\ +\ \mathrm{w1}^{2/3}\ \mathrm{w2}^{4/3}]}{\mathrm{w1}^{1/3}\ \mathrm{Sqrt}[\mathrm{w1}^{2}\ +\ \mathrm{w2}^{2}]\ \mathrm{y}},$$

Out[4](cont.)

$$z1 \rightarrow \frac{\mathrm{Sqrt}[w1^2 - w1^{4/3} w2^{2/3} + w1^{2/3} w2^{4/3}]}{\mathrm{Sqrt}[w1^2 + w2^2] \, y}\}$$

Now it is easy to solve for the factor demand functions and the cost function:

In[5]:= `{x1,x2} = Simplify[{1/z1,1/z2}/.solution]`

Out[5]:=

$$\{\frac{\mathrm{Sqrt}[w1^2 + w2^2] \, y}{\mathrm{Sqrt}[w1^2 - w1^{4/3} w2^{2/3} + w1^{2/3} w2^{4/3}]},$$

$$\frac{w1^{1/3} \, \mathrm{Sqrt}[w1^2 + w2^2] \, y}{w2^{1/3} \, \mathrm{Sqrt}[w1^2 - w1^{4/3} w2^{2/3} + w1^{2/3} w2^{4/3}]}\}$$

In[6]:= `c[w1_,w2_,y_] := (w1 /z1 + w2 /z2)/.solution`

In[7]:= `Simplify[c[w1,w2,y]]`

Out[7]:=

$$\frac{w1^{1/3} \, (w1^{2/3} + w2^{2/3}) \, \mathrm{Sqrt}[w1^2 + w2^2] \, y}{\mathrm{Sqrt}[w1^2 - w1^{4/3} w2^{2/3} + w1^{2/3} w2^{4/3}]}$$

1.3.1.4 Monopoly Behavior

As a final example, consider the following comparative statics calculation that arose in a problem involving quality choice of a monopolist. A profit-maximizing monopolist chooses a, b, and x to maximize the following expression

In[1]:= `profit[a_,b_,x_] := a R[x] + b x - (1-sa)ca[a] -`
`                              (1-sb) cb[b]`

In this expression, a R[x] + b x is revenue, while sa and sb are subsidies on the "quality" variables a and b. We want to know how this monopolist will respond to "small" subsidies sa and sb.

In[2]:= `effects=Sensitivity[profit[a,b,x], {a,b,x}]`

Out[2]:=

$$\{Dt[a] \rightarrow -(\frac{Dt[sb] \, \frac{dcb}{db} \frac{dR}{dx}}{\mathrm{detHessian}}) -$$

$$\frac{Dt[sa] \, \frac{dca}{da} \, (-1 - a \, \frac{d^2 cb}{db^2} \frac{d^2 R}{dx^2} + a \, sb \, \frac{d^2 cb}{db^2} \frac{d^2 R}{dx^2})}{\mathrm{detHessian}},$$

Out[2] (cont.)

$$Dt[b] \rightarrow -\left(\cfrac{Dt[sa]\ \cfrac{dca}{da}\ \cfrac{dR}{dx}}{detHessian}\right) -$$

$$\cfrac{Dt[sb]\ \cfrac{dcb}{db}\ \left(-\left(\cfrac{dR}{dx}\right)^2 - a\ \cfrac{d^2 ca}{da^2}\ \cfrac{d^2 R}{dx^2} + a\ sa\ \cfrac{d^2 ca}{da^2}\ \cfrac{d^2 R}{dx^2}\right)}{detHessian},$$

$$Dt[x] \rightarrow -\left(\cfrac{Dt[sb]\ \cfrac{dcb}{db}\ \left(\cfrac{d^2 ca}{da^2} - sa\ \cfrac{d^2 ca}{da^2}\right)}{detHessian}\right)$$

$$\cfrac{Dt[sa]\ \cfrac{dca}{da}\ \left(\cfrac{dR}{dx}\ \cfrac{d^2 cb}{db^2} - sb\ \cfrac{dR}{dx}\ \cfrac{d^2 cb}{db^2}\right)}{detHessian}\}$$

We want to evaluate this derivative at sa=sb=0. However, if we simply make this substitution, *Mathematica* wrongly decides that Dt[sa]=Dt[sb]=0. To get around this, we'll first redefine Dt[sa] and Dt[sb] and then make the substitution. While we're at it, we'll make a few more changes of notation.

In[3]:= **result=effects/.{Dt[sb]->dsb,Dt[sa]->dsa,sb->0,sa->0,
    "detHess"->H}**

Out[3]:=

$$\{Dt[a] \rightarrow -\left(\cfrac{dsb\ \cfrac{dcb}{db}\ \cfrac{dR}{dx}}{detHessian}\right) - \cfrac{dsa\ \cfrac{dca}{da}\ \left(-1 - a\ \cfrac{d^2 cb}{db^2}\ \cfrac{d^2 R}{dx^2}\right)}{detHessian},$$

$$Dt[b] \rightarrow -\left(\cfrac{dsa\ \cfrac{dca}{da}\ \cfrac{dR}{dx}}{detHessian}\right) - \cfrac{dsb\ \cfrac{dcb}{db}\ \left(-\left(\cfrac{dR}{dx}\right)^2 - a\ \cfrac{d^2 ca}{da^2}\ \cfrac{d^2 R}{dx^2}\right)}{detHessian},$$

Out [3] (cont.)

$$Dt[x] \rightarrow -(\frac{dsb\frac{dcb}{db}\frac{d^2ca}{da^2}}{detHessian}) - \frac{dsa\frac{dca}{da}\frac{dR}{dx}\frac{d^2cb}{db^2}}{detHessian}\}$$

In this case the second-order conditions imply that detHess is negative, and it is easy to verify that R'[x] is positive at the equilibrium. Under the usual assumptions of increasing marginal cost, increasing either sa or sb will increase output.

1.4   Graphics

I mentioned earlier that Hessian conditions for verifying that a matrix is positive or negative definite are often difficult to apply. However, with *Mathematica* we can always draw a picture. This is especially convenient for contour plots. For example, we can draw a standard utility maximization problem with the following sequence of commands.

```
In[1]:= indiffCurves=ContourPlot[Log[x1] + Log[x2],
           {x1,1,10},{x2,1,10},ContourShading->False,
           DisplayFunction -> Identity]
        budgetLine=ContourPlot[x1 + x2 -11,{x1,1,10},{x2,1,10},
           Contours->{0},ContourShading->False,
           DisplayFunction -> Identity]
        Show[indiffCurves,budgetLine,
        DisplayFunction->$DisplayFunction]
```

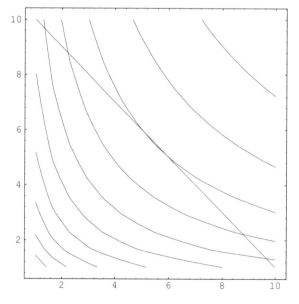

The routine `ConsumerPlot[u,p1,p2,m]` in `SymbOpt.m` will draw a picture of a consumer optimization problem given a utility function, two prices, and income. It calculates the optimal utility using a numerical routine in *Mathematica*.

```
In[2]:= u[x1_,x2_] := x1*x2
        ConsumerPlot[u,2,1,50]
```

1.5   Integrability

We can also use *Mathematica* to solve "inverse optimization problems." That is, given a function that is the answer to an optimization problem, find out what it is that was being optimized. Economists refer to this as "integrability theory." Generally this sort of task will require solving a system of partial differential equations which will usually have to be done numerically. However, in some low dimensional cases, such systems of PDE's may reduce to a single ODE. The classic case is consumer demand theory with two goods.

Normally we think of the two goods as being the good we're interested in and "all other goods." This composite commodity is the numeraire good and both price and income are measured relative to the price of the numeraire.

1.5.1   Linear Demand

Consider the case of a linear demand

```
In[1]:= x[p_,m_] := a*p + b*m + c
```

This is the demand for one of the two goods. The demand for "all other goods" comes from the budget constraint; it is given by $m - p*x[p,m]$.

The integrability equation for this system can be solved using *Mathematica*'s **SolveD** function.

```
In[2]:= solution=DSolve[{mu'[p]==a p + b mu[p] + c,mu[q]==m},
              mu[p],p][[1]]
```

Out[2]:=

$$\{mu[p] \to -(\frac{a + b\ c}{b^2}) - \frac{a\ p}{b} + \frac{E^{b\ (p - q)}\ (a + b\ c + b^2\ m + a\ b\ q)}{b^2}\}$$

Substitute into mu[p] to get the money-metric utility function.

```
In[3]:= mm[p_,q_,m_] := mu[p]/.solution
        mm[p,q,m]
```

Out[3]:=

$$-(\frac{a + b\ c}{b^2}) - \frac{a\ p}{b} + \frac{E^{b\ (p - q)}\ (a + b\ c + b^2\ m + a\ b\ q)}{b^2}$$

Let's see if we can figure out what the indifference curves for this indirect utility function looks like. The easiest way to do this is to solve for the Hicksian demand functions.

```
In[4]:= h1[p_,q_,m_,a_,b_,c_] :=
           Evaluate[x[p,income]/.{income->mm[p,q,m]}]
        h1[p,q,m,a,b,c]
```

Out[4]:=

$$c + a\ p + b\ (-(\frac{a + b\ c}{b^2}) - \frac{a\ p}{b} +$$

$$\frac{E^{b\ (p - q)}\ (a + b\ c + b^2\ m + a\ b\ q)}{b^2})$$

This is one Hicksian demand; the other one comes from the budget constraint.

```
In[5]:= h2[p_,q_,m_,a_,b_,c_] := Evaluate[(income -
                     p x[p,income])/.{income->mm[p,q,m]}]
        h2[p,q,m,a,b,c]
```

Out[5]:=

$$-(\frac{a + b\ c}{b^2}) - \frac{a\ p}{b} + \frac{E^{b\ (p - q)}\ (a + b\ c + b^2\ m + a\ b\ q)}{b^2} -$$

$$p\ (c + a\ p + b\ (-(\frac{a + b\ c}{b^2}) - \frac{a\ p}{b} +$$

Out[5] (cont.)

$$E^{\frac{b \ (p - q)}{b}} \quad \frac{(a + b \ c + b^2 \ m + a \ b \ q)}{b^2}))$$

Now we'll fix q and m, so that utility is held fixed, pick some values for (a,b,c) and then plot these functions as p varies

```
In[6]:= hh1[p_] := Simplify[Evaluate[h1[p,1,10,-10,1,1]]]
        hh2[p_] := Simplify[Evaluate[h2[p,1,10,-10,1,1]]]
        Simplify[{hh1[p],hh2[p]}]
```

Out[6]:=

$$\{\frac{10 \ E - 9 \ E^p}{E}, \frac{9 \ (E - E^p + E^p \ p)}{E}\}$$

```
In[7]:= ParametricPlot[{hh1[p],hh2[p]},{p,0,1.5},
        AxesOrigin->{0,0}, PlotRange->{0,12},AspectRatio->1]
```

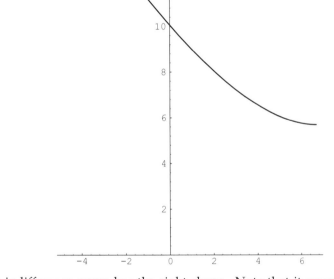

The indifference curve has the right shape. Note that it crosses the vertical axis, which is not meaningful economically. This shows how useful it is to plot a picture of what you are doing before blindly accepting a calculation.

1.5.2   Log-Linear Demand

Suppose that demand takes the linear-in-logs form

```
In[1]:= x[p_,m_] := p^a m^b E^c
```

We estimate the demand function and find that a=-0.2, b=1.2, and c=0.0. Initially, the consumer faces prices p=2 and has income of m=1. If the price rises to p=3, how much income would the consumer need to make her as well off as she was before the price increase?

We'll answer this question using integrability theory. Before the price change, e[2,u]=1. We want to know what e[3,u] equals. First we find a numerical solution to the integrability equation.

```
In[2]:= a=-0.2
        b=1.2
        c=0.0
        solution2=
          NDSolve[{e'[p]==(p^a)* (e[p]^b), e[2]==1},e, {p,1,4}]
```

```
Out[2]:= -0.2
```

```
Out[2]:= 1.2
```

```
Out[2]:= 0.
```

```
Out[2]:= {{e -> InterpolatingFunction[{1., 4.}, <>]}}
```

We can plot the function e[p] that *Mathematica* found for us using the following expressions. Note that e[2]=1, as required by the boundary condition.

```
In[3]:= Plot[Evaluate[e[p]/.solution2], {p,1,4}]
```

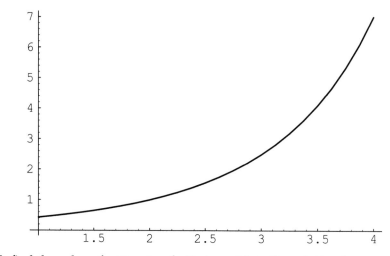

To find the value of e[3,u], substitute p=3 into the solution for e[p].

```
In[4]:= e[3]/.solution2
```

```
Out[4]:= {2.49004}
```

1.6   Symbolic Dynamic Programming

One of the more amazing things that *Mathematica* can do is to solve dynamic programming problems symbolically. For example, let's look at a simple intertemporal portfolio problem. The consumer's utility function is Log[c] and the discount factor is `alpha`. We use `w` to denote wealth and `R` is the total return on savings. If the consumer chooses to consume `c` this period, she will save `(w-c)` which will yield `(w-c) R` next period.

1.6.1 Two-period Case

```
In[1]:= V[c_] := Log[c] + alpha Log[(w-c)R]
        solution1=Simplify[Solve[D[V[c],c]==0,c][[1]]]
Out[1]:=              w
            {c -> ───────────}
                   1 + alpha
```

Substituting back into `V[c]` gives us the indirect utility function.

```
In[2]:= Simplify[V[c]/.solution1]
Out[2]:=          w                              alpha R w
         Log[───────────] + alpha Log[───────────]
             1 + alpha                    1 + alpha
```

1.6.2 Calculating the Value Function by Recursion

Let's try to program *Mathematica* to do the dynamic programming recursion all by itself. As it turns out the only thing that we have to do is to make the consumption variable, `c`, local to the routine where it is being calculated. Otherwise, *Mathematica* gets confused by all the values of `c` that are floating around. To do this, we use the **Module** construction. Here's how it works for a 3-period problem.

```
In[1]:= V3[w_,t_]:=
        Module[{c},
        Log[c] + alpha*V3[(w-c)*R,t+1]/.Solve[D[Log[c]
              + alpha*V3[(w-c)*R,t+1],c]==0,c][[1]]]

        V3[w_,3]  := Log[w]
In[2]:= TableForm[{V3[w,3],V3[w,2],Simplify[V3[w,1]]}]
Out[2]:= Log[w]
```

```
              w                            w
     Log[───────────] + alpha Log[R (w - ───────────)]]
         1 + alpha                        1 + alpha


              w                                  alpha R w
     Log[─────────────────] + alpha Log[─────────────────]
                        2                                2
         1 + alpha + alpha                1 + alpha + alpha


                                      2  2
                          2      alpha  R  w
          +   alpha  Log[─────────────────]
                                          2
                         1 + alpha + alpha
```

1.6.3   Solving for Consumption

Once we have the value function, it is easy to solve for consumption in a given period. First let's check that we get the same values in the next-to-last period.

```
In[1]:= V3[w,2]
        Solve[D[Log[c] + alpha*V3[(w-c)*r,3],c]==0,c][[1]]
```

$$
Out[1]:= \quad \mathrm{Log}\left[\frac{w}{1 + alpha}\right] + alpha\ \mathrm{Log}\left[R\ \left(w - \frac{w}{1 + alpha}\right)\right]
$$

$$
Out[1]:= \quad \{c \rightarrow \frac{w}{1 + alpha}\}
$$

Note that we get the same answer as before. Here's the first period consumption in a 3-period problem.

```
In[2]:= Solve[D[Log[c] + alpha*V3[(w-c)*r,2],c]==0,c][[1]]
```

$$
Out[2]:= \quad \{c \rightarrow \frac{w}{1 + alpha + alpha^2}\}
$$

To solve for first-period consumption in, say, a 5-period problem, we have to go back and define a new value function for that problem.

```
In[3]:= V5[w_,t_]:=
        Module[{c},
        Log[c] + alpha*V5[(w-c)*R,t+1]/.Solve[D[Log[c]
               + alpha*V5[(w-c)*R,t+1],c]==0,c][[1]]]

        V5[w_,5]  := Log[w]

In[4]:= Solve[D[Log[c] + alpha*V5[(w-c)*r,2],c]==0,c][[1]]
```

$$
Out[4]:= \quad \{c \rightarrow \frac{w}{1 + alpha + alpha^2 + alpha^3 + alpha^4}\}
$$

Note that consumption is independent of the rate of return, a feature special to the log utility function.

1.6.4   Speeding Things Up

Actually, we should define the value function a little bit differently if we want to use *Mathematica* efficiently. When we calculate V[w,1], we have to calculate all the other values of V[w,t]. When we calculate V[w,2] we have to calculate

those values all over again. We can tell *Mathematica* to "remember" the values
of the V[w,t] function by using the following construction.

```
In[1]:= V5f[w_,t_]:= V5f[w,t] =
          Module[{c},
          Log[c] + alpha*V5f[(w-c)*R,t+1]/.Solve[D[Log[c]
                    + alpha*V5f[(w-c)*R,t+1],c]==0,c][[1]]]

          V5f[w_,5] := Log[w]

In[2]:= Timing[V5[w,1];]
          Timing[V5[w,2];]

Out[2]:= {2.48333 Second, Null}

Out[2]:= {0.683333 Second, Null}

In[3]:= Timing[V5f[w,1];]
          Timing[V5f[w,2];]

Out[3]:= {1.26667 Second, Null}

Out[3]:= {0.4 Second, Null}
```

Note that the second way of calculating the value function is a lot faster.

1.6.5   Stochastic Dynamic Programming

One of the strengths of dynamic programming is that it is easy to handle stochastic problems. Consider the savings problem discussed above. Suppose that R
takes value Ru with probability p and Rd with probability 1-p. Then the expected value function is

```
In[1]:= V3s[w_,t_]:= V3s[w,t] =
          Module[{c},
          Log[c] + alpha*(p*V3s[(w-c)*Ru,t+1]+
                      (1-p)*V3s[(w-c)*Rd,t+1])/.Solve[D[Log[c]
                      + alpha*(p*V3s[(w-c)*Ru,t+1]+
                        (1-p)*V3s[(w-c)*Rd,t+1]),c]==0,c][[1]]]
          V3s[w_,3] := Log[w]
```

We solve for optimal consumption in period 1:

```
In[2]:= Solve[D[Log[c] + alpha*(p*V3s[(w-c)*Ru,2]+
              (1-p)*V3s[(w-c)*Rd,2]),c]==0,c][[1]]

Out[2]:=                        w
              {c ->  ---------------------}
                                   2
                      1 + alpha + alpha
```

Note that even in the stochastic case, consumption doesn't depend on p. That
is, optimal consumption is independent of the probability distribution of the
rate of return in the case of log utility.

1.7 Numeric Dynamic Programming

1.7.1 By the Numbers

Of course only a few dynamic programming problems have explicit closed-form expressions. However, we can use exactly the same techniques to solve problems numerically. First we'll try the problem we've already investigated since we can check the numerical formula against the symbolic one. The *Mathematica* function **FindMinimum[f[x],{x,x0}]** returns a list {fmax,{x->xmax}} where fmax is a (local) minimum value of f[x] starting at the value x0.

Here's the expression for the optimal consumption with wealth w at time t in a 3-period problem.

```
In[1]:= c3n[w_,t_]  := c3n[w,t] =
                c/.FindMinimum[-Log[c] - alpha*V3n[(w-
c)*R,t+1],{c,1}][[2]]
        c3n[w_,3]  := w
```

Here's the expression for the value function:

```
In[2]:= V3n[w_,t_]:= V3n[w,t] =
                Log[c3n[w,t]] + alpha*V3n[(w-c3n[w,t])*R,t+1]
        V3n[w_,3]  := N[Log[w]]
```

Set the parameters so that we can do this numerically.

```
In[3]:= R=1.5
        alpha=.9
```

```
Out[3]:= 1.5
```

```
Out[3]:= 0.9
```

Now let's calculate

```
In[4]:= {V3n[100,1],V3n[100,2],V3n[100,3]}
```

```
Out[4]:= {10.533, 7.8004, 4.60517}
```

Compare this to the values found by the symbolic calculation:

```
In[5]:= {V3[100,1],V3[100,2],N[V3[100,3]]}
```

```
Out[5]:= {10.5345, 7.8004, 4.60517}
```

Pretty close! Now let's try the same calculation for a 5-period problem:

```
In[6]:= c5n[w_,t_]  := c5n[w,t] =
                c/.FindMinimum[-Log[c] -
                    alpha*V5n[(w-c)*R,t+1],{c,1}][[2]]
        c5n[w_,5]  := w
        V5n[w_,t_]:= V5n[w,t] =
                Log[c5n[w,t]] + alpha*V5n[(w-c5n[w,t])*R,t+1]
        V5n[w_,5]  := N[Log[w]]
```

```
In[7]:= {V5n[100,3],V5n[100,4],V5n[100,5]}

Out[7]:= {10.533, 7.8004, 4.60517}
```

1.8 Summary

Mathematica can be used to automate a number of the tedious tasks involved in analyzing optimization problems. These include solving algebraic examples, graphing solutions, doing comparative statics calculations, solving integrability equations and solving algebraic and numeric dynamic programming problems.

1.9 References

Varian, Hal (1992) *Microeconomic Analysis*, W. W. Norton & Co., New York.
Wolfram, Stephen (1991) *Mathematica: a System for Doing Mathematics by Computer*, Addison-Wesley, Reading, MA.

2 Designing an Incentive-Compatible Contract

Todd Kaplan and Arijit Mukherji

2.1 Description of the Problem and a Summary of the Theory

One of the most important problems in modern economics is concerned with the interaction of incentives, information, and economic mechanisms that solve them. This is typically posed as the problem of designing an optimal mechanism using game theory. The solution concept that is used is that of Bayesian-Nash equilibrium (or refinements of that concept).

One player, typically referred to as the Principal, proposes a scheme or mechanism to the other party/parties. The other parties respond with messages, and the result is agreement on the implementation of the mechanism. Generally speaking, a mechanism is a function, and a particular realization is the function evaluated at a particular value of the environment. The Principal recognizes that the other parties will act in accordance with their private information and that their incentives may only be incompletely aligned with his own. Mechanism design thus involves trade-offs between the costs of potential distortions from relying on false statements made by different parties and the gains from coordination. For a review of the mechanism design literature see [Myerson 1991, Chapter 6] or [Fudenberg and Tirole 1991, Chapter 7].

Typically, communication in such a game is in the form of **menus of contracts**, one for each possible state of nature or the environment. A contract specifies the actions to be taken and the money that is to be transferred between various parties involved as a function of the environment. A menu of contracts is a sequence of functions indexed over some set of environments, commonly referred to as types t. Note that t may be a member of a finite set, or a continuum. If there are many players with private information, a problem that is not modelled here, then the set of types will mean the cross-product of their individual sets. In most applications, the types are ordered in the sense that one type t_1 will be "better" than another type t_2. For instance, good types may be more productive or more likely to produce the same good at a lower cost or less likely to suffer an accident. We will discuss this ordering below when we discuss the **single-crossing property**.

Suppose a menu of contracts $\{r(t), y(t)\}$ is offered where t is an element of T. Then if an Agent chooses the pair $\{r(t), y(t)\}$ that is equivalent to a claim that the state was t: in other words, the contract will enforce a performance of an action $y(t)$ and a transfer of $r(t)$ to the Agent.

While the above discussion has been fairly abstract, we will now explain the nature of the mechanism design problem in relation to two specific examples: the Maskin-Riley screening problem and the Sappington employee-incentives problem.

2.2 Preferences: the Single-Crossing Property

In this section we will explain a property, the Single-Crossing Property, that is crucial for imposing structure on mechanism design problems. We will use this property to solve different examples of designing incentive compatible contracts. We will first consider an application to industrial organization and then another application to the internal environment of the firm.

In [Maskin and Riley 1984], a monopolist faces consumers with different preferences for a commodity. Let q represent quality and p represent price. A consumer of type t has a preference relation represented by a utility function $U(p, q, t)$ which we shall assume has a separable representation $V(t, q) - p$. Preferences are thus **quasilinear** i.e. they are linear in money, the price p. Assume V is increasing in q (so that higher quality is desired by all consumers) but that the marginal value of quality varies with type t. In a situation where consumers of higher types value more quality more highly, the mixed-partial of V with respect to t and q will be positive. More abstractly, the marginal rate of substitution between quality and price will be increasing in t. To see this, note that marginal rate of substitution between quality and price is

$$-\frac{\partial U(p, q, t)/\partial a}{\partial U(p, q, t)/\partial p}.$$

```
In[1]:= U[p_,q_,t_]:=V[t,q] - p; V[t_,q_]=t^(1/2) q;
        MRS[p_,q_,t_]:=-D[U[p,q,t],q]/D[U[p,q,t],p];
        Table[MRS[p,q,t],{t,1,5}]
        MixPart[t_,q_]:=D[D[V[t,q],t],q]
        MixPart[t,q]

Out[1]:= {1, Sqrt[2], Sqrt[3], 2, Sqrt[5]}

Out[1]:=        1
         -----------
         2 Sqrt[t]
```

The Marginal Rates of Substitution (**MRS**) are increasing in t, and the mixed partial (**MixPart**) is positive. The indifference curves in the (q, p) plane are as shown below, for four distinct levels of utility, with the dashed ones representing those for a higher type $t = 4.7$ and the plain ones for those of a lower type $t = 1.2$. Notice that at the points of intersection, the dashed indifference curve for the higher type has a higher slope. Higher levels of utility are in the South-East portion of the diagram.

```
In[2]:= SetOptions[ContourPlot,ContourShading->False,
        Contours->4,DisplayFunction->Identity];
      g1=ContourPlot[U[p,q,1.2],{q,0,100},{p,0,100}];
      g2=ContourPlot[U[p,q,4.7],{q,0,100},{p,0,100},
        ContourStyle->Dashing[{.01,.01}]];
      SetOptions[ContourPlot, DisplayFunction->$DisplayFunction];
      Show[{g1,g2},DisplayFunction->$DisplayFunction,
        PlotLabel->"Single-Crossing of Utility Functions"]
```

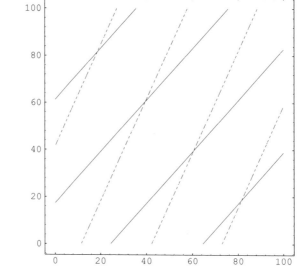

```
Out[2]:= -Graphics-
```

In [Sappington's 1983] model, an employer hires an Agent to produce a level of output, but the cost of production varies with the state of nature: for instance, in bad states of nature, the costs of production are much higher. As costs of production are private information, the employee has an incentive to shirk by underproducing. Let r represent wages and y represent output. The employee, or Agent, has a preference relation represented by a utility function $U(r, y, t)$ which we shall assume is represented by $r - V(y, t)$ where r is the wage, t is the state and y is the level of production. Thus $V(y, t)$ is the Agent's cost of producing y units in state t: one could think of this as the disutility of production. Preferences are thus quasilinear i.e. they are linear in money, the wage r. Assume V is increasing in y (so that higher output is more costly to produce regardless of the state) but that the marginal cost of production varies with state t. In a situation where marginal costs of producing the same level of output are higher in worse states, the mixed partial of V will be positive. Just as before, the marginal rate of substitution between output and wage will be decreasing in state. To see this, note that marginal rate of substitution between quality and price is

$$-\frac{\partial U_A(p,q,t)/\partial q}{\partial U_A(p,q,t)/\partial p}.$$

```
In[3]:= Clear[V]; UA[r_,y_,t_]:=r-V[t,y]; V[t_,y_]=t^(2) y;
        MRS[r_,y_,t_]:=-D[UA[r,y,t],y]/D[UA[r,y,t],r];
        Table[MRS[r,y,t],{t,1,5}]
        MixPart[t_,y_]:=D[D[V[t,y],t],y]
        MixPart[t,y]
```

```
Out[3]:= {1, 4, 9, 16, 25}
```

```
Out[3]:= 2 t
```

Again in this problem, the marginal rates of substitution (**MRS**) between output and wage are increasing in the state for the Agent. The mixed partial (**MixPart**) of the cost or disutility function is positive. So the indifference curves in the (y, r) plane are as below, as shown for four distinct levels of utility, with the dashed ones representing those for a higher type $t = 1$ and the plain ones for those of a lower type $t = .7$. Notice that at the points of intersection, the dashed indifference curve for the higher type has a higher slope. Higher levels of utility are in the North West portion of the diagram.

```
In[4]:= SetOptions[ContourPlot,ContourShading->False,
        Contours->4,DisplayFunction->Identity];
        g1=ContourPlot[UA[r,y,.7],{y,0,50},{r,0,50}];
        g2=ContourPlot[UA[r,y,1],{y,0,50},{r,0,50},
        ContourStyle->Dashing[{.01,.01}]];
        SetOptions[ContourPlot, DisplayFunction->$DisplayFunction];
        Show[{g1,g2}, DisplayFunction->$DisplayFunction,
        PlotLabel->"Single-Crossing of Utility Functions"]
```

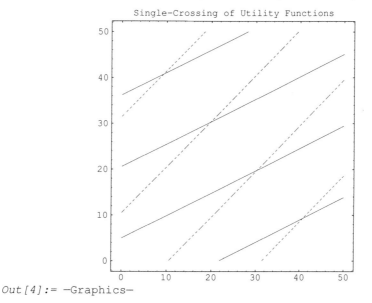

```
Out[4]:= -Graphics-
```

2.3   Incentive Compatible Contracts with Finitely Many Types

2.3.1   Formulating the Finite Problem

In this section, we will present the formulation of the problem with finitely many types. We now present an example of a model of an incentive problem as formulated by David Sappington. A risk neutral Principal and a risk neutral effort-averse Agent contract on a menu. After the Agent learns the state, he selects one of the items on the menu: i.e. an output target and a wage level. Risk neutrality implies that the preferences of the Agent are quasilinear: i.e his preferences are separable in his utility for money income and his disutility or cost from producing various levels of output in different states. Before we clarify what this means in terms of the indifference curves graphed above, we need to introduce the notation.

The notation is as follows: there are n states $i = 1, 2, \ldots n$; the menu of contracts requires the Agent to produce output $y[i]$ and receive wage $r[i]$. Now define $p[i]$ to be be the prior probability of state i. The contract menu must have the self-selection property, i.e. be incentive compatible (or IC). The Revelation Principle allows us to impose these constraints without loss of generality. It should also be individually rational (or IR) ex-post for the Agent i.e. the contract should offer more than his reservation utility (normalized to zero). Thus the Agent is free to leave the firm rather than work, and we must provide enough incentives for him to work for the firm in each state. These generate a series of

IC constraints: in state i, the Agent must prefer $\{y[i], r[i]\}$ to $\{y[j], r[j]\}$

IR constraints: in state i, the Agent must receive at least zero utility from $\{y[i], r[i]\}$

The Agent's cost (or disutility) of production is $v[y[j], t]$ where t is the true state and output $y[j]$ is produced. He has separable quasilinear preference $r[j] - v[y[j], t]$ from accepting $\{y[j], r[j]\}$ in state t. Order the states $i = 1, 2, \ldots n$ so that 1 is the worst state, and n is the best (i.e. least costly). In the general problem, there will be $n(n-1)$ IC constraints; in each of the n states, the Agent should prefer to report the true state rather than report any of the other $(n-1)$ states there will also be n IR constraints: in each of the n states, truthfully declaring the state should guarantee at least the reservation utility.

This generates a messy problem with n^2 constraints and $2n$ First Order Conditions on $y[i]$ and $r[i]$: these have to be solved for n^2 Lagrange multipliers and $2n$ decision variables $\{y[i], r[i]\}$. Fortunately we do not have to search over all possible sets of binding constraints to derive an optimal contract. Under appropriate conditions, namely Single-Crossing, the constraints will be well-behaved and we can solve a less messy problem.

2.3.2   Kuhn-Tucker conditions and kuhntuck.m

The accompanying package `kuhntuck.m` solves the Kuhn Tucker conditions to an optimization problem. The Kuhn-Tucker program is provided for illustrative purposes. It is not particularly efficient: it considers **all possible sets** of binding constraints, and finds the solution that maximizes the objective function. This does not utilize any economic intuition about the problem. Later we will discuss an alternative approach: solving the first order conditions and the binding constraints on a reduced program. The latter approach is valid if preferences satisfy the single-crossing property.

At this point load the Kuhn-Tucker package

```
In[1]:= <<kuhntuck.m
```

2.3.3   Examples of Kuhn Tucker Maximization

```
In[1]:= KTMax[x^2+y^2,{-( 3 x + 5 y - 4 ),-(7 x + 10 y - 9),
          x,y},{x,y}]
       KTMax[x^2+y^2,{-(7 x + 10 y - 9),x,y},{x,y}]
       KTMax[x^3+y^2,{-(7 x + 10 y - 9),x,y-.5},{x,y}]
```

$$Out[1]:= \{\frac{81}{49}, \{\{x \to \frac{9}{7}, y \to 0, lam[1] \to 0, lam[2] \to \frac{18}{49},$$

$$lam[3] \to 0, \quad lam[4] \to \frac{180}{49}\}\}\}$$

$$Out[1]:= \{\frac{81}{49}, \{\{x \to \frac{9}{7}, y \to 0, lam[1] \to \frac{18}{49}, lam[2] \to 0,$$

$$lam[3] \to \frac{180}{49}\}\}\}$$

$$Out[1]:= \{0.81, \{\{x \to 0., y \to 0.9, lam[1] \to 0.18,$$
$$lam[2] \to 1.26, lam[3] \to 0\}\}\}$$

The package uses **NSolve**. One could have used **Solve** but it doesn't always work. In the following example, **NSolve** works but **Solve** doesn't.

```
In[2]:= KTMax[.5x y^2,{-(x^2+y^2-1),x,y-.5},{x,y}]
Out[2]:= {0.19245, {{x -> 0.577350269189626,
       y -> 0.816496580927726, lam[1] -> 0.288675134594813,
       lam[2] -> 0, lam[3] -> 0}}}
```

2.3.4   An Application to the Principal Agent Problem

We present an example with a quadratic disutility function for the agent and two equally likely states. The IR constraints are Individual Rationality constraints for the Agent; the Incentive Compatibility Constraints are represented by IC. Using **KTMax** to solve this, we have,

```
In[1]:= n=2;v[y_,t_]:=y*y/t;t[i_]=i; p[i_]=.5;
        IR=Table[r[i]-v[y[i],t[i]],{i,1,2}];
        IC={r[1]-v[y[1],t[1]]-r[2]+v[y[2],t[1]],
               r[2]-v[y[2],t[2]]-r[1]+v[y[1],t[2]]};
        Constraints=Join[IR,IC];
        Obj=Sum[p[i]*(y[i]-r[i]),{i,1,2}];
        KTMax[Obj,Constraints,{r[1],r[2],y[1],y[2]}]
Out[1]:= {0.333333, {{r[1] -> 0.111111, r[2] -> 0.555556,
         y[1] -> 0.333333, y[2] -> 1., lam[1] -> 1.,
         lam[2] -> 0, lam[3] -> 0, lam[4] -> 0.5}}}
```

The above numerical solution provides a lot of intuition: first, notice the IR constraint in state 1, the worse state, is binding. The only other constraint that is binding is the IC constraint on the Agent reporting in the better state, state 2. This follows from `lam[1] > 0` and `lam[4] > 0`. In a more general problem with more than 2 states, we will see that under suitable regularity conditions on the preferences (the Single Crossing Property), the only constraints that are binding are the **IR constraint in the worst state**, and the **downward adjacent IC constraints**.

How about trying the **KTMax** function for three states and the uniform distribution and trying to solve the Kuhn Tucker conditions for this problem? That is probably too much for most computers, but maybe you have access to *Mathematica* on a Cray? The **KTMax** procedure would involve searching over $2^9 = 512$ possibilities! (In general there will be $2^{(n^2-1)}$ possibilities.) We suggest you run the program in the next cell only if you are confident about your computing resources.

```
In[2]:= n=3;v[y_,t_]:=y*y/t;t[i_]=i; p[i_]=1/n;
        IR=Table[r[i]-v[y[i],t[i]],{i,1,n}];
        IC=Table[r[i]-v[y[i],t[i]]-r[Mod[j+i-1,n]+1]+
             v[y[Mod[j+i-1,n]+1],t[i]],{i,1,n},{j,1,n-1}];
        constraints=Flatten[Join[IR,IC]];
        Obj=Sum[p[i]*(y[i]-r[i]),{i,1,n}];
        KTMax[Obj,constraints,Flatten[Table[{r[i],y[i]},
           {i,1,n}]]]
Out[2]:= {0.416666666666667, {{r[1] -> 0.0625, y[1] -> 0.25,
         r[2] -> 0.3125, y[2] -> 0.75, r[3] -> 0.875,
         y[3] -> 1.5, lam[1] -> 1., lam[2] -> 0,
         lam[3] -> 0, lam[4] -> 0, lam[5] -> 0, lam[6] -> 0,
         lam[7] -> 0.666666666666667, lam[8] -> 0,
         lam[9] -> 0.333333333333333}}}
```

The numerical solution to the above three state problem has the same two features as the solution in the two state problem. For the remainder of this chapter, we will assume that these are the only relevant constraints. We can do this if the Single-Crossing Property holds. This is really without loss of generality as one can compute the solution to the **relaxed problem** dropping the other constraints, and then show that the solution to the **relaxed problem** does in fact satisfy the constraints that were relaxed, and is thus feasible and optimal in the **original problem**. This will be shown graphically at the end.

We now show how to solve the two state problem symbolically. The success of this program for higher values of n depends upon the computational capacity of the machine. The next three sub-sub-sections display the idea behind the programs in the package for three cases: three states (symbolic solution) and two states (symbolic and numeric solutions). For a numeric solution, one can use the package directly. For a symbolic solution, one needs to use **Solve** rather than **NSolve** as was used in the package.

2.3.5 Two States, Numerical Solution.

```
In[1]:= s=.4;n=2;v[y_,t_]:=y*y/t;t[i_]=i;
        p[i_]=Binomial[n,i] (sî) ((1-s)^(n-i));
```

The above statements set up the quadratic disutility function v and the prior probability, for which alternative functional forms are of course available. Next we generate a vector of Lagrange multipliers lamv and **IC** and **IR** which represent the constraints; finally we set up the **Obj**ective function and then the **Lagran**gian. **Focs** represent the set of first order conditions. **Eqns** represent the union of first order conditions and the sets of binding constraints. Notice that IR is only for the bad state, state 1; also notice that IC is only for the good state where the Agent has to be restrained from reporting the bad state. This is our attempt to use the intuition we received from the numerical solution above.

```
In[2]:= s=.3;lamv=Table[lam[i],{i,1,n}];
        IC=Table[r[i]-v[y[i],t[i]]-r[i-1]+v[y[i-1],
        t[i]],{i,2,n}];
        IR={r[1]-v[y[1],t[1]]};
        Constraints=Join[IR,IC];
        Obj=Sum[p[i]*(y[i]-r[i]),{i,1,n}];
        Lagran=Obj+lamv.Constraints;
        Focs=Flatten[Table[{D[Lagran,y[i]]==0,
        D[Lagran,r[i]]==0},{i,1,n}]];
        eqns=Join[Focs,Table[Constraints[[i]]==0, {i,1,n}]]
        NSolve[eqns,Flatten[Join[Table[y[i],{i,1,n}],
        Table[r[i],{i,1,n}],Table[lam[i],{i,1,n}]]]]
```

```
Out[2]:= {0.48 - 2 lam[1] y[1] + lam[2] y[1] == 0,

          -0.48 + lam[1] - lam[2] == 0,

          0.16 - lam[2] y[2] == 0,
                                                     2
          -0.16 + lam[2] == 0, r[1] - y[1]  == 0,

                                   2        2
                               y[1]     y[2]
          -r[1] + r[2] +      ------ - ------ == 0}
                                  2        2
```

```
Out[2]:= {{lam[1] -> 0.64, lam[2] -> 0.16, r[2] -> 0.591837,

          r[1] -> 0.183673, y[2] -> 1., y[1] -> 0.428571}}
```

2.3.6   Two States, Binomial, Symbolic Solution.

Next, we present an example which provides the more general symbolic solution to the two state problem. The statements are the same as before except that **Solve** is used instead of **NSolve**.

```
In[1]:= Clear[s];n=2;v[y_,t_]:=y*y/t;t[i_]=i;
        p[i_]=Binomial[n,i] (s^i) ((1-s)^(n-i));
        lamv=Table[lam[i],{i,1,n}];
        IC=Table[r[i]-v[y[i],t[i]]-r[i-1]+v[y[i-1],
        t[i]],{i,2,n}]; IR={r[1]-v[y[1],t[1]]};
        Constraints=Join[IR,IC];
        Obj=Sum[p[i]*(y[i]-r[i]),{i,1,n}];
        Lagran=Obj+lamv.Constraints;
        Focs=Flatten[Table[{D[Lagran,y[i]]==0,
        D[Lagran,r[i]]==0},{i,1,n}]];
        eqns=Join[Focs,Table[Constraints[[i]]==0,{i,1,n}]]
        Solve[eqns,Flatten[Join[Table[y[i],{i,1,n}],
        Table[r[i],{i,1,n}],Table[lam[i],{i,1,n}]]]]
```

Out[1]:= {2 (1 − s) s − 2 lam[1] y[1] + lam[2] y[1] == 0,

−2 (1 − s) s + lam[1] − lam[2] == 0,

s^2 − lam[2] y[2] == 0,

$-s^2$ + lam[2] == 0,   r[1] − y[1]^2 == 0,

$$-r[1] + r[2] + \frac{y[1]^2}{2} - \frac{y[2]^2}{2} == 0\}$$

Out[1]:=

$$\{\{lam[1] \to (2 - s) \, s, \ lam[2] \to s^2,$$

$$r[2] \to \frac{39 - \dfrac{24}{4 - 3s} + \dfrac{16}{(4 - 3s)^2} - \dfrac{4}{(4 - 3s) \, s}}{54},$$

$$r[1] \to \frac{12 - \dfrac{24}{4 - 3s} + \dfrac{16}{(4 - 3s)^2} - \dfrac{4}{(4 - 3s) \, s}}{27},$$

$$y[2] \to 1, \ y[1] \to \frac{2 - \dfrac{2}{4 - 3s}}{3}\}\}$$

2.3.7 Three States, Binomial, Symbolic Solution.

In this section, we present the symbolic solution to the same problem, but with three states. The solution is more complex, and for more states, *Mathematica* might fail to find a solution. Further, with more states, *Mathematica*'s command **Simplify** does not always reduce the solution to its simplest form. An example of simplification using special rules is described in the last section of this chapter (on non-linear pricing). Another caveat is that sometimes there will be multiple solutions. One should check if they satisfy the second-order conditions, which the reader should be able to develop by analogy to the way FOCs are developed below.

```
In[1]:= n=3;v[y_,t_]:=y*y/t;t[i_]=i;
        p[i_]=Binomial[n,i] (sî) ((1-s)^(n-i));
        lamv=Table[lam[i],{i,1,n}];
        IC=Table[r[i]-v[y[i],t[i]]-r[i-1]+v[y[i-1],
        t[i]],{i,2,n}]; IR={r[1]-v[y[1],t[1]]};
        Constraints=Join[IR,IC];
        Obj=Sum[p[i]*(y[i]-r[i]),{i,1,n}];
        Lagran=Obj+lamv.Constraints;
        Focs=Flatten[Table[{D[Lagran,y[i]]==0,
        D[Lagran,r[i]]==0},{i,1,n}]];
        eqns=Join[Focs,Table[Constraints[[i]]==0, {i,1,n}]]
        Solve[eqns,Flatten[Join[Table[y[i],{i,1,n}],
        Table[r[i],{i,1,n}],Table[lam[i],{i,1,n}]]]]
```

$$Out[1]:=$$

$$\{3\ (1-s)^2\ s\ -\ 2\ lam[1]\ y[1]\ +\ lam[2]\ y[1]\ ==\ 0,$$

$$-3\ (1-s)^2\ s\ +\ lam[1]\ -\ lam[2]\ ==\ 0,$$

$$3\ (1-s)\ s^2\ -\ lam[2]\ y[2]\ +\ \frac{2\ lam[3]\ y[2]}{3}\ ==\ 0,$$

$$-3\ (1-s)\ s^2\ +\ lam[2]\ -\ lam[3]\ ==\ 0,$$

$$s^3\ -\ \frac{2\ lam[3]\ y[3]}{3}\ ==\ 0,$$

$$-s^3\ +\ lam[3]\ ==\ 0,\ \ r[1]\ -\ y[1]^2\ ==\ 0,$$

$$-r[1]\ +\ r[2]\ +\ \frac{y[1]^2}{2}\ -\ \frac{y[2]^2}{2}\ ==\ 0,$$

$$-r[2]\ +\ r[3]\ +\ \frac{y[2]^2}{3}\ -\ \frac{y[3]^2}{3}\ ==\ 0\}$$

$Out[1]:=$

$$\{\{lam[3] \rightarrow s^3, \quad lam[1] \rightarrow s(3 - 3s + s^2),$$

$$lam[2] \rightarrow (3 - 2s)s^2,$$

$$r[3] \rightarrow (636 + \frac{108}{(9 - 8s)^2} - \frac{216}{9 - 8s} -$$

$$\frac{207}{(6 - 9s + 4s^2)^2} +$$

$$\frac{378}{s(6 - 9s + 4s^2)^2} - \frac{540}{6 - 9s + 4s^2} -$$

$$\frac{63}{s(6 - 9s + 4s^2)} + \frac{288s}{6 - 9s + 4s^2}) \ / \ 512,$$

$$r[2] \rightarrow (468 + \frac{324}{(9 - 8s)^2} - \frac{648}{9 - 8s} -$$

$$\frac{207}{(6 - 9s + 4s^2)^2} + \frac{378}{s(6 - 9s + 4s^2)^2} -$$

$$\frac{540}{6 - 9s + 4s^2} - \frac{63}{s(6 - 9s + 4s^2)} +$$

$$\frac{288s}{6 - 9s + 4s^2}) \ / \ 512,$$

$$r[1] \rightarrow (144 - \frac{207}{(6 - 9s + 4s^2)^2} +$$

$$\frac{378}{s(6 - 9s + 4s^2)^2} -$$

Out[1] (cont.)

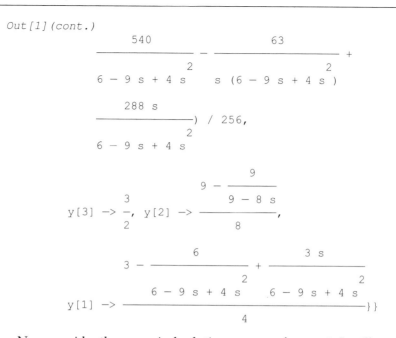

$$\frac{540}{6 - 9\,s + 4\,s^2} - \frac{63}{s\,(6 - 9\,s + 4\,s^2)} +$$

$$\frac{288\,s}{6 - 9\,s + 4\,s^2}) \; / \; 256,$$

$$y[3] \;\rightarrow\; \frac{3}{2}, \quad y[2] \;\rightarrow\; \frac{9 - \dfrac{9}{9 - 8\,s}}{8},$$

$$y[1] \;\rightarrow\; \frac{3 - \dfrac{6}{6 - 9\,s + 4\,s^2} + \dfrac{3\,s}{6 - 9\,s + 4\,s^2}}{4}\}\}$$

Now consider the numerical solution program for $n = 3$. It will work, assuming as before that it is valid to work with a reduced set of constraints. The only difference is the use of **NSolve** rather than **Solve**.

```
In[2]:= n=3; s=.25; v[y_,t_]:=y*y/t;t[i_]=i;
        p[i_]=Binomial[n,i] (sî) ((1-s)^(n-i));
        lamv=Table[lam[i],{i,1,n}];
        IC=Table[r[i]-v[y[i],t[i]]-r[i-1]+v[y[i-1],
        t[i]],{i,2,n}];
        IR={r[1]-v[y[1],t[1]]}; Constraints=Join[IR,IC];
        Obj=Sum[p[i]*(y[i]-r[i]),{i,1,n}];
        Lagran=Obj+lamv.Constraints;
        Focs=Flatten[Table[{D[Lagran,y[i]]==0,
        D[Lagran,r[i]]==0},{i,1,n}]];
        eqns=Join[Focs,Table[Constraints[[i]]==0,{i,1,n}]]
        NSolve[eqns,Flatten[Join[Table[y[i],{i,1,n}],
        Table[r[i],{i,1,n}],Table[lam[i],{i,1,n}]]]]]
```

Out[2]:= {0.421875 − 2 lam[1] y[1] + lam[2] y[1] == 0,

$$-0.421875 + lam[1] - lam[2] == 0,$$

$$0.140625 - lam[2]\ y[2] + \frac{2\ lam[3]\ y[2]}{3} == 0,$$

$$-0.140625 + lam[2] - lam[3] == 0,$$

$$0.015625 - \frac{2\ lam[3]\ y[3]}{3} == 0,$$

Out[2] (cont.)

$$-0.015625 + \text{lam}[3] == 0, \quad r[1] - y[1]^2 == 0,$$

$$-r[1] + r[2] + \frac{y[1]^2}{2} - \frac{y[2]^2}{2} == 0,$$

$$-r[2] + r[3] + \frac{y[2]^2}{3} - \frac{y[3]^2}{3} == 0\}$$

Out[2]:= {{lam[3] -> 0.015625, lam[1] -> 0.578125,

   lam[2] -> 0.15625, r[3] -> 0.993964,

   r[2] -> 0.553913, r[1] -> 0.177979, y[3] -> 1.5,

   y[2] -> 0.964286, y[1] -> 0.421875}}

2.3.8 Using the Single-Crossing Property to Simplify the Problem

We now justify our use of the procedure presented above for $n = 2$ and $n = 3$. A standard result (see for instance [Matthews and Moore 1987] or [Cooper 1984]) is that with appropriate conditions on $v(.,.)$ the only constraints that are binding are $n - 1$ IC constraints where the Agent is indifferent between choosing $\{y[i], r[i]\}$ and $\{y[i-1], r[i-1]\}$ and the IR constraint for the worst state $i = 1$.

Add to these n equations the $2n$ First-Order Conditions on y[i] and r[i] and define lam[i] to be the Lagrange multipliers for the above constraints with lam[1] being the multiplier for the IR constraint, and lam[2],..,lam[i], ..lam[n-1], lam[n] being those for the indifference between declaring the true state $i + 1$ and claiming state i.

The appropriate conditions are essentially the Single-Crossing Property: the indifference curves of lower and higher types should cross only once, and at the point of crossing the indifference curve the higher type should have a steeper slope. With quasilinear preferences, this reduces to requiring that the marginal cost of production will be increasing in the state. A sufficient condition is that the disutility function $V[y, t]$ is **supermodular**: the mixed partial is positive. Generalizations of this are found in [Milgrom and Shannon 1991]. This is also the intuition behind [Spence's 1974] model of signalling and [Mirrlees' 1971] model of optimal taxation.

For the numerical results presented here, either p[i]=1/n i.e. uniform or p[i_]=Binomial[n,i] (s^i)((1-s)^(n-i)); we have not experimented with functional forms other than v[y,t]=1/t y^2 i.e. quadratic. It is important to check that other functional forms that one might use do satisfy the Single-Crossing Property above.

2.4   A Comprehensive Illustration of the Finite Case

At this point load the package

In[1]:= **<<finite.m**

We will assume that there are n states, the default being 5. We will also impose the default that there is a quadratic cost function and a binomial distribution with default parameter 0.6.

Other functions could be chosen if neccessary. OptimalContract[n,p,v,t] finds the optimal wage and output levels and multipliers for a n state problem with distribution p, with disutility function v(y,t(i)) for producing output y in state i. Let's find the solution with the default values, obtained by asking for **OptimalContract[]**. This takes about 14 seconds on a Macintosh IIfx.

2.4.1   The Numerical Solution

In[1]:= **OptimalContract[]**

Out[1]:= {{lam[5] —> 0.07776, lam[4] —> 0.33696,
            lam[3] —> 0.68256, lam[1] —> 0.98976,
            lam[2] —> 0.91296, r[5] —> 1.59399,
            r[4] —> 1.05599, r[3] —> 0.529621,
            r[2] —> 0.12917, r[1] —> 0.00518504,
            y[5] —> 2.5, y[4] —> 1.88679, y[3] —> 1.20603,
            y[2] —> 0.503145, y[1] —> 0.0720072}}

The above list (call it, say, data) captures the solution from the equations for n states. We will first **ListPlot** the data: output y, wages r and multipliers lambda unsmoothed. This plots r[i], y[i], and lam[i] against i, and joins the points using the option.

PlotJoined -> True. This is done to show monotonicities. The way we have set up the problem, lam[1] (i.e. the cost of meeting the IR constraint in the lowest state) is the highest, for if it were not binding all other IC constraints could be relaxed as well by reducing wages by an equal amount in each state. Since the incentive is to underreport the state, the IC constraint is **most binding** in the highest state, so we should expect lam[i] to be decreasing. We would expect outputs and wages to increase with the states, and also rents and profits to be increasing as well as i increases. Also for some specifications, one can show that r will be convex in the states. It is easy to do this with the package loaded.

2.4.2   Graphical Presentations of the Solution

In[1]:= **Graphs[%]**

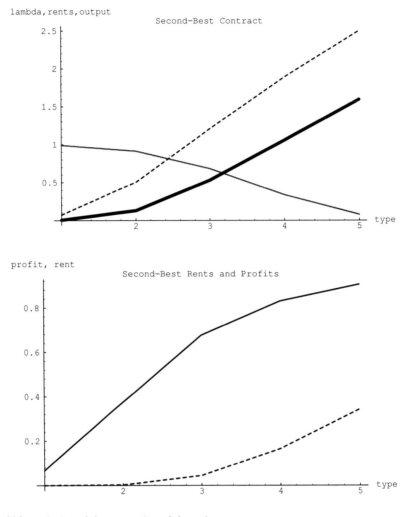

Out[1]:= {-Graphics-, -Graphics-}

From the last graph, one can see that the rents earned by the Agent start from zero and increase in subsequent states. First notice that the only IR constraint which binds is for the first state and all other IR constraints are satisfied. Second notice that the Principal earns positive profits in all states and so would always wish to hire the Agent.

2.4.3   Verifying the Relaxation of the Other Constraints

In the next section, we show that relaxing the program by dropping all constraints other than downward binding incentive compatibility constraints is valid. We present a series of 5 (or more generally n) graphs which show for each state i $(i = 1, \ldots n)$ the utility to the agent from choosing the contract meant for state j $(j = 1, \ldots n)$ i.e. $r[j]-v[y[j]]$. This graph is plateau shaped, and is flat between state $i - 1$ and state i, representing the Downward Binding Adjacent Incentive Compatibility Constraint. Everywhere else it is below the plateau. Thus in state i, the agent's best response is to announce either state i or state $i - 1$. As only these incentives matter, the other constraints can be dropped without loss of generality. We will impose some definitions used in the package: namely

```
In[1]:= data=OptimalContract[]
```

```
Out[1]:= {{lam[5] -> 0.07776, lam[4] -> 0.33696,
          lam[3] -> 0.68256, lam[1] -> 0.98976,
          lam[2] -> 0.91296, r[5] -> 1.59399,
          r[4] -> 1.05599, r[3] -> 0.529621,
          r[2] -> 0.12917, r[1] -> 0.00518504,
          y[5] -> 2.5, y[4] -> 1.88679,
          y[3] -> 1.20603, y[2] -> 0.503145,
          y[1] -> 0.0720072}}
```

and

```
In[2]:= data=Flatten[data/.{"r"->r,"y"->y,"lam"->lam}]
```

```
Out[2]:= {lam[5] -> 0.07776, lam[4] -> 0.33696,
          lam[3] -> 0.68256, lam[1] -> 0.98976,
          lam[2] -> 0.91296, r[5] -> 1.59399,
          r[4] -> 1.05599, r[3] -> 0.529621,
          r[2] -> 0.12917, r[1] -> 0.00518504,
          y[5] -> 2.5, y[4] -> 1.88679,
          y[3] -> 1.20603, y[2] -> 0.503145,
          y[1] -> 0.0720072}
```

The previous statement is needed because labels such as r, y, and lam are defined as **Private** within the package.

```
In[3]:= n=5;v[y_,t_]:=y^2/t;t[i_]:=i;
        rentgraph=ListPlot[Flatten[Table[
            r[i]-v[y[i],t[i]]/.data,{i,1,n}]],
        PlotStyle->Dashing[{.01,.01}],
        PlotJoined->True,
        DisplayFunction->Identity];
```

This generates a plot of how rents vary with states. The next statement finds the maximal rent which will help us scale the graphs when they will be shown together. Notice that the agent's rents, as a function of the true type i, are plateau-shaped, and attain their maximum value at $i - 1$ and i. The graph is flat between these maxima, which causes the downward adjacent incentive compatibility constraints to be binding. To save space, we have included only the graph for type 3, and the one that superimposes all the graphs.

```
In[4]:= rentmax=N[r[n]-v[y[n],t[n]]/.data];
```

```
In[5]:= Show[rentgraph,Table[
        ListPlot[Flatten[Table[(r[j]-v[y[j],t[i]])/.data,{j,1,n}]],
            PlotLabel->StringJoin["Rent if type ",ToString[i],
            " claims to be j"],
            AxesLabel->{"Claim j=1,2...5","Rent"}
            ,PlotJoined->True],{i,1,n}],
        DisplayFunction->$DisplayFunction,
        PlotLabel->"Rents if i claims to be j",
        AxesLabel->{"Claim j=1,2...5","Rent"}]
```

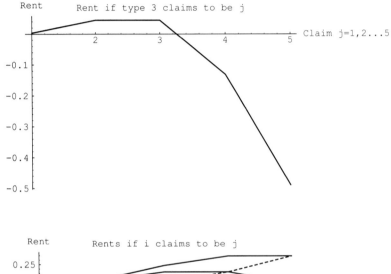

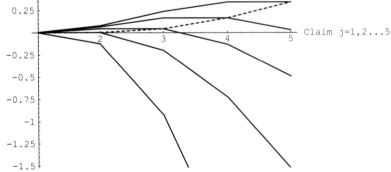

Out[5]:= —Graphics—

One could zoom in on this with the following statement:

```
In[6]:= Show[%,PlotRange->{-.1,rentmax+.1}]
```

The parameters used above are specific to the problem, so some modifications may be needed for another example. This illustrates that the solution we obtained by ignoring the other constraints is feasible.

2.5   Approximating the Continuous Problem through Interpolation

One way to solve a problem where the states are on a continuum is to approximate the solution to the continuous problem by taking the limit of the solution to the discrete problem. Another way is to use interpolation e.g. with polynomials. Even though the above problem does have only five states, one can use *Mathematica's* inbuilt functions to understand the problem with a continuum of states. We will show how the solution to the above problem can be "smoothed", i.e. we will join the discrete points as an approximation to the continuous case. The suffix s (used below for outputs, wages, rents, multipliers, etc.) indicates it is a smoothed value of the variable. In the graph below, we plot rents, outputs and the Lagrange multiplier against the state. The gray line represents multipliers; the dashed one represents output.

```
In[1]:= ys=Interpolation[Flatten[Table[y[i]/.data,{i,1,n}]]];
        rs=Interpolation[Flatten[Table[r[i]/.data,{i,1,n}]]];
        lams=Interpolation[Flatten[Table[lam[i]/.data,{i,1,n}]]];
        Plot[{ys[i],rs[i],lams[i]},{i,1,n},
        AxesLabel->{"type","lambda,rents,output"},
        PlotLabel->"Smoothed Second-Best Contract",
        PlotStyle-> {Dashing[{.01,.01}],Thickness[.01],
        GrayLevel[0.5]}]
```

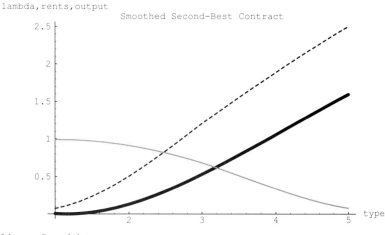

```
Out[1]:= —Graphics—
```

Now that we've seen outputs, wages and lagrange multipliers smoothed, let's view smoothed profits and rents, to confirm whether they are also monotonic with states. Profits are plotted as the plain black line. Rents are represented by the thicker line.

```
In[2]:= Plot[{ys[i]-rs[i],rs[i]-v[ys[i],t[i]]}, {i,1,n},
        PlotStyle->{Dashing[{.01,.01}],Thickness[.01]},
        AxesLabel->{"type",     "profit, rent"},
        PlotLabel->"Smoothed Second-Best Rents and Profits"]
```

profit, rent

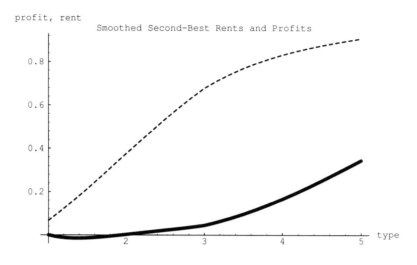

Out[2]:= —Graphics—

In[3]:= **Plot[rs[i]-v[ys[i],t[i]],{i,1,n},**
         AxesLabel->{"type","rents"},
         PlotLabel->"Smoothed Rents a Closer Look"]

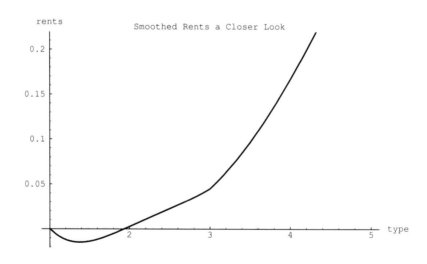

Out[3]:= —Graphics—

This is clearly not right. First, the "smoothed rents" are **decreasing** over a subset of [1,2]! Second, they are actually negative over the same subset. This means that the "smoothed" contract is not individually rational over that region and probably fails to be incentive compatible as well. Therefore one needs to explicitly model the continuous problem which we do in the next section.

2.6   Continuous Screening Problems

2.6.1   Incentive-Compatible Contracts with a Continuum of Types

2.6.1.1   Notation and Discussion

So far we have analysed the case where the agent could be one of finitely many types. We now discuss the case where the Agent's types are represented by a continuum. More specifically, both the Principal and the Agent share common prior beliefs about the Agent's types which are represented by a strictly increasing Cumulative Distribution Function $F(.)$ on an interval $[a, b]$. Denote the density function by $f(.)$. Let t represent the type of the generic agent. Higher types can be thought of as representing more productive agents. Then a contract is a pair of functions $\{y(t), r(t)\}$ where $y(t)$ represents production levels for an agent of type t and $r(t)$ represents the wage of an agent of type t. Let p represent the price of a unit of output. The principal's problem is to design a mechanism, i.e. select a pair of functions $\{y(t), r(t)\}$, so as to maximize $E[p \cdot y(t) - r(t)]$ subject to IR constraints in each state t IC constraints in each state t such that the agent prefers the contract $\{y(t), r(t)\}$ to the contract $\{y(t'), r(t')\}$ for all $t't$

We assume the principal's utility function is defined on output, types and wages and is defined by `Vp[y,t]` $-$ `r`. Similarly we assume the agent's utility is **quasilinear** in transfers $r(.)$ and **separable** in transfers and cost/disutility as `r` $-$ `Va[y,t]`.

Consider a cost function $-V_a(y, t)$ which is typically increasing in output, decreasing in t, and having the property that the marginal cost of production is decreasing in t. (Further restrictions on $-V_a(y, t)$ may be required: for a list of sufficient conditions and more technical details see [Fudenberg and Tirole 1991 p. 263] we use the same notation.) It can be shown that the continuum of IC constraints can be replaced by a single equation IC' defined in terms of the derivative of the agent's indirect utility function. Essentially, the IC constraint is equivalent to monotonicity of $y(t)$ and the monotonicity of the agent's indirect utility in type t. As for the IR constraint, it can be shown that, as for finitely many types, the least productive type will be held to his reservation utility, and the other IR constraints will have slack. One can then substitute IC' into the objective function and solve for the optimal production schedule $y(t)$.

2.6.2   First-best and Second-best Solutions

In the first best, the first-order condition on $y(t)$ will equate `D[Vp[y,t],y]` the marginal benefit of producing an extra unit of output to `D[-Va[y,t],y]` the marginal cost to the Agent of producing the extra unit of output. Private information causes a distortion: typically the agent will tend to understate his productivity to earn rents: this causes the marginal cost of producing the extra unit of output to be overstated to `D[-Va[y,t],y]` + `D[D[Va[y,t],y],t]*(1-F[t])/f[t]`. Thus now $y(t)$ solves

```
D[Vp[y,t],y] + D[Va[y,t],y] == D[D[-Va[y,t],y],t]*(1-F[t])/f[t].
```

The quantity

```
D[-Va[y,t],y] + D[D[Va[y,t],y],t]*(1-F[t])/f[t]
```

is called the marginal virtual cost: the expression `(1-F[t])/f[t]` is called the inverse hazard rate. Note that for the best type $F(t) = 1$ so "there is no distortion at the top". We first solve the program below for the optimal production schedule $y(t)$.

2.6.2.1   An example with the Uniform Distribution

We first set up the uniform distribution on $[a, b]$ and define the inverse hazard rate and the payoffs of the parties. In this example a unit of output sells for twenty dollars; the agent's cost or disutility function is quadratic and is defined by `Va(.,.)`

```
In[1]:=  a=1; b=1+a;
         F[t_]:=(t-a)/(b-a); f[t_]:=Evaluate[D[F[t],t]];
         hazard[t_]:=f[t]/F[t]; invhazard[t_]:=(1-F[t])/f[t];
         Vp[y_,t_]:=20 y; Va[y_,t_]:=-y*y/t;
```

The output of the most productive agent will be undistorted and will equal the first-best level.

```
In[2]:=  undistorted=y[b]==(y/.Solve[D[Vp[y,t],y]+
         D[Va[y,t],y]==0,y][[1]]/.{t->b})
```

```
Out[2]:= y[2] == 20
```

The LHS sets up marginal benefit minus marginal cost. The RHS represents the agent's rents which arise from private information. In the first-best, the distortion is zero and the optimal first-best schedule solves for equality of marginal revenue and marginal cost as above. In the second-best, for all agents other than the most productive agent, there will be a decrease in the level of output compared to the first-best.

```
In[3]:=  LHS[t_,y_]:=D[Vp[y,t],y]+D[Va[y,t],y]
         RHS[t_,y_]:=D[D[Va[y,t],y],t]*(invhazard[t])
         firstbest=Solve[LHS[t,y]==0,y];
         eqns={LHS[t,y]==RHS[t,y]}
         secondbest=Solve[eqns,y];
         schedules=Flatten[{y/.firstbest,y/.secondbest}]
         Plot[Evaluate[schedules],{t,1,2},
           AxesLabel->{"type","output"},
           PlotStyle->{Thickness[.008],Dashing[{.01,.01}]},
           PlotLabel->"First/Second output schedules"]
```

```
Out[3]:=            2 y      2 (2 - t) y
         {20 -  ---   ==  -----------}
                 t             2
                              t
```

```
Out[3]:=              2
         {10 t, 5 t }
```

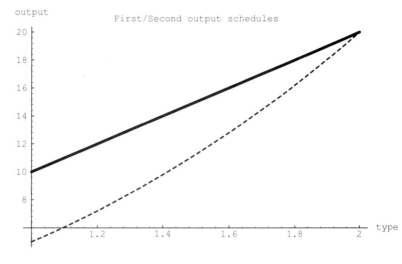

Out[3]:= —Graphics—

Next we calculate the agent's wage as a function of his type, given that the least productive type will be held to his reservation utility and will therefore earn no rents. The first graph is his utility, the second his wage.

```
In[4]:= Ua[t_]:=0+Integrate[D[Va[y,t1],t1]/.
          secondbest, {t1,a,t}]
       Plot[{Ua[t],Ua[t]-Va[y,t]/.secondbest},{t,1,2},
       PlotStyle->{Dashing[{.03,.03}],Thickness[.008]},
       PlotLabel->"Wages and Agent Utility",
       AxesLabel->{"type","utility"}]
```

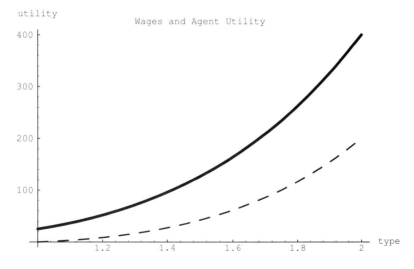

Out[4]:= —Graphics—

One could ask "Can we implement the first-best in an incentive-compatible way"? Yes, but it will be too costly! What is the cost of implementing the first-best output schedule under private information? Agents have incentives to underreport their types: to discourage productive agents from claiming to be less productive, the principal has to compensate them by paying them "informational rents". These rents are so large that it is not optimal to implement the first-best output level under private information.

```
In[5]:= FBUa[t_]:=0+Integrate[D[Va[y,t1],t1]/.firstbest,
        {t1,a,t}]
        Plot[{Ua[t],FBUa[t]},{t,1,2},
        PlotStyle->{Thickness[.003],
            Thickness[.008]},
        PlotLabel->"Agent Utility given FB/SB output",
        AxesLabel->{"type","utility"}
        ]
```

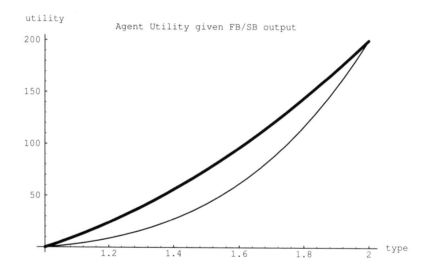

```
Out[5]:= -Graphics-
```

The agent not only produces more than he would have in the "second-best optimum", but also requires a higher utility. Now we wonder if the extra output is worth the extra wages.

```
Plot[{Va[y,t]+Vp[y,t]-Ua[t]/.secondbest,
Va[y,t]+Vp[y,t]-FBUa[t]/.firstbest},
{t,1,2},
PlotLabel -> "Profit under FB/SB outputs",
AxesLabel -> {"type","profit"},
PlotStyle -> {Thickness[.003],Thickness[.008]}
]
```

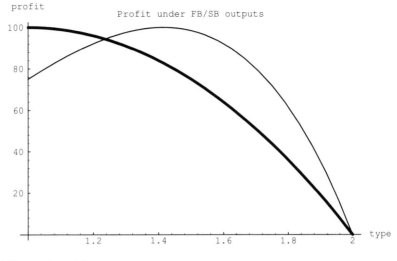

Out[5]:= —Graphics—

The reason why it is not optimal to implement the first-best output schedule in the second-best is that the principal can do better strictly by adjusting the production or output level as well. By asking less productive agents to produce less, he can reduce the attractiveness of underreporting by the more productive agents. So the rents that have to be paid to the more productive agents are reduced and the principal can increase his profits if he uses **both instruments**, wages and outputs, to control the agent rather than if he uses only one, i.e. wages.

Notice from the graph that the profit for lower types is lower in the second-best. This is because higher types must be paid more to discourage them from claiming to be lower types the more lower types are paid. Which has the greater area? Expected profits from implementing the second-best are given first, followed by the expected profit from producing the first-best.

```
In[6]:= {NIntegrate[Flatten[(Va[y,t]+Vp[y,t]-Ua[t])*f[t]
           /.secondbest][[1]],{t,1,2}],
           NIntegrate[Flatten[(Va[y,t]+Vp[y,t]-FBUa[t])*f[t]
           /.firstbest][[1]],{t,1,2}]}
```

Out[6]:= {78.3333, 66.6667}

Next we look at aggregate welfare, which ought to be lower in the second best because of distortions and rents arising from private information.

```
In[7]:= Plot[{(Va[y,t]+Vp[y,t])/.firstbest,
           (Va[y,t]+Vp[y,t])/.secondbest},{t,1,2},
           PlotLabel->"Welfare in FB/SB",
           AxesLabel->{"type","Welfare"},
           PlotStyle->{Thickness[.003],Thickness[.008]}
           ]
```

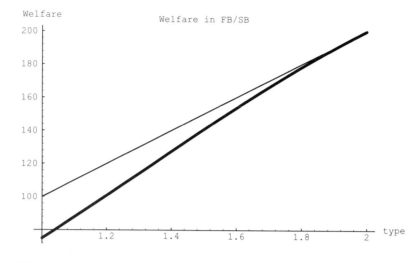

Out[7]:= -Graphics-

How much does the total welfare decrease? The first number is the total welfare in the first-best, the second is the total welfare in the second-best. The difference is the welfare loss from private information.

```
In[8]:= {NIntegrate[Flatten[(Va[y,t]+Vp[y,t])*f[t]/.firstbest][[1]],
        {t,1,2}],
        NIntegrate[Flatten[(Va[y,t]+Vp[y,t])*f[t]/.secondbest][[1]],
        {t,1,2}]}
```

Out[8]:= {150., 139.583}

2.7   Non-linear Pricing with Two Types of Consumers

2.7.1   An Application to Non-linear Pricing

In this section, we present an example of non-linear pricing by a monopolist facing a distribution of consumers. For simplicity we assume consumers can be of two types: high and low, represented by subscripts 2 and 1 respectively. The preferences of a type i consumer for wealth, m, and q units of the good are given by a utility function $U_i(q,m) = t_i V(q) + m_i$ where V is an increasing and concave function and $t_1 > 0$. The two types of consumers differ in the preference parameter which is t_1 for the low type and t_2 for the high type. We assume $t_2 > t_1$, so that the high type consumer values a unit of the good more than the low type consumer. The fraction of t_1 consumers is f, while the fraction of t_2 consumers is $1 - f$. The monopolist can produce the good at constant marginal cost c. The monopolist offers bundles (q_1, p_1) and (q_2, p_2) to the consumers, where a consumer of type i gets quantity q_i and pays the **non-linear price** p_i.

We next introduce the objective function of the monopolist; i.e., he maximizes expected profits subject to constraints on the consumer's selection from the bundles offered to the market. The consumer's type is private information, so the monopolist must price the bundles to prevent t_2 consumers mimicking t_1 consumers (and vice versa, but we know that with Single-Crossing the reverse is not a major problem). This is represented by the IC or incentive compatibility constraints. Consumers will refuse to buy the product if the purchase offers them a negative utility: this is represented by the IR or individual rationality constraints. We assume the reservation utility is zero for both types. It is a standard result that in these models the t_2 consumer earns rents, that $q[2]$ is full-information efficient (first-best), that the t_1 consumer is held to his reservation utility and that $q[1]$ is reduced to make mimicking less attractive to t_2 consumers. The Lagrangean introduces Lagrange multipliers for the Incentive Compatibility constraint for type t_2 and Individual Rationality constraint for type t_1, respectively `lam[2]` and `lam[1]`.

2.7.1.1 Formulation and Solution

```
In[1]:= Profit=f*(p[1]-c q[1]) + (1-f)(p[2]-c q[2]);
        U[q_,m_,i_]:=t[i] V[q] + m;
        IC[i_,j_]:=U[q[i],-p[i],i]-U[q[j],-p[j],i];
        IR[i_]:=U[q[i],-p[i],i];
        Lagrange=Profit+lam[1]*IC[2,1]+lam[2]*IR[1]
Out[1]:= f (p[1] − c q[1]) + (1 − f) (p[2] − c q[2]) +
            lam[2] (−p[1] + t[1] V[q[1]]) +
            lam[1] (p[1] − p[2] − t[2] V[q[1]] + t[2] V[q[2]])
```

We differentiate the Lagrangean with respect to the prices, quantities and the Lagrange multipliers. This yields the binding constraints, and the first-order conditions on the decision variables. Notice that this is in terms of constants such as t_1 and t_2, and also involves functions such as $V(.)$ whose functional form has not yet been specified.

```
In[2]:= Focs=Map[D[Lagrange,#]==0 &,
           {q[1],p[1],q[2],p[2],lam[1],lam[2]}]
Out[2]:= {−(c f) + lam[2] t[1] V′[q[1]] − lam[1] t[2] V′[q[1]]
             == 0,
             f + lam[1] − lam[2] == 0,
             −(c (1 − f)) + lam[1] t[2] V′[q[2]] == 0,
             1 − f − lam[1] == 0,
             p[1] − p[2] − t[2] V[q[1]] + t[2] V[q[2]] == 0,
             −p[1] + t[1] V[q[1]] == 0}
```

We now choose specific parametric values for preferences and restrict the functional form of the agent's utility, in order to get a closed form solution. The set **conditions** represents the specific substitutions to be made in the general **Focs** above. Substituting these we have a set of equations `focs`, whose solution is stored in `ans`.

```
In[3]:= conditions={V->Sqrt,t[1]->2 ,t[2]->5};
        focs=Focs/.conditions
        ans=Solve[focs,{q[1],p[1],q[2],p[2],lam[1],lam[2]}]
```

Out[3]:=
$$\left\{-(c\ f) - \frac{5\ \text{lam}[1]}{2\ \text{Sqrt}[q[1]]} + \frac{\text{lam}[2]}{\text{Sqrt}[q[1]]} == 0,\right.$$

$$f + \text{lam}[1] - \text{lam}[2] == 0,$$

$$-(c\ (1 - f)) + \frac{5\ \text{lam}[1]}{2\ \text{Sqrt}[q[2]]} == 0,$$

$$1 - f - \text{lam}[1] == 0,\ p[1] - p[2] - 5\ \text{Sqrt}[q[1]] +$$

$$5\ \text{Sqrt}[q[2]] == 0,\ -p[1] + 2\ \text{Sqrt}[q[1]] == 0\}$$

Out[3]:=
$$\{\{\text{lam}[2] \to 1,\ \text{lam}[1] \to 1 - f,$$

$$p[2] \to \frac{9 + 10\ f}{2\ c\ f},\ q[2] \to \frac{25}{4\ c},$$

$$p[1] \to \frac{-3 + 5\ f}{c\ f},\ q[1] \to \frac{9 - 30\ f + 25\ f^2}{4\ c^2\ f^2}\}\}$$

2.7.1.2 Simplification and Verification of Assumptions

Given the symbolic solution above, we would like to verify that the constraints that we assumed were binding do in fact hold as equalities, and that there is slack on the other constraints. To do this we need to substitute the solution we obtained above. However *Mathematica* does have some problems in simplifying the complicated expressions, so we have to assign some (problem specific) simplification rules.

```
In[1]:= rules={Sqrt[x_/(c^2 f^2)]->Sqrt[x]/(c f),
          Sqrt[x_^2]->x,Sqrt[x_^(-2)]->1/x,
          Sqrt[(x_)^2/(y_)^2]->x/y,
          Sqrt[x_]:>Sqrt[Factor[x]]};
```

We now use the **rules** to simplify the constraints evaluated at the discriminating solution. Notice that the second and third constraints are binding and the other two have slack, as we assumed. We also evaluate the objective function at the discriminating solution and store the function as Value[c,f]. Also notice the fourth constraint is violated for some positive values of f, e.g. if $5f < 3$.

```
In[2]:= constraints=Chop[Simplify[
          {IC[1,2],IC[2,1],IR[1],IR[2]}/.ans/.
          conditions//.rules]]
```

Out[2]:=
$$\left\{\left\{\frac{9}{2\ c\ f},\ 0,\ 0,\ \frac{3\ (-3 + 5\ f)}{2\ c\ f}\right\}\right\}$$

```
In[3]:= Value[c_,f_]:=Simplify[Profit/.ans]
        Value[c,f]
Out[3]:=   9 - 5 f
        {---------}
          4 c f
```

2.7.1.3 Should the Monopolist Serve the Entire Market?

When is it optimal to not discriminate and serve only the high type?

The above problem was solved assuming an interior solution: that in fact it was optimal to serve both types of customers. If the parameters of the problem are such that an interior solution does in fact exist, then the contract we derived above is the optimal contract.

However it may so happen that an interior solution to the problem does not exist. For instance if there are too few consumers of type t_1, then it might be better for the monopolist to concentrate only on the t_2 segment. In that case the monopolist will offer only one bundle. He will sell the first-best quantity to type t_2 and charge the first-best price. This is because when the market is not "covered", type t_2 has no alternative except to buy from the monopolist. As the monopolist has specifically excluded type t_1 from the market, type t_2 cannot pretend to be type t_1. Thus the monopolist can extract the entire surplus from t_2, and if there are enough t_2 types, that is sufficiently profitable.

It will, of course, never be optimal to serve only the low end of the market. Suppose the monopolist did choose to serve only type t_1. At the margin, selling to a type t_2 would dominate selling to a type t_1. As type t_2 values the good more than a type t_1 consumer, so the monopolist can extract at least as much surplus from type t_2.

Therefore the only relevant decision for the monopolist in deciding whether or not to discriminate between the two types, and if so how to design the contract, is the comparison of two contracting problems: one in which he serves both types, and one in which he serves only the high type. We now present the solution to the latter problem. We first set up the **Profit2** function and form the Lagrangean **Lagrange2** for this problem. The monopolist sells only to the high type t_2, providing quality q[2] for a price p[2].

```
In[1]:= Profit2=(1-f)(p[2]-c q[2]); Lagrange2=Profit2+lam*IR[2]
Out[1]:= (1 - f) (p[2] - c q[2]) + lam (-p[2] + t[2] V[q[2]])
```

Here IR[2] is the Individual Rationality Constraint for type t_2 and lam is the Lagrange multiplier for that constraint. The optimal contract solves the first order conditions **Foc2s** for the specifications **conditions**. We store the solution in **ans2**.

```
In[2]:= Foc2s=Map[D[Lagrange2,#]==0 &, {q[2],p[2],lam}];
        foc2s=Foc2s/.conditions
        ans2=Simplify[Solve[foc2s,{q[2],p[2],lam}]//.rules]
Out[2]:=                       5 lam
        {-(c (1 - f)) + --------------- == 0, 1 - f - lam == 0,
                          2 Sqrt[q[2]]

         -p[2] + 5 Sqrt[q[2]] == 0}
```

$Out[2]:=$

$$\{\{lam \to 1 - f,\ p[2] \to \frac{25}{2\,c},\ q[2] \to \frac{25}{4\,c}\}\}$$

$In[3]:=$ **Value2[c_,f_]:=Simplify[Profit2/.ans2]**
        Value2[c,f]//.rules

$Out[3]:=$ $\{125.\ (1 - f)\}$

Now we verify that for various values of the parameters, one solution form dominates the other. We plot **Value[c,f]** and **Value2[c,f]** as functions of f for a given value of c.

$In[4]:=$ **c=.05; p1=Plot[{Value[.05,f],**
        Value2[.05,f]},{f,.005,.995},PlotRange->{0,150},
        AxesLabel->{"f","Profit"}]

$Out[4]:=$ $-Graphics-$

It might appear that the upper envelope of the curves drawn above represents the value function of the monopolist. That would be so if we ignored feasibility constraints. In particular, when we solved the program under the assumption that both segments of the market were served, we needed to assume that the IR constraint of the high type was not violated. If there are too few t1 types, it will not be optimal for the monopolist to sell to both types. To find the threshold level of low types **fstar** such that it is profitable for the monopolist to offer two commodity bundles, we solve for the point where the two schedules are equal to one another. For the parameters of the problem, **fstar**=0.6. There are two roots to the quadratic. We define the monopolist's profit function to lie along the **Value2** curve for f $<$ **fstar** and along the **Value** curve for f $\geq$ **fstar**. This defines a new function **Value3[c,f]** which is the red curve in the figure.

$In[5]:=$ **fstar=Solve[Value[c,f]==Value2[c,f],{f}]**

$Out[5]:=$ $\{\{f \to 0.6\},\ \{f \to 0.6\}\}$

In[6]:= **Value3[c_,f_]:=Value[c,f] /; f>=(f/.fstar[[1]])**
         Value3[c_,f_]:=Value2[c,f] /; f<(f/.fstar[[1]])

In[7]:= **p2=Plot[Value3[.05,f],{f,0,1},PlotRange->{0,150},**
         PlotStyle->Thickness[.006],AxesLabel->{"f","Profit"}];
         Show[p1,p2]

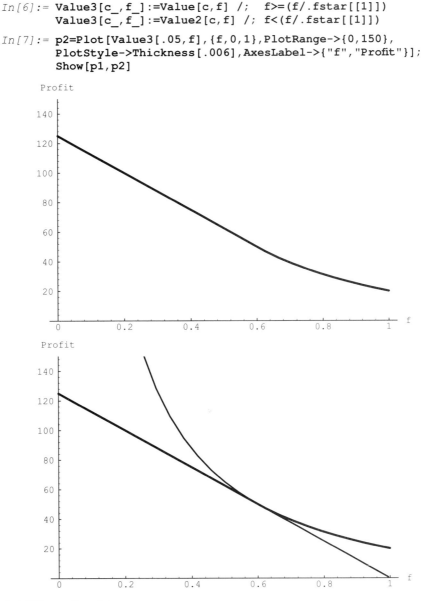

Out[7]:= —Graphics—

To explain exactly what happens in a neighborhood of **fstar**, we will show another graph: this displays the rents of type t_2 from the discriminating contract as f changes. Notice that these are positive only for f > **fstar**, so if f < **fstar**, type t_2 will reject the contract that the monopolist would offer if he planned to serve both types of consumers. So as long as f < **fstar**, the monopolist will have to serve only one section of the market, the high type t_2, and extract the first-best price from them. As f > **fstar**, discrimination becomes a possibility and the monopolist offers two commodity bundles. We derive **fstar** by noting the point where the IR constraint of type t_2 intersects the horizontal axis: a vertical line from there intersects the graph of **value3** where it shifts from the linear function **value2** (one segment) to the curve **value** (two segments).

```
In[8]:= IR2[c_,f_]:=constraints[[1,4]]
```

```
In[9]:= p3=Plot[IR2[.05,f],{f,0.1,.9},
         PlotStyle->Dashing[{.01,.005}],
         AxesLabel->{"f","Rents of t2"}]
```

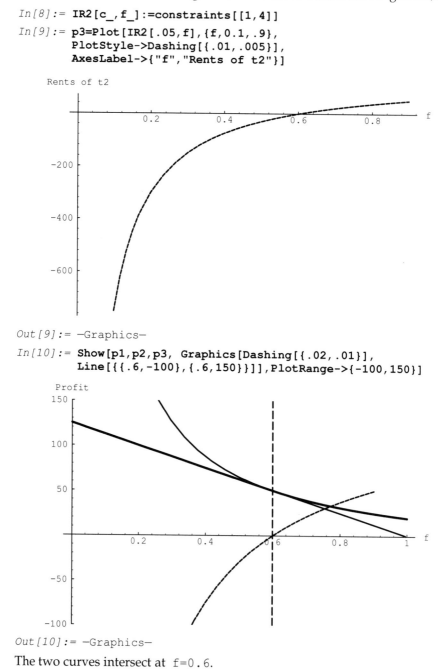

```
Out[9]:= —Graphics—
```

```
In[10]:= Show[p1,p2,p3, Graphics[Dashing[{.02,.01}],
          Line[{{.6,-100},{.6,150}}]],PlotRange->{-100,150}]
```

```
Out[10]:= —Graphics—
```

The two curves intersect at f=0.6.

This concludes the section on Nonlinear Pricing. A more detailed discussion can be found in [Maskin and Riley 1984], [Tirole 1989] or [Wilson 1992, forthcoming].

2.8 References

Cooper, R. "On Allocative Distortions in Problems of Self-Selection." Rand Journal of Economics 1984 15:568–577.

Fudenberg, D. and J. Tirole *Game Theory*. MIT Press 1991.

Maskin, E. and J. Riley "Monopoly with incomplete information." Rand Journal of Economics, 15:171–196 1984.

Matthews, S. and J. Moore "Monopoly Provision of Quality and Warranties: An Exploration in the Theory of Multidimensional Screening" Econometrica 1987 52:441–468.

Milgrom, P. and C. Shannon "Monotone Comparative Statics." Stanford Institute of Theoretical Economics Technical Report May 1991.

Mirrlees, J. "An Exploration in the Theory of Optimal Income Taxes." Review of Economic Studies, 1971 38:175–208.

Myerson, R. "Game Theory" Harvard University Press 1991.

Sappington, D. "Limited Liability Contracts between Principal and Agent." Journal of Economic Theory, 1983 29:1–21.

Spence, A. M. "Job Market Signalling" Quarterly Journal of Economics 1973 87:355–374.

Wilson, R. "Non-Linear Pricing." Electric Power Research Institute, Oxford University Press, NY 1992.

3 Economic Dynamics

John C. Eckalbar

If you had asked an economist twenty years ago to outline the study of dynamics, he or she would probably have said that there are three main questions: existence—does the system have an equilibrium; uniqueness—does it have only one equilibrium; and stability—do all paths converge to the equilibrium as time goes to infinity? Though more exotic questions were raised by some (Goodwin is an example), existence, uniqueness and stability were certainly the basic issues in dynamics. These were, for example, the main questions raised in the famous series of articles from the 1950's by Arrow-Block-Hurwicz-Debru, or one might note the contents of Arrow and Hahn's *General Competitive Analysis*.

Today the questions are much more exotic. Economists are quite likely to find themselves studying systems with multiple equilibria, limit cycles, discontinuous right-hand-sides, and chaotic time paths.

Mathematica can be an invaluable aid in the study of dynamics. As a symbol manipulator, it can help one accurately and quickly move through the necessary algebra and calculus. This affords the investigator the opportunity to ask more questions and to deal with "messier" systems. And as a numerical processor, *Mathematica* can quickly yield phase diagrams or simulated time paths for specific systems. For instance, a 25 MHz 80486 using *Mathematica* 2.0 takes only 2 minutes 15 seconds to compute the first 20000 points visited by a chaotic system. (Figure 7 shows the first 2000 such points.) Again, this gives the researcher a chance to cover much more ground than was possible back in the dark ages (only twenty years ago) of key-punched cards and central main-frame computer centers. And one only has to page through Danby's *Computing Applications to Differential Equations* to see the vast advantage *Mathematica* has over Fortran or Basic as a means of exploring dynamical systems.

In the present chapter, I am interested in displaying a wide range of applications of *Mathematica* techniques useful in the study of dynamical systems. Given the versatility of *Mathematica*, there are often several ways of achieving the same end result. In the following I make no pretense of finding the most efficient method, in fact, if I have a choice, I will give a novel solution (i.e., one that I have not yet described) in place of a more efficient method that has already been covered. This will give the reader exposure to a maximum number of alternative techniques.

Space limitations preclude an exhaustive tutorial on dynamics concurrent with the programming discussions. Some readers may find it handy to keep a copy of Hirsch and Smale or Beltrami nearby for general reference.

3.1 Systems with One Dynamic Variable

3.1.1 Linear Difference Equations

We will begin our exploration by investigating one of the oldest and simplest dynamical systems in economics—the cobweb model. The cobweb model postulates that today's demand depends upon today's price, while today's supply depends upon yesterday's price. (For an elaboration, see Archibald and Lipsey, p. 308. We follow their notation here.) We will suppose that demand at time t is given by $a + b * p(t)$, and supply is $c + d * p(t-1)$. a, b, c, and d are constants. a is negative, and b is positive. If the price at time t adjusts to equate demand at t with supply at t, we have

$$p(t) = \frac{(c-a)}{b} + \left(\frac{d}{b}\right) * p(t-1)$$

In equilibrium, $p = p^* = (c-a)/(b-d)$. If we let $p' = p - p^*$, and define $A = d/b$, then we easily see the following

$$p'(1) = Ap'(0)$$
$$p'(2) = Ap'(1) = A^2 * p'(0)$$
$$\vdots$$
$$p'(t) = A^t * p'(0)$$

where $p'(t)$ is price at time t. It is obvious that $p'(t)$ approaches zero, or p approaches p^*, as t goes to infinity, iff $|A| < 1$.

In *Mathematica*, we can define `p[t_]:=A^t*p0`, where the initial point, `p0`, and A are already given numerically. Then `Table[p[t],{t,0,20}]` will list the first 20 prices following `p0`. Since this constitutes a list, we can get a graphical look at the result by typing `ListPlot[Table[p[t],{t,0,20}],` `PlotJoined -> True]`. It is instructive to note that there are alternative ways of obtaining the same result. For instance, we could define `pt1[pt_]:=A*pt`, which gives the price at time $(t+1)$, i.e., "pt1" as a function of the price at time t, "pt". Then `NestList[pt1,1,20]` will give a list of the first twenty points following the initial point $p = 1$. And **ListPlot** will give a graph of the result. If one wants to experiment with a variety of starting points and time periods, it is handy to create a function which generates graphs without requiring any editing or retyping of previous lines. For instance, cobweb[t_,p0_] := ListPlot[NestList[pt1,p0,t],PlotJoined -> True] will let one simply type cobweb[20,1] to generate a graph like Figure 1, where A has been set to −.7. It is now simple to compare this result with the one we would see if $A = .9$—we simply type A = .9 followed by cobweb[1,20], and then use the **Show** command to superimpose the graphs.

In[1]:= **A=-.7**

Out[1]:= −0.7

In[2]:= **pt1[pt_]:=A*pt**

In[3]:= **cobweb[t_,p0_]:=ListPlot[NestList[pt1,p0,t],**
        PlotJoined->True]

In[4]:= **cobweb[20,1]**

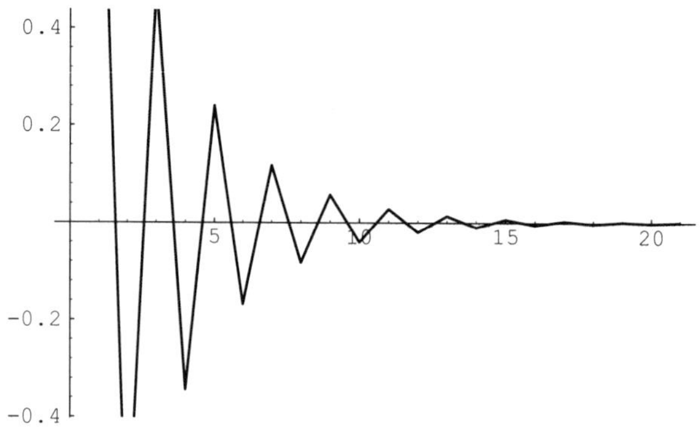

Figure 1

Out[4]:= −Graphics−

Mathematica can also be used to generate the more conventional "cobweb" picture showing price and quantity moving from demand to supply to demand repeatedly in price-quantity space. We illustrate that general method in the following section.

3.1.2 Non-linear Differential Equations in One Variable

The big story in dynamics over the past fifteen years is that incredibly complicated time paths can be created by very simple equations. Systems which have this property are called "chaotic." All of this has its origin in a paper [May, 1976] exploring the simple logistic equation $x(t+1) = w * x(t) * (1 - x(t))$. Already, a number of economic models have been "cut to fit" on this Procrustean bed, with the result that chaos is now a rapidly growing sub-field in economics. (See Baumol and Benhabib for a survey.)

It is very simple to program *Mathematica* to explore the logistic equation. First, we can define a function, f, which gives us $x(t + 1)$ as a function of $x(t)$:

```
f[x_] := w*x*(1 - x)
```

Once we type in a value for parameter w, the following command will give us a graph showing the time path for $x(t)$, with x on the vertical axis and t on the horizontal.

```
pathf[x0_,T_]:=ListPlot[NestList[f,x0,T],PlotJoined->True]
```

An alternative presentation of the system is a graph in $(x(t), x(t + 1))$ space. If we graph f together with a 45 degree line, we can trace out the evolution of $x(t)$ from any starting point. Suppose, for example that

```
w = 3.9; x0=.6
```

Refer to Figure 2. Now x(1) = f[x(0)] = .936, and we can draw in our initial point as (x(0),f[x(0)]) = (.6,.936), which is shown as A in Figure 2. Moving ahead one period in time, we slide to point B with co-ordinates (x(1),x(1)) = (f[x(0)],f[x(0)]) = (.936,.936). Now x(2) = f[x(1)] = f[f[x(0)]] = .233626, and this moves us to point C, which has coordinates (f[x(0)],f[f[x(0)]]) = (.936,.233626). It is handy to be able to trace out the evolution of such a system, with the points A, B, C, . . .connected by line segments. Once we have specified parameter w, the following "logistic" function will accomplish this:

```
logistic[x0_, T_] := Show[Plot[{x, f[x]}, {x, 0, 1}],
ListPlot[Rest[Partition[Flatten[Transpose[{NestList[f, x0, T],
   NestList[f, x0, T]}]], 2, 1]], PlotJoined -> True]]
```

In[1]:= **logistic[.6,3]**

In[2]:= **Show[Graphics[{Text["A",{.6,.936}], Text["B",{.936,.936}],
         Text["C",{.936,.233626}]}]]**

In[3]:= **Show[%,%%]**

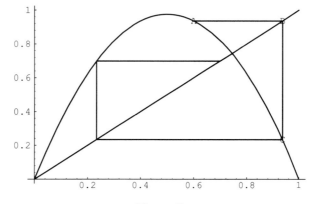

Figure 2

Out[3]:= *−Graphics−*

Now, with parameter w set at 3.9, simply typing `logistic[.6,50]` will cause *Mathematica* to draw a graph (shown here in Figure 3) giving the first 50 points visited after starting at x(0) = .6 with w = 3.9. It is now simple to make rapid explorations of the ways in which the system changes as the parameter w is varied.

In[4]:= **logistic[.6,50]**

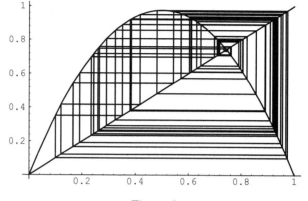

Figure 3

Out[4]:= —Graphics—

An example might best show why this definition for "**logistic**" works. First we set w = 3.9, and note that, for example,

{NestList[f,.6,3],NestList[f,.6,3]}

returns the matrix

{{.6,.936,.233626,.698274}, {.6,.936,.233626,.698274}}.

Now typing Transpose[%] returns

{{.6,.6}, {.936,.936}, {.233626,.233626}, {.698274,.698274}}.

Flatten[%] now gives

 {.6, .6, .936, .936, .233626, .233626, .698274, .698274}

and Partition[%,2,1] yields

{{.6,.6}, {.6,.936}, {.936,.936}, {.936,.233626},
{.233626,.233626}, {.233626,.698724},
{.698724,.6987}}.

Finally, Rest[%] deletes the first item from the previous list. (Wagon, p. 120, was helpful in constructing the logistic function.)

   Looking for two (and, with appropriate modifications, also higher) period cycles in a graph is now as simple as typing Plot[{x,f[x],f[f[x]]},{x,0,1}]. To get numerical values for the x's defining the cycle, one can simply use

`Solve[x==f[f[x]],x]`. For example, with w = 3.43, there is a stable two period cycle with $x(t)$ = .44458, $x(t+1)$ = .846965, and $x(t+2)$ = .44458.

3.1.3 Linear Differential Equations in One Variable

Linear autonomous differential equations of a single variable are easily analyzed with Mathematica. Consider the following differential equation derived from the simple Aggregate Demand plus 45 degree line income/expenditure macro model.

$$\left(\frac{dy}{dt}\right) = k_1(X + c*y - y)$$

where k_1 is the adjustment speed, X is autonomous spending, c is the marginal propensity to consume, and y is national income. We can use the following strategy to find the solution path for y over time, $y[t]$.

In[1]:= **AA=DSolve[{y'[t]==k1(X+c*y[t]-y[t]),y[0]==y0},y[t],t]**

Out[1]:=

$$\{\{y[t] \rightarrow \frac{X}{1-c} + \frac{E^{(-1+c) \ k1 \ t} \ (X - y0 + c \ y0)}{-1+c}\}\}$$

Now we can define the function $y[t]$ with the replacement rule `y[t_]=y[t] /.AA[[1]]`. If we specify numerical values for `k1`, `y0`, `X`, and `c`, then we can plot `y[t]` or obtain `Limit[y[t], t->Infinity]`. It is easy to see that as long as $0 < c < 1$, the limit is the equilibrium value for y, $X/(1-c)$, and that `y[t]` approaches this limit asymptotically.

We dispense with a non-linear differential equation example. Simple cases can be handled with **DSolve** as shown above, and more complicated cases can use **NDSolve**, which will be illustrated below.

3.2 Systems with Two Dynamic Variables

3.2.1 Linear Difference Equations in Two Variables

Suppose we are interested in the following discrete time dynamical system:

`{delta x,delta y} = A.{x,y} + B`

where `delta x` and `delta y` are the first differences in the dynamic variables `x` and `y`, `A` is a real two-by-two parameter matrix, and `B` is a real two-by-one column vector. If the determinant of `A` is non-zero, then the equilibrium for this system exists and is given by (x,y) = `-Inverse[A].B`. Alternatively, one might use `Solve[A.{x,y}+B==0,{x,y}]` to find the equilibrium.

Since `delta x = x(t+1) - x(t)`, the above system could be written as

```
{x(t+1),y(t+1)} = (A + IdentityMatrix[2]).{x(t),y(t)} + B
```

It can be shown that the equilibrium is asymptotically stable if and only if the absolute values of the eigenvalues of $(A + I)$ are less than one. (See Lakshmikantham and Trigiante, p. 93). For a numerical problem, this is easily checked in *Mathematica* by the command

```
Abs[Eigenvalues[(A+IdentityMatrix[2])]].
```

Often we are interested in seeing a graph showing the history of the points visited by the system over time. Does the system follow a "beeline" to the equilibrium, does it spiral in, cycle around, or what? *Mathematica* is also quite adept at displaying the answers to questions like these.

To add interest, consider the following simple IS-LM model.

```
delta y = k1(X + c*y - r*i - y)
delta i = k2(k*y - h*i - M)
```

or

```
{delta y,delta i} = A1.{y,i} + B1
```

where

```
A1={{k1(c-1),-k1*r},{k2*k,-k2*h}}
```

and

```
B1={k1*X,-k2*M}
```

X is autonomous spending, y is income, i is the interest rate, M is the money supply, c, r, k, and h are positive parameters, k1 and k2 are speed of adjustment parameters. (X + c*y - r*i is aggregate demand for goods, k*y - h*i is money demand.)

We can use *Mathematica* to define the IS and LM curves as follows:

```
In[1]:= ISS=Solve[X + c*y - r*i - y== 0,i]
```
```
Out[1]:=              X - y + c y
          {{i -> -------------}}
                       r
```

```
In[2]:= IS[y_]:=i/.ISS[[1]]
```

```
In[3]:= LMM=Solve[k*y-h*i-M==0,i]
```
```
Out[3]:=              -M + k y
          {{i -> -----------}}
                      h
```

```
In[4]:= LM[y_]:=i/.LMM[[1]]
```

One can find the equilibrium values for y and i with either of the following instructions: `-Inverse[A1].B1` or `Solve[A1.{y,i}+B1==0,{y,i}]`.

To get a picture of the dynamics of this system, we will define a function `H[{y,i}]` which gives `{y,i}` at time t+1 as a function of `{y,i}` at time t.

```
H[{y_,i_}]:= (A1+IdentityMatrix[2]).{y,i}+B1
```

The following `path[ ]` function can then be used to generate the first T points visited after a starting point at `{y0,i0}`, e.g., `path[1900,10,100]` gives the first 100 points following an initial value for `y` and `i` (i.e., `y0,i0`) of 1900 and 10, respectively.

```
path[y0_, i0_, T_] := ListPlot[NestList[H, {y0, i0}, T],
   PlotRange -> All, AxesLabel -> {y, i}]
```

Figure 4 was generated using the **Show** command to superimpose `path[1900, 10,100]` over `Plot[{IS[y],LM[y]},{y,1700,2100}]`. (The parameter values are X=400, r=3, c=.8, M=450, h=1, k=.25, k1=.4, k2=.5.)

In[5]:= **X=400; r=3; c=.8; M=450; h=1; k=.25; k1=.4; k2=.5;**

In[6]:= **path[1900,10,100]**

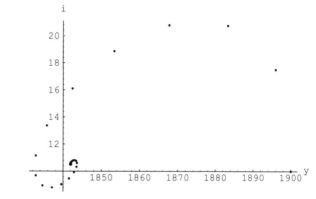

Out[6]:= —Graphics—

In[7]:= **Plot[{IS[y],LM[y]},{y,1700,2100}]**

Out[7]:= —Graphics—

In[8]:= **Show[%,%%]**

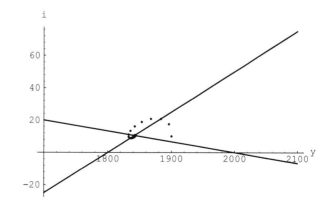

Figure 4

Out[8]:= —Graphics—

3.2.2   Linear Differential Equations

Consider now a continuous time linear differential equation system defined as follows:

```
{x'[t],y'[t]}=Q.{x[t],y[t]}+R
```

Again, the equilibrium is found by `-Inverse[Q].R`. The equilibrium is asymptotically stable iff the real parts of the eigenvalues of `Q` are negative. For any numerical example, one can easily check this in *Mathematica* with the command `Eigenvalues[Q]`. (The eigenvalues reveal much about the nature of the paths of the variables over time: if the eigenvalues are real and negative, the equilibrium is a stable node; if they are real with one positive and one negative, we have a saddle point, if they are complex conjugates with negative real parts, all paths spiral into the equilibrium. See Beltrami p. 21.) But often we are interested in seeing a sketch of the graph of the path itself.

Mathematica's **DSolve** command can be used to generate the desired graphs of trajectories. To illustrate, let

```
In[1]:= Q={{-.4,4},{-2,-.3}}; R={0,0}; x0=y0=1;
```

```
In[2]:= Clear[x,y]
```

The following will give the solution functions x[t] and y[t].

```
In[3]:= aa=DSolve[{x'[t]==-.4x[t]+4y[t],y'[t]==- 2x[t] -.3y[t],
        x[0]==1,y[0]==1},{x[t],y[t]},t]
```

```
Out[3]:=                                  (-0.35 - 2.82799 I) t
        {{x[t] -> (0.5 + 0.698377 I) E                          +

                          (-0.35 + 2.82799 I) t
        (0.5 - 0.698377 I) E                          ,

                          (-0.35 - 2.82799 I) t
        y[t] -> (0.5 - 0.344768 I) E                          +

                          (-0.35 + 2.82799 I) t
        (0.5 + 0.344768 I) E                          }}
```

Now we use the replacement rules `/.` to define the functions x[t] and y[t].

```
In[4]:= x[t_]=x[t]/.aa[[1]]
```

```
Out[4]:=                                  (-0.35 - 2.82799 I) t
        (0.5 + 0.698377 I) E                          +

                          (-0.35 + 2.82799 I) t
        (0.5 - 0.698377 I) E
```

```
In[5]:= y[t_]=y[t]/.aa[[1]]
```

```
Out[5]:=                                  (-0.35 - 2.82799 I) t
        (0.5 - 0.344768 I) E                          +

                          (-0.35 + 2.82799 I) t
        (0.5 + 0.344768 I) E
```

Now the `ParametricPlot` command can be used to display the path of x and y through time.

```
In[6]:= twist =ParametricPlot3D[{t,x[t],y[t]},{t,0,10},
        Boxed->False,BoxRatios->{5,1,1},AxesLabel->{t,x,y}]
```

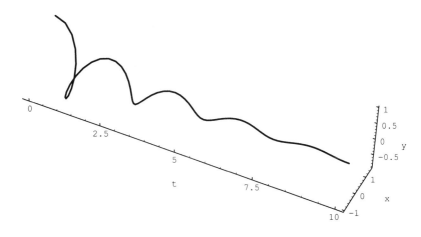

Figure 5

```
Out[6]:= —Graphics3D—
```

It is often convenient to compress or project this graph onto two dimensions— the phase space (x, y). We will once again use the IS-LM example. We now have

```
{y'[t],i'[t]}=A1.{y[t],i[t]} + B1,
```

where A1 and B1 are as defined above.

Again, we can use *Mathematica*'s **DSolve** routine to obtain explicit solutions for y[t] and i[t] under the various parameter assumptions. We use

```
In[7]:= Short[ans2=DSolve[{y'[t]==k1(X+(c-1)y[t]-r*i[t]),
        i'[t]==k2(k*y[t]-h*i[t]-M),y[0]==y0,
        i[0]==i0},{y[t],i[t]},t]]
```

```
Out[7]:= {{y[t] —> (1.84376 + <<1>>) <<2>>, <<1>>}}
```

Now to generate the y[t] and i[t] functions we use the replacement rule "/." as follows.

```
In[8]:= Short[y[t_]=y[t]/.ans2[[1]]]
```

```
Out[8]:=                              -16
           (1.84376 + 2.22045 10    I) <<2>>
```

```
In[9]:= Short[i[t_]=i[t]/.ans2[[1]]]
```

```
Out[9]:= (0.5 + 0.322657 I) <<1>> (—326.705 + <<1>> + <<6>>)
```

With these functions we might check `Limit[y[t],t->Infinity]` and `Limit[i[t],t->Infinity]` to explore convergence. Or to get a picture of a trajectory coming from some specific point, we might specify, for example, `i0=15` and `y0=1800` and then use **ParametricPlot** as follows:

`ParametricPlot[{y[t],i[t]},{t,0,20}].`

One can also type

`<<Graphics'PlotField'`

to input a package which can draw a vector field for this system. Then the command `pvf = PlotVectorField[{k1(X+(c-1)y-r*i),k2(k*y-h*i-M)},{y,1780,1900},{i,0,20}]` will generate a graph of the vector field in `(y,i)`-space. Figure 6, which gives a fairly complete picture of the dynamics around the equilibrium, was generated using **ParametricPlot**, **PlotVctorField**, **Plot[IS[y],LM[y],y,1780,1900]**, and **Show[ ]**.

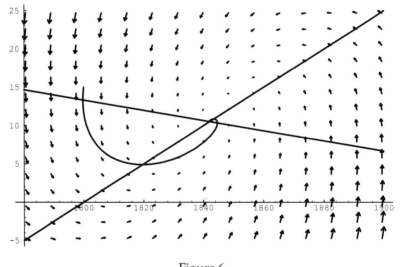

Figure 6

3.2.3 Non-linear Difference Equations in Two Variables

Here is a piecewise linearized difference equation version of a problem which arises in a wide class of disequilibrium economic models. (See Eckalbar 1980 for details on why this problem arises.)

```
{x(t+1),y(t+1)} =  MA.{x(t),y(t)}, if y(t) > m*x(t) + e
{x(t+1),y(t+1)} =  MB.{x(t),y(t)}, if y(t) <= m*x(t) + e,
```

where `MA` and `MB` are distinct real two by two matrices, `m` and `e` are scalars. The locus `y = m*x + e` is called the "switching line". If the point `{x,y}` is above the line, the movement of the system is governed by `MA`, otherwise the system is driven by MB. The system is non-linear, though piecewise linear. A differential equation version of the problem has received considerable attention (see Varian (1977), Eckalbar (1980), Honkapohja and Ito (1983), for instance), but the difference equation version remains relatively unexplored. (Brief history: Simonovits (1982) conjectured that chaos might be an outcome, Hommes and Nusse showed that in certain cases this may not be so. Tim Poston using a program known as "Kaos" written by Guckenheimer and Kim demonstrated in a private correspondence to the author that it could. The following owes much to Poston.) We set up *Mathematica* as follows:

```
In[1]:= MA={{.8,-.4},{.7,.5}}; MB={{.7,-1},{.9,.8}};
        m=-1; e=1; size=.005;
        q[{x_,y_}]:=If[y>m*x + e, MA.{x,y},MB.{x,y}]
        graph[x_,y_,T_]:=ListPlot[NestList[q,{x,y},T],
        PlotRange->All,
        Prolog->PointSize[size]]
        graph2[x_,y_,T_]:=ListPlot[NestList[q,{x,y},T],
        PlotRange->All,
        PlotJoined->True]
```

The function graph[1,2,3], for instance, shows the points visited over 3 periods with initial point at {1,2}, while graph2[ ] connects the points. Figure 7 was generated by graph[0,2,2000], with MA, MB, m, and e as shown above.

```
In[2]:= graph[0,2,2000]
```

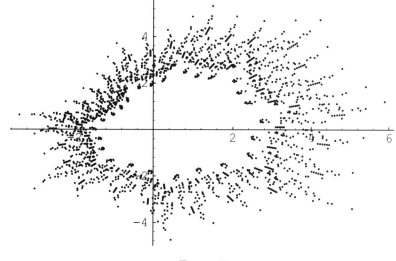

Figure 7

```
Out[2]:= —Graphics—
```

Figure 8, produced by graph2[ ] shows the counter-clockwise flow of the first 200 points. The pattern is clearly chaotic.

In[3]:= **graph2[0,2,200]**

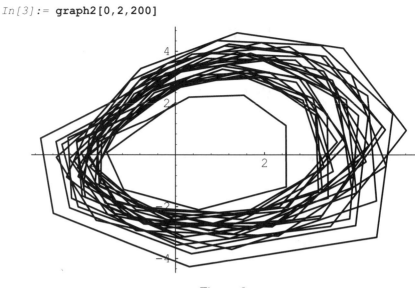

Figure 8

Out[3]:= —Graphics—

We seem to get this result because the equilibrium {0,0} is on the lower side of the switching line, where the system is driven by MB. And MB is unstable (check this with Abs[Eigenvalues[MB]]). The flow from MB produces a counter-clockwise spiral away from the origin. But once the path crosses the switching line, MA takes over and pushes the variables back toward equilibrium and across the switching line once again, whereupon the pattern can repeat—apparently indefinitely—neither converging to the origin, nor escaping a bounded set. Here we find chaos arising naturally from the switching problem inherent in disequilibrium. This is novel.

The general technique of defining functions like q[ ] above to deal with dynamical systems with discontinuous right-hand sides works well even with fairly complex cases. We illustrate with a more difficult inventory model due to Honkapohja and Ito, Simonovits, and further explored by Hommes and Nusse. Labor, L, is supplied in fixed quantity, d. Current output is given by delta*L. Current demand for goods is a + b*L(t), with a > 0, b => 0, and delta > b. Desired inventory holding by firms is beta*[a + b*L(t-1)], i.e., it is a multiple of last period's sales. Firms hire labor (up to a maximum of d) on the basis of expected sales and current inventory levels, I(t). Inventory change is governed by the difference between current output and actual sales. We have the following dynamical system: (See Hommes and Nusse p. 162, and for a continuous time version see Eckalbar, 1985.)

```
L(t+1)  =    0, if I(t)>=(beta+1)[a+b*L(t)]=I1(t)
L(t+1)  =    [(beta+1){a+b*L(t)}-I(t)]/delta, if I2(t)<=I(t)<=I1(t)
```

```
L(t+1) =    d, if I(t)<=I1(t)−delta*d=I2(t)
I(t) =      I(t) − a, if L(t+1) = 0
I(t) =      [b(beta+1){(delta−b)L(t)−a}+b*I(t)+a*beta*delta]/
                delta,   if 0<L(t+1)<d
I(t) =      I(t)+(delta−b)d−a, if L(t+1)=d
```

The following *Mathematica* code sets up the system for simulation:

```
In[4]:= beta = 0.3; a=8; b=9; delta=10; d=10; thick=.0002;
        size=.005;
        NI[L_, I_] := Which[I >= (beta + 1)*(a + b*L), I - a,
        (beta + 1)*(a + b*L) - delta*d <= I<=(beta+1)*(a + b*L),
        (b*(beta + 1)*((delta - b)*L - a) + b*I + a*beta*delta)/
        delta, I <= (beta + 1)*(a + b*L) - delta*d,
        (I+ (delta - b)*d) - a]

        NL[L_, I_] := Which[I >= (beta + 1)*(a + b*L), 0,
        (beta + 1)*(a + b*L) - delta*d <= I
        <= (beta+1)*(a + b*L), ((beta + 1)*(a + b*L) - I)/delta,
        I <= (beta + 1)*(a + b*L) - delta*d, d]

        F[{L_, I_}] := {NL[L, I], NI[L, I]}

        trail[I_, L_, T_] := ListPlot[NestList[F, {I, L}, T],
        Prolog->PointSize[size], PlotRange->All,
        AxesLabel -> "I","L"]

        trail2[I_, L_, T_] := ListPlot[NestList[F, {I, L}, T],
        Prolog -> Thickness[thick], PlotRange -> All,
        AxesLabel -> {"I","L"}, PlotJoined -> True]

In[5]:= trail2[8,24.5,200]
```

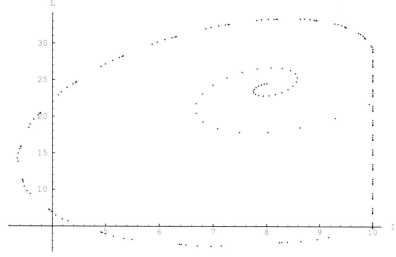

Figure 9

Figure 9 was generated using `trail[8,24.5,200]`, i.e., it shows the first 200 points visited after the initial point `{I,L} = {8,24.5}`. The result may appear to be convergence to a chaotic-looking quasi-cycle; but as Hommes and Nusse shows, we have a 28 period cycle. We can verify this by noting that `NestList[F,{10,28.7902},28]` returns the point `{10,28 .7902}`, that is, there is a 28 period cycle through the point `{10,28.7902}`.

3.2.4   Non-linear Differential Equations in Two Variables

Consider the following Van der Pol system (See Beltrami, p. 149):

$$\frac{dx}{dt} = x' = -y$$

$$\frac{dy}{dt} = y' = x - e\left(\frac{y^3}{3} - m*y\right)$$

where parameter e is taken to be positive and m is yet to be discussed. (Goodwin's famous model is of this general type, see also Lorenz, 1987.)   If we define `v={-y,x-e(y^3/3-m*y)}`, then `Jac[v_]:= Transpose[{D[v,x],` `D[v,y]}]` defines the Jacobian of v. (An equivalent instruction is `Jac[v_]:=` `Outer[D,v,{x,y}].`)   Clearly $x = y = 0$ is the unique equilibrium for this system, and at this point, the Jacobian is `{{0,-1},{1,e*m}}`.

`Determinant[Jac]=1` and `Trace(Jac)=Sum[Jac[[i,i]],{i,2}]` `=e*m`. Now with $e > 0$, local stability of the system depends critically upon the sign of m. It turns out (see Beltrami, p. 149ff) that for $0 < m < 1$, there is a stable limit cycle surrounding the origin. We can employ **NDSolve** to get a picture of this limit cycle. We set `e = 1` and `m = .5` and then define `sol` and use **ParametricPlot** to get a picture of the path coming out of the point $(2,2)$. Figure 10 shows this path plus another coming out of the point $(.01,.01)$. The stable limit cycle is clearly visible.

```
In[1]:= e=1;m=.5;
```

```
In[2]:= Clear[x,y]
```

```
In[3]:= sol=NDSolve[{x'[t]==-y[t],
        y'[t]==x[t]-e((y[t]^3)/3-m*y[t]),
        x[0]==2,y[0]==2},{x,y},{t,20}]
```

```
Out[3]:= {{x -> InterpolatingFunction[{0., 20.}, <>],
          y -> InterpolatingFunction[{0., 20.}, <>]}}
```

```
In[4]:= ParametricPlot[Evaluate[{x[t],
        y[t]}/.sol],{t,0,20},
        PlotRange->All]
```

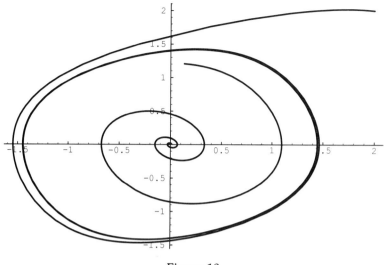

Figure 10

3.3 Three Dimensional Systems

We will illustrate the study of three dimensional problems with a look at the
Lorenz system: (See Holden, p. 19ff.)

$$x' = -s*x + s*y$$
$$y' = -x*z + p*x - y$$
$$z' = x*y - u*z$$

Parameters s, p, and u are set at 10, 60, and 8/3, respectively. The following
NDSolve expression will generate solutions for x[t], y[t], and z[t], given
initial values for x0, y0, and z0 of $(1, 1, 1)$. And then **ParametricPlot** will
will give a three-D view of the path of the system, shown here in Figure 11.

```
In[1]:= {s,p,u}={10,60,8/3}
```

```
In[2]:= Clear[x,y]
```

```
In[3]:= sol2=NDSolve[{x'[t]==-s*x[t]+s*y[t],
        y'[t]==-x[t]*z[t]+p*x[t]-y[t],
        z'[t]==x[t]*y[t]-u*z[t],x[0]==1,
        y[0]==1,z[0]==1},{x,y,z},{t,5}]
```

```
Out[3]:= {{x -> InterpolatingFunction[{0., 3.36044}, <>],
          y -> InterpolatingFunction[{0., 3.36044}, <>],
          z -> InterpolatingFunction[{0., 3.36044}, <>]}}
```

```
In[4]:= ParametricPlot3D[Evaluate[{x[t],y[t],z[t]}/.sol2],{t,0,3.3}
        PlotPoints->1000,PlotRange->All,
        AxesLabel->{"x","y","z"}]
```

```
Out[4]:= —Graphics3D—
```

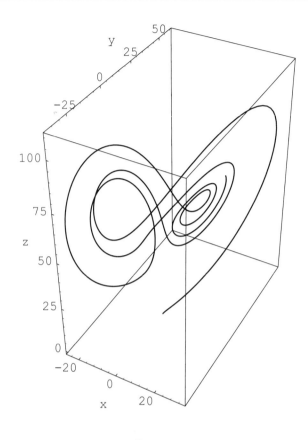

Figure 11

Out[4]:= −Graphics3D−

Experiments with **ViewPoint** can then display the system from a variety of angles. Or if we type <<Graphics `Graphics3D` to load a graphics package, we can then use Show[Project[%XX,{a,b,c}]] to project the three-D image onto two dimensions. (The "XX" term would be the output line on which the 3-D graph was displayed, and the plane of projection is normal to a line from the center of the %XX object to the point {a,b,c}.) Experiments with {a,b,c} will afford one a variety of views of the trajectory.

If we define Lor={-10x + 10y, -x*z + 60x - y, x*y -8/3z}, then Solve[Lor=={0,0,0},{x,y,z}] returns three equilibrium points—{0,0,0}, {12.5433,12.5433,59}, and {-12.5433,-12.5433,59}. The Jacobian for the system is JL=Transpose[{D[Lor,x],D[Lor,y],D[Lor,z]}]. Setting {x,y,z} equal to the three equilibrium values in turn while checking Eigenvalues[JL] shows that all three of the equilibria are locally unstable. It can be shown (see Sparrow, Appendix c) that all trajectories for the Lorenz system are bounded, so there is a trapping region containing the three unstable equilibria—hence the endless flow around the equilibria without convergence.

3.4 Lyapunov Functions

Finding a Lyapunov function is more a matter of intuition, perseverence, and luck than of science. Though *Mathematica* cannot constructively find Lyapunov functions, it can make it relatively painless to check candidates. For example, one might define

```
In[1]:= V[x_,y_]:=x^2 + y^2/W
```

For positive values of `W`, the level sets of `V` will be elipses around the origin, whose shapes can be "tuned" by the `W` parameter. Now if we have a dynamical system `ss = {dx/dt,dy/dt}`, then `dV/dt ={D[V[x,y],x], D[V[x,y],y]}.ss`. We can then specify a value for `W` and use

```
In[2]:= Vdot = Simplify[{D[V[x,y],x],D[V[x,y],y]}.ss]
```

```
Out[2]:=        2 y
          {2 x, ---} . ss
                 W
```

to compute the time derivative of `V`. For example, let

```
In[3]:= ss = {-x -y,x - y^3}
```

Now we need only type `Vdot` to check the sign of the change in `V`:

```
In[4]:= Vdot
```

```
Out[4]:=                          3
                        2 y (x - y )
          2 x (-x - y) + ------------
                              W
```

We note that if `W = 1`, this reduces to `-2(x^2 + y^4)`, which is negative. Hence, we have a Lyapunov function for this system whenever `W = 1`.

Here is another example. This time we let

```
In[5]:= ss = {-y,x + y - y^3/3}
```

```
In[6]:= Vdot
```

```
Out[6]:                          3
                                y
                      2 y (x + y - ---)
                                   3
          -2 x y + -------------------
                            W
```

With `W = 1` we have `Vdot = 2y^2(3 - y^2)/3`. Now for all `y < Sqrt[3]`, `Vdot` is positive. This shows the local instability of the origin. Results such as this are used to clarify behavior of van der Pol systems. We give a final example:

```
In[7]:= ss = {-x+2y,-4x-y}
```

```
Out[7]:= {-x + 2 y, -4 x - y}
```

We now have a Lyapunov function whenever `W = 2`. To further explore this system, we load the following package and display the vector field.

```
In[8]:= <<Graphics`PlotField`
In[9]:= PlotVectorField[{-x+2y,-4x-y},{x,-4,4},
        {y,-5,5},DisplayFunction->Identity]

Out[9]:= —Graphics—
```

Now we can use **ContourPlot** to look at the level curves of V.

```
In[10]:= ContourPlot[x^2+y^2/2,{x,-4,4},{y,-5,5},
         ContourShading->False,DisplayFunction->Identity]

Out[10]:= —ContourGraphics—

In[11]:= Show[%,%%,DisplayFunction->$DisplayFunction]
```

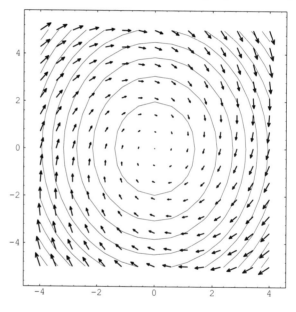

Figure 12

```
Out[11]:= —Graphics—
```

Figure 12 seems to verify the one way flow across these level curves.

3.5   Catastrophe

In this section we show how the **ParametricPlot** command can be used to generate a picture of the cusp catastrophe discussed in Varian (1979). The reader is referred to Varian for details. The **II[ ]** function shows investment, II, to be dependent upon current income, Y, and the level of the capital stock, K. The II function is sigmoid over the relevant range. Both the `mpc` and the consumption function intercept, **dd[ ]**, are functions of the level of wealth, `W`.

The **Solve** command is used to derive a function `K[Y,W]` giving, for each `(Y,W)` pair, the level of `K` at which savings, `S`, equals investment, `II`. Finally, **ImplicitPlot** is used to show the locus of `(K,Y,W)` points at which `S=II`. The cusp is clearly visible in Figure 13.

```
In[1]:= II[Y_,K_]:=(-.1Y^3+50Y^2+100Y)/
            10000-.25K+500
```

```
In[2]:= mpc[W_]:=W/(100+W)
```

```
In[3]:= dd[W_]:=5W/(10+W)
```

```
In[4]:= S[Y_,W_]:=Y-mpc[W]*Y-dd[W]
```

```
In[5]:= Solve[S[Y,W]==II[Y,K],K]
```

$$Out[5]:=$$
$$\{\{K \to -((-500000. - 55500.\ W - 505.\ W^2 + 990.\ Y +$$
$$98.9\ W\ Y - 0.01\ W^2\ Y - 5.\ Y^2 - 0.55\ W\ Y^2 -$$
$$0.005\ W^2\ Y^2 + 0.01\ Y^3 + 0.0011\ W\ Y^3 +$$
$$0.00001\ W^2\ Y^3)$$
$$/\ (250. + 27.5\ W + 0.25\ W^2))\}\}$$

```
In[6]:= K[Y_,W_]=K/.%[[1]]
```

$$Out[6]:=$$
$$-((-500000. - 55500.\ W - 505.\ W^2 + 990.\ Y +$$
$$98.9\ W\ Y - 0.01\ W^2\ Y - 5.\ Y^2 - 0.55\ W\ Y^2 -$$
$$0.005\ W^2\ Y^2 + 0.01\ Y^3 + 0.0011\ W\ Y^3 + 0.00001\ W^2\ Y^3)$$
$$/\ (250. + 27.5\ W + 0.25\ W^2))$$

```
In[7]:= ParametricPlot3D[{K[Y,W],W,Y},{W,0,500},{Y,-300,700},
        BoxRatios->{3,3,1},
        Boxed->False,
        AxesLabel->{"K","W","Y"},
        ViewPoint->{1.3,-2.4,1}]
```

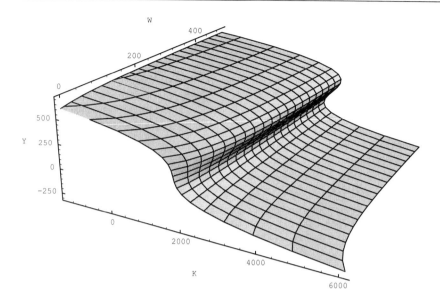

Figure 13

Out[7]:= —Graphics3D—

The full dynamics of the system is not radically different from that of the Lorenz model, so we will dispense with a further analysis.

3.6   Conclusion

Fifty years of econometrics has not revealed much about the true form (linear, cubic, logarithmic,. . .) of the economy's underlying dynamic equations, let alone about the numerical values of the parameters in such equations. Given our curent level of ignorance, it seems desirable to explore a vast range of plausible dynamic systems in order to gain an appreciation for the often bizarre behaviors that complex systems are capable of exhibiting. The purpose of this chapter is to demonstrate that Mathematica can be an invaluable aid in this inquiry.

3.7   References

Archibald, G. and R. Lipsey, *An Introduction to Mathematical Economics*, Harper and Row, New York, 1976.

Arrow, K. and F. Hahn, *General Competitive Analysis*, Holden-Day, San Francisco, 1971.

Baumol, W. and J. Benhabib, "Chaos: Significance, Mechanism, and Economic Applicationss," *Journal of Economic Perspectives*, Vol 3 No. 1, Winter, 77–106, 1989.

Beltrami, E., *Mathematics for Dynamic Modeling*, New York, Academic Press, 1987.

Danby, M., *Computing Applications to Differential Equations*, Reston Publishing, Reston, VA, 1985.

Eckalbar, J. "The Stability of Non-Walrasian Processes: Two Examples," *Econometrica*, **48**, 371–386, 1980.

Eckalbar, J., "Inventory Fluctuations in a Disequilibrium Macro Model," *Economic Journal*, 95, pp. 976–991, Dec. 1985.

Goodwin, R., "The NonLinear Accelerator and the Persistence of Business Cycles," *Econometrica* **19**, 1–17, 1951.

Hirsch, M. and S. Smale, *Differential Equations, Dynamical Systems, and Linear Algebra*, New York: Academic Press. 1974.

Holden, A. *Chaos*, Princeton: Princeton Univ. Press, 1986.

Hommes, C. and H. Nusse, "Does an Unstable Keynesian Unemployment Equilibrium in a non-Walrasian Dynamic Macroeconomic Model Imply Chaos?," *Scandinavian J. of Economics* **91** (1), pp. 161–167, 1989.

Honkapohja, S. and T. Ito, "Stability with Regime Switching," *Journal of Economic Theory*, 29, p. 22–48, 1983.

Honkapohja, S. and T. Ito, "Inventory Dynamics in a Simple Disequilibrium Macroeconomic Model," *Scandinavian Journal of Economics* **82**, pp. 184–198, 1980.

Lakshmikantham, V. and D. Trigiante, *Theory of Difference Equations*, Boston, Academic Press, 1987.

Lorenz, H. "Goodwins non-linear accelerator," *J. of Economics*, Vol. 47, No. 4, p. 413–418, 1987.

May, R. M., "Simple Mathematical models with very Complicated Dynamics," *Nature*, **261**, pp. 459–467, 1976.

Simonivits, A. "Buffer Stocks and Naive Expectations in a non-Walrasian Dynamic Macro-Model," *Scandinavian Journal of Economics*, **82**, p. 569–581, 1982.

Sparrow, C., *The Lorenz Equations*, New York: Springer-Verlag, 1982.

Varian, H., "Non-Walrasian Equilibria," *Econometrica* **45**, p. 573–590, 1977.

Varian, H. "Catastrophe Theory and the Business Cycle," *Economic Inquiry*, **17,1**, Jan. 1979, pp. 14–28.

Wagon, S. *Mathematica in Action*, New York, W. H. Freeman, 1991.

4 Perturbation Solution Methods for Economic Growth Models

Kenneth L. Judd and Sy-Ming Guu

4.1 Introduction

Economic growth is one of the most important macroeconomic phenomena. With economic growth comes the possibility of improving the living standards of all in a society. Economic growth has been studied by all generations of economists. Economists have used optimal control theory and dynamic programming to formalize the study of economic growth, yielding many important insights. Unfortunately, most of these methods are generally qualitative and do not yield the kind of precise quantitative solutions necessary for econometric analysis and policy analysis.

There are many ways to compute numerical solutions to economic growth models; see Taylor and Uhlig (1990) and Judd (1991) for a discussion of standard numerical analytic methods applied to a simple stochastic growth model. In this paper, we will focus on solutions arising from perturbation methods. Perturbation methods are distinct from standard numerical analytic procedures in that they use algebraic manipulations of equilibrium equations to derive information about a solution at a point, producing a local solution. In contrast, numerical analytic procedures take a more global approach, using information about the solution at several points and linking that information to form an approximate solution. The advantage of perturbation solutions is that they produce solutions which are, in some sense, the best possible near some point, and can be quickly computed. The supposed weakness of perturbation methods is that their quality falls as one moves away from the starting point. We will show how to compute perturbation solutions in simple growth models, and demonstrate that they often produce approximate solutions of high quality globally.

This chapter will examine methods based on the analyses of Bensoussan, Judd, and Judd and Guu; the reader should see those papers for the formal mathethematical results which underly the formal procedures described below. Section 4.2 will discuss both Taylor series and Padé approximation methods.

Section 4.3 will outline a simple optimal growth model in continuous time, show how to produce perturbation solutions, and discuss a way to evaluate their quality. Section 4.4 extends the continuous-time analysis to uncertainty and section 4.5 applies the same method to a discrete-time optimal growth model. While perturbation methods can be used for a much wider variety of models, these examples provide a good introduction to the techniques.

4.2 Approximations

Perturbation methods of approximation begin by computing a function and its derivatives at a point. We should therefore begin with a discussion of approximation methods based on such information. If we have a function, $f(x)$, and we want to study it near the point x_0, we compute f and several of its derivatives at x_0, and then use this information to construct good approximations for f in the neighborhood of x_0. We only assume that these derivatives exist. We will discuss two basic methods using this point-based information: Taylor series and Padé approximants.

4.2.1 Taylor Series Approximations

The most basic local approximation method is based on Taylor's Theorem:
Taylor's Theorem: If $f \in C^{n+1}[a, b]$ and x, $x_0 \in [a, b]$, then

$$f(x) = f(x_0) + (x - x_0) f'(x_0) + \frac{(x - x_0)^2}{2} f''(x_0)$$

$$+ \cdots + \frac{(x - x_0)^n}{n!} f^{(n)}(x_0) + R_{n+1}(x)$$

where

$$R_{n+1}(x) = \frac{1}{n!} \int_{x_0}^{x} (x - t)^n f^{(n+1)}(t) \, dt$$

$$= \frac{(x - x_0)^{(n+1)}}{(n + 1)!} f^{(n+1)}(\xi),$$

for some ξ between x and x_0.

A Taylor series approximation of $f(x)$ based at x_0 is the degree n polynomial in Taylor's Theorem. It uses only derivative information at x_0 and the error of this approximation is proportional to the $n + 1$'th derivative of f and

$$\frac{(x - x_0)^{(n+1)}}{(n + 1)!}.$$

It is therefore valid to a high order near x_0, and asymptotically exact if f is an analytic function. Generally, this approximation is good only near x_0 and decays rapidly away from x_0. The hope is that we are only interested in values of x sufficiently close to x_0 or that we are "lucky" and the approximation is good away from x_0.

4.2.2   Padé Approximations

Taylor series approximations construct a polynomial to approximate f. An alternative way to use the same information is to construct a rational function, that is, a ratio of two polynomials, which agrees with f and its first n derivatives at x_0. The basic rational approximation method based at a point is called *Padé Approximation*.

The (m, n) Padé approximant of f at x_0 is a rational function

$$r(x) = \frac{p(x)}{q(x)}$$

where $p(x)$ and $q(x)$ are polynomials, the degree of p is m, the degree of q is n, and

$$\frac{d^k}{dx^k}(p - f\,q)(x_0), \quad k = 0, \cdots, m + n$$

This definition says that if $f(x)$ is approximated by $p(x)/q(x)$, then the first n derivatives of $q(x)f(x) - p(x)$ will be zero. Such derivative conditions impose linear constraints on the coefficients of p and q. The only restriction on p and q is that the degrees of p and q add up to at most n. This implies that there are $n + 2$ unknown coefficients of p and q. The n derivatives of f at x_0 and the value of f at x_0 provide $n+1$ conditions. Since we are interested only in p/q, we can set the leading coefficient of q equal to 1 without loss of generality. Hence, the ratio p/q can be uniquely specified. (See Cuyt and Wuytack (1986) for a more rigorous demonstration of the critical properties of Padé approximation.) Usually we take p and q to be of equal degree, or make p one degree greater.

Theory and experience say that Padé approximants are better global approximants than Taylor series approximations, that is, the error grows less rapidly as we move away from x_0. For this reason, computers typically use Padé approximants to compute trigonometric, exponential, and other functions. We will use both Padé and Taylor approximants in our calculations below.

4.3   Optimal Growth Models

The solution of optimal growth models is important for dynamic modelling in economics. In this section, we will show how one can compute high-order polynomial and rational approximations to optimal policy functions in simple growth models.

The basic focus in economic growth models is how a country allocates resources and income between current consumption and investment. By foregoing current consumption, a country increases its wealth, its future output and income, and its future potential consumption. The more a country allocates to investment, the more rapidly income and potential consumption grows. However, that growth comes at the sacrifice of consumption today. Intuitively, the choice between consumption and investment depends on how important current consumption is today relative to the return on the investment. Economic growth models allow us to formalize these ideas.

We will first examine a simple continuous-time growth problem. We will assume that $f(k)$ is a concave production function, $u(c)$ is a concave utility function of consumption, c, and that the capital stock, k, obeys the law of motion

$$\frac{dk}{dt} = f(k) - c.$$

This law says that the rate of increase in capital equals current output minus current consumption. We will allow consumption to exceed output, permitting decreases in k. This is a very simple model, assuming that there is only one good produced in the economy and that it is used for both consumption and investment purposes. However, it will allow us to simply display perturbation methods, which, as shown in Judd (1991), can also be used to study models with several goods and several kinds of capital stocks.

The basic growth problem is choosing a consumption path, $c(t)$, which is feasible—that is, it keeps the capital stock nonnegative at all times, and maximizes the discounted sum of utility. This is represented by the control problem

$$V(k_0) = \max_c \int_0^\infty e^{-\rho t} u(c)\, dt$$
$$\frac{dk}{dt} = f(k) - c$$
$$k(0) = k_0$$

$V(k_0)$ will denote the total value when one follows the optimal dynamic consumption plan when k_0 is the initial capital stock.

Dynamic programming methods study the value function by constructing a Bellman equation. The Bellman equation for this dynamic programming problem is

$$\rho V(k) = u\big(C(k)\big) + V'(k)\big(f(k) - C(k)\big) \tag{1}$$

The first-order condition for the indicated maximization is

$$0 = u'\big(C(k)\big) - V'(k) \tag{2}$$

This equation implies that consumption can be expressed as a function of capital, $c = C(k)$. Note that calendar time plays no role here, as is expected since the horizon is infinite and neither the utility function nor the production function depends on time in any crucial way.

When we substitute the first-order condition into the Bellman equation, we get a pair of equations in the two unknown functions:

$$0 = u(C(k)) + V'(k)(f(k) - C(k)) - \rho V(k)$$
$$u'C(k) = V'(k)$$

These equations describe our problem. We will simplify the problem by eliminating V and V' and reducing the problem to one equation in one unknown function, $C(k)$. If we differentiate the Bellman equation with respect to k we get

$$0 = u'(C(k))C'(k) + V''(k)(f(k) - C(k)) + V'(k)(f'(k) - C'(k)) - \rho V'(k)$$

If we differentiate the first-order condition with respect to k, we get

$$u''(C(k))C'(k) = V''(k)$$

which allows us to eliminate V'' and arrive at a single equation for C:

$$0 = C'(k)(f(k) - C(k)) - (u'(C(k))/u''(C(k)))(\rho - f'(k)) \tag{3}$$

It is this equation which will be the basis for our perturbation solution for various choices of $f(k)$ and $u(c)$.

In particular, we will assume a Cobb-Douglas production function with capital share .25, and an isoelastic utility function with intertemporal elasticity of substitution equal to .1. Our first *Mathematica* instructions will clear various variables and specify tastes and technology:

```
In[1]:= Clear[f,u,kss,gamma,rho,alpha,ctay,ccoef,
        cpade,numcoef,dencoef]
        rho = .05;
        alpha = .25;
        f[k_] = (rho/alpha) k^alpha;
        gamma = -10;
        u[c_] = c^(1+gamma)/(1+gamma);
```

Our objective is to find the first n derivatives of $C(k)$ at kss. This can be accomplished by defining the policy function in terms of the parameters `ccoef(i)`:

```
In[2]:= n = 5;
        ctay[k_] := Sum[ccoef[i] (k-kss)^i/i!, {i,0,n}]
```

where kss will serve as the starting point of our approximation, and will be determined below.

We next define the critical function of equation (3), which for our choice of utility function reduces to:

```
In[3]:= bellman[k_] = - rho*ctay[k] -
                      gamma*ctay[k]*Derivative[1][ctay][k]+
                      gamma*f[k]*Derivative[1][ctay][k]+
                      ctay[k]*Derivative[1][f][k];
```

Equation (3) says that bellman[k] is always zero at all capital stocks k. It is this fact which we will now exploit, since this implies that all derivatives are also zero at all k, a condition which in turn imposes identifying conditions on the derivatives of C.

4.3.1   Steady State Determination

Our basic equation, (3), is a first-order differential equation. Such differential equations need an initial condition to define a unique solution, that is, we need to find a k where we know the solution to C. We shall determine an initial condition by computing the steady state. The steady state capital stock is that k where there is no savings, that is, where $f(k) = C(k)$. From equation (3), saving is zero if and only if

$$f'(k) = \rho$$

The solution to this condition, denoted kss, is the steady state capital stock. We have defined the production function so that

```
In[1]:= kss = 1;
```

At the steady state, net invesment is zero, and consumption equals output, implying the conditions

```
In[2]:= ctay[kss] = f[kss];
        ccoef[0] = f[kss]
```

```
Out[2]:= 0.2
```

The steady state capital stock will serve as the point on which we base our perturbation procedures. Economically, this is a special point. If the country is at kss, then it will stay there forever. This implies that if $k_0 = kss$, then we know the entire future path of consumption and capital, and that we know both $C(k_0)$ and $V(k_0)$.

From this beginning, we can compute the necessary derivatives of $C(k)$ near kss and construct our approximation.

4.3.2   Computing C'(kss):

Computing the first derivative of the consumption policy function is a linearization procedure, commonly used in analyzing these models. However, the usual procedure revolves around linearizing a system of differential equations and is limited by this ODE perspective. We will pursue a more general approach, not limited to problems with an ODE formulation.

The key fact for our procedure is that `bellman[k] = 0` at all k, which in turn implies that all derivatives of `bellman[k]` are also zero at all k. Therefore, we first differentiate the Bellman equation with respect to k,

```
In[1]:= xbellman[k_] = D[bellman[k],k];
```

We then evaluate the resulting expression at kss,

```
In[2]:= xbellman[kss]
Out[2]:=
                                                          2
         -0.0075 - 0.5 ccoef[1] + 10 ccoef[1]
```

Since `xbellman[kss]` = 0, we can solve this quadratic equation for the possible values of $C'(kss) =$ `ccoef[1]`,

```
In[3]:= root = Solve[xbellman[kss]==0,ccoef[1]]

Out[3]:= {{ccoef[1] -> 0.062081}, {ccoef[1] -> -0.012081}}
```

This equation has two roots of opposite sign, but we can select one. In particular, only the positive root is consistent with V being concave at kss. Therefore,

```
In[4]:= ccoef[1] = root[[1]][[1]][[2]]

Out[4]:= 0.062081
```

This derivative corresponds to the usual linearization procedure widely used to study these models. Analysis usually stops with this linearization. However, we will go on to compute higher-order derivatives.

4.3.3   Computing Higher Derivatives:

In order to compute higher derivatives of C at kss, we need only to take more derivatives of `bellman[k]` evaluate them at kss, and solve out for the appropriate derivative of C, as in the following:

```
In[1]:= For[j=2, j<n+1, j++,
          xbellman[k_] = D[xbellman[k],k];
          root=Solve[xbellman[kss]==0,ccoef[j]];
          ccoef[j] = root[[1]][[1]][[2]]
          ]
```

This procedure will, in succession, compute the first $n-1$ derivatives of C. Note that we constantly redefine `xbellman[k]`; this is done to save space since these expansions can grow rapidly. Each new derivative of xbellman produces a higher derivative of `bellman[k]`, and introduces a new, and unknown, derivative of C. When `xbellman[kss]` is computed, that new derivative of C at kss is the only unknown. Furthermore, as shown in Judd (1991), the new derivative of C at kss appears linearly. More precisely, at stage j, the first $j-1$ derivatives of C are known, `xbellman[kss]` involves only the first j derivatives of C, and the unknown derivative, the j'th, appears linearly in the equation `xbellman[kss]` == 0. Therefore, we have reduced the problem of computing the higher-order derivatives of C to a sequence of linear problems.

With the first several derivatives of C at kss computed, we have computed the Taylor series approximation. We can plot the consumption function:

In[2]:= **Plot[ctay[x],{x,.1,2}]**

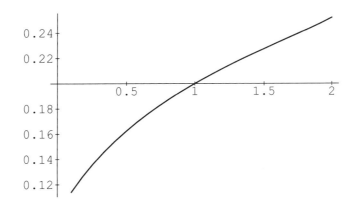

Out[2]:= —Graphics—

and the saving ratio function,

In[3]:= **Plot[(f[x]-ctay[x])/f[x],{x,.1,2.}]**

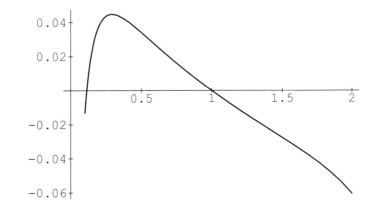

Out[3]:= —Graphics—

From the saving rate function, we can see that the approximation is not good at small capital stocks since we know from theory that savings is positive at all capital stocks below the steady state, which equals 1 here. However, near the steady state, the policy function appears to be sensible, implying stable dynamics near the steady state. Unfortunately, this tells us little about how good the approximation is.

4.3.4   Computing the Padé Approximation

An alternative use of these derivatives is to compute a Padé approximation. This is accomplished by finding a pair of polynomials such that their ratio has the same derivative properties at kss as C. The degree of the numerator will be mpade,

```
In[1]:= mpade = Floor[n/2];
```

npade will be the degree of the denominator,

```
In[2]:= npade = n - mpade;
```

and we choose them so that the numerator is the same degree or one degree greater than the denominator.

We next define the numerator and denominator, and compute the coefficients of the Padé approximation. We first define a function centered at k=1:

```
In[3]:= c1[k_] = ctay[k+1]
```

$$Out[3]:= 0.2 + 0.062081\ k - 0.0184069\ k^2 + 0.0103787\ k^3 -$$

$$0.00702861\ k^4 + 0.00522644\ k^5$$

Next we define the numerator and denominator polynomials:

```
In[4]:= numpol[x_] = Sum[numcoef[i] x^(i-1),{i,npade+1}];
        denpol[x_] = Sum[dencoef[i] x^(i-1),{i,mpade+1}];
```

We expand the function, c1, to be approximated at $x = 0$:

```
In[5]:= taylor[x_] = Series[c1[x],{x,0,npade+mpade}]
```

$$Out[5]:= 0.2 + 0.062081\ x - 0.0184069\ x^2 + 0.0103787\ x^3 -$$

$$0.00702861\ x^4 + 0.00522644\ x^5 + O[x]^6$$

We next express the error in the rational approximation:

```
In[6]:= diff = numpol[x] - taylor[x] denpol[x];
```

It is obvious that we can multiply both numpol[x] and denpol[x] by a common constant and have an equivalent rational function. We need to eliminate this degree of indeterminacy. Without loss of generality, we can normalize the representation by

```
In[7]:= dencoef[1] = 1;
```

We now solve for the polynomial coefficients by invoking the linear derivative conditions which define a Padé approximation:

```
In[8]:= s1 = Solve[LogicalExpand[diff==0]];
        Do[numcoef[i]=numcoef[i]/.s1[[1]],{i,npade+1}]
        Do[dencoef[i]=dencoef[i]/.s1[[1]],{i,mpade+1}]
        pade[x_]=numpol[x]/denpol[x]
```

Out[8]:=
$$\frac{0.2 + 0.276831\ x + 0.0929694\ x^2 + 0.00449471\ x^3}{1 + 1.07375\ x + 0.223585\ x^2}$$

   This direct procedure is not the most efficient way to compute the coefficients of a Padé expansion. See Cuyt and Wuytack (1986) for a discussion of superior procedures. We choose this procedure for its directness and simplicity.

   To get a policy function for consumption, we shift the Padé approximation so that the resulting function is centered on the steady state:

In[9]:= **cpade[k_] = pade[k-1];**

We next plot the difference between the Taylor and Padé approximations:

In[10]:= **Plot[(ctay[x]-cpade[x])/f[x],{x,.1,2.}, PlotRange->All]**

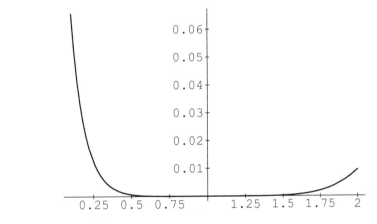

Out[10]:= —Graphics—

   We see that the two approximations are very similar except for the outer values of capital. At this point one wonders which is better. We next consider a procedure for making a judgment on that issue.

4.3.5   Evaluating the Quality of the Approximations

We next examine the quality of the approximations over a wide range of capital stocks. To do this we substitute the Taylor and Padé approximations into equation (3), yielding functions of k which measure the error in equation (3) generated by these approximations. Since this error is not unit-free, we then normalized the error function, commonly referred to as the *residual*, by rho and the steady-state consumption. We define residtay[k] to be the residual function of the Taylor approximation,

In[1]:= **residtay[k_] := Abs[((f'[k]-rho)*ctay[k]+**
                    gamma*(f[k]-ctay[k])*ctay'[k])/(rho*ctay[kss])]

and `residpade[k]` is the residual function for the Padé approximation,

```
In[2]:= residpade[k_] := Abs[((f'[k]-rho)*cpade[k]+
            gamma*(f[k]-cpade[k])*cpade'[k])/(rho*cpade[kss])]
```

Both of these residuals are small near the steady state; for example,

```
In[3]:= {residtay[.98], residtay[1.02],residpade[.98],
        residpade[1.02]}
```

```
Out[3]:=                    -11              -11               -13
           {3.62898 10    , 3.46191 10    , 6.80142 10    ,

                        -13
           6.01198 10      }
```

We will examine the relative quality of the two approximations by examining which has the smaller residual function. To do this we plot the residuals on a logarithmic scale. To avoid underflow, we will plot the base 10 logarithm of the residual's magnitude, plus, to prevent overflow, a small number.

```
In[4]:= eps = 0.000000000001;
        Plot[{Log[residpade[x]+eps]/Log[10.],
            Log[residtay[x]+eps]/Log[10.]}, {x,.1,2.5},
            PlotStyle->{{Dashing[{.05,.05}]}, {}}]
```

```
Out[4]:= -Graphics-
```

These plots show that both expansions are excellent near the steady state, but that the Padé approximation, represented by the solid line, is substantially better away from the steady state. In fact the Padé approximation remains an excellent approximation, with an error of less than one part in a thousand, even for capital stocks more than double the steady state, whereas the Taylor approximation has unacceptable errors at those capital stocks.

Considerations from complex analysis indicate the limitations of the Taylor series expansion. Because of the singularity in the production function at $k = 0$, one expects that the consumption policy function is also singular at $k = 0$; this would be the case if consumption is roughly proportional to output. From complex analysis, this would imply that the Taylor series approximation centered at $k = 1$ cannot be valid outside of $[0, 2]$. Therefore, the poor performance of the Taylor series for $k > 2$ is not surprising. The good performance of the Padé approximation is not limited by the singularity at $k = 0$, and performs very well even for $k = 2.5$.

In this section we have shown how to compute a high order approximation of $C(k)$ for a simple continuous-time growth model. In the sections below we show how to extend this to discrete time, uncertainty, and labor supply.

4.3.6 A Perturbation Package

We will now collect the basic functions above into a set of functions which will allow us to compactly compute the important functions. We will define a function which will automatically compute the Taylor series expansion of the consumption policy function around the steady state:

```
In[1]:= ctayfunc[alpha_,gamma_,rho_,n_] :=
        Block[{f,u,kss,ccoef,c,root,bellman,xbellman},
               f[k_] = (rho/alpha) k^alpha;
               u[c_] = c^(1+gamma)/(1+gamma);
               c[k_] := Sum[ccoef[i] (k-kss)^i/i!, {i,0,n}];
               bellman[k_] = - rho*c[k] -
                          gamma*c[k]*Derivative[1][c][k]+
                          gamma*f[k]*Derivative[1][c][k]+
                          c[k]*Derivative[1][f][k];
               kss = 1;
               c[kss] = f[kss];
               ccoef[0] = f[kss];
               xbellman[k_] = D[bellman[k],k];
               root = Solve[xbellman[kss]==0,ccoef[1]];
               rt1=root[[1]][[1]][[2]];
               rt2=root[[2]][[1]][[2]];
               If[rt1>0,rt=rt1,rt=rt2];
               ccoef[1] = rt;
               For[j=2,j<n+1,j++,
                   xbellman[k_] = D[xbellman[k],k];
                   root=Solve[xbellman[kss]==0,ccoef[j]];
                   ccoef[j] = root[[1]][[1]][[2]]
                   ];
               Sum[ccoef[i] (x-kss)^i/i!, {i,0,n}]
              ]
```

To use `ctayfunc`, we invoke it as part of a function definition, as in the following application which replicates the example above:

```
In[2]:= ctay[x_] = ctayfunc[.25,-10.,.05,5]
Out[2]:=
                                                  2
        0.2 + 0.062081 (-1 + x) - 0.0184069 (-1 + x)  +

                       3                         4
        0.0103787 (-1 + x)  - 0.00702861 (-1 + x)  +

                       5
        0.00522644 (-1 + x)
```

The Padé expansion of a function C around a point, xpt, using the first n derivatives of C can be computed by cpadefunc:

```
In[3]:= cpadefunc[c_,xpt_,n_] :=
        Block[{mpade,npade,numpol,numcoef,denpol,
                dencoef,taylor,pade,c1},
            mpade = Floor[n/2];
            npade = n - mpade;
            c1[x_] = c[x+xpt];
            numpol[x_] = Sum[numcoef[i] x^(i-1),
                             {i,npade+1}];
            denpol[x_] = Sum[dencoef[i] x^(i-1),
                             {i,mpade+1}];
            taylor[x_] = Series[c1[x],{x,0,npade+mpade}];
            diff = numpol[x] - taylor[x] denpol[x];
            dencoef[1] = 1.;
            s1 = Solve[LogicalExpand[diff==0]];
            Do[numcoef[i]=numcoef[i]/.s1[[1]],{i,npade+1}];
            Do[dencoef[i]=dencoef[i]/.s1[[1]],{i,mpade+1}];
            pade[x_]=numpol[x]/denpol[x];
            pade[x-xpt]
            ]
```

We check cpadefunc by asking it to repeat the example above:

```
In[4]:= cpadefunc[ctay,1,5]
```

$$Out[4]:= \frac{0.2 + 0.276831\ (-1+x) + 0.0929694\ (-1+x)^2 + 0.00449471\ (-1+x)^3}{1. + 1.07375\ (-1+x) + 0.223585\ (-1+x)^2}$$

We now demonstrate just how fast these expansions can be computed and how good they can be by repeating these operations with $n = 15$, thereby generating 15'th degree approximations.

```
In[5]:= n = 15;
```

```
In[6]:= Clear[ctay,cpade]
        Timing[ctay[x_] = ctayfunc[alpha,gamma,rho,n];]
```

```
Out[6]:= {28.9167 Second, Null}
```

```
In[7]:= Timing[cpade[x_] = cpadefunc[ctay,1,n]]
```

$$Out[7]:= \{1.71667\ Second,\ (0.2 + 0.778477\ (-1+x) + 1.22781\ (-1+x)^2 + $$
$$1.00546\ (-1+x)^3 + 0.454781\ (-1+x)^4 + 0.111466\ (-1+x)^5 + $$
$$0.0134483\ (-1+x)^6 + 0.000634302\ (-1+x)^7 + $$
$$0.00000625817\ (-1+x)^8\ )\ /$$

Out[7] (cont.)

$$(1. + 3.58198 \ (-1 + x) + 5.11923 \ (-1 + x)^2 + 3.71602 \ (-1 + x)^3$$

$$+ \ 1.44084 \ (-1 + x)^4 + 0.286181 \ (-1 + x)^5 + 0.0250533 \ (-1 + x)^6$$

$$+ \ 0.000638291 \ (-1 + x)^7 \ )\}$$

When we plot the residuals, we find that both expansions are excellent:

```
In[8]:= eps = 0.000000000001;
        Plot[{Log[residpade[x]+eps]/Log[10.],
              Log[residtay[x]+eps]/Log[10.]},{x,.1,2.5},
              PlotStyle -> {{Dashing[{0.05,0.01}]},{}},
              PlotRange -> All]
```

Out[8]:= —Graphics—

Note that in this case the Padé expansion is excellent over a very large range of capital stocks; in fact, the residual is of the order 10^{-7} or better over almost all capital stocks examined. The Taylor expansion is better near the steady state, as it should be since it is the best possible local expansion. However, its advantage in that region is truly trivial, existing only past the seventh significant digit, whereas the Taylor expansion becomes of questionable value outside of $[.5, 1.5]$.

We have seen that perturbation methods can be used to compute two kinds of approximation to the continuous-time deterministic growth problem, and that *Mathematica* programs can automate the necessary algebra. We will next turn to other models which can also be analyzed in this way.

4.4   Continuous-Time Stochastic Growth

For many interesting questions concerning economic growth and dynamics, it is necessary to add uncertainty to the analysis. We will next show how to use the approximation to $C(k)$ around kss in the deterministic case to compute an approximate policy function in a similar model with small amounts of uncertainty. While the assumption of small shocks may seem limiting, we will find that the approximations do well with empirically relevant levels of risk.

The problem we will examine is just the stochastic version of the previous problem:

$$V(k_0) = \max_c E\left\{ \int_0^\infty e^{-\rho t} u(c)\, dt \right\}$$

$$dk = \left(f(k) - c \right) dt + \frac{1}{2}\, \sqrt{\sigma}\, k\, dz$$

$$k(0) = k_0$$

We define the value function to be

$$V(k) = \sup_{c \in \mathcal{F}} E\left\{ \int_0^\infty e^{-\rho t} u(c)\, dt \right\}$$

where $\mathcal{F}$ is the set of feasible consumption processes with $k(0) = k_0$. If $V(k)$ is C^2, then stochastic optimization theory demonstrates that the value function solves the partial differential equation

$$0 = \max_c \left[-\rho V(k) + u(c) + V'(k)\left(f(k) - c \right) + \sigma k^2 V''(k) \right]$$

Again, the optimal choice of consumption depends solely on the current capital stock. While the dependence of V and C on σ is normally suppressed in the notation, we will add σ as a parameter and express the policy function as $C(k, \sigma)$. This emphasizes the fact that we are using the $\sigma = 0$ case as the basis of our approximation. Formally, we are looking for the terms of the Taylor expansion of C:

$$C(k, \sigma) \doteq C(kss, 0) + C_k(kss, 0)(k - kss) + C_\sigma(kss, 0)\sigma$$
$$+ C_{kk}(kss, 0)(k - kss)^2/2 + C_{\sigma k}(kss, 0)\sigma(k - kss) + C_{\sigma\sigma}(kss, 0)\sigma^2/2 + \cdots$$

The Bellman equation implies that the policy and value functions satisfy the system

$$0 = -\rho V + u(C) + V_k \left(f - C \right) + \sigma k^2 V_{kk} \tag{4}$$
$$0 = u'(C) - V_k \tag{5}$$

Differentiating (4,5) with respect to k and using (5), we find a single equation for the consumption policy function, C:

$$0 = u'(f' - \rho) + u'' C_k (f - C) + 2\sigma k u'' C_k + \sigma k^2 (u'' C_k C_k + u'' C_{kk}) \tag{6}$$

Equation (6) will be the centerpiece of our analysis. We know that at $\sigma = 0$ and $k = kss$

$$C(kss, 0) = f(kss).$$

Our earlier analysis has computed all of the derivatives

$$\frac{\partial^i C}{\partial k^i}(kss, 0),\ i = 1, \cdots, n.$$

We will next move our derivatives

$$\frac{\partial}{\partial \sigma} \left(\frac{\partial^i C}{\partial k^i} \right) (kss, 0)$$

We first differentiate (6) with respect to σ, yielding

$$
\begin{aligned}
0 = \ & u'' C_\sigma (f' - \rho) + u''' C_\sigma (f - C) C_k + u'' C_{k\sigma} (f - c) + u'' (-C_\sigma) C_k \\
& + 2ku'' C_k + 2\sigma k u''' C_\sigma C_k + 2\sigma k u'' C_{k\sigma} \\
& + k^2 (u''' C_k C_k + u'' C_{kk}) \\
& + \sigma k^2 (u'''' C_\sigma C_k C_k + 2u''' C_{k\sigma} C_k + u''' C_\sigma C_{kk} + u'' C_{kk\sigma})
\end{aligned}
\tag{7}
$$

At $(kss, 0)$ this reduces to

$$0 = -u'' C_\sigma C_k + 2ku'' C_k + k^2 (u''' C_{kk} + u'' C_{kk})$$

showing that C_σ can be solved linearly in terms of C, C_k, and C_{kk} at kss.

Subsequent differentiation of (4) with respect to k will yeild similar expressions for $C_{\sigma k}$, $C_{\sigma kk}$, etc.

However, note that C_σ needs C_{kk}, $C_{\sigma k}$ needs C_{kkk}, etc. Hence, if we know only the first n derivatives of C with respect to k, we can only compute the first $n - 2$ derivatives of C_σ with respect to k. This restricts what σ derivatives can be computed. For example, the following is a maximal collection of computable derivatives if we only know up to C_{kkkk}:

$$
\begin{array}{cccc}
C & C_k & C_{kk} & C_{kkkk} \\
C_\sigma & C_{\sigma k} & C_{\sigma kk} & \\
C_{\sigma\sigma} & & &
\end{array}
$$

This tableau is maximal since $C_{\sigma kkk}$ needs C_{kkkkk}, which is absent, and the resulting absence of $C_{\sigma kkk}$ then makes it infeasible to compute $C_{\sigma\sigma k}$.

We now implement this procedure in *Mathematica*. We first initialize the critical parameters,

```
In[1]:= kss=1; alpha = .25; rho = .05; gamma = -2;
```

define the production function,

```
In[2]:= f[k_] = rho/alpha k^alpha;
```

define the utility function,

```
In[3]:= u[c_] = c^(1+gamma)/(1+gamma);
```

define some useful auxiliary functions,

```
In[4]:= u1[c_] = Simplify[u'[c]/u''[c]];
```

```
In[5]:= u2[c_] = Simplify[u'''[c]/u''[c]];
```

and set the desired degree of approximation,

```
In[6]:= n = 4;
```

The following procedure builds a function, `conss[k,s]`, which approximates $C(k, \sigma)$:

```
In[7]:= Block[{sbell,root,cons},
         Clear[conss];
       For[j=0,j<=n,j++,
         For[p=0,p<=n,p++,
          Derivative[j,p][cons][kss,0] = .;
            ];
            ];
         sbell[0,0,k_,s_] = (f'[k] - rho) u1[cons[k,s]] +
            D[cons[k,s],k] (f[k]-cons[k,s]) +
            s k k (u2[cons[k,s]] (D[cons[k,s],k])^2 +
            D[cons[k,s],{k,2}]);
         sbell[1,0,k_,s_] = D[sbell[0,0,k,s],k];
         cons[kss,0] = f[kss];
         conss[k_,s_] = cons[kss,0];
         root = Solve[sbell[1,0,kss,0]==0,
         Derivative[1,0][cons][kss,0]];
         Print[root];
         Derivative[1,0][cons][kss,0] = root[[2]][[1]][[2]];
         conss[k_,s_] = cons[k,s]
                         + Derivative[1,0][cons][kss,0] (k-kss);
         For[j=2,j<n+1,j++,
            sbell[j,0,k_,s_] = D[sbell[j-1,0,k,s],k];
            root = Solve[sbell[j,0,kss,0]==0,
            Derivative[j,0][cons][kss,0]];
            Print[root];
            Derivative[j,0][cons][kss,0] = root[[1]][[1]][[2]];
            conss[k_,s_] = cons[k,s] +
              Derivative[j,0][cons][kss,0] (k-kss)^j / j!
            ];

         For[p=1,p<=n/2,p++,
            sbell[0,p,k_,s_] = D[sbell[0,p-1,k,s],s];
            root = Solve[sbell[0,p,kss,0]==0,
            Derivative[0,p][cons][kss,0]];
            Print[root];
            Derivative[0,p][cons][kss,0] = root[[1]][[1]][[2]];
            conss[k_,s_] = cons[k,s] +
              Derivative[0,p][cons][kss,0] s^p / p!;
            For[j=1, j <= n - 2 p,j++,
               sbell[j,p,k_,s_] = D[sbell[j-1,p,k,s],k];
               root = Solve[sbell[j,p,kss,0]==0,
               Derivative[j,p][cons][kss,0]];
               Print[root];
               Derivative[j,p][cons][kss,0] = root[[1]][[1]][[2]];
               conss[k_,s_] = cons[k,s] +
               Derivative[j,p][cons][kss,0]
                  (k-kss)^j s^p/(j! p!)
               ];
            ]
         ]
```

$$\{\{cons^{(1,0)}[1, 0] \to 0.0911438\}, \{cons^{(1,0)}[1, 0] \to -0.0411438\}\}$$

$$\{\{cons^{(2,0)}[1, 0] \to 0.0293714\}\}$$

```
        (3,0)
{{cons      [1,  0] -> -0.0481816}}

        (4,0)
{{cons      [1,  0] -> 0.127661}}

        (0,1)
{{cons      [1,  0] -> -0.0967163}}

        (1,1)
{{cons      [1,  0] -> 0.0617278}}

        (2,1)
{{cons      [1,  0] -> 0.0392422}}

        (0,2)
{{cons      [1,  0] -> -5.30455}}
```

To evaluate the quality of the approximation, we substitute it into the stochastic bellman equation,

```
In[8]:= sbells[0,0,k_,s_] = (f'[k] - rho) u1[conss[k,s]] +
            D[conss[k,s],k] (f[k]-conss[k,s]) +
            s k k (u2[conss[k,s]] (D[conss[k,s],k])^2 +
            D[conss[k,s],{k,2}]);
```

and define a unit-free residual function,

```
In[9]:= resid[k_,s_] = sbells[0,0,k,s]/(rho u1[conss[kss,0]]);
```

We plot a three-dimensional surface of `resid`:

```
In[10]:= Plot3D[Log[Abs[resid[k,s]]+.0000000001]/Log[10],
            {k,.8,1.2}, {s,0,.001}]
```

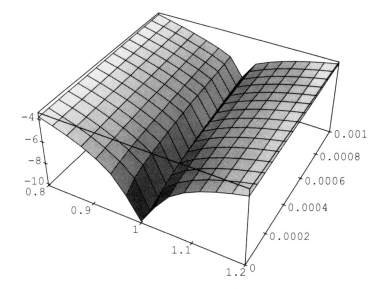

```
Out[10]:= -SurfaceGraphics-
```

This graph shows that the residual function is quite small over a wide range of capital stocks and an economically significant range of s values. To get some perspective on what s means, recall that the standard deviation of output in the U.S. economy is on the order of 2% of GNP and that capital-output ratio is about 2, implying that the standard deviation of output is 1% of wealth and implying a variance, s, equal to .0001.

We next plot the residual function for some specfic values of s which are similar to output variability in U.S. aggregate data:

```
In[11]:= eps = .0000000001;
         Plot[{Log[Abs[resid[k,0]]+eps]/Log[10],
              Log[Abs[resid[k,.0001]]+eps]/Log[10],
              Log[Abs[resid[k,.0004]]+eps]/Log[10]},
             {k,.5,1.5},
             PlotStyle -> {{Dashing[{.06,.0}]},
                           {Dashing[{.05,.01}]},
                           {Dashing[{.01,.01}]}}]
```

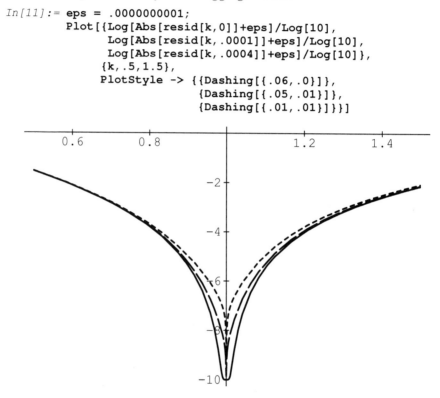

```
Out[11]:= -Graphics-
```

Note that the residuals are quite small, considering the low degree of approximation and the wide range of capital stocks. Also note that the residuals are practically equal for all three values of the variance, s.

4.5   Discrete-Time Growth

In some problems, it is more natural to use a discrete-time formulation of the problem. We will next apply these ideas to a discrete-time growth model. In this model, we assume that at the beginning of each period the current stock of capital, k, is split between consumption uses, c, and investment, $k - c$, which is used to produce gross output, $f(k - c)$, which will be available the next period. More specifically,

$$k(t + 1) = f(k(t) - c(t))$$

is the law of motion.

The optimal growth problem is expressed as

$$\max_{c_t} \sum_{t=0}^{\infty} \beta^t\, u(c_t)$$

$$k(t + 1) = f(k(t) - c(t))$$
$$k(0) = k_0$$

We make the standard assumptions that $u(c)$ is a concave utility function and $f(k)$ is a concave gross production function.

Because of the stationarity of the problem, the optimal consumption in each period is given by a policy function, $C(k)$, satisfying the Euler Equation

$$u'\big(C(k)\big) = \beta\, u'\Big(C\big(f(k - C(k))\big)\Big)\, f'(k - C(k)) \qquad (8)$$

At the steady state, kss, we have $f(kss - C(kss)) = kss$, implying

$$u'\big(C(kss)\big) = \beta\, u'\big(C(kss)\big)\, f'(kss - C(kss))$$

which in turn implies

$$1 = \beta\, f'(kss - C(kss))$$

all of which uniquely determines kss. Furthermore

$$kss = f(kss - C(kss))$$

Taking the derivative of (8) with respect to k implies

$$u''\big(C(k)\big)\, C'(k) = \beta u''\Big(C\big(f(k - C(k))\big)\Big)\, C'(f(k - C(k)))$$
$$\times\, f'(k - C(k))(1 - C'(k))\, f'(k - C(k))$$
$$+\, \beta\, u'\Big(C\big(f(k - C(k))\big)\Big)\, f''(k - C(k))\, (1 - C'(k))$$

At $k = kss$, this reduces to (we will now drop all arguments)

$$u''C' = \beta u''C'f'(1 - C')\, f' + \beta u'\, f''(1 - C')$$

This is a quadratic equation with the solution

$$C' = \frac{1}{2}\left(1 - \beta - \beta^2\, \frac{u'}{u''}\, f'' + \sqrt{\left(1 - \beta - \beta^2\, \frac{u'}{u''}\, f''\right)^2 + 4\, \frac{u'}{u''}\, \beta^2\, f''}\right)$$

We now define the critical functions and parameters:

```
In[1]:=  n=7; Clear[cd]; kss=1.;beta=0.96;alpha=0.25;
         gamma=-10.0; a=kss/(alpha beta kss)âlpha;
         f[k_]=a kâlpha; u[y_]=y^(1+gamma)/(1+gamma);
         u1[y_]=u'[y]; u2[k_]=u'[cd[f[k-cd[k]]]];
         cd[kss]=kss*(1-alpha beta);
```

The Euler equation for this model is

```
In[2]:=  euler[0,k_]=beta*u2[k]*f'[k-cd[k]]-u'[cd[k]]
```

$$Out[2]:= \quad \frac{-1.}{cd[k]^{10.}} + \frac{0.342893}{(k-cd[k])^{0.75} \; cd[1.42872 \; (k-cd[k])^{0.25}]^{10.}}$$

This equation states that the utility from saving one unit of capital and consuming the gross proceeds tomorrow has the same marginal yield as consuming that unit today.

While this equation is intuitive, this form of the Euler equation generates unnecessarily complex algebraic expressions. More efficient is the equivalent form which follows from the CRRA specification of the utility function which we specified above:

```
In[3]:=  euler1[0,k_]=cd[f[k-cd[k]]]*(beta f'[k-cd[k]])^(1/gamma)-
         cd[k]
```

$$Out[3]:= \quad -cd[k] + 1.11297 \; (k-cd[k])^{0.075} \; cd[1.42872 \; (k-cd[k])^{0.25}]$$

The gain in simplicity is seen by examining the output cells of euler and euler1. The denominator of the second term in euler involves the tenth power of cd[k] composed with itself raised to a power. In euler1, the tenth power is missing from the comparable term. Rewriting the Euler equation so as to minimize the complexity of the most complex term will help us keep down the complexity of the computation.

We sequentially solve for the Taylor series solution around the steady state. Successive differentiation and solving for derivatives yields these series:

```
In[4]:= Derivative[1][cd][kss] = .;
        euler1[1,k_]=D[euler1[0,k],k]; euler1[0,k] = .;
        root=Solve[euler1[1,kss]==0, Derivative[1][cd][kss]];
        r1=root[[1]][[1]][[2]]; r2=root[[2]][[1]][[2]];
        If[r1>0,rt=r1,rt=r2]; Derivative[1][cd][kss]=rt;
        For[j=1,j<n,j++,
            Derivative[j][cd][kss] = .;
            euler1[j,k_]=D[euler1[j-1,k],k];
            euler1[j-1,k] = .;
            sol=Solve[euler1[j,kss]==0,
                    Derivative[j][cd][kss]];
            vt=Derivative[j][cd][kss]/.sol[[1]];
            Derivative[j][cd][kss]=vt;];
        Do[cee[ii]=1/(ii!)
                Derivative[ii][cd][kss],{ii,1,n-1}]
        Do[cd[k_]=cd[kss]+
                Sum[cee[iii] (k-kss)îii,{iii,1,jj}],
                {jj,1,n-1}]
        cd[k]
```

Out[4]:=
$$0.76 + 0.392658\ (-1. + k) - 0.286785\ (-1. + k)^2\ +$$

$$0.195456\ (-1. + k)^3\ - 0.0727102\ (-1. + k)^4\ -$$

$$0.0639789\ (-1. + k)^5\ + 0.166206\ (-1. + k)^6$$

In this code, we eliminate `euler1[j,k]`, the *j*th derivative of the Euler equation, as soon as we have finished using it. This is done to economize on space.

We can again solve for the Padé approximation.

```
In[5]:= mpade = Floor[n/2];
        npade = n-mpade;
        fcn[x_] = cd[x+1];
        numpol[x_] = Sum[numcoef[i] x^(i-1),{i,npade+1}];
        denpol[x_] = Sum[dencoef[i] x^(i-1),{i,mpade+1}];
        taylor[x_] = Series[fcn[x],{x,0,npade+mpade}];
        diff = numpol[x] - taylor[x] denpol[x];
        dencoef[1] = 1;

In[6]:= s1 = Solve[LogicalExpand[diff == 0]];
        Do[numcoef[i]=numcoef[i]/.s1[[1]],{i,npade+1}];
        Do[dencoef[i]=dencoef[i]/.s1[[1]],{i,mpade+1}];
        pade[x_] = numpol[x]/denpol[x];
        cdpade[k_] = pade[k-1]
```

Out[6]:=
$$(0.76 + 6.9806\ (-1 + k) + 13.9395\ (-1 + k)^2 + 8.83725\ (-1 + k)^3\ +$$

$$0.397994\ (-1 + k)^4\ )\ /$$

$$(1 + 8.66834\ (-1 + k) + 14.2402\ (-1 + k)^2 + 7.28448\ (-1 + k)^3\ )$$

We can again compute residual functions to represent the error of our approximation. In this case, the residual will be `euler1[0,k]/cd[kss]`. This expresses the Euler equation error as a fraction of steady state consumption. While this is similar to what we did in the continuous-time case, the meaning of the residual is more clear here. If the residual is .01 at some k, then we conclude that the difference between what our approximation says current consumption should be and what it would be if an agent optimized today believing that our approximation would be used in the future equals `.01*c[kss]`. This is therefore a one-period error. Over the life of an economic agent he may make several such errors. However, if this relative error is on the order of, say, 10^{-6}, then this one-period error is so small that the cumulative error is also small given the ability of the human brain to do intricate calculations.

We next compute and plot the residual functions for both the Taylor and Padé approximations:

```
In[7]:= cdtay[k_] = cd[k];
        residtay[k_]=Abs[
        (cdtay[f[k-cdtay[k]]]*(beta f'[k-cdtay[k]])^(1/gamma)-
           cdtay[k]) / cdtay[kss]];
        residpade[k_]=Abs[
        (cdpade[f[k-cdpade[k]]]*(beta f'[k-cdpade[k]])^(1/gamma)-

           cdpade[k]) / cdpade[kss]];
In[8]:= eps = 0.0000000001;
        Plot[{Log[residpade[x]+eps]/Log[10.],
             Log[residtay[x]+eps]/Log[10.]},{x,.1,2.5},
           PlotStyle -> {{},{Dashing[{.01,.01}]}}]
```

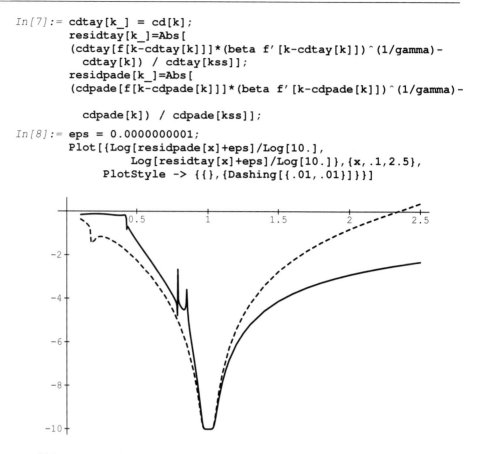

```
Out[8]:= -Graphics-
```

Again we find that the Euler equation errors are quite small. The difference in the discrete-time case is that the Taylor expansion slightly dominates for capital stocks below the steady state, but is much worse above the steady state.

Overall, we conclude that our approximations are as good as one could reasonably expect real-life individuals to compute. We also find that the Padé approximation is good over a wider range of capital stocks than the Taylor expansion.

4.6   Extensions and Conclusions

We have demonstrated that perturbation methods can be implemented in *Mathematica*, and can produce excellent approximate solutions to simple economic growth models. Other applications are under development. Adding taxes to our analysis is straightforward and will facilitate analysis of the effects of taxation on growth and welfare. In Judd [1991], there are discussions of, for example, applications with several state variables and applications to dynamic games.

In our examples, we have focussed on computing particular examples. *Mathematica* is rather slow if we wanted to compute hundreds of examples, as would be the case inside a maximum likelihood estimation procedure. These methods could still be used. Using the same procedures, one can compute the derivatives in terms of the underlying parameters, ρ, α, γ and any others, and then, using **FortranForm** commands, write Fortran statements which could be used in Fortran programs to rapidly compute the coefficients. In this way one can combine the symbolic tools of *Mathematica* with the computational power and software base of Fortran.

In general, we anticipate that perturbation methods will become as useful in economics as they have been in science generally, particularly when symbolic manipulation software becomes more powerful and widespread.

4.7 References

Bensoussan, A. *Perturbation Methods in Optimal Control.* John Wiley and Sons, 1988.

Cuyt, A. and L. Wuytack, *Nonlinear Numerical Methods: Theory and Practice,* Amsterdam: North-Holland, 1986.

Judd, K. L. *Numerical Methods in Economics,* December, 1991, Hoover Institution.

Judd, K. L. *Perturbation Methods for Solving Dynamic Economic Models,* November, 1991, Hoover Institution.

Judd, K. L., and Sy-Ming Guu, "Asymptotic Methods in Aggregate Growth Models," *Journal of Economic Dynamics and Control* (forthcoming).

Taylor, J., and H. Uhlig. "Solving Nonlinear Stochastic Growth Models: A Comparison of Alternative Solution Methods," *Journal of Business and Economic Statistics* 8 (January, 1990): 1–18.

5 General Equilibrium Models

Asahi Noguchi

Since the time of Leon Walras (1834–1910), describing the economy as systems of simultaneous equations has been a customary task of economists. They are broadly called general equilibrium models, though there are several variations among them. In this chapter we describe a method of obtaining numerical solutions of these models with *Mathematica*. In addition, we show how *Mathematica* can depict various aspects of these models graphically.

5.1 The Basic Model

First we present the basic model with multi-sectors and multi-factors in production corresponding to multi-commodities in consumption.

5.1.1 The Production Condition

Each sector is assumed to produce one specific commodity. The production function of the i-th sector is

$$X[i] = F[i](L[i, 1], \ldots, L[i, m]) \qquad i = 1, \ldots, n, \tag{1}$$

where $X[i]$ is the physical amount of the i-th commodity produced in a year, say; $L[i, 1], \ldots, L[i, m]$ are the amounts of production factors allocated to i-th sector. It is assumed that there are n-production sectors all of which require m-production factors. The production function $F[i]$ is an arbitrary homogeneous function of degree one; this means that if all the inputs to it double, for example, the output also doubles.

The total amounts of each input are assumed fixed:

$$Ltot[j] = \sum_{i=1}^{n} L[i, j] \qquad j = 1, \ldots, m, \tag{2}$$

where $Ltot[j]$ is the total factor supply of j-th input. In other words, all the production factors are always fully employed.

Next we set

$$w[i,j] = \delta F[i]/\delta L[i,j] \qquad i = 1,\ldots,n; j = 1,\ldots,m, \tag{3}$$

We call $w[i,j]$ the marginal productivity of the j-th factor in the i-th sector. The production condition for competitive equilibrium is

$$w[l,j]/w[1,1] = w[i,j]/w[i,1] \qquad i = 2,\ldots,n; j = 2,\ldots,m, \tag{4}$$

that is, the ratio of marginal productivities between any pair of the factors is the same across all the sectors. If these conditions are not satisfied, then the economy is not on the efficiency locus in the sense that some of the production can be increased without the decrease of any through the inter-sectoral shifts of production factors.

5.1.2   The Consumption Condition

Second, we proceed to the consumption side. The representative consumer in the economy is assumed to maximize his utility function

$$U = U(Co[1],\ldots,Co[n]) \tag{5}$$

under the budget constraint. Here $Co[1],\ldots,Co[n]$ are the consumptions of the commodities. We call it the social utility function. The first-order condition for this maximizing problem is that the relative prices of the commodities must coincide with the marginal rates of substitution in the consumptions. If the first of the commodities is selected as numéraire, that is to set $p[1] = 1$, this condition is transformed as follows:

$$p[i] = (\delta U/\delta Co[i])/(\delta U/\delta Co[1]) \qquad i = 1,\ldots,n, \tag{6}$$

Here $p[i]$ is the price of the i-th commodity.

We denote accompanying social budget constraint, or the national income, again expressed in terms of the first commodity, by

$$Y = \sum_{i=1}^{n} p[i]Co[i], \tag{7}$$

5.1.3   The Equilibrium Condition

Now that the respective equilibrium conditions of the scissors in the economy, that is the production and the consumption, are settled, we can set forth the overall equilibrium conditions of the economy. The following two conditions must be satisfied: 1) all the consumptions of commodities must be equal to their productions; 2) all the prices in (6), thus the marginal rates of substitution in the consumptions, must be equal to the marginal rates of substitution in the productions.

The first condition is simply set as

$$Co[i] = X[i] \qquad i = 1,\ldots,n, \tag{8}$$

Before attaining the second condition, we set

$$vp[i] = w[i,1]p[i] \qquad i = 1,\ldots,n, \tag{9}$$

Here $vp[i]$ is the marginal value productivity of the first factor in the i-th sector. If the condition (4) is satisfied, then the ratios of marginal productivities between a pair of the sectors are the same across all the factors. Thus any one of them, say $w[i,1]/w[1,1]$, represents the marginal rate of substitution in the productions between the first commodity and the i-th commodity. If all the marginal value productivities in the first factor are the same across all the sectors, therefore, the above condition for the overall equilibrium 2) is satisfied. It leads to

$$vp[1] = vp[i] \qquad i = 2,\ldots,n, \tag{10}$$

Equations (1)–(10), then, define our model; there are $2ij + 4i + 2$ equations, and also $2ij + 4i + 2$ variables, $L[i,j]$, $w[i,j]$, $X[i]$, $Co[i]$, $p[i]$, $vp[i]$, U, and Y ($Ltot[j]$ is fixed), so the system is fully determined.

5.2   Solving the Model

5.2.1   The Functional Form

In order to compute numerical solutions, both the production functions and the social utility function must be specified. The functional forms commonly used in the economic researches are either Cobb-Douglas or the constant elasticity of substitution (CES) function.

Cobb-Douglas production function with m-factor inputs is

$$X = A \prod_{j=1}^{m} L[j]^{a[j]} \text{ with } A > 0, \sum_{j=1}^{m} a[j] = 1 \tag{11}$$

where X is the output, $L[j]$ is the factor inputs, A is the units parameter, and $a[j]$ is the distribution parameter. Similarly CES production function is

$$X = A \left(\sum_{j=1}^{m} a[j]L[j]^{-e} \right)^{-1/e} \text{ with } A > 0, \sum_{j=1}^{m} a[j] = 1, e > -1 \tag{12}$$

where the elasticity parameter e is added. By eliminating the units parameter A, and designating X as the utility and $L[j]$ as the consumptions, both of these functions can also be thought of as the utility functions.

5.2.2   Setting the Dimensions of the Model

Before calculating an actual solution of the basic model presented above, we must determine the dimensions of the model, that is how many sectors are in existence and how many factors are is use. In presenting the solution procedure, we tentatively adopt the simplest case of this model, that is the two-sector and two-factor case. This special case is frequently referred to in the economic literature as the two-sector general equilibrium model. As for the functional form, we first apply the Cobb-Douglas function both to the productions and the utility.

The boundary of the model is then set as

```
In[1]:= TSectors=2;
        TFactors=2;
```

Here `TSectors` and `TFactors` are respectively the total number of the sectors in existence and the production factors in use.

5.2.3   Assigning the Variables

Before applying *Mathematica*'s solution function to the model, it is necessary to reduce the total number of the unknown variables by substitutions. To this end we set

```
In[1]:= Do[X[i] = A[i] Product[L[i,j]^a[i,j], {j,1,TFactors}],
             {i,1,TSectors}];
        Do[w[i,j] = D[X[i],L[i,j]], {i,1,TSectors},
             {j,1,TFactors}];
        U = Product[Co[i]^s[i], {i,1,TSectors}];
        Do[p[i] = D[U,Co[i]]/D[U,Co[1]], {i,1,TSectors}];
        Y = Sum[p[i] Co[i], {i,1,TSectors}];
        Do[Co[i] = X[i], {i,1,TSectors}];
        Do[vp[i] = w[i,1] p[i], {i,1,TSectors}];
```

These assignments correspond with (1), (3), (5), (6), (7), (8), and (9) in the basic model. Thereafter all these variables, the productions (`X[i]`), the marginal productivities of the production factors (`w[i,j]`), the social utility (`U`), the prices (`p[i]`), the national income (`Y`), the consumptions (`Co[i]`), and the marginal value productivities (`vp[i]`) are eliminated by substitutions.

5.2.4   Assigning the Parameters

The resulting expressions depend on the units parameters of the commodities ($A[i]$), the parameters of the production functions ($a[i,j]$) and the utility function ($s[i]$), also with the factor endowments $Ltot[j]$ in (2). We won't assign values to these variables, in order to be able to use the same model repeatedly with different parameters. Instead, when we want to solve a specific instance of the model, we use transformation rules. To this end we set

```
In[1]:= $unitspars=Array[A, TSectors];
        $prodpars=Array[a, {TSectors, TFactors}];
        $utilpars=Array[s, TSectors];
        $extpars=Array[Ltot, TFactors];
        Assign[{unitspars_,prodpars_,utilpars_,extpars_}] :=
          Join[Thread[Rule[$unitspars,unitspars]],
               Thread[Rule[Flatten[$prodpars],Flatten[prodpars]]],
               Thread[Rule[$utilpars,utilpars]],
               Thread[Rule[$extpars,extpars]]];
```

Now, for example,

```
In[2]:= Assign[{{1,1},{{0.8,0.2},{0.2,0.8}},{0.6,0.4},{400,600}}]
Out[2]:= {A[1] -> 1, A[2] -> 1, a[1, 1] -> 0.8, a[1, 2] -> 0.2,
          a[2, 1] -> 0.2, a[2, 2] -> 0.8, s[1] -> 0.6,
          s[2] -> 0.4, Ltot[1] -> 400, Ltot[2] -> 600}
```

5.2.5 Solving the Equations

We express the equations that must be satisfied at equilibrium by symbolic
names, to make it easier to manipulate them. The remaining equations in the
basic model, the factor availability condition (2), the production equilibrium
condition (4), and the marginal value productivities equality (10), are called
FactorConstraints, **MPRatioEqualities**, and **MVProEqualities** respectively.

```
In[1]:= FactorConstraints =
            Table[Ltot[j]==Sum[L[i,j], {i,1,TSectors}],
                        {j,1,TFactors}];
        MPRatioEqualities =
            Flatten[
              Table[w[1,1] w[i,j]==w[1,j] w[i,1], {i,2,TSectors},
                          {j,2,TFactors}]
            ];
        MVProEqualities = Table[vp[1]==vp[i],{i,2,TSectors}];
        Equations =
            Join[FactorConstraints, MPRatioEqualities,
              MVProEqualities];
```

We are now ready to write a function to solve the model. Because the built-in
FindRoot function is inadequate to deal with our problem, we use a function
MyFindRoot written by Silvio Levy. To this end we load a package **MyFind-
Root.m**

```
In[2]:= <<MyFindRoot.m
```

The **MyFindRoot** function can be used similarly to **FindRoot**, and therefore
requires initial guesses for the values of the variables. Choosing an initial guess
is one of the most difficult tasks in the numerical solution of equations; for our
functions it turns out that starting very close to the maximum allowed value
for each variable is a reasonable strategy, because of the production function's
convexity properties. In any case, we isolate the guesses in separate definitions,
to make the equilibrium-finding function model-independent.

```
In[3]:= eps=1. 10^-6;
        Do[LGuess[i,j] = Ltot[j]-eps, {i,1,TSectors},
           {j,1,TFactors}];
        Vars = Flatten[
          Table[{L[i,j],LGuess[i,j],0,Ltot[j]}, {i,1,TSectors},
                {j,1,TFactors}],1];
```

As `L[i,j]` should only take values between `0` and `Ltot[j]`, we limit the search in **MyFindRoot** in that range.

Here then is the equilibrium-finding function:

```
In[4]:= Equilibrium[pars_] := Equilibrium[pars] =
          MyFindRoot @@ (Prepend[Vars, Equations] /. Assign[pars])
```

Notice the common trick of using a `:=` assignment that contains a `=` assignment; this causes *Mathematica* to remember the value of **Equilibrium** for any particular set of arguments, thus avoiding recomputations.

Now all the equilibrium allocations are obtained when **Equilibrium** is called with appropriate arguments:

```
In[5]:= Equilibrium[{{1,1},{{0.8,0.2},{0.2,0.8}},{0.6,0.4},
                     {400,600}}]
```

```
Out[5]:= {L[1, 1] -> 342.857, L[1, 2] -> 163.636,
           L[2, 1] -> 57.1429, L[2, 2] -> 436.364}
```

Since **Equilibrium** returns a list of transformation rules, it is easy to obtain the value of the remaining endogenous variables by substitution. For instance, the value of `X[1]` at equilibrium is given by the function `XEq[1][pars]`, defined by

```
In[6]:= XEq[i_][pars_] := X[i] /. Equilibrium[pars] /.
          Assign[pars]
```

```
In[7]:= XEq[1][{{1,1},{{0.8,0.2},{0.2,0.8}},{0.6,0.4},{400,600}}]
```

```
Out[7]:= 295.71
```

Similarly we define `L[i,j]`, `w[i,j]`, `Co[i]`, `p[i]`, `vp[i]`, `U`, and `Y` as

```
In[8]:= LEq[i_,j_][pars_] := L[i,j] /. Equilibrium[pars] /.
          Assign[pars]
        wEq[i_,j_][pars_] := w[i,j] /. Equilibrium[pars] /.
          Assign[pars]
        CoEq[i_][pars_] := Co[i] /. Equilibrium[pars] /.
          Assign[pars]
        pEq[i_][pars_] := p[i] /. Equilibrium[pars] /.
          Assign[pars]
        vpEq[i_][pars_] := vp[i] /. Equilibrium[pars] /.
          Assign[pars]
        UEq[pars_] := U /. Equilibrium[pars] /. Assign[pars]
        YEq[pars_] := Y /. Equilibrium[pars] /. Assign[pars]
```

5.3 Presenting the Graph

Since the time of Alfred Marshall (1842–1924) and Francis Edgeworth (1845–1926), geometrical tools have been used as a means of explaining the economy. Here we use *Mathematica*'s graphics facilities to implement two tools useful for the visualization of the model described above: the Edgeworth-Bowley box diagram and the production-possibilities curve.

5.3.1   The Edgeworth-Bowley Box Diagram

The Edgeworth-Bowley box diagram displays the allocation of resources between two agents of an economy—in our case, between sectors 1 and 2. The diagram contains several types of curves: typically isoquants for the two commodities, an isocost and a contract curve. The meaning of these terms is explained below.

5.3.1.1   The Isoquants Map

An isoquant for a commodity shows all possible combinations of inputs that can be used to produce a fixed amount of the commodity. In other words, an isoquant for commodity i is a level curve of the production function $X[i]$ ($L[i,1]$, $L[i,2]$). Therefore a function to draw a number of isoquants for commodity i can be written very simply using **ContourPlot**:

```
In[1]:= Isoquants[i_][pars_,opts___] :=
          ContourPlot[Release[X[i]/.Assign[pars]],
            Release[{L[i,1],eps,Ltot[1]-eps}/.Assign[pars]],
            Release[{L[i,2],eps,Ltot[2]-eps}/.Assign[pars]],
            opts]
```

For example,

```
In[2]:= Isoquants[1][{{1,1},{{0.8,0.2},{0.2,0.8}},{0.6,0.4},
          {400,600}}]
```

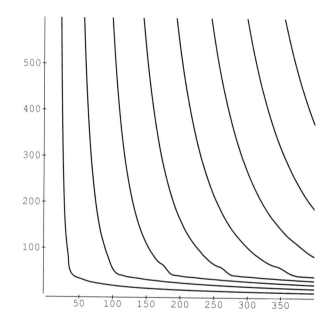

```
Out[2]:= —ContourGraphics—
```

A function to plot the isoquants of commodity 2 in terms of `L[2,1]` and `L[2,2]` would be exactly analogous, but it is advantageous to show the isoquants of commodity 2 also as a function of `L[1,1]` and `L[1,2]`, so the two graphs can be superimposed. With this in mind, we write

```
In[3]:= FactorRules =
          Table[L[TSectors,j] -> Ltot[j]-Sum[L[i,j],
              {i,1,TSectors-1}], {j,1,TFactors}];

In[4]:= Isoquants2[pars_,opts___] :=
          ContourPlot[Release[X[2]/.FactorRules/.Assign[pars]],
              Release[{L[1,1],eps,Ltot[1]-eps}/.Assign[pars]],
              Release[{L[1,2],eps,Ltot[2]-eps}/.Assign[pars]],
              opts]
```

For example,

```
In[5]:= Isoquants2[{{1,1},{{0.8,0.2},{0.2,0.8}},{0.6,0.4},
              {400,600}}]
```

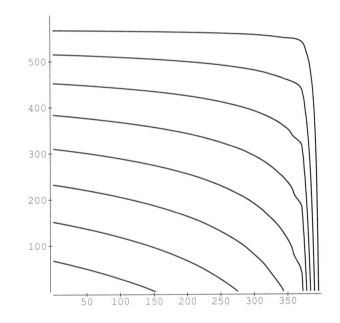

```
Out[5]:= -ContourGraphics-
```

5.3.1.2   The Contract Curve

In the two-sector, two-factor case addressed so far, the two factors are usually called labor and capital, whose remunerations are called wage and rental respectively. Then there is one production equilibrium condition, as can be easily seen from (4), implying that the wage-rental ratios of both the industries must be equalized at the equilibrium.

In the box diagram, this wage-rental equality condition is shown in that the isoquants for the two commodities are tangent at the equilibrium point. If we superimposed `Isoquants[1]` and `Isoquants2`, we would notice that each isoquant of commodity 1 is tangent to exactly one isoquant of commodity 2, at exactly one point. The set of tangency points is the locus of possible equilibria, given the production functions. This locus is the so-called contract curve.

Since we formerly designated the wage-rental equality condition as **MPRatioEqualities**, the function to draw the contract curve is written as follows:

```
In[1]:= ContractCurve[pars_,opts___] :=
          Plot[capital /. MyFindRoot @@
            ({MPRatioEqualities /. FactorRules /.
              L[1,2]->capital,
              {capital,LGuess[1,2],0,Ltot[2]}}
                /. Assign[pars]/. L[1,1]->labor),
            Release[{labor,eps,Ltot[1]-eps}
                /. Assign[pars]],
            opts]
```

5.3.1.3   The Isoquant Curve at the Equilibrium

Similar to the above, we can define functions to draw the single isoquants going through the equilibrium point as follows:

```
In[1]:= Isoquant[i_][pars_,opts___] :=
          Block[{eqn, lims},
            eqn = X[i] == XEq[i][pars] /. Assign[pars];
            Lmin = labor/.MyFindRoot[
              Release[eqn/.L[i,2]->Ltot[2]-eps/.Assign[pars]/.
              L[i,1]->labor],
              {labor,LGuess[i,1],0,Ltot[1]}/.Assign[pars]];
            Lmax = Ltot[1]-eps/.Assign[pars];
            Plot[capital/.MyFindRoot[Release[eqn
                /.{L[i,1]->labor, L[i,2]->capital}],
              {capital,LGuess[i,2],0,Ltot[2]}
                /.Assign[pars]],{labor,Lmin,Lmax},
              opts]]
In[2]:= Isoquant2[pars_,opts___] :=
          Block[{eqn, lims},
            eqn = X[2] - XEq[2][pars] /. FactorRules
                /. Assign[pars];
            Lmin = eps;
            Lmax = labor/.MyFindRoot[Release[eqn
                /.{L[1,2]->eps,L[1,1]->labor}],
              {labor,LGuess[1,1],0,Ltot[1]}/.Assign[pars]];
            Plot[capital/.MyFindRoot[
              Release[eqn/.{L[1,1]->labor,L[1,2]->capital}],
              {capital,LGuess[1,2],0,Ltot[2]}
                /.Assign[pars]],{labor,Lmin,Lmax},
              opts]]
```

5.3.1.4   The Isocost Line

Finally, the tangent to the isoquant curves at the equilibrium point is itself an isocost: it shows the amounts of the inputs that can be obtained at a fixed cost.

```
In[1]:= Isocost[pars_,opts___] := Block[{slope, yint},
            slope = -wEq[2,1][pars]/wEq[2,2][pars];
            yint = slope LEq[1,1][pars] - LEq[1,2][pars];
            Lmin = Max[0,(Ltot[2]+yint)/slope] /. Assign[pars];
            Lmax = Min[Ltot[1],yint/slope] /. Assign[pars];
            Plot[slope labor - yint,{labor,Lmin,Lmax},opts]]
```

5.3.1.5 Integrating to the Box Diagram

Before unifying the above figures into the box diagram, we should define a
function to plot its frame.

```
In[1]:= FrameBox[pars_,opts___] := Graphics[
            {Line[{{0,Ltot[2]},{Ltot[1],Ltot[2]}}],
             Line[{{Ltot[1],0},{Ltot[1],Ltot[2]}}]}
             /.Assign[pars],opts]
```

Then we collect all five graphics into a single routine:

```
In[2]:= EdgeworthBowley[args__] := Show[{
            Isoquant[1][args,DisplayFunction->Identity],
            Isoquant2[args,DisplayFunction->Identity],
            ContractCurve[args,DisplayFunction->Identity],
            Isocost[args,DisplayFunction->Identity],
            FrameBox[args,DisplayFunction->Identity]},
            DisplayFunction->$DisplayFunction]
```

The example command is

```
In[3]:= EdgeworthBowley[{{1,1},{{0.8,0.2},{0.2,0.8}},{0.6,0.4},
        {400,600}}, AxesLabel->{"labor","capital"},
        AspectRatio->Automatic]
```

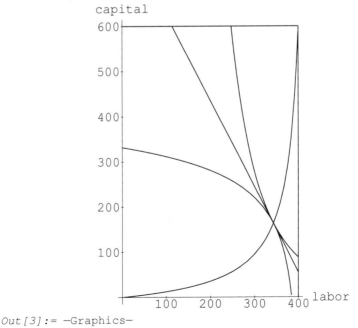

```
Out[3]:= —Graphics—
```

5.3.2   The Production-possibilities Curve

The production-possibilities curve (PPC) depicts the efficient-production locus, that is, it plots the maximum obtainable amount of one commodity for each amount of the other. The PPC can be obtained by allocating the factors along the contract curve, so essentially the same code can be reused:

```
In[1]:= PPC[pars_,opts___]  :=
          Block[
            {PP={X[1],X[2]} /.FactorRules /. Assign[pars]},
            ParametricPlot[
              PP /. L[1,2]->capital /. MyFindRoot @@
                ({MPRatioEqualities /. FactorRules/.
                  L[1,2]->capital,
                  {capital,LGuess[1,2],0,Ltot[2]}}
                  /. Assign[pars]/. L[1,1]->labor) /.
                L[1,1]->labor,
              Release[{labor,eps,Ltot[1]-eps} /. Assign[pars]],
              opts]]
```

The equilibrium productions on the production-possibilities curve is the point where both the PPC and the social-indifference curve are tangent to the social budget line. The social-indifference curve is a level curve of the utility function, that is equation (5) in the basic model. The social budget line, that is equation (7), is the combination of commodity amounts ($Co[i]$) that can be afforded by the economy given a national income (Y) and prices ($p[i]$).

As in the case of the Edgeworth-Bowley diagram, we can easily write **Plot**-based functions to illustrate the indifference curve and the budget line:

```
In[2]:= IndifferenceCurve[pars_,opts___]  :=
          Block[{eqn,slope,yint},
            {slope,yint} = {-1,YEq[pars]}/pEq[2][pars];
            eqn = UEq[pars] == De[1]^s[1] De[2]^s[2]/.Assign[pars];
            D1min = De1 /. MyFindRoot[Release[eqn /.
              {De[2]->yint,De[1]->De1}],
                {De1,CoEq[1][pars]}];
            D1max = -yint/slope;
            Plot[D2 /. MyFindRoot @@
              ({eqn, {De[2],CoEq[2][pars]}}/.
                {De[2]->D2,De[1]->D1}),
              {D1, D1min, D1max},
              opts]]
In[3]:= BudgetLine[pars_,opts___]  :=
          Block[{yint,slope},
            {slope,yint} = {-1,YEq[pars]}/pEq[2][pars];
            Plot[slope De[1] + yint /. De[1]->De1,
              {De1, 0, -yint/slope}, opts]]
In[4]:= PPCDiagram[args__]  :=
          Show[{
            PPC[args,DisplayFunction->Identity],
            IndifferenceCurve[args,DisplayFunction->Identity],
            BudgetLine[args,DisplayFunction->Identity]},
          DisplayFunction->$DisplayFunction]
```

The example command is

```
In[5]:= PPCDiagram[{{1,1},{{0.8,0.2},{0.2,0.8}},{0.6,0.4},
                {400,600}},
          AxesLabel->{"food","clothing"},
          AspectRatio->Automatic]
```

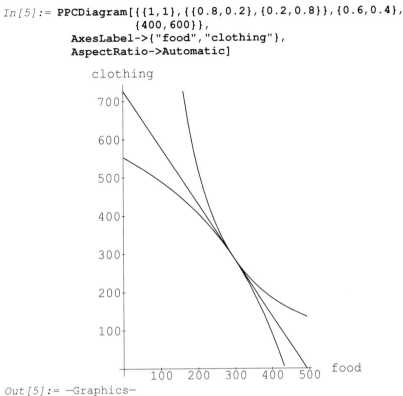

```
Out[5]:= -Graphics-
```

5.4   Program Extensions

So far we have proceeded on the simple two-sector and two-factor economy with the Cobb-Douglas production functions and the Cobb-Douglas utility function. These specifications are, however, only for simplicity's sake, and can be modified in many directions. In this section we describe some examples of these extensions.

5.4.1   The Model with CES Functions

Replacing the Cobb-Douglas functions with the CES functions on the productions and/or the utility is simple and straightforward. In order to apply the CES production functions (12) to the model, it is necessary to alter the definition of X[i] as

```
In[1]:= Do[X[i] =
          A[i] Sum[a[i,j] L[i,j]^-a[i,TFactors+1],
          {j,1,TFactors}]^(-1/a[i,TFactors+1]), {i,1,TSectors}];
```

where the elasticity parameter, e in equation (12), of the i-th sector is designated as $a[i, \text{TFactors+1}]$, that is $(1 + m)$th production parameter of $a[i, j]$.

Therefore the dimension of $\text{\$prodpars}$ must be increased to include it.

In[2]:= **\$prodpars=Array[a, {TSectors, TFactors+1}];**

By replacing the respective definitions and rerunning the assignments to the variables that depend on them, the model is changed to use the CES production functions. The package **GEModels.m** gives a general mechanism to do this.

In[3]:= **<<GEModels.m**

After loading the above package, one must choose between models with **SetModel** command. The following command gives the default two-sector and two-factor model with Cobb-Douglas production functions and Cobb-Douglas utility function.

In[4]:= **SetModel[]**

The command to change for CES production functions is

In[5]:= **SetModel[ProductionFunctions->CES]**

The example command is

In[6]:= **PPCDiagram[{{1,1},{{0.8,0.2,0.3},{0.2,0.8,0.5}},**
          {0.6,0.4},{400,600}},
       AxesLabel->{"food","clothing"},
       AspectRatio->Automatic]

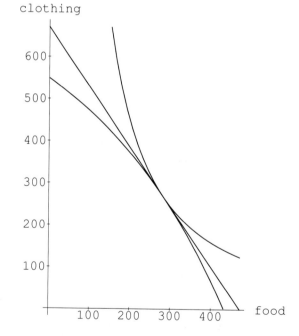

Out[6]:= —Graphics—

Similarly, we can set the model with the CES utility function by redefining as

```
In[7]:= U = Sum[s[i] Co[i]^-s[TSectors+1],
          {i,1,TSectors}]^(-1/s[TSectors+1]);
```

and

```
In[8]:= $utilpars=Array[s, TSectors+1];
```

The command to do this is

```
In[9]:= SetModel[UtilityFunction->CES]
```

The example command is

```
In[10]:= PPCDiagram[{{1,1},{{0.8,0.2},{0.2,0.8}},
              {0.6,0.4,4},{400,600}},
         AxesLabel->{"food","clothing"}, AspectRatio->Automatic]
```

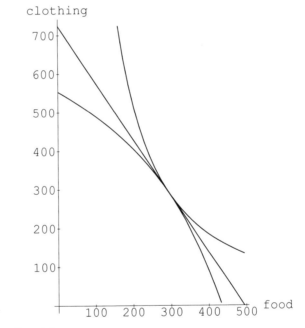

```
Out[10]:= -Graphics-
```

5.4.2   The Multi-sector and/or Multi-factor Model

The next extension we discuss is to a model with more than two commodities and/or more than two production factors. Since our program has been constructed to correspond to the basic model with n-sector and m-factor, such extensions need no modifications in the code except the dimensional setting of the model at the outset. In the case of a three-commodity and two-factor economy, for example, the initial setting must be

```
In[1]:= TSectors=3; TFactors=2;
```

On using the package **GEModels.m**, the command to do this is

In[2]:= **SetModel[TSectors->3]**

Though there are no limits on the dimensional sizes of the model in using the numerical solution functions we have defined, most of the graphical functions are valid only in the two-sector and two-factor setting. It is always possible, however, to visualize a two dimensional production-possibilities curve however many production factors are in use. To make our former PPC function effective for multi-factor cases, therefore, we modify it as follows.

```
In[3]:= PPC[pars_,opts___] := Block[
          {PP={X[1],X[2]} /.FactorRules /. Assign[pars]},
          ParametricPlot[PP /. MyFindRoot @@
            (Prepend[Take[Vars,{2,TFactors}],
             MPRatioEqualities /. FactorRules]
          /. Assign[pars]/. L[1,1]->labor) /. L[1,1]->labor,
            Release[{labor,eps,Ltot[1]-eps} /. Assign[pars]],
          opts]]
```

To obtain a PPC graph for the two-commodity and three-factor case, for example, the initial setting must be

In[4]:= **TSectors=2; TFactors=3;**

On using the package **GEModels.m**, it is necessary to set initially as

In[5]:= **SetModel[TFactors->3]**

Then the following command gives a PPC graph.

In[6]:= **PPC[{{1,1},{{0.6,0.2,0.2},{0.1,0.1,0.8}},{0.6,0.4},** **{400,600,100}}]**

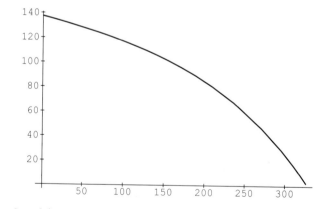

Out[6]:= —Graphics—

5.4.3   The Ricardian Model

Similarly, we can modify the model into the opposite direction by reducing the total number of the sectors and/or the factors to one.

Although the one-sector model isn't interesting within our modelling, a little attention should be paid to one-factor model. In the economic literature, the model which requires labor as the sole production factor is often called the Ricardian model, and has long been used as an efficacious framework in international trade theories.

To make the model appropriate for such Ricardian cases, it is necessary to set the total number of the factors in use to one. On the package **GEModels.m**, it is done by

In[1]:= **SetModel[TFactors->1]**

Then an equilibrium allocation of the labor between the two sectors is obtained by

In[2]:= **Equilibrium[{{2,3},{{1},{1}},{0.6,0.4},{200}}]**

Out[2]:= {L[1, 1] -> 120., L[2, 1] -> 80.}

In this command it must be noted that all the distribution parameters (a[i,1]) are set to one, thus giving linear production functions. Then the units parameter (A[i]), given A[1]->2 and A[2]->3 respectively in the above command, represents the physical productivity of labor in the i-th sector.

As previously argued, the production-possibilities curve can be plotted irrespective of the dimensional size of the production factors. It is so with this one-factor case. The following is an example command to visualize an equilibrium on the Ricardian production-possibilities, a figure familiar in international trade textbooks.

In[3]:= **PPCDiagram[{{2,3},{{1},{1}},{0.6,0.4},{200}},**
            AxesLabel->{"food","clothing"}, AspectRatio->Automatic]

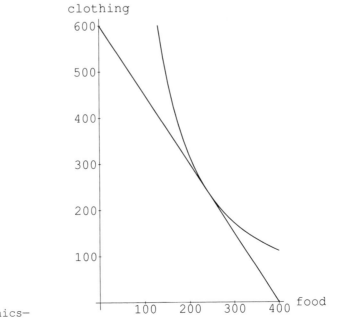

Out[3]:= —Graphics—

5.4.4   The Specific Factor Model

On the Cobb-Douglas production functions, it is assumed that the summation of all the distribution parameters is one. Otherwise the linear homogeneity of the production functions can't be guaranteed. If we set it to be less than unity, the production functions are under decreasing returns to scale. We can easily examine this with the isoquant map.

In[1]:= **Isoquants[1][{{1,1},{{.4,.2},{.2,.8}},{.6,.4},{400,600}}]**

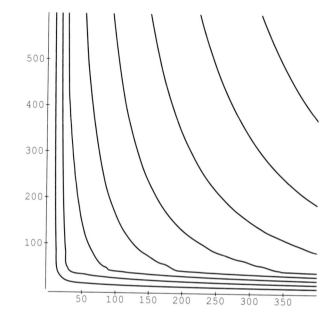

Out[1]:= −ContourGraphics−

Here the distribution parameters in the first sector are set to 0.4 (=a[1,1]) and 0.2 (=a[1,2]) so that the summation of them is 0.6 (<1).

We can interpret this as a specific factor model, whose assumption is that the productions are under decreasing returns (= increasing costs) owing to the existence of the sector-specific factor that cannot be increased.

5.4.5   The Model with Intermediate Inputs

If we want to apply our program to research of the actual economy, it must be modified to include the intermediate inputs. Since we don't assume the existence of the intermediate inputs in the basic model, this extension requires a slight modification to it.

According to the usual Leontief-Sraffa model, we assume that all the intermediate inputs' coefficients are fixed. Then equation (8) in the basic model is replaced by

$$Co[i] = X[i] - \sum_{k=1}^{n} X[k]ic[i,k] \qquad i = 1,\ldots,n, \qquad (13)$$

Here $ic[i,k]$ is the physical amount of i-th goods requisite for producing one unit of k-th goods. Equation (13) means that all the consumptions of commodities are equal to their net productions.

We also replace equation (9) with

$$vp[i] = w[i,1](p[i] - \sum_{l=1}^{n} p[l]ic[l,i]) \qquad i = 1,\ldots,n, \qquad (14)$$

Here $vp[i]$ is the net marginal value productivity of the first factor in the i-th sector. Then equation (10) can represent the equilibrium condition on this model as before. In view of this extended model, our former basic model is thought to be a special case where all the intermediate inputs' coefficients are zero.

Corresponding to the extension, we alter the definitions of Co[i] and vp[i] in the program as follows:

```
In[1]:= Do[Co[i] = X[i]-Sum[X[k] ic[i,k], {k,1,TSectors}],
          {i,1,TSectors}];
        Do[vp[i] = w[i,1](p[i]-Sum[p[l] ic[l,i], {l,1,TSectors}]),
          {i,1,TSectors}];
```

Also, the intermediate inputs' coefficients matrix is added next to the production function parameters.

```
In[2]:= $intcoffs=Array[ic, {TSectors, TSectors}];
```

As argued above, the introduction of intermediate inputs into the model necessitates a divergence between the gross productions and the net productions. Therefore we have a net production-possibilities curve (NPPC) besides PPC. We can define NPPC function in the same manner as PPC.

```
In[3]:= NPPC[pars_,opts___] := Block[
          {NPP={Co[1],Co[2]} /. FactorRules /. Assign[pars]},
          ParametricPlot[NPP /. MyFindRoot @@
            (Prepend[Take[Vars,{2,TFactors}],
              MPRatioEqualities /. FactorRules]
          /. Assign[pars] /. L[1,1]->labor) /. L[1,1]->labor,
            Release[{labor,eps,Ltot[1]-eps} /. Assign[pars]],
            opts]]
```

We also define a function to draw edge lines of the net production-possibilities.

```
In[4]:= NPPCLines[pars_,opts___] := Block[
          {Lim1={Co[1],Co[2]} /. FactorRules
          /. Table[Rule[L[1,j],0],{j,1,TFactors}]
          /. Assign[pars], Lim2={Co[1],Co[2]} /. FactorRules
          /. Table[Rule[L[1,j],Ltot[j]],{j,1,TFactors}]
          /. Assign[pars]},
          Graphics[{Line[{{0,0},Lim1}],
                    Line[{{0,0},Lim2}]}, opts]]
```

Finally we define a function to plot all the associated objects.

```
In[5]:= NPPCDiagram[args__] := Show[{
            PPC[args,DisplayFunction->Identity],
            NPPC[args,DisplayFunction->Identity],
            NPPCLines[args,DisplayFunction->Identity],
            IndifferenceCurve[args,DisplayFunction->Identity],
            BudgetLine[args,DisplayFunction->Identity]},
         DisplayFunction->$DisplayFunction]
```

The example command is

```
In[6]:= NPPCDiagram[{{1,1},{{.8,.2},{.2,.8}},{{.1,.3},{.4,.1}},
         {.6,.4},{400,600}},
         AxesLabel->{"food","clothing"},
         AspectRatio->Automatic]
```

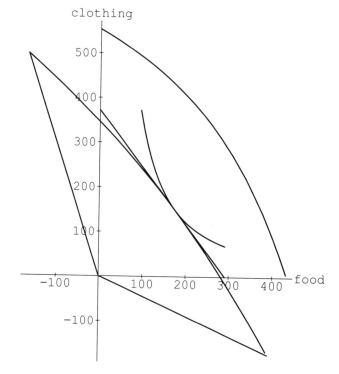

```
Out[6]:= -Graphics-
```

5.4.6   The Leontief-Sraffa Model

Similar to the Ricardian model, we can think of a case in which there is only one production factor in this intermediate production model. Then we obtain a model known as the Leontief-Sraffa model. The initial setting of this is

```
In[1]:= SetModel[TFactors->1, Intermediates->True]
```

The example command is

```
In[2]:= NPPCDiagram[{{2,3},{{1},{1}},{{.1,.3},{.4,.1}},
            {.6,.4},{400}}, AxesLabel->{"food","clothing"},
            AspectRatio->Automatic]
```

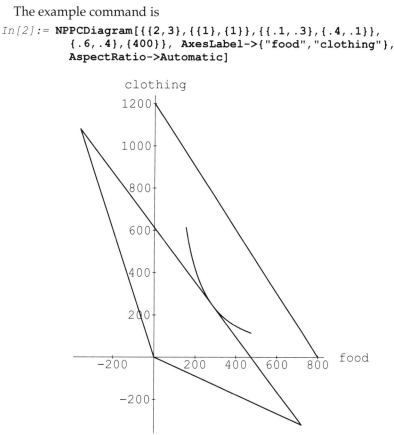

```
Out[2]:= —Graphics—
```

5.5 Acknowledgment

The contents of this chapter depends largely on [Noguchi 1991]. Most of the code accompanying the previous article, for which I am greatly indebted to Silvio Levy, are reused with or without modifications. I am also indebted to Senshu University for the financial assistance in carrying out the research.

5.6 References

Afriat, S. N. 1987. *Logic of Choice and Economic Theory.* Oxford, Clarendon Press.

Chacholiades, M. 1985. *International Trade Theory and Policy.* McGraw-Hill, Inc.

Dinwiddy, C. L. and F. J. Teal. 1988. *The Two-Sector General Equilibrium Model: A New Approach.* Oxford, Phillip Allan.

Katzner, D. W. 1989. *The Walrasian Vision of the Microeconomy: an Elementary Exposition of the Structure of Modern General Equilibrium Theory.* Ann Arbor, The University of Michigan Press.

Noguchi, A. 1991 "The Two-Sector General Equilibrium Model: Numerical and Graphical Representations of an Economy," *The Mathematica Journal*, Volume 1, Issue 3 Winter, 96–103

6 ▷ Symbolic Algebra Programming for Analyzing the Long Run Dynamics of Economic Models

Gary S. Anderson

6.1 Introduction

Economists have long used nonlinear mathematical models to explore important empirical and theoretical issues in public finance, development, international trade, savings and monetary policy. Recently, some researchers have criticized the way these and other models characterize the long run tendency of the economy. If the equations which codify the assumptions in the models can display bizarre behavior, the models could give misleading forecasts of the behavior of the economy.

This paper shows how symbolic algebra programs can facilitate the analysis of the dynamics of these nonlinear equation systems. I have used the symbolic algebra capabilities of *Mathematica* to develop a collection of programs for analyzing the asymptotic behavior of economic models. These symbolic programming algorithms implement a set of algorithms originally designed for numerical processing. The paper shows how to use these tools to derive formulae for characterizing the long run dynamics of economic models.

The powerful symbolic and algebraic manipulation tools make it possible to analytically explore the subtle transitions between generic classes of long run behavior for these models. The paper develops formulae for characterizing the asymptotic behavior of an overlapping generations model for plausible ranges of the parameters. These results provide insights about features of these models which are useful for both theoretical and empirical economists.

Nonlinear dynamic models have served as important tools for much of modern macroeconomics [8, 24]. The Ramsey neoclassical growth model, and overlapping generation models are but two examples of mainstream macroeconomic models which posit a nonlinear specification of the relationship between economic variables over time. Economists use these models in the classroom, in theoretical and empirical analysis of important aggregate relationships, and for investigating the potential impact of monetary, and fiscal policy. The continued increase in computing speed and declining cost of computing for economists probably means nonlinear models will become even more important for future econometric and policy analysis.

Some of these nonlinear models come from dynamic optimization of the choice problem facing individual economic agents or a central planner. Economists often use first order conditions from dynamic optimization problems and a simplifying certainty equivalence assumption to characterize the behavior of economic agents. This approach leads to models which possess the "saddle point property." Simulation and estimation of these models involves solving a nonlinear two point boundary value problem with one endpoint arbitrarily far off in the future.

Although dynamic nonlinear models can have very complicated behavior [14], economists who use these models often implicitly assume that these mainstream economic models have a fixed point to which model solutions converge. Unfortunately, it is difficult to guarantee that a given nonlinear specification will have the appropriate asymptotic properties for all plausible values of model parameters. It is becoming clear that it is important to be aware of and accommodate a more comprehensive set of possible asymptotic solutions when applying these models or while searching parameter space when estimating the coefficients in such models.

6.2   Numerical Routines vs Symbolic Routines

The art of modeling is an integral part of all scientific study. There are many approaches to and types of models used in the sciences. Intrilligator [15] identifies four important types of models:

- Verbal/logical models: The "Invisible Hand" and the "Division of Labor" are prominent examples of the use of verbal analogies to codify important systemic phenomena.

- Physical models: Economists have used analog computers and fluid flow models to codify important interactions between economic agents.

- Geometric models: The traditional ISLM model of the relationship between interest rates and output presented in undergraduate macroeconomics courses exemplifies the use of a diagrammatic characterization of the important interactions between markets and economic agents.

- Algebraic models: These models use algebraic relations forming a system of equations to codify the interactions between agents and markets. The system of equations contains variables, both *endogenous* (jointly determined by the equation system) and *exogenous* (determined by factors outside the modeled system), and *parameters* (quantities which the modeler must set at particular values in order to completely characterize the interactions between components of the model). The variables typically correspond to stocks or flows of quantities which economic agents own and exchange and vary over time. Parameters typically are fixed at particular values and allow a specific algebraic model to accommodate a range of behaviors within the same algebraic framework.

6.2.1   An Example ISLM Model

Modeling of complicated real world phenomena entails developing simplified representations of the important interactions between components of the system under study. Consider a model of the determination of the level of output and interest rates in a macro economy. A simple ISLM model can be described in several ways:

Verbal Model   The verbal model posits that

- for equilibrium in financial markets, real money balances must be lower if interest rates are higher for a given level of real output, but must be higher if real output is higher for a given level of interest rates.

- for equilibrium in product markets, higher interest rates correspond to lower levels of output

Graphical Model   We can graph equilibrium combinations of interest rates and output in the financial markets to construct an LM curve and then in product markets to construct an IS curve as was done to create Figure 1.

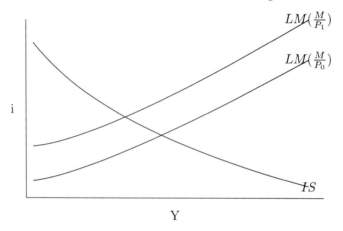

Figure 1: Graphical Representation of the ISLM Model

Algebraic Model   The algebraic model asserts [8]:

$$\frac{M}{P} = L(i, Y)$$

with $\partial L/\partial i < 0, \partial L/\partial Y > 0$.

$$Y = A(i)$$

with $\partial A/\partial i < 0$. Where M represents the level of money held by economic agents, P represents the general price level, i represents the level of interest rates, and Y represents the level of gross domestic product.

Thus, we have three different characterizations of the same conceptual model.

Economists often write down systems of equations which codify the qualitative aspects of the verbal, physical, and geometric models. They use the

symbolic representations of the models to investigate generic, qualitative properties of the models. Indeed, before computers were widely available, this was
the most effective way to use algebraic models.

With the advent of computers, numerical processing became much easier and
it became possible to employ data in calibrating relationships embodied in the
conceptual models. In order to bring data to bear in the context of these models,
the economist must typically commit to a specific set of equations and a specific
parameterization of those equations. Economists use these parameters to help
them characterize the strength of qualitative relationships. Thus, these parameters play a special role in the linkage between the algebraic characterization
of the models and the verbal, physical or geometric model counterparts. In
some contexts the particular parameter values are not as important as the fact
that the parameters lie in some range of values consistent with some important
qualitative relationship. For example, the following system of equations and
parameterization of the ISLM model would constitute a particular econometric
model.

Econometric Model   The econometric model posits specific functional forms
with parameters [8]:

$$\log\left(\frac{M}{P}\right) = b_0 + b_i i + b_Y Y$$

$$Y = c_o + c_i i$$

In this context, one expects, and hopes the data confirms, that $\partial L/\partial i = b_i < 0$,
$\partial L/\partial Y = b_y > 0$. $\partial A/\partial i = c_i < 0$.

In this particular model there is a simple direct relationship between the
parameters of the econometric model and the conceptual/qualitative properties of the corresponding economic model. In most econometric models, the
relationship is not nearly so transparent.

The power of computers for carrying out numerical calculations is well known
and widely available. The complexity of the relationship between parameter
values and the qualitative properties of the equation systems have led some to
apply numerical techniques for exploring the properties of the models in specific
regions of the parameter space. Unfortunately with numerical approaches, one
must often leave the question of robustness of the results unresolved. One
typically cannot try all valid values of the parameters for a given model. Even
if one did, one would still need a way of summarizing the results in a coherent
and accessible way.

6.2.2   A New Tool For an Old Problem

Economists have developed theory and techniques for exploring the relationship
between the parameters and the qualitative properties of models. Lancaster [20]
describes an algorithm for determining the qualitative impact of changes in endogenous variables given the sign of coefficients in a simultaneous equation
system. Samuelson's "Correspondence Principle" is another example of a tech-

nique which explores the relationship between particular parameter values and the qualitative properties of an economic model. More recently, Berndsen and Daniels [7] and Farley and Lin [11] describe a formal approach for constructing and manipulating algebraic models in which the modeler only specifies the sign of the impact of changes in endogenous variables.

However, even for small relatively simple models, these approaches have been difficult to apply. Relatively simple equation systems can lead to scores of equations that are difficult to manipulate and intractable using traditional approaches carried out by hand without computers.

However, it is now possible to use computer programs to assist the economist in carrying out the analysis of equation systems. Symbolic algebra analysis of economic models is not new—indeed such analysis preceded numerical analysis of economic models. Programming languages like Maple and *Mathematica* allow their users to enter symbols representing an equation and to analytically add, multiply, differentiate, and integrate these equations. Using computers to manipulate the equation systems can push back the frontier of tractability and produce useful insights into the connection between the parameter values and the qualitative behavior of the economic models. Economists will likely find that some models which have closed form solutions that were difficult to obtain will now be tractable.

Symbolic algebra programs are not a substitute for human ingenuity. The computer provides a useful tool for accurately transforming an equation system, but the economist will likely have to direct the computer to carry out the appropriate transformations and simplifications just as he would using the traditional pencil and paper approach to solving economic models. In effect, the symbolic algebra programs provide a "smart sheet of paper." In addition, they also provide a mechanism for preserving results and for recording and communicating the steps required to get the results. If the steps that one applies for a particular model are useful for a class of models, these steps are easy to reapply for the new model. When one reapplies these steps on the new model, one will be executing a symbolic algebra program.

Numerical techniques for analyzing models often have corresponding symbolic implementations. If one can write down a sequence of numerical transformations to be applied to a model, one often can write down an analogous symbolic transformation. In order to apply the numerical routine, one will have to substitute specific parameter values into a given model. The successful completion of the numerical routine will produce a specific numerical result for that specific set of parameter values. In order to apply a symbolic approach, one need not make these specific parameter value substitutions. The successful completion of the symbolic routine will produce a more general symbolic result analogous to the result of solving the system of equations by hand.

6.2.3   Symbolic Algebra Analysis of Example ISLM Model

For example, one may be interested in the equilibrium level of the interest rate and income in the simple ISLM model, and how these quantities are affected by the level of real balances. In a numerical approach to investigating this problem, one would select specific reasonable parameter values for c_0, c_i, b_0, b_i, b_Y, and M/P. Given these numerical values, one could use a package like MATLAB to solve for the equilibrium interest rate and level of output. One could construct a table of values in order to empirically investigate the relationship between the level of real money balances and the equilibrium interest rate and output. See Figure 2.

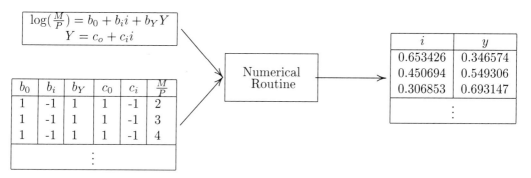

Figure 2: Numerical Routine Inputs and Outputs

Alternatively, in a symbolic approach, one would solve the system of equations for i and y in terms of the coefficients and the level of real money balances:

$$i^* = \frac{-b_o - b_y c_o + \log(\frac{M}{P})}{b_i + b_y c_i}$$

$$y^* = \frac{b_i c_o - b_o c_i + c_i \log(\frac{M}{P})}{b_i + b_y c_i}$$

It would be relatively easy to infer important qualitative properties from the closed form solution.

One could use a symbolic algebra program to obtain the closed form solutions above. Having done so, one has a template for solving similar equation systems. See Figure 3.

Figure 3: Symbolic Routine Inputs and Outputs

Symbolic algebra programs provide a means of obtaining traditional closed form solutions for some problems whose solutions may have been difficult to obtain analytically. This template can be transformed into a symbolic algebra program which obtains closed form solutions for a specific set of models. Section 6.8 applies this simple idea in a more useful context.

6.3 Complicated Dynamics are Potentially Present in Traditional Economic Models

Recently, some economists have begun to embrace the potentially complex non-linear asymptotic behavior of nonlinear dynamic economic models as an important topic of investigation. Gale first pointed out the existence of equilibrium cycles in overlapping generations models [12]. Benhabib and Rustichini [6] describe a neoclassical growth model with equilibrium limit cycles with the idea of convincing their colleagues that this is not unusual for dynamic nonlinear models. Jullien [16] investigates bifurcations of solutions of a nonlinear model to establish the existence of cycles. Jullien demonstrates the equivalence of an overlapping generations model and a one dimensional system to prove that equilibrium cycles and chaotic solutions are possible.

Grandmont [13] studies the existence of sunspot equilibria in nonlinear models by investigating their potentially complex asymptotic dynamics. Laitner describes how complicated dynamics is a prerequisite for the existence of sunspot equilibria [19]. James Peck performs a similar analysis on overlapping generations models to identify situations where there are sunspot equilibria [22].

The possible existence of complicated long run dynamics has several potentially important implications for the use of nonlinear models in economics.

6.3.1   Implications for Econometrics

The existing methodologies for simulating and estimating these models often encounter problems which are hard to diagnose. During the model development process, economists conceive models with appropriate asymptotic properties; but during estimation, hill climbing routines control the parameters *and* the asymptotic properties. A fixed point with the appropriate stability property may evolve into a periodic point, or disappear or lose the saddle point property frustrating the function evaluation phase of the estimation process.

A robust method for simulating and estimating these models must carefully investigate the asymptotic behavior of the models in order to identify problems caused by a failure of the solution methodology, poor model specification, bad parameter selection, or programmer error.

6.3.2   Implications for Our Basic Understanding of a Competitive System

Analysis of the overlapping generations model and neoclassical growth models suggests that a competitive system may have an endogenous business cycle. Benhabib and Rustichini [6] describe a neoclassical growth model with equilibrium limit cycles. They show that the perfect competition assumption does not rule out persistent endogenous cycles.

There is a close relationship between the existence of multiple solutions, indeterminacy of perfect foresight paths and bifurcations of fixed points on the one hand and the existence of sunspot equilibria on the other [19, 21, 22]. When there are sun spot equilibria, self fulfilling expectations are often insufficient to uniquely determine the future values of economic variables. In this case, it may be impossible for individual agents to learn the underlying fundamental parameters of the model by observing economic timeseries. In such a world, "animal spirits" can play an important role in conditioning economic agents' expectations of the evolution of economic variables.

6.3.3 Tools and Methodology From Dynamic Systems Analysis Useful in Diagnosing or Exploiting Complicated Dynamic Behavior of Nonlinear Economic Systems

When nonlinear models possess fixed points or limit cycles, a linear algebraic analysis of asymptotic properties can often determine the local existence and uniqueness of convergent paths. The local analysis of a nonlinear dynamical system should begin with a study of the first order or linear behavior of the equation system [10, 14].[1]

For "saddle point" models, linear algebraic analysis of the asymptotic behavior provides linear restrictions on the solution paths that are useful for computing nonlinear solutions. Economically meaningful solutions require appropriate asymptotic convergence properties. Laitner [18] provides a definition of stability for nonlinear perfect foresight models. Anderson and Moore [2] describe a technique for checking the appropriateness of the asymptotic properties of linear models. The Anderson-Moore technique is easily extended to nonlinear systems, and *Mathematica*, a symbolic algebra program, provides powerful tools for automating the symbolic computations involved in applying these asymptotic stability checks.

6.4 Nonlinear Dynamic Economic Model Specification

6.4.1 General Formulation

Consider the model

$$h(x_{t-\tau}, x_{t-\tau+1}, ..., x_{t+\theta-1}, x_{t+\theta}) = 0$$
$$t = 0, ..., \infty \tag{1}$$

where $x \in \Re^L$ and $h : \Re^{L(\tau+1+\theta)} \to \Re^L$. We want to determine the solutions to equation system (1) with initial conditions

$$x_i = \bar{x}_i \ for \ i = -\tau, ..., -1$$

---

[1] Terms higher than first order must be considered at nonhyperbolic periodic points.

satisfying

1. **A fixed point**

$$\lim_{t \to \infty} x_t = x^*.$$

or

2. **A Limit Cycle**

$$\lim_{k \to \infty} \begin{bmatrix} x_{pk} \\ x_{pk+1} \\ \vdots \\ x_{pk+(p-1)} \end{bmatrix} = \begin{bmatrix} x_0^* \\ x_1^* \\ \vdots \\ x_{p-1}^* \end{bmatrix}$$

Where p is the periodicity of the limit cycle.

The literature contains many models which are special cases of equation system (1).

6.4.2   Several Example Dynamic Nonlinear Economic Models

6.4.2.1   The Overlapping Generations Model of Benhabib and Laroque

Benhabib and Laroque [5] present an overlapping generations model with money, labor, and a good which workers can consume or store as capital. Benhabib and Laroque demonstrate that there is a one to one correspondence between competitive equilibria of this model and solutions to the three equation system

$$f_k(k_t, l_{t+1}) f_l(k_{t-1}, l_t) U_1'(f_k(k_t, l_{t+1}) f_k(k_{t-1}, l_t) l_t) - U_2'(l_t) = 0$$
$$k_t + M q_t - f_l(k_{t-1}, l_t) = 0 \qquad (2)$$
$$q_{t+1} - f_k(k_t, l_{t+1}) q_t = 0$$

Benhabib and Laroque use this model to demonstrate that cyclical equilibria exist, and to develop an interpretable parameterization of the model. They study the behavior of their model near the golden rule equilibria and apply results from bifurcation theory to show the existence of limit cycles.

6.4.2.2   The Overlapping Generations Model of Jullien

Jullien [16] also studies an overlapping generations model with production where m_t represents real money balances, k_t represents capital, $W(k_t)$ is a wage function reflecting the marginal product of labor from a constant returns production function, and $S(W(k_t), f'(k_t))$ is a savings function obtained from intertemporal utility maximization. His system is also of the form of equation system (1).

$$m_t + k_t = S(W(k_{t-1}), f'(k_t))$$
$$m_{t+1} = f'(k_t) m_t$$

He demonstrates the possibility of cyclical and chaotic behavior by recasting the model as a one dimensional system and using well known results characterizing the global properties of one dimensional maps.

6.4.2.3   A Certainty Equivalence Formulation of a Real Business Cycle Model

McCallum [3] describes a real business cycle model:

$$c_t + k_t = z_t f(n_t, k_{t-1}) + (1 - \delta)k_{t-1}$$
$$u_1(c_t, 1 - n_t) - \lambda_t = 0$$
$$u_2(c_t, 1 - n_t) = \lambda_t z_t f_1(n_t, k_{t-1})$$
$$\lambda_t = \beta \lambda_{t+1} [z_{t+1} f_2(n_{t+1}, k_t) + 1 - \delta]$$
$$(z_t - z^*) = \rho(z_{t-1} - z^*)$$

This model is also of the form of equation system (1).

6.4.2.4   A Money Demand Model

Consider the three equation nonlinear system

$$\ln \frac{m_t}{p_t} = \alpha + \beta \ln(\rho + (\frac{p_{t+1} - p_t}{p_t}))$$
$$m_t - m_{t-1} = \gamma(m_{t-1} - \mu) + \delta s_t$$
$$s_t = \lambda s_{t-1}(1 - s_{t-1})$$

Where $0 \leq \lambda$, $\alpha < 0$, $\beta < 0$, $\rho > 0$, $\gamma < 0$, and $m^* > 0$ exogenously given.

This example augments a simple forward looking money demand model with a quadratic map. The quadratic map is a much studied nonlinear function whose asymptotic properties are well known [10]. As we vary the parameter λ we can study a model with fixed points, limit cycles, and with more complicated invariant sets.

There are several widely known techniques for computing solutions to equation system (1) when h is linear [9]. This paper adopts the method of Anderson and Moore [2] to determine the existence, and local uniqueness of the solutions to equation system (1).

6.5   A General Methodology for Analyzing the Asymptotic Properties of Nonlinear Dynamic Economic Models

6.5.1   The Anderson-Moore Linear Algebraic Technique for Solving Linear Perfect Foresight Models

Anderson and Moore [2] present a fail-safe method for analyzing any linear perfect foresight model. They describe a procedure which either computes the reduced form solution or indicates why the model has no reduced form.

6.5.1.1   A Useful Theorem

Anderson and Moore [2] outline a procedure that computes solutions for structural models of the form

$$\sum_{i=-\tau}^{\theta} H_i\, X_{t+i} = 0\,,\, t \geq 0 \tag{3}$$

with initial conditions

$$X_i\, =\, x_i\,,\, i = -\tau\,,\ldots,\, -1$$

where both τ and θ are non-negative, and X_t is an L dimensional real vector.

Anderson-Moore [1] provides a constructive proof of the following theorem.

Theorem 1   If the L by L real coefficient matrices $H_i : i = -\tau,\ldots,\theta$ satisfy the following two restrictions:

1. The origin is the unique steady state of equation (3). That is, if

$$\left(\sum_{i=-\tau}^{\theta} H_i\right) X^* = 0,\, \Rightarrow\, X^* = 0$$

2. Corresponding to any initial conditions $X_i = x_i : i = -\tau, \ldots, -1$, equation (3) has a unique solution $X_t : t \geq 0$ such that

$$\lim_{t\to\infty} X_t\, =\, 0$$

then the model has a reduced-form representation

$$X_t\, =\, \sum_{i\,=\,-\tau}^{-1} B_i X_{t+i}\,,\, t\, >\, 0$$

generating the unique solution $X_t : t \geq 0$ such that

$$\lim_{t\to\infty} X_t\, =\, 0.$$

Anderson-Moore [2] presents a constructive procedure for analyzing linear perfect foresight models. Given the coefficient matrix

$$[\,H_{-\tau} \ldots H_\theta\,]$$

the procedure computes the reduced form coefficient matrix

$$[\,B_{-\tau} \ldots B_{-1}\,]$$

for any model satisfying assumptions 1 and 2. If the model does not satisfy assumptions 1 and 2, the procedure indicates whether there are no convergent solutions or a multiplicity of convergent solutions.

In order to compute the matrix B the algorithm first computes a matrix Q which embodies constraints which come from computing a state space transition matrix and linear constraints that guarantee asymptotic convergence to the saddle point. The algorithm described in Section 6.5.2 uses this matrix Q.

6.5.1.2   Summary of the Procedure

This section summarizes the procedure presented in Anderson and Moore [2].

Initialization

1. Verify that $\left(\sum_{i=-\tau}^{\theta} H_i \right)$ is full rank. If it is singular, the steady state is not unique; stop.

2. If it is non-singular, initialize

$$H^{(0)} := [\, H_{-\tau} \ldots H_{\theta} \,]$$
$$Q^{(0)} := \text{null matrix,}$$

Auxiliary Initial Conditions

1. Compute the singular values, $\{\mu_i : i = 1, \ldots, L\}$, and singular vectors, V, of $H_{\theta}^{(k^*)}$. Sort the μ_i small-to-large and order the columns of V conformably. If $\mu_i \neq 0$, $i = 1, \ldots, L$, then $H_{\theta}^{(k^*)}$ is non-singular; go to step 1 of the paragraph on stability conditions below.

2. $H_{\theta}^{(k^*)}$ is singular. Premultiply the coefficient matrix by V^T to annihilate L-rank $(H_{\theta}^{(k^*)})$ rows of $H_{\theta}^{(k^*)}$.

$$\tilde{H}^{(k)} := V^T H^{(k)}$$

3. Partition the coefficient matrix as

q	0
r	

$:= \tilde{H}^{(k)}$

The matrix q has L-rank $(H_{\theta}^{(k^*)})$ rows and $L(\tau + \theta)$ columns; r has rank $(H_{\theta}^{(k)})$ rows and $L(\tau + 1 + \theta)$ columns.

4. Include q among the auxiliary initial conditions

$Q^{(k)}$
q

Now, shift the sub-matrix qL columns to the right in H,

0	q
r	

Repeat these four steps until $H_{\theta}^{(k)}$ is non-singular. Let k^* denote this final value of k

Stability Conditions

1. $H_{\theta}^{(k^*)}$ is non-singular. Solve for coefficients expressing $X_{t+\theta}$ in terms of $X_{t-\tau} \ldots X_{t+\theta-1}$.

$$\Gamma := -(H_{\theta}^{(k^*)})^{-1} \left[H_{-1}^{(k^*)} \ldots H_{(\theta-1)}^{(k^*)} \right]$$

2. Construct the first order state space transition matrix

$$A := \begin{bmatrix} 0I \\ \Gamma \end{bmatrix}$$

3. Compute W, a matrix of row vectors spanning the left invariant subspace of A associated with roots outside the open unit disk. One can use the routine HQR3 presented by G. Stewart [25]. The matrix W contains the stability conditions which guarantee the saddle point property [1].

Reduced Form

1. Concatenate the auxiliary initial conditions with the stability conditions.

$$Q := \boxed{\begin{array}{c} Q^{(k^*)} \\ \hline W \end{array}}$$

2. Partition Q.

$$[Q_L \quad Q_R] := Q$$

where Q_L has $L\tau$ columns and Q_R has $L\theta$ columns.

3. Let n be the number of rows in Q.

   (a) If $n < L\theta$, then assumption 2 is violated; there are many solutions converging to the origin for any initial condition. Stop.

   (b) If $n > L\theta$ or $n = L\theta$ and Q_R is singular, then assumption 2 is violated; there exist initial conditions for which there are no solutions converging to the steady state. Stop.

   (c) If $n = L\theta$ and Q_R is non-singular, then set

   $$[\, B_{-\tau} \ldots B_{-1} \,] := \text{the first L rows of } -Q_R^{-1}Q_L \text{ and}$$

   $$X_t = \sum_{i=-\tau}^{-1} B_i X_{t+i}, t \geq 0$$

   is the unique solution converging to the steady state for any initial conditions. Stop. End.

6.5.2 A Nonlinear Extension of the Anderson-Moore Technique

An investigation of the asymptotic dynamics of nonlinear difference equations can usefully begin with an analysis of the asymptotically linear behavior near fixed points and limit cycles [14, 17, 18].

Since h is nonlinear, we will compute approximate solutions to equation system (1) by linearizing the nonlinear h constraints in equation system (1) at the fixed point or limit cycle.

6.5.2.1 Fixed Points

Compute the steady state value x^* satisfying

$$h(x^*, ..., x^*) = 0$$

Near the steady state, the linear first-order Taylor expansion of h about x^* provides a good approximation to the function h.

$$h(x_{t-\tau}, ..., x_{t+\theta}) \approx \sum_{i=-\tau}^{\theta} H_i\big|_{x^*} (x_{t+i} - x^*)$$

We can apply the techniques presented in [2] to determine the existence and uniqueness of perfect foresight solutions near the steady state.

That stability analysis will produce a matrix Q which restricts values of the endogenous variables to the stable subspace of the linearized system. For trajectories which approach a steady state, we can ultimately replace the nonlinear system with the constraints codified in the matrix Q.

$$Q \begin{bmatrix} x_{T-\tau} - x^* \\ \vdots \\ x_T - x^* \\ \vdots \\ x_{T+\theta} - x^* \end{bmatrix} = 0$$

6.5.2.2   Limit Cycles

Compute the periodic points $x_1^*, x_2^*, \ldots, x_p^*$ satisfying

$$\begin{bmatrix} h(x_{-\tau}^*, \ldots, x_1^*, \ldots, x_\theta^*) \\ h(x_{1-\tau}^*, \ldots, x_2^*, \ldots, x_{1+\theta}^*) \\ \vdots \\ h(x_{p-\tau}^*, \ldots, x_p^*, \ldots, x_{p+\theta}^*) \end{bmatrix} = 0$$

Near a limit cycle, the linear first-order Taylor expansion of h about x_t^* provides a good approximation to the function h.

$$h(x_{t-\tau}, ..., x_{t+\theta}) \approx \sum_{i=-\tau}^{\theta} H_i\big|_{x_{i-\tau}^* \ldots x_{i+\theta}^*} (x_{t+i} - x_i^*)$$

Define $(\bar{\theta} + 1)$ matrices of dimension $pL \times pL$

$$\bar{H}_0 = \begin{bmatrix} H_{-\tau}\big|_{x_{1-\tau}^* \ldots x_{1+\theta}^*} & \cdots & H_{p-\tau}\big|_{x_{1-\tau}^* \ldots x_{1+\theta}^*} \\ & \ddots & \vdots \\ & & H_{-\tau}\big|_{x_{p-\tau}^* \ldots x_{p+\theta}^*} \end{bmatrix} \tag{4}$$

$$\bar{H}_1 = \begin{bmatrix} H_{p-\tau+1}\big|_{x_{1-\tau}^* \ldots x_{1+\theta}^*} & \cdots & H_{p-\tau+p}\big|_{x_{1-\tau}^* \ldots x_{1+\theta}^*} \\ \vdots & \vdots & \vdots \\ H_{-\tau+1}\big|_{x_{p-\tau}^* \ldots x_{p+\theta}^*} & \cdots & H_{p-\tau+1}\big|_{x_{p-\tau}^* \ldots x_{p+\theta}^*} \end{bmatrix} \tag{5}$$

$$\vdots$$

$$\bar{H}_{\bar{\theta}} = \begin{bmatrix} H_{-\theta}|_{x^*_{1-\tau} \cdots x^*_{1+\theta}} & & \\ \vdots & \ddots & \\ H_{\theta-p}|_{x^*_{p-\tau} \cdots x^*_{p+\theta}} & \cdots & H_{\theta}|_{x^*_{p-\tau} \cdots x^*_{p+\theta}} \end{bmatrix} \quad (6)$$

where $\bar{\theta}$ is the smallest integer greater than $(\tau + \theta + p)/p$. The $\bar{H}_0, \ldots, \bar{H}_{\bar{\theta}}$ make up a linear system of the form explored in [2].

Analysis of this system will produce a matrix of constraints, Q, which guarantee that the trajectories near the limit cycle converge to the limit cycle. For trajectories of the original system which converge to this limit cycle, we can ultimately replace the nonlinear system of equations with the matrix of constraints, Q.

$$Q \begin{bmatrix} x_{-\tau} - x^*_{-\tau} \\ \vdots \\ x_0 - x^*_0 \\ \vdots \\ x_{p\theta} - x^*_{p\theta} \end{bmatrix} = 0$$

Although the algorithm and all the models presented here are discrete time models, the technique is easily modified to accommodate continuous time models.

The asymptotic linearization of a nonlinear system provides a succinct characterization of evolution of trajectories so long as the magnitudes of the eigenvalues are not equal to one. The asymptotic behavior of nonlinear models at so-called non hyperbolic points is more subtle [14]. Methods for characterizing the asymptotic behavior still rely on identifying hyperbolic points by linear algebraic means and renormalizing the system to analyze the behavior of higher order terms in the subspace associated with the unit modulus eigenvectors. Nonhyperbolic points are important in dynamic economic models because, as Laitner [17] and Peck [22] have noted, there is a close association between nonhyperbolicity and the existence of sunspot equilibria. In addition, Benhabib and Laroque [4], and Reichlin [23] have emphasized the role of nonhyperbolicity in constructing equilibrium cycles at the critical bifurcation values of model parameters.

6.6 Numerical Implementation

There are several numerical implementations of the algorithms described in Section 6.5. A numerical implementation of the technique outlined in Section 6.5.1 has, over the years, been programmed in computer languages including SPEAKEZ, MATLAB, FORTRAN, C, and *Mathematica*. The code has been used for estimating stochastic linear equation systems and certainty equivalence non-linear equation systems.

6.7   Symbolic Implementation

6.7.1   Symbolic Processing Routines

This section describes the several symbolic processing routines developed to carry out the analysis of non-linear economic models.

6.7.1.1   derivativesOfVectorFunction

This routine takes a list of functions and a list of variables as inputs and returns a matrix of derivatives.

$$\texttt{derivativesOfVectorFunction}[f, x] \to \frac{\partial f}{\partial x}$$

6.7.1.2   makeSymbolicAsymptoticHMatrix

This routine takes a non linear model specification, and a periodicity as input and generates a symbolic matrix representing the asymptotic $\bar{H}_i$ described in equations (4)–(6).

$$\texttt{makeSymbolicAsymptoticHMatrix}[(f, x, \alpha, (\tau, \theta)), p] \to \left[\bar{H}_0 \dots \bar{H}_{\bar{\theta}} \right]$$

6.7.1.3   stateSpaceTransitionMatrix

This routine takes a matrix of coefficients corresponding to the H_i matrices of equation (3) and returns the three matrix results of the auxiliary initial conditions phase of the Anderson-Moore algorithm: the matrix A, the matrix $Q^{(k^*)}$, and the matrix $H^{(k^*)}$

$$\texttt{stateSpaceTransitionMatrix}[[H_{-\tau} \dots H_{\theta}]] \to (A, Q^{(k^*)}, H^{(k^*)})$$

6.7.1.4   eliminateInessentialLags

This routine identifies superfluous columns and rows in the transition matrix thereby reducing the dimension of the state vector. It takes a transition matrix and an indicator vector of the same dimension as input. The routine returns a reduced dimension transition matrix with the corresponding elements deleted from the indicator vector.

$$\texttt{eliminateInessentialLags}[(A, i)] \to (\bar{A}, \bar{i})$$

6.8   The Analytic Implementation of the Anderson-Moore Saddle Point Analysis Routine Applied to the Example Nonlinear Models

The algorithm described above was originally designed for use in estimation of linear rational expectations models and for estimation of nonlinear certainty equivalence models. In that context, it is usually necessary and appropriate to use numerical linear algebra routines to compute the required matrices. However, here *Mathematica* provides tools for automating symbolic computation. In the present context it has proven worthwhile to use this symbolic algebra program to compute the matrices analytically.

6.8.1   The Money Demand Model

We have

$$
H_{-1} = \begin{bmatrix} 0 & 0 & 0 \\ -(1+\gamma) & 0 & 0 \\ 0 & 0 & \lambda(2s_{t-1}-1) \end{bmatrix}
$$

$$
H_0 = \begin{bmatrix} \dfrac{1}{m_t} & \dfrac{\beta p_{t+1} - \rho p_t - (p_{t+1} - p_t)}{p_t(\rho p_t + (p_{t+1} - p_t))} & 0 \\ 1 & 0 & -\delta \\ 0 & 0 & 1 \end{bmatrix}
$$

$$
H_1 = \begin{bmatrix} 0 & \dfrac{-\beta}{\rho p_t + (p_{t+1} - p_t)} & 0 \\ 0 & 0 & 0 \\ 0 & 0 & 0 \end{bmatrix}
$$

We want to investigate the model with initial conditions

$$
m_0 = \bar{m}_0
$$
$$
p_0 = \bar{p}_0
$$
$$
s_0 = \bar{s}_0
$$

and terminal conditions

$$
\lim_{t\to\infty} \begin{bmatrix} m_t \\ p_t \\ s_t \end{bmatrix} = \begin{bmatrix} m^* \\ p^* \\ s^* \end{bmatrix}
$$

with $s^* = 0, (\lambda - 1/\lambda)\, m^* = \mu - (-\delta s^*)\gamma\, p^* = m^* \exp^{-(\alpha + \beta \ln(\rho))}$, so that when $|\delta| < 1$ we have:

$$
H_{-1}|_{x^*} = \begin{bmatrix} 0 & 0 & 0 \\ -(1+\gamma) & 0 & 0 \\ 0 & 0 & \lambda(2s^*-1) \end{bmatrix}
$$

$$
H_0|_{x^*} = \begin{bmatrix} \dfrac{1}{m^*} & \dfrac{\beta - \rho}{\rho p^*} & 0 \\ 1 & 0 & -\delta \\ 0 & 0 & 1 \end{bmatrix}
$$

$$
H_1|_{x^*} = \begin{bmatrix} 0 & \dfrac{-\beta}{\rho p^*} & 0 \\ 0 & 0 & 0 \\ 0 & 0 & 0 \end{bmatrix}
$$

so that applying the methods of [2] near the fixed point, the state space transition matrix is

$$
A = \begin{bmatrix} (1+\gamma) & 0 & -\delta\lambda(2s^* - 1) \\ \dfrac{\rho/\beta}{m^*/p^*} & \dfrac{\beta - \rho}{\beta} & 0 \\ 0 & 0 & -\lambda(2s^* - 1) \end{bmatrix}
$$

The Q matrix consists of two shifted equations and one unstable left eigenvector if $\lambda > 1$

$$
Q = \begin{bmatrix} -(1+\gamma) & 0 & 0 & 1 & 0 & -\delta \\ 0 & 0 & \lambda(2s^* - 1) & 0 & 0 & 1 \\ 0 & 0 & 0 & \dfrac{-\rho/\beta}{m^*/p^*} & \left(\dfrac{(\beta - \rho)}{\beta} + (1+\gamma) \right) & -\delta\dfrac{\frac{\rho/\beta}{m^*/p^*}}{(\frac{\beta-\rho}{\beta} + \delta)} \end{bmatrix}
$$

So that

$$
B = \begin{bmatrix} 1+\gamma & 0 & \delta\lambda - 2\delta\lambda s^* \\ \dfrac{(1+\gamma)\,\rho p^*}{(\beta\gamma + \rho)\,m^*} & 0 & \dfrac{\delta\lambda\rho\,(-\beta + \rho)\,p^*\,(-1 + 2s^*)}{(\beta\gamma + \rho)\,m^*\,(\beta - \beta\lambda - \rho + 2\beta\lambda s^*)} \\ 0 & 0 & \lambda - 2\lambda s^* \end{bmatrix}
$$

In this simple example I have grafted a nonlinear equation with known asymptotic properties onto a simple model which typically has only fixed points in order to demonstrate how the numerical and symbolic tools can be applied to determine the asymptotic behavior of a nonlinear model. We find that this simple model inherits the asymptotic properties of the quadratic map. There are typically two fixed points, only one of which is an attracting fixed point.[2]

6.8.2 A Certainty Equivalence Formulation of McCallum's Real Business Cycles Model

McCallum [3] describes a real business cycle model

$$
c_t + k_t = z_t f(n_t, k_{t-1}) + (1 - \delta)k_{t-1}
$$
$$
u_1(c_t, 1 - n_t) - \lambda_t = 0
$$
$$
u_2(c_t, 1 - n_t) = \lambda_t z_t f_1(n_t, k_{t-1})
$$
$$
\lambda_t = \beta\lambda_{t+1}\left[z_{t+1}f_2(n_{t+1}, k_t) + 1 - \delta\right]
$$
$$
(z_t - z^*) = \rho(z_{t-1} - z^*)
$$

One can obtain an analytic expression for the state space transition matrix for solutions near a fixed point. The general expression is rather complicated, but particular functional forms would produce more easily interpretable expressions.

---

[2] When $\lambda = 3.5$, for example, neither fixed point has the appropriate saddle point property. This does not mean that the model has no plausible perfect foresight solution. Then, the solution with the appropriate saddle point properties is a limit cycle of period three.

6.8.3   The Jullien Overlapping Generations Model

$$H_{-1} = \begin{bmatrix} -(S_w W') & 0 \\ 0 & 0 \end{bmatrix}$$

$$H_0 = \begin{bmatrix} 1 - S_r f'' & 1 \\ -(f'' m^*) & -r^* \end{bmatrix}$$

$$H_1 = \begin{bmatrix} 0 & 0 \\ 0 & 1 \end{bmatrix}$$

$$A = \begin{bmatrix} \dfrac{-(S_w W') + f'' m^*}{-1 + S_r f''} & \dfrac{r^*}{-1 + S_r f''} \\ f'' m^* & r^* \end{bmatrix}$$

The eigenvalues are

$$\frac{r^* + \frac{-(S_w W') + f'' m^*}{-1 + S_r f''} \pm \sqrt{\left(-r^* - \frac{-(S_w W') + f'' m^*}{-1 + S_r f''}\right)^2 - 4\left(-\frac{f'' m^* r^*}{-1 + S_r f''} + \frac{r^*(-(S_w W') + f'' m^*)}{-1 + S_r f''}\right)}}{2}$$

One and only one of these must be greater than 1 for a unique solution converging to the steady state. If both are larger than one, then the trajectory of capital and money would converge to a limit cycle or behave chaotically.[3]

6.9   Symbolic Algebra Programming Facilitates a Deeper Analysis of an Overlapping Generations Model

The Benhabib-Laroque model provides a vehicle for demonstrating how symbolic programming techniques can push back the limits of tractability and facilitate the exploration of the properties of economic models.

6.9.1   The Overlapping Generations Model of Benhabib and Laroque

The Benhabib and Laroque equation system 1.1 consists of:
Consumer budget constraint:

$$k_t - F_L(k_{t-1}, l_t) l_t + M q_t = 0 \tag{7}$$

Consumer arbitrage condition:

$$-(F_K(k_t, l_{t+1}) q_t) + q_{t+1} = 0 \tag{8}$$

Consumer maximization first-order condition:

$$F_K(k_t, l_{t+1}) F_L(k_{t-1}, l_t) U'(F_K(k_t, l_{t+1}) F_L(k_{t-1}, l_t) l_t) - V'(l_t) = 0 \tag{9}$$

---

[3] Jullien [16] transforms this small dimensional system into a one dimensional system to prove that cycles and chaotic trajectories are possible. His global analysis exploits what is known about one dimensional maps to characterize the asymptotic properties of OLG models.

We need assumptions similar to those in Benhabib and Laroque to guarantee the existence of a fixed point.

Assumption 1 U is a strictly increasing concave function from $\Re_+$ to $\Re$ and

$$\lim_{C \to 0} U(C) = +\infty.$$

V is a strictly increasing convex function from $[0, \bar{L}]$ into $\Re$. It is smooth on $[0, \bar{L})$ and

$$V'(0) = 0, \lim_{L \to \bar{L}} V'(L) = +\infty$$

Assumption 2 F is a strictly concave function from $\Re_+^2$ into $\Re_+$. It is homogeneous of degree 1. It is smooth on the interior of $\Re_+^2$ and

$$\lim_{K \to \infty} F(K, L)/K \le (1 - \delta) < 1$$

$$\lim_{K \to 0} F_K(K, L) = \infty \; \forall \; L > 0$$

$$\lim_{L \to 0} F_L(K, L) = \infty \; \forall \; K > 0$$

6.9.2   Fixed Points

6.9.2.1   Existence and Uniqueness

The fixed points for the system given by equations (8)–(9) are given by the solution to:[4]

$$-V' + U'r^*w^* = 0$$

$$k^* + Mq^* - l^*w^* = 0$$

$$q^* - q^*r^* = 0$$

where

$$w^* = F_L[k^*, l^*]$$

$$r^* = F_K[k^*, l^*]$$

Thus there are two types of fixed point solutions.

• Monetary Solutions: $q^* \ne 0, r^* = 1$

• Non-Monetary Solutions: $q^* = 0$

I will illustrate the use of the symbolic processing techniques by analyzing the monetary solutions.

Monetary Solutions: $r^* = 1$ Assuming constant returns to scale we can find the marginal product of labor and the capital labor ratio corresponding to a marginal product of capital equal to one. In addition there exists a $\bar{K}$ such that $F_K(\bar{K}, \bar{L}) = 1$. As a result, we can express $\mu_1(k) = w^*U'$ and $\mu_2(k) = V'$ as

---

[4] Lines 20 through 40 develop the equations presented here.

functions of k. Figure 4 presents graphs illustrating the functions μ_1 and μ_2. $\mu_1(k)$ will be monotonically downward sloping with an asymptote for small values of k and low consumption while $\mu_2(k)$ will be monotonically upward sloping with an asymptote at large values of k and high labor.

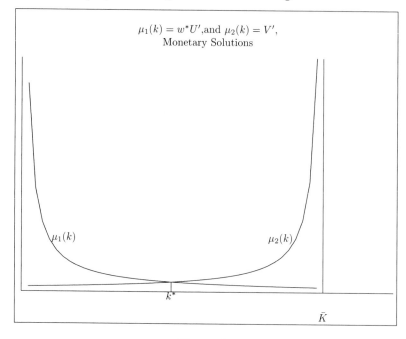

Figure 4:

The value of the capital stock where the functions μ_1 and μ_2 cross constitutes a fixed point. Uniqueness follows from the convexity of V and the concavity of U.

Asymptotic Stability of Monetary Fixed Points $U' + U''l^*w^* \neq 0$ Assuming constant returns to scale so that $F_{KL} \to (w^*/\sigma y^*)$ and after making the simplifying substitutions $U' + U''l^*w^* \to \phi$ and $V'' - U''w^{*2} \to \tau$ we can write the minimal dimension OLG System transition matrix when $\phi \neq 0$ as:

$$\begin{bmatrix} 0 & 1 & 0 & 0 \\ \dfrac{k^* + Mq^* - \sigma y^*}{\sigma y^*} & \dfrac{l^*w^*}{k^*} & -\dfrac{(k^* + Mq^* - \sigma y^*)(k^*\phi w^* + l^*\sigma\tau y^*)}{l^*\phi\sigma w^*y^*} & -M \\ -\dfrac{1}{w^*} & \dfrac{l^*}{k^*} & \dfrac{k^*\phi w^* + l^*\sigma\tau y^*}{l^*\phi w^{*2}} & 0 \\ -\dfrac{q^*}{\sigma y^*} & 0 & \dfrac{q^*(k^*\phi w^* + l^*\sigma\tau y^*)}{l^*\phi\sigma w^*y^*} & 1 \end{bmatrix}$$

$$\begin{bmatrix} k_{t-2} \\ k_{t-1} \\ l_{t-1} \\ q_{t-1} \end{bmatrix}$$

The characteristic polynomial is λ times

$$1 + \frac{l^*\tau}{\phi w^*} \tag{10}$$

$$\lambda \left(-1 - \frac{k^*}{l^* w^*} - \frac{l^*\tau}{\phi w^*} - \frac{Ml^* q^*\tau}{k^* \phi w^*} - \frac{l^* w^*}{k^*} - \frac{\sigma\tau y^*}{\phi w^{*2}} \right)$$

$$\lambda^2 \left(1 + \frac{k^*}{l^* w^*} + \frac{l^* w^*}{k^*} + \frac{\sigma\tau y^*}{\phi w^{*2}} \right)$$

$$- \lambda^3$$

Since the characteristic equation, equation (10), is a cubic, we can obtain a closed form expression for each of the eigenvalues. Because such an expression would be rather long and complicated, subsection 6.9.2.2 will explore properties of the solutions by determining bifurcation values for the linearized system.

We can make further simplifications for monetary solutions. We can write the minimal dimension OLG System transition matrix as:

$$\begin{bmatrix} 0 & 1 & 0 & 0 \\ -\dfrac{-1+\kappa+\sigma}{\sigma} & -1+\dfrac{1}{\kappa} & -\dfrac{(-1+\kappa+\sigma)(\kappa+\alpha\sigma)w^*}{(-1+\kappa)\sigma} & -M \\ -\dfrac{1}{w^*} & -\dfrac{-1+\kappa}{\kappa w^*} & -\dfrac{\kappa+\alpha\sigma}{-1+\kappa} & 0 \\ \dfrac{-1+2\kappa}{M\sigma} & 0 & \dfrac{(-1+2\kappa)(\kappa+\alpha\sigma)w^*}{M(-1+\kappa)\sigma} & 1 \end{bmatrix}$$

where $\kappa = (k^*/y^*)$ when the marginal product of capital is 1.

The characteristic polynomial is λ times[5]

$$1 + \alpha$$

$$\lambda \left(\alpha - \frac{1}{\kappa} - \frac{\alpha}{\kappa} - \frac{\kappa}{1-\kappa} - \frac{\alpha\sigma}{1-\kappa} \right)$$

$$\lambda^2 \left(\frac{1}{\kappa} + \frac{\kappa}{1-\kappa} + \frac{\alpha\sigma}{1-\kappa} \right)$$

$$- \lambda^3$$

6.9.2.2 Bifurcations

The asymptotic dynamics of the system near the fixed point are determined by the three parameters α, κ, and σ. So long as there are exactly two roots outside the unit circle, there are unique trajectories which converge to the steady state. Combinations of parameters which correspond to unit roots are important because they trace out the border between regions where the fixed point has the appropriate stability properties and those regions where the stability properties are inappropriate.

---

[5] This is the same as Benhabib and Laroque's equation 3.1 if we set $\{r^* \to 1\}$ and $\{\tau \to -(\alpha\phi w^*/l^*), \sigma \to (l^* w^*/\epsilon y^*)\}$

We can use symbolic algebra programming to solve for combinations of the parameters which correspond to roots of unit modulus. Flip bifurcations occur when $\lambda = -1$. This occurs when $\alpha = (-2/1 - \kappa + 2\kappa\sigma)$. Hopf bifurcations occur for values of $\kappa > (1/2)$ when $\alpha = (1 - 2\kappa/\kappa + \sigma - 1)$. When $\kappa = (1/2)$ or $\alpha = 0$ there is a root $\lambda = 1$. Table 1 summarizes these results. The table generalizes the results Benhabib and Laroque obtained for a specific production to any constant returns to scale production function.

Table 1

Bifurcations of Monetary Solutions $r^* = 1$ Constant Returns to Scale	
$\lambda = (1)$	$-1 + 2\kappa \neq 0 \wedge \alpha = 0 \vee 2\kappa = 1$
$\lambda = (-1)$	$1 - \kappa + 2\kappa\sigma \neq 0 \wedge \alpha = \dfrac{-2}{1 - \kappa + 2\kappa\sigma}$
λ complex $|\lambda| = 1$	$\left(\dfrac{1}{2} < \kappa < 1\right) \wedge \left(\alpha = \dfrac{1 - 2\kappa}{-1 + \kappa + \sigma}\right) \vee (\kappa = 1 \wedge \alpha\sigma = -1)$

6.10   References

1. G. Anderson and G. Moore, *An Efficient Procedure for Solving Linear Perfect Foresight Models*, 1983, Unpublished Manuscript, Board of Governors of the Federal Reserve System.
2. _____, *A Linear Algebraic Procedure For Solving Linear Perfect Foresight Models*, Economics Letters **17** (1985), 247–252.
3. R. Barro, *Modern Business Cycle Theory*, Harvard University Press, 1989.
4. J. Benhabib, S. Jafarey and K. Nishimura, *The Dynamic Efficiency of Intertemporal Allocations with Many Agents, Recursive Preferences, and Production*, Journal of Economic Theory **44** (1988).
5. J. Benhabib and G. Laroque, *On Competitive Cycles in Productive Economies*, Journal of Economic Theory **45** (1988).
6. J. Benhabib and A. Rustichini, *Equilibrium Cycling With Small Discounting: A Note*, 1989, CV Starr Center for Applied Economics.
7. R. Berndsen and H. Daniels, *Qualitative Dynamics and Causality in a Keynesian Model*, Journal of Economic Dynamics and Control **14** (1990), 435–450.
8. O. J. Blanchard and S. Fischer, *Lectures on Macroeconomics*, The MIT Press, 1989.
9. O. J. Blanchard and C. Kahn, *The Solution of Linear Difference Models Under Rational Expectations*, Econometrica **48** (1980).
10. R. Devaney, *An Introduction to Chaotic Dynamical Systems*, Addison-Wesley, Inc. 1987.
11. A. M. Farley and K. P. Lin, *Qualitative Reasoning in Economics*, Journal of Economic Dynamics and Control **14** (1990), 465–490.
12. D. Gale, *Pure Exchange Equilibrum of Dynamic Economic Models*, Journal of Economic Theory (1973).
13. J-M. Grandmount, *Nonlinear Economic Dynamics*, Academic Press, 1986.
14. J. Guckenheimer and P. Holmes, *Nonlinear Oscillations, Dynamical Systems, and Bifurcations of Vector Fields*, Springer-Verlag, 1983.
15. M. Intrilligator, *Economic and Econometric Models*, In Handbook of Econometrics, vol. I, North Holland, 1983, 182–221.

16. B. Jullien, *Competitive Business Cycles in an Overlapping Generations Economy with Productive Investment*, Journal of Economic Theory **46** (1988).

17. J. Laitner, *The Stability of Steady States in Perfect Foresight Models*, Econometrica (1981).

18. _____, *The Definition of Stability in Models with Perfect Foresight*, Journal of Economic Theory (1982).

19. _____, *Dynamic Determinacy and the Existence of Sunspot Equilibria*, Econometrica (1989).

20. K. Lancaster, *The Scope of Qualitative Economics*, Review of Economic Studies (1962).

21. W. J. Muller and M. Woodford, *Determinacy of Equilibrium in Stationary Economies with Both Finite and Infinite Lived Consumers*, Journal of Economic Theory **46** (1988).

22. J. Peck, *On the Existence of Sunspot Equilibria in an Overlapping Generations Model*, Journal of Economic Theory (1988).

23. P. Reichlin, *Equilibrium Cycles in an Overlapping Generations Economy With Production*, Journal of Economic Theory **44** (1986).

24. T. Sargeant, *Dynamic Macroeconomic Theory*, Harvard University Press, 1987.

25. G. W. Stewart, *Algorithm 506, HQR3 and EXCHNG: FORTRAN Subroutines for Calculating and Ordering the Eigenvalues of a Real Upper Hessenburg Matrix*, ACM Transactions on Mathematica Software **2** (1976), 275–280.

7 A Program for Finding Nash Equilibria

John Dickhaut and Todd Kaplan

We describe two-player simultaneous-play games. First, we use a zero-sum game to illustrate minimax, dominant, and best-response strategies. We illustrate Nash equilibria in the Prisoners' Dilemma and the Battle of the Sexes Games, distinguishing among three types of Nash equilibria: a pure strategy, a mixed strategy, and a continuum (partially) mixed strategy. Then we introduce the program, Nash.m, and use it to solve sample games. We display the full code of Nash.m; finally, we discuss the performance characteristics of Nash.m.

7.1   Introduction

Simple parlour games such as tic-tac-toe and stone-paper-scissors can serve as references for elements of two-player games. Such games have two specific players, distinct choices for each player, and some notion of implicit payoffs for each player. In these cases, it is convenient to think of one player's gain (or win) as the other's loss. Two-player parlour games can become quite complex, as in Chess or Go. Yet, these games retain two essential properties: first, all moves are well-defined; second, one expects the players to use some intelligent strategy. Other choice settings are similar such as pricing in the market place, taking a particular political position, and deciding on the level of nuclear capacity. In such examples, however, the strategy set may be both large and ill-defined; also, one person's gain need not be the other's loss.

Game theory is used to analyze environments in which there are distinct players, each with a set of well-defined actions, and a payoff function which associates that player's payoff with each possible combination of actions. By means of examples, we provide a brief introduction to the fundamentals of game theory, and focus on those elements of game theory that relate to the program, Nash.m, our main contribution. The roots of the game theory used here are in [von Neumann and Morgenstern, 1953] and [Nash, 1951], but the literature is extensive and employed in many diverse disciplines such as Economics, Statistics, Political Science, Finance, and Accounting. A very readable introduction is provided by [Rapoport, 1970]. More advanced applications are in [Kreps, 1990] and [Friedman, 1986].

We represent the two person games as tensors which we will also call the Normal Form of the game. (See for example Figure 1.) This representation reflects the idea that for each player the moves are simultaneous. The entries in the cells show the payoffs to both players. The outcome of the Game-Theoretic analysis is to identify the equilibria of the game; that is, game theory tells us what each intelligent player would do, given that each person know's the other's strategies. Informally, an equilibrium is a set of plans of action for each player such that neither player would change plans given the plan of the other player. Our examples demonstrate several games with equilibria based on several different types of strategies: minimax, dominant strategy, and best-response (Nash). We begin with a simple zero-sum game in which we intuitively demonstrate all three of these concepts (minimax, dominant strategy, and best-response); we then clarify the assumptions we make about payoffs and define mixed strategies. We examine non-zero-sum games and illustrate the different types of Nash equilibria: pure-strategy Nash equilibria, mixed-strategy Nash equilibria, and partially-mixed-strategy Nash equilibria. We then present the program `Nash.m`, apply it to example games, and discuss the robustness of `Nash.m`.

7.1.1   Definitions

Consider the simple zero-sum game in Figure 1. Each player has two choices, 1 or 2, which could be represented by each player hiding the choice of one finger or two behind the back. Player A's payoffs are the left entry in the cells while Player B's are the right entry. When each player's choice is simultaneously revealed, payoffs are made. For the time being, assume that these numbers are dollars and that the entries in the cells reflect the amount one player pays to the other. (Positive numbers represent money received; negative, money surrendered.)

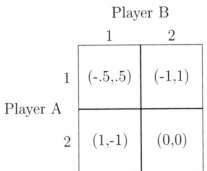

Figure 1: Simple Parlour Game

What might an equilibrium for this game be? One approach, the minimax approach, determines a player's choice based on minimizing the maximum damage that the opponent might cause. Thus, Player A will wish to avoid a loss of −1 and will choose action 2, while Player B will likewise attempt to avoid −1 and choose action 2. An alternative approach is to base the choice of an action on dominant strategies, that is an action that is best given any action of the opponent. Note that Player A is better off choosing strategy 2 regardless of the action choice of Player B, and similarly for Player B. A **Nash equilibrium** is one in which the play of each player is a best response to the play of the other player. Each player choosing action 1 could not be a Nash equilibrium, since Player A's best response to Player B's play would not be action 1. Player A choosing action 2 is a best response to Player B's choosing strategy 2, and vice-versa. In this example, the three different criteria governing strategy choice all lead to the same equilibrium outcome (each player choosing action 2), although this need not always be the case. Before illustrating this point, let us elaborate on the fundamental properties of payoffs and introduce the concept of a mixed strategy:

We take the numbers representing payoffs to have several properties. First, each player prefers a higher payoff to a lower payoff. Furthermore, some transformations of the payoffs will not result in distortions. In particular, we assume that positive linear transformations of the form, $f[x] = ax + b$, $a > 0$, do not distort the inherent relationships between the payoff numbers. It should be clear that if in Figure 1, one or both of the players' payoffs were multiplied by 4, and 3 were subtracted, the same equilbrium would emerge regardless of whether the minimax, dominant strategy, or best-response approach was used to find equilibria. Measuring payoffs is a rich topic in its own right and beyond the scope of the present paper. We follow [von Neumann and Morgenstern, 1953] and refer to these payoffs as utilities.

Figure 2 is the basis for introducing the idea of mixed strategies. Figure 2 represents a two-player game, each player having two pure strategies. Player A has strategies $\{a_1, a_2\}$; Player B has strategies $\{b_1, b_2\}$. The cells in the matrix represent utilities of the players that result from simultaneous choices. When A chooses a_1 and B chooses b_1, A gets x_{11} and B gets y_{11}. We assume that each

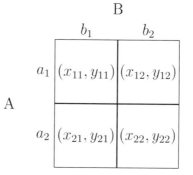

Figure 2: A Two-Player, Two-Strategy Game

player has not only the opportunity to a play single strategy, but can mix his strategies by assigning probability weights. We denote the sets of such mixtures for players A and B by

$$M_A = \{(p_1, p_2) | p_1 + p_2 = 1, p_1, p_2 \geq 0\} \text{ and}$$
$$M_B = \{(q_1, q_2) | q_1 + q_2 = 1, q_1, q_2 \geq 0\}.$$

Pure strategies are mixed strategies with the entire probability mass on one strategy. The value of the game to player i, $V_i : M_A \times M_B \mapsto \Re$ (where $i \in \{A, B\}$), is that player's expected utility, given the strategies of both players. So for example, given $\{(\hat{p}_1, \hat{p}_2), (\hat{q}_1, \hat{q}_2)\}$, the value of the game to player A is $V_A((\hat{p}_1, \hat{p}_2), (\hat{q}_1, \hat{q}_2)) = \hat{p}_1 \, \hat{q}_1 \, x_{11} + \hat{p}_1 \, \hat{q}_2 \, x_{12} + \hat{p}_2 \, \hat{q}_1 \, x_{21} + \hat{p}_2 \, \hat{q}_2 \, x_{22}$. In a **Nash equilibrium**, each player chooses his probability mixture to maximize his value conditional on the other player's selected probability mixture; in other words, his probability mixture is a best response to the other player's probability mixture. Thus, $\{(p_1^*, p_2^*), (q_1^*, q_2^*)\}$ is a Nash Equilibrium if and only if it satisfies

$$V_A((p_1^*, p_2^*), (q_1^*, q_2^*)) \geq V_A((p_1, p_2), (q_1^*, q_2^*)) \quad \forall \, (p_1, p_2) \in M_A \text{ and}$$
$$V_B((p_1^*, p_2^*), (q_1^*, q_2^*)) \geq V_B((p_1^*, p_2^*), (q_1, q_2)) \quad \forall \, (q_1, q_2) \in M_B$$

A Nash equilibrium $\{(p_1^*, p_2^*), (q_1^*, q_2^*)\}$ is totally mixed if and only if $\{(p_1^*, p_2^*), (q_1^*, q_2^*)\}$ $\in \overset{\circ}{M}_A \times \overset{\circ}{M}_B$, where

$$\overset{\circ}{M}_A = \{(p_1, p_2) | p_1 + p_2 = 1, p_1, p_2 > 0\} \text{ and}$$

$$\overset{\circ}{M}_B = \{(q_1, q_2) | q_1 + q_2 = 1, q_1, q_2 > 0\}.$$

In our notation, a strictly dominant strategy, $\{(p_1^*, p_2^*), (q_1^*, q_2^*)\}$, is represented by

$$V_A((p_1^*, p_2^*), (q_1, q_2)) > V_A((p_1, p_2), (q_1, q_2))$$
$$\forall \, (p_1, p_2) \in M_A , (p_1, p_2) \neq (p_1^*, p_2^*) , \forall \, (q_1, q_2) \in M_B \text{ and}$$

$$V_B((p_1, p_2), (q_1^*, q_2^*)) > V_B((p_1, p_2), (q_1, q_2))$$
$$\forall \, (q_1, q_2) \in M_B , (q_1, q_2) \neq (q_1^*, q_2^*) \, \forall \, (p_1, p_2) \in M_A$$

The minimax strategy is represented by

$$(p_1^*, p_2^*) = \arg \max_{(p_1, p_2)} \min_{(q_1, q_2)} V_A((p_1, p_2), (q_1, q_2))$$
$$(q_1^*, q_2^*) = \arg \max_{(q_1, q_2)} \min_{(p_1, p_2)} V_B((p_1, p_2), (q_1, q_2))$$

In the remainder of the paper, the main focus is on Nash equilibria. This focus is motivated by the generality of the Nash concept. For example in zero-sum games, the case in which a pessimistic approach such as minimax seems most appropriate, the Nash concept and minimax concept lead to the same equilibria. In any game in which there is an equilibrium in dominant strategies, that equilibrium will also be a Nash equilibrium.

7.2 Examples

7.2.1 Prisoners' Dilemma

To illustrate the Nash equilibrium concept, we present three games whose solutions increase in complexity.

Consider the Prisoners' Dilemma in Figure 3. Two software pirates are held in separate interrogation cells. They are suspected of having deleted a large amount of disk space prior to capture; however, enough evidence was recovered to convict each pirate for 6 months. Interrogators offer to cut the following deal with the prisoners: If each prisoner rats on the other, they both get 5 years. On the other hand, if one prisoner rats and the other doesn't, then the squealer gets off on probation while the other spends 10 years hard time.

Figure 4 represents the outcome in utilities rather than in years. Utilities represent an individual's preference for outcomes. A less preferred outcome receives a lower utility. In this game, it can be seen that the only Nash equilibrium is $\{a_2, b_2\} (\equiv \{(p_1 = 0, p_2 = 1), (q_1 = 0, q_2 = 1)\})$, since Player A would choose a_2 regardless of the choice of Player B; similarly, Player B would choose b_2. The choice of rat is a dominant strategy as well as minimax strategy for both players; however this is not a zero-sum setting.

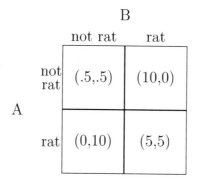
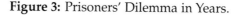

Figure 3: Prisoners' Dilemma in Years.

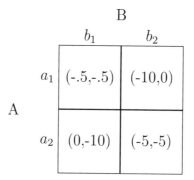
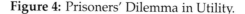

Figure 4: Prisoners' Dilemma in Utility.

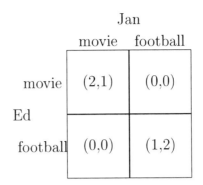

Figure 5: Battle of the Sexes.

7.2.2   Battle of the Sexes

Now consider the "Battle of the Sexes" depicted in Figure 5. Ed, Player A, prefers movies to football, while Jan, Player B, prefers football to movies. They prefer being together to being separate. There are two obvious Nash equilibria, $(movie, movie)$ and $(football, football)$, but there is a third, a mixed strategy equilibrium, $\{(2/3, 1/3), (1/3, 2/3)\}$. To demonstrate that this is an equilibrium, assume that Ed chooses movie with probability 2/3 and football with probability 1/3. Then Jan's expected utility is

$$V_B\left(\left(\frac{2}{3}, \frac{1}{3}\right), (q_1, q_2)\right) = (2)\frac{1}{3}q_1 + \frac{2}{3}q_2 = \frac{2}{3}(q_1 + q_2) = \frac{2}{3}$$

Jan cannot affect her value of the game, so $(1/3, 2/3)$ is an optimal strategy for Jan. A similar argument leads Ed to choose $(2/3, 1/3)$, when Jan chooses $(1/3, 2/3)$.

To derive mixed strategy equilibria, we use the following fact: if $\{(p_1^*, p_2^*), (q_1^*, q_2^*)\}$ is a totally mixed strategy Nash equilibrium, (p_1^*, p_2^*) must make Player B indifferent across all mixtures of strategies in M_B and (q_1^*, q_2^*) must make Player A indifferent. Thus, $(p_1^*, p_2^*), (q_1^*, q_2^*)$ must solve

$$V_B((p_1, p_2), (1, 0)) = V_B((p_1, p_2), (0, 1)) \text{ and } (p_1, p_2) \in \overset{\circ}{M}_A \text{ ; and}$$

$$V_A((1, 0), (q_1, q_2)) = V_A((0, 1), (q_1, q_2)) \text{ and } (q_1, q_2) \in \overset{\circ}{M}_B \text{ .}$$

$$\Longrightarrow (1)p_1 + (0)p_2 = (0)p_1 + (2)p_2 \text{ and } (p_1, p_2) \in \overset{\circ}{M}_A$$

$$(2)q_1 + (0)q_2 = (0)q_1 + (1)q_2 \text{ and } (q_1, q_2) \in \overset{\circ}{M}_B$$

The only solution to these equations is $\{(p_1^* = \frac{2}{3}, p_2^* = \frac{1}{3}), (q_1^* = \frac{1}{3}, q_2^* = \frac{2}{3})\}$.

When there are only two players, each with 2 strategies, it is possible to graph (Figure 6) the best response functions of each of the players, and the intersection of the two functions represents the equilibria. None of the Nash Equilibria contain either dominant strategies or minimax strategies.

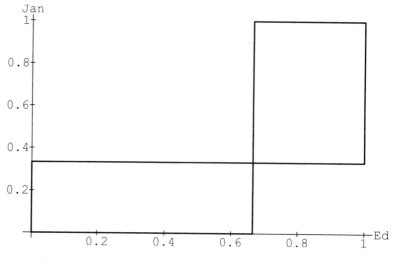

Figure 6: Best Response Function for Jan and Ed

7.2.3 Modified Battle of the Sexes

Now we modify the original "Battle of the Sexes" game, Figure 5, by changing the payoff to Ed from 0 to 2, when Ed chooses *football* and Jan chooses *movie*.

The pure strategy equilibria of the game are the same as before, (*movie, movie*) and (*football, football*). The new twist this game illustrates is the existence of a continuum of (partially) mixed equilibria, where one player chooses a mixed strategy and the other player chooses a pure strategy. If Jan chooses *movie*, then Ed is indifferent among any mixture of strategies. The mixtures of Ed's strategies that cause Jan to choose *movie* are (p_1^*, p_2^*) that solve

$$V_B((p_1, p_2), (1, 0)) \geq V_B((p_1, p_2), (0, 1)) \text{ and } (p_1, p_2) \in M_A.$$
$$\implies (1)p_1 + (0)p_2 \geq (0)p_1 + (2)p_2 \text{ and } (p_1, p_2) \in M_A$$

So $\{(p_1, p_2), (1, 0)|1 \geq p_1 \geq (2/3) \text{ and } p_2 = 1 - p_1\}$ are Nash Equilibria.

7.3 Sessions

7.3.1 Solving the Example Games

Nash.m finds the pure, mixed, and any continuum of mixed Nash equilibria for all two person Normal Form games with a finite number of strategies. The representation of the Prisoners' Dilemma game in Figure 4 is **In[1]** in the following session:

```
In[1]:= game1={{{-1/2,-1/2},{-10,0}},{{0,-10},{-5,-5}}}
```

Out[1]:=
$$\{\{\{-(\tfrac{1}{2}),\ -(\tfrac{1}{2})\},\ \{-10,\ 0\}\},\ \{\{0,\ -10\},\ \{-5,\ -5\}\}\}$$

The payoffs to individual players can be extracted from `game1` by standard list operations. For example, `In[2]` illustrates how to extract player 2's (B's) payoff, given that player 1 (A) has chosen action 2 and player 2 has chosen action 1.

In[2]:= **game1[[2]][[1]][[2]]**

Out[2]:= −10

In general, `game1[[i]][[j]][[k]]` gives player k's payoff, given that player 1 chooses i and player 2 chooses j. The Normal Form can be recovered by the command in `In[3]`:

In[3]:= **MatrixForm[Transpose[game1]]**

Out[3]:=
−0.5	−0.5	−10	0
0	−10	−5	−5

We use the program `Nash.m` to find the Nash equilibria.

In[4]:= **<<Nash.m**

In[5]:= **Nash[game1]**

Out[5]:= {{{0, 1}, {0, 1}}}

The output is the set of probability mixtures for players 1 and 2. Each player puts the full probability weight on the second strategy.

In the next part of the session, we find equilibria for the Battle of the Sexes game, Figure 5, and its extension, Figure 7.

In[6]:= **game2={{{2,1},{0,0}},{{0,0},{1,2}}};**

In[7]:= **Nash[game2]**

Out[7]:=
$$\{\{\{0,\ 1\},\ \{0,\ 1\}\},\ \{\{\tfrac{2}{3},\ \tfrac{1}{3}\},\ \{\tfrac{1}{3},\ \tfrac{2}{3}\}\},\ \{\{1,\ 0\},\ \{1,\ 0\}\}\}$$

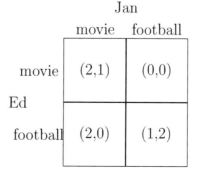

Jan

Ed	movie	football
movie	(2,1)	(0,0)
football	(2,0)	(1,2)

Figure 7: Modified Battle of the Sexes.

For games with only 2 strategies per player and mixed strategy equilibria Nash.m can present the graphical solution of the problem

In[8]:= **Brgraph[{{{2,1},{0,0}},{{0,0},{1,2}}}]**

Out[8]:= −Graphics−

In[9]:= **game3={{{2,1},{0,0}},{{2,0},{1,2}}};**

In[10]:= **Nash[game3]**

Out[10]:=   2   1
$$\{\{\{0, 1\}, \{0, 1\}\}, \{\{\tfrac{2}{3}, \tfrac{1}{3}\}, \{1, 0\}\}, \{\{1, 0\}, \{1, 0\}\}\}$$

Notice that Out[7] is equal to the Nash equilibria we previously found, but Out[10] is a subset of the Nash equilibria we found. We can find the full set of Nash equilibria by using the following rule: Any time one player plays the same strategy in two equilibria, then any convex combination of these two equilibria is also an equilibrium. Using Out[10], {{2/3, 1/3},{1, 0}} and {{1, 0},{1, 0}} are equilibria where Player 2 has the same strategy. This implies that any convex combination of these strategies is also an equilibrium. In other words,

In[11]:= **ans=%10;**

In[12]:= **t*ans[[2]]+(1-t)*ans[[3]]**

Out[12]:=   t   t
$$\{\{1 - \tfrac{t}{3}, \tfrac{t}{3}\}, \{1, 0\}\}$$

Out[12] is a Nash equilibrium for all t between 0 and 1.

In the package Nash.m the command Convex will transform observed solutions to solutions in terms of convex combinations directly.

In[13]:= **Convex[{{{0,1},{0,1}},{{2/3,1/3},{1,0}},{{1,0},{1,0}}}]**

Out[13]:=   2   1
$$\{\{\{0, 1\}, \{0, 1\}\}, \{\{\tfrac{2}{3}, \tfrac{1}{3}\}, \{1, 0\}\}, \{\{1, 0\}, \{1, 0\}\},$$

$$> \quad \{\{1 - \tfrac{t1}{3}, \tfrac{t1}{3}\}, \{1, 0\}\}, \{\{\tfrac{2 + t1}{3}, \tfrac{-(-1 + t1)}{3}\}\},$$

$$\{1, 0\}\},$$

$$> \quad \{\{1 - \tfrac{t2}{3}, \tfrac{t2}{3}\}, \{1, 0\}\}, \{\{\tfrac{2 + t2}{3}, \tfrac{-(-1 + t2)}{3}\}\},$$

$$\{1, 0\}\},$$

$$> \quad \{\{\tfrac{2 + t1 + t2 - 2\,t1\,t2}{3}, \tfrac{1 - t1 - t2 + 2\,t1\,t2}{3}\}\},$$

$$\{1, 0\}\},$$

Out[13] (cont.)

$$> \quad \{\{\frac{2 + t1 - t1\ t2}{3}, \frac{1 - t1 + t1\ t2}{3}\}, \{1,\ 0\}\},$$

$$> \quad \{\{\frac{2 + t2 - t1\ t2}{3}, \frac{1 - t2 + t1\ t2}{3}\}, \{1,\ 0\}\},$$

The problem here is that the convex combinations are not in the most simplified form. To eliminate redundancies the function ReduceSoln is provided. The second argument of ReduceSoln[] corresponds to there being two "t"'s, t1 and t2, in the output of Convex[].

In[14]:= **ReduceSoln[%13,2]**

Out[14]:=
$$\{\{\{\{0,\ 1\},\ \{0,\ 1\}\}\},\ \{\{\{\frac{2}{3},\ \frac{1}{3}\},\ \{1,\ 0\}\}\},\ \{\{\{1,\ 0\},$$

$$\{1,\ 0\}\}\},$$

$$> \quad \{\{\{1 - \frac{t1}{3},\ \frac{t1}{3}\},\ \{1,\ 0\}\}\}\}$$

7.3.2   The Package: Nash.m

Figure 8 displays the code of the package Nash.m. The procedures of the package Nash.m fall into two categories, housekeeping and computational. To insure correct inputs the procedure **Nash[]** determines if the tensor representation of the two person game has been input correctly. If the inputs are not a square game, Nash.m uses the procedure **Square[]** to convert a non-square game to a square game with an equivalent solution. If necessary, Nash.m converts the solution back to the solution of a non-square game. Also, with the procedure, **Convex[]**, we give the user the chance to get a symbolic representation of all the partially mixed strategy games. To see how this works we use a *Mathematica* session.

First let's consider an input that is not a two-person game.

In[1]:= **Nash[random input]**

Out[1]:= Not a two—player game!

Now consider a different game,

In[2]:= **a={{{2,3,4},{5,4,9}},{{4,5,6},{7,8,9}}}**

Out[2]:= {{{2, 3, 4}, {5, 4, 9}}, {{4, 5, 6}, {7, 8, 9}}}

In[3] and Out[3] indicate that if payoffs are input for three or more players then Nash will indicate that it is not a two player game.

In[3]:= **Nash[a]**

Out[3]:= Payoffs aren't defined for two players

```
BeginPackage["Nash`"]

Nash::usage ="Nash[game_] finds the Nash Equilibria of game, a
game in normal form. Example input:
Nash[{{{2,1},{0,0}},{{0,0},{1,2}}}].
Nash returns the probability weights on the different pure
strategies."

IsNash::usage ="IsNash[game_,strategies_] returns True if
strategies is a Nash Equilibrium of game and False otherwise.
Example input: IsNash[game,{{2/3,1/3},{1/3,2/3}}]."

Brgraph::usage="Brgraph[game_,step_:.01] plots the best response
graph of a 2 by 2 by 2 game. It plots the best response of
player 1 on the x—axis given the action of player 2 on the
y—axis. It then plots the best response of player 2 on the
y—axis given the action of player 1 on the x—axis. The intersection
points of the two are the equilibria. Step is the interval size
for plotting. (Note that this doesn't show the shaded area in
the best response correspondence when it exists in a continuum
of equilibria .)"

Convex::usage="Convex[solns_] takes the solutions of Normal Form
game generated by Nash.m and generates the convex combinations
that are also Nash equilibria. Convex will output the entire
set of Nash equilibria of the original game; however, the
output won't be in the simplest form."; ReduceSoln::usage
="ReduceSoln[solns_,highestt_] eliminates redundant representations
of Nash equilibria from the output of Convex (solns). highestt
is the highest numbered t in the output of Convex. For example,
t4 is valued 4."

Begin["`Private`"]

Convex[solns_]:=Block[{t1,i,x,t2,t3,t4,t5,t6,doit,conv1,convex,
                       make,representation},

representation[{z_, s_},i_] := ToExpression[
                               StringJoin["t",ToString[i]]]
z + (1 — ToExpression[StringJoin["t",ToString[i]]] ) s;

  make[{a_, b_}] := Function[x, x[[2]] == b || x[[1]] == a];

  convex[solutionset_] :=
    Table[Select[solutionset, make[solutionset[[i]]]],
    {i, 1, Length[solutionset]}];
         conv1[a_,b_,ii_]:=Table[Map[Function[
                          x,representation[{a[[i]],x},ii]],
  b[[i]] ],{i,1,Length[a]}];

  conversion[solnns_,ii_]:=Union[Simplify[Flatten[conv1[solnns,
    convex[solnns],ii],1]]];

  doit[solnns_,0]:=solnns;
  doit[solnns_,x_]:=doit[conversion[solnns,x],x—1];
```

Figure 8: The **Nash** package

```
        doit[solns, Length[solns[[1,1]]]+Length[solns[[1,2]]]-2] ];

   ReduceSoln[solns_,hightestt_]:=Block[{x,i,j,k,z1,endlist,expand},
      expand[x_,j_]:= Union[Table[x/.Table[
      ToExpression[StringJoin["t",ToString[i]]]->
        Mod[Floor[k/2^(i-1)],2],{i,1,j}],{k,0,2^j-1}]];
   endlist=Map[Function[x,expand[x,hightestt]],solns];
   uendlist=Union[endlist];
   Table[solns[[Position[endlist,uendlist[[z1]] ][[1]]]],
         {z1,1,Length[uendlist]}]
      ];

   Brgraph[game_,step_:.01]:=Block[{V,BR,l1,l2,pl1,pl2},
      If[Length[Dimensions[game]]!=3 || Dimensions[game][[1]]!=2 ||
        Dimensions[game][[2]]!=2,
        Return["The game is not a 2 by 2 by 2 list"]];

      V[i_,{p1_,p2_}]:={p1,1-p1}.Transpose[game,{2,3,1}]
                        [[i]].{p2,1-p2};

      BR[1,p2_]:=ConstrainedMax[V[1,{p1,p2}],{p1<=1},{p1}];
      BR[2,p1_]:=ConstrainedMax[V[2,{p1,p2}],{p2<=1},{p2}];

      l1=Table[{p1/.BR[1,p2][[2]],p2},{p2,0,1,step}];
      l2=Table[{p1,p2/.BR[2,p1][[2]]},{p1,0,1,step}];

      SetOptions[ListPlot,DisplayFunction->Identity];
      pl1= ListPlot[l1,PlotJoined->True];
      pl2= ListPlot[l2,PlotJoined->True];
      SetOptions[ListPlot,DisplayFunction->$DisplayFunction];

      Show[pl1,pl2,DisplayFunction->$DisplayFunction]
   ];

   IsNash[a_,S_]:=Block[{l},
      l=Dimensions[a][[1]];
      Isnash[a,S]
   ];

   Isnash[a_,S_]:=Block[{m1,m2,Eu,br1,br2,t},
      Eu[2,st_]:=N[S[[1]].a[[Range[1,l],st,2]]];
      Eu[1,st_]:=N[S[[2]].a[[st,Range[1,l],1]]];
      m1=Max[Table[Eu[1,t],{t,1,l}]];
      m2=Max[Table[Eu[2,t],{t,1,l}]];
      br1=Table[If[Eu[1,t]==m1,0,1],{t,1,l}];
      br2=Table[If[Eu[2,t]==m2,0,1],{t,1,l}];
      If[br1.S[[1]]+br2.S[[2]]==0,True,False]
   ];

   Square[a_]:=Block[{n,l},
    n[i_]:=Dimensions[a][[i]];
    l=Max[n[1],n[2]];
   Table[ If[i<=n[1] && j<=n[2],a[[i,j]],
         {Min[a]-1,Min[a]-1}],{i,1,l},{j,1,l}]]
```

Figure 8: The **Nash** package (cont.)

```
Nash[a_]:=Block[{n,l,anew,MapD,Dropd,solns},

   If[Length[Dimensions[a]]!=3,
      Return["Not a two-player game!"]];
   n[i_]:=Dimensions[a][[i]];
   l=Max[n[1],n[2]];
   If[2!=Dimensions[a][[3]],
      Return["Payoffs aren't defined for two players"]];
   If[n[1]!=n[2],anew=Square[a];
      solns=Nash[anew];
      Dropd[i_][x_]:=Drop[x,n[i]-l];
      MapD[x_]:=MapAt[Dropd[1],MapAt[Dropd[2],x,{{2}}],{{1}}];
      Return[Map[MapD,solns]]
   ,Return[NashSq[a]]];
]

NashSq[a_]:=Block[{t1,t2,t3,l,p,pp,a1list,a2list,blist,
                   f,pos,nq,pn,nlist,eqn1,eqn2,eqns1,eqns2,ans1,
                   ans2,i,j,NashE},
   l=Dimensions[a][[1]];
   pp=Table[p[i],{i,1,l}]; a1list={}; a2list={};
   blist=Table[Mod[Floor[j/2î],2],{j,1,2^l-1},{i,0,l-1}];
   For[t1=1,t1<=Length[blist],t1++,
   { num=Apply[Plus,blist[[t1]]];
     f[x_]:=If[Apply[Plus,x]==num,True,False];
     slist=Select[blist,f];
     For[t2=1,t2<=Length[slist],t2++,
     { pos=Flatten[Position[slist[[t2]],1]];
       eqn1=Table[(pp*blist[[t1]]).
                  a[[Range[1,l],pos[[t3]],2]],{t3,1,num}];
       eqn2=Table[(pp*blist[[t1]]).a[[pos[[t3]],
                  Range[1,l],1]],{t3,1,num}];
       eqns1=Table[eqn1[[i]]==eqn1[[i+1]],{i,1,num-1}];
       eqns2=Table[eqn2[[i]]==eqn2[[i+1]],{i,1,num-1}];
       ans1=Solve[Join[eqns1,{Apply[Plus,pp*blist[[t1]]]==1}],pp];
       ans2=Solve[Join[eqns2,{Apply[Plus,pp*blist[[t1]]]==1}],pp];
       AppendTo[a1list,Flatten[(pp*blist[[t1]])/.ans1]];
       AppendTo[a2list,Flatten[(pp*blist[[t1]])/.ans2]];
   }}}];

   nq[x_]:=Apply[And,Table[NumberQ[N[x[[i]]]],{i,1,Length[x]}]];
   pn[x_]:=Apply[And,Table[N[x[[i]]]>=0 &&
               N[x[[i]]]<=1,{i,1,Length[x]}]];
   a1list=Union[Select[Select[a1list,nq],pn]];
   a2list=Union[Select[Select[a2list,nq],pn]];
   nlist=Flatten[Table[{a1list[[i]],a2list[[j]]},
               {i,1,Length[a1list]},
               {j,1,Length[a2list]}],1];
   INash[S_]:=Isnash[a,S];
   NashE=Select[nlist,INash]
];
End[]

EndPackage[]
```

Figure 8: The **Nash** package (cont.)

The following example shows how the procedure **Square[]** works to augment the game to be an equal number of strategies per player by adding strategies that would not be played.

In[4]:= **a={{{2,3},{4,5},{6,1}},{{1,3},{2,9},{1,8}}}**

Out[4]:= {{{2, 3}, {4, 5}, {6, 1}}, {{1, 3}, {2, 9}, {1, 8}}}

In[5]:= **Square[a]**

Out[5]:= {{{2, 3}, {4, 5}, {6, 1}}, {{1, 3}, {2, 9}, {1, 8}},

{{0, 0}, {0, 0}, {0, 0}}}

The computational procedures of the package are **IsNash[]** and **NashSq[]**. To demonstrate how **IsNash[]** and **NashSq[]** work we will mimic the actual code, but simplify it in such a way as to better illustrate the key ideas of these procedures. First we consider **IsNash[]**. **IsNash[]** takes a game and a candidate for the equilibrium for the game and determines if the candidate is in fact an equilibrium. In what follows, a will be the game and S the candidate for an equilibrium.

In[6]:= **a={{{2,4},{1,3}},{{3,5},{1,2}}}**

Out[6]:= {{{2, 4}, {1, 3}}, {{3, 5}, {1, 2}}}

In[7]:= **S={{.5,.5},{.2,.8}}**

Out[7]:= {{0.5, 0.5}, {0.2, 0.8}}

To arrive at the conclusion that S is not a Nash equilibrium, **IsNash[]** finds what would be the maximum that could be obtained by responding optimally to the other player's strategy.

First it computes the expected utility which would be achieved by responding with each of the strategies. The function defining this calculation is

In[8]:= **Eu[1,st_]:=N[S[[2]].a[[st,Range[1,2],1]]];**

For Player 1, the expected utility of choosing action1 given Player 2's choice of S[[2]] is

In[9]:= **Eu[1,1]**

In[10]:= **1.2**

For strategy 2, the expected utility is

In[11]:= **Eu[1,2]**

Out[11]:= 1.4

We find the maximum by the following:

In[12]:= **m1=Max[Table[Eu[1,t],{t,1,2}]]**

Out[12]:= 1.4

Next **IsNash[]** asks which pure strategies yield the maximum payoff to Player 1 in response to Player 2.

```
In[13]:= br1=Table[If[Eu[1,t]==m1,0,1],{t,1,2}]
```

```
Out[13]:= {1, 0}
```

Note that those that yield the maximum receive weight zero. The reason for this is that we want to check which if any sub-optimal strategies receive any positive weight in the candidate strategy. For example, strategy 1 in game a receives .5 from Player 1 which is not optimal. The following calculation allows us to determine if non-zero weight is placed on an optimal strategy by Player 1.

```
In[14]:= If[br1.S[[1]]==0,True,False]
```

```
Out[14]:= False
```

The procedure **IsNash[]** duplicates these operations for Player 2 to attempt to establish mutual best response properties for each of the player strategies.

NashSq[] uses the principle that a player is indifferent between playing any pure strategy that is given positive weight in a mixed strategy that is a best response. **NashSq[]** considers every subset of pure strategies of Player 2 and asks what play of Player 1 would make Player 2 indifferent among playing each strategy in that subset. **NashSq[]**, similarly, determines a set of such strategies for Player 2. The Cartesian Cross Product of Player 2's set of such strategies with Player 1's become the sets of strategies tested by **IsNash[]**.

To see how this works we use the battle of the sexes game.

```
In[15]:= a={{{2,1},{0,0}},{{0,0},{1,2}}}
```

```
Out[15]:= {{{2, 1}, {0, 0}}, {{0, 0}, {1, 2}}}
```

First, the number of strategies for each player is determined.

```
In[16]:= l=Dimensions[a][[1]]
```

```
Out[16]:= 2
```

Then a list of symbols representing potential probability weights is generated.

```
In[17]:= pp=Table[p[i],{i,1,l}]
```

```
Out[17]:= {p[1], p[2]}
```

The term, blist, will generate a representation of the set of subsets of strategies. Since we are talking about a square matrix, such a representation will be the same for both players.

```
In[18]:= blist=Table[Mod[Floor[j/2î,2],{j,1,2^l-1},{i,0,l-1}]
```

```
Out[18]:= {{1, 0}, {0, 1}, {1, 1}}
```

Note here {1,0} would be the case when all the weight is placed on the 1st strategy, {0,1}, all weight placed on strategy 2, and {1,1}, some weight placed on both strategies.

Thus, there are as many equations to create to solve for `p[1]` and `p[2]` as there are subsets, namely 3 subsets.

In[19]:= **Length[blist]**

Out[19]:= 3

NashSq works separately with pure strategies, mixtures with 2 pure strategies, mixtures with 3 pure strategies, etc. To identify which type of strategy to work with we used the function, f,

In[20]:= **f[x_]:=If[Apply[Plus,x]==num,True,False];**

We will show how determining equations works for one member of `blist`, namely the third member, since this is the mixed strategy. In what follows, num refers to the number of strategies which will receive positive weight; thus, for mixed strategies it is two.

In[21]:= **num=2;**

Out[21]:= slist=Select[blist,f]

In[22]:= **{{1, 1}}**

The following two expressions calculate the expected utility to Player 2 for strategies 1 and 2 separately, given Player 1 plays {p[1],p[2]}

In[23]:= **pos=Flatten[Position[slist[[1]],1]]**

Out[23]:= {1, 2}

In[24]:= **eqn1=Table[(pp*blist[[3]]).a[[Range[1,1],pos[[t3]],2]],
                {t3,1,num}]**

Out[24]:= {p[1], 2 p[2]}

Note that `p[1]` is the expected utility for Player 2 if Player 2 plays strategy 1 while 2 `p[2]` is the expected utility for Player 2 if Player 2 plays strategy 2.

For Player 2 to be indifferent these strategies must be set equal.

In[25]:= **eqns1=Table[eqn1[[i]]==eqn1[[i+1]],{i,1,num-1}]**

Out[25]:= {p[1] == 2 p[2]}

We then add the restriction that p[1] + p[2] = 1 and solve for p[1] and p[2].

In[26]:= **ans1=Solve[Join[eqns1,{Apply[Plus,
                pp*blist[[3]]]==1}],pp]**

Out[26]:=
$$\{\{p[1] \rightarrow \frac{2}{3}, \ p[2] \rightarrow \frac{1}{3}\}\}$$

This is a candidate for a solution and `Nash.m` will also generate strategies Player 1 might play to get Player 2 to follow the pure strategies, and then repeat the process to find strategies Player 2 might play relative to all subsets of Player 1.

	b1	b2	b3	b4
a1	(-1,-1)	(-1,-1)	(1,1)	(-1,-1)
a2	(-1,-1)	(-1,-1)	(0,2)	(0,2)
a3	(0,2)	(0,2)	(1,1)	(-1,-1)
a4	(0,2)	(0,2)	(0,2)	(0,2)

Figure 9: Harsanyi and Selten game

7.4 Performance

Nash.m can solve two-player games that have more than two strategies per player. For example, the game in Figure 9 has four strategies per player. The game is found in Harsanyi and Selten, and applying Nash.m reveals one pure equilibrium strategy they omit and numerous mixed strategies they omit.

Harsanyi and Selten (4×4):

```
In[1]:= a={{{-1,-1},{-1,-1},{1,1},{-1,-1}},
             {{-1,-1},{-1,-1},{0,2},{0,2}},
             {{0,2},{0,2},{1,1},{-1,-1}},
             {{0,2},{0,2},{0,2},{0,2}}};

In[2]:= Nash[a]
Out[2]:= {{{0, 0, 0, 1}, {0, 0, 0, 1}}, {{0, 0, 0, 1},

                     1   1
              {0, 0, -, -}},
                     2   2

                                  1       1
    >     {{0, 0, 0, 1}, {0, -, 0, -}}, {{0, 0, 0, 1},
                              2       2

          {0, 1, 0, 0}},

                                 1          1
    >     {{0, 0, 0, 1}, {-, 0, 0, -}}, {{0, 0, 0, 1},
                          2          2

          {1, 0, 0, 0}},
```

```
Out[2](cont.)
      >      {{0, 0, 1, 0}, {0, 1, 0, 0}}, {{0, 0, 1, 0},

             {1, 0, 0, 0}},

      >      {{0, 1, 0, 0}, {0, 0, 0, 1}}, {{0, 1, 0, 0},

                        1   1
             {0, 0,  -,  -}},
                        2   2

                 1       2
      >      {{-,  0,  -,  0}, {0, 0, 1, 0}}, {{1, 0, 0, 0},
                 3       3

             {0, 0, 1, 0}}}
```

In general, the length of time required to solve a game by Nash.m increases exponentially in the number of strategies per player. We used ShowTime in conjunction with

```
game[n_]:=Table[{Random[Integer,10],Random[Integer,10]},
                {i,1,n},{j,1,n}].
```

game[n_] generates random two player games with n strategies and utilities ranging in the integers 0 to 10. Figure 10 graphs the natural log of the time Nash.m requires on a Sun 4 against the number of pure strategies per player.

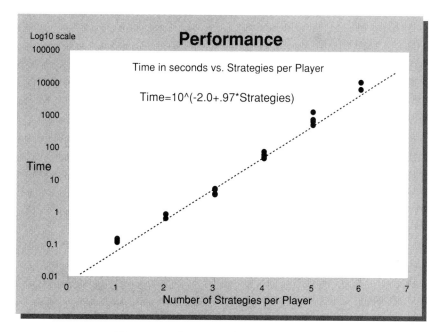

Figure 10: Sun 4 Performance Graph

7.5 Conclusion

`Nash.m` should prove useful to both the novice, who is learning the theory and mechanics of discovering equilibria, and the expert, who can never be completely sure he has isolated all the equilibria of a complex game. Jack Stecher's and two anonymous referees' suggestions significantly improved this paper.

7.6 References

[Friedman, 1986] Friedman, J. W. *Game Theory with Applications to Economics.* Oxford University Press, New York, NY, 1986.

[Harsanyi and Selten, 1988] Harsanyi, J. and R. Selten, *A General Theory of Equilibrium Selection in Games.* The MIT Press, Cambridge, MA, 1988.

[Kreps, 1990] Kreps, D. M. *A Course in Microeconomic Theory.* Princeton University Press, Princeton, N.J, 1990.

[Nash, 1951] Nash, J. Non-Cooperative Games. *Annals of Mathematica*, 54:286–295, 1951.

[Rapoport, 1970] Rapoport, A. *Two-Person Game Theory.* University of Michigan Press, Ann Arbor, Michigan, 1970.

[von Neumann and Morgenstern, 1953] von Neumann, J. and O. Morgenstern, *Theory of Games and Economic Behavior.* Princeton University Press, Princeton, N.J., 1953.

8 Cooperative Games

Michael Carter

Game theory has two major branches—cooperative and non-cooperative. Co-operative games have been used extensively in both economics and political science. One notable practical application of cooperative game theory is to problems of cost allocation and the division of common property, which are ubiquitous in economics. As an example, consider the problem of allocating the cost of a lecture tour amongst the institutions visited. Cooperative games provide a fruitful model for the analysis of allocation problems, and the various solution concepts which have been proposed for cooperative games can be interpreted as alternative solutions to an allocation problem. These solutions can be used to evaluate the rules-of-thumb which are used in practice and to prescribe allocations embodying particular normative principles.

In this notebook, we present tools for representing and solving cooperative games in *Mathematica*. We derive some fundamental solutions, including the core, the Shapley value and the nucleolus. We apply these tools to a number of examples, including applications to some problems of cost allocation.

This Notebook was developed while visiting the Universities of Mannheim and Southampton. I gratefully acknowledge their hospitality and the invaluable assistance of Tim Coffey (The Math Shop), Volker Boehm, Ulrich Schwalbe, and Hartmut Stein.

8.1 Modelling Cooperative Games

To introduce the necessary ideas of game theory, let us consider an example.

A bankrupt firm has assets totally $100. Three creditors come forward, claiming debts of $30, $40 and $50 respectively. The debts total $120 so clearly the creditors cannot be fully recompensed. How should the assets of $100 be divided between the three claimants so as to satisfy their different claims in the most equitable manner?

In an attempt to answer this question, let us consider how the problem might be resolved if it was left to the parties themself to reach some agreement. Let us assume that it is legally possible for any creditor to assume control of the assets of the firm, reimburse in full the other creditors and retain the residual for themselves. Under this procedure, creditor 1 could realise $10, creditor 2 $20 and creditor 3 $30. Creditor 3 is least disadvantaged by this procedure. Although no creditor is likely to seize the initiative in the manner, this conjecture suggests that creditor 3 has a relatively stronger position and this should be recognised in any final settlement.

Taking this idea a step further, any two creditors could combine in taking over the assets of the firm, paying out the remaining creditor, and retaining the balance. In this settlement, creditors 1 and 2 could expect to retain $50, creditors 1 and 3 $60 and creditors 2 and 3 $70. This indicates that creditors 2 and 3 are in the stronger bargaining position and could expect a relatively larger share than creditor 1. We can summarize these conclusions in the following table.

```
Creditors          Residual

1                    $10
2                     20
3                     30
1,2                   50
1,3                   60
2,3                   70
1,2,3                100
```

This example is typical of the circumstances which are modelled as cooperative games. A group of individual agents, called players, has available a sum of "money" to distribute amongst themselves in some agreed fashion. Subgroups of the players, called coalitions, may have lesser sums which they could distribute amongst themselves if they proceeded alone without the other players. A solution to the game is a distribution of the overall sum which in some way reflects the opportunities available to the players in sub-groups or coalitions. Let us model this division problem mathematically.

Given a set of players T, the set of coalitions is the set of all subsets of T. The strength of the various coalitions is measured by the characteristic function $v[]$ which ascribes to every coalition its worth, that is the sum which is available to it if it acts alone. Thus a cooperative game $G = (T, v)$ comprises

- A set T of players

- A function $v: 2^T \mapsto \Re$ defined on the set of all coalitions.

We make a number of remarks on this definition.

1. Strictly speaking, we have defined a particular subclass of games called games with transferable utility, namely the money to be distributed.

2. The empty coalition $\{\}$ and the grand coalition T are coalitions in every game. By convention, the worth of the empty coalition $\{\}$ is always taken to be zero, that is

$$v[\{\}] = 0$$

3. In most circumstances, distinct coalitions cannot lose by acting jointly, so that the characteristic function is *superadditive*, that is for all disjoint coalitions M, N

$$v[M \cup N] \geq v[M] + v[N]$$

4. To make the game interesting, there needs to be some surplus to distribute, so that

$$v[T] > \sum_{i \in T} v[\{i\}]$$

Such a game is called *essential*.

It is straightforward to represent a cooperative game in *Mathematica*. Let us do so for the preceding example.

The set of players is

```
In[1]:= T = {1,2,3};
```

The set of coalitions is the set of subsets of T.

```
In[2]:= Coalitions := Subsets[T]
```

It will be convenient to refer to the set of proper coalitions—namely the set of coalitions excluding the grand coalition T and the empty set { }.

```
In[3]:= ProperCoalitions := Rest[Drop[Coalitions,-1]]
```

The characteristic function can be represented directly.

```
In[4]:= v[{1}]    = 10;
        v[{2}]    = 20;
        v[{3}     = 30;
        v[{1,2}] = 50;
        v[{1,3}] = 60;
        v[{2,3}] = 70;
        v[T]      = 100;
```

Good general references on cooperative game theory include Luce and Raiffa (1957), Owen (1982) and Shubik (1982).

8.2 Some Examples

We now present a number of illustrative examples.

8.2.1 The Bankruptcy Game

```
In[1]:= BankruptcyGame := (
        T = {1,2,3};
        Clear[v];
        v[{}]     = 0; v[{1}]    = 10;
        v[{2}]    = 20; v[{3}]    = 30;
        v[{1,2}] = 50; v[{1,3}] = 60;
        v[{2,3}] = 70; v[T]      = 100;
        )
```

8.2.2   The Three-way Market (Shubik)

A farmer, f, owns a block of land which is worth $1 million as a farm. There are two potential buyers

1. a manufacturer to whom it is worth $2 million as a plant site.

2. a subdivider to whom it is worth $3 million.

```
In[1]:= ThreeWayMarketGame := (T = {f,m,s};
        Clear[v];
        v[{}] = 0; v[{f}] = 1;
        v[{m}] = v[{s}] = 0; v[{f,m}] = 2;
        v[{f,s}] = 3; v[{m,s}] = 0;
        v[T] = 3;
        )
```

8.2.3   The Three Person Majority Game

The allocation of $1 amongst three persons is to be decided by majority vote. This can be represented as a cooperative game with

```
In[1]:= ThreePersonMajorityGame := (
        T = {1,2,3};
        Clear[v];
        v[{}] = 0;
        v[{i_}] = 0;
        v[{i_,j_}] = 1;
        v[T] = 1;
        )
```

8.2.4   The Corporation (Owen)

A game, such as the preceding example, for which $v[S] = 0$ or 1 for all S is called a simple game. Such games can be concisely represented by the set of winning coalitions

$$W = \{S \in T | v[S] = 1\}$$

Simple games are often a convenient model for situations involving the exercise of voting power. This is illustrated in the following example.

A corporation has four shareholders, holding respectively 10, 20, 30 and 40 shares each. Voting rights are proportional to share holdings with decisions made according to majority rule. This can be modelled as the following game:

```
In[1]:= CorporationGame := (T = {1,2,3,4};
        Clear[v];
        W = {{2,4},{3,4},{1,2,3},{1,2,4},{1,3,4},{2,3,4},
            {1,2,3,4}};
        v[S_] := 1 /; MemberQ[W,S];
        v[S_] := 0 /; FreeQ[W,S];
        )
```

8.2.5   The Lecture Tour

A distinguished English game theorist has been invited to present seminars in Frankfurt, Paris and Vienna. Airfares are as follows:

```
London—Frankfurt—London                   750
London—Paris—London                       750
London—Vienna—London                     1800
London—Frankfurt—Paris—London            1200
London—Frankfurt—Vienna—London           1950
London——Paris—Vienna—London              1800
London—Frankfurt—Vienna—Paris—London     2400
```

How should the round trip airfare be allocated amongst the three institutions? We can model this as a game where the payoffs are the cost savings which result from cooperating rather than proceeding alone.

$$v[S] = \sum_{i \in S} c[\{i\}] - C[S]$$

```
In[1]:= LectureTourGame := (T = {Frankfurt, Paris, Vienna};
        Clear[v]; v[{}] = 0; v[{i_}] = 0;
        v[S_List] := Plus @@ (c[{#}] & /@ S) - c[S];
        c[{Frankfurt}]=750; c[{Paris}]=750; c[{Vienna}]=1800;

        c[{Frankfurt,Paris}]   = 1200;
        c[{Frankfurt,Vienna}]  = 1950;
        c[{Paris,Vienna}]      = 1800;

        c[{Frankfurt,Paris,Vienna}] =2400;)
```

PROGRAMMING NOTE: Particular games are stored as unevaluated definitions. Citing the game evaluates the set T and the characteristic function for that game. This then becomes the current game until replaced. By default, all functions refer to the current game unless another game is explicitly cited. Note that the list of defined games can obtained by ?*Game and the characteristic function of the current game by ??v. At the moment, the package contains no error checking for a validly defined game. If an undefined game is cited, the then current game will be retained as the current game.

8.3   Imputations and Solutions

An outcome of a cooperative game consists of an allocation of the available sum $v[T]$ to each of the players. It is vector $x = (x_1, x_2, \ldots, x_n)$, called a payoff vector, whose components sum to $v[T]$. Each component of this vector is the payoff or allocation to player i. In effect, a payoff vector is a mapping from the set of players to the real numbers, and is defined by

```
In[1]:= PayoffVector := x /@ T;
```

For example, for the three player game with $T = 1, 2, 3$, an allocation is the payoff vector

```
In[2]:= T={1,2,3}; PayoffVector
```

```
Out[2]:= {x[1], x[2], x[3]}
```

It will be useful to extend the definition of the allocation $x[]$ to include coalitions as well as individual players, so that

$$x[S] = \sum_{i \in S} x[i]$$

represents the total sum accruing to members of S under the allocation x. This is straightforward to achieve with the following definition

```
In[3]:= x[S_List] := Plus @@ x /@ S
```

Thus for

```
In[4]:= S = {1,2}; x[S]
```

```
Out[4]:= x[1] + x[2]
```

and

```
In[5]:= x[T]
```

```
Out[5]:= x[1] + x[2] + x[3]
```

We can represent the requirement that an allocation exhaust the available sum by the equation

```
In[6]:= ParetoOptimality := x[T] == v[T];
```

which is conventionally called Pareto Optimality.

On the grounds that no player will be willing to settle for any outcome which gives her less than her worth $v[\{i\}]$, we focus our attention on the subset of allocations for which $x[i] \geq v[\{i\}]$ for all i. This restriction on allowable allocations, which is called individual rationality, is given by

```
In[7]:= IndividualRationality := x[#] >=v[{#}] & /@ T;
```

which uses a pure function to map the inequality $x[i] \geq v[\{i\}]$ over the set of players, T.

PROGRAMMING NOTE: We use delayed assignment (:=) in these and other definitions so that they are only evaluated in the context of a particular game.

Allocations which are Pareto Optimal and Individually Rational are called imputations. The set of imputations for a game G, denoted $I[G]$, is

$$I[G] = \{x \in \Re^n | \sum_{i \in T} x_i = v[T] \text{ and } x_i \geq v[i] \; \forall i\}$$

which can be defined as the set of solutions to the system of inequalities

```
In[8]:= Imputations[game_] :=
            Append[IndividualRationality, ParetoOptimality];
```

For example, in the three player game we have

```
In[9]:= ParetoOptimality
```

```
Out[9]:= x[1] + x[2] + x[3] == 100
```

```
In[10]:= IndividualRationality // TableForm
Out[10]:= x[1] >= 10
          x[2] >= 20
          x[3] >= 30
```

The set of imputations is defined by the system of inequalities

```
In[11]:= Imputations[ ]//TableForm

Out[11]:= Imputations
```

For example, for the Bankruptcy game, the set of imputations is

```
In[12]:= Imputations[BankruptcyGame] //TableForm
Out[12]:= x[1] >= 10
          x[2] >= 20
          x[3] >= 30
          x[1] + x[2] + x[3] == 100
```

The extreme points of the set of imputations are readily seen to be

```
In[13]:= extremepoints = {{10,20,70}, {10,60,30}, {50,20,30}};
```

This is illustrated in the following picture where we see that the set of imputations for a three player game is a subset of the 2 dimensional simplex in $\Re^3$.

```
In[14]:= Show[Graphics3D[{{Hue[0.4],Polygon[v[T]
          IdentityMatrix[3]]},
          {Hue[0.6],Polygon[extremepoints]}}],
          Lighting -> False,
          Axes -> True, ViewPoint -> {2.627,-1.122,1.310}]

Out[14]:= —Graphics3D—
```

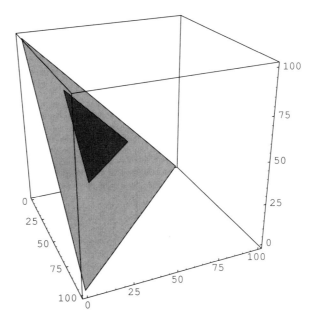

```
In[15]:= Show[%, Axes -> False, ViewPoint -> {2,2,1.8}]
Out[15]:= —Graphics3D—
```

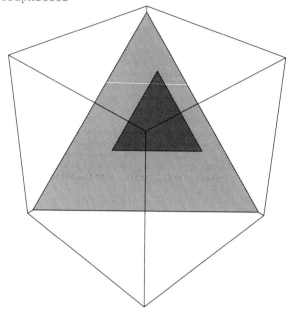

A more concise pictorial representation of the set of imputations can be obtained by projecting the 2 dimensional simplex onto the plane from a suitable viewpoint. This gives us a 2 dimensional representation of the set imputations. This is illustrated in the following figure. Each of the vertices is labelled with one of the players. The payoff to each player is measured from the baseline opposite the vertex corresponding to the player. Each point in the simplex has the property that the sum of its coordinates is a constant, which the sum available for distribution, $v[T]$. The shaded area is the set of imputations.

```
In[16]:= toSimplex = {x1_?NumberQ, x2_?NumberQ, x3_?NumberQ} ->
              {(x2-x1) Sqrt[3]/2, x3-(x1+x2)/2};
         Show[Graphics[{CooperativeGames`Private`Simplex[],
              {Hue[0.6],Polygon[extremepoints]}} /. toSimplex]]

Out[16]:= —Graphics—
```

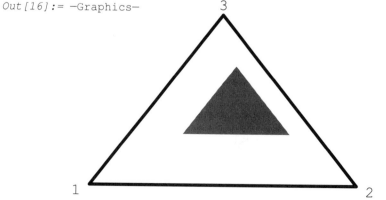

In general the imputation space for any n-player game is an $n - 1$ dimensional simplex. Consequently, it is conventional to illustrate solution concepts for 3 player games in the 2 dimensional simplex, and solution concepts for four player games in the 3 dimensional simplex. This is a practice which will be followed here. In viewing a representation of the imputation space of a 3 player game, as in the preceding figure, the reader should keep in mind that this is a planar representation of the relevant part of a three dimensional space.

A solution to a game comprises either a particular outcome (imputation) or a set of outcomes (imputations). A solution concept defines a solution for every game. It defines a function on the set of all games. Solution concepts for cooperative games thus fall into two classes

1. Point valued—a function from the set of games to the set of imputations

2. Set valued—a correspondence from the set of games to the set of imputations.

The pre-eminent example of a point-valued solution concept is the Shapley value. The most important example of a set-valued solution concept is the core. We examine each of these in turn, starting with the core.

8.4   The Core

One of the most intuitive of solution concepts, the core extends the idea of excluding outcomes which are less favourable than acting alone to coalitions as well as individuals. An allocation x is coalitionally rational if no coalition receives less than its worth, that is

$$x[S] \geq v[S] \ \forall S$$

Analogous to the requirement of individual rationality, this can be implemented by

```
In[1]:= CoalitionalRationality := x[#] >= v[#] & /@
        ProperCoalitions;
```

The core of a game, $Core[T, v]$, is simply the set of all Coalitionally Rational and Pareto Optimal allocations

$$Core[T, v] = \{x \in \Re^n \mid \sum_{i \in T} x_i = v[T] \text{ and } x[S] \geq v[S] \ \forall S\}$$

Since Coalitional Rationality implies Individual Rationality, the core is always a subset of the set of imputations. In *Mathematica*, the core can be defined as the solution to the following system of inequalities

```
In[2]:= Core[game_] :=
            Append[CoalitionalRationality, ParetoOptimality]
```

In the bankruptcy example, the core is defined by the following system of inequalities

```
In[3]:= Core[BankruptcyGame] // MatrixForm
```

```
Out [3] := x[1] >= 10
           x[2] >= 20
           x[3] >= 30
           x[1] + x[2] >= 50
           x[1] + x[3] >= 60
           x[2] + x[3] >= 70
           x[1] + x[2] + x[3] == 100
```

The easiest way to appreciate the nature of the core is to depict it graphically, which is feasible in the case of three and four player games. The function **Draw[]** depicts the various solution concepts on the appropriate simplex.

```
In[4] := Draw[Core[BankruptcyGame]]
```

```
Out [4] := —Graphics—
```

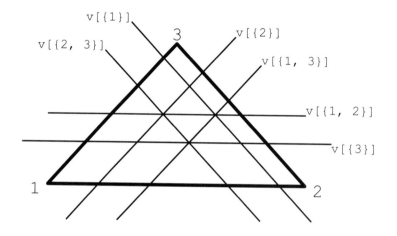

By default, **Draw[]** labels the various constraints defining the core. Sometimes this can be messy; it can be turned off with the option ConstraintLabels -> False.

The core of the Three Way Market Game is

```
In[5] := Core[ThreeWayMarketGame] // MatrixForm
```

```
Out [5] := x[f] >= 1
           x[m] >= 0
           x[s] >= 0
           x[f] + x[m] >= 2
           x[f] + x[s] >= 3
           x[m] + x[s] >= 0
           x[f] + x[m] + x[s] == 3
```

which is illustrated in the following figure.

```
In[6] := Draw[Core[ThreeWayMarketGame]]
```

```
Out [6] := —Graphics—
```

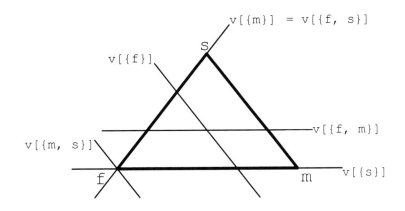

In this case, the core is the line segment from $\{3,0,0\}$ to $\{2,0,1\}$ which is highlighted in the following diagram.

```
In[7]:= Draw[{Core[],{{3,0,0},{2,0,1}}},
        ConstraintLabels->False]
```

```
Out[7]:= —Graphics—
```

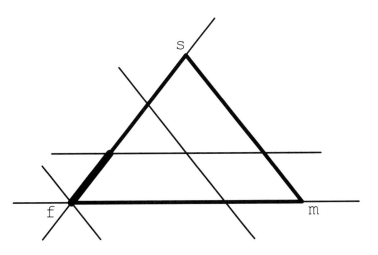

Checking whether or not a particular point belongs to the core is straightforward. For example, proportional division is a common practice in many problems. In the Bankruptcy game, proportional division gives the allocation

```
In[8]:= proportionalDivision = {30,40,50} 100/120
```

```
Out[8]:=        100   125
        {25,  ———, ———}
               3     3
```

The function **Payoff[]** transforms a payoff into a set of allocation rules.

```
In[9]:= BankruptcyGame; Payoff[proportionalDivision]
```

Out[9]:=
$$\{x[1] \to 25,\ x[2] \to \frac{100}{3},\ x[3] \to \frac{125}{3}\}$$

which can then be tested against the core.

In[10]:= **Core[BankruptcyGame] /. %**

Out[10]:= {True, True, True, True, True, True, True}

The result confirms that proportional division satisfies all the demands of all the coalitions and is Pareto optimal. Hence it is in the core. We summarize this procedure in the function **InCoreQ[]**.

In[11]:= **InCoreQ[y_List,game_] := And @@**
        Core[game] /. Payoff[y]

In[12]:= **InCoreQ[proportionalDivision, BankruptcyGame]**

Out[12]:= True

On the other hand, equal division is not in the core.

In[13]:= **equalDivision = Table[100/3,{3}]**

Out[13]:=
$$\{\frac{100}{3},\ \frac{100}{3},\ \frac{100}{3}\}$$

In[14]:= **InCoreQ[equalDivision, BankruptcyGame]**

Out[14]:= False

We might want to know which coalitions are in a position to "block" a particular allocation. This question is answered by the function **Blocking[]**, which uses the list of violated constraints to identify the blocking coalitions.

In[15]:= **Blocking[y_List,game_] := Module[{violated},**
     violated = Flatten @
     Position[Core[game] /. Payoff[y], False];
     Part[Rest[Coalitions], violated]
   ]

In the Bankruptcy game, it is coalition

In[16]:= **Blocking[equalDivision,BankruptcyGame]**

Out[16]:= {{2, 3}}

which can block equal division. Before proceeding, we should clear the particular values equalDivision and proportionalDivision.

In[17]:= **Clear[equalDivision, proportionalDivision]**

For a particular game, there may be no allocation which is Pareto Optimal and Coalitionally Rational, in which case we say that the core is empty. Emptyness of the core is straightforward to test. Let m be the smallest allocation that satisfies all the coalitions, that is

$$m = \min_x x[T]$$

subject to

$$x[S] \geq v[S] \; \forall S$$

If m is feasible, that is

$$m \leq v[T]$$

then m belongs to the core and the core is nonempty. Conversely, if m is not feasible ($m > v[T]$), there can be no feasible allocation which is coalitionally rational and the core is empty. This minimization is a linear programming problem, which can be solved using the *Mathematica* built-in linear programming function, **ConstrainedMin[]**. Thus we can define the function **CoreQ[]** which returns True if the core is nonempy and false otherwise.

```
In[18]:= CoreQ[game_] := v[T] >=
             ConstrainedMin[x[T],
                 CoalitionalRationality,
                 PayoffVector][[1]]
```

Thus we can verify that the Bankruptcy Game has a non-empty core

```
In[19]:= CoreQ[BankruptcyGame]
```

```
Out[19]:= True
```

Conversely, the core of the Three Person Majority Game, and indeed any simple game, is empty.

```
In[20]:= CoreQ[ThreePersonMajorityGame]
```

```
Out[20]:= False
```

The core seems an eminently reasonable condition to impose on the solutions of a game and is particularly apposite in certain applications. For example, in the theory of cost allocation, core allocations can be identified with the absence of cross-subsidization, implying that core allocations are proof against succession. The limitation of the core is that, in many games of interest, the core is either too big (that is, not sufficiently discriminating) or two small (that is, empty). We are left with the problem of choosing a solution for these games. One interesting refinement of the core, the nucleolus, yields a unique solution to every game and a solution which belongs to the core if the core in nonempty.

The core exemplifies one fundamental approach to the solution of cooperative games, which is directed at selecting a set of imputations which in some sense contains the reasonable outcomes to the game. Other examples of this approach include the von Neuman-Morgenstern solution, the bargaining set, and the kernel.

8.5   The Nucleolus

The size of the core of a game depends upon the strength of the coalitions, as measured by $v[S]$, relative to the total available, $V[T]$. A large core means that the coalitions are relatively weak. Conversely, an empty core means that the coalition demands are excessive given the available sum. We can investigate the impact of adjusting the worth of all coalitions uniformly by means of the ϵ-core, which is defined as the set of all imputations which satisfy

$$x[S] \geq v[S] - \epsilon \, \forall S \subset T$$

We add to our definition of the core

```
In[1]:= Core[game_:Null, epsilon] :=
            Append[Relax[CoalitionalRationality,epsilon],
            ParetoOptimality]
```

where

```
In[2]:= Relax[ineq_, epsilon_] :=  ineq /.
            lhs_ >= rhs_ -> lhs >= rhs - epsilon
```

relaxes a system of inequalities uniformly by `epsilon`.

Reducing the worth of the each of the coalitions in the Bankruptcy game by 10 produces

```
In[3]:= Core[BankruptcyGame, 10] // TableForm
Out[3]:= x[1] >= 0
         x[2] >= 10
         x[3] >= 20
         x[1] + x[2] >= 40
         x[1] + x[3] >= 50
         x[2] + x[3] >= 60
         x[1] + x[2] + x[3] == 100
```

which is bigger than the core of the original game. Conversely, strengthening the coalitions ($\epsilon < 0$) reduces the core.

Starting with a non-empty core, if we gradually reduce the size of the core by strengthening the coalitions, we eventually reach a value of ϵ at which the core is about to become empty. We can do this by solving the linear programming problem

$$\min_{x} \epsilon$$

subject to

$$x[S] \geq v[S] - \epsilon$$
$$x[T] = v[T]$$

At this critical value, the ϵ-core is called the least core. For the Bankruptcy Game, we have

```
In[4]:= ConstrainedMin[e-f, Append[
            Relax[CoalitionalRationality,e-f],
            ParetoOptimality], Join[PayoffVector,{e,f}]]
```

Out[4]:=
$$\{-(\frac{20}{3}),\ \{x[1]\ ->\ \frac{70}{3},\ x[2]\ ->\ \frac{100}{3},\ x[3]\ ->\ \frac{130}{3},$$

$$e\ ->\ 0,\ f\ ->\ \frac{20}{3}\}\}$$

PROGRAMMING NOTE: We use e-f in place of ϵ to allow for $\epsilon < 0$.

In this case, the least core is the ϵ-Core with $\epsilon = -20/3$, containing the single point

In[5]:= **PayoffVector /. %[[2]]**

Out[5]:=
$$\{\frac{70}{3},\ \frac{100}{3},\ \frac{130}{3}\}$$

In general, the least core is a convex set containing more than a single point. It can be characterized by a mixed system of equations and inequalities. The function **LeastCore[]** provides the least core for any game. The real work is delegated to the function **LeastCoreAux[]** which solves the above linear programming problem and then attempts to simplify the resulting inequalities.

In[6]:= **LeastCore[game_] := LeastCoreAux[Prepend[**
CoalitionalRationality,
ParetoOptimality]]

To illustrate, consider the following game.

In[7]:= **example = (T = {1,2,3};**
Clear[v]; v[{}] = 0;
v[{i_}] = 0;
v[{1,2}] = 50;
v[{1,3}] = 20;
v[{2,3}] = 10;
v[{1,2,3}] = 60;)

In[8]:= **Draw[Core[example]]**

Out[8]:= —Graphics—

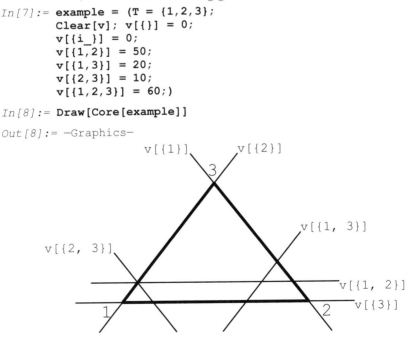

The least core is found by tightening all the constraints at a uniform rate until some meet. For example, the `Core[-4]` of this game is

```
In[9]:= Draw[Core[-4]]
Out[9]:= —Graphics—
```

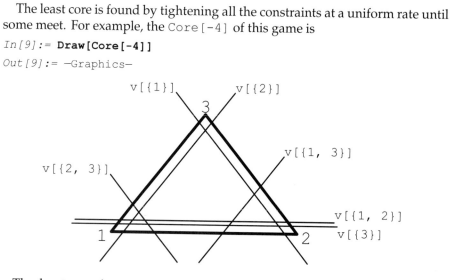

The least core is `Core[-5]`, the line segment between $\{20,35,5\}$ and $\{45,10,5\}$. Here, the two constraints $v[1,2]$ and $v[3]$ collide.

```
In[10]:= Draw[{Core[-5],  {{20,35,5},{45,10,5}}}]
Out[10]:= —Graphics—
```

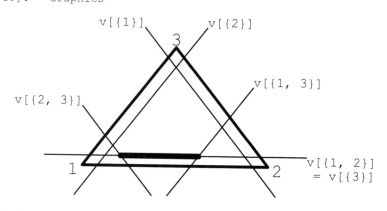

In the Three Way Market Game, the core is in fact the least core, namely the line segment from $\{3,0,0\}$ to $\{2,0,1\}$.

```
In[11]:= LeastCore[ThreeWayMarketGame] // TableForm
Out[11]:= x[m]  ==  0
          x[f] + x[s]  ==  3
          x[f] + x[m] + x[s]  ==  3
          x[s]  >=  0
          x[m] + x[s]  >=  0
          x[f]  >=  1
          x[f] + x[m]  >=  2

In[12]:= Solve[%[[{1,2,3}]]]
Out[12]:= {{x[m] -> 0,  x[f] -> 3 - x[s]}}
```

```
In[13]:= %%[[7]] /. %
Out[13]:= {3 - x[s] >= 2}
```

A game with an empty core has coalitions which are too strong for the available resources. In such a game, the least core corresponds to the core which would emerge if the coalitions were sufficiently weakened.

```
In[14]:= Solve[Cases[LeastCore[ThreePersonMajorityGame],_Equal],
            PayoffVector]
```

$$Out[14]:= \quad \{\{x[1] \to \frac{1}{3}, \ x[2] \to \frac{1}{3}, \ x[3] \to \frac{1}{3}\}\}$$

A least core exists for every game. Furthermore, the dimension of the least core is always a convex set of dimension less than the dimension of the core. Starting with a least core which contains more than one point, we can consider repeating the process by strengthening further those coalitions which are not constrained in the least core. This yields a subset of the least core which is of still lower dimension. Continuing in this way, we will eventually leave only a single point. This point is called the nucleolus. It is found by repeated application of **LeastCoreAux[]**.

```
In[15]:= Nucleolus[game_:Null] := Module[{equations},
            equations = FixedPoint[LeastCoreAux,
              Prepend[CoalitionalRationality, ParetoOptimality],
              Length[T]];
            equations = Cases[equations,_Equal];
            PayoffVector /. Solve[equations,PayoffVector]
              [[1]]]
```

In the above example, the Nucleolus is the midpoint of the least core (which is the case for all three player games.)

```
In[16]:= Nucleolus[example]
```

$$Out[16]:= \quad \{\frac{65}{2}, \ \frac{45}{2}, \ 5\}$$

```
In[17]:= Draw[{Core[-5], {{20,35,5},{45,10,5}},Nucleolus[]}]
```

```
Out[17]:= -Graphics-
```

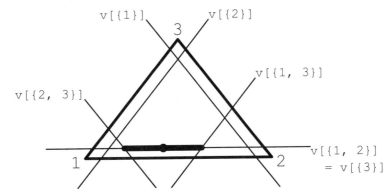

Since the least core Bankruptcy Game contains a single point, this must be the nucleolus of this game.

```
In[18]:= Nucleolus[BankruptcyGame]
```

$$Out[18]:= \{\frac{70}{3}, \frac{100}{3}, \frac{130}{3}\}$$

The nucleolus of the Three Way Market Game is the midpoint of the line segment which comprises the core.

```
In[19]:= Nucleolus[ThreeWayMarketGame]
```

$$Out[19]:= \{\frac{5}{2}, 0, \frac{1}{2}\}$$

In higher dimensional games, the relationship between the least core and the nucleolus is subtle. The nucleolus is not necessarily the midpoint of the least core even if the least core is a line. This is illustrated by the following game.

```
In[20]:= FourPlayerGame := (
        T = {1,2,3,4};
        Clear[v]; v[{}] = 0; v[T] = 2;
        v[{1,2,3}] = v[{1,2,4}] = v[{1,3,4}] = v[{2,3,4}] = 1;
        v[{1,2}] = v[{3,4}] = v[{1,4}] = v[{2,3}] = 1;
        v[{1,3}] = 1/2; v[{2,4}] = 0; v[{i_}] = 0;
        )
```

The least core is the line segment between $\{1,0,1,0\}$ and $\{1/4,3/4,1/4,3/4\}$. The nucleolus is the symmetric solution, not the midpoint.

```
In[21]:= Nucleolus[FourPlayerGame]
```

$$Out[21]:= \{\frac{1}{2}, \frac{1}{2}, \frac{1}{2}, \frac{1}{2}\}$$

However, if we amend the game slightly by strengthening one of the coalitions, the nucleolus shifts to the midpoint of the least core. The nucleolus is very sensitive to the parameters of the game.

```
In[22]:= v[{1,2,3}] = 5/4;
        Nucleolus[]
```

$$Out[22]:= \{\frac{5}{8}, \frac{3}{8}, \frac{5}{8}, \frac{3}{8}\}$$

The nucleolus has many desirable properties as a solution concept. It is defined uniquely for every game. It always belongs to the core provided the core is non-empty. It is, in a precisely defined sense, the center of the core. It is a strong candidate for the solution of cost allocation games. However, it has a major rival in the Shapley value, to which we now turn.

8.6   The Shapley Value

A point valued solution concept essentially defines a function on the set of games which yields a unique outcome for every game. Obviously, there are an infinity of possible functions. One way to select a particular function is to specify a list of properties or axioms which the function must satisfy and which are sufficient to produce a unique function. This is the approach underlying the Shapley value.

We must first define some terms. Recall that a permutation Π of a finite set S is a one-to-one mapping from S to itself. Given any game (T, v), we define the permuted game $(\Pi T, \Pi v)$ by

$$\Pi v(S) = v(\Pi S) \; \forall S.$$

A permuted game is the game obtained by relabelling all the players. Similarly, for any allocation x,

$$\Pi x[i] = x[\Pi i].$$

We say that a solution is anonymous (symmetric) if the names of the players do not matter, that is it is invariant to a relabelling of the players. Formally, a point-valued solution concept F is anonymous if

$$F[\Pi v] = \Pi F[v]$$

We say that a player is a null player if his contribution to every coalition is zero, that is

$$v[S \cup \{i\}] = v[S] \; \forall S.$$

A value is a point valued solution concept $F[v]$ which is

1. Linear $F[v + w] = F[v] + F[w]$

2. Anonymous $F[\Pi v] = \Pi F[v]$

3. Pareto Optimal $F[v][T] = v[T]$

4. $F[v][i] = 0$ for every null player.

Shapley (1953) showed that there was a unique value on every game which is given by

$$\phi v_i = \sum_{S \subset T} \gamma_S(v[S] - v[S - \{i\}])$$

where

$$\gamma_S = (|S| - 1)!(n - |S|)!/n!$$

This can be directly expressed in *Mathematica*.

```
In[1]:= gamma[S_List] :=
            (Length[S] - 1)! ( Length[T] - Length[S])! /
                Length[T] !
```

```
In[2]:= ShapleyValue1[game_,i_] :=
            Plus @@
              (gamma[#] (v[#] - v[DeleteCases[#,i]] )&
                  /@ Rest[Coalitions])
```

```
In[3]:= ShapleyValue1[BankruptcyGame,2]
```

$$Out[3]:= \frac{100}{3}$$

If we make the function Listable

```
In[4]:= Attributes[ShapleyValue1] = {Listable};
```

and define a pattern for the case in which we do not specify a player

```
In[5]:= ShapleyValue1[game_] := ShapleyValue1[game,T]
```

we can extend the function to provide Shapley values for the whole game.

```
In[6]:= ShapleyValue1[BankruptcyGame]
```

$$Out[6]:= \{\frac{70}{3}, \frac{100}{3}, \frac{130}{3}\}$$

It is trivial to verify that the Shapley value satisfies the requirement of Pareto Optimality.

```
In[7]:= Plus @@ % == v[T]
```

```
Out[7]:= True
```

Using some other examples

```
In[8]:= ShapleyValue1[ThreeWayMarketGame]
```

$$Out[8]:= \{\frac{13}{6}, \frac{1}{6}, \frac{2}{3}\}$$

```
In[9]:= ShapleyValue1[ThreePersonMajorityGame]
```

$$Out[9]:= \{\frac{1}{3}, \frac{1}{3}, \frac{1}{3}\}$$

```
In[10]:= ShapleyValue1[CorporationGame]
```

$$Out[10]:= \{\frac{1}{12}, \frac{1}{4}, \frac{1}{4}, \frac{5}{12}\}$$

The Shapley value does not necessarily yield a core allocation, even when the core is non-empty.

```
In[11]:= InCoreQ[ShapleyValue1[BankruptcyGame],BankruptcyGame]
```

```
Out[11]:= True
```

```
In[12]:= InCoreQ[ShapleyValue1[ThreeWayMarketGame],
                 ThreeWayMarketGame]
```

```
Out[12]:= False
```

The function **ShapleyValue1[]** is inefficient, especially for large games. It can be improved dramatically by recognising that the value of the function gamma[S] depends only on the size of the coalition S. By redefining this function and caching its values, we obtain a more efficient version, **ShapleyValue2**.

```
In[13]:= g[s_Integer] := g[s] = Module[{n=Length[T]},
                          (s - 1)! ( n-s)! / n !
                          ]
```

```
In[14]:= ShapleyValue2[game_,i_] :=
                Plus @@
                   (g[Length[#]] (v[#] - v[DeleteCases[#,i]] )&
                      /@ Rest[Coalitions])
```

```
In[15]:= Attributes[ShapleyValue2] = {Listable};
```

```
In[16]:= ShapleyValue2[CorporationGame,T]
```

$$Out[16]:= \{\frac{1}{12}, \frac{1}{4}, \frac{1}{4}, \frac{5}{12}\}$$

The catch is that we must clear the cached values of $g[]$ before any further calculation.

```
In[17]:= g[#] = . & /@ Range @ Length[T];
```

The improvement in efficiency can be seen by comparing

```
In[18]:= Timing[ShapleyValue1[CorporationGame]]
```

$$Out[18]:= \{0.45 \text{ Second}, \{\frac{1}{12}, \frac{1}{4}, \frac{1}{4}, \frac{5}{12}\}\}$$

```
In[19]:= Timing[ShapleyValue2[CorporationGame,T]]
```

$$Out[19]:= \{0.333333 \text{ Second}, \{\frac{1}{12}, \frac{1}{4}, \frac{1}{4}, \frac{5}{12}\}\}$$

```
In[20]:= g[#] = . & /@ Range @ Length[T];
```

There is an alternative approach based on recent work of Hart and Mas-Colell (1989) which offers even more efficient computation in some games.

The potential function for a game $G = (T, v)$ can be defined recursively as follows:

$$p[S] = (v[T] + \sum_{i \in S} p[S \setminus \{i\}])/|S|$$

where

$$p[\{i\}] = v[\{i\}]$$

This is readily expressed in *Mathematica* as:

```
In[21]:= p[{i_}]  := p[{i}] = v[{i}];

        p[S_]    := p[S] =
                  (v[S] + Plus @@ Map[p[Complement[S,{#}]] &,S])/
                               Length[S]
```

The Shapley value of player *i* is given by her marginal contribution, which is defined to be

$$\phi v_i = \text{MarginalContribution} = p[T] - p[T \setminus \{i\}]$$

Again, this is straightforward to express in *Mathematica*, so that the function **ShapleyValue3** returns the vector of Shapley values.

```
In[22]:= ShapleyValue3[game_,S_List:T]  := Module[{value},
              value = p[T] - (p[DeleteCases[T,#]] & /@ S);
              p[#] = . & /@ Rest[Coalitions];
              Return[value]
         ]
```

```
In[23]:= ShapleyValue3[BankruptcyGame]
```

$$Out[23]:= \left\{\frac{70}{3}, \frac{100}{3}, \frac{130}{3}\right\}$$

```
In[24]:= ShapleyValue3[CorporationGame]
```

$$Out[24]:= \left\{\frac{1}{12}, \frac{1}{4}, \frac{1}{4}, \frac{5}{12}\right\}$$

Since computing the Shapley value via the potential function essentially requires dealing with all the players together, we have utilized this in the definition of **ShapleyValue3**. Consequently, we can incorporate the clearing of the cached values of $p[]$ into the function. Since, in large games, it may be desirable to calculate the Shapley value for the subset of the players, we have allowed for this option.

```
In[25]:= ShapleyValue3[CorporationGame,{1,2}]
```

$$Out[25]:= \left\{\frac{1}{12}, \frac{1}{4}\right\}$$

By adding the pattern

```
In[26]:= ShapleyValue3[game_,i_?AtomQ]  :=
              ShapleyValue3[game,{i}]
```

we can provide for the calling convention of the preceding definitions.

```
In[27]:= ShapleyValue3[CorporationGame,1]
```

$$Out[27]:= \left\{\frac{1}{12}\right\}$$

ShapleyValue3[] provides a dramatic improvement in performance.

In[28]:= **Timing[ShapleyValue3[CorporationGame]]**

Out[28]:=
$$\{0.133333 \text{ Second}, \{\frac{1}{12}, \frac{1}{4}, \frac{1}{4}, \frac{5}{12}\}\}$$

In view of this, we use **ShapleyValue3** in the package Cooperative.m.

8.7 Conclusion

We conclude by comparing the various solutions to the Lecture Tour Game. The major solutions are

In[1]:= **Core[LectureTourGame] // TableForm**

Out[1]:= x[Frankfurt] >= 0
 x[Paris] >= 0
 x[Vienna] >= 0
 x[Frankfurt] + x[Paris] >= 300
 x[Frankfurt] + x[Vienna] >= 600
 x[Paris] + x[Vienna] >= 750
 x[Frankfurt] + x[Paris] + x[Vienna] == 900

In[2]:= **Nucleolus[LectureTourGame]**

Out[2]:= {100, 250, 550}

In[3]:= **ShapleyValue[LectureTourGame]**

Out[3]:= {200, 275, 425}

Recall that these payoffs are cost savings from cooperation. We can convert them into cost shares by subtracting them from the costs of individual action, which are

In[4]:= **c[{#}]& /@ T**

Out[4]:= {750, 750, 1800}

The corresponding cost shares are

In[5]:= **% - Nucleolus[]**

Out[5]:= {650, 500, 1250}

In[6]:= **%% - ShapleyValue[]**

Out[6]:= {550, 475, 1375}

Both concepts award relatively more of the cost savings to Paris than Frankfurt, reflecting the savings from combining Paris with Vienna. We see that, compared to the Shapley value, the nucleolus favours Vienna at the expense of

Frankfurt and Paris. How do we choose between these alternatives, or indeed other possible allocations? A picture gives some insight.

In[7]:= **Draw[{Core[],{Nucleolus[],"N"},{ShapleyValue[],"S"}},**
                        ConstraintLabels -> False]

Out[7]:= —Graphics—

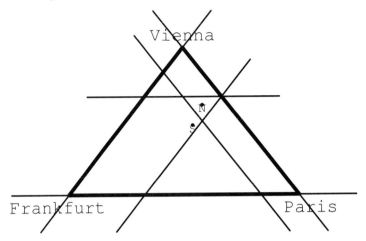

We see immediately that the Shapley Value does not belong to the core, which can be confirmed by

In[8]:= **InCoreQ[ShapleyValue[]]**

Out[8]:= False

The difficulty with a non-core allocation is that one or more of the coalitions would find it profitable to act on their own and opt out of the collective agreement. In this case

In[9]:= **Blocking[ShapleyValue[]]**

Out[9]:= {{Paris, Vienna}}

Paris and Vienna can arrange a tour excluding Frankfurt at a cost of 1800, where as their share under the Shapley value is 1850. They have no incentive to agree.

Since the nucleolus always belongs to the core, it might seem that this is the best solution to any cost allocation problem. However, the nucleolus lacks another desirable property which the Shapley value exhibits. This property is called monotonicity, and it means that, if the worth of a coalition increases, it share should not decrease.

To illustrate monotonicity, suppose that a bargain airfare between London, Frankfurt and Paris of 900 suddenly becomes available. It seems that this should not be to their disadvantage. However, we can demonstrate that the cost share attributed to Paris under the nucleolus actually rises as result of taking account of the bargain airfare.

In[10]:= **c[{Frankfurt,Paris}] = 900;**

In[11]:= **c[{#}]& /@ T - Nucleolus[]**

Out[11]:= {550, 400, 1450}

In[12]:= **c[{#}]& /@ T - ShapleyValue[]**

Out[12]:= {500, 425, 1475}

Paris' share under the nucleolus is now 520, compared to 500 previously. It does not look like a bargain for Paris.

Monotonicity is especially important where the costs are under the control of the participants. If the cost allocation procedure is not monotonic, the participants do not always have an incentive to economise. On the other hand, it we choose the Shapley value, which is monotonic but not always in the core, the participants do not necessariy have an incentive to participate.

This example illustrates that there is no single best answer to the problem of cost allocation. However, an analysis along the preceding lines can help clarify the essence of a particular problem and the characteristics of any proposed solution.

8.8 References

Hart, S., and A. MasColell(1989): "Potential, Value, and Consistency," *Econometrica*, **57**, 589–614.

Luce, R. D., and H. Raiffa (1957): *Games and Decisions*. New York: Wiley.

Maschler, M., Peleg, B., and Shapley, L. S. (1979): "Geometric Properties of the Kernel, Nucleolus and Related Solution Concepts," *Mathematics of Operations Research*, **4**, 303–338.

Owen, G. (1982): *Game Theory*. 2nd. ed. New York: Academic Press.

Shapley, L. S. (1953): "A Value for n-Person Games," in: *Contributions to the Theory of Games II (Annals of Mathematics Studies 28)*, ed. by H. W. Kuhn and A. W. Tucker. Princeton: Princeton University Press, 307–317.

Shubik, M. (1982): *Game Theory in the Social Sciences. Concepts and Solutions*. Cambridge, MA: MIT Press.

Young, H. P. (1988): *Cost Allocation: Methods, Principles, Applications*. Amsterdam: North Holland.

9 Mathematica and Diffusions

J. Michael Steele and Robert A. Stine

9.1   Introduction

A central aim of this chapter is to illustrate how symbolic computing can simplify or eliminate many of the tedious aspects of the stochastic calculus. The package `Diffusion.m` included with this book provides a suite of functions for manipulating diffusion models, and individuals with a basic knowledge of *Mathematica* should be able to use this package to expedite many of the routine calculations of stochastic calculus. After demonstrating the basic features of this package, we give an extensive example that applies the functions of the package to a problem of option-pricing.

This application offers a derivation of the well-known Black-Scholes formula for options pricing. The derivation exploits the idea of a self-financing portfolio (Duffie 1988). Our goal is show how *Mathematica* simplifies the *derivation* of the central expression in this problem. This task is to be distinguished from that engaged in Miller (1990) which shows a variety ways to describe and use the Black-Scholes formula.

In the next section we give a brief overview of the central idea of diffusions as required by options pricing theory, and we introduce the notation that is needed. This section is indeed very brief, and readers unfamiliar with diffusions should consider a text like that of Arnold (1974) or Duffy (1988) for the missing details and intuition. Section 9.3 introduces the new *Mathematica* functions that will be needed in Section 9.4 where we present a *Mathematica* derivation of the Black-Scholes formula. Section 9.5 demands more knowledge of *Mathematica* since it describes issues of implementation and includes further examples of the methods used in the extended example.

This package uses features found in Version 2 of *Mathematica*. Since some of these features are not available in earlier versions of the software, problems will occur if one attempts to use the package without having upgraded to at least Version 2.0.

9.2   Review of Diffusions and Itô's Formula

Diffusions form a class of stochastic processes that allow one to apply many of the modeling ideas of differential equations to the study of random phenomena. In simplest terms, a diffusion X_t is a Markov process in continuous time $t \geq 0$ that has continuous sample paths. A key feature of diffusions is that there exist two functions μ and σ which together with an initial value X_0 completely characterize each diffusion. Moreover, in many applications μ and σ have physical or financial interpretations.

For this article we will assume that the scalar-valued functions μ and σ are locally bounded, and let W_t denote the standard Weiner process. Under these conditions, a fundamental result of the Itô calculus is that there exists a well-defined process X_t having the suggestive representation

$$X_t = X_0 + \int_0^t \mu(X_s, s)ds + \int_0^t \sigma(X_s, s)dW_s. \tag{1}$$

The intuition behind this representation for X_t is that the function μ determines the instantaneous drift of X_t whereas σ controls its disperson or variability. If, as in later examples, X_t denotes the price of a stock at time t, then μ and σ may be interpreted as the rate of return and the instantaneous risk.

Since the process W_t is not of bounded variation, the second integral on the right-hand side of (1) cannot be interpreted naively. For example, suppose that we were to attempt to evaluate $\int_0^t W_s dW_s$ as the limit of an approximating sum over partitions of the interval $[0, t]$,

$$\sum_i W_{s_i}(W_{t_i} - W_{t_{i-1}}), 0 \leq t_{i-1} \leq s_i \leq t_i \leq t.$$

Since W_t is not of bounded variation, the value for the integral suggested by such approximation turns out to depend upon how we choose to locate s_i in the interval $[t_{i-1}, t_i]$. Throughout this chapter, we adopt the convention $s_i = t_{i-1}$. The resulting stochastic integral has a unique solution known as the Itô integral. A very important reason for choosing $s_i = t_{i-1}$ is that with this choice a stochastic integral with respect to W_t is always a martingale.

One of the most common and convenient ways to express a diffusion is to use a notation that is analogous to that of differential equations. Rather than use the stochastic integral to represent X_t as in (1), one often uses a shorthand notation:

$$dX_t = \mu(X_t, t)dt + \sigma(X_t, t)dW_t. \tag{2}$$

This compact description of the process X_t resembles a differential equation, but it must be interpreted appropriately as just shorthand for (1).

An important property of diffusions is their behavior under smooth transformations. Perhaps the central result in the theory of diffusions is that a smooth function of a diffusion produces another diffusion. Moreover, an explicit formula due to Itô identifies the new process by giving expressions for the drift and disperson functions. Suppose that the function f maps $(\Re, \Re^+) \rightarrow \Re$, and consider applying this function to a diffusion, say $Y_t = f(X_t, t)$. Under modest conditions on f, the process Y_t is also a diffusion. One set of sufficient conditions is to require continuous first and second derivatives of f in its first argument and a single continuous derivative in the second. Denote these derivatives by $f_x = \partial f(x, t)/\partial x$, $f_{xx} = \partial^2 f(x, t)/\partial x^2$, and $f_t = \partial f(x, t)/\partial t$.

Under these restrictions on f, Itô's formula guarantees that Y_t is a diffusion and gives the functions that characterize this new diffusion. Specifically, the stochastic differential for $Y_t = f(X_t, t)$ is

$$dY_t = \{f_t(X_t, t) + \mu(X_t, t)f_x(X_t, t) + f_{xx}\sigma^2(X_t, t)/2\}dt + \{f_x(X_t, t)\sigma(X_t, t)\}dW_t. \tag{3}$$

This expression is not in the canonical form of (2) since the drift and dispersion functions of Y_t are functions of X_t rather than Y_t, but this problem is easily remedied. If the transformation f has an inverse g so that

$$y = f(x, t) \Leftrightarrow x = g(y, t),$$

then we can use this inverse to obtain the desired form. Substitution in (3) gives

$$dY_t = \{f_t(g(Y_t, t), t) + \mu(g(Y_t, t), t)f_x(g(Y_t, t), t) + $$
$$f_{xx}\sigma^2(g(Y_t, t), t)/2\}dt + \{f_x(g(Y_t, t), t)\sigma(g(Y_t, t), t)\}dW_t$$

So indeed,

$$dY_t = \bar{\mu}(Y_t, t)dt + \bar{\sigma}(Y_t, t)dW_t \tag{4}$$

for the indicated values of $\bar{\mu}$ and $\bar{\sigma}$. The complexity of (4) suggests that we can avoid some tedium if we put *Mathematica* to work managing the transformation of the pair $\{\mu(x, t), \sigma(x, t)\}$ into $\{\bar{\mu}(x, t), \bar{\sigma}(x, t)\}$

Itô's formula (3) can be made more revealing if one also introduces the notion of the infinitesimal generator of the diffusion X_t. The infinitesimal generator of a diffusion measures the instantaneous rate of change in the expected value of a transformation of a diffusion as a function of its starting value. Under some natural conditions on the function f, we can define the infinitesimal generator as

$$A_X f(x) = lim_{t \to 0} \frac{E_x f(X_t, t) - f(x, 0)}{t},$$

where E_x denotes the expectation conditional on the starting value $X_0 = x$. This limit turns out to be closely related to the drift expression in Itô's formula, and one can show under mild conditions that A_X is the differential operator that has the explicit form

$$A_X = \frac{\partial}{\partial t} + \mu(x, t)\frac{\partial}{\partial x} + \frac{1}{2}\sigma(x, t)\frac{\partial^2}{\partial x^2}. \tag{5}$$

By using the infinitesimal generator associated with the diffusion X_t, we obtain a more compact form of Itô's formula,

$$dY_t = df(X_t, t) = A_X f dt + f_x(X_t, t)\sigma(X_t, t)dW_t.$$

9.3 Basic Mathematica Operations

9.3.1 Introduction to the Package

This section introduces basic functions that permit us to build and manipulate diffusions. In order to follow the operations described here, one must first import the package that defines the needed functions. The package itself is located in the file named "Diffusion.m" which should be placed in a directory which is easily, if not automatically, searched. The following command imports the package.

```
In[1]:= << Diffusion`
```

The names of most of the functions in this package begin "Diffusion", though some *also* have shorter, more convenient names. This convention allows for an easy listing of the available functions via the built-in **Names** function.

```
In[2]:= Names["Diffusion*"]

Out[2]:= {DiffusionA, DiffusionChangeSymbol, DiffusionDispersion,
          DiffusionDrift, DiffusionExpand, DiffusionExpandRules,
          DiffusionFeynmanKac, DiffusionInitialValue,
          DiffusionIto, DiffusionLabel, DiffusionMake,
          DiffusionPrint, DiffusionSimulate, DiffusionSymbol,
          DiffusionWeinerProcess, DiffusionWeinerProcessMake,
          DiffusionWeinerProcessSymbol}
```

A brief synopsis of each function is available via the standard *Mathematica* request for help; one precedes the name of the function of interest with a question mark. For example, the following command reveals the syntax and a brief description of the function which prints diffusions.

```
In[3]:= ?DiffusionPrint

DiffusionPrint[d] prints a formatted version of the
     diffusion object d using subscripts and symbolic names.
```

The next section describes how to build the diffusion objects that this function requires as arguments.

9.3.2 Building a Diffusion

The first order of business in building a diffusion is to specify a Weiner process. In this and many other examples, we begin by calling the **Clear** function. This function removes any value that might already be bound to the named symbol, as might occur when experimenting with *Mathematica* outside of the range of commands shown here. Thus, we first clear the name W which we intend to use to represent a Wiener process.

In[1]:= **Clear[W]**

The next command associates the name W with a Weiner process. Until we say otherwise, the name W will denote a Weiner process to the system.

In[2]:= **WeinerProcessMake[W]**

We can now use this Weiner process to define more complex diffusions. To build each diffusion, our convention requires a symbolic identifier (or name) for the diffusion and for the underlying Weiner process, two expressions (the drift μ and the dispersion σ), and an initial value. As an example, we first consider the lognormal diffusion. This process is used extensively in financial modeling and it will play a central role in Section 9.4 when we derive the Black-Scholes formula. In the classical notation of the stochastic calculus, a lognormal diffusion can be specified by

$$dX_t = \alpha X_t dt + \beta X_t dW_t, X_0 = v,$$

for scalars α and $\beta > 0$. To represent this diffusion in *Mathematica*, use the command **DiffusionMake**. Again, we clear the name X before we make the new process.

In[3]:= **Clear[X]**
In[4]:= **DiffusionMake[X, W, alpha X, beta X, v]**

To test the success of this command, we recall that typing the name of any object in *Mathematica* reveals the value of that object. In the case of a diffusion, the value is a list that holds the definition of the process.

In[5]:= **X**
Out[5]:= diffusion[X, W, alpha X, beta X, v]

While revealing to the *Mathematica* programmer, this form is probably not very appealing to one more familiar with the standard mathematical notation. The function **DiffusionPrint** ameliorates this problem by producing a more familiar rendering of a diffusion, complete with subscripting. Here are examples for the two diffusions created so far. The printed form for a Weiner process is pretty simple.

In[6]:= **DiffusionPrint[W]**
```
W  = Weiner Process with scale 1
 t
```

The format in general for printing a diffusion matches the notation of equation (2).

In[7]:= **DiffusionPrint[X]**
```
dX  = alpha X  dt + beta X   dW   ; X  = v
  t          t          t   t     0
```

9.3.3 Simulating Diffusions

In order to experiment with a diffusion model, it is often useful to simulate realizations of the process. The function **DiffusionSimulate** generates simulated realizations by building a discrete-time approximation to the continuous-time process. The method implemented in this software is a little naive—it resembles Euler's method for approximating solutions of a differential equation—but it functions quite usefully in most instances. To illustrate, we begin by asking *Mathematica* to reveal its summary of **DiffusionSimulate**.

```
In[1]:= ?DiffusionSimulate
DiffusionSimulate[d_diffusion, n, dt] simulates a
   diffusion.  It returns a list of n pairs
   {,,,{i*dt,x[i*dt]},,,} of the  diffusion d. Each realized
   series is an independent realization.  Responds with an
   error if the diffusion contains symbolic paramters.
```

As a simple example of the use of this function, we will simulate 100 values of a Weiner process at times $\{0, 0.01, \ldots, 0.99\}$. Assuming that we are simulating a diffusion labelled X_t, the simulated realization begins with the pair $\{0, X_0\}$ and adds $n-1$ pairs of the form $\{i\,dt, X_{idt}\}, i = 1, 2, \ldots, n-1$, separated in time by the chosen step size dt which is the last argument to the function. In this example, the semicolon at the end of the command suppresses the printing of the complete simulated realization. The function **Short** reveals the start and end of the list, and the bracketed number indicates that 97 of the items in the list are hidden.

```
In[2]:= simW = DiffusionSimulate[W,100,0.01];
```

```
In[3]:= Short[simW]
```

```
Out[3]:= {{0, 0}, {0.01, 0.0984664}, <<97>>, {0.99, -1.55817}}
```

The list structure of the simulated diffusion makes it quite easy to have *Mathematica* plot this artificial realization versus time.

```
In[4]:= ListPlot[simW, PlotJoined -> True]
```

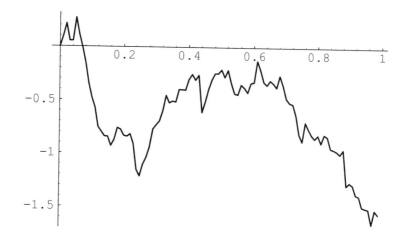

```
Out[4]:= -Graphics-
```

Simulations of other diffusions can be obtained just as easily. For example, suppose that we wished to plot the simulation of the diffusion

$$dY_t = Y_t dt + Y_t dW_t, Y_0 = 10.$$

First we build the diffusion using **DiffusionMake**.

In[5]:= **DiffusionMake[Y,W, Y,Y,10]**

Next we generate the partial realization using **DiffusionSimulate**, and again we note that **Short** reveals just the extremes of the list. Since the time spacing is not specified in the call to **DiffusionSimulate**, this program sets the spacing to a default value of 0.01.

In[6]:= **simY = DiffusionSimulate[Y,100];**
            Short[simY]

Out[6]:= {{0, 10.}, {0.01, 9.99454}, <<97>>, {0.99, 37.4779}}

In[7]:= **ListPlot[simY,**
              PlotJoined -> True]

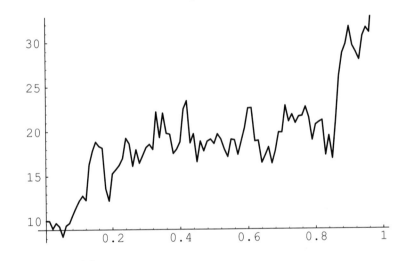

Out[7]:= —Graphics—

The function **RandomSeed** makes it possible to generate correlated realizations. By default, each realization of a diffusion is independent of other realizations. This structure may not be desired for many problems. As an example, consider the relationship of the Weiner process realization and the diffusion for the process $dY_t = Y_t dt + Y_t dW_t$ considered above. Independent realizations fail to capture the relationship between the series and suggest little relationship between the two. After all, these simulated realizations are independent. Here is a plot of Y_t on W_t with the plots joined in time sequence order.

In[8]:= **ListPlot[Table[{simW[[i,2]], simY[[i,2]]},{i,1,100}],**
              AxesLabel -> {"W[t]", "Y[t]"},
              PlotJoined -> True]

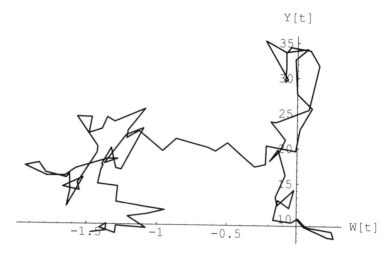

Out[8]:= −Graphics−

By explicitly setting the random seed used by *Mathematica*, we force the realization of Y_t to be based on the same random values used to simulate the Weiner
process W_t. This connection gives the realizations we would have expected.

```
In[9]:= SeedRandom[732712];
        simW = DiffusionSimulate[W,100];
        SeedRandom[732712];
        simY = DiffusionSimulate[Y,100];
```

The plot of Y_t on W_t now exhibits the strong relationship between the two
simulated realizations that is missing without matching the simulation seeds.

```
In[10]:= ListPlot[Table[{simW[[i,2]], simY[[i,2]]},{i,1,100}],
             AxesLabel->{"W[t]", "Y[t]"},
             PlotJoined -> True]
```

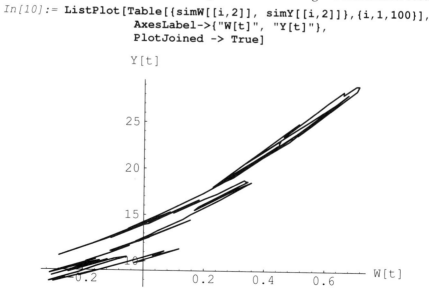

Out[10]:= −Graphics−

9.4 Deriving the Black-Scholes Formula

To illustrate the use of these tools in a problem of considerable historical interest, we will use our tools to derive the Black-Scholes option-pricing formula. Our approach parallels the development in Duffie (1988) and uses the notion of a self-financing trading strategy. Following the tradition in elementary option pricing theory, we will ignore the effects of transaction costs and dividends. Readers who are curious for further details and intuition should consider Duffie (1988) for a more refined discussion than space permits here.

The model begins with a simple market that consists of two investments, a stock and a bond. The bond is taken to be a risk free asset with rate of return ρ, so in our differential notation the bond price B_t at time t obeys $dB_t = \rho B_t dt$. The stock is assumed to have rate of return μ as well as some risk, so we can model the stock price S_t as a diffusion for which $dS_t = \mu S_t dt + \sigma S_t dW_t$ with the scalar $\sigma > 0$. We can set up these processes and clear the needed symbols as follows:

```
In[1]:= Clear[W, S,S0, B,B0, V, mu,sigma,rho, g,P]

        WeinerProcessMake[W]
        DiffusionMake[S, W, mu S, sigma S, S0]
        DiffusionMake[B, W, rho B, 0, B0]
```

Before continuing, we should perhaps view our processes in more conventional form by getting the printed version of each of the three diffusions.

```
In[2]:= DiffusionPrint[W]
        DiffusionPrint[S]
        DiffusionPrint[B]

W   = Weiner Process with scale 1
 t
dS   = mu S  dt + sigma S  dW  ; S  = S0
  t      t            t   t    0
dB   = rho B  dt ; B  = B0
  t       t        0
```

With these processes as building blocks, we can define the equations that permit us to give the explicit value of the European option. Suppose that there exists a function $V(s,t)$ such that $V(S_t,t)$ is the value at time $t, 0 \le t \le T$, of an option to purchase the stock modeled by S_t at a terminal time T at the strike price P. Our goal is to find an expression for this function in terms of μ, σ, P, T, and t. Since the value of the option is a function of the diffusion S_t, Itô's formula gives an expression for $V(S_t,t)$. Even though we do not explicitly know $V(S_t,t)$, we can use the **Ito** function to identify this new diffusion symbolically in terms of derivatives of V. In this case, we want to avoid putting the diffusion into the canonical form (4) since doing so would conceal how $V(S_t,t)$ depends upon S_t. The use of the **ItoInvert** option avoids the inversion to the canonical diffusion form, thereby retaining the stock symbol S in the expressions for the drift and dispersion of the new diffusion.

```
In[3]:= Ito[V[S,t], ItoInvert->False];

             (0,1)                      (1,0)
dV[S, t] = (V      [S, t] + mu S V         [S, t] +

        2   2  (2,0)
    sigma  S  V     [S, t]
    ----------------------- ) dt + (sigma S V(1,0) [S, t]) dW
             2                                              t
```

Now equate the value of the option to that of a self-financing trading portfolio. That is, assume that the value $V(S_t, t)$ of this stock option can be reproduced by a portfolio consisting of a_t shares of stock and b_t shares of bond, $V(S_t, t) = a_t S_t + b_t B_t$. Here, of course, we are assuming that a_t and b_t are both stochastic processes. An argument for the existence of such a portfolio in this problem appears in Duffy (1988). The matching of the value of the option to that of a portfolio gives a second expression for V in addition to that from Itô's formula. If we equate these two expressions for $V(S_t, t)$, we can solve for a_t and b_t. The manipulations that support the elimination of a_t and b_t are very easy in *Mathematica* since the diffusion package defines some simple algebraic operations for diffusions.

By default, diffusions retain their symbolic form in algebraic expressions. For example, if we enter a sum of two diffusions, the sum is retained and no attempt is made to combine the drift of one with that of the other.

```
In[4]:= at S + bt B

Out[4]:= bt B + at S
```

This behavior is consistent with the way *Mathematica* handles many other symbolic expressions, such as the way a product is not expanded unless the user makes an explicit request:

```
In[5]:= (a + b) (c + d)

Out[5]:= (a + b) (c + d)

In[6]:= Expand[%]

Out[6]:= a c + b c + a d + b d
```

The analogous behaviour is needed in the algebra of diffusions. In order to equate the two expressions for $V(S_t, t)$, we require the drift and dispersion of a diffusion that is the sum of two diffusions. The function **DiffusionExpand** combines several diffusions, though the resulting "diffusion" is not of the canonical form. Since we are only interested in the drift and dispersion, the absence of the canonical form is not a problem.

```
In[7]:= diff = DiffusionExpand[V - (at S + bt B)]
```

```
Out[7]:=                                                            (0,1)
        diffusion[$3, W, -(bt rho B) - at mu S + (V)      [S, t]

                                             2  2   (2,0)
                    (1,0)                sigma  S  (V)     [S, t]
        + mu S (V)      [S, t] +        ───────────────────────────── ,
                                                       2

                                                     (1,0)
        -(at sigma S) + sigma S (V)      [S, t],

        -(bt B0) - at S0 + V[S0, t]]]
```

In order for the difference $V(S_t, t) - (a_t S_t + b_t B_t)$ to be zero, both the drift and dispersion of this new diffusion must be identically zero. This gives two equations in two unknowns, and thus the number of stock and bond shares in the matching portfolio, a_t and b_t. The built-in function **Solve** gives a set of rules that define the solution of the system of two equations.

```
In[8]:= roots = Solve[{DiffusionDrift[diff]==0,
            DiffusionDispersion[diff]==0}, {at,bt}]
Out[8]:=              (1,0)
        {{at -> (V)      [S, t], bt ->

                      (1,0)
            mu S (V)      [S, t]
        -(─────────────────────) +
                 rho B

            (0,1)                        (1,0)
        (2 (V)     [S, t] + 2 mu S (V)      [S, t] +

              2  2   (2,0)
         sigma  S  (V)     [S, t]) / (2 rho B)}}
```

For convenience, we next extract the values of a_t and b_t implied by these rules and assign them appropriately. The additional simplification eases later manipulations and seems unavoidable in some implementations of *Mathematica*. The function **First** in the next two expressions extracts the solution from the single-element list in which it is embedded.

```
In[9]:= at = Simplify[ First[at /. roots] ]
Out[9]:=     (1,0)
        (V)      [S, t]

In[10]:= bt = Simplify[ First[bt /. roots] ]
Out[10]:=      (0,1)                 2  2   (2,0)
         2 (V)      [S, t] + sigma  S  (V)     [S, t]
        ───────────────────────────────────────────────
                        2 rho B
```

In more conventional notation,

$$a_t = V_x(S_t, t), b_t = \frac{V_t(S_t, t) + \frac{1}{2}\sigma^2 S_t^2 V_{xx}(S_t, t)}{2\rho B_t},$$

where V_x denotes the partial derivative of $V(x, u)$ with respect to its first argument, and V_{xx} denotes the second partial derivative in the first argument. Similarly, V_t is the first partial in the second argument.

To find a partial differential equation for the value of the option, we substitute these expressions for a_t and b_t back into the relation $V(S_t, t) = a_t S_t + b_t B_t$. The use of the function **Expand** assures that the function **Coefficient** extracts the proper term.

```
In[11]:= pde = Expand[ at S + bt B - V[S,t] ]
```

```
Out[11]:=                    (0,1)
                        (V)      [S, t]              (1,0)
           -V[S, t] + ──────────────────── + S (V)       [S, t] +
                              rho


                   2   2    (2,0)
             sigma  S   (V)      [S, t]
           ──────────────────────────────
                         2 rho
```

To set things up for the next step, normalize this PDE so that the coefficient of V_t is 1.

```
In[12]:= pde = Expand[ pde / Coefficient[pde, D[V[S,t],t]] ]
```

```
Out[12]:=                          (0,1)                        (1,0)
          -(rho V[S, t]) + (V)      [S, t] + rho S (V)      [S, t]


                   2   2    (2,0)
             sigma  S   (V)      [S, t]
         + ──────────────────────────────
                         2
```

These equations and the boundary conditions discussed shortly are sufficient to determine V, thus solving the option pricing problem. The problem now faced is the purely mathematical one of solving our PDE. A variety of tools exist for solving PDE's that arise in the application of diffusions, and one of the most powerful is based upon the Feymann-Kac theorem. For our purposes, the Feynman-Kac theorem expresses the solution of a certain second-order PDE as an expectation with respect to a related diffusion. The first question one has to resolve before applying this method is whether the PDE of interest is of the appropriate type. The second issue is to make an explicit correspondence between one's PDE and the form of the Feynman-Kac result. The function **FeynmanKac** performs both of these tasks. As a side-effect, it also prints out the terms used in its matching using the notation of Duffie (1988).

The use of this function also requires identifying boundary conditions. Let $g(x)$ denote the payout function for the option. For example, the payout function for a European option with exercise price P is the piecewise linear function $g(x) = (x - P)^+$ where $(x - P)^+ = x - P$ if $x > P$ and is zero otherwise. The payout function determines the needed boundary condition, $V(x, T) = g(x)$. Here we apply the **FeynmanKac** function, using the symbol g to denote the payout function. In the following output, the symbol `Ave` stands for the expected value operator since the symbol `E` denotes the base of the natural log e in *Mathematica*.

```
In[13]:= soln = FeynmanKac[pde,g]

f = V;   rho = rho;   u = 0
dX  = rho X   dt + sigma X   dW   ; X  = x
  t        t             t.   t.    0
Out[13]:=        g[X[-t + T]]
          Ave[---------------]
               rho (-t + T)
             E
```

The "solution" given by the Feynman-Kac theorem is rather abstract and the task of rendering it concrete is not always easy. The result of this function indicates that the solution of our PDE is the expected discounted payout

$$e^{-\rho(T-t)} E g(X_{T-t}),$$

where X_t is the diffusion that satisfies $dX_t = \rho X_t dt + \sigma X_t dW_t$ with initial value $X_0 = x$ and Weiner process W_t. The process X_t is just the familiar lognormal diffusion, as confirmed by use of Itô's formula.

We will next confirm that the exponential of the normal diffusion $dY_t = a\, dt + b\, dW_t$ is indeed a lognormal diffusion, and we use *Mathematica* to make the required identification of coefficients in both drift and dispersion.

```
In[14]:= Clear[Y];
         DiffusionMake[Y,W, a,b,0];
         Ito[Y][Exp[Y]]

                   2    Y
   Y      (2 a + b ) E              Y
 dE   = (----------------) dt + (b E ) dW
                2                        t

Inversion rule... {Y -> Log[Z]}
Out[14]:=                              2
                          (2 a + b ) Z
           diffusion[Z, W, ----------------, b Z, 1]
                                 2
```

Clearly, b corresponds to σ. Equating the drift coefficients $(2a + b^2/2) = \rho$ shows that $a = \rho - (s^2/2)$.

```
In[15]:= a = Simplify[a/.First[ Solve[(2 a+sigma^2)/2 == rho,
         a]]]
Out[15]:=                 2
                      sigma
             rho - --------
                      2
```

This calculation implies that the diffusion X_t in the solution from the Feynman-Kac theorem is the exponential of a normal diffusion with constant drift $\rho -$

$(\sigma^2/2)$ and dispersion σ. Recalling that $X_0 = x$, at any time $t \geq 0$ X_t satisfies

$$X_t = xe^{(\rho - \frac{\sigma^2}{2})t + \sigma W_t}.$$

Hence for any t, X_t has the same distribution as $xe^{(\rho - (\sigma^2/2))t + \sigma\sqrt{T}Z}$ where Z is a standard normal random variable with mean zero and variance one. Finally we see that the value of the option at time $t = 0$ is

$$V(x,0) = e^{-\rho T} Eg(X_T) = \frac{e^{-\rho T}}{\sqrt{2\pi}} \int_{-\infty}^{\infty} g(xe^{(\rho - \frac{\sigma^2}{2})T + \sqrt{T}\sigma z})e^{-z^2/2}dz.$$

For the European option with exercise price P, we have $g(x) = (x - P)^+$ and this integral becomes

$$\frac{e^{-\rho T}}{\sqrt{2\pi}} \int_{z_0}^{\infty} (xe^{(\rho - \frac{\sigma^2}{2})T + \sqrt{T}\sigma z} - P)e^{-z^2/2}dz,$$

where z_0 solves

$$xe^{(\rho - \frac{\sigma^2}{2})T + \sqrt{T}\sigma z_0} = P.$$

Calculation of this integral is somewhat tedious, but its evaluation makes for a nice illustration of the integral solving capabilities of *Mathematica*. To make the coding a little more modular, we first define a function $h(z) = xe^{(\rho - (\sigma^2/2))T + \sqrt{T}\sigma z} - P$ and use it to locate the lower bound z_0.

```
In[16]:= h[z_] := x Exp[(rho-sigma^2/2.)T+Sqrt[T] sigma z] - P
         rule = Solve[ h[z]==0, z];
         z0 = Simplify[ First[z /. rule] ]
```

```
Out[16]=                       2           P
           -(rho T) + 0.5 sigma  T + Log[-]
                                         x
          ────────────────────────────────
                    sigma Sqrt[T]
```

To simplify the input further, we define the Gaussian kernel gauss$(z)=e^{-z^2/2}/\sqrt{2\pi}$.

```
In[17]:= gauss[z_] := E^(-(z^2)/2)/Sqrt[2 Pi]
```

Given these definitions of the functions **h** and **gauss**, it is quite simple to describe the needed integral. We call the integration function with specific limits a and b rather than symbolic infinite limits. The integration routines seem to behave more robustly in this application with these limits rather than infinite limits.

```
In[18]:= Clear[a,b]
         intab = Integrate[E^(-rho T) h[z] gauss[z], {z,a,b}]
```

```
Out[18]=        a                    b
         P Erf[─────]          P Erf[─────]
              Sqrt[2]               Sqrt[2]
         ─────────────    -    ─────────────    -
             rho T                 rho T
           2 E                    2 E
```

Out [18] (cont.)

$$(E^{-(\text{rho } T) + (\text{sigma}^2 T)/2 + (\text{rho} - 0.5 \text{ sigma}^2) T} x$$

$$\text{Erf}[\dfrac{a - \text{sigma Sqrt}[T]}{\text{Sqrt}[2]}]) / 2 +$$

$$(E^{-(\text{rho } T) + (\text{sigma}^2 T)/2 + (\text{rho} - 0.5 \text{ sigma}^2) T} x$$

$$\text{Erf}[\dfrac{b - \text{sigma Sqrt}[T]}{\text{Sqrt}[2]}]) / 2$$

Now we can apply two substitution rules that specify the range of integration, $a = z_0$ and $b = \infty$, and we have the desired integral.

In[19]:= **int = intab /. {a->z0, b->Infinity};**
          Simplify[int]

Out[19]:=

$$\dfrac{-P}{2 E^{\text{rho } T}} + \dfrac{x}{2} - \dfrac{x \text{ Erf}[\dfrac{-(\text{rho } T) - 0.5 \text{ sigma}^2 T + \text{Log}[\frac{P}{x}]}{\text{Sqrt}[2] \text{ sigma Sqrt}[T]}]}{2}$$

$$+ \dfrac{P \text{ Erf}[\dfrac{-(\text{rho } T) + 0.5 \text{ sigma}^2 T + \text{Log}[\frac{P}{x}]}{\text{Sqrt}[2] \text{ sigma Sqrt}[T]}]}{2 E^{\text{rho } T}}$$

This expression involves the error function defined in *Mathematica* as $\text{erf}(z) = \int_0^z e^{-x^2} dx$. We get a more familiar result by using the equivalence $\text{erf}(z) = 2\Phi(\sqrt{2}z) - 1$, where $\Phi(z)$ denotes the cumulative standard normal distribution, $\Phi(z) = \int_{-\infty}^z (e^{(-x^2/2)}/\sqrt{2\pi}) dx$.

In[20]:= **bs = Simplify[int /. Erf[x_] ->**
          (2 NormalCDF[Sqrt[2]x] - 1)]

Out[20]:=

$$-(\dfrac{P}{E^{\text{rho } T}}) + x - x \text{ NormalCDF}[\dfrac{-(\text{rho } T) - 0.5 \text{ s}^2 T + \text{Log}[\frac{P}{x}]}{\text{s Sqrt}[T]}] +$$

```
Out[20](cont.)
                                         2          P
                      -(rho T) + 0.5 s   T + Log[-]
                                                  x
        P NormalCDF[------------------------------]
                              s Sqrt[T]
        _____
                           rho T
                          E
```

We can express this result in yet more familiar form by using a rule that expresses the relationship $\Phi(x) = 1 - \Phi(-x)$.

```
In[21]:= Simplify[ bs/.NormalCDF[x_]->1-NormalCDF[-x]]
Out[21]:=                                  2          P
                        -(rho T) - 0.5 s   T + Log[-]
                                                    x
        x NormalCDF[-(------------------------------)] -
                                s Sqrt[T]

                                           2          P
                        -(rho T) + 0.5 s   T + Log[-]
                                                    x
        P NormalCDF[-(------------------------------)]
                                s Sqrt[T]
        _____
                              rho T
                             E
```

This is the Black-Scholes formula for pricing the European option (Duffie, 1988, p. 239). Miller (1990) discusses this function at length and shows various manipulations of it using *Mathematica*.

9.5   More Mathematica Details and Examples

The material of this section focusses on some issues that can be omitted at a first reading, but that might prove useful for the user who wishes to extend the methods or examples. The discussion begins with the underlying data structure used to represent a diffusion. Many of the ideas come from object-oriented programming. We next consider in some detail the use of our functions that produce the infinitesimal and Itô's formula. Further programming details appear as comments embedded in the code of the package itself.

The examples in this section use both of the *Mathematica* diffusion objects built in Section 9.3. In case these are not available, the following command rebuilds the Weiner process W_t and the associated lognormal diffusion X_t.

```
In[1]:= Clear[X,W];
        WeinerProcessMake[W];
        DiffusionMake[X,W,alpha X, beta X, v];
```

The data structure we use to represent a diffusion parallels the notation of Section 9.2. To represent an arbitrary diffusion, one must describe each of the distinguishing components: drift, dispersion, Weiner process, and initial value. In addition, we need to supply a symbol that names the diffusion itself. As a result, the list that we use to represent a diffusion has these five items: name of the diffusion, name of Weiner process, drift expression, dispersion expression, and initial value. This data structure is particularly simple for a Weiner process. The first two symbols which are the names of the diffusion and its underlying Weiner process match for a Weiner process. The drift and dispersion are the constants 0 and 1, respectively. The matching of the leading symbols identifies in the software the presence of a Weiner process.

Several accessor functions permit one to extract components of a diffusion without requiring detailed knowledge of its data structure. Although these functions simply index the list that holds the components of the diffusion, use of these accessors frees one from having to remember the arrangement of the list. Such abstraction offers the opportunity to change the data structure at a later point without having to rewrite code that uses accessor functions. Here are a few examples of the accessor functions.

```
In[2]:= DiffusionWeinerProcessSymbol[X]
```

```
Out[2]:= W
```

Notice that this function results in the symbol associated with the Weiner process rather than the Weiner process itself. A different accessor extracts the process.

```
In[3]:= DiffusionWeinerProcess[X]
```

```
Out[3]:= diffusion[W, W, 0, 1, 0]
```

The next three examples extract the remaining components of the diffusion.

```
In[4]:= DiffusionDrift[X]
```

```
Out[4]:= alpha X
```

```
In[5]:= DiffusionDispersion[X]
```

```
Out[5]:= beta X
```

```
In[6]:= DiffusionInitialValue[X]
```

```
Out[6]:= v
```

It is important to notice that the results of some of these functions include the symbol X which represents the diffusion. A sleight of hand is needed to obtain this behavior, and all is not quite as it appears. The built-in function **FullForm** reveals that the results of both **DiffusionDrift** and **DiffusionDispersion** contain so-called "held expressions" that one must use in order to keep the system from trying to evaluate the diffusion symbols that appear in the drift and dispersion expressions.

```
In[7]:= DiffusionDrift[X] // FullForm
```

```
Out[7]:= Times[alpha, HoldForm[X]]
```

Were it not for holding the evaluation of the symbol X in this expression, *Mathematica* would descend into an endless recursion, continually substituting the list representing the diffusion each time it encountered the symbol X in the list. Further discussion of this recursion appears in Steele and Stine (1991).

We have found that it is most easy to manipulate the drift and dispersion functions as expressions rather than *Mathematica* functions. Still, occasions arise when one wants a function. For example, one might want to differentiate or plot the drift. The accessors normally extract these components in a manner that preserves their symbolic content. That is, they return an expression which includes the symbol for the diffusion. When a function is desired, the accessors **DiffusionDrift** and **DiffusionDispersion** have an optional argument that forces the output to be returned as a function. The returned function has two arguments, the first for the diffusion and the second for time, as in $\mu(x,t)$ and $\sigma(x,t)$ respectively.

As example, consider generating a plot of the drift from the lognormal diffusion. First, extract the drift as a *Mathematica* function and give it a suggestive name.

In[8]:= **mu = DiffusionDrift[X,Function]**

Out[8]:= Function[{x\$, t\$}, alpha x\$]

We can treat this function just like any other, differentiating or plotting as we choose.

In[9]:= **D[mu[x,t],x]**

Out[9]:= alpha

Of course, if we expect to plot the drift function, we have to make sure that all of the symbolic terms have a value. Here we set $\alpha = 2$ so that $\mu(x,t) = 2x$.

In[10]:= **Plot[mu[x,t]/.alpha->2, {x,0,5}]**

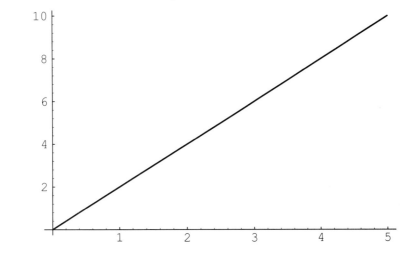

Out[10]:= —Graphics—

In general, we would need to plot the drift $\mu(x, t)$ as a surface over the plane, but in this and many other common circumstances this elaborate plot is not needed.

As we noted in our review of Itô's formula, the infinitesimal generator of a diffusion process has an intimate relationship to the stochastic differential representation of the diffusion. The argument given to the function which finds the infinitesimal is an expression involving a diffusion. For example, the next example determines the infinitesimal of the process defined by an arbitrary function g of W_t. We see that the infinitesimal is half of the second derivative of g.

```
In[11]:= A[g[W]]

Out[11]:= g''[W]
          ———————
            2
```

For the lognormal diffusion X_t, the result is somewhat more complex, but the syntax of the commands is the same. We saw this expression in Section 9.4 in the option-pricing problem.

```
In[12]:= A[g[X]]

Out[12]:=
                                  2   2
                              beta  X  g''[X]
           alpha X g'[X] + ————————————————————
                                     2
```

The function associated with Itô's formula provided in the accompanying package is more potent than the other functions of the package. The function **Ito** (or more elaborately, **DiffusionIto**) builds the new diffusion associated with the input expression which again is an expression which includes a diffusion. The program also assigns a default name to the new diffusion unless a new name is chosen.

As an example we show how to use Itô's formula to find the diffusion associated with half the square of a Weiner process, $Y_t = W_t^2/2$. The optional argument sets the name of the new diffusion to be the symbol Y which has been cleared of any prior value.

```
In[13]:= Clear[Y]
         Ito[1/2 W^2, ItoSymbol->Y]

   2
  W      1
 d—— = (—) dt + (W) dW
   2     2              t

Inversion rule... {W -> Sqrt[2] Sqrt[Y]}

Out[13]:=                        1
             diffusion[Y, W, —, Sqrt[2] Sqrt[Y], 0]
                             2
```

Two pieces of intermediate output precede the final result in this example. The first portion of the output shows the diffusion associated with the transformation in the form of (3) before conversion to canonical form. This portion of the output is occasionally useful in solving various stochastic integrals. In this example, the output expression $dW_t^2/2 = (1/2)dt + W_t dW_t$ suggests the solution to a stochastic integral,

$$\int_0^t W_s dW_s = W_t^2/2 - 1/2$$

Of course, one would have to know to look at Itô's formula applied to W_t^2 in order to find $\int_0^t W_s dW_s$ in this way. However, since $\int_0^t x dx = t^2/2$, this is not such a bad place to start looking for an answer.

The second piece of intermediate output in the example beginning "Inversion rule. . ." (above) gives the inverse transformation used to convert the result of Itô's formula (which is a function of W_t) into a function of Y_t. This is the inverse function g described in the introductory review.

Here is another example. This example shows that the exponential of a Weiner process is a lognormal diffusion. Notice as always that it is important to begin with an unbound symbol to use for the new diffusion.

```
In[14]:= Clear[Y]
         Ito[Exp[W],ItoSymbol->Y]

           W
   W      E              W
  dE   = (—)  dt + (E )  dW
           2              t


Inversion rule... {W -> Log[Y]}

Solve::ifun:
   Warning: Inverse functions are being used by Solve, so
      some solutions may not be found.
Out[14]:=                      Y
            diffusion[Y, W, —, Y, 1]
                            2
```

The warning message in this example will often suggest a problem in the inversion process. In this example the inversion via logarithms works since $Y_t = e^{W_t}$ implies $W_t = \log_e Y_t$. Were the process W_t complex, for example, such inversion might not be appropriate. Since *Mathematica* does not assume W_t is real-valued, it displays a warning.

9.6   Summary and Concluding Remarks

This chapter began by reviewing some of the basic notions of the theory of diffusions such as the local drift μ, the local dispersion σ, and the specification of a diffusion process though the formalism of stochastic integraton. We then illustrated how the fundamental formula of Itô for functions of diffusions can lead to calculations that can be profitably performed by symbolic methods.

Much of the chapter served to illustrate how our package for stochastic calculus can be applied.

The problem chosen for this illustration was that of the *derivation* of the famous Black-Scholes formula for pricing of European options. This problem offers a natural first hurdle for any stochastic calculus package, and the successful clearing of that hurdle provides honest reassurance that the package implementation is rich enough and robust enough to engage problems of genuine interest. Since the practical and theoretical success of the Black-Scholes theory has served as a central motivation for much of the spreading of the technology of stochastic calculus, any symbolic system for stochastic calculus must sooner or later meet the challenge offered by this theory.

The implementational details given in Section 9.5 provide some of the design criteria that were used in the development of our stochastic calculus package, but it should be clear that even this second formulation (cf. Steele and Stine 1991) leaves room for further work. One immediate concern is that any serious stochastic calculus package needs to be able to handle the multivariate versions of Itô's formula. The most recent version of our package does handle multivariate diffusion, and, in fact, the current distribution of the package owes much of its design to the demands of multivariate diffusions. Because we chose to provide the easiest possible introduction to symbolic stochastic calculus, we have kept this chapter and the accompanying software focused on one-dimensional diffusions. Even these diffusions offer many important applications, and for those with pressing need for mutivariate tools the best recourse is to go directly to the package internals.

One natural development that has not been addressed in any version of the package is that of integrating the tools of stochastic differential equations with the differential-equation-solving features of *Mathematica*. This issue is more complex than it might seem at first thought, and at the very minimum one needs to come to grips with the fact that even simple problems in stochastic differential equations can lead to partial differential equations that test the limits of modern theory. One twist that could evolve to be of considerable interest is that of reversing the natural course of investigation and using the stochastic calculus to assist in the development of symbolic tools for PDE's. This may seem an unlikely turn of events, but the use of the Feynman-Kac formula here to solve the key PDE provides a hint of the practicality of the process.

Symbolic computation has been available in some special environments for a good number of years, but the widespread use of symbolic computation is still rather new. The number of users of symbolic computation is growing at more than 50% per year, and the community of sophisticated users is already many times larger than one could have imagined just a few years ago. The vital importance of diffusion processes in many areas of scientific and social modelling teamed with the explosive growth in symbolic computation virtually guarantee that symbolic stochastic calculus can expect to have many subsequent developments of far reaching influence.

9.7 References

Arnold, L. (1974). *Stochastic Differential Equations: Theory and Applications.* Wiley, New York.

Duffie, D. (1988). *Security Markets.* Academic Press, New York.

Steele, J. M. and R. A. Stine (1991). "Applications of *Mathematica* to the stochastic calculus." In *American Statistical Association, Proceedings of the Statistical Computing Section.*, 11–19, Amercian Statistical Association, Washington, D.C.

Miller, R. (1990). "Computer-aided financial analysis: an implementation of the Black-Scholes model." *Mathematica Journal*, **1**, 75–79.

10 Itovsn3: Doing Stochastic Calculus with Mathematica

Wilfrid S. Kendall

10.1 Introduction

This chapter describes the construction and use of `Itovsn3`, a *Mathematica* package which implements stochastic calculus (also known as Itô calculus). Stochastic calculus is of great use in mathematical finance (see for example Duffie, 1988) and therefore its implementation within computer algebra packages is likely to be of considerable interest to readers of this volume. `Itovsn3` is a direct descendant of a collection of procedures (also called `Itovsn3`) which implement stochastic calculus in the REDUCE computer algebra language. The two implementations are similar, differing mainly in the use of the package concept (for the *Mathematica* version) and in the use of global substitution rules (for the REDUCE version), but both providing a simple and direct implementation based around the renowned Itô formula.

In this chapter we expound neither stochastic calculus nor its application to finance theory. However the current section (section 10.1) describes a brief heuristic approach to stochastic calculus, supported by simulations within *Mathematica* based on approximating random walks. Sections 10.2 and 10.3 respectively describe the principles underlying `Itovsn3` and document its application in practice. Section 10.4 gives an example of the use of `Itovsn3` to perform calculations in continuous-time hedging theory following Duffie & Richardson (1991). Further examples of `Itovsn3` in use are to be found in the notebooks `itoexp.ma` and `itoarea.ma` in the disk accompanying the volume. Readers who already know stochastic calculus should find enough information here to make effective use of `Itovsn3` in their own researches. Readers who are new to stochastic calculus should be able to pick up an informal and intuitive understanding, but will need to consult the further reading in 1.5 below if they intend substantial use of stochastic calculus. All the same, `Itovsn3` should be a helpful companion in such reading.

10.1.1   The Brownian path

First recall some details about the path of Brownian motion, since these motivate the constructions of stochastic calculus. The Brownian path may be viewed as the limiting case of a random walk which is equally likely to move by plus or minus $\sqrt{\delta}$ at time points located at multiples of δ. Here are two simulations of such approximating random walks based on $\delta = 0.1$ and $\delta = 0.01$ respectively:

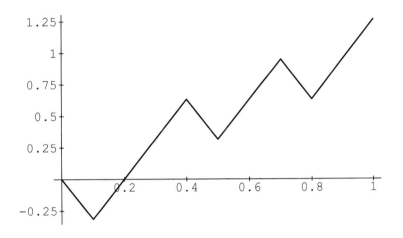

Simulation of Brownian motion   b   (coarse)

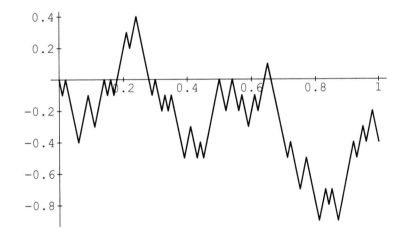

Simulation of Brownian motion   b   (fine)

It is evident that the limiting path will be continuous but very irregular. The following points are plausible from the figures (and could be checked heuristically by further investigation within *Mathematica*):

10.1.1.1   Ordinary Calculus Will Not Work on b:

This is because the limiting path will be continuous but not differentiable.

10.1.1.2   Conditional Mean Forward Increments:

It is possible to measure the drift, or trend of the path, via the mean of small forward increments, conditioned on the past. In the Brownian case this is zero, and is expressed in infinitesimal terms by `Drift[db]=0`.

10.1.1.3   Conditional Mean-square Forward Increments:

It is possible to measure the rate of diffusion, or infinitesimal variance, via the second-order quantity which is the mean value of squares of small forward increments, conditioned on the past. In the Brownian case this is proportional to the length of the corresponding time increment; this is expressed in infinitesimal terms by $db^2 = dt$. (In the particular case of the approximating random walks used in the simulations above, this relationship is exact even before the limit is attained!)

In the limiting case of the Brownian path all these observations are exact, not just approximate. Although ordinary calculus cannot be applied to the Brownian path nevertheless a generalization will work using a second-order theory based on observations (1.1.2) and (1.1.3). This is the stochastic calculus. In essence it captures those aspects of the calculus of finite differences for random walks *et cetera* which carry over to continuous Brownian-like limits.

10.1.2   Semimartingales

Of course the stochastic calculus applies to a much larger class of random processes, known as the (continuous) semimartingales. A continuous semimartingale X may be characterized as admitting a "signal-plus-noise" decomposition $X = X[0] + V + M$, where V is a process (the signal or trend) whose sample paths are continuous and of locally bounded variation (hence classical calculus applies) while M is a continuous local martingale (the noise), a process with zero conditional mean forward infinitesimal increments. Informally one can think of a semimartingale as the sum of a solution V of an ordinary differential equation (perhaps with random coefficients) and a much more erratic random function M which is similar to Brownian motion in that it possesses a zero average trend.

The semimartingale decomposition is unique if we require V and M to be zero at time zero. Consequently the statistical behaviour of a given semimartingale X may be determined by giving stochastic calculus formulae for its conditional mean forward infinitesimal increment dV (the "drift differential" `Drift[dX]` of X) and for the conditional mean square forward infinitesimal increment of the remainder or "martingale part" $dM = dX - dV$. The information in this second part can be summarized by a second-order "Itô multiplication table" of stochastic differentials dX, specifying formulae for drift differentials `Drift[dX]` (infinitesimal conditional means) and squares and cross-products of stochastic differentials dX^2 and $dX\,dY$ (infinitesimal conditional variances and covariances). Note that bounded variation differentials dV^2 and dt^2 are zero, in accordance with the rules of classical calculus, as are products $dbdV$ and $dbdt$ of bounded variation differentials with general semimartingale differentials.

In particular Brownian motion b is characterized by its initial value and the requirements `Drift[db]=0, db^2=dt`, leading to an Itô multiplication table

```
        db      dt

db      dt      0
dt      0       0
```

If stochastic differentials are viewed as the infinitesimal limits of finite differences then this characterization (essentially due to Paul Lévy) appears entirely reasonable, since b is constructed by summing the increments db and we may expect that a Central Limit Theorem effect will apply.

Larger Itô multiplication tables arise when dealing with several semimartingales rather than just one. For n semimartingales the Itô multiplication table has $n + 1$ rows and $n + 1$ columns; the extra row and column arising from the time differential dt. (However the dt row and column are always composed entirely of zeros, since time t generates a process of bounded variation.) The cross terms correspond to "infinitesimal covariances" between two different semimartingales.

In summary, we often describe the statistical behaviour of a collection of semimartingales by listing the values of `Drift[dX]` and by displaying the Itô multiplication table.

10.1.3   The Itô Formula

The central computational tool for stochastic calculus is the celebrated Itô formula, which gives a semimartingale-type decomposition for smooth functions of Brownian motion and other semimartingales. Suppose that f is a function, at least twice-differentiable. The second-order Taylor series expansion of finite differences

```
Y[t] - Y[t+Delta] =
f'[X] (X[t] - X[t+Delta])
  + (1/2) f''[X]  (X[t] - X[t+Delta])^2 + error
```

suggests that the stochastic differential dY of $Y = f[X]$ for a semimartingale X should be given by

```
dY  =  f'[X] dX  +  (1/2) f''[X]   dX^2
```

since the error obtained by summing the discrete approximations should vanish in the limit. Here dX^2 is the infinitesimal conditional variance differential of X, obtained from the "Itô multiplication table" described above.

Simulations indicate that this holds in practice: consider the case $f[b] = b^3$ for b a Brownian motion and the two discrete approximations given above. The graphs below display together the path b^3 (light path) and also the path Y (dark

path) obtained by adding up the finite differences approximating the Itô formula
for b^3:

```
Y[t] - Y[t+Delta] = 3 b[t]^2 (b[t] - b[t+Delta])
            + 3 b[t]  (b[t] - b[t+Delta])^2
```

It is clearly plausible from the figures that the two paths agree in the limit:
the paths are very close for the coarse simulation and are indistinguishable in
the figure for the fine simulation!

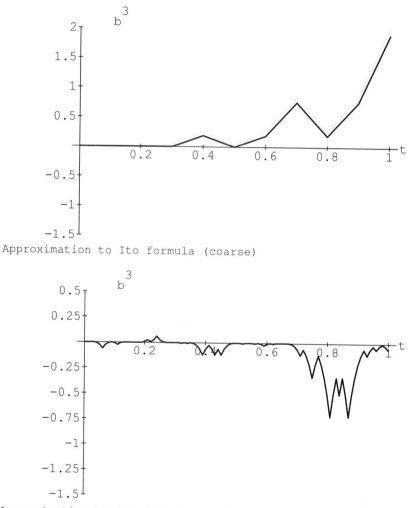

Approximation to Ito formula (coarse)

Approximation to Ito formula (fine)

The reason for taking $f[x] = x^3$ in the above is that it is the simplest non-
trivial case: the finite difference analogue of the Itô formula is essentially exact
for $f[x] = x^2$!

To prove Itô's formula for the limiting case of Brownian motion it is necessary
to make sense of integrating the stochastic differential $f'[X]dX$ and also to show

that the correction terms for the second-order Taylor series expansion really do have a sum which is asymptotically vanishing. Integrating the stochastic differential uses the theory of the stochastic or Itô integral, based on the second-order remark (1.1.3) above and using the fact that $f'[X]$ does not anticipate the future. The substance of the proof of the Itô formula is to show that the correction term vanishes asymptotically. See the monographs mentioned in subsection 10.1.5 below for proofs, and also Kendall (1992b) for a geometrically based proof of the Itô formula.

Note that integration of a stochastic differential $H\,dX$ has an intrinsic economic and financial interest as the limiting case of trading in a financial security of time-varying price X according to a strategy of holding a time-varying amount H units of the security. Thus the non-anticipating condition on H required by Itô integral theory is actually a "no insider-trading" kind of condition—the strategy H must depend only on (publicly) available information at the present!

10.1.4   Applications

The Itô formula together with the formalism of stochastic differentials provides a powerful and expressive way of talking about semimartingale random processes. One may define a semimartingale by giving equations for its stochastic differential (in terms of stochastic differentials of other semimartingales), as for example in the linear case

```
dX = f X db + g dt
```

(but also including nonlinear cases). The solution exists and is unique under reasonable conditions on the coefficients of the stochastic differentials. Any such stochastic differential equation can be interpreted by integration using stochastic calculus, which is the infinitesimal analog of summing both sides of a finite difference equation.

Again, under reasonable conditions the statistical behaviour of collection of semimartingales is defined by the "second-order structure" of the Itô multiplication table and the drifts. This means that the behaviour of a new semimartingale X is specified by giving formulae for its initial value X_0, its infinitesimal conditional mean (or drift differential) `Drift[dX]`, and its infinitesimal conditional variance (or quadratic variation or bracket differential) dX^2. If other semimartingales Y are being considered then it is also necessary to specify the infinitesimal conditional covariance (or quadratic covariation) $dX\,dY$.

Finally, the Itô formula provides a way of re-expressing semimartingales under nonlinear changes of parametrization—this is particularly useful in searching for associated processes for which the drift is zero, which is to say local martingales. The reason for this is that if an integrability condition is satisfied then a local martingale is actually a genuine martingale, so that its expectation at any subsequent time is equal to its initial value. This provides a very powerful way of computing expectations of some random quantities. The reader is referred to the monographs described in the next subsection for more details, but a related example is given in section 10.4 as an illustration of the use of `Itovsn3`.

Note that the theoretical justification of all this in the limiting case requires some work, but reasonable intuition may be acquired simply by considering simulations and replacing stochastic differentials by finite differences as above. In fact this naïve procedure can be immensely refined, leading to a considerable and rapidly developing theory of numerical solutions of stochastic differential equations; see several of the articles in Bouleau & Talay (1992).

10.1.5   Further Reading

There are now many monographs on stochastic calculus. Karatzas & Shreve (1988) provide a treatment oriented towards finance theory. Chung & Williams (1983) and Øksendal (1989) give succinct treatments. Among more extensive treatments we mention Rogers & Williams (1987), and the remarkable coverage in depth by Revuz & Yor (1991). Stochastic integration for general (discontinuous) semimartingales is covered in Rogers & Williams (1987) but also by Protter (1990) in a new approach based on recent theoretical developments in general stochastic integration.

Applications of computer algebra to stochastic calculus date back to Kendall (1985, 1988, 1990a,b), using the computer algebra language REDUCE to develop a package which is the direct ancestor of the *Mathematica* package `Itovsn3` described here. The REDUCE version is documented in Kendall (1991, 1992a). Other implementations, differing from each other and from `Itovsn3` in interesting and nontrivial ways, are described by Valkeila (1991) for the Macsyma computer algebra language, and Steele & Stine (1991) for *Mathematica*.

The `Itovsn3` approach has links with an approach to stochastic calculus via second-order differential geometry due to L. Schwartz. See Emery (1989), and Barndorff-Nielsen *et al.* (1991) for other geometrical relationships.

10.1.6   Acknowledgements

I want to record my thanks to Chris Burdzy (Department of Mathematics, University of Washington) for very properly insisting that I obey the *Mathematica* capitalization convention for reserved identifiers (in particular for suggesting `ItoD` in place of d), and to Martin Cripps (Economics, University of Warwick) for arranging access to a Macintosh running *Mathematica* notebooks.

10.2   Basic Implementation of Itovsn3

10.2.1   Introduction

In the following we demonstrate the principles underlying symbolic Itô calculus by implementing a simple version of the Itô formula in *Mathematica*, namely the version which holds for a single Brownian motion b.

Note that throughout the following the identifiers t and dt stand for time and its differential respectively.

10.2.2   Building Up to Itô's Formula

We have seen that Itô's formula can be viewed simply as a formal expansion of db as a second-order Taylor series, using the Itô multiplication rules ($db^2 = dt$ et cetera) to reduce the second-order differentials such as db^2 to more conventional differentials. We will now build up a procedure `ItoD[f]` which returns the Itô differential of a semimartingale expression f. It first constructs a formal second-order Taylor series in time t for f (using the total derivative procedure `Dt[f,t]` and its second iterate `Dt[f,{t,2}]`), and then applies an auxiliary procedure `ItoExpand` to simplify the result using a substitution list `ItoMultiplications` which corresponds to the Itô multiplication table.

Because of the interactive nature of *Mathematica* we can develop `ItoD` and `ItoExpand` progressively. In fact the top-level definition of `ItoD` is very simple:

```
In[1]:= ItoD[f_] :=
        ItoExpand[ Dt[f,t] dt + (1/2) Dt[f,{t,2}] dt^2 ]
```

`ItoExpand[sd]` must be defined as applying the Itô multiplication table listed in `ItoMultiplications` in order to simplify the stochastic differential expression `sd`. `Expand` is used first in order to cancel out any occurrences of `dt` in both numerator and denominator (we will shortly arrange for `Dt[b,t]` to yield the FORMAL result db/dt, so this cancellation will be very important!)

```
In[2]:= ItoExpand[sd_] := Expand[sd] /. ItoMultiplications
```

Now we must find out what extra structure we need in order for `ItoD` to work as advertized. We start off with an empty `ItoMultiplications` list, because we can then find out experimentally what more has to be done.

```
In[3]:= ItoMultiplications = {};
```

A general Itô differential shows what must be done next!

```
In[4]:= Print["Ito differential of  f[b]  is ",
              ItoD[f[b]]               ];
Ito differential of  f[b]  is


                      2
                    dt   Dt[b, {t, 2}] f'[b]
    dt Dt[b, t] f'[b] + ───────────────────────── +
                                  2


      2        2
    dt   Dt[b, t]   f''[b]
    ──────────────────────
              2
```

We see straight away that basic semimartingales need to be related to their stochastic differentials in some fashion; in order to implement this we introduce rules for taking formal time differentials of basic semimartingales. Note that these rules are attached to the corresponding basic semimartingales in order to avoid having to deal with the Protected status of the total derivative operator `Dt`.

```
In[5]:= t/:      Dt[t,t]  =  dt/dt;
        b/:      Dt[b,t]  =  db/dt;
```

Of course `db/dt` makes no sense mathematically, but the `dt` in the denominator will cancel with the `dt` terms produced in `ItoD`. This produces the required final effect, so that the results produced for the user by `ItoD` do indeed make mathematical sense.

We also now set up the Itô multiplication table for the basic semimartingales time `t` and Brownian motion `b`. Notice that it is stored as a list of *Mathematica* substitutions, though we think of it as a table.

```
In[6]:= ItoMultiplications = {db^2->dt, db dt->0, dt^2->0};
```

Were we to try the general Itô differential again we would see that it is almost correct, except that some total time derivatives of stochastic differentials intervene! The final step in making `ItoD` behave properly is to ensure that all the basic stochastic differentials have zero total time differentials:

```
In[7]:= dt/:      Dt[dt,t]  =  0;
        db/:      Dt[db,t]  =  0;
```

A final try now shows that our general Itô differential comes out the way that theory says it should:

```
In[8]:= Print["Ito differential of  f[b]  is ",
             ItoD[f[b]]              ];
```

$$\text{Ito differential of f[b] is db f'[b] + } \frac{\text{dt f''[b]}}{2}$$

10.2.3   Implementing Drift

The concept of the `Drift` of a stochastic differential (its "conditional mean infinitesimal forward increment") is important in applications, as noted in the introductory section.

Careful examination of theory from stochastic calculus shows that the drift of a stochastic differential expression is obtained by the following steps:

1. express the stochastic differential expression as a linear combination of basic stochastic differentials multiplied by scalars,

2. replace each of the basic stochastic differentials by the corresponding drift differential (its "conditional mean infinitesimal forward increment")

To do this we need to maintain a list of current stochastic differentials.

```
In[1]:= CurrentDifferentials  = {db, dt};
```

The description above shows how to implement `Drift`, and we only need to translate the description into the language of *Mathematica*:

```
In[2]:= Drift[sd_]  := Apply[Plus,
            Map[Coefficient[Expand[sd],#]
               Drftbydt[#] dt &,CurrentDifferentials]
                 ]
         Drftbydt[dt] = 1;
         Drftbydt[db] = 0;
```

Here `dt Drftbydt[dx]` represents the stochastic differential expression which is the drift of the basic stochastic differential dx. We have set it up so that `db` has zero drift. (To deal instead with Brownian motion of constant drift 2 (say) it is only necessary to arrange for `Drftbydt[db]` = 2.) Observe now that we can calculate the drift of the general function of Brownian motion:

```
In[3]:= Drift[ItoD[f[b]]]
```

$$Out[3]:= \frac{dt\ f''[b]}{2}$$

10.2.4 Summary

It is of course rather tedious to carry out all the above steps each time we want to do stochastic calculus in *Mathematica*. Thus it would be very desirable to automate and package the process of setting up the structures (such as `Ito-Multiplications`) and of introducing semimartingales. Moreover it would be useful to use the context facility of *Mathematica* to hide the fundamental structures from public access, so as to avoid unwitting changes. This is all done in `Itovsn3`, in the package named `"Itovsn3`"`. It contains procedures to do the following:

A: To set up the basic time semimartingale t and its stochastic differential dt.

B: To implement the Itô formula using `ItoD` and `ItoExpand`.

C: To package the process of introducing new semimartingales and associated stochastic differentials, which involves the following tasks:

   C.1: connecting semimartingales to their stochastic differentials,

   C.2: setting formal time derivatives of stochastic differentials to zero,

   C.3: maintaining the list `CurrentDifferentials`, as well as another list of `CurrentSemimartingales`.

   C.4: maintaining the structure `ItoMultiplications` carrying information about second-order structure,

   C.5: maintaining information about the first-order structure via `Drftbydt`.

D: To display and to reset the fundamental structures.

E: To provide further procedures to record and to construct initial values, to deal with Itô integrals, to define multidimensional Brownian motions, and to define semimartingales by means of (currently single-variable) stochastic differential equations.

Of course step A is just a special case of step C, although it is carried out in a procedure `ItoInit` which accomplishes other initialization tasks as well. Moreover steps C.4, C.5 can only be carried out provisionally in the general packaged operation, and must be supplemented by special knowledge in a particular application. In the rest of this article we document the use of the package `Itovsn3` and give an example of its use.

10.3 Documentation for Itovsn3

The purpose of this section is to demonstrate the use of `Itovsn3`, the package of *Mathematica* procedures for symbolic Itô calculus. The first task is to load in the package:

```
In[1]:= Needs["Itovsn3`"];
```

The various publicly available procedures of `Itovsn3` are as follows:

```
In[2]:= ?Itovsn3`*
```

AddDrift	BrownSingle	Introduce	ItoReset
AddFixed	Drftbydt	ItoD	ItoStatus
AddQuadVar	Drift	ItoExpand	Itosde
Brktbydt	Fixed	ItoInit	RandomQ
BrownBasis	InitialValue	ItoIntegral	

In this section we discuss each of these in turn, with brief examples of usage. Note that a succinct online description of usage can be obtained using ? as usual: for example

```
In[3]:= ?ItoInit
```

```
ItoInit[t,dt] starts things off with basic structures, using the
identifier t for time variable and the identifier  dt for its
differential.
```

10.3.1 Initialization with ItoInit

At the start of any session the `Itovsn3` structures must be initialized using `ItoInit[t,dt]`. The two arguments t and dt signal which identifiers represent time (t) and the time differential (dt).

```
In[1]:= ItoInit[t,dt]
```

```
Out[1]:= Itovsn3  initialized
            with time semimartingale t
            and time differential dt
```

10.3.2   Setting Up with BrownSingle

The simplest set-up for stochastic calculus requires the introduction of just one single Brownian motion. This can be done in one step by using the procedure `BrownSingle[b,b0]`. Its two arguments give the identifier b for the semimartingale which is to be declared as Brownian motion (the corresponding stochastic differential will be obtained from this by prefixing "d") and the initial value b0 at time zero. (See subsection 10.3.9 for how to deal with initial values).

```
In[1]:= BrownSingle[b,0];
```

10.3.3   Reporting with ItoStatus

To see what has been done at any stage one may invoke `ItoStatus[]`, which reports on the current structures of `Itovsn3`.

```
In[1]:= ItoStatus[]
```

```
Summary of current structure of
current stochastic differentials.
{db, dt}
— — — — — — —
Current second—order structure:
dt    0

0     0
— — — — — — —
Current first—order structure:
0

dt
— — — — — — —
Current initial values:
0

0
```

`Itovsn3` is now in a state very similar to that achieved in section 10.2. Note that `ItoStatus` provides a display of the Itô multiplication table (second-order information) and a list of the values of `Drift` (first-order structure) as well as other information.

10.3.4   Calculations with ItoD

Calculating the Itô differential of an expression `exprn` is a matter of a simple invocation of `ItoD[exprn]`. We give two examples. First consider the simplest possible non-trivial case, Itô's formula for the square of Brownian motion:

```
In[1]:= Print["Ito differential of  b^2  is ",
            ItoD[b^2]                ];
```

$$\text{Ito differential of } f[b] \text{ is db } f'[b] + \frac{dt\ f''[b]}{2}$$

Now consider the most general case for this set-up, a general function of both b and time t:

```
In[2]:= Print[
          "Ito differential of  f[b,t] is ",
            ItoD[f[b,t]]              ];
```

Ito differential of f[b,t] is

$$dt\ f^{(0,1)}[b,\ t] + db\ f^{(1,0)}[b,\ t] + \frac{dt\ f^{(2,0)}[b,\ t]}{2}$$

Notice that ItoD requires a semimartingale expression as its argument (departures from this may have unpredictable effects!).

Note that the effect of the Itô multiplication table is revealed by applying the auxiliary procedure ItoExpand to a stochastic differential (an example of this is to be found in subsection 10.3.12 below).

10.3.5   Calculating the Drift

The procedure Drift[sd] calculates the drift differential for the semimartingale differential sd which is its argument. It is often used in conjunction with ItoD. Consider the two examples used above:

```
In[1]:= Print["Drift of differential of  b^2  is ",
            Drift[ ItoD[b^2] ]        ];
```

Drift of differential of b^2 is dt

```
In[2]:= Print["Drift of differential of  f[b,t]  is ",
            Drift[ ItoD[f[b,t]] ]           ];
```

Drift of differential of f[b,t] is

$$dt\ (f^{(0,1)}[b,\ t] + \frac{f^{(2,0)}[b,\ t]}{2})$$

It is interesting to note that this vanishes if f solves a heat differential equation—an elementary example of an important connection between stochastic calculus and partial differential equations.

Notice that `Drift` requires a semimartingale differential as its argument (departures from this may have unpredictable effects!).

10.3.6   Introducing General Semimartingales

In the above we used `BrownSingle` to introduce the Brownian motion b. Below we will describe how to introduce multidimensional Brownian motions (10.3.11) and semimartingales defined by stochastic differential equations (10.3.12). All these methods are based on a primitive procedure `Introduce` which introduces an entirely general semimartingale:

```
In[1]:= Introduce[x,dx];
```

Here the first argument x is the identifier for the new semimartingale and the corresponding stochastic differential is given by the second argument.

Attempting to reintroduce a semimartingale or a stochastic differential incurs an error—but notice that no check is made as to whether you have already used the semimartingale or stochastic differential symbol for some other purpose (so make sure you don't do this!).

```
In[2]:= Print["Trying  x   again: ",Introduce[x,dy]];

        Print["Trying  dx   again: ",Introduce[y,dx]];


Trying  x   again: Attempt to re—introduce a semimartingale
                   or a stochastic differential!
Trying  dx   again: Attempt to re—introduce a semimartingale
                   or a stochastic differential!
```

10.3.7   Specifying Structure with AddQuadVar and AddDrift

A semimartingale x introduced as above has entirely general second- and first-order structure, as is apparent from `ItoStatus`:

```
In[1]:= ItoStatus[]

_____

Summary of current structure of
current stochastic differentials.
{dx, db, dt}
- - - - - - - -

Current second—order structure:
???   ???   0

???   dt    0

0     0     0
```

```
_ _ _ _ _ _ _ _
Current first—order structure:
dt Drftbydt[dx]

0

dt
_ _ _ _ _ _ _ _
Current initial values:
Fixed[0, x]

0

0
```
_____

The elements `Brktbydt[dx^2]` (here replaced by `???` in the `ItoStatus[]` display), `Drftbydt[dx]`, `Fixed[0,x]` can be specified. For `Fixed[0,x]` see below. The differential structure is best specified using special procedures `AddQuadVar[dxdy,udt]`, `AddDrift[dx,udt]`. These each have two arguments. The first argument specifies the product of differentials `dxdy` or differential `dx` to which the relevant structure applies, while the second argument `udt` gives the (classical) differential which replaces it.

```
In[2]:= AddQuadVar[dx^2,a2 dt];
        AddDrift[dx,a3 dt];
        AddQuadVar[dx db,rho dt];
```

Note that we also specify the "infinitesimal covariance" expression for `dx db`. This is necessary if we are to investigate the joint behavior of x and b.

Users of `Itovsn3` are recommended to use `AddQuadVar` and `AddDrift` rather than manipulate the `Itovsn3` structures directly, since these structures are deliberately hidden away in the private part of the `Itovsn3` package! (This is done to protect the user from the consequences of inadvertently altering or overwriting these structures.)

10.3.8   Itô Integral with ItoIntegral

Given a stochastic differential we can use the theory of Itô integration to integrate it to recover the original semimartingale, at least up to initial value. In `Itovsn3` such an Itô integral is represented by the operator `ItoIntegral[sd]`, taking a stochastic differential `sd` as argument:

```
In[1]:= ItoIntegral[dx]
```

```
Out[1]:= x — Fixed[0, x]
```

Furthermore the implementation of `ItoD` in `Itovsn3` is adjusted so that `ItoIntegral` will behave well in, for example, exponential martingales. Stochastic calculus experts know that the following is the correct output:

```
In[2]:= ItoD[Exp[ItoIntegral[f db]
            - (1/2)ItoIntegral[f^2 dt]]]
```

Out[2]:=

$$\mathrm{E}^{\mathrm{ItoIntegral[db\ f]} - \frac{\mathrm{ItoIntegral[dt\ f}^2]}{2}} \qquad \mathrm{db\ f}$$

Incidentally we can check that the above is a local martingale:

In[3]:= **Drift[ItoD[**
        Exp[ItoIntegral[f db] - (1/2)ItoIntegral[f^2 dt]]]]

Out[3]:= 0

See the notebook `itoexp.ma` for other simple manipulations with semi-martingales involving exponentials and Itô integrals.

It is possible to add still further properties to `ItoIntegral`, for example to allow `Itovsn3` to perform basic simplifications such as `ItoIntegral[2 b db] -> 2 ItoIntegral[b db] -> b^2 - t` and their generalizations. These are not included in the current version of `Itovsn3` (although they would be easy to add), essentially because their invariable application would not always be useful.

10.3.9   Initial Values with InitialValue and AddFixed

Recall that `ItoStatus` reports initial values. It is possible to add specifications for initial values at a prescribed time t_0 and then to compute the initial value of an expression `exprn` at t_0 by using `InitialValue[t0,exprn]`. This can be very useful for computing the expectation of a quantity given by a martingale evaluated at a time $t > t_0$. Take for example the semimartingale

In[1]:= **expmgl =**
        Exp[ItoIntegral[f db] - (1/2)ItoIntegral[f^2 dt]]

Out[1]:=

$$\mathrm{E}^{\mathrm{ItoIntegral[db\ f]} - \frac{\mathrm{ItoIntegral[dt\ f}^2]}{2}}$$

We have seen that the `Drift` of this expression vanishes, and this means that the expectation of `expmgl` at time `t` is the same as the initial value of `expmgl` (actually this assumes that `expmgl` is not just a local martingale (`Drift = 0`) but a full martingale, but theory tells us this is true if f is well-behaved, certainly for example if f is bounded).

In[2]:= **Print["Expectation of the following"];**
        Print[expmgl]; Print[" is ",InitialValue[0,expmgl]];

Expectation of the following

$$\mathrm{E}^{\mathrm{ItoIntegral[db\ f]} - \frac{\mathrm{ItoIntegral[dt\ f}^2]}{2}}$$

 is   1

We can alter the initial value of a given semimartingale x by using `AddFixed[t0,x,x0]` to alter the value of `Fixed[t0,x]` to x_0. For example the following sets `Fixed[0,x]` to equal 1:

In[3]:= **AddFixed[0,x,1];**

These procedures can be used as part of a computer algebra treatment of Janson's derivation of the distribution of the Lévy stochastic area (see Kendall, 1993, for a version of this using the REDUCE implementation of `Itovsn3`, and the notebook `itoarea.ma` for a version using the present implementation).

10.3.10   Resetting Structures with ItoReset

It is often useful to reset `Itovsn3` to forget all the previously established structures (for example, to prevent the output from `ItoStatus` from growing too large!). `ItoReset[t,dt]` takes two arguments t and dt specifying time and its differential, as with `ItoInit[t,dt]`.

In[1]:= **Print[ItoReset[u,du]]**

```
Itovsn3  resetting . . .

Itovsn3  initialized

with time semimartingale u

and time differential du
```

For the purposes of demonstration we have taken the opportunity to change the symbols for the time process and its stochastic differential to u and du.

Note that `ItoReset` does NOT cause *Mathematica* to forget any previous assignments! (you have been warned . . .)

10.3.11   Multidimensional Brownian Motions with BrownBasis

In the above we used `BrownSingle` to introduce a single Brownian motion (in 10.3.2) and `Introduce` to introduce an entirely general semimartingale (in 10.3.6). Now we shall see how to introduce a multidimensional Brownian motion, or more strictly a sequence of independent and identically distributed Brownian motions. This is done via a procedure `BrownBasis[slist,ivlist]` which takes two list arguments. The first argument `slist` lists the symbols representing the coordinate Brownian motions. The second argument `ivlist` lists their initial values.

For example we now introduce a 2-dimensional Brownian motion starting at the origin (0,0).

In[1]:= **BrownBasis[{b1,b2},{0,0}];**
       ItoStatus[]

```
Summary of current structure of
current stochastic differentials.
{db2, db1, du}
- - - - - - -
Current second-order structure:
du   0    0

0    du   0

0    0    0
- - - - - - -
Current first-order structure:
0

0

du
- - - - - - -
Current initial values:
0

0

0
```

10.3.12   Itô Stochastic Differential Equations with Itosde

We can define a semimartingale x as a solution to a stochastic differential equation with an initial value x_0, using Itosde[x,sde,x0]. For example:

```
In[1]:= Itosde[x,dx==b2 db1 - b1 db2,0]
        ItoStatus[]
```

```
Summary of current structure of
current stochastic differentials.
{dx, db2, db1, du}
- - - - - - -
Current second-order structure:

    2        2
b1  du + b2  du          -(b1 du)              b2 du      0

-(b1 du)                 du                    0          0

b2 du                    0                     du         0

0                        0                     0          0
- - - - - - -
Current first-order structure:
0

0
```

```
0

du
_ _ _ _ _ _ _
Current initial values:
0

0

0

0
```

(Note that the output of ItoStatus here may be too large to fit comfortably on your computer screen . . .!) This defines the famous Lévy stochastic area, the signed area mapped out by a line segment from the origin to the planar Brownian point (b1,b2). It is of great importance both in the theory of numerical solutions to stochastic differential equations and also in applications of stochastic calculus to differential geometry! Aspects such as its quadratic variation differential can either be read off from the output of ItoStatus above or else computed directly as follows:

```
In[2]:= ItoExpand[ItoD[x]^2]

Out[2]:=    2          2
         b1   du + b2   du

In[3]:= ItoExpand[db1 ItoD[x]]

Out[3]:= b2 du

In[4]:= Drift[ItoD[x]]

Out[4]:= 0

In[5]:= InitialValue[0,x]

Out[5]:= 0
```

Note here the use of ItoExpand[sd] to find out the effect of applying the Itô multiplication table to the stochastic differential sd.

See the notebook itoarea.ma for more manipulations with the stochastic area.

10.3.13   Other Features

RandomQ[u] is a predicate procedure which returns the value True if its argument u is a stochastic differential or a semimartingale. This facility is maintained by the various procedures for introducing semimartingales (BrownSingle, Introduce, BrownBasis, Itosde). At present it is not used, but it is expected to be useful in later extensions of Itovsn3.

10.3.14   Caveats for Users!

Itovsn3 assumes that the user is familiar with stochastic calculus and that the user is responsible for maintaining distinctions between semimartingales, stochastic differentials, and other expressions. For example no check is made as to whether ItoD is being applied to an expression which truly represents a semimartingale, nor to whether Drift is being applied to an expression which truly represents a stochastic differential. (Indeed the user can check that if ItoD is applied to a stochastic differential then the result is related to the so-called Stratonovich correction term, while if Drift is applied to a non-stochastic differential then the result is zero, but the user is encouraged scrupulously to avoid such abuses!). Similarly it is left to the user to ensure that the unbound identifiers for basic semimartingales and their stochastic differentials are not subjected to assignments. These checks are omitted for the sake of computational efficiency and also because their inclusion would lead to much more complicated *Mathematica* code, obscuring the basic simplicity of the Itovsn3 procedures.

Note also that Itovsn3 provides no facility for distinguishing between local martingales and genuine martingales. This is an important distinction but one which is essentially to do with the analytic notion of integrability rather than any algebraic concepts. Consequently it is left to the user to use knowledge from stochastic analysis to determine when a drift-free stochastic differential is actually the differential of a genuine martingale (though indeed it can be the case that *Mathematica* manipulations will aid the user in this task).

Consider these examples of the above abuses, based on the set-up of subsection 10.3.12 on Itosde:

10.3.14.1   ItoD (mis-)Applied to a Stochastic Differential Expression

The result of ItoD[b1 dx] is the same as ItoExpand[ItoD[b1] dx], and is the time-differential term in ItoD[b1 x]:

```
In[1]:= ItoD[b1 dx]

Out[1]:= b2 du

In[2]:= ItoExpand[ItoD[b1] dx]

Out[2]:= b2 du

In[3]:= ItoD[b1 x]

Out[3]:= b2 du + b1 dx + db1 x
```

10.3.14.2   Drift (mis-)Applied to a Semimartingale Expression

Drift applied to a semimartingale expression gives zero:

```
In[1]:= Drift[b1^2]

Out[1]:= 0
```

```
In[2]:= Drift[ItoD[b1^2]]
```

```
Out[2]:= du
```

```
In[3]:= Drift[b1^2 + ItoD[b1^2]]
```

```
Out[3]:= du
```

10.3.14.3 Subjecting a Stochastic Differential to an Assignment

Suppose that y is to stand for a basic semimartingale satisfying the stochastic differential equation dy==y db1, where db1 is the stochastic differential of (say) a Brownian motion b1, and has already been introduced. The correct way to proceed is to use Itosde to introduce y and to set up the correct structure. The incorrect way is to try making an assignment to dy:

```
In[1]:= Introduce[y,dy]; dy = y db1;
```

The consequence of this error is that dy will no longer behave as an Itô stochastic differential but rather as some strange hybrid quantity, for which correct behavior is no longer guaranteed!

```
In[2]:= ItoD[y^2]
```

```
Out[2]:=        2
         2 db1 y  + 2 du Brktbydt[db1 y, db1 y]
```

So avoid making assignments to basic stochastic differentials.

10.4 Application to a Hedging Problem

This section discusses an application of Itovsn3 to a problem from mathematical finance as discussed in Duffie & Richardson (1991). As in section 10.3, we begin by loading the Itovsn3 package:

```
In[1]:= Needs["Itovsn3`"];
```

10.4.1 The Simplest Finance example

Suppose we wish to consider an asset price process S with appreciation rate μ and volatility rate σ. That is to say, over an infinitesimal time-step dt the price S should change by $\mu S dt + \sigma S dB$, where B is a standard Brownian motion. Obviously this has to be justified by limit considerations, supposing first that the change of S over a short time interval is proportional to S times a random walk, and we do not enter into these theoretical considerations here. However given these considerations we obtain a stochastic differential equation for S and can by this means introduce it to Itovsn3.

```
In[1]:= ItoInit[t,dt]; BrownBasis[{B,Xi},{0,0}];
        AddQuadVar[dB dXi, rho dt];
        Itosde[S,dS == mu S dt + si S dB,   S0 ]
```

Here we have also introduced a second Brownian motion `Xi` which is correlated to `B` (the effect of the `AddQuadVar` invocation), because we will next want
to introduce a correlated asset price process.

In the case where μ and σ are constant in time it is possible to solve this
stochastic differential equation to obtain a closed form expression for S. Here
however we allow μ and σ (and ρ) to vary with time; however we do suppose
them to be deterministic, not random.

10.4.2   Another Correlated Asset Price Process, and the Problem

We now introduce a correlated asset price process `F` using the correlated Brownian motion `Xi`.

```
In[1]:= Itosde[F,dF == m  F dt + v  F dXi, F0 ]
```

The problem is as follows: suppose one is committed to k units of S at time
T, and wishes to hedge this by trading in F. Given a target L for wealth at
time T one is required to minimize the expectation of $[kS - W_\theta - L]^2$ at time T,
where W_θ arises from choosing a trading strategy θ for F, so that `W[theta] =
ItoIntegral[theta dF]`. Here L and k are constants, so have to be declared
explicitly as such to *Mathematica*.

```
In[2]:= SetAttributes[L,Constant];
        SetAttributes[k,Constant];
```

10.4.3   The Proposed Optimal Strategy

The solution to the problem is based on a "tracking process" Z defined as
follows. Suppose `Total = ItoIntegral[gamma dt]` evaluated at time T,
where
```
In[1]:= SetAttributes[Total,Constant];
        gamma = m si rho / v - mu;
        Z = k Exp[ - Total + ItoIntegral[gamma dt]] S
Out[1]:=                                        m rho si
              -Total + ItoIntegral[dt (-mu + ———————)]
                                                v
        E                                              S k
```

`Total` is introduced here because we have no notation for an Itô integral with
varying lower limit. Note that with this interpretation of `Total` the term in the
exponential vanishes at time `T`, so that `Z` equals `k  S` at time `T`.

Now introduce an operator `Phi` using `Z`:
```
In[2]:= Phi[x_] =
        ( (m / v^2) (L - Z - x) - (si rho / v) Z )/ F;
```

The optimal strategy in `F` is defined recursively using `Phi` as `Phi[Gs]` leading
to holding `Gs` units of `F`, where `Gs` is zero at time zero:
```
In[3]:= Itosde[Gs, dGs == Phi[Gs] dF, 0]
```

We now have to show that `Phi[Gs]` is indeed the optimal strategy.

10.4.4   Proof of Optimality

A Hilbert space projection argument shows that `Phi[Gs]` will be optimal if `(L
- k S - Gs) G` is of zero expectation at time `T` for all `G` resulting from trading
strategies in `F`. Let `G` arise from such a strategy `theta`:

```
In[1]:= Itosde[G,  dG  == theta   dF, 0]
```

Recall that `Z` is equal to `k S` at time `T`. Hence if we define `H` by

```
In[2]:= H = (L - Z - Gs) G ;
```

(we omit output of `H` as it cannot be displayed comfortably on a Macintosh
SE/30 screen!) then it suffices to show that `H` is of zero expectation at time `T`.
    To do this we compute `Esd`, the drift differential `Drift[ItoD[H]]` of the
deficit `H`:

```
In[3]:= Esd = Drift[ItoD[H]] ;
```

This is apparently complicated, but is really a rather simple expression, as can
be seen by dividing it by `H` and manipulating it within *Mathematica*!

```
In[4]:= logderiv=Cancel[Together[Esd]/H]
```
```
Out[4]:=            2
             dt m
          -(------)
              2
              v
```

Subject as usual to checking the mathematical niceties of integrability, we
can deduce that `EofH`, the expectation of `H`, satisfies the ordinary differential
equation `EofH'[t]==logderiv EofH[t]/dt` with the boundary condition
`EofH[0]==0`. (Formally speaking, this is because we have found `Drift[
ItoD[H]]` is linear in `H`. The mathematical niceties involve checking that we are
permitted to interchange expectation and differentiation.) Solving this ordinary
differential equation in *Mathematica*, or by using the general theory of ordinary
differential equations, one deduces that `EofH` vanishes for all time and hence in
particular at time `T`:

```
In[5]:= Print["Expectation[H]  at time  t  is equal to ",
        EofH[t]/.(DSolve[{EofH'[t]==logderiv EofH[t]/dt
              EofH[0]==0},EofH[t],t])]
        (*   Users of Mathematica 2.xx should replace   *)
        (*   the DSolve  invocation by                  *)
        (*                                              *)
        (*   DSolve[                                    *)
        (*   {EofH'[t]==logderiv EofH[t]/dt,            *)
        (*   EofH[0]==0}, EofH, t ]                     *)

Expectation[H]  at time  t  is equal to {0}
```

Subject to the mathematical niceties mentioned above, this proves the required
optimality.

10.4.5   Further Work

The reader is invited as an exercise to use `Itovsn3` to explore the calculation of the variance of the total wealth of an optimal policy (see Duffie & Richardson, 1991, where it is "calculated (tediously)"!).

10.5   Conclusion

In this article we have described in some detail the principles and basics of using `Itovsn3` to do stochastic calculus in *Mathematica*. Computer algebra packages in general are friendly environments for stochastic calculus, since so much can be achieved using the formalism of stochastic differentials and the Itô formula, and yet the complexity of the resulting calculations begs for some automatic assistance. It will have become clear to the reader that `Itovsn3` does not obviate the need for a good grounding in the theory and analytical aspects of stochastic calculus—this is most notably evident in the requirement to be able to check when a local martingale is really a martingale, and in the similar requirement to check mathematical niceties when dealing with `EofH` in the section above.

There are many directions in which `Itovsn3` might be developed. For example its REDUCE ancestor contains procedures which automatically compute the Riemannian geometry associated to a diffusion, which have been used to good effect in research problems to do with statistical shape diffusions (Kendall, 1988, 1990a,b, Barndorff Nielsen et al, 1991). The REDUCE ancestor also has experimental procedures allowing automatic simulation of semimartingales defined within the package, and these could easily be extended to provide a similar facility for the *Mathematica* version. (However such exercises raise important issues both in classical numerical analysis and in the methodology of numerical solution of stochastic differential equations, so that the task of doing this extension properly would be highly non-trivial!) Other experimental procedures in the REDUCE ancestor include automatic determination of Lie algebras associated to stochastic differential equations, and automatic solution of (strongly limited!) classes of stochastic differential equations and Itô integrals. The possibilities are wide-ranging, but even the simple implementation described above is able to support researchers in non-trivial problems.

10.6   References

Barndorff Nielsen, O. E., P. E. Jupp, & W. S. Kendall, (1991), "Stochastic Calculus, Statistical Asymptotics, Strings and Phyla", Warwick University Department of Statistics Research Report 222.

Bouleau, N. & D. Talay, (1992), *Probabilités Numeriques*. INRIA, Rocquencourt, France.

Chung, K. L. & R. J. Williams, (1983), *Introduction to Stochastic Integration*. Birkhauser, Boston.

Duffie, D. (1988), *Security markets: Stochastic Models*. Academic Press, New York.

Duffie, D. & H. R. Richardson, (1991), "Mean-variance hedging in continuous time", *Annals of Applied Probability*, **1**, 1–15.

Emery, M. (1989) *Stochastic Calculus in Manifolds, with an appendix by P. A. Meyer*, Springer-Verlag, New York.

Karatzas, I. & S. Shreve, (1988), *Brownian motion and Stochastic Calculus*. Springer-Verlag, New York.

Kendall, W. S. (1985), Discussion of read paper by Clifford, Green and Pilling, *Journal of the Royal Statistical Society* **49**, 286–287.

Kendall, W. S. (1988) "Symbolic computation and the diffusion of shapes of triads," Advances in *Applied Probability* **20**, 775–797.

Kendall, W. S. (1990a), "The Euclidean Diffusion of Shape" in *Disorder in Physical Systems* Editors D. Welsh & G. Grimmett, Oxford University Press, Oxford, 203–217.

Kendall, W. S. (1990b), "Computer Algebra and Stochastic Calculus," *Notices of the American Mathematical Society* **37**, 1254–1256.

Kendall, W. S. (1991), "Symbolic Itô calculus: an introduction," Warwick University Department of Statistics Research Report 217.

Kendall, W. S. (1992a), "Symbolic Itô calculus: an overview" in *Probabilités Numeriques* Editors N. Bouleau & D. Talay, INRIA, Rocquencourt, France, 186–192.

Kendall, W. S. (1992b), "A remark on the proof of Itô's formula for C^2 functions of continuous semimartingales", *Journal of Applied Probability* **29**, 216–221.

Kendall, W. S. (1993), "Computer Algebra in Probability and Statistics", *Statistica Neerlandica* (1), 9–25.

Øksendal, B. (1989), *Stochastic Differential Equations*, Second edition. Springer-Verlag, New York.

Protter, P. (1990), *Stochastic Integration and Differential Equations: a new approach*. Springer-Verlag, New York.

Revuz, D. & M. Yor, (1991), *Continuous martingales and Brownian motion*. Springer-Verlag, New York.

Rogers, L. C. G. & D. Williams, (1987), *Diffusions, Markov Processes and Martingales, volume 2: Itô calculus*. Wiley & Sons, New York.

Steele, J. M. & R. A. Stine, (1991), *Applications of Mathematica to the Stochastic Calculus*, ASA Proceedings.

Valkeila, E. (1991), "Computer algebra and stochastic analysis—some possibilities", *CWI Newsletter* **4**, 229–238.

11 Bounded & Unbounded Stochastic Processes

Colin Rose

In recent years, economic modelling has seen a significant shift from deterministic models to stochastic ones. Because of the prevalence of imperfect information and rational expectations, bounded and unbounded stochastic models now play an important role in both micro- and macro-economics, as well as the full ambit of financial models. This chapter illustrates how *Mathematica* can be used to model and simulate a variety of stochastic problems. Particular attention is focused upon exchange rate target zones and the theory of irreversible investment under uncertainty.

11.1 Overview

- The Normal Distribution: a toolkit
  — pdf, cdf, quantiles
  — lower, upper and doubly truncated normal distributions
  — lower, upper and doubly censored normal distributions
- An Application: Exchange Rate Target Zones
- An Application: Irreversible Investment under Uncertainty
- Simulating Stochastic Processes
  — Markov Chains, stochastic (bursting) speculative bubbles, absorbing barriers and the gambler's ruin, reflecting barriers, Gaussian random walks, AR(1) processes, random walks with drift.

This chapter makes use of functions defined in the custom package `Bounded`. The package should be loaded into *Mathematica* before working through the chapter.

11.2   The Normal Distribution

It is easy to set up functions for the probability density function (pdf) and cumulative distribution function (cdf) of any normal distribution. Note that the parameters are the mean *mu* and the standard deviation *sig* (and not the variance, as per convention). The functions **g[]** and **G[]** denote the pdf and cdf respectively.

```
In[1]:= g[s_] := PDF[NormalDistribution[mu, sig], s]
        G[s_] := CDF[NormalDistribution[mu, sig], s]
```

Because they are functions of the variable *s*, we can plot them after specifying any *mu* and *sig*:

```
In[2]:= mu = 100;   sig = 16;

        XX = Plot[g[s], {s, mu - 3sig, mu + 3sig}, DisplayFunction ->
            Identity, PlotLabel -> "Probability Density Function"]
        YY = Plot[G[s], {s, mu - 3sig, mu + 3sig}, DisplayFunction ->
            Identity, PlotLabel -> "Distribution Function"]
        Show[GraphicsArray[{XX, YY}], DisplayFunction -> $DisplayFunction]
```

Out[2]:= —Graphics—

Out[2]:= —Graphics—

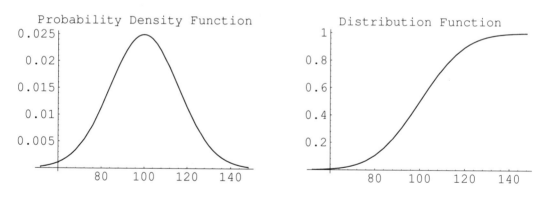

Out[2]:= —GraphicsArray—

To calculate the density at a point s^*, or to calculate the $Prob[S < s^*]$, *Mathematica* must evaluate these functions at the point s^*. In this example, *Mathematica* calculates the pdf and cdf at the point $s^* = 105$, for the same mean and standard deviation as above. Of course, you can specify any *mu* and *sig*. This certainly beats using the tables at the back of your statistics text.

```
In[3]:= mu = 100;   sig = 16;
        g[105] G[105]
```

Out[3]:= 0.0237457

Out[3]:= 0.62267

One can also calculate the qth quantile. In other words, we can calculate the value of s at which the $Prob[S < s] = q$, given mu and sig. In this example, we calculate the 98th quantile.

```
In[4]:= mu = 100;   sig = 16;
        Q[q_] := Quantile[NormalDistribution[mu, sig], q]
        Q[0.98]

Out[4]:= 132.86
```

A vast number of economic models assume that relevant variables follow (Gaussian) random walks. This tendency is especially common in financial asset-pricing models as a consequence of weak-form notions of market efficiency. If a variable follows a random walk, then its domain is unbounded. In reality though, many of these economic variables are constrained. For instance, inventories, prices and quantities are all positive variables, and thus have lower bounds at zero. The explicit inclusion of bounds becomes particularly important when the variable is constrained by government (or central) intervention. Examples include the prices of some primary products such as wool in Australia and corn in the USA, and significantly, exchange rates in Europe. In this section, we provide some tools for analyzing bounded normal random variables (in particular, truncated and censored normal distributions). The use of these tools is illustrated later with two working applications: namely, exchange rate target zones and the theory of irreversible investment under uncertainty.

11.2.1   Truncated Normal Distributions

11.2.1.1   Lower Truncated Normal Distributions

If a normal random variable is bounded below, then it may follow a lower truncated normal distribution. Truncated normal distributions are really quite intuitive. Suppose we want to find out what the probability density function of IQ looks like at a selective university. By convention, IQ is simply the normal random variable with mean of 100. The standard deviation of IQ depends on which IQ test is used, but for most IQ tests, it is about 16, yielding a distribution similar to that plotted above. If a university/department is selective, then it must set minimum criteria to enforce the selection process. In the US, selection is often done on the basis of SAT scores. For any given SAT score, there corresponds an IQ that has the same quantile as the SAT score. For example, a combined SAT score of 1250 and an IQ score of 132 both correspond to the 98th quantile of the population. If a department sets its *equivalent* lower bound at say $IQ = 105$, then generally only those with $IQ \geq 105$ are accepted so that our pdf will consist only of the points, in the diagram above, that are in excess of 105. We know from the calculations above that 62% of the distribution lies below 105, and hence 62% of the distribution has been truncated. The 38% of the population that remain do not constitute a pdf, for after all, the area under a pdf must equal 1, and the area under our pdf is just .38. To convert it into a "proper" pdf, simply divide the relevant region of the old pdf by .38 so that the area under it will now equal 1. More generally, when a distribution has a lower truncation at s^{Low}, the new pdf is $g[\ ]/(1 - G[s^{\text{Low}}])$. Because this is a function, it can be plotted. It is always useful to compare a truncated distribution with the "parent" distribution that generated it. In the diagram below, the thick line represents the truncated distribution, whilst the thin line is the untruncated parent distribution. The diagram is generated by the function **LowerPlot** which is included in the package Bounded. The plot will take a few moments. . .

$In[1]:=$ **mu = 100; sig = 16; sLow = 105;**
            LowerPlot

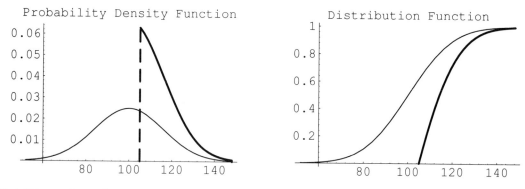

$Out[1]:=$ —GraphicsArray—

The above diagram probably gives a fairly good indication of the distribution of IQ at universities (set s^{Low} as required for your department). It is interesting to note that the resulting distribution is in no sense bell-shaped when $s^{\text{Low}} > mu$. If we are willing to believe that IQ and examination results are strongly correlated, then the mark distribution at our universities should have a similar shape to that shown here, and not the bell-shape so loved by those who mark strictly to a curve.

By definition, the expectation of a normal random variable is the mean mu. By contrast, the expectation of a lower truncated normal random variable will always exceed mu, since the lower values have been truncated. For instance, the average IQ at a selective university cannot possibly be 100 if the minimum entry criterion is 105. The expectation of a lower truncated normal random variable is calculated by the function **TruncLowerMean** which is included in the package Bounded. As shown below, it suggests that the average IQ at a selective university is 116.11, when the entry criterion is IQ of 105. Similarly, a truncated variable always has a smaller variance than an untruncated variable, for by truncating a variable, we are limiting its freedom. The function **TruncLowerVAR** calculates the conditional variance. In this example, the unconditional variance is $16^2 = 256$, whilst the conditional variance $Var[s|s > s^{\text{Low}}]$ is just 77.

```
In[2]:= mu = 100;   sig = 16;   sLow = 105;
        TruncLowerMean
        TruncLowerVAR
```

Out[2]:= 116.11

Out[2]:= 77.0108

11.2.1.2   Upper Truncated Normal Distributions

Just as a lower truncated normal distribution has a lower bound s^{Low}, an upper truncated normal distribution has an upper bound at s^{Up}. All values in excess of s^{Up} get truncated, leaving behind $\mathbf{G}[s^{\text{Up}}]\%$ of the distribution. A diagram like the one above can be generated by the function **UpperPlot** after specifying mu, sig and s^{Up}.

```
In[1]:= mu = 12;   sig = 5;   sUp = 8;
        UpperPlot
```

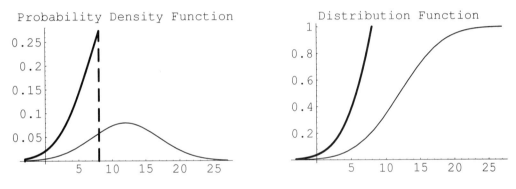

Out[1]:= —GraphicsArray—

The expectation of an upper truncated distribution will always lie below mu, since the upper values have been truncated. The expectation and variance of the upper truncated normal random variable are calculated by the functions **TruncUpperMean** and **TruncUpperVAR** as included in the package Bounded.

```
In[2]:= mu = 12;   sig = 5;   sUp = 8;
        TruncUpperMean
        TruncUpperVAR
```

Out[2]:= 5.16299

Out[2]:= 5.60332

11.2.1.3   Doubly Truncated Normal Distributions

If a normal random variable is bounded both above and below, then it is said to have a doubly truncated normal distribution. This will prove most useful in the analysis of exchange rate target zones. All values above s^{Up} are now truncated, as are all values below s^{Low}. A diagram like those above can be generated by the function **DoublePlot** after specifying mu, sig, s^{Low} and s^{Up}. The following example uses a standard normal distribution with symmetric bounds:

```
In[1]:= mu = 0;   sig = 1;   sLow = -1;   sUp = 1;
        DoublePlot
```

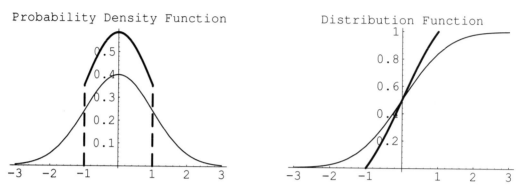

```
Out[1]:= -GraphicsArray-
```

The expectation and variance of the doubly truncated normal random variable are calculated by the functions **TruncDoubleMean** and **TruncDoubleVAR** which are included in the package Bounded.

```
In[2]:= mu = 0;   sig = 1;   sLow = -1;   sUp = 1;
        TruncDoubleMean
        TruncDoubleVAR
```

```
Out[2]:= 0.
```

```
Out[2]:= 0.291125
```

11.2.2   Censored Normal Distributions

11.2.2.1   Lower Censored Normal Distributions

Instead of truncating a random variable s at some lower bound s^{Low}, one can censor it instead, in which case all values smaller than s^{Low} get collapsed onto the point s^{Low}. The censored variable s^* takes the following form:

$$s^* = \begin{cases} s & \text{if } s > s^{\text{Low}} \\ s^{\text{Low}} & \text{if } s \leq s^{\text{Low}} \end{cases}$$

The expectation of s^* (a lower censored normal random variable) is calculated by the function **CensLowerMean** which is included in the package Bounded. This conditional expectation should always be at least as great as the unconditional expectation mu. The variance of s^* should always be smaller than sig^2, for by censoring a variable, we have constrained its freedom. The function **CensLowerVAR** calculates this conditional variance.

```
In[1]:= mu = 100;   sig = 20;   sLow = 80;
        CensLowerMean
        CensLowerVAR
```

Out[1]:= 101.666

Out[1]:= 300.435

Lower censored variables have many important applications in economics, and perhaps the most famous of these is option pricing, for the value of a call option is given precisely by the expectation of a lower censored random variable (but with lognormal distribution).

11.2.2.2 Upper Censored Normal Distributions

Just as a lower censored normal distribution has a lower bound at s^{Low}, an upper censored normal distribution has an upper bound at s^{Up}. All values in excess of s^{Up} get collapsed onto the point s^{Up}, so that the censored variable s^* takes the following form:

$$s^* = \begin{cases} s^{\text{Up}} & \text{if } s \geq s^{\text{Up}} \\ s & \text{if } s < s^{\text{Up}} \end{cases}$$

The expectation of s^* will always be smaller than (or equal to) mu, since the uppermost values have been censored. The expectation and variance of the upper censored normal random variable are calculated by the functions **CensUpperMean** and **CensUpperVAR**, as included in the package Bounded. An example illustrates:

```
In[1]:= mu = 12;   sig = 5;   sUp = 8;
        CensUpperMean
        CensUpperVAR
```

Out[1]:= 7.39896

Out[1]:= 2.531

11.2.2.3 Doubly Censored Normal Distributions

A random variable s^* is said to have a doubly censored normal distribution if s^* takes the following form:

$$s^* = \begin{cases} s^{\text{Up}} & \text{if } s \geq s^{\text{Up}} \\ s & \text{if } s^{\text{Low}} < s < s^{\text{Up}} \\ s^{\text{Low}} & \text{if } s \leq s^{\text{Low}} \end{cases}$$

The expectation and variance of the doubly censored normal random variable are calculated by the functions **CensDoubleMean** and **CensDoubleVAR** which are included in the package Bounded.

```
In[1]:= mu = 0;   sig = 1;   sLow = -1;   sUp = 1;
        CensDoubleMean
        CensDoubleVAR
```

Out[1]:= 0.

Out[1]:= 0.516059

11.3 Exchange Rate Target Zones

An exchange rate target zone is simply an announced band within which the exchange rate is allowed to float freely. If s denotes the exchange rate, then the concept of an exchange rate target zone may be expressed algebraically as: $s^{\text{Low}} < s < s^{\text{Up}}$, where s^{Low} and s^{Up} denote the lower and upper bounds respectively of a perfectly credible band. What makes exchange rate target zones so interesting is that the very presence of the zone influences the value of the exchange rate through expectations, even when the band is not binding —that is, even when the exchange rate lies within its band. The intuition behind this is that, if the exchange rate was close to its lower (upper) bound, it could not fall (rise) by much, yet it could rise (fall) a lot, so roughly speaking, the expectation is that it will rise (fall). Most of the member nations of the European Monetary System (EMS) now operate under a target zone regime. Over the last year, exchange rate target zones have become very popular, and there is now a booming literature spearheaded by the work of Paul Krugman (Quarterly Journal of Economics 1991). Exchange rate target zone models tend to be somewhat complex. By contrast, when *Mathematica* is applied to the analysis, the problem really becomes quite simple.

We proceed by comparing a free-float regime with a target zone regime.

A Under a Free-Float Regime
In the international finance literature, it is now widely accepted that even a random walk will outperform structural models in forecasting nominal exchange rates. This is not to say that exchange rates *should* follow random walks, but merely that it is empirically difficult to distinguish them from random walks. Indeed, the random walk has become the benchmark to beat, yet structural models consistently fail to do so. Thus, it has become standard to assume that, under a free float, the exchange rate follows a random walk with or without drift:

$$s_{t+1} = s_t + k + \epsilon_{t+1} \text{ and } \epsilon \sim N(0, sig^2) \qquad \text{(Gaussian White Noise)}$$

where s_t denotes the known spot exchange rate (domestic price of foreign currency, and measured in natural logarithms), s_{t+1} denotes next-period's spot rate, k denotes a constant drift term that may be zero, and ϵ denotes Gaussian white noise. The above equation may immediately be written as:

***
$$s_{t+1} \sim N(s_t + k, sig^2)$$

Note that, as s_t varies, the whole distribution shifts with it.

B Under a Target-Zone Regime
We now establish a perfectly credible target zone which places lower and upper bounds on the exchange rate so that $s \in (s^{\text{Low}}, s^{\text{Up}})$. If the announcement of these bands is the only difference between the free-float information set and the target-zone information set, then in our calculations, we must replace the unconditional pdf of *** with the conditional pdf (conditional on $s \in (s^{\text{Low}}, s^{\text{Up}})$),

and this yields a doubly truncated normal distribution. That is, s now follows a **doubly-truncated** normal distribution. The properties of this distribution are briefly discussed above. Let s_0 denote the point halfway between these bounds, at the centre of the band. For simplicity it is usually assumed that $s_0 = 0$. Thus, if $s^{\text{Up}} = b$, then $s^{\text{Low}} = -b$.

Our aim is to derive a diagram with the current exchange rate s_t on the horizontal axis, and the expected future exchange rate on the vertical axis. In other words, we wish to derive the expected future rate as a function of the current rate, under each regime.

- Under a **FreeFloat**: $E[s_{t+1}] = s_t + k$ (follows immediately from ***)

- Under a **TargetZone**: $E[s_{t+1}|\ s^{\text{Low}} < s < s^{\text{Up}}]$ is given by simply calculating the expectation of a random variable with doubly truncated normal distribution, given mu, sig, and of course the bounds (where $mu = s_t + k$ as per ***). This is exactly what the function **TruncDoubleMean** does for us (as introduced above).

- Finally, let **EquiLine** denote a 45 degree line passing through the origin. At any point on this line, the expected future exchange rate would simply be equal to the present exchange rate.

First we specify the **parameters**:

```
In[1]:=    b = 0.25; k = 0.00; sig = 0.12;
```

Note that we have made the band just over 4 standard deviations wide. Then we note the following **definitions**:

```
In[2]:= mu = s + k;   sLow = -b;   sUp = b;
```

Next, we specify the **functions**, as discussed above:

```
In[3]:= FreeFloat  = s + k; TargetZone = TruncDoubleMean;
        EquiLine   = s;
```

If you want to see what the function **TargetZone** looks like after *Mathematica* has had a go at manipulating it, remove the semi-colon after the word Trunc-DoubleMean, and then evaluate the cell. We can plot the above functions, and then embellish the picture by putting a box around it. The box represents the bounds of the target zone, within which the exchange rate is defined.

The **graphics cell** follows:

```
In[4]:= q = 2.5;
        PW  = Plot[{TargetZone, FreeFloat}, {s, -b q, b q},
              PlotPoints -> 90, DisplayFunction -> Identity,
              PlotStyle -> { {AbsoluteThickness[1.5]},
              {AbsoluteThickness[0.2], AbsoluteDashing[{7, 5}]} }];
        Box = Graphics[{AbsoluteDashing[{7, 5}],
              AbsoluteThickness[0.2], Line[{{-b, b},
              {-b, -b}, {b, -b}, {b, b},{-b, b}}]}];
        PP  = Plot[EquiLine, {s, -b 1.2, b 1.2},
              DisplayFunction -> Identity,
              PlotStyle -> {AbsoluteThickness[1]}];
        Show [PW, Box, PP, AspectRatio -> (1.2)/Max[q,1.2],
              AxesLabel -> {"Current S","Expected Future S"},
              PlotRange -> {{-b Max[q, 1.2], b Max[q,1.2]},
              {-b 1.2, b 1.2}}, DisplayFunction -> $DisplayFunction]
```

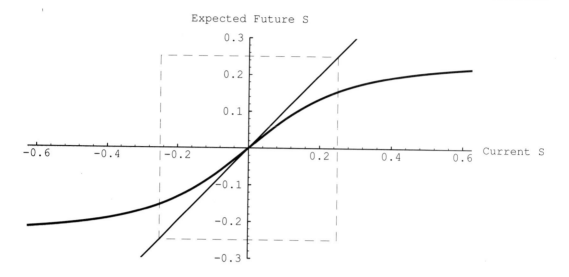

Out[4]:= —Graphics—

In this zero-drift case ($k = 0$), the **free-float** line is just a 45 degree line passing through the origin. Stated differently, under a free-float regime, the expectation of next period's exchange rate is simply the present exchange rate, as is quite standard for a random walk.

But under a **target zone**, we obtain the S-shaped curve. The vertical gap between the free-float line and the S-shaped curve is the expected depreciation/appreciation of the exchange rate due to the very presence of the target zone. From the diagram, it is easy to see that this gap increases as the present exchange rate approaches its bounds (on the left and right), which will tend to push the exchange rate away from the edge of its band and towards the centre of the band, at least intertemporally.

In summary, we see that an exchange rate target zone has 2 manifestations, namely:

a) the S-curve

b) a **feasible zone** within which both the present and future exchange rates must be found (this is represented by the square box in the above diagram).

The part of the S-curve that lies within the feasible zone defines the **relevant segment** of the S-shaped curve. This is why the parameter q was added to the first line of the graphics cell: it allows us to view only the **relevant segment** of the S-curve, and to do so, simply set $q = 1$, and then re-evaluate the Graphics Cell. Try it! It gives us a somewhat different interpretation of S-curves. More generally, by changing q, we can view as little or as much of the S-curve as we desire. Note that the tails of the S-curve do not lie within the feasible zone.

11.3.1   Playing with the Parameters

What happens if a target zone is made wider? What happens if we include a drift term in the random walk? And what happens if there is an increase in the variance of the random process?

Such questions are easily modelled by changing the parameters in the parameter box above. A word of caution is due: after changing a parameter, you must re-evaluate the definitions cell and the functions cell before proceeding to the graphing cell, for otherwise, *Mathematica* does not know that you have made the changes.

- To make the target zone wider, increase the size of b. Since a free-float is just a target zone with an infinitely wide band, increasing b should simply pull the S-curve towards the free-float line, thus reducing the non-linearity of the S-curve. Contrariwise, as b approaches zero, the band gets smaller and smaller, until in the limit we obtain a fixed exchange rate. Thus, as b approaches zero, the S-curve should flatten out into the horizontal axis, which is the fixed-exchange rate solution. Try it: but don't set $b = 0$, because that will yield an undefined expression.

- To model the effect of an increase in the variance of the free-float random walk, simply increase the size of the term sig. For the same bounds, an increase in the variance is tantamount to saying that the band is more restrictive, so that we would expect an increase in sig to pull the S-curve towards the fixed-exchange rate solution: that is, towards the horizontal axis. A few mouse clicks will verify this intuition.

- The above diagram provides the zero-drift case when $k = 0$. Determining the shape of the S-curve with non-zero drift is quite important, and of course, is easily done with *Mathematica*, by changing the parameter k. In setting k, make sure that $|k| < 2b$, which in economic terms means that the drift is smaller than the zone itself. At significantly larger values of k, *Mathematica* may be unable to evaluate the function. When $k > 0$, the free-float line is still a 45° line, but it will no longer pass through the origin: it will appear on the screen as a dashed 45° line. As you can test for yourself, when $k > 0$, the shape of the S-curve does NOT change: it simply shifts k units to the left (that is, when $k > 0$, it shifts to the left, and when $k < 0$, it shifts to the right). However, as k varies, the shape of the **relevant segment** of the S-curve does change, and may not resemble an 'S'-shape at all. To see this clearly, set $q = 1$ in the graphics cell, and set a large value for k, say $k = 1.5b$. The result is perhaps somewhat surprising.

11.3.2   Iteration and the Convergent Exchange Rate

The graph of the S-curve plots the variable **TargetZone** (the expected future rate as defined above) as a function of the present rate. Under a rational expectations hypothesis,

$$s_{t+1} = \textbf{TargetZone} + \text{a serially uncorrelated error term}$$

Thus, the future rate s_{t+1} has both a deterministic component (**TargetZone**) and a stochastic component (the error term). In this section we demonstrate the convergence of the deterministic component. To do so, we ignore the stochastic component so that $s_{t+1} = $ **TargetZone**. This is equivalent to saying that the S-curve depicts a (non-linear) first-order difference equation; indeed, the diagram above is then just a phase diagram. Since the slope of an S-curve is clearly always positive, and by observation smaller than 1, it follows from simple dynamic analysis that under this rational expectations hypothesis, the target-zone exchange rate follows a convergent non-oscillatory time path to an equilibrium. This can be illustrated numerically with iteration, as now shown.

As above, first specify the **parameters**:

```
In[1]:=   b = 0.25;
          k = 0.00;
        sig = 0.12;
```

Then list the **definitions**:

```
In[2]:= mu = s + k;   sLow = -b;   sUp = b;
```

Instead of plotting a graph of the future exchange rate, we can calculate its value given any exchange rate. If the present exchange rate is 0.25, then the future exchange rate is:

```
In[3]:= FutureRate[s_] = N[TargetZone];
        FutureRate[0.25]
```

```
Out[3]:= 0.154267
```

So if $s_t = 0.25$, then $s_{t+1} = 0.154$, for the given parameters. But now we can calculate s_{t+2}, using s_{t+1} as the input:

```
In[4]:= FutureRate[0.154267]
```

```
Out[4]:= 0.110232
```

And now we can calculate s_{t+3}, and so on . . . . But instead of doing this manually, we can get *Mathematica* to do the iteration for us. To do so, use the **NestList** function, which will apply the function **FutureRate** n times, given some starting value. Here, n has been set to 30, and the starting value has been set to 0.25.

```
In[5]:= n = 30; L1 = NestList[FutureRate, 0.25, n]
Out[5]:= {0.25, 0.154267, 0.110233, 0.0831209, 0.0643385,
        0.0505211, 0.0400063, 0.0318424, 0.025425, 0.0203416,
        0.0162953, 0.0130644, 0.0104796, 0.00840894, 0.0067489,
        0.00541732, 0.00434885, 0.00349131, 0.00280298,
        0.00225041, 0.0018068, 0.00145065, 0.00116471,
        0.000935132, 0.000750811, 0.000602822, 0.000484003,
        0.000388604, 0.000312009, 0.000250511, 0.000201135}
```

Plotting the list yields a visual representation of s_{t+n} ($n = 0, 30$). As hinted above, we see that under this rational expectations hypothesis, the exchange rate converges under a target-zone regime. The dashed lines once again represent the bounds of the target zone.

```
In[6]:= ListPlot[L1, PlotStyle -> {AbsolutePointSize[4.5]},
       AxesLabel -> {" Time Period", "Exchange Rate"},
       Epilog -> {AbsoluteDashing[{7, 7}], AbsoluteThickness[.4],
       Line[{ {0,-b}, {n+1,-b} }], Line[{ {0,b}, {n+1,b} }] },
       PlotRange -> { {0, n+1}, {-1.1 b, 1.1 b} }]
```

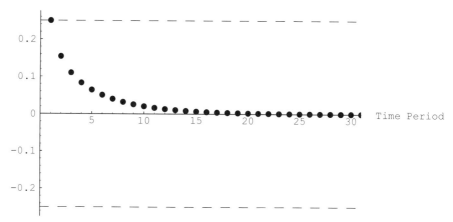

```
Out[6]:= -Graphics-
```

So, when $k = 0$, the exchange rate converges to the centre of the band. Try it out for $k > 0$, but be sure to evaluate all the intermediate cells before plotting again.

11.3.3 A Target-Zone Exchange Rate is Heteroskedastic

Not only is the exchange rate non-linear in a target zone regime, but it is also heteroskedastic. With *Mathematica*, this can be easily illustrated by plotting the variance of the exchange rate under both a free-float and a target zone. Once again, we first specify the **parameters**:

```
In[1]:=  b = 0.25; k = 0.00; sig = 0.12;
```

. . .and then list the **definitions**:

```
In[2]:= mu = s + k;   sLow = -b;   sUp = b;
```

Let **FreeVariance** denote the variance of the exchange rate s under a free-float.

From ***, we see that **FreeVariance** $= sig^2$, which is a constant. Similarly, let **TargetVariance** denote the variance of s under a target-zone. This is derived by calculating the variance of a doubly-truncated normal random variable, which is exactly what the function **TruncDoubleVAR** does for us (as introduced in the section on doubly truncated distributions). Hence. . .

```
In[3]:= FreeVariance    = sig^2;
        TargetVariance = TruncDoubleVAR;
```

We can now plot the variance under each regime as a function of the current
exchange rate *s*. The dashed lines represent the bounds of the target zone. To
plot **TargetVariance** for exchange rates outside the band, set $q > 1$.

```
In[4]:= q = 1;
        AA    =  Plot[FreeVariance, {s, -b 1.2, b 1.2},
                 DisplayFunction -> Identity]
        BB    =  Plot[TargetVariance, {s, -b q, b q},
                 PlotPoints -> 90, DisplayFunction -> Identity,
                 PlotStyle -> {AbsoluteThickness[1.5]}]
        Band =   Graphics[{AbsoluteDashing[{7,5}],
                 AbsoluteThickness[0.2], Line[{{-b, sig^2 1.2},
                 {-b, 0}}], Line[{{b, 0}, {b, sig^2 1.2}}]}]
        Show [AA, BB, Band, DisplayFunction -> $DisplayFunction,
              AxesLabel -> {"S", "Variance"},
              AspectRatio -> 1,
              PlotRange -> {{-b Max[q, 1.2], b Max[q,1.2]},
                            {0, 1.2 sig^2} }]
```

Out[4]:= —Graphics—

Out[4]:= —Graphics—

Out[4]:= —Graphics—

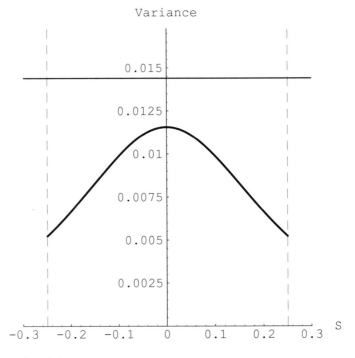

Out[4]:= —Graphics—

This result is also intuitive: a target zone places bounds on the freedom of the
exchange rate. Thus, the variance of a target-zone exchange rate must always
be smaller than the variance of an unbounded free-floating exchange rate, and

this is clear from the plot above. Moreover, the target-zone exchange rate has most freedom when it is at the centre of the band, and has least freedom when it is near the edge of the band, as is also apparent from the diagram. If drift was added to the model by setting $k > 0$, the point of maximum freedom would shift k units to the left (from the centre of the band). Try this out, but remember to re-evaluate all of the intermediate cells after changing k.

In concluding the section on target zones, we stress once again that the above model is developed on the assumption that the zone is perfectly credible. Given the recent European exchange rate crisis, it is of interest to model imperfectly credible bands as well. Of course, this can be done with *Mathematica*; readers wishing to pursue this further are referred to the author.

11.4   Irreversible Investment Under Uncertainty

According to almost every finance textbook, it is optimal for a risk neutral agent to invest in a project when the net present value (NPV) of that project is positive. Recently the theory of irreversible investment under uncertainty has shown this rule to be sub-optimal. Moreover, it has been able to explain the existence of inertia in an amazing variety of examples (see for instance Dixit 1992). For the uninitiated, these models can often be quite difficult to grasp at first. However, by using *Mathematica*, the essence of the theory of irreversible investment can be derived and illustrated quite easily.

Models of irreversible investment typically have 3 central elements. Firstly, the investment must involve an irreversible expenditure, the nominal size of which is K. This expenditure then yields an infinite sequence of nominal net revenues $< R_t >$. Secondly, there is uncertainty because R_t is stochastic, and here it is assumed that net revenues follow a discrete time random walk:

$$R_{t+1} = R_t + \epsilon_{t+1} \quad \text{and} \quad \epsilon \sim N(0, \sigma^2) \quad \text{so that} \quad R_{t+1} \sim N(R_t, \sigma^2).$$

Thirdly, the firm can delay its investment. In particular, we will consider the case where the firm is able to delay its investment by a single period of time, of arbitrary length. The decision to invest then becomes an intertemporal one: *either* invest today *or* wait one period and then decide again given the new information set. We can devise a decision rule to solve this dilemma as follows:

Let I_0 denote the expected NPV of investing today;

Let I_1 denote the expected NPV of investing tomorrow, given that we only invest tomorrow if it is still worthwhile to do so, AND given tomorrow's information set;

Let I_{1E} denote I_1 conditional on today's information set.

To emphasize that the results have nothing to do with risk preferences, it is assumed that agents are risk neutral. This also serves to simplify the analysis. It is then clear that the optimal investment rule is to:

$$\text{Invest Today} \quad \text{iff} \quad I_0 > I_{1E}$$
$$\text{Wait 1 Period} \quad \text{iff} \quad I_{1E} > I_0$$

By contrast, the textbook firm always invests today if $I_0 > 0$.

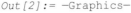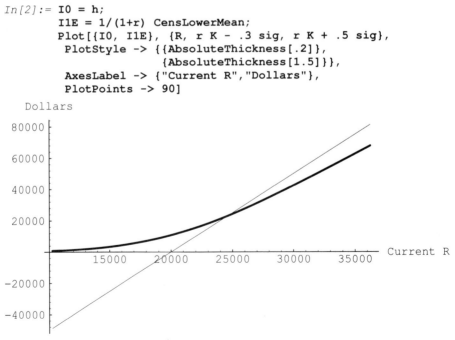

Let r denote a positive discount rate, and let $h_t = R_t/r - K$, so that $h_{t+1} = R_{t+1}/r - K$.

Then I_0 and I_1 may be neatly expressed as:

$$I_0 = h_t \quad \text{AND} \quad I_1 = \frac{1}{1+r}\begin{cases} h_{t+1} & \text{If } h_{t+1} > 0 \\ 0 & \text{If } h_{t+1} \leq 0 \end{cases}$$

Note that I_1 is unknown at time t because R_{t+1} is unknown at time t (only its distribution is known). Indeed, this is precisely the reason our investment rule compares I_{1E} with I_0, rather than I_1 with I_0. Given I_1, how does one calculate I_{1E}? Simply note that I_1 has exactly the same form as a lower censored random variable (as discussed above) with $s^{\text{Low}} = 0$, and where the random variable is $h_{t+1} \sim N(h_t, \sigma^2/r^2)$, since $R_{t+1} \sim N(R_t, \sigma^2)$. Then, the expectation at time t of I_1 (ie I_{1E}) is given by the present value of the function **CensLowerMean**, where $mu = h_t$, and where $sig = \sigma/r$.

We can now consider a numerical example: the following project has $K = \$100,000$, $r = .2$, and $\sigma = 6500$. In the next cell, we let sd denote the standard deviation σ.

```
In[1]:= K = 100000;     r = .2;     sd = 6500;
        h = R/r - K;    mu = h;     sig = sd/r;    sLow = 0;
```

Given these parameters and definitions, all that remains for us to do is to tell *Mathematica* what I_0 and I_{1E} look like. They can then be plotted (I_{1E} is the bold line).

```
In[2]:= I0 = h;
        I1E = 1/(1+r) CensLowerMean;
        Plot[{I0, I1E}, {R, r K - .3 sig, r K + .5 sig},
          PlotStyle -> {{AbsoluteThickness[.2]},
                        {AbsoluteThickness[1.5]}},
          AxesLabel -> {"Current R","Dollars"},
          PlotPoints -> 90]
```

Out[2]:= —Graphics—

The optimising firm will be indifferent between investing today and investing tomorrow when $I_{1E} = I_0$. Since I_{1E} is necessarily positive, I_0 must also be positive at this point of indifference. Then there must exist a non-empty set $S = \{R_t : I_0 > 0, I_0 < I_{1E}\}$ within which textbook rules are strictly sub-optimal. For instance, in the above example, the set S is given approximately by $S = \{R_t : 20000 < R_t < 25000\}$. Within this range, textbook investment rules state "invest today", whereas optimality prescribes waiting one period and then evaluating the problem again given the new information set. Inertia then results as a consequence of optimality in an uncertain environment. Indeed, the more uncertain the environment, the greater will be the inertia before investment occurs. This can be shown by plotting I_{1E} with various values of σ, which we once again denote by sd.

```
In[3]:= K = 100000;      r = .2;     sd = .;
        h = R/r - K;      mu = h;     sig = sd/r;    sLow = 0;
        I0    =    h;
        aaI1E = 1/(1+r) CensLowerMean /. sd -> 100;    (* bold *)
        bbI1E = 1/(1+r) CensLowerMean /. sd -> 10000;  (* plain *)
        ccI1E = 1/(1+r) CensLowerMean /. sd -> 20000;  (* dash *)
        Plot[{I0, aaI1E, bbI1E, ccI1E}, {R, -7000, 50000},
            AxesLabel -> {"Current R","Dollars"}, PlotPoints -> 90,
            PlotRange -> {{-7000, 50000}, {-1/2 K, 1.5 K}},
            PlotStyle -> {{AbsoluteThickness[.2]}, {AbsoluteThickness[1.5]},
                          {AbsoluteThickness[.2]},
                          {AbsoluteThickness[.2], AbsoluteDashing[{7,5}]} }]
```

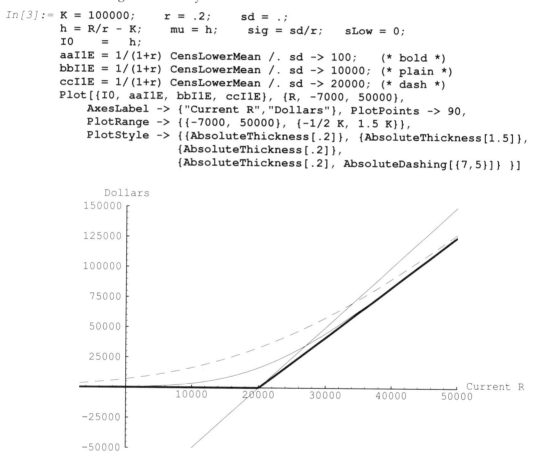

Out[3]:= —Graphics—

Note how the size of set S increases as σ increases. Similarly, as σ approaches 0, set S approaches an empty set. This can be seen above in the case when $\sigma = 100$ (small) which yields the bold line with the kink in it (the bold line starts out on the horizontal axis; at $R_t = 20000$, there is a kink and the bold line moves off the horizontal axis). This bold line serves as an asymptote which the other curves approach.

The essence of the above is that there are both benefits and costs to waiting. Roughly speaking, the benefit is that by waiting, one can avoid potentially poor investments, at least in the light of the newly received information. Naturally, the more uncertain the environment, the greater is this benefit, and this is apparent in the above diagram.

11.5 Simulating Random Processes

The simple random walk $x_{t+1} = x_t + \epsilon_{t+1}$ where ϵ is a white noise process, has left an indelible mark on economic analysis. Its prominence most likely stems from its empirical relevance in financial markets, its theoretical elegance in economic modelling, and the predominance of weak-form notions of market efficiency. The special case of Gaussian white noise is especially important in economic models. In this section, we simulate a whole variety of random processes, starting with a simple Markov Chain, and then add more complex forms, as used in the binomial option pricing model. This is then used to simulate stochastic (or bursting) speculative rational bubbles with both exogenous and endogenous probability of bursting. Absorbing barriers and reflecting barriers are added, and allow us to simulate the gambler's ruin problem, and to derive the asymptotic distribution of bounded random variables. Finally, Gaussian random walks are considered, with and without drift, with AR(1) processes as a special case.

11.5.1 Markov Chains

A Markov chain is a discrete time, discrete state system, in which the transition from any state to any other is a fixed probability that is independent of the past, since by the so-called Markov property, the past and future are statistically independent when the present is known. Markov chains thus have 2 essential charactersitics: the set of states, and the set of transition probabilities which define the probability of moving from the present state to any other state. A simple example of such a chain is the random walk with discrete steps. Freddy, who is our random walker, starts out at time t at point x on a line; his state and time may thus be denoted x_t. He flips a fair coin to decide his direction: if heads, he takes one step to the right in which case $x_{t+1} = x_t + 1$; if tails, he goes to the left so that $x_{t+1} = x_t - 1$. The one-step transition probabilities are of course 1/2 each for a fair coin. To model such a scenario, we can make use of the **If[a, b, c]** function. This simply means "IF a is true, THEN do b; ELSE do c". Other than being simple, it turns out that this is a particularly efficient random walk generator. Moreover, as shown below, it is quite easy to adapt it so as to simulate more complex Markov chains. The function **Random[]** generates a pseudorandom real number between 0 and 1, with uniform distribution over $(0, 1)$. Consequently, the event "Tails" can be represented by "**Random[]** < .5". The cell immediately below thus reads: If it is Tails, Then let $x_{t+1} = x_t - 1$; Else let $x_{t+1} = x_t + 1$. The starting value is $x = 0$, and there are 1000 time periods. The resulting time series gets recorded in a data list called Fred1:

```
In[1]:= t = 1000; x = 0;
        Fred1 = Table[If[Random[] < 0.5, x--, x++], {t}];
```

By adding the semicolon to the end of the last line, *Mathematica* keeps the output in memory, rather than cluttering up the screen with the generated time series. This is particularly important when generating large data sets—indeed, when working with the asymptotic properties of a distribution, we might specify several million time periods. Nevertheless, we may want to take a look at the first few (say 50) values of our data set:

```
In[2]:= Take[Fred1, 50]
```

```
Out[2]:= {0, 1, 2, 3, 2, 1, 0, -1, 0, 1, 0, 1, 0, 1, 2, 1, 2, 1,
          2, 1, 2, 3, 2, 3, 4, 5, 4, 3, 4, 5, 6, 7, 6, 7, 6, 5,
          4, 5, 4, 5, 6, 5, 4, 3, 4, 5, 4, 3, 2, 1}
```

In economic applications, the Markov chain often takes a slightly more general form. If x denotes the present asset price, then next period the asset price may go down to dx (i.e. d times x) with probability p, or go up to ux with probability $1 - p$. Indeed, this specification is the basis of none other than the binomial option pricing model. By comparing **Fred1** above with **Fred2** below, it is easy to see how the above simulation has been adapted to generate this more general scenario. We now start out with $x = 100$; the other parameters are self-explanatory:

```
In[3]:= t = 1000;  x = 100;  d = .9;  u = 1.2;  p = .65;
        Fred2 = Table[If[Random[]< p, x = d x, x = u x],{t}];
```

This can yield some amazingly volatile time series plots (you may have to try more than once to get a really exciting series):

```
In[4]:= ListPlot[Fred2, PlotJoined -> True, PlotRange -> All]
```

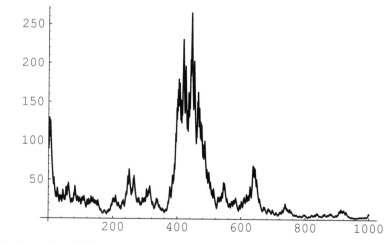

```
Out[4]:= -Graphics-
```

11.5.1.1 Stochastic Speculative Bubbles

Financial markets often seem *prima facie* to be irregular, with the volatility of prices in such markets far exceeding any underlying movement in fundamental determinants. Although some may attribute this irregularity purely to mania and euphoria, considerable effort has been devoted to show that such behaviour is consistent with a rational expectations hypothesis in the presence of rational speculative bubbles. In the presence of such a bubble, the price of an asset p_t will be the sum of a market fundamentals component P^*, and a rational bubbles component b_t: in other words, $p_t = P^* + b_t$. Of course, the bubble component is the interesting part and is derived as the solution to an expectational difference equation. The saddle path solution is obtained when $b_t = 0$; for all $b_t \neq 0$, the asset price is driven by a rational bubbles component. If b_t were a deterministic bubble, the asset price would have to increase (or decrease) indefinitely which renders such bubbles unrealistic in most asset markets. By contrast, in a stochastic bubble, there is a probability q that the bubble will continue each period, and a probability $(1-q)$ that it will burst. Under this scenario, the bubble component typically takes the following form (where r denotes the return on a riskless asset, and ϵ denotes a white noise process):

$$b_{t+1} = \begin{cases} (1+r)q^{-1}b_t + \epsilon_{t+1} & \text{with probability } q \\ \epsilon_{t+1} & \text{with probability } 1-q \end{cases}$$

We shall take care of the error term ϵ first, by letting it take a Gaussian form with known standard deviation:

```
In[1]:= sig = 10; e = NormalDistribution[0, sig];
```

The bubble can now be simulated by using the Markov structure discussed above. In the following example, we start the bubble out at $b_t = 0$ (no bubble at time t), simulate it for 500 time periods given that it continues each period with a probability of $q = .80$. The result is plotted immediately.

```
In[2]:= t = 500; b = 0; r = .05; q = .80; u = (1+r)(q^-1);
        Bubble1 = Table[If[Random[] < q, b = u b + Random[e],
                                          b = Random[e]], {t}];
        ListPlot[Bubble1, PlotJoined -> True, PlotRange -> All]
```

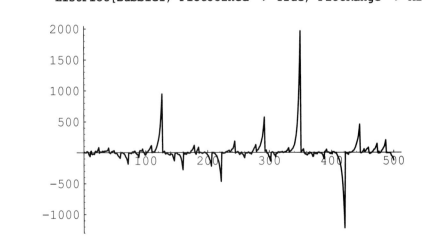

```
Out[2]:= -Graphics-
```

In the above example, the probability of a crash was a constant. Instead, the probability that the bubble survives can be modelled as a function of the absolute size of the bubble itself. Specifically, it seems plausible to let $q \to 1$ as $|b_t| \to 0$, AND for $q \to 0$ as $|b_t| \to \infty$. The hyperbolic secant function satisfies these conditions and thus we let $q = Sech[\alpha \, b_t]$ where α is a scalar constant. Note that if q is endogenous, then so is u (see the cell above), and thus both must be specified within the table structure itself, as shown below.

```
In[3]:= t = 500;    b = 0;     r = .05;
        Bubble2 = Table[q = Sech[.01 b]; u = (1+r)(q^-1);
                        If[Random[] < q, b = u b + Random[e],
                                         b = Random[e]], {t}];
        ListPlot[Bubble2, PlotJoined -> True, PlotRange -> All]
```

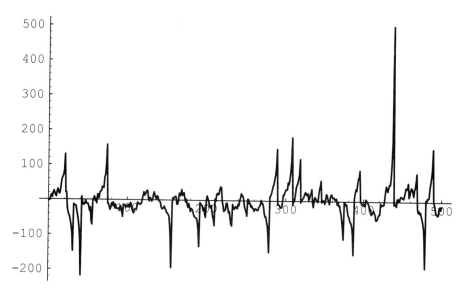

```
Out[3]:= -Graphics-
```

11.5.1.2   Markov Chains with Absorbing Barriers—
Simulating the Gambler's Ruin Problem

Consider the simple discrete random walk example: if heads, Freddy moves right one step; if tails, he moves left. We now add absorbing barriers at x^{Lo} and x^{Up}. As before, Freddy starts out at $x = 0$, and moves about by flipping a fair coin. But now, should he reach either barrier, he gets absorbed by it and the walk ends. This scenario is identical to the well-known problem of the gambler's ruin. Here, Player A starts with say \$3, and Player B starts with say \$6. They repeatedly toss a fair coin. For each tail, A gives B one dollar, and for each head, B gives A one dollar. This continues until either A or B runs out of money; that is, until one gambler is in a state of ruin. Drawing a picture may make it clearer:

In[1]:= **xLo = -3; xUp = 6;**

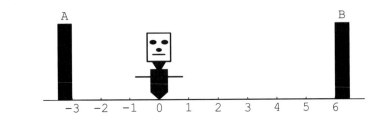

Out[1]:= —Graphics—

At any given moment, Player A's wealth is just the distance between Freddy and barrier A. If the coin is heads, Freddy moves one unit to the right, and Player A's wealth rises by 1 dollar. Player A wins the game if Freddy reaches barrier B. This scenario can be modelled in 2 stages. First we specify the Markov Chain, now written as a function. The following assumes that they play with a fair coin, so that $p = .5$. Of course, you can set any value:

In[2]:= **f[x_] := If[Random[] < .5, x-1, x+1]**

Then, we tell *Mathematica* to evaluate this function only **While** x lies within its barriers, that is only for $x > x^{Lo}$ AND $x < x^{Up}$. The resulting time-series will be recorded in a list called L.

In[3]:= **SimSalabim := (While[x > xLo && x < xUp, x = f[x];**
                         AppendTo[L, x]]; Length[L])

An Example: suppose Player A starts out with $3, and Player B starts out with $6.

In[4]:= **x = 0;   xLo = -3;   xUp = 6;   L = {x};**
         SimSalabim;
         L

Out[4]:= {0, −1, −2, −1, −2, −1, 0, −1, 0, 1, 2, 3, 4, 5, 6}

In the problem of the gambler's ruin, it is often of interest to calculate the expected duration of play. That is, on average, how many tosses will occur before Freddy walks into a barrier. We can get *Mathematica* to simulate the result for us, without knowing anything about difference equations. This is done by evaluating the function **SimSalabim** several thousand times, (each time measuring how long the list is), and then rounding off the average of all these values. In this example, we do so just 500 times: it may take a minute or two to evaluate. Obviously, accuracy increases with the number of trials.

In[5]:= **xLo = -3;   xUp = 6;**
         Q = Table[x=0; L={}; SimSalabim, {500}];
         Round[Mean[Q]]

Out[5]:= 18

Well, the correct answer is 18 tosses, although it is quite possible that you may have got 17 or 19 or even 16 or 20, because of the small sample size. More generally, for a fair coin, the expected duration is equal to x^{Lo} times x^{Up}, in absolute values. In other words, if Player A starts out with $2000, and Player B starts with $1, it will take on average 2000 tosses before either is ruined!! Of even greater interest is the frequency distribution of the length of play. Recall that the list Q contains 500 elements, each giving the length of one random walk (i.e. the duration of one play). To derive the frequency distribution of the length of play, we simply tell *Mathematica* to count the number of times the length of play was 1, to count the number of times it was 2, and so on. ... We start the count at 1, and end at 100.

```
In[6]:= Freq = Table[Count[Q, i], {i, 1, 100}]
Out[6]:= {0, 0, 66, 0, 39, 6, 30, 10, 26, 15, 25, 16, 12, 17,
         20, 13, 4, 11, 20, 8, 7, 9, 9, 11, 7, 10, 7, 9, 7, 7,
         4, 6, 6, 5, 3, 3, 4, 2, 4, 3, 3, 2, 0, 1, 2, 1, 0, 0,
         3, 0, 1, 2, 1, 0, 3, 1, 0, 2, 1, 0, 3, 2, 0, 0, 1, 0,
         0, 0, 0, 0, 1, 1, 1, 1, 0, 1, 0, 0, 0, 0, 1, 0, 0, 0,
         0, 0, 1, 0, 0, 0, 0, 0, 1, 0, 0, 0, 1, 0, 0, 0}
```

We will plot this as a histogram; that is, we will plot a bar graph of the frequency distribution. This requires a special package, which we will have to load. We need do so only once.

```
In[7]:= <<Graphics`Graphics`
```

We can now plot our histogram, with frequency on the vertical axis, and the length of play on the horizontal axis.

```
In[8]:= BarChart[Take[Freq, 25],
         AxesLabel -> {"","Frequency"}, AspectRatio -> .5]
```

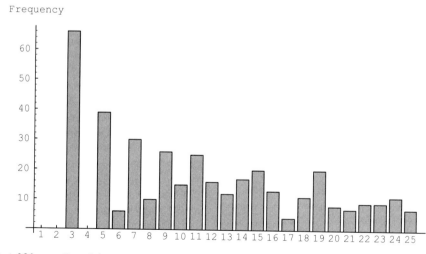

```
Out[8]:= —Graphics—
```

Note how there are really 2 distributions here; one for odd numbers, and one for even numbers. Now set both x^{Lo} and x^{Up} to even numbers and try it out again. Note that the random walk now never ends after an odd number of tosses! Of course, if we were doing this seriously, we would have to take many more trials than 500.

Some Fun Things: Freddy comes alive!
Let's generate a new walk, just as we did above:

```
In[9]:= x = 0;    xLo = -3;    xUp = 6;    L = {x};
        SimSalabim;
        L
```

```
Out[9]:= {0, -1, 0, -1, -2, -1, 0, -1, -2, -1, -2, -3}
```

So these are the actual steps taken by Freddy this time. Let's liven things up and make Freddy actually walk this path. The code to make Freddy do this may be found in the demonstration notebook that accompanies this chapter. Simply open the notebook, and then work through the section on "Markov Chains with Absorbing Barriers".

11.5.1.3 Markov Chains with Reflecting Barriers

Instead of the barriers absorbing Freddy, they can reflect him instead. Suppose Freddy is at the upper barrier. He flips a coin. If it is tails, he simply moves back into the band. If it is heads, he stays at the upper barrier, and stays there until he gets a tails. A Markov Chain random walk with reflecting barriers has a variety of aliases, among which are the regulated random walk, the ergodic random walk, and the regulated Markov Chain. In its continuous state-space form, it usually goes by the name of regulated brownian motion or regulated Wiener process.

It is often of interest to calculate the distribution of a variable which has lower and upper bounds. In even the simplest cases, this can be somewhat nasty to do theoretically. Instead, *Mathematica* can simulate the asymptotic distribution for us, and for any given scenario. First we generate a time series for a heads/tails style random walk starting at zero, with lower bound at -2, upper bound at 3, and with a fair coin ($p = .5$). In this example, our random walk will consist of 30000 coin flips. If we were doing this seriously, we would want to generate at least a million coin flips. Nevertheless, 30000 will suffice for the moment. It should take about 60 seconds:

```
In[1]:= t = 30000; x = 0;   xLo = -2;   xUp = 3;   p = .5;

        Fred3 = Table[If[Random[] < p,
          If[x > xLo, x--, x],   If[x < xUp, x++, x] ], {t}];
```

To get a clearer idea of what a regulated random walk might look like, we can take a look at the first 50 points in the time series:

```
In[2]:= Take[Fred3, 50]
```

```
Out[2]:= {0, 1, 0, -1, 0, -1, -2, -2, -2, -1, 0, 1, 0, -1, 0,
          -1, -2, -1, 0, 1, 0, 1, 0, 1, 0, 1, 2, 1, 2, 1, 2, 1,
          2, 1, 2, 1, 0, -1, 0, -1, 0, 1, 0, 1, 0, 1, 0, -1, -2,
          -1}
```

Next, we tell *Mathematica* to count the number of times it landed at each x value. This gives us the frequency distribution of x over its band.

```
In[3]:= Frequency = Table[Count[Fred3, i], {i, xLo, xUp}]
```

```
Out[3]:= {4853, 4923, 5045, 5087, 5098, 4994}
```

Now we can plot our barchart:

```
In[4]:= BarChart[Frequency, Ticks -> {Table[{j+1-xLo, j}, {j,
        xLo,xUp}],Automatic}, AxesLabel -> {"X","Frequency"}]
```

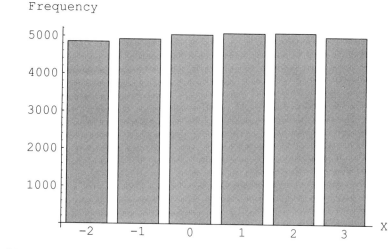

```
Out[4]:= —Graphics—
```

You should obtain something that resembles a uniform distribution, which is the correct result. Try it out for a biased coin: that is, change the probability to say $p = .4$, and get a strikingly different result.

11.5.2   Gaussian Random Walks

Thus far, only discrete state random walks have been considered. Naturally, the continuous state-space random walk is also of considerable interest. Because *Mathematica* can model the normal distribution, it is remarkably easy to simulate a random walk with Gaussian white noise of form $x_{t+1} = x_t + \epsilon_{t+1}$ and $\epsilon \sim N(0, sig^2)$. We first specify the error term which is standard normal in the following example:

```
In[1]:= sig = 1;
        Gauss = NormalDistribution[0, sig]
```

```
Out[1]:= NormalDistribution[0, 1]
```

The rest is easy: the following random walk has 150 time periods, and starts out with x at 0:

In[2]:= **t = 150; x = 0;**

DATA = Table[x = x + Random[Gauss], {t}];

We can take a look at the first few (say 15) values of our data set:

In[3]:= **Take[DATA, 15]**
Out[3]:= {0.847667, 0.175568, −0.611004, −2.39858, −2.1605,
          −2.94318, −2.63926, −2.64874, −4.42722, −3.96331,
          −4.59483, −4.10965, −5.17403, −4.88958, −5.39126}

Of course, since the data is pseudo-random, we will get different results every time we generate a new data set. To plot the entire data set. . .

In[4]:= **ListPlot[DATA, PlotJoined -> True]**

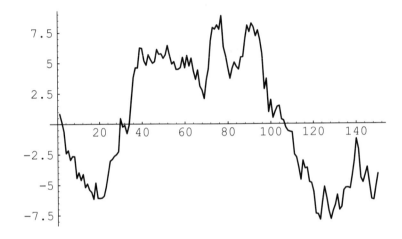

Out[4]:= −Graphics−

Adding a Drift Term:

The specification of a random walk with constant drift depends on how variable x is measured. If x is measured in levels, then a random walk with drift is written $x_{t+1} = (1 + b')x_t + \epsilon_{t+1}$. If x is measured in logs, then a random walk with drift is written $x_{t+1} = a + x_t + \epsilon_{t+1}$. Both of these scenarios can be nested as follows:

$$x_{t+1} = a + bx_t + \text{Random[Gauss]} \qquad \text{where } b = 1 + b'$$

Setting $a = 0$ yields the levels scenario, whilst setting $b = 1$ yields the log scenario. The random walk without drift is obtained with $a = 0$, $b = 1$. More generally, the entire class of AR(1) processes is obtained when $a = 0$. The following generates the first 150 values of the stationary AR(1) process with $b = 0.5 < 1$.

In[5]:= **t = 150; x = 0; a = 0; b = .5;**

DATA1 = Table[x = a + b x + Random[Gauss], {t}];

Once again, this can be plotted. Notice how the series converges stochastically upon zero, and now with a much smaller range:

In[6]:= **ListPlot[DATA1, PlotJoined -> True]**

Out[6]:= −Graphics−

Further Reading

Readers whose interest has been stimulated by exchange rate target zones or irreversible investment under uncertainty might consider expanding their knowledge... In particular, Krugman (1991) is the obvious starting choice for someone new to exchange rate target zones. The literature is now quite extensive and a survey of its present state may be found in Svensson (1993). Those interested in irreversible investment should consult Dixit (1992) for an excellent introduction, and Pindyck (1991) for a thorough review of the literature.

11.6 References

Dixit, Avinash (1992), "Investment and Hysteresis", *Journal of Economic Perspectives*, Volume 6, No.1, Winter 1992, 107–132.

Krugman, Paul (1991), "Target Zones and Exchange Rate Dynamics", *The Quarterly Journal of Economics*, August 1991, 669–682.

Pindyck, Robert (1991), "Irreversibility, Uncertainty, and Investment", *Journal of Economic Literature*, September 1991, 1110–1148.

Svensson, Lars (1993), "Recent Research on Exchange Rate Target Zones: an interpretation", *Journal of Economic Perspectives*, forthcoming.

11.7 Acknowledgements

This chapter would be incomplete without my thanking Jeff Sheen for some helpful insights, and it is with considerable pleasure that I do so now.

12 Option Valuation

Ross M. Miller

12.1   Introduction

Although financial computation is often viewed as an exercise in number crunching, the emergence of a new breed of financial "rocket scientists" has expanded the role of computers in finance to include not only numerical manipulations, but also structural manipulations. Investment houses now routinely "slice and dice" securities such as mortgages, government bonds, and even the infamous "junk bonds," to engineer their cash flows to meet particular risk/return criteria. While spreadsheet programs and traditional programming languages (e.g., FORTRAN and C) continue to play an important role in financial computation, symbolic programming languages, i.e., languages that manipulate both the numbers and the symbols with which financial structures are represented, are taking hold as a way of dealing with the increasing complexity of the financial world. Indeed, some of the more innovative investment houses around the world have been using LISP and Smalltalk since the mid-1980's to handle a variety of difficult valuation and design problems.

This chapter contains a redesigned version of a suite of option valuation tools that the author originally developed in LISP as part of a comprehensive textbook on the application of object-oriented and artificial intelligence technology to finance analysis (Miller, 1990a), and some of which were included in the premiere issue of the *Mathematica Journal* (Miller, 1990b). It is a testament to *Mathematica*'s flexibility that even the most complex LISP-based tool developed in conjunction with that textbook ports easily to *Mathematica*. This chapter contains a brief introduction to option valuation; however, a more complete introduction to the topic can be found in any of several sources. The original exposition of the Black-Scholes model appears in Black and Scholes, 1973 and an excellent adaptation of the Cox-Ross-Rubinstein binomial model appears in Cox and Rubinstein, 1985. An excellent textbook that covers a wide range of topics in option valuation is Hull, 1990.

This chapter takes a very general approach to the problem of financial valuation, utilizing object-oriented design methods to the extent that they are possible within *Mathematica* to achieve this generality. The traditional approach that economists have taken to computing has been to create completely separate programs or procedures for each model. In the object-oriented approach to computing the goal is to create general valuation procedures, called methods, that can operate on many different types of objects, in this case options. The advantage to the object-oriented approach is that the development of new financial instruments does not require programming new, ad hoc valuation procedures. Instead, existing objects that represent related financial instruments are updated to reflect any innovations in the newly-created instrument. Furthermore, once an object has been formally defined, other methods can be created to perform other functions, such as accounting, without starting from scratch.

The *Mathematica* functions developed in this chapter were designed with their pedagogical utility foremost in mind, especially when used interactively as a *Mathematica* notebook. Although we have tried to make them as computationally efficient as possible, in some instances speed has been sacrificed in favor of simplicity or elegance. In particular, the binomial model has been developed within a very general framework that is readily extensible to more complex valuation problems, but is in no way optimized for the binomial model. In addition, the tendency in this chapter is to use *Mathematica*'s built-in algorithms even in cases where user-defined alternatives would be far more efficient. Finally, the functions developed in this chapter have been designed for interpreted rather than compiled use.

12.2   The Black-Scholes Model

The Black-Scholes model provides a direct way of valuing a *call option* for common stock. A call option is an option to buy stock at a pre-specified *exercise* or *strike price* prior to a given expiration date. (An option which can only be exercised on its expiration date is known as a *European* option, while one that can be exercised at any time prior to expiration is known as an *American* option. Most exchange-traded stock options in the U.S. are American options. Except in special cases, the Black-Scholes model must be modified to deal with the possibility of early exercise.)

If the market price of the stock is greater than the exercise price when the expiration date arrives, then the value of the option will be equal to the payoff that can be created by buying the stock at the exercise price and then immediately selling the stock at its market price. Otherwise, it will not pay to exercise the option, and so it will expire with zero value. The payoff pattern of an option is easily modeled in *Mathematica* by the function **CallPayoff** as follows:

```
In[1]:= CallPayoff[price_,strike_] = Max[0,price-strike]

Out[1]:= Max[0, price - strike]
```

For example, consider the payoff function for a call option that gives the holder the option to buy a share of DEC stock at a price of $60 on the third Friday in

June. If the price of DEC stock is $80 on expiration in June, then the option will pay off $20; however, if DEC stock is below $60, the option will be worth $0 as it will not pay to exercise it. This payoff function is readily plotted as follows:

In[2]:= **Plot[CallPayoff[x,60],{x,0,120}]**

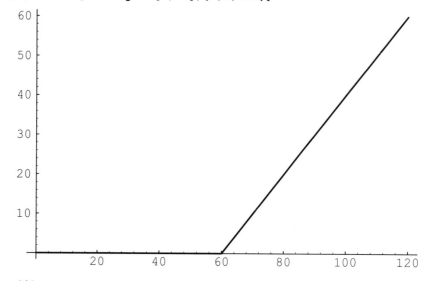

Out[2]:= —Graphics—

Similiarly, the payoff function for a *put option*, i.e., an option to sell a share of stock at a predetermined exercise price (in this case, $60) can be defined and plotted as follows:

In[3]:= **PutPayoff[price_,strike_] = Max[0,strike-price]**

Out[3]:= Max[0, -price + strike]

In[4]:= **Plot[PutPayoff[x,60],{x,0,120}]**

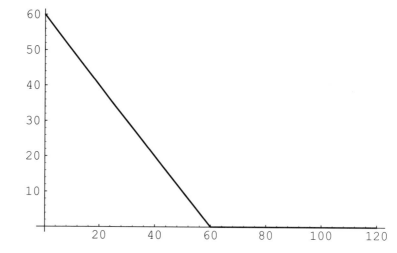

Out[4]:= —Graphics—

Hence, at a price below the exercise price, it will pay to purchase the stock and then use the put option to sell it at the exercise price; otherwise, the put option is worthless.

A payoff diagram, such as those shown above, only provides the value of an option at a boundary—the moment the option expires at the close of trading on the expiration date. Determining the value of the option prior to expiration can be reduced to taking the current price of the stock, which is presumably known, and projecting it forward in time to the expiration date. Because of the many factors that can affect the price of a stock, this projection must be made probabilistically rather than deterministically. In the Black-Scholes model, it is assumed that the percentage change in the stock price (its rate of return when no dividends are paid) follows a Weiner process (i.e., a random walk) with a known drift and standard deviation, so that on the expiration date, the stock prices have a lognormal distribution with a known mean and variance.

Although the lognormality assumption of the Black-Scholes model cannot be expected to hold in any but the most contrived situations, the model (and its variants) can be used to predict option prices with great accuracy under a broad range of real-world situations. Indeed, most traders on the floors of options exchanges carry computerized "crib sheets" with them that give the theoretical value of the options in which they trade so that they may identify options whose prices are temporarily mispriced relative to the model.

Under the further assumptions that the stock pays no dividends and will only be exercised, if at all, upon expiration, the Black-Scholes model yields a closed-form equation for the value of the call option that is easily modelled in *Mathematica*. Although this derivation was a notable technical feat when it was first derived around 1970, it is now a standard application of stochastic calculus. (The use of *Mathematica* to do stochastic calculus appears elsewhere in this book.)

Because it is relatively complex, the Black-Scholes formula is best expressed in terms of an auxiliary function. Both the Black-Scholes formula and the auxiliary functions take five arguments as follows:

```
p   = current price of the stock
k   = exercise price of the option
sd  = volatility of the stock (standard deviation of annual
      rate of return)
r   = continuously compounded risk-free rate of return, e.g.,
      the return on U.S. Treasury bills with very short maturities
t   = time (in years) until the expiration date
```

The critical feature of the Black-Scholes and related option valuation models is that the value of the option depends only on the standard deviation of the stock's rate of return and not upon its expected value. That is because the model is based on an arbitrage argument in which any risk premium above the risk-free rate of return is cancelled out.

Using the five variables given above, we can define the auxiliary function, **AuxBS**, and the Black-Scholes valuation function, **BlackScholes**, as follows:

```
In[5]:= AuxBS[p_,k_,sd_,r_,t_] = (Log[p/k]+r t)/
                                 (sd Sqrt[t])+
                                 .5 sd Sqrt[t]
```

$$Out[5]:= \; 0.5 \; sd \; Sqrt[t] + \frac{r \; t + Log[\frac{p}{k}]}{sd \; Sqrt[t]}$$

```
In[6]:= BlackScholes[p_,k_,sd_,r_,t_] =
           p Norm[AuxBS[p,k,sd,r,t]]-
           k Exp[-r t] (Norm[AuxBS[p,k,sd,r,t]-sd Sqrt[t]])
```

$$Out[6]:= \; -\left(\frac{k \; Norm[-0.5 \; sd \; Sqrt[t] + \frac{r \; t + Log[\frac{p}{k}]}{sd \; Sqrt[t]}]}{E^{r \; t}}\right) +$$

$$p \; Norm[0.5 \; sd \; Sqrt[t] + \frac{r \; t + Log[\frac{p}{k}]}{sd \; Sqrt[t]}]$$

The function **Norm** is the cumulative normal distribution function and can be defined for numerical arguments as follows:

```
In[7]:= Norm[z_?NumberQ] := N[0.5 + 0.5 Erf[z/Sqrt[2]]]
```

A separate definition of the derivative of **Norm** used for symbolic valuation will be given in the following section on risk management.

Notice that because **BlackScholes** is defined using the immediate assignment operator, =, it contains the full Black-Scholes formula with the actual values from **AuxBS** appropriately substituted as shown by the output given above.

We are now ready to compute the dollar value for stock options by calling the function **BlackScholes** with numerical arguments. For example, to continue the above dialog, we might wish to find the value of a call option on DEC stock with an exercise price of 60 assuming that the current price of DEC is 58 1/2, the time until expiration is 0.3 years, the volatility of DEC stock is 29%, and the continuously compounded risk-free rate of return is 4% as follows:

```
In[8]:= BlackScholes[58.5,60.,0.29,0.04,0.3]
```

```
Out[8]:= 3.34886
```

Using the graphic capabilities of *Mathematica* one can easily explore the various qualitative properties of the Black-Scholes formula and even go so far as to animate them. Two parameters of the model that are certain to change as time passes are the stock price and, trivially, the time to expiration. The instantaneous dependence of the option value on the stock price for the DEC option can be shown as follows:

In[9]:= **Plot[BlackScholes[x,60.,0.29,0.04,0.3],{x,50,70}]**

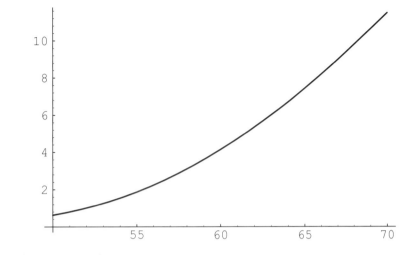

Out[9]:= —Graphics—

Looking at the following 3D plot of option value as a function of both stock price and time until expiration, one can see how the curvature of the above graph diminishes as expiration approaches:

In[10]:= **Plot3D[BlackScholes[x,60.,0.29,0.04,y],{x,50.,70.},**
{y,0.01,0.5},
ViewPoint->{1.450, -2.900, 0.810}]

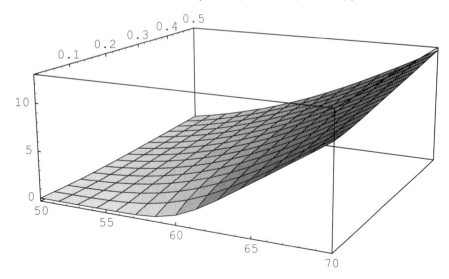

Out[10]:= —SurfaceGraphics—

The sensitivity of the Black-Scholes model to the two parameters that characterize the "financial state of the world" can also be explored graphically using *Mathematica*. For example, although the Black-Scholes model assumes the volatility of the stock is constant, it will tend to fluctuate over the life of the option. The sensitivity of the value of an option to changes in volatility can be graphed as follows:

In[11]:= **Plot[BlackScholes[60.,60.,x,0.04,0.3],{x,0.2,0.4}]**

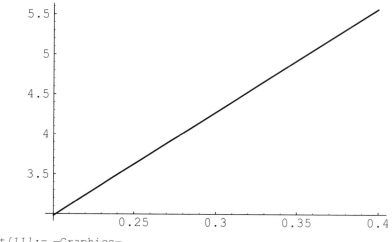

Out[11]:= —Graphics—

This graph is not particularly exciting because over a broad range of volatilities the option value is nearly perfectly linear. Nonetheless, it is evidence of an important feature of the Black-Scholes model, i.e., that it provides an excellent approximation to the value of an option with variable volatility as long as the mathematical expectation of the volatility is known.

Although *Mathematica*'s powerful and convenient graphics provide a qualitative insight into the Black-Scholes, the quantitative application of the model, especially to the area of risk management, is facilitated by applying the symbolic manipulation capabilities of *Mathematica* directly to the Black-Scholes formula. Such risk management applications are the focus of the next section.

12.3   Risk Management Using the Black-Scholes Model

The Black-Scholes model is useful not only because it provides a closed-form expression for the value of an option, but also because the sensitivity of the model to changes in its parameters, as represented by (partial) derivatives of the option valuation formula, can be expressed in closed form. The most important parameter that affects the value of an option is the price of the underlying stock. The partial derivative of option value with respect to stock price is known as *delta*.

Delta is a useful measurement of risk for an option because it indicates how much the price of the option will respond to a $1 change in the price of the stock.

For call options, delta can range from 0 to 1, i.e., the option may be insensitive to change in the stock price, may track it exactly, or may lie somewhere in between. Delta is a particularly useful gauge of the risk contained in a portfolio that contains more than one option on a given stock. In particular, the theoretical risk associated with the holding of a stock will be completely neutralized (in the very short run) if the overall dollar-weighted delta of a portfolio of options on that stock is equal to zero. This is because the portfolio delta gives change in portfolio value for a $1 change in stock price, which is zero in this case. However, because delta is a partial derivative it assumes that all other variables are held constant and the change in stock price is relatively small, which will usually not be the case over even a short period of time. Additional measures of risk that either are derived later in this section or are contained in the accompanying *Mathematica* package can help the reader to get a handle on other changes that can influence option value.

Using the derivative function, **D**, that is built into *Mathematica*, it is easy to calculate symbolically any derivative of the **BlackScholes** function, including delta. Before these derivatives can be defined, however, it is first necessary to supply *Mathematica* with the derivative of the **Norm** function, since only the numerical value of Norm was provided above and its derivative frequently figures into derivatives of **BlackScholes**. In *Mathematica*, the derivative of Norm is defined as follows:

```
In[1]:= Norm'[z_] = N[(1/Sqrt[2 Pi])] Exp[-z^2/2]
Out[1]:= 0.398942
           ─────────
                2
              z /2
             E
```

The leading constant in the definition of this derivative is expressed as a number rather than being left in terms of **Pi** to ensure that full numerical conversion occurs when derivatives of the Black-Scholes formula are evaluated for a particular set of parameter values.

Then, the function that computes delta, **Delta**, becomes:

```
In[2]:= Delta[p_,k_,sd_,r_,t_] = D[BlackScholes[p,k,sd,r,t],p]
Out[2]:=
        0.398942 / (E (0.5 sd Sqrt[t] + (r t + Log[p/k]) /

                                  2
          (sd Sqrt[t])) /2

        sd Sqrt[t]) - (0.398942 Power[E, -(r t) -

                                             p
                              r t + Log[-]
                                             k   2
          (-0.5 sd Sqrt[t] + ──────────────)
                              sd Sqrt[t]
        ──────────────────────────────────────────] k) /
                            2
```

Out[2] (cont.)

$$(p\ sd\ Sqrt[t]) + Norm[0.5\ sd\ Sqrt[t] + \frac{r\ t + Log[\frac{p}{k}]}{sd\ Sqrt[t]}]$$

The assignment statement that defines **Delta**, like the one that defined **BlackScholes**, generates a formula for delta directly. It should be noted that the evaluation mechanism in *Mathematica* does not always generate formulas in their simplest form and, indeed, the expression output for **Delta** (and some other derivatives of **BlackScholes**) could be further simplified in the interests of computational efficiency as it is actually equal to Norm[AuxBS[p,k,sd, r,t].

When **Delta** is applied to the situation given above, we get the following:

In[3]:= **Delta[58.5,60.,0.29,0.04,0.3]**
Out[3]:= 0.498235

Hence, for a $1 increase in DEC stock, the price of this call option will increase by about 50 cents.

A plot of **Delta** against stock price provides a fundamental insight into option valuation as follows:

In[4]:= **Plot[Delta[x,60.,0.29,0.04,0.3],{x,20.,100.}]**

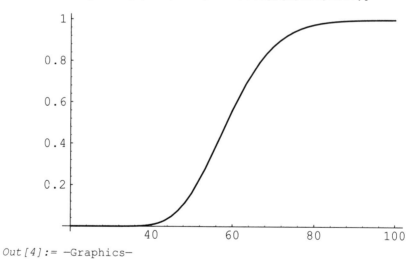

Out[4]:= —Graphics—

For very low stock prices, i.e., when the call option is very much *out of the money*, delta is virtually zero indicating that the value of the option, which is also virtually zero, is insensitive to changes in the stock price because even a modest increase will have little effect of the likely outcome that the option will expire worthless. For very high stock prices, i.e., when the option is very much *in the money*, delta approaches one because the increase in the stock price dollar for dollar translates into an expected increase in the value of the option at expiration.

Other aspects of option value are as easy to investigate as delta using the symbolic math features of *Mathematica*. The sensitivity of the value of an option to time, *theta*, is derived as easily as delta was as follows:

$In[5]:=$ **Theta[p_,k_,sd_,r_,t_] = -D[BlackScholes[p,k,sd,r,t],t]**

$Out[5]:=$

$$0.398942 \; \text{Power}\left[E, \; -(r\,t) - \frac{\left(-0.5\;sd\;\text{Sqrt}[t] + \frac{r\,t + \text{Log}[\frac{p}{k}]}{sd\;\text{Sqrt}[t]}\right)^2}{2}\right] k$$

$$\left(\frac{r}{sd\;\text{Sqrt}[t]} - \frac{0.25\;sd}{\text{Sqrt}[t]} - \frac{r\,t + \text{Log}[\frac{p}{k}]}{2\;sd\;t^{3/2}}\right) -$$

$$\frac{0.398942\;p\;\left(\frac{r}{sd\;\text{Sqrt}[t]} + \frac{0.25\;sd}{\text{Sqrt}[t]} - \frac{r\,t + \text{Log}[\frac{p}{k}]}{2\;sd\;t^{3/2}}\right)}{E^{(0.5\;sd\;\text{Sqrt}[t] + (r\,t + \text{Log}[p/k])/(sd\;\text{Sqrt}[t]))^2/2}} -$$

$$\frac{k\;r\;\text{Norm}\left[-0.5\;sd\;\text{Sqrt}[t] + \frac{r\,t + \text{Log}[\frac{p}{k}]}{sd\;\text{Sqrt}[t]}\right]}{E^{r\,t}}$$

$In[6]:=$ **Plot[Theta[x,60.,0.29,0.04,0.3],{x,20.,100.}]**

$Out[6]:=$ *-Graphics-*

By convention theta is taken to be the negative of the derivative with respect to time to expiration because moving forward in clock time decreases the time to expiration, hence theta gives the instantaneous change in the value of the option as time passes and all other parameters are unchanged. Because an option is more valuable the greater the time until expiration, theta is always negative. As the above plot clearly demonstrates, the time decay in the value of an option tends to be greatest when the stock price is close to the exercise price; however, as time passes this decay becomes more uniform across stock prices as the following 3D graph demonstrates:

```
In[7]:= Plot3D[Theta[x,60.,0.29,0.04,y],{x,20.,100.},
                                          {y,0.01,0.5},
              ViewPoint->{0.520, -3.420, 1.810}]
```

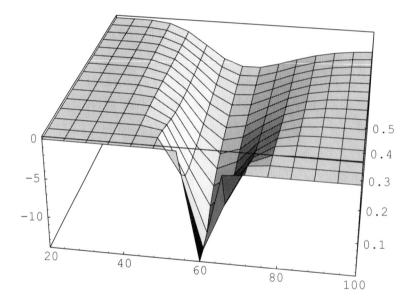

```
Out[7]:= —SurfaceGraphics—
```

As was mentioned at the beginning of this section, the partial derivatives of the Black-Scholes formula can also be applied to an entire portfolio of options to determine the sensitivity of the value of the portfolio to changes in any or all of the variables that underlie the formula.

On a related note, in situations where an option's price is believed to be an accurate indication of its value, it can be desirable to "reverse engineer" the volatility of an option from its market price. The function **ImpliedVolatility** uses the built-in function **FindRoot** to solve numerically for the volatility of an option given its price as follows:

```
In[8]:= ImpliedVolatility[p_,k_,r_,t_,optionprice_] :=
            sd /. FindRoot[BlackScholes[p,k,sd,r,t]==
                           optionprice,{sd,0.2}]
```

Hence, if we knew the price of the DEC option given above was 3.34886 we could verify that the volatility is 0.29 as follows:

```
In[9]:= ImpliedVolatility[58.5,60.,0.04,0.3,3.34886]

Out[9]:= 0.29
```

Implied volatility is an extremely useful way of looking at options; indeed, some options on foreign currencies and other financial instruments are frequently quoted in terms of their implied volatility rather than by price, much as bonds are quoted by yield rather than price. There are many trading strategies that are designed to go either long or short volatility while limiting risk using the techniques described above.

As with any other group of related functions in *Mathematica*, the functions associated with the Black-Scholes model can be collected into a single *Mathematica* package that accompanies this book. The public part of this package, which appears before the `Begin["`private`"]` statement, provides access to these functions, as well as to a small database described later. This package includes not only the functions defined in this chapter but additional functions for popular measures of option value sensitivity—`theta`, `kappa`, `rho`, `gamma`, and (stock price) `elasticity`.

12.4   Options as Objects

Mathematica provides not only numerical and symbolic manipulation capabilities for formulas, it also provides the basic tools needed to treat options and option-based securities as self-contained objects and to make the action of function depend on the type of object to which it is applied. Although the object manipulation capabilities of *Mathematica* fall short of those provided by object-oriented design toolkits, the core facilities for object creation and data abstraction are contained within *Mathematica*. This section will develop the tools for representing options as objects and the following section will exploit this representation to develop the technology for having a single **Value** function that is capable of evaluating a variety of options and other securities.

We will start by showing how the DEC call option (and its underlying DEC stock) can be represented as objects in *Mathematica*. The distinguishing features of a computational object are its *properties*. For example, the properties of the DEC option, `DECFL`, are that it is a call option on DEC stock, has an exercise price of $60 and expires in June, which we have assumed to be 0.3 of a year away. In *Mathematica*, we can link these properties to the symbol `DECFL` as follows:

```
In[1]:= Type[DECFL]         ^= "call" ;
        Asset[DECFL]        ^= DEC ;
        ExercisePrice[DECFL] ^= 60. ;
        ExpirationTime[DECFL] ^= 0.3 ;
```

The operator `^=` is the known as **UpSet** and is used to make sure that *Mathematica* associates the value assignment with the "upvalue" `DECFL` rather than the head of the left-hand side of the assignments as it normally would. It is easy to check that these properties have been associated with DECFL as follows:

```
In[2]:= ?DECFL
Global`DECFL

Asset[DECFL] ^= DEC

ExercisePrice[DECFL] ^= 60.

ExpirationTime[DECFL] ^= 0.3

Type[DECFL] ^= "call"
```

As a convenience we will define an object constructor function, **ConsObj**, that takes a symbol and property list as its arguments:

```
In[3]:= ConsObj[obj_,proplist_] :=
            Do[Block[{propname=proplist[[2*i-1]],
                      propval=proplist[[2*i]]},
                     propname[obj]^=propval],
               {i,Length[proplist]/2}]
```

The object, DECFL, can now be constructed as follows:

```
In[4]:= ConsObj[DECFL,{Type,"call",
                       Asset,DEC,
                       ExercisePrice,60.,
                       ExpirationTime,0.3}]
```

Notice that not all of the information needed to value the DECFL option is contained in its object description. In particular, the price and volatility of DEC stock are properties that must be "inherited" from the object representation of the stock. This object, DEC, can be constructed as follows:

```
In[5]:= ConsObj[DEC,{Type,"stock",
                     Price,58.5,
                     Volatility,0.29}]
General::spell1:
   Possible spelling error: new symbol name "Price"
     is similar to existing symbol "Prime".
```

The properties of the DEC object are stored in *Mathematica* as follows:

```
In[6]:= ?DEC
Global`DEC

Price[DEC] ^= 58.5

Type[DEC] ^= "stock"

Volatility[DEC] ^= 0.29
```

Of course, these properties of the DECFL option that come from the underlying stock are not inherited automatically; *Mathematica* needs assignment rules to facilitate this inheritance as follows:

```
In[7]:= AssetPrice[option_] := (AssetPrice[option] ^=
                                   Price[Asset[option]]);
        AssetVolatility[option_] := (AssetVolatility[option] ^=
                                   Volatility[Asset[option]])
```

This form for the assignment ensures that *Mathematica* associates the value with the option rather than the function. We can now test that these two new properties of the DECFL option have been properly inherited:

```
In[8]:= AssetPrice[DECFL]
```

```
Out[8]:= 58.5
```

```
In[9]:= AssetVolatility[DECFL]
```

```
Out[9]:= 0.29
```

Checking the values now associated with DECFL, we can see that these two new properties are listed:

```
In[10]:= ?DECFL
Global`DECFL

Asset[DECFL] ^= DEC

AssetPrice[DECFL] ^= 58.5
   OptionValue`private`Price[OptionValue`private`Asset[DECFL]]

AssetVolatility[DECFL] ^= 0.29
   OptionValue`private`Volatility[OptionValue`private`Asset[DECFL]]

ExercisePrice[DECFL] ^= 60.

ExpirationTime[DECFL] ^= 0.3

Type[DECFL] ^= "call"
```

As noted above, *Mathematica* does not provide a full object-oriented design environment so these new "properties" are not generated automatically, but become part of the object description after their first use.

The final piece of information necessary to evaluate DECFL is the risk-free rate of return. Because this rate is assumed to be constant and can be applied to all options, it makes sense to define it as a global variable as follows:

```
In[11]:= RiskFreeRate = 0.04
```

```
Out[11]:= 0.04
```

It is now a simple matter to define a value function that takes an option's symbol as its argument and retrieves the necessary information to apply the Black-Scholes function defined above:

```
In[12]:= Value[option_] := BlackScholes[AssetPrice[option],
                              ExercisePrice[option],
                              AssetVolatility[option],
                              RiskFreeRate,
                              ExpirationTime[option]]
```

```
General::spell1:
   Possible spelling error: new symbol name "Value"
      is similar to existing symbol "ValueQ".
```

We can now demonstrate that **Value** actually works when applied to DECFL:

In[13]:= **Value[DECFL]**

Out[13]:= 3.34886

Of course, the Black-Scholes formula only applies to a limited number of options. In the next section we will look at other option valuation methods that can be applied to options in general, including put options, and see how the Value function can be appropriately extended.

12.5   Valuing Options with Financial Decision Trees

When considering options for which the Black-Scholes model is not designed, e.g., American put options (options to sell that can be exercised early), there is usually no closed-form solution and closed-form approximations are frequently inadequate. The source of the problem is that the continuous-time techniques used to derive the Black-Scholes formula no longer apply when the option valuation path can be disrupted by early exercise. Nonetheless, the symbol manipulation features of *Mathematica* can still be used to great advantage. This section will contain a brief survey of these techniques and how they might be implemented in *Mathematica*. These methods are sufficiently general that they may not only be applied to virtually any kind of option, but also apply to securities with embedded options, such as callable and convertible bonds and many kinds of mortgage-backed securities. Less ambitious extensions, such as options on dividend-paying stocks, can be readily incorporated into this framework. A more detailed survey of these techniques is contained in the author's book *Computer-Aided Financial Analysis*, where they were originally developed in LISP (Miller, 1990a).

The key to solving general financial valuation problems that is introduced in this chapter is what the author has called *financial decision trees*. These trees are a generalization of the decision trees used in traditional decision analysis. The key extension of decision trees that is introduced in this section is dynamic discounting that is applied as one traverses the tree. A further extension (Miller, 1990a) also handles cash flows that occur at any node in the decision tree. The advantage that financial decision trees hold over traditional decision trees is both representational and computational. Imbedding discounting and cash flows in the tree itself rather than imputing them to terminal nodes, which is the only way to take them into account in the traditional approach, minimizes the amount of computation required to both represent and evaluate the decision tree that represents a given option or financial instrument.

In this section we will focus on an American put option on DEC stock with identical properties to those of the DECFL call option presented earlier except for the fact that it is a put option and has the symbol, DECQL. Recall that a put option is an option to sell stock at a given exercise price, in this case $60. As we saw earlier, the payoff function for a put is the opposite of that for a call; it is zero for prices above the exercise price and it has a slope of -1 for prices below the exercise price. The **ConsObj** function can be used to create the object DECQL as follows:

```
In[1]:= ConsObj[DECQL,{Type,"put",
                Asset,DEC,
                ExercisePrice,60.,
                ExpirationTime,0.3}]
```

```
General::spell1:
   Possible spelling error: new symbol name "DECQL"
      is similar to existing symbol "DECFL".
```

Of course, if we were to apply the **Value** function in its current form to DECQL it would have no way of dealing with the fact that it was a put and not a call; therefore, it is good to create a property for options that affects how they are valued. We will use **ExerciseFunction** to store the payoff function and define it as follows:

```
In[2]:= ExerciseFunction[option_] := CallPayoff /;
                                Type[option]=="call"

        ExerciseFunction[option_] := PutPayoff /;
                                Type[option]=="put"
```

Hence, for our new put option we have:

```
In[3]:= ExerciseFunction[DECQL]
```

```
General::spell1:
   Possible spelling error: new symbol name "DECQL"
      is similar to existing symbol "DECFL".
```

```
Out[3]:= ExerciseFunction[DECQL]
```

With an American put option it is quite possible that the value of the underlying stock can drop low enough that the natural upward drift of the stock price will make it profitable to exercise the option early. Indeed, a significant component of the put option's value can be associated with the potential for early exercise. The simplest way to model the option that enables one to consider the possibility of early exercise explicitly is the *binominal model*. The binomial model divides the time until expiration into a number of equal time periods and over each time segment considers two possibilities, that the stock move either up in price by a fixed proportion or down in price by a fixed proportion. The size of the up and down movements as well as their probability can be chosen so that in the limit as the number of periods approaches infinity, the distribution of prices will converge to the lognormal distribution used in the Black-Scholes model. The derivation of these up and down movements and their probabilities is given in Hull (1989) and are used here within further discussion.

As with the Black-Scholes model, the value of the option is known at expiration and can be determined recursively by working backwards until the present is reached. The difference is that at each point in time the potential advantage of exercising the option immediately must be considered.

The approach that we will take to computing the binomial model is to embed it in a more general framework that can handle far more complex options. This framework casts the process by which stock prices change and the option holder considers his or her alternatives at each point in time as a financial decision tree. Although every option valuation method may generate a different financial decision tree, every tree can be evaluated using the same **TreeValue** function. Hence, the process for valuing an option will be to convert it into a tree and then evaluate that tree.

The conversion of an American option into a financial decision tree is performed with the **MakeAmerTree** function which is defined as follows:

```
In[4]:= MakeAmerTree[option_,n_:4] :=
              Block[{ChanceSymbol = Unique["cnode"],
              DecisionSymbol = Unique["dnode"],
              s  = AssetPrice[option],
              k  = ExercisePrice[option],
              ex = ExerciseFunction[option],
              t  = ExpirationTime[option],
              sd = AssetVolatility[option] Sqrt[t/n] // N,
              a  = Exp[RiskFreeRate t/n] // N,
              u  = Exp[sd],
              d  = 1/u},
              ConsObj[Evaluate[ChanceSymbol],
                    {Type,"chance",
                    Dfactor,1/a,
                    Upamt,u,
                    Downamt,d,
                    Upprob,(a-d)/(u-d) // N,
                    ExercisePrice,k,
                    ExerciseFunction,ex,
                    Succsym,DecisionSymbol}];
              ConsObj[Evaluate[DecisionSymbol],
                    {Type,"decision",
                     ExercisePrice,k,
                     ExerciseFunction,ex,
                     Succsym,ChanceSymbol}];
              node[ChanceSymbol,s,n,1]]
```

This rather imposing function is essentially a list of ingredients needed to build a financial decision tree for an American option. It starts by using the built-in *Mathematica* function **Unique** to create symbols for the two types of nodes in the tree, chance nodes, which reflect the up and down movement in the stock price, and decision nodes, which reflect the ability of the optionholder to choose whether or not to exercise the option. The **ConsObj** function is then used to assign the properties needed by chance and decision nodes to their symbols, ChanceSymbol and DecisionSymbol, respectively. Finally, it creates the seed of the tree as an expression with **node** as its head and the beginning state of the financial decision tree, including the stock price and period remaining as its body. For expository purposes, **MakeAmerTree** defaults to four periods, which is enough to understand what it is doing, but not enough for an accurate valuation, which can require ten or more periods.

Let us dive into things by applying **MakeAmerTree** to DECQL as follows:

```
In[5]:= DECQLTree = MakeAmerTree[DECQL]

Out[5]:= node[cnode1, 58.5, 4, 1]
```

Hence, we start the tree at a chance node called cnode1 at a stock price of 58.5 with 4 periods to go and a "weight" of 1. (The weight only provides useful information at decision nodes, as we shall see.) To find out where we can proceed from this *root node*, we need a **Successors** function that derives a list of successors to both chance and decision nodes. Here is the definition of that function for each type of node:

```
In[6]:= Successors[node[symbol_,price_,left_,weight_]] :=
        {node[Succsym[symbol],
              Upamt[symbol]*price,left-1,
              Upprob[symbol]],
         node[Succsym[symbol],
              Downamt[symbol]*price,left-1,
              1-Upprob[symbol]]}  /;   Type[symbol]=="chance" ;

        Successors[node[symbol_,price_,left_,weight_]] :=
        {node[Succsym[symbol],
              price,
              left,
              1],
         node[Succsym[symbol],
              price,
              0,
              1]}                      /; Type[symbol]=="decision"
```

We can then simply apply the **Successors** function to the root node, DEC-QLTree and see what happens:

```
In[7]:= Successors[DECQLTree]
Out[7]:= {node[dnode1, 63.3355, 3, 0.499051],
          node[dnode1, 54.0336, 3, 0.500949]}
```

The successors of this chance node are two decision nodes, both with the symbol dnode1, but reflecting different states of nature. The first decision node corresponds to a DEC stock price of 63.3355, which will occur with a probability/weight of 0.499051. The second decison node corresponds to a DEC stock price of 54.0336 which will occur with a probability/weight of 0.5000949. The "rolling of the dice" associated with the chance node also consumed one period, leaving three to go.

As a quick exercise we can also look directly at the successors of the first decision node as follows:

```
In[8]:= Successors[First[Successors[DECQLTree]]]
Out[8]:= {node[cnode1, 63.3355, 3, 1],
          node[cnode1, 63.3355, 0, 1]}
```

At a decison node, we are given a choice of continuing to hold the option, leaving periods left set to three, or exercising the option by setting the periods left to zero.

The function **TreeValue** automates the process of generating successors and simultaneously computes the mathematical expectation for each chance node and chooses the maximum expected payoff for each decision node. This function and its two auxiliary functions, **Prob** and **Expectation**, are defined as follows:

```
In[9]:= TreeValue[node[symbol_,price_,left_,weight_]] :=
        (TreeValue[node[symbol,price,left,weight]]
          = Which[left==0,
             ExerciseFunction[symbol] [price,ExercisePrice[symbol]],
            Type[symbol]=="chance",
             Dfactor[symbol] *
              Expectation[Successors[node[symbol,price,left,weight]]],
            Type[symbol]=="decision",
             Max[TreeValue[Successors[node[symbol,price,left,weight]]]]]);

        SetAttributes[TreeValue,Listable]

        Prob[node_] := node[[4]] ; SetAttributes[Prob,Listable]

        Expectation[nodelist_] := Dot[Prob[nodelist],
                                      TreeValue[nodelist]]
```

The **TreeValue** function uses **Which** to distinguish three situations, terminal nodes (left==0), chance nodes, and decision nodes. **TreeValue** is designed to remember old values so that dynamic programming is employed to reduce the number of evaluations that are required. The downside of this approach is that without additional memory management, memory will tend to fill with the results of old option valuations.

Now that **TreeValue** has been defined we can apply it to DECQLTree as follows:

```
In[10]:= TreeValue[DECQLTree]

Out[10]:= 4.27628
```

We can get a more accurate value by expanding the size of the tree that is generated as follows:

```
In[11]:= TreeValue[MakeAmerTree[DECQL,8]]

Out[11]:= 4.26538
```

Finally, we can return to the **Value** function introduced at the end of the previous section and extend its definition to handle all American options on stock that do not pay dividends as follows:

```
In[12]:= Value[option_] := BlackScholes[AssetPrice[option],
                                        ExercisePrice[option],
                                        AssetVolatility[option],
                                        RiskFreeRate,
                                        ExpirationTime[option]] /;
                           Type[option]=="call"

          Value[option_] := TreeValue[MakeAmerTree[option,8]] /;
                                      Type[option]=="put"
```

This function will now simply apply the Black-Scholes formula to call options and will grow and evaluate a binomial tree for put options. Hence, we can apply it to the two DEC options as follows:

```
In[13]:= Value[DECFL]

Out[13]:= 3.34886

In[14]:= Value[DECQL]

Out[14]:= 4.27374
```

12.6   Concluding Remarks

This chapter has provided an extensive introduction to closed-form and numerical approaches to option valuation using *Mathematica*. Because of its versatile nature, *Mathematica* is well-suited to the large variety of techniques that may be needed to value options and securities with option components to them. The motivated reader will find it easy to use *Mathematica* to extend the basic methods developed here to the wide range of option valuation techniques that have been developed in the financial literature. Elsewhere (Miller, 1991) the author has addressed the problem of additional ways of using rule-based methods to extend and build a more "intelligent" object-oriented valuation function.

12.7   References

Black, Fisher, and Myron Scholes. 1973. "The Pricing of Options and Corporate Liabilities," *Journal of Political Economy*, **81**, 637–659.

Cox, John C., and Mark Rubinstein. 1985. *Options Markets*: Englewood Cliffs, NJ, Prentice-Hall.

Hull, John. 1989. *Options, Futures and Other Derivative Securities*: Englewood Cliffs, NJ, Prentice-Hall.

Miller, Ross M. 1990a. *Computer-Aided Financial Analysis*: Reading, MA, Addison-Wesley.

Miller, Ross M. 1990b. "Computer-Aided Financial Analysis: An Implementation of the Black-Scholes Model," *Mathematica Journal*, **1**, 75–79.

Miller, Ross M. 1991. "An Intelligent Approach to Financial Valuation," *Proceedings of the First International Conference on Artificial Intelligence Applications on Wall Street*, IEEE Press.

13 Nonlinear Systems Estimation: Asset Pricing Model Application

Stephen J. Brown

13.1 Introduction

In this chapter we consider the application of *Mathematica* in the context of estimating a simultaneous system of nonlinear equations. The particular application involves the estimation of asset pricing models. This subject is a staple of the financial economics literature. The objective is not to show how *Mathematica* can be used to solve problems of this type. Indeed, the program is not well suited to this kind of large scale numerical optimization. Rather, the intent is to show how *Mathematica* can be used in conjunction with more specialized software products for this purpose.

13.2 Nonlinear Systems Estimation

A simultaneous system of nonlinear equations can be represented as

$$y_{it} = h_i(X_t, \theta_i) + e_{it}, \quad 1, \ldots, M \tag{1}$$

A straightforward approach to estimating the vector of parameters, θ, is nonlinear least squares. A quadratic criterion function in the errors, e_t is defined

$$Criterion_{LS} = \sum_{t=1}^{T} e_t' W e_t \tag{2}$$

and minimized for choice of parameters θ. The resulting estimator is consistent and asymptotically normal. If we choose the weighting matrix W to be the inverse of the covariance matrix of the errors e_t the estimator is also efficient.[1]

The nonlinear least squares estimator is also the maximum likelihood estimator where we assume that the vector of errors is multivariate normal and

---

[1] Both this and other properties of the nonlinear least squares estimator are discussed in Goldfeld and Quandt [1972].

independent through time. The logarithm of the likelihood function for a particular observation is

$$\ln \mathcal{L}(\theta \,|e) = -\frac{M}{2} \ln(2\pi) - \frac{1}{2} \ln |\Sigma| - \frac{1}{2} e_t' \Sigma^{-1} e_t \tag{3}$$

Assuming independence, the logarithm of the likelihood function is then

$$\ln \mathcal{L}(\theta \mid e) = -\frac{MT}{2} \ln(2\pi) - \frac{T}{2} \ln |\Sigma| - \frac{1}{2} \sum_{t=1}^{T} e_t' \Sigma^{-1} e_t \tag{4}$$

which is maximized by minimizing the criterion function (2).[2]

We can relax the distributional assumptions and estimate the parameters using the Generalized Method of Moments. In this case the criterion function is given by

$$Criterion_{GMM} = g'Wg \tag{5}$$

where

$$g = \frac{1}{T} \sum_{t=1}^{T} e_t \otimes Z_t \tag{6}$$

is a vector of moments conditional on a set of instruments, Z_t, and W is an appropriately designed weighting matrix.[3]

Similar computational procedures are used to evaluate maximum likelihood and generalized method of moments estimators. First, initial values of the weighting matrix W are specified. This matrix is assumed either to be proportional to the identity matrix, or to equal the inverse of the covariance matrix estimated without imposing the overidentifying restrictions of the model. Nonlinear optimization procedures are used to minimize the respective criterion functions over the space of the parameters. Resulting estimates of the parameters are used to evaluate the errors e_t which are then used to obtain second pass estimates of the weighting matrix. The sequence of nonlinear estimation and updating of weighting matrices proceeds until convergence is reached.

There are many numerical optimization algorithms that can be used to minimize (2) or (5).[4] A general characteristic of such algorithms is that they are iterative in nature. An initial value of the parameter vector is specified, and is successively updated according to the formula

$$New\ \theta \ = \ Old\ \theta \ + \ stepsize \ \times \ direction[Old\ \theta] \tag{7}$$

---

[2] This is true where the covariance matrix Σ is given. The necessary conditions for a full information maximum likelihood estimator of this parameter establish that it is proportional to the residual covariance matrix evaluated at the maximum likelihood estimators of the other parameters. This justifies the use of iterated seemingly unrelated regression procedures which successively update the covariance matrix on the basis of parameter estimates from the previous iteration.

[3] For a discussion of this estimator see Hansen and Singleton [1982].

[4] For an excellent introduction to these methods, see Greene [1990] pp. 363–377. A standard text is Luenberger [1984].

while at each step, a convergence test is applied. A common algorithm used for maximum likelihood problems is Newton's method. If we write the first order conditions for a minimum criterion function

$$\frac{\partial Criterion}{\partial \theta} = 0 \tag{8}$$

in a first order Taylor expansion around some arbitrary value of the parameter vector

$$\frac{\partial Criterion}{\partial \theta} \simeq \left. \frac{\partial Criterion}{\partial \theta} \right|_{\bar{\theta}} + \left. \frac{\partial^2 Criterion}{\partial \theta \partial \theta'} \right|_{\bar{\theta}} (\theta - \bar{\theta}) = 0, \tag{9}$$

this implies the iteration given in Equation (7) for unit stepsize, and direction

$$direction[\bar{\theta}] = H \left. \frac{\partial Criterion}{\partial \theta} \right|_{\bar{\theta}} \tag{10}$$

where

$$H = - \left\{ \left. \frac{\partial^2 Criterion}{\partial \theta \partial \theta'} \right|_{\bar{\theta}} \right\}^{-1}. \tag{11}$$

The required matrix of second order partial derivatives is often difficult to compute. Moreover, it may even not be positive definite for an arbitrary choice of the parameter vector. There are a variety of derivative-based procedures that approximate this matrix in such a way as to ensure that it is positive definite. Some do not use the second derivatives at all. These derivatives are approximated by outer products of the sequence of first-order derivatives computed in the course of the iterations. Still other procedures modify the step size in Equation (7). No one procedure is guaranteed to be optimal for the class of all nonlinear estimation problems. Fortunately, most econometric software packages offer the user a choice of algorithms. One package, GAUSS$_{TM}$,[5] allows the user to change the algorithm in the course of the iterations.

There remains the problem of evaluating a vector of partial derivatives, perhaps many times. Most econometric software products that provide for estimation of nonlinear systems of equations allow these derivatives to be computed numerically. For some packages, this is the only option.[6] GAUSS$_{TM}$ provides the user the option of specifying the analytic derivatives. While it is generally recognized that analytic derivatives are to be preferred, both for accuracy and speed, these derivatives are usually very tedious to compute for most nonlinear systems estimation problems. An example of some practical significance arises in the estimation of equity asset pricing models. The required derivatives are many in number and are complicated expressions involving parameters and data. The task of computing these derivatives is an ideal application of *Mathematica*.

---

[5] The version we shall be referring to is the Optimization and Maximum Likelihood Applications Package, Version 2.01, Aptech Systems (1990).

[6] For example, the SYSNLIN procedure of SAS/ETS®, SAS Institute 1984, and the NLSYSTEM instruction of RATS, Thomas A. Doan 1992.

13.3 Equity Asset Pricing Models

13.3.1 Introduction

The purpose of estimating asset pricing models is to describe the tradeoff of risk for return in the capital market in such a way as to characterize the cross sectional dispersion in returns investors require from investment in different equity securities. This exercise has relevance for measuring and controlling for risk in an investment management context, as well as for determining the required return on equity in a corporate financial planning context.

The general approach to estimating asset pricing models usually proceeds in three stages. In the first stage, pervasive factors that influence returns on all securities are either specified or estimated. In early work,[7] the pervasive factor was the return on a value weighted index of traded securities, such as the S&P500 market index. Later work expanded the set of factors to consider factors specified by factor analysis (Roll and Ross, 1980), principle components (Connor and Korajczyk, 1988), and innovations from macroeconomic time series (Chen, Roll, and Ross, 1986). In the second stage, time series analysis is used to determine the sensitivity of security returns to the pervasive factor or factors. In an asset pricing model framework, these sensitivities are measures of exposure to risk. In the third stage, cross section analysis is used to estimate risk premia, the compensation in return per unit risk measured by factor sensitivity.

Since the output of each stage is used as the input to the succeeding stage, it is natural to be concerned about the effect of measurement errors on the analysis. Brown and Weinstein (1983) suggest that a systems estimation approach would resolve this issue. This approach has been implemented by McElroy and Burmeister (1988). They estimate factors using innovations from macroeconomic time series, and then apply a systems estimation approach to estimate factor sensitivities and risk premia simultaneously. The systems estimation can be performed using standard nonlinear seemingly unrelated regression algorithms available in the SAS/ETS® econometric software package.

The systems estimation approach can be extended to consider estimating the innovations process and the asset pricing model simultaneously. This would combine all three stages into one. In this way, information from asset prices as well as macroeconomic time series can be used to identify the factors. The model can be further extended to consider deterministic changes in risk premia. These extensions are quite straightforward.

13.3.2 An Example

The equity asset pricing model we use as an example is a generic form of the asset pricing model. It is consistent with both Capital Asset Pricing Model and

---

[7] Representative examples being Black, Jensen, and Scholes (1971) and Fama and MacBeth (1974).

Arbitrage Pricing Theory paradigms, and in addition, allows for the possibility of time-varying risk premia. In this model, the observed risk premium for a security is made up of two components: the expected risk premium and risk factors. The risk factors are further subdivided into macrofactor risk and security specific components. The sensitivity to these sources of macrofactor risk (or β) determine the expected risk premium:

$$R_{ti} = \lambda_{t0} + \lambda_{t1}\beta_{1i} + \cdots + \lambda_{tk}\beta_{ki} + f_{t1}\beta_{1i} + \cdots + f_{tk}\beta_{ki} + \nu_{ti} \qquad (12)$$

where f_{kt} is the kth source of macrofactor risk, and λ_{kt} is the expected risk premium in period t per unit of exposure to the kth source of macrofactor risk. The factors f_{it} are understood to have zero mean as of the start of period t. If we consider the rate of return on the ith security rate of return to be in excess of the return on some reference asset, the risk factors β are interpreted as in excess of the reference asset, and the λ_{t0} shall equal zero. The intertemporal version of the asset pricing model implies that the risk premium elements will themselves depend on macroeconomic factors (or *instruments*) known at the beginning of period t. If these relationships are linear

$$\lambda_{tj} = \alpha_{1j}X_{t1} + \alpha_{2j}X_{t2} + \cdots + \alpha_{mj}X_{tm} \qquad (13)$$

then the relationship between equity returns and factors can be represented

$$R_{ti} = \rho_{1i}X_{t1} + \cdots + \rho_{mi}X_{tm} + f_{t1}\beta_{1i} + \cdots + f_{tk}\beta_{ki} + \nu_{ti} \qquad (14)$$

Equation (14) provides a very simple representation of the process generating security returns. The β_{ji} coefficients describe the exposure of equity index i to macro factor risk j, and the ρ coefficients describe the way that expected returns vary systematically through time. Ordinary least squares provides efficient estimates of these parameters given a set of predefined factors f, and vector of instruments X.

To understand the nature of the asset pricing constraints, it is helpful to express equations (12) through (14) in a convenient matrix notation:

$$R_t = \lambda_{0t} + \lambda_t B + f_t B + \nu_t \qquad (15)$$
$$\lambda_t = X_t \alpha \qquad (16)$$

and

$$R_t = X_t \rho + f_t B + \nu_t \qquad (17)$$

where we set λ_{t0} equal to zero. The asset pricing model implies

$$\rho = \alpha B \qquad (18)$$

In addition, the factors f_t are not known but have to be estimated. Suppose we represent these factors as the innovations derived from a vector of macro variables y_t

$$f_t = y_t - Z_t \gamma \qquad (19)$$

where Z_t represents a vector of instruments known as of the start of period t.

The constraints of the asset pricing model, combined with the necessity to estimate the factors, f, implies the following nonlinear system of equations[8] obtained by substituting Equations (18) and (19) into (17):

$$y_t = Z_t\gamma + f_t$$
$$R_t = [X_t\alpha + y_t - Z_t\gamma]B + \nu_t \tag{20}$$

This system of equations can be estimated using maximum likelihood assuming that the errors f_t and ν_t are joint-Normally distributed. It is possible to relax this assumption and estimate the system of equations using the Generalized Method of Moments, at some loss in the precision of the estimates obtained.

McElroy and Burmeister (1988) suggest incorporating a residual market factor f_0 as the 0th factor. This factor can be thought of as a residual factor not explained by the set of predefined macro variables. The existence of such a factor allows the Capital Asset Pricing Model and related Multibeta models to be consistent with the Arbitrage Pricing Model estimated using such a multi-factor model. This factor can be defined by aggregating Equation (17) using an appropriate set of market weights

$$f_{0t} = R_{mt} - [X_t\rho_m + f_tB_m] \tag{21}$$

The inclusion of a residual market factor defines the equation system:

$$y_t = Z_t\gamma + f_t$$
$$R_{mt} = X_t\rho_m + [y_t - Z_t\gamma]B_m + f_{0t} \tag{22}$$
$$R_t = X_t[\alpha B + \alpha_m\beta_0] + [y_t - Z_t\gamma]B + (R_{mt} - X_t\rho_m - [y_t - Z_t\gamma]B_m)\beta_0 + \nu_t$$

where f_t, f_{0t}, and ν_t are zero mean errors. This is the system of equations that we estimate. The first and second equations define the macro factors and residual market factors respectively, where Z_t represents the set of instruments X_t augmented by past values of y_t. The third equation shows how equity returns relate to instrumental variables and the various risk factors. The first term gives the risk premium as a function of the instrumental variables X. The second shows how returns depend on the risk factors defined in the first equation. The third term gives the influence of the residual market factor on individual security returns.

13.3.3   Systems Estimation Considerations

While the equation system (22) is a general representation of an asset pricing model that allows for a time varying component to the risk premiums, we

---

[8] This system of equations is similar to one provided by Ferson [1990]. The one difference is that Ferson prefers the reduced form given as Equation (17) and defined in terms of k reference assets, k being defined as the number of factors. This parameterization involves the inverse of a matrix of the reference asset coefficients. Numerical nonlinear least squares procedures (in a likelihood or GMM framework) require conditions to guarantee that the inverse matrix exists, and thus violate the standard convergence criteria. While formally identical, equation system Equation (20) is simpler to estimate using standard numerical maximum likelihood or GMM procedures.

shall illustrate how to estimate the system of equations in a simplified example consisting of just four assets, two factors, and two instruments. A more realistic problem might have many hundreds of assets. The system of equations can be estimated using either the method of maximum likelihood, or generalized method of moments. For illustrative purposes we concentrate on maximum likelihood methods here.[9]

It is relatively straightforward to set the system of equations (22) up to estimate using the SAS/ETS®SYSNLIN package, the NLSYSTEM command in RATS, or in the OPTMUM or MAXLIK applications in GAUSS$_{TM}$. However, the process to convergence can be very time consuming unless analytic derivatives are provided to the nonlinear optimization algorithms. In this particular example, these derivatives represent a simple exercise in linear algebra. However for large systems of nonlinear equations, these derivatives are excessively tedious to code and difficult to code correctly. The alternative is to use *Mathematica* for this purpose.

The general procedure is as follows. First, the model is set up using arrays of data and parameters. The derivatives are defined in terms of individual observations which are later combined to obtain the appropriate derivatives of the likelihood function. For this reason, the arrays that represent the data have only one row. The criterion function is defined, and derivatives taken with respect to a list containing all of the parameters. These derivatives are simplified, expressed in **FortranForm** and then printed out to a file.

The first step is to define the equation system (22) in *Mathematica* using the **ARRAY** statement and standard matrix operations, collecting residuals and parameters into two separate lists:

```
In[1]:= (*   First, define the innovation equations          *)

        yt = Array[y,{1,2}];
        zt = Array[z,{1,6}];
        gmat = Array[g,{6,2}];
        ft = yt - zt . gmat;

        (*  Then, define the residual market equation          *)

        xt = Array [ x , {1,3}];
        rhovec = Array[rho,{3,1}];
        bmvec = Array[bm,{2,1}];
        f0 = rmt - xt.rhovec - ft . bmvec;

        (*   Finally, the equity return equations              *)

        rt = Array[r,{1,4}];
        amat = Array[a,{3,2}];
        amvec = Array[am,{3,1}];
```

[9] The computational issues are very similar for the generalized method of moments. However, in the GAUSS$_{TM}$ implementation computational efficiency requires that the derivatives of the criterion function be inferred from the derivatives of the moment conditions. In addition the OPTMUM package should be used in place of the MAXLIK package to minimize the criterion function.

```
bmat = Array[b,{2,4}];
b0vec = Array[b0,{1,4}];
et = rt  - xt . ( amat . bmat + amvec . b0vec ) -
         ft . bmat - f0 . b0vec;

(*    Collect residuals and parameters                  *)

residuals = Flatten[{ft, f0, et}];
parameters = Flatten [ { gmat, rhovec, bmvec,
         amvec, amat, b0vec, bmat }];
```

```
Short[parameters,5]
General::spell1:
  Possible spelling error: new symbol name "amat"
    is similar to existing symbol "gmat".
General::spell1:
  Possible spelling error: new symbol name "amvec"
    is similar to existing symbol "bmvec".
General::spell:
  Possible spelling error: new symbol name "bmat"
    is similar to existing symbols {amat, gmat}.
```

Out[1]:= //Short=

```
{g[1, 1], g[1, 2], g[2, 1], g[2, 2], g[3, 1], g[3, 2],

 g[4, 1], g[4, 2], g[5, 1], g[5, 2], g[6, 1], g[6, 2],

 rho[1, 1], rho[2, 1], <<17>>, b[1, 2], b[1, 3],

 b[1, 4], b[2, 1], b[2, 2], b[2, 3], b[2, 4]}
```

The weighting matrix W is symmetric. There are several ways of creating such a matrix in *Mathematica*. Perhaps the simplest method is to use the matrix manipulation procedures found in the standard *Mathematica* LinearAlgebra package:

In[2]:= **(*   Create a symmetric weighting matrix   *)**

```
<<LinearAlgebra`MatrixManipulation`
wmat = UpperDiagonalMatrix[w,7];
wmat = wmat + Transpose[wmat] - wmat*IdentityMatrix[7]
```

```
General::spell:
  Possible spelling error: new symbol name "wmat"
    is similar to existing symbols {amat, bmat, gmat}.
```

Out[2]:= {{w[1, 1], w[1, 2], w[1, 3], w[1, 4], w[1, 5], w[1, 6],

   w[1, 7]}, {w[1, 2], w[2, 2], w[2, 3], w[2, 4],

   w[2, 5], w[2, 6], w[2, 7]},

   {w[1, 3], w[2, 3], w[3, 3], w[3, 4], w[3, 5], w[3, 6],

   w[3, 7]}, {w[1, 4], w[2, 4], w[3, 4], w[4, 4],

Out[2](cont.)
```
      w[4, 5], w[4, 6], w[4, 7]},

    {w[1, 5], w[2, 5], w[3, 5], w[4, 5], w[5, 5], w[5, 6],

    w[5, 7]}, {w[1, 6], w[2, 6], w[3, 6], w[4, 6],

    w[5, 6], w[6, 6], w[6, 7]},

    {w[1, 7], w[2, 7], w[3, 7], w[4, 7], w[5, 7], w[6, 7],

    w[7, 7]}}
```

Then the least squares criterion function is defined using standard matrix operations:

In[3]:= **(*   Define the criterion function   *)**

```
        ssq = residuals . wmat . Transpose[residuals] ;
        Short[ssq,5]
```
Out[3]:= //Short=

```
    (y[1, 1] − g[1, 1] z[1, 1] − g[2, 1] z[1, 2] −

        g[3, 1] z[1, 3] − g[4, 1] z[1, 4] −

        g[5, 1] z[1, 5] − g[6, 1] z[1, 6])

    (w[1, 1] (y[1, 1] − g[1, 1] z[1, 1] + <<4>> −

        g[6, 1] z[1, 6]) + <<6>>) + <<6>>
```

The first derivatives are, unfortunately, somewhat complicated

In[4]:= **(*   Take the first derivative   *)**

```
        deriv1 = D[ssq, parameters[[1]] ]; Short[deriv1,5]
```
Out[4]:= //Short=
```
        (−(w[1, 1] z[1, 1]) + bm[1, 1] w[1, 3] z[1, 1] +

            w[1, 4] (b[1, 1] z[1, 1] −

                bm[1, 1] b0[1, 1] z[1, 1]) + <<1>> +

            w[1, 6] <<1>> + w[1, 7]

            (b[1, 4] z[1, 1] − bm[1, 1] b0[1, 4] z[1, 1]))

        <<1>> + <<12>>
```

They can be simplified considerably by replacing expressions for the residuals wherever they appear. Notice that Replace (/.) does not necessarily recognize the negative of expressions that are to be replaced. For this reason the replacement rules specified in factors includes the negative of residuals

```
In[5]:= factors =   {ft[[1,1]] -> f1, ft[[1,2]] -> f2,
        f0[[1,1]] -> fm, et[[1,1]] -> e1, et[[1,2]] -> e2,
        et[[1,3]] -> e3, et[[1,4]] -> e4,-ft[[1,1]] -> -f1,
          -ft[[1,2]] -> -f2,
        -f0[[1,1]] -> -fm, -et[[1,1]] -> -e1,
          -et[[1,2]] -> -e2,
        -et[[1,3]] -> e3, -et[[1,4]] -> -e4} ;

        deriv1 = deriv1 /. factors; Short [deriv1,5]
Out[5]:= //Short=

        -((f1 w[1, 1] + f2 w[1, 2] + fm w[1, 3] + e1 w[1, 4] +

            e2 w[1, 5] + e3 w[1, 6] + e4 w[1, 7]) z[1, 1]) +

          <<11>> + e4 (-(w[1, 7] z[1, 1]) + <<4>> +

            w[7, 7] (b[1, 4] z[1, 1] - bm[1, 1] <<1>> z[1, 1]))
```

The resulting expressions are still complicated. Given how many terms are involved, it is very time consuming to simplify the expressions directly using *Mathematica*. However, some simplification is possible by collecting terms involving the symmetric matrix W:

```
In[6]:= w1 = Union[Flatten[wmat] ];
        simplify = Flatten[{xt,zt,{f1,f2,fm,e1,e2,e3,e4},
                    parameters,w1}];

        deriv1 = Collect[Expand[deriv1],simplify] ;
Short[deriv1,5]
General::spell1:
   Possible spelling error: new symbol name "simplify"
     is similar to existing symbol "Simplify".
Out[6]:= //Short=

          (f1 (-2 w[1, 1] + 2 b[1, 1] w[1, 4] +

            2 b[1, 2] w[1, 5] + <<2>> +

            bm[1, 1] (2 w[1, 3] - 2 b0[1, 1] w[1, 4] -

              2 b0[1, 2] w[1, 5] - 2 b0[1, 3] w[1, 6] -

              2 b0[1, 4] w[1, 7])) + <<6>>) z[1, 1]
```

Notice that collecting terms involving the data suggest some simple common factors

```
In[7]:= factor1 = deriv1[[1]];
        deriv1 =  deriv1 /. factor1 -> fct1
        deriv2 = D[ssq,parameters[[2]] ]  /.  factors ;
        deriv2 = Collect[Expand[deriv2],simplify ] ;
        factor2 = deriv2[[1]];
        deriv2 = deriv2 /. factor2 -> fct2
```

```
Out[7]:= fct1 z[1, 1]

Out[7]:= fct2 z[1, 1]
```

Once we are satisfied that we have the simplest versions of the derivatives, we then put them into a file. To do this we convert the FORTRAN forms of the expressions into strings and directly Put them into a file. Note that the **>>** notation writes the expression to a file (erasing the previous contents) and **>>>** appends to an existing file

```
In[8]:= ToString[StringForm["fct1 = ``  ",FortranForm[factor1] ]
          ] >> deriv.prn
        ToString[StringForm["fct2 = ``  ",FortranForm[factor2] ]
          ] >>> deriv.prn

        For[i=1,i<=6,i++, Print[i];
           deriv =  D[ssq,parameters[[i]] ]  /. factors ;
           deriv = Collect[Expand[deriv],simplify]  /.
           {factor1 -> fct1, factor2 -> fct2};
           ToString[StringForm["deriv(``) =
                     ``",i,FortranForm[deriv]]
             ] >>> deriv.prn
           ]
        1
        2
        3
        4
        5
        6
```

which we can inspect:

```
In[9]:= !!deriv.prn
```

```
"fct1 = f1*(-2*w(1,1) + 2*b(1,1)*w(1,4) + 2*b(1,2)*w(1,5) + 2*b(1,3)*w(1,6) +
    2*b(1,4)*w(1,7) + bm(1,1)*(2*w(1,3) - 2*b0(1,1)*w(1,4) - 2*b0(1,2)*w(1,5) -
    2*b0(1,3)*w(1,6) - 2*b0(1,4)*w(1,7))) + f2*(-2*w(1,2) + 2*b(1,1)*w(2,4) +
    2*b(1,2)*w(2,5) + 2*b(1,3)*w(2,6) + 2*b(1,4)*w(2,7) + bm(1,1)*(2*w(2,3) -
    2*b0(1,1)*w(2,4) - 2*b0(1,2)*w(2,5) - 2*b0(1,3)*w(2,6) - 2*b0(1,4)*w(2,7)))
    + fm*(-2*w(1,3) + 2*b(1,1)*w(3,4) + 2*b(1,2)*w(3,5) + 2*b(1,3)*w(3,6) +
    2*b(1,4)*w(3,7) + bm(1,1)*(2*w(3,3) - 2*b0(1,1)*w(3,4) - 2*b0(1,2)*w(3,5) -
    2*b0(1,3)*w(3,6) - 2*b0(1,4)*w(3,7))) + e1*(-2*w(1,4) + 2*b(1,1)*w(4,4) +
    2*b(1,2)*w(4,5) + 2*b(1,3)*w(4,6) + 2*b(1,4)*w(4,7) + bm(1,1)*(2*w(3,4) -
    2*b0(1,1)*w(4,4) - 2*b0(1,2)*w(4,5) - 2*b0(1,3)*w(4,6) - 2*b0(1,4)*w(4,7)))
    + e2*(-2*w(1,5) + 2*b(1,1)*w(4,5) + 2*b(1,2)*w(5,5) + 2*b(1,3)*w(5,6) +
    2*b(1,4)*w(5,7) + bm(1,1)*(2*w(3,5) - 2*b0(1,1)*w(4,5) - 2*b0(1,2)*w(5,5) -
    2*b0(1,3)*w(5,6) - 2*b0(1,4)*w(5,7))) + e3*(-2*w(1,6) + 2*b(1,1)*w(4,6) +
    2*b(1,2)*w(5,6) + 2*b(1,3)*w(6,6) + 2*b(1,4)*w(6,7) + bm(1,1)*(2*w(3,6) -
    2*b0(1,1)*w(4,6) - 2*b0(1,2)*w(5,6) - 2*b0(1,3)*w(6,6) - 2*b0(1,4)*w(6,7)))
    + e4*(-2*w(1,7) + 2*b(1,1)*w(4,7) + 2*b(1,2)*w(5,7) + 2*b(1,3)*w(6,7) +
    2*b(1,4)*w(7,7) + bm(1,1)*(2*w(3,7) - 2*b0(1,1)*w(4,7) - 2*b0(1,2)*w(5,7) -
    2*b0(1,3)*w(6,7) - 2*b0(1,4)*w(7,7)))    "
"fct2 = f1*(-2*w(1,2) + 2*b(2,1)*w(1,4) + 2*b(2,2)*w(1,5) + 2*b(2,3)*w(1,6) +
    2*b(2,4)*w(1,7) + bm(2,1)*(2*w(1,3) - 2*b0(1,1)*w(1,4) - 2*b0(1,2)*w(1,5) -
    2*b0(1,3)*w(1,6) - 2*b0(1,4)*w(1,7))) + f2*(-2*w(2,2) + 2*b(2,1)*w(2,4) +
```

```
2*b(2,2)*w(2,5) + 2*b(2,3)*w(2,6) + 2*b(2,4)*w(2,7) + bm(2,1)*(2*w(2,3) −
2*b0(1,1)*w(2,4) − 2*b0(1,2)*w(2,5) − 2*b0(1,3)*w(2,6) − 2*b0(1,4)*w(2,7)))
+ fm*(−2*w(2,3) + 2*b(2,1)*w(3,4) + 2*b(2,2)*w(3,5) + 2*b(2,3)*w(3,6) +
2*b(2,4)*w(3,7) + bm(2,1)*(2*w(3,3) − 2*b0(1,1)*w(3,4) − 2*b0(1,2)*w(3,5) −
2*b0(1,3)*w(3,6) − 2*b0(1,4)*w(3,7))) + e1*(−2*w(2,4) + 2*b(2,1)*w(4,4) +
2*b(2,2)*w(4,5) + 2*b(2,3)*w(4,6) + 2*b(2,4)*w(4,7) + bm(2,1)*(2*w(3,4) −
2*b0(1,1)*w(4,4) − 2*b0(1,2)*w(4,5) − 2*b0(1,3)*w(4,6) − 2*b0(1,4)*w(4,7)))
+ e2*(−2*w(2,5) + 2*b(2,1)*w(4,5) + 2*b(2,2)*w(5,5) + 2*b(2,3)*w(5,6) +
2*b(2,4)*w(5,7) + bm(2,1)*(2*w(3,5) − 2*b0(1,1)*w(4,5) − 2*b0(1,2)*w(5,5) −
2*b0(1,3)*w(5,6) − 2*b0(1,4)*w(5,7))) + e3*(−2*w(2,6) + 2*b(2,1)*w(4,6) +
2*b(2,2)*w(5,6) + 2*b(2,3)*w(6,6) + 2*b(2,4)*w(6,7) + bm(2,1)*(2*w(3,6) −
2*b0(1,1)*w(4,6) − 2*b0(1,2)*w(5,6) − 2*b0(1,3)*w(6,6) − 2*b0(1,4)*w(6,7)))
+ e4*(−2*w(2,7) + 2*b(2,1)*w(4,7) + 2*b(2,2)*w(5,7) + 2*b(2,3)*w(6,7) +
2*b(2,4)*w(7,7) + bm(2,1)*(2*w(3,7) − 2*b0(1,1)*w(4,7) − 2*b0(1,2)*w(5,7) −
2*b0(1,3)*w(6,7) − 2*b0(1,4)*w(7,7)))   "
"deriv(1) = fct1*z(1,1)"
"deriv(2) = fct2*z(1,1)"
"deriv(3) = fct1*z(1,2)"
"deriv(4) = fct2*z(1,2)"
"deriv(5) = fct1*z(1,3)"
"deriv(6) = fct2*z(1,3)"
```

This output can be used with only minor revision to create a FORTRAN sub-routine to compute the required derivatives. However, some modification is needed to create a procedure to compute the derivatives in GAUSS$_{TM}$. That language is similar to *Mathematica* in that array elements are denoted by square brackets and exponentiation by carets (^). A major difference is that the multiplication sign "*" in GAUSS$_{TM}$ corresponds to the matrix product operator "." in *Mathematica*. Element-by-element multiplication is represented as ".*". Along with a few other minor modifications,[10] any standard text editor can be used to construct a derivative procedure for GAUSS$_{TM}$.

```
In[10]:=            !edit deriv.prn

In[11]:=            !!deriv.prn
```

```
fct1 = f1 .* (−2 .* w[1,1] + 2 .* b[1,1] .* w[1,4] + 2 .* b[1,2] .*
w[1,5] + 2 .* b[1,3] .* w[1,6] + 2 .* b[1,4] .* w[1,7] + bm[1,1] .* (2
.* w[1,3] − 2 .* b0[1,1] .* w[1,4] − 2 .* b0[1,2] .* w[1,5] − 2 .*
b0[1,3] .* w[1,6] − 2 .* b0[1,4] .* w[1,7])) + f2 .* (−2 .* w[1,2] + 2 .*
.
.
.
b0[1,4] .* w[7,7])) ;
fct2 = f1 .* (−2 .* w[1,2] + 2 .* b[2,1] .* w[1,4] + 2 .* b[2,2] .*
w[1,5] + 2 .* b[2,3] .* w[1,6] + 2 .* b[2,4] .* w[1,7] + bm[2,1] .* (2
.* w[1,3] − 2 .* b0[1,1] .* w[1,4] − 2 .* b0[1,2] .* w[1,5] − 2 .*
b0[1,3] .* w[1,6] − 2 .* b0[1,4] .* w[1,7])) + f2 .* (−2 .* w[2,2] + 2 .*
.
.
.
```

---

[10] In particular, the use of periods within square brackets to denote all elements in that array dimension (useful for denoting time series). Statements are terminated using a semicolon.

```
b0[1,4] .* w[7,7])) ;
deriv[.,1] = fct1 .* z[.,1];
deriv[.,2] = fct2 .* z[.,1];
deriv[.,3] = fct1 .* z[.,2];
deriv[.,4] = fct2 .* z[.,2];
deriv[.,5] = fct1 .* z[.,3];
deriv[.,6] = fct2 .* z[.,3];
```

The GAUSS$_{TM}$ code to estimate this simplified model using the MAXLIK application package is available in the software appendix.[11] The model is estimated on the basis of equity return data for the United States, United Kingdom, Japan, and Germany for the period February 1981 through March 1992.[12] After the data is read into the program, initial values are computed on the basis of ordinary least squares estimates, which also provides the weighting matrix. The maximum likelihood program is then called. The algorithm used is the derivative-based procedure of Broyden, Fletcher, Goldfarb, and Shanno (see Luenberger [1984] p. 268).

Analytic derivatives give two major advantages over the use of corresponding numerically-defined derivatives. In the first place, they are computationally efficient. In the example above, the algorithm takes 25.088 minutes to converge on a 25MHz 386 DOS-based machine. This represents a total of 303 iterations, at 4.97 seconds per iteration. Using numerically defined derivatives, the algorithm takes 19.03 seconds per iteration. In the second place, the resulting derivatives are more accurate. The algorithm failed to converge using numerically defined derivatives.

On a problem of a more realistic scale, the differences can be quite substantial. With 21 countries, four factors, and as many instruments, the time to convergence is 5 hours and 20 minutes. This calculation is not feasible without analytically-defined derivatives.

13.4 Summary

In this chapter we show how to use *Mathematica* in conjunction with other more specialized econometric software packages to provide efficient algorithms for estimating simultaneous systems of nonlinear equations. The particular advantage of *Mathematica* is its ability to compute large numbers of derivatives that are tedious to code and difficult to code correctly. These analytic derivatives are computationally more efficient and more accurate than their numerical counterparts. This is particularly important in the asset pricing example, which involves estimating systems of many equations.

---

[11] The file nlml.m contains a *Mathematica* package to compute all derivatives. The GAUSS$_{TM}$ code is contained in nlml.g which uses data contained in nlml.dat and produces the output file nlml.out.
[12] This example is a simplified verison of the model described in Brown and Otsuki [1992]. The nature and sources of data are described in that paper.

13.5 References

Black, Fischer, Michael Jensen, and Myron Scholes, 1972. "The Capital Asset Pricing Model: Some Empirical Tests," in Jensen, Michael C. (ed.) *Studies in the Theory of Capital Markets*, New York: Praeger.

Brown, Stephen and Toshiyuki Otsuki, 1992. "Risk Premia in Pacific Rim Capital Markets," (Unpublished working paper, Department of Finance, Stern School, NYU.)

Brown, Stephen and Mark Weinstein, 1983. "A New Approach to Testing Asset Pricing Models: The Bilinear Paradigm," *Journal of Finance* **38**, 711–743.

Chen, N-F., R. Roll, and S. Ross, 1986. "Economic Forces and the Stock Market," *Journal of Business* **59**, 383–404.

Connor, Gregory and Robert Korajczyk, 1988. "Risk and Return in an Equilibrium APT: Application of a New Test Methodology," *Journal of Financial Economics*, **21**, 255–290.

Fama, Eugene and James MacBeth, 1973. "Risk, Return and Equilibrium: Empirical Tests," *Journal of Political Economy* **81**, 607–636.

Ferson, Wayne, 1990. "Are the Latent Variables in Time-varying Expected Returns Compensation for Consumption Risk?" *Journal of Finance* **45**, 397–430.

Goldfeld, S., and Richard Quandt, 1972. *Nonlinear Methods in Econometrics*, Amsterdam: North Holland.

Greene, William, 1990. *Econometric Analysis*, New York: Macmillan Publishing Company.

Hansen, Lars and Kenneth Singleton, 1982. "Generalized Instrumental Variables Estimation of Nonlinear Rational Expectations Models," *Econometrica* **50**, 1269–1286.

Luenberger, D. G, 1984. *Linear and Nonlinear Programming*, Reading, MA: Addison-Wesley.

McElroy, Margery and Edwin Burmeister, 1988. "Arbitrage Pricing Theory as a Restricted Nonlinear Regression Model," *Journal of Business and Economic Statistics* **6**, 29–42.

Richard Roll and Stephen Ross, 1980. "An Empirical Investigation of the Arbitrage Pricing Theory," *Journal of Finance* **35**, 1073–1102.

14 Econometrics.m: A Package for Doing Econometrics in Mathematica

David A. Belsley

14.1 Introduction

Econometrics is an area of applied statistics that has developed with a very strong individual flavor—although its techniques are also widely used in such disciplines as biometrics, psychometrics, and sociometrics, and, to be somewhat polemical, are applicable to a far wider statistical audience than seems aware of their need.

One of its main differences from other areas of applied statistics is its use of simultaneous-equations estimation, a subject pioneered by econometricians in the '40s and early '50s. Here it is recognized that models describing complex, interrelated phenomena cannot properly be described and estimated by a single regression equation relating a "dependent" variate to a set of "independent" variates, but rather must be described by a set of equations in which dependent or, more properly, endogenous variates determined in one equation can also act as determinants in other equations in the system. Special estimation techniques are required to handle such models since ordinary least squares (OLS), the popular and ubiquitous linear regression estimation technique, is incapable of providing unbiased, or even consistent, estimation when some of the regressors are endogenous, that is, when they are not independent of the error structure.

In principle, *Mathematica* is a marvelous environment in which to conduct econometric analyses. Its data (matrix) manipulation, transformational, and graphical facilities allow many of the operations common to econometrics to be done quickly, cleanly, and efficiently. But the basic elements of Mathematica do not contain the requisite estimation facilities. Indeed, even the built-in line-fitting functions, "`Fit`" and "`LinearSolve`," are inadequate for the econometrician's simplest need for an ordinary least-squares routine. These procedures are able to return the least-squares coefficients of the parameters β of the linear model $y = X\beta + \epsilon$, but they cannot return the estimates of the coefficient standard errors or their variance-covariance matrix $V(b)$.

Further, without additional transformations, these procedures do not return the estimated regression residuals which are so basic to much econometric analysis. Thus, they are procedures adequate to descriptive statistics but not to inferential statistics. And these procedures are clearly not at all adapted to the econometrician's more sophisticated need for an estimator suitable for simultaneous equations.

The *Mathematica* package, Econometrics.m, that accompanies this chapter achieves many of these needs. It contains functions for ordinary least-squares (OLS), block regression (sets of regressions), mixed-estimation (ME), two-stage least-squares (2SLS), and instrumental-variables (IV) estimation. It is assumed the reader is already familiar with these techniques. For those wishing more information on them, see Theil (1971) or Johnston (1984). The first two functions provide a complete econometrics regression routine for accomplishing ordinary least squares, and the last two mentioned estimators are suitable for limited-information estimation of simultaneous equations. The mixed-estimation routine provides one means for including prior information in a least-squares estimation context.

Each of these functions returns the estimated coefficients, the estimated variance, the estimated coefficient standard errors, the coefficient variance-covariance matrix, the residuals, and the predicted values for the response variate. Further, options exist that allow one to select either the standard estimate of the variance-covariance matrix or the White (1980) heteroskedasticity-consistent estimator. Options also allow the level of the output to be varied, the screen display to be suppressed, and the collinearity diagnostics of Belsley, Kuh, and Welsch (1980) and Belsley (1991) to be effected.

Econometrics.m is by no means a complete econometrics package such as SAS or RATS and, at least at the moment, is not intended to be—indeed, it is not clear that *Mathematica* is ready yet for such large-scale packages. Rather, its purpose is to place some basic econometric facilities directly within the *Mathematica* environment so that the econometric user need not constantly be communicating with other econometric packages in order to accomplish the relatively straightforward estimation tasks that frequently arise in the conduct of econometric research.

On the other hand, in comparison to some of these gargantuan statistical packages, Econometrics.m is not as limited as it may first appear. Because of *Mathematica*'s data-handling, transformational, and graphics facilities, and the ease with which functions may be defined to accomplish complex operations, the regression output returned by Econometrics.m can frequently become the input to many more advanced econometric operations.

Documentation for Econometrics.m comprises the next section. The third section contains a number of self-contained, hands-on examples that illustrate many of the facilities contained in Econometrics.m. Elements in the user's guide that pair up with specific examples will be so noted by [§n], where n gives the example number. The fourth section examines some of the design issues relating to this package that will be of interest to those wondering how it works or how to extend it.

A fifth section provides a description of two experimental packages that can be used in conjunction with `Econometrics.m` and which greatly expand its serviceability. Specifically, the package `BlockMatrix.m` provides the tools needed for the user to construct his own large-scale, simultaneous-equations packages, such as three-stage least squares or full-information maximum likelihood. In this regard, the user may also be interested in Belsley (1992). The package `StatUtilities.m` adds a number of often-needed utility routines for data massaging and for conducting statistical tests. It bears repeating that these latter two notebooks are experimental. While they contain some error-handling facilities, they do not approach `Econometrics.m` in this regard. The user is more nearly on his own in making sure the routines are correctly employed and return what is expected.

14.2   User's Guide

14.2.1   Basic Overview

`Econometrics.m` is a *Mathematica* package containing some basic econometric operations. This version, 2.2.5, includes

- basic regression (or ordinary least squares—OLS) [§1,§2],

- block regression (sets of OLS regressions) [§9],

- mixed-estimation (ME) [§10],

- two-stage least squares (2SLS) [§11], and

- instrumental-variables (IV) estimation [§11].

The regression results are displayed on the screen (a default option) and the regression output, including predicted values, residuals, coefficient estimates, estimated standard errors, and the variance-covariance matrix are returned through output options [§2].

Labels for the screen display are readily applied [§6].

The estimated variance-covariance matrix can be either the standard estimate or the White (1980) heteroskedasticity-consistent estimate.

Collinearity diagnostics are optionally available for all estimators [§9]. There are additional utility programs[§6,§7].

`Econometrics.m` operates in its own *Mathematica* context, so the variates used by it will not conflict with those in the user's own context. The only names that are introduced into the user's context are

- those of the main functions, `Reg[ ]`, `MixedEstimation[ ]`, `TwoStage[ ]`, and `IV[ ]`,

- those of the utility functions `Name[ ]`, `Call[ ]`, `UnName[ ]`, `lag[ ]`, and `delta[ ]`,

- those of the options (displayOutput, returnValues, varDCom, Level1, Level2, varCovMatrix, White, Standard, QR, SVD, displayDigits, algorithm, labels, lagValue), and

- the symbol @ (which may be changed by the user) acting as a postfix shorthand for labeling.

Additional utility functions are provided in two accompanying packages, StatUtilities.m and BlockMatrix.m. Briefly, the former contains numerous standard statistical routines (means, correlations, and the like), Gaussian and multivariate Gaussian generation routines, and hypothesis testing procedures. The latter contains routines to carry out operations on block matrices and to construct the various Kronecker products of block matrices necessary for creating full-information systems estimators such as FIML or 3SLS. The contents of these packages are described in detail in the section Related Experimental Packages.

14.2.2   Functional Formats for the Estimators

The relevant functional formats for the OLS, ME, 2SLS, and IV estimators, respectively, are

```
Reg[y, x, opts];
MixedEstimation[y, X, c, R, SigR, SigX:Null, opts];
TwoStage[y, includedy, includedx, excludedx, opts];
IV[y, includedVariates, instrumentalVariates, opts];
```

Note: special care is needed in specifying the MixedEstimation[] function when options are used along with a default SigX. If no options are specified and SigX is to default at Null, then use

```
MixedEstimation[y, X, c, R, SigR];
```

If, however, an option is to be specified along with SigX defaulted to Null, its space must be maintained (a place holder) with commas as

```
MixedEstimation[y, X, c, R, SigR, , opts];
```

14.2.3   Data Input

Specifying the input data is very easy and flexible in Econometrics.m. For each function, the first argument, y, is the dependent variable. In all cases but standard OLS, y must be a single vector (or a $1 \times n$ or $n \times 1$ matrix) [§1]. In Reg[] (without the White variance-covariance matrix), y may also be a list. If y is a list, each variate in y is separately regressed on the x variates (block regression or sets of regressions [§9]) with appropriate screen displays.

All other non-option arguments are lists whose elements may be any combination of vectors, matrices, or tensor arrays of data series. Illustrations will be given shortly to make this clear [§1]. Furthermore, matrices can be either $n \times p$

or $p \times n$; Econometrics.m assumes the larger dimension relates to the number of observations n and the smaller to the number of variables p. The first data element in each variate is assumed to refer to the same case (the same period or observation)—a special initial non-data element containing a label may, however, be present (see labeling) [§6]. There may be missing observations, denoted by any non-numeric entry in the data series [§7].

14.2.3.1   Specifying Data Input

Data entry for Econometrics.m is extremely flexible [§1]. Consider as an example a regression of Consumption on an intercept, GNP, IntRate, Wealth, and Expectations. If these variates were all separately defined, this could be effected as

```
Reg[Consumption, {"const", GNP, IntRate, Wealth, Expectations}];
```

The argument y is the single variable Consumption, and x is the list {"const", GNP, IntRate, Wealth, Expectations}. If this latter list had already been defined as

```
ConsumptionData = {"const", GNP, IntRate, Wealth, Expectations}
```

then the same regression would result from

```
Reg[Consumption, ConsumptionData];
```

This works even if the individual data series in ConsumptionData are of different lengths. Econometrics.m determines the number of observations as the minimum of the lengths of the included data series (less any missing observations—see below). You are apprised of any situation in which the number of observations becomes less than the number of variates—negative degrees of freedom.

To continue, let us suppose GNP, IntRate, and Expectations were the same length (not necessarily equal to that of Wealth) so

```
myData = {GNP, IntRate, Expectations}
```

is a matrix. And define

```
dataBlock = {Wealth, Transpose[myData]}.
```

Then one could obtain the same regression as above with any of the following:

```
Reg[Consumption, {myData, Wealth, "const"}];
Reg[Consumption, {Transpose[myData], Wealth, "Const"];
Reg[Consumption, {"const", {myData, Wealth}}];
Reg[Consumption, {"Constant", dataBlock}];
Reg[{Consumption}, {"Const", dataBlock}];
Reg[Consumption, {{{Wealth, {myData}}, "const"}}];
Reg[Consumption, {{"Const", Wealth}, {IntRate,
                {GNP, Expectations}}}];
```

That is, the x argument in Reg[] can be any list containing any combination of nested lists of vectors, matrices, or tensors of data series, each in any size or orientation. Thus, one could have a tensor of matrices of data. `Econometrics.m` will determine from these only possible $n \times p$ data matrix, assuming for each matrix that its longer dimension is a number of observations. The same is true for the non-optional, non-y arguments (such as `includedy`) of `TwoStage[]`, `IV[]`, and `MixedEstimation[]`. Note in the last three cases above that excess braces do not matter.

14.2.3.2 Specifying the Intercept or "Constant" Term

Despite the belief held by many statisticians that all regressions have constant terms, a little thought will lead to the realization that the presence of an intercept term in a regression is a matter of specification that requires as much consideration as the inclusion of any other variate. So, `Econometrics.m` assumes by default that there will be no intercept term, and its inclusion requires a conscious entry. There are two ways of doing this

- one can either define a vector of ones (`Constant = Table[1.0, {n}]`) to be included just like any other variate, or
- one can let `Econometrics.m` automatically generate such a variate.

This latter is accomplished simply by including the string term `"const"` in the list, as seen in the examples above or in [§1]. This string may take any of the forms `"const"`, `"Const"`, `"constant"`, or `"Constant"`, but, in all cases, it must contain the quotes. The `"const"` may occur anywhere in the list (not just at the beginning). Regression through the origin (without a constant term) is clearly accomplished simply by omitting to specify the presence of an intercept.

14.2.3.3 NonSeries

Naturally, if any of the arguments contains a name that has not been defined or refers to a data series with zero length, `Reg[]`, `MixedEstimation[]`, `TwoStage[]`, or `IV[]` cannot proceed and will return an error message. This will occur if the quotes are left off `"const"` and no variate `const` has otherwise been defined in the current session.

14.2.3.4 Using Mathematica's Built-in Transformations

It is very simple to transform the variates used in `Reg[]`, `MixedEstimation[]`, `TwoStage[]`, and `IV[]`; simply use the built-in *Mathematica* operations [§3]. Thus, if one wished to examine a "logged" version of the above model, one need only use

```
Reg[Log[Consumption], {"const", Log[ConsumptionData]}];
```

Here the `"const"` must be separated, for `Log["const"]` could not be correctly interpreted by *Mathematica*.

Similarly, linear or nonlinear combinations of the data can be introduced directly. Thus,

```
Reg[Consumption, {"const",Wealth*IntRate+0.5*GNP, Expectations}];
```

has the desired effect.

Transformations for lags, leads, and deltas are also available in `Economet-rics.m` [§7]. They are described in greater detail below.

14.2.3.5   Series Alignment and Missing Observations

Whereas the various data series may be of unequal lengths, it is assumed that the first data element of each data series refers to the same case index or period; that is, the data series are aligned through the first data element. Labels (described below and in §6) occupying the first element of a variate are not considered to be a data element and will be disregarded in any subsequent calculations done by `Econometrics.m` (but not by other built-in *Mathematica* routines).

Any non-numeric entry for a given data series will be treated as a missing observation, and once encountered, that case will be removed from all data series in subsequent calculations. In any output that is returned, a non-numeric entry "na" will occur for each missing case [§5].

When adding non-numeric elements, it is usually safest to use string literals (with quotes), such as "na" rather than just the symbol na. If the symbol na has not been defined (or has been defined non-numerically) during the existing session, its use will produce the desired result. But if na has been assigned a numerical value, this value will be substituted and used in the subsequent regression calculations, producing undesired results. Thus, if na has been defined as `2.0`, attempting to remove the data `3.5` by writing `3.5na` will instead produce the value `7.0`. Use `3.5"na"` instead [§5].

Troubles can even arise using strings if the variates are to undergo certain mathematical transformations. Thus, if two variates had "na" in the same observation, and the difference between these two lists were calculated, the resulting observation would be the numerical value `0` (`"na"-"na"`) and would no longer be considered missing. If there is any doubt on this score, simply use the somewhat longer and more awkward *Mathematica* symbol `Indeterminate`, which will always produce the desired result.

14.2.3.6   Regression on Subsets

The preceding feature for missing observations can be used to accomplish regression analyses on arbitrary subsets of the data merely by doctoring any data series to have non-numeric entries in those cases to be excluded [§5]. This can be done without danger of loosing data simply by placing a letter before or after existing data so that the original data can readily be retrieved. This, of course, need only be done for one data value for a given observation, since a non-numeric entry in any one entry will cause all data for that case to be ignored.

If the regression has a constant term, subset regression can also be accomplished quite generally by defining an indicator variable which has value 1 for all cases to be included and any non-numeric value, such as "na", for cases to be excluded. This variate may then be specified in place of "const". This will have some minor side effects as noted below in the section describing screen display output and in §5. If there is no constant term, the same indicator can be used multiplicatively to achieve the same effect.

14.2.3.7   Limitations

As already mentioned, the first argument, y, in `MixedEstimation[]`, `Two-Stage[]`, and `IV[]` must be a vector or an $n \times 1$ matrix (or its transpose). Also, for `TwoStage[]`, there must be at least as many variates in the argument "excludedx" as in "includedy". This is the basic order condition for identification. And `IV[]` requires that the number of variates in the two arguments "includedVariates" and "instrumentalVariables" be the same.

14.2.4   Options

There are six options that apply to all estimators:

```
displayOutput  -> True
returnValues   -> Level1
varDCom  ->      False
displayDigits  -> 3
algorithm  -> QR
varCovMatrix  -> Standard
```

These options, shown with their default values, are briefly described here. Further information relevant to their effects occurs in subsequent sections. There are also several options that apply specifically to the functions `lag[]` and `delta[]`. These are described later in the sections devoted to these functions.

14.2.4.1   displayOutput

Setting `displayOutput -> True` causes the screen display of the regression analysis to be suppressed [§2]. This affects the screen display only; the regression output is still returned to *Mathematica* in a form determined by the `returnValues` option [§2]. The default here is `True`, so unless the user specifies otherwise, there will be a screen display.

Note: to prevent the `returnValues` from also being displayed on the screen, be sure a semicolon follows the estimator function call.

14.2.4.2   returnValues

At the moment there are two levels for the items returned by `Reg[]`, `MixedEstimation[]`, `TwoStage[]` and `IV[]`:

- `Level1` (default) includes coefficient estimates, residuals, predicted ys (y hats) and sigma-squared [§2]: {beta, err, yhat, sig2}

- `Level2` includes all of the above plus the estimated coefficient standard errors and the estimated coefficient variance-covariance matrix [§2, §5]:
  {beta, err, yhat, sig2, se, vcMat}

The estimated variance-covariance matrix `vcMat` that is returned differs in nature depending on estimator. For all estimators except standard OLS, the actual variance-covariance matrix is returned, and sigma square `sig2` contains $e'e/(n - p)$. In the case of standard OLS, the inverse of $X'X$ is returned. Thus, to get the estimated variance-covariance matrix in this case, one must multiply this by sigma squared `sig2` [§2]. This modest inconvenience allows a single matrix to be returned in the event that sets of regressions (block regression) [§9] are run (as occurs automatically when `y` is a list of "dependent" variates).

Note: to prevent the `returnValues` from also being displayed on the screen, be sure a semicolon follows the estimator function call.

14.2.4.3   varDCom

This option, when made `True`, causes a collinearity analysis to be run and a matrix of condition indexes and variance-decomposition proportions to be displayed on the screen after the normal regression output [§9]. For further information on these diagnostics and their interpretation, see Belsley, Kuh, and Welsch (1980) or Belsley (1991).

14.2.4.4   displayDigits

This option stipulates the number of digits to the right of the decimal point to be reported in the output display [§3]. The default is 3. This option affects the screen display only; any regression output is still returned with full precision. This option also does not affect the number of digits reported in the `varDCom` tableau, which need not be greater than the three that are printed.

14.2.4.5   algorithm

This option allows one to chose between using the QR decomposition or the singular-value decomposition (SVD) in calculating the regression coefficients and the variance-covariance matrix.

The default is to use the QR decomposition, which, when it works, is very much faster than the SVD. With highly ill-conditioned data, however, one might wish to force the use of the SVD, and setting `algorithm -> SVD` will accomplish this. Further, when the data become so ill-conditioned that they are, for all intents and purposes, perfectly collinear, the QR decomposition will fail to return an R matrix of full rank, and, in this instance, `Econometrics.m` will inform the user of the situation and automatically switch to using the SVD. There is more on this in the section Development Notes below.

There are several related matters in this regard. First, the collinearity diagnostics must always use the information obtained from the SVD. Thus, when the `varDCom -> True` option is chosen and the QR decomposition is used, the collinearity diagnostics are based on a subsequent SVD of the (scaled) R matrix. This provides the needed information, but at computational savings over applying the SVD to the original data matrix. If the SVD is used instead of the QR, then the `varDCom` routine is fed an appropriately scaled version of the output of the SVD. In all cases, the collinearity diagnostics produce the appropriate scaled condition indexes and variance-decomposition proportions. [See Belsley, (1991)].

Second, the means for checking when the QR decomposition should be replaced by the SVD requires the *Mathematica* error messages `Inverse::invc` and `Inverse::matsq`. Be sure, therefore, not to turn off the reporting of these two messages when using `Econometrics.m`, or it will not operate properly in these extreme situations.

14.2.4.6   varCovMatrix

This option allows one to choose between the standard (`varCovMatrix -> Standard`) estimator of the coefficient standard errors (and variance-covariance matrix), which is the default, and the heteroskedasticity-consistent (`varCov-Matrix -> White`) version described in White (1980).

14.2.5   Screen Display and Output

Unless one specifies `displayOutput -> False`, the basic results of a regression and its associated statistics will be displayed on the screen after a regression is run [§2]. This display includes

• R square

• Rbar square (corrected R square)

• uncentered R square

• sigma square

• Durbin-Watson (along with a statement of the number of missing observations)

• number of observations

• degrees of freedom, and an

• indication when the White variance-covariance estimator has been opted for, followed by,

• each estimated coefficient, estimated standard error, and t ratio, and, in the case of the `TwoStage[]` and `IV[]` estimators,

• a list of the instrumental variables employed.

   The order of the coefficients is that in which the variates are entered, except that an internally generated constant term (one specified by `"const"` as noted above) will always be listed first and will be so labeled. A user-defined constant term will be placed in the order of its occurrence in the input list.

   Although it is not necessary to do so, I have found that `Econometrics.m` responds best when the options "Place Print output as it is generated" and "Place each Print line in a separate cell" are turned off (left unchecked). On the Macintosh, these are found in the Action preferences in the Edit menu. Also, no effort has been made to "page" output displays. For the most part, the screen displays fit easily in a standard 80 column line. Lengthy labels, however, may produce lines longer than 80 columns, a problem that can also occur with the display of variance-decomposition proportions in a collinearity analysis when there are many variates. If you anticipate such situations, merely use the Action preferences to set a longer line length, say, 150 characters, and use the horizontal and vertical scroll bars to view the display.

Each regression will also return an output list whose contents depend upon the value of the `returnValues` option [§2]. The default `returnValues ->` `Level1` returns the list

```
{beta, err, yhat, sig2},
```

where `beta` is a list of the estimated coefficients, `err` is a list of the residuals, `yhat` is a list of the predicted values of `y`, and `sig2` is the scalar-valued estimate of sigma square (although, see below in the section on Block regression how to deal with these when running sets of regressions). These lists can be used for subsequent analyses. Thus the statements

```
{beta, err, yhat, sig2} = Reg[Consumption, ConsumptionData];
forecasts = beta.forecastData
```

would result in a set of forecasts based on a matrix of `forecastData` corresponding to `ConsumptionData` for the forecast period. Or one could examine a residual plot such as

```
ListPlot[err]
```

or a scatter plot such as

```
ListPlot[Transpose[{yhat,err}]].
```

The option `returnValues -> Level2` causes these functions to return the list

```
{beta, err, yhat, sig2, se, vcMat}
```

where, added to the `Level1` items, are `se`, the estimated coefficient standard errors, and `vcMat`, the variance-covariance matrix [§2, §5].

In the case of `Reg[]` using the standard (non-White) definition of the variance-covariance matrix, the matrix `vcMat` is the inverse of $X'X$, and the estimated variance-covariance matrix can be obtained as `sig2*vcMat`. In all other cases, `vcMat` is the estimated variance-covariance matrix.

Recall that, if there are missing observations, `yhat` and `err` will have non-numeric entries in the corresponding missing-case positions. Thus it may be necessary to take precautions in using these lists in subsequent calculations. The plotting routines seem to work fine without further adjustment, although one will receive *Mathematica* messages indicating the presence of non-numeric values. You might want to turn this message off if it gets annoying.

Recall also that one can suppress the printing of the values returned by the function to the screen simply by placing a semicolon after the function call; thus,

```
TwoStage[y, yhat, myX, otherX, varDCom->True];
```

will perform a 2SLS regression and its attendant screen display and collinearity analysis, but will not print the values returned by the function `TwoStage[]` to the screen [§11].

14.2.6   Labels

Econometrics.m's flexible data entry requires special steps be taken to supply labels (variate names) to appear in the screen displays. In the absence of such action, these labels default to appropriately suggestive indexed symbols. In Reg[], for example, the different variates are labeled X[1], X[2], etc. Dependent variates are noted by y[i]'s. In TwoStage[] and IV[], X[i]'s and Y[i]'s are used for the exogenous and endogenous variates, respectively, and Z[i]'s are used to indicate various instrumental variates: the excluded exogenous variates for TwoStage[] (the included exogenous variates are always used as well) and the full set of instrumental variables for IV[].

More informative labels [§6-§11] may be introduced as follows: Econometrics.m will interpret any material in the first element of a data vector as a label for that variate in the screen display *as long as that entry contains somewhere at least one underscore character*. First elements not containing an underscore will be considered data, whether numeric or not. Underscores occurring in elements other than the first have nothing to do with labeling (but will cause that observation to be considered missing—see Section 14.2.3, Data Input). The underscore may appear anywhere in the first element, and there may be multiple underscores. Variates that are not explicitly labeled receive default labels as noted above.

Thus, suppose it is desired that the output relating to the estimated coefficient of the data series

```
Consumption = {1.1, 1.2, 1.3}
```

be labeled Consumption in the screen display. This will occur if the string "_Consumption" is prepended to the list as, for example, {_Consumption, 1.1, 1.2, 1.3}. An initial underscore will be dropped in the screen display, so that _Consumption will produce Consumption as a label, but underscores in other positions will be retained, so that the label derived from {Cons_78, 1.1, 1.2, 1.3} will be Cons_78.

It is important to note that this modified Consumption series will still be treated by Econometrics.m as a three-element data vector; the labeling will be stripped off before any regression calculations are done. When labeled and unlabeled variates are mixed as input, the data are aligned with respect to their first non-label elements. If, however, these label elements are made a permanent part of the list, care must be taken in using them in other operations with *Mathematica* functions. The expression

```
Consumption + Income
```

will clearly not have the desired effect if one variate is labeled and the other not, as

```
Consumption = {_Consumption, 1.1, 1.2, 1.3}
Income = {2.1, 2.3, 3.4}.
```

On the other hand, if Income also has a label, such as {_Income, 2.1, 2.3, 3.4}, this sum will be

```
{_Consumption + _Income, 3.2, 3.5, 4.7},
```

and will receive the label

```
Consumption + _Income.
```

Likewise, using a function like `Log[Consumption]` will produce

```
{Log[_Consumption], 0.095310, 0.182321, 0.262364}
```

which will in turn produce a not inappropriate label of `Log[_Consumption]`.

Perhaps the safest labeling strategy to adopt until one gains more experience is simply to enter variates separately into `Econometrics.m` "at run time" using techniques that provide temporary labels for the regression at hand but that do not permanently affix the label to the variate. There are several utility functions defined in `Econometrics.m` that make both temporary and permanent labeling and unlabeling easy. We describe them now.

14.2.6.1   Name[]

`Name[x_]` is a function [§6–§11] that prepends to the data x a label which is the same as its *Mathematica* symbol. If x is a vector, the symbol x is used. If x is a matrix or tensor of vectors, the *i*-th such vector in x is labeled with `x[i]`. Thus, for the data vector

```
Income = {1, 2, 3}
```

`Name[Income]` will produce `{_Income, 1, 2, 3}`. For the data tensor

```
Rates = {{1, 2, 3}, {4, 5, 6, 7}}
```

`Name[Rates]` gives `{{_Rates[1], 1, 2, 3}, {_Rates[2], 4, 5, 6, 7}}`.

If the data vector x (or any vector in the array x) is already labeled, the new label will replace the existing one. This (re)labeling will be temporary; that is, it will not alter the actual object `Income`, which will remain defined as before. But giving `Name[x]` as an argument to `Reg[]` will have the desired effect of introducing the label x in the appropriate parts of the screen display. To permanently affix this label to the list x use

```
x = Name[x].
```

This function works only on vectors, matrices, or tensors of vectors. Thus, it does not have the fully flexible input facility of `Econometrics.m` (which works also, for example, on tensors of matrices). Further, it is intended to be used only on a symbol name and not the data list itself. If, for example, one used the list itself, as in `Name[{1, 2, 3}]`, the result would be `{_{1, 2, 3}, 1, 2, 3}`, and the label `{1, 2, 3}` would appear in the screen display. This would clearly prove awkward for a long list. `Name[]` has the attribute `HoldAll`.

It may be easier to use the function suffix `//Name` to name variates as arguments in the functions of `Econometrics.m`. For example, one could enter

```
Reg[Name[Consumption],{"const",Name[Income]}];
```

or, equivalently, one could use

```
Reg[Consumption//Name,{"const",Income//Name}];
```

which is easier for the eye to comprehend quickly.

Indeed, facility has been added to make life easier yet. Specifically, the symbol @ has been defined in $PreRead to act as a labeling suffix so that variate@ and Name[variate] are equivalent. Thus, the same labeling as above can be effected simply by entering

```
Reg[Income@, {"const",Consumption@}];
```

The @ will not become part of the label.

Warning: this convenience could be troublesome, for the symbol @ becomes committed to this special meaning and cannot be used otherwise. The @ symbol, for example, is also used in *Mathematica* as a metacharacter for string matches (meaning zero or more characters excluding upper-case letters) and as an operator in various other contexts. If you commonly employ these other uses of @, you should choose any other symbol (or combination of symbols) that does not conflict with your style and use it instead. To do this, open the package Econometrics.m and scroll down a short way until you find the statement defining $PreRead. The last entry of this statement is "@" -> "//Name". Simply replace the @ with your newly chosen symbol, being sure to retain the quotes. Now this symbol will automatically be used as a labeling suffix each time you open Econometrics.m.

14.2.6.2 Call[]

Call[x_, name_] assigns the names listed in name as the labels for the data x [§6, §9]. If you wish to label a variate with a name other than its symbol name, this is the function to use.

x may be a vector, a matrix, or a tensor of vectors. The argument name accommodates a variable number of entries. There must be exactly as many names in name as there are data vectors in x. Thus, for the single data vector

```
Income = {1, 2, 3}
```

Call[Income, GNP] will produce {_GNP, 1, 2, 3}. For the two-element data tensor

```
Rates = {{1, 2, 3}, {4, 5, 6, 7}}
```

Call[Rates, 3MonthBills, 30YearBonds] will produce

```
{{_3MonthBills, 1, 2, 3}, {_30YearBonds, 4, 5, 6, 7}}.
```

If the data vector x (or any vector in the array x) is already labeled, the new label will replace the existing one. This (re)labeling will be temporary; that is, it will not alter the actual object x, which will remain defined as before. But giving `Call[x, name]` as an argument to `Reg[]` will have the desired effect of introducing the label(s) name in the appropriate parts of the screen display. To permanently affix this label to the list x use

```
x = Call[x,name]
```

Each name is entered as a separate parameter (name is not a list of names). Typically there is no need to place the names in quotes, but this is necessary if you wish to include parentheses in the name. `Call[]` has the attribute `HoldRest`.

14.2.6.3 UnName[]

`UnName[x_]` simply strips away any label from the data vector x. If x has no label, no change occurs. This effect is temporary; that is, it will not alter the actual object x. To permanently remove the label from the list x, use

```
x = UnName[x]
```

14.2.7 Collinearity Diagnostics

Specifying the option `varDCom -> True` causes a collinearity analysis to be run and a matrix of scaled condition indexes and variance-decomposition proportions to be displayed on the screen [§9]. These tools and their use are described in *Regression Diagnostics: Identifying Influential Observations and Sources of Collinearity*, Wiley (1980) by Belsley, Kuh, and Welsch or in *Conditioning Diagnostics: Collinearity and Weak Data in Regression*, Wiley (1991) by D. A. Belsley.

The condition indexes are listed across the first row, and, in each succeeding row, the variance-decomposition proportions for each included variate are listed in turn. These are listed in the same order as the regression display: if there is an internally generated constant, it comes first, but otherwise the variates are in the order in which they are entered. It is worth noting that the screen display form given here is the mirrored transpose of that given in Belsley (1991) and Belsley, Kuh, and Welsch (1980). As noted above, the collinearity diagnostics reported here are always based on scaled condition indexes and variance-decomposition proportions.

If the number of variates p is large, say, greater than 7 or 8, the variance-decomposition proportion display may not fit within the width of one screen, depending on the *Mathematica* preference settings for the screen display. If this occurs, the output will be placed in staggered blocks, vertically down the screen, and will typically be difficult to read. To avoid this, use the action preferences in the Edit menu to set the window break at some large number of characters, say, 150 or more as needed. The variance-decomposition display will then be placed as a single array, and you may use the horizontal and vertical scroll bars to move to the desired spot in it.

In forming the auxiliary regressions that so often are useful complements to the variance-decomposition proportions in conducting a collinearity analysis, see the next section dealing with block regression (sets of regressions) [§9].

14.2.8   Block Regression (Sets of Regressions)

If the first argument of the Reg[y, x] function is a list of variates instead of a single variate and if the default variance-covariance matrix is chosen (var-CovMatrix -> Standard), Reg[] will perform an OLS regression of each variate in the list on the set of variates specified in x [§9].

In this case, screen displays for each regression will fall one after the other, and the returned output elements will be matrices instead of vectors. Thus the "beta" portion will be a matrix whose first element is the list of coefficient estimates for the first regression, whose second element will be the list of coefficient estimates for the second regression, etc. Likewise, sig2 will be a list of sigma squares for all the regressions. vcMat will, of course, remain a single matrix, pertaining identically to the inverse of the matrix $X'X$ common to all of the regressions [§2].

The block regression facility is only available for Reg[] when using the standard (non-White) estimate of the variance-covariance matrix. For all other estimator functions, the first argument must be a single vector. This facility can be used very effectively in conjunction with the collinearity diagnostics to conduct the set of auxiliary regressions described in Belsley (1991) or Belsley, Kuh, and Welsch (1980) [§9].

14.2.9   Lags, Leads, and Differences

Two utility functions, lag[] and delta[], provide Econometrics.m with remarkable power and flexibility for generating lags, leads, and differences of arbitrary orders.

14.2.9.1   lag[]

lag[] is a lag/lead function with great flexibility [§7]. lag[] is a function with an optional number of arguments to achieve different results. Suppose, then, a variate called pickle.

- With one argument, lag[pickle] returns a list of pickle with a non-numeric entry prepended so that it will align correctly in Reg[], MixedEstimation[], TwoStage[], and IV[] as pickle lagged once. To regress y on lagged pickle, then, one merely writes

Reg[y, lag[pickle]];

The non-numeric entries at the beginning, combined with Econometrics.m's ability to handle missing observations, allows this statement automatically to produce the intended result without any further adjustment by the user.

- With two arguments, lag[pickle, n] returns the n-th lag of pickle if n is positive and the n-th lead of pickle if n is negative. lag[pickle, 0] is equivalent to lag[pickle]. When n is positive, n non-numeric values are prepended to pickle, thus preserving the proper alignment. When n is negative, the first n observations are removed (and n non-numeric values appended), thus preserving the proper alignment. Regressing y on the 4-th lead of `pickle`, then, is simply effected by

```
Reg[y, lag[pickle, -4]];
```

- With three arguments, `lag[pickle, n, m]` returns an array with the n-th through m-th lags/leads of `pickle` [§7]. m and n may be positive or negative, but n must be less than m. The resulting array is exactly that that would be produced by `{lag[pickle, n], . . . , lag[pickle,m]}` and is directly suitable for use in `Reg[]`, `MixedEstimation[]`, `TwoStage[]`, or `IV[]`. Thus, to regress y on `pickle`, its first lead, and its first two lags, use

```
Reg[y, lag[pickle, -1, 2]];
```

If an intercept is desired, use

```
Reg[y, {"const", lag[pickle, 1, 2]}];
```

The `lag[]` function has the labeling [§6, §7] facility `Name[]` built in (see Section 14.2.6, Labels). That is, when you use `lag[pickle]`, the label indicator `_pickle(-1)` is automatically prepended to the resulting list so that its output will be labeled `pickle(-1)` in the screen display. Likewise, appropriate labels are automatically prepended for other lags and leads. `lag[pickle,-1,2]`, for example, will produce respective labels of `pickle(1), pickle, pickle(-1), pickle(-2)`. If the vector `pickle` already contains a label in its first element, that label will be used (with appropriate indexing for lags and leads) instead of the *Mathematica* symbol name.

When using the `lag[]` function directly as an argument to the `Econometrics.m` functions [§6], the preceding labeling rules will usually produce the desired result. Occasionally, however, it may be desirable to prevent `lag[]` from attaching labels. This is accomplished using the option `labels -> False`. This option must be the fourth argument to `lag[]`, so if defaults for other arguments are used, appropriate place holders are required. Thus, to produce `lag[pickle]` with no labels, one would use `lag[pickle, 1, , labels -> False]`. For convenience, and to prevent inadvertent errors, the `lag[]` function is defined so that `lag[pickle, , , labels -> False]` also works correctly, although normally this would not be true of *Mathematica* functions. (Those who are just learning the inner mysteries of *Mathematica*'s parameter default methods might want to pursue this case in greater detail as an exercise.) The default is `labels -> True`. Thus, suppression of automatic labeling in the `lag[]` function requires the insertion of `labels -> False` in each instance of the function for which no labeling is desired. Global suppression of automatic labeling can be achieved by redefining the default option with `SetOptions[lag, labels -> False]`.

By default, `lag[]` fills in the missing cases created by either lagging or leading with the *Mathematica* symbol `Indeterminate`. Thus, `lag[{1, 2, 3}]` is `{Indeterminate, 1, 2}`. This convention has been adopted because it usually produces the desired result and avoids other unexpected problems. If, for example, the letter `"a"` were used for the missing observation, `lag[{1,`

2, 3}] - lag[{4, 5, 6}] would produce {a, 1, 2} - {a, 4, 5} = {0, 3, 3}, and there would no longer be a missing observation. With In-determinate, however, this result would be {Indeterminate, 3, 3} as desired.

Occasionally, however, it is desirable to use some other value for the missing observation. In some tests for serial correlation, for example, one uses lags of regression residuals for which it is permissible to employ the value zero for these missing cases [§8]. To accommodate this, lag[] has an option lagValue to allow any symbol to be used. Thus, lag[err,,,lagValue -> 0] would produce the residuals lagged once with a zero in the first position. Be sure to use place holders for any missing default parameters. The default is lagValue -> Indeterminate.

14.2.9.2 delta[]

The delta[x_, n_] function returns x - lag[x, n]. (Actually, it returns lag[x, 0, , opts] - lag[x, n, , opts] to provide consistent label-ing, data alignment, and options specification.)

To take an n-th difference of the r-th lag of x, use delta[lag[x, r], n]. This automatically produces the label Delta[n]_x(-r) for the screen display.

delta[] uses the same options and defaults as lag[]. Thus, delta[] au-tomatically labels its output unless the option labels -> False is used, and it replaces newly created missing observations with Indeterminate unless another symbol is specified using the option lagValue -> symbol.

In using either of these options, remember to use place holders if other pa-rameter defaults are used. Thus, to take the first difference of a series x without labels, use either delta[x, 1, labels -> False] or delta[x, , la-bels -> False].

Global suppression of automatic labeling in both delta[] and lag[] can be achieved by resetting the default option by entering SetOptions[lag, labels -> False].

14.3   Examples

14.3.1   Do This before Doing Any of the Examples

Before doing anything, the Econometrics.m package must be loaded. We do this first (you may be asked to help *Mathematica* find the Econometrics.m package).

In[1]:= **<<Econometrics.m**

Next, we define some basic data that will be used in the subsequent examples. All of the examples given below require these data and will not work unless they are defined first. So before proceeding to any example, enter all the cells in this subsection. The examples are otherwise self contained and can be worked in any order. But, within any example, be sure to enter all input steps in order to be sure that everything that needs to be defined for that example is defined.

Here we have some basic economic data related to estimating a consumption function. These are annual observations, 1948–1974, on consumption (`Con`), its first lag (`Clag`), disposable personal income (`dpi`), its first difference `deldpi`, and the rate of interest (`r`).

```
In[2]:= Con = {210.775, 216.5, 230.5, 232.825, 239.425,
        250.775, 255.725, 274.2, 281.4, 288.15, 290.05, 307.3,
        316.075, 322.5, 338.425, 353.3, 373.725, 397.7, 418.1,
        430.1, 452.725, 469.125, 477.55, 496.425, 527.35,
        552.075, 539.45};

        Clag = {206.275, 210.775, 216.5, 230.5, 232.825,
        239.425, 250.775, 255.725, 274.2, 281.4, 288.15, 290.05,
        307.3, 316.075, 322.5, 338.425, 353.3, 373.725, 397.7,
        418.1, 430.1, 452.725, 469.125, 477.55, 496.425,
        527.35, 552.075};

        r = {2.81667, 2.66, 2.6225, 2.86, 2.95583, 3.19917,
        2.90083, 3.0525, 3.36417, 3.885,3.7875, 4.38167, 4.41,
        4.35, 4.325, 4.25917, 4.40417, 4.49333, 5.13, 5.50667,
        6.175, 7.02917, 8.04, 7.38667, 7.21333, 7.44083,
        8.56583};

        dpi = {229.7, 230.925, 249.65, 255.675, 263.25, 275.475,
        278.4, 296.625, 309.35, 316.075, 318.8, 333.05, 340.325,
        350.475, 367.25, 381.225, 408.1, 434.825, 458.875,
        477.55, 499.05, 513.5, 534.75, 555.425, 580.45, 619.5,
        602.875};

        deldpi = {11.625, 1.225, 18.725, 6.025, 7.575, 12.225,
        2.925, 18.225, 12.725, 6.725, 2.725, 14.25, 7.275,
        10.15, 16.775, 13.975, 26.875, 26.725, 24.05, 18.675,
        21.5, 14.45, 21.25, 20.675, 25.025, 39.05, -16.625};
```

When you return to these examples in the future, you can quickly re-enter everything in this section with one keystroke simply by selecting its encompassing bracket to the right and pressing the enter key. Indeed, if the section is closed, you need not reopen it. Simply select it and hit enter.

Also, while we are setting things up, if your front end allows for these things, you might want to be sure that the options "Place Print output as it is generated" and "Place each Print line in a separate cell" are turned off (left unchecked) in the Action options of the Preference item in the Edit menu. You may prefer to set these otherwise, but, for what it's worth, I find it better to leave them off when using `Econometrics.m`.

14.3.2 Basic Regression, Input [§1]

Begin with a basic consumption function regression

```
In[1]:= Reg[Con,{"const",Clag,dpi,r,deldpi}];
```

```
Dependent variable is y[1]
RSquared = 0.999079  RBarSquared = 0.998911
R2uncentered = 0.999924  SER = 3.55721
Num of Observations = 27    Degrees of Freedom = 22
dw = 1.88922 with 0 missing obs.

                  coef.       st. err.           t

Const            6.724        3.827           1.757
X[2]             0.245        0.237           1.033
X[3]             0.698        0.208           3.363
X[4]            -2.210        1.838          -1.202
X[5]             0.161        0.183           0.877
```

Or, if the data were grouped, say, as

In[2]:= **Data = {Clag,dpi,r,deldpi};**

the same regression is effected by

In[3]:= **Reg[Con,{"Constant", Data}];**

```
Dependent variable is y[1]
RSquared = 0.999079  RBarSquared = 0.998911
R2uncentered = 0.999924  SER = 3.55721
Num of Observations = 27    Degrees of Freedom = 22
dw = 1.88922 with 0 missing obs.

                  coef.       st. err.           t

Const            6.724        3.827           1.757
X[2]             0.245        0.237           1.033
X[3]             0.698        0.208           3.363
X[4]            -2.210        1.838          -1.202
X[5]             0.161        0.183           0.877
```

or, if

In[4]:= **X1 = {Clag,dpi};**
         X2 = {r,deldpi};
         X3 = {Table[1.0,{Length[Con]}],X1};

In[5]:= **Reg[Con,{"Const",X1,X2}];**

```
Dependent variable is y[1]
RSquared = 0.999079  RBarSquared = 0.998911
R2uncentered = 0.999924  SER = 3.55721
Num of Observations = 27    Degrees of Freedom = 22
dw = 1.88922 with 0 missing obs.

                  coef.       st. err.           t

Const            6.724        3.827           1.757
X[2]             0.245        0.237           1.033
X[3]             0.698        0.208           3.363
X[4]            -2.210        1.838          -1.202
X[5]             0.161        0.183           0.877
```

or

```
In[6]:= Reg[Con,{Transpose[X3],X2}];
```

```
Dependent variable is y[1]
RSquared = 0.999079  RBarSquared = 0.998911
R2uncentered = 0.999924  SER = 3.55721
Num of Observations = 27    Degrees of Freedom = 22
dw = 1.88922 with 0 missing obs.
```

	coef.	st. err.	t
X[1]	6.724	3.827	1.757
X[2]	0.245	0.237	1.033
X[3]	0.698	0.208	3.363
X[4]	−2.210	1.838	−1.202
X[5]	0.161	0.183	0.877

Note two things in this latter case: First, the orientation of the input matrices makes no difference. X3 has been transposed here, but you may try it without the Transpose[] to see that you will get the same result. And second, since the intercept term is not generated internally here, its estimate is not labeled Const in the output display. Of course, the intercept could be suppressed simply by not including it, as:

```
In[7]:= Reg[Con, {X1,X2}];
```

```
Dependent variable is y[1]
RSquared = 0.998999  RBarSquared = 0.998868
R2uncentered = 0.999914  SER = 3.7151
Num of Observations = 27    Degrees of Freedom = 23
dw = 2.06571 with 0 missing obs.
```

	coef.	st. err.	t
X[1]	0.531	0.181	2.939
X[2]	0.476	0.172	2.768
X[3]	−3.724	1.696	−2.196
X[4]	0.325	0.165	1.967

14.3.3   Basic Regression, Output [§2]

There are two forms of output for the results of a regression: the informative screen display and the actual regression output data, suitable for further processing.

14.3.3.1   Screen Display

As we have seen above, a screen display giving the standard regression estimates and summary statistics follows a regression by default. The information in this display is for the user's convenience and is not in a form that can be readily processed in *Mathematica*. In many cases, such as Monte Carlo studies, interest may center on the usable output, and it may be desirable to suppress this purely informative display. This is accomplished with the `displayOutput` option. Thus

```
In[1]:= Reg[Con, {"const",Clag,dpi,r,deldpi},
                         displayOutput -> False];
```

runs the regression but suppresses the screen display.

14.3.3.2 Regression Output

The usable output of the function `Reg[]` is returned as a list. The semicolon following the function call above prevents these values from cluttering up the screen. (Try redoing the preceding function call after removing the final semicolon). But this output is readily trapped and put to use.

```
In[1]:= Regout = Reg[Con, {"const",Clag,dpi,r,deldpi},
                         displayOutput -> False];
```

Now we can get the separate elements as:

```
In[2]:= {beta, err, yhat, sig2} = Regout;
```

```
In[3]:= beta
```

```
Out[3]:= {6.7242, 0.245374, 0.698421, -2.20966, 0.160812}
```

```
In[4]:= sig2
```

```
Out[4]:= 12.6538
```

Additional output is obtained by using the `returnValues` option. Level1, given above, is the default. Setting `returnValues -> Level2` adds the estimated standard errors of the coefficients and the inverse of $X'X$, from which the variance-covariance matrix can be derived. Thus,

```
In[5]:= {beta, err, yhat,sig2, se, vcMat} =
              Reg[Con,{"const",Clag,dpi,r,deldpi},
                   displayOutput -> False,
                   returnValues -> Level2];
```

```
In[6]:= TableForm[sig2 vcMat]
```

Out[6]:= 5.42751	-0.0641088	0.0380621	0.544892	-0.0337922
-0.0641088	0.00534083	-0.00446465	-0.0131057	0.00262157
0.0380621	-0.00446465	0.00395103	-0.00280783	-0.00251163
0.544892	-0.0131057	-0.00280783	1.03585	0.00944224
-0.0337922	0.00262157	-0.00251163	0.00944224	0.00492143

To test the hypothesis that the true betas are

```
In[7]:= TrueBeta = {6.0, 0.25, 0.7, -1.0, 0.2};
```

we need only calculate the F-statistic

```
In[8]:= (beta-TrueBeta).Inverse[vcMat].(beta-TrueBeta)/(5 sig2)
```

```
Out[8]:= 29.1662
```

With the 5% critical value for $F(5, 22) = 2.66$, we would certainly reject this hypothesis.

14.3.4 Transformations [§3]

Complex data transformations for regressions in Econometrics.m are made simple in *Mathematica*. Consider, for example, a respecification using a squared term in dpi in place of the deldpi term.

```
In[1]:= Reg[Con,{"const",Clag,dpi,r,dpi^2}];
Dependent variable is y[1]
RSquared = 0.999305  RBarSquared = 0.999179
R2uncentered = 0.999943  SER = 3.08901
Num of Observations = 27    Degrees of Freedom = 22
dw = 1.97767 with 0 missing obs.
```

	coef.	st. err.	t
Const	−13.467	8.167	−1.649
X[2]	0.039	0.097	0.399
X[3]	0.990	0.084	11.721
X[4]	−1.325	1.623	−0.816
X[5]	−0.000	0.000	−2.862

Here the default of 3 digits beyond the decimal is inadequate for the report on X[5], so

```
In[2]:= Reg[Con,{"const",Clag,dpi,r,dpi^2},
                displayDigits -> 6];
Dependent variable is y[1]
RSquared = 0.999305  RBarSquared = 0.999179
R2uncentered = 0.999943  SER = 3.08901
Num of Observations = 27    Degrees of Freedom = 22
dw = 1.97767 with 0 missing obs.
```

	coef.	st. err.	t
Const	−13.466974	8.167300	−1.648889
X[2]	0.038552	0.096696	0.398691
X[3]	0.989560	0.084429	11.720636
X[4]	−1.324900	1.623281	−0.816187
X[5]	−0.000146	0.000051	−2.862462

Or consider estimating the partially logged model,

```
In[3]:= Reg[Log[Con],{"const", Log[Clag], Log[dpi], r,
            deldpi}];
Dependent variable is y[1]
RSquared = 0.999199  RBarSquared = 0.999054
R2uncentered = 0.999998  SER = 0.00933427
Num of Observations = 27    Degrees of Freedom = 22
dw = 1.76025 with 0 missing obs.
```

	coef.	st. err.	t
Const	−0.112	0.119	−0.934
X[2]	0.164	0.191	0.860
X[3]	0.848	0.190	4.471
X[4]	−0.006	0.004	−1.710
X[5]	0.000	0.000	0.408

14.3.5 Plots [§4]

Mathematica's plotting facilities can be employed directly on the output of `Reg[]`
to produce many standard regression plots. Thus, a residual plot

```
In[1]:= {beta,err,yhat,sig2} =
           Reg[Con,{"const",Clag,dpi,r,deldpi},
           displayOutput->False];
```

```
In[2]:= ListPlot[err]
```

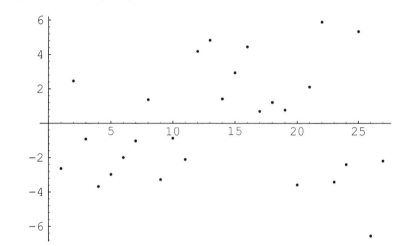

```
Out[2]:= —Graphics—
```

Or a plot of `yhat` vs. `y`

```
In[3]:= ListPlot[Transpose[{yhat,Con}]]
```

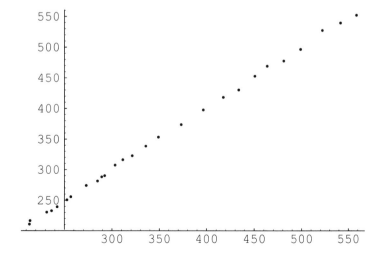

```
Out[3]:= —Graphics—
```

Or r vs. residuals

In[4]:= **ListPlot[Transpose[{r,err}]]**

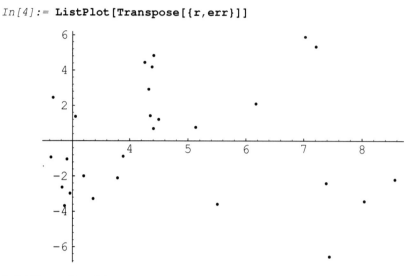

Out[4]:= —Graphics—

14.3.6   Regressions on Subsets and Hypothesis Testing [§5]

Regressions on subsets of the data are easily done in Econometrics.m. Since Econometrics.m ignores all the data for any observation that contains any non-numeric characters, one can place non-numeric entries in any element of those observations that are to be ignored. Two simple ways exist for this:

1. Substitute non-numeric entries, say "na", for those elements of the constant term (if there is one) corresponding to observations that are to be ignored; or

2. Add non-numeric entries to any element of the data for those observations that are to be ignored. This can be done without danger of losing numeric information simply by placing a letter after any piece of numeric data, say by changing 3.445 to 3.445"na".

   In using either of these techniques, it is safer to use a string character like "na" rather than just the letters themselves. If for some reason na had previously been defined, say, na = 2, then 3.445na would be treated just like the numeric data 6.890, and the wrong effect would be achieved.

14.3.6.1   Using an Indicator Variate

Thus, one can run a regression without the first three observations by constructing a new indicator "constant term" as follows:

In[1]:= **const3 = ReplacePart[Table[1.0,{Length[Con]}],**
                          "na",{{1},{2},{3}}]

Out[1]:= {na, na, na, 1., 1., 1., 1., 1., 1., 1., 1., 1., 1.,
           1., 1., 1., 1., 1., 1., 1., 1., 1., 1., 1., 1., 1., 1.}

```
In[2]:= Reg[Con,{const3,Clag,dpi,r,deldpi}];
```
```
Dependent variable is y[1]
RSquared = 0.99891  RBarSquared = 0.998681
R2uncentered = 0.999926  SER = 3.7192
Num of Observations = 24    Degrees of Freedom = 19
dw = 1.95068 with 3 missing obs.
```

	coef.	st. err.	t
X[1]	6.939	4.365	1.590
X[2]	0.291	0.252	1.154
X[3]	0.651	0.222	2.930
X[4]	−1.811	1.994	−0.908
X[5]	0.219	0.200	1.096

Note that there are now 24 instead of 27 observations; the na's in the first three elements cause these to become "missing observations".

14.3.6.2 Testing Coefficient Equality

To do a test of coefficient equality between, say, the first 12 and the last 15 periods [See, for example, Johnston (1984)]

```
In[1]:= Const1 = Flatten[{Table["na",{12}],Table[1.0,{15}]}];
        Const2 = Flatten[{Table[1.0,{12}],Table["na",{15}]}];
In[2]:= Output = Reg[Con,{"const",Clag,dpi,r,deldpi},
                    displayOutput->False];
        Output1 = Reg[Con,{Const1,Clag,dpi,r,deldpi},
                    displayOutput->False];
        Output2 = Reg[Con,{Const2,Clag,dpi,r,deldpi},
                    displayOutput->False];
In[3]:= SSR = Output[[4]] (27-5);
        SSU = Output1[[4]] (15-5) + Output2[[4]] (12-5);
In[4]:= ((SSR-SSU)/5)/(SSU/(27-10))
Out[4]:= 2.83957
```

With a 5% critical value of $F(5,17) = 2.70$, we would reject the hypothesis of coefficient equality between these two periods.

14.3.6.3 Using Rules to Remove Specific Data

Previously we exemplified using Log[] transformations in Reg[]. The entire equation was not logged because there are negative entries in the deldpi variate. One can remove the negative valued observations and estimate the fully logged equation on the rest as

```
In[1]:= PosDeldpi = deldpi /. z_:>"na" /; z<0
Out[1]:= {11.625, 1.225, 18.725, 6.025, 7.575, 12.225, 2.925,

          18.225, 12.725, 6.725, 2.725, 14.25, 7.275, 10.15,

          16.775, 13.975, 26.875, 26.725, 24.05, 18.675, 21.5,

          14.45, 21.25, 20.675, 25.025, 39.05, na}
```

```
In[2]:= Reg[Log[Con],{"const", Log[Clag], Log[dpi], Log[r],
              Log[PosDeldpi]}];
```

```
Dependent variable is y[1]
RSquared = 0.999044   RBarSquared = 0.998862
R2uncentered = 0.999998   SER = 0.00993143
Num of Observations = 26     Degrees of Freedom = 21
dw = 1.59372 with 1 missing obs.
```

	coef.	st. err.	t
Const	−0.079	0.154	−0.514
X[2]	0.151	0.212	0.709
X[3]	0.856	0.202	4.250
X[4]	−0.024	0.027	−0.891
X[5]	0.001	0.005	0.102

14.3.7   Labels [§6]

The examples until now have used the default labels for the screen displays. Here are two examples providing a montage of more informative labeling techniques. They make use of the Name[] and Call[] functions which, respectively, use the *Mathematica* symbol name or a user-specified name as the given variate's label. For convenience, the symbol @ has been defined in $PreRead to act exactly as the postfix function application //Name. If this conflicts with your typical use of @ (which has many other uses in *Mathematica*), simply change its assignment rule to your preference in the statement defining $PreRead in Econometrics.m.

```
In[1]:= Reg[Name[Con],{"Const",Clag//Name,dpi,
              Call[r,Interest],deldpi@}];
```

```
Dependent variable is Con
RSquared = 0.999079   RBarSquared = 0.998911
R2uncentered = 0.999924   SER = 3.55721
Num of Observations = 27     Degrees of Freedom = 22
dw = 1.88922 with 0 missing obs.
```

	coef.	st. err.	t
Const	6.724	3.827	1.757
Clag	0.245	0.237	1.033
X[3]	0.698	0.208	3.363
Interest	−2.210	1.838	−1.202
deldpi	0.161	0.183	0.877

Notice that X[3] retains its default label here since no other label was applied.

```
In[2]:= Reg[Call[Con-Clag,DeltaConsumption],{"Constant",
              Clag+dpi//Name,Name[Log[r]],Call[r deldpi,Wierd],
              Sin[deldpi]@}];
```

```
Dependent variable is DeltaConsumption
RSquared = 0.715001   RBarSquared = 0.663183
R2uncentered = 0.901828   SER = 5.29022
Num of Observations = 27     Degrees of Freedom = 22
dw = 2.32769 with 0 missing obs.
```

	coef.	st. err.	t
Const	12.101	5.417	2.234
Clag + dpi	0.016	0.022	0.740
Log[r]	−12.497	12.861	−0.972
Wierd	0.100	0.015	6.493
Sin[deldpi]	−0.162	1.626	−0.100

Or, for labeling elements of matrices or tensors,

In[3]:= **Data = {Clag,dpi,r,deldpi};**

In[4]:= **Reg[Con//Name,{"const",Data//Name}];**

```
Dependent variable is Con
RSquared = 0.999079   RBarSquared = 0.998911
R2uncentered = 0.999924   SER = 3.55721
Num of Observations = 27   Degrees of Freedom = 22
dw = 1.88922 with 0 missing obs.
```

	coef.	st. err.	t
Const	6.724	3.827	1.757
Data[1]	0.245	0.237	1.033
Data[2]	0.698	0.208	3.363
Data[3]	−2.210	1.838	−1.202
Data[4]	0.161	0.183	0.877

In[5]:= **Reg[Con@,{"const",Call[Data,"Con(-1)",DisPerInc,Interest,**
              ChangeDPI]}];

```
Dependent variable is Con
RSquared = 0.999079   RBarSquared = 0.998911
R2uncentered = 0.999924   SER = 3.55721
Num of Observations = 27   Degrees of Freedom = 22
dw = 1.88922 with 0 missing obs.
```

	coef.	st. err.	t
Const	6.724	3.827	1.757
Con(−1)	0.245	0.237	1.033
DisPerInc	0.698	0.208	3.363
Interest	−2.210	1.838	−1.202
ChangeDPI	0.161	0.183	0.877

Note: If you want to use parentheses in the labels, it is necessary to place the name inside quotes.

14.3.8   Lags, Leads, and Deltas [§7]

The data we have used so far (defined in §1) contain separate series for Con and its lag Clag. But Econometrics.m has powerful facilities for forming leads, lags, and changes: the functions lag[] and delta[]. Thus, suppose instead of using the original 27-term data series (1948–1974), let us prepend to each series its 1947 observation so we have 28-term data series containing the full history for (1947–1974):

```
In[1]:= Consumption = Prepend[Con,206.275];
        Income = Prepend[dpi,218.075];
        Interest = Prepend[r,2.61083];
```

Now our previous regression can be achieved as

```
In[2]:= Reg[Consumption, {"const",lag[Consumption],Income,
                Interest,delta[Income]}];
Dependent variable is y[1]
RSquared = 0.999079  RBarSquared = 0.998911
R2uncentered = 0.999924   SER = 3.55721
Num of Observations = 27    Degrees of Freedom = 22
dw = 1.88922 with 1 missing obs.
```

	coef.	st. err.	t
Const	6.724	3.827	1.757
Consumption(−1)	0.245	0.237	1.033
X[3]	0.698	0.208	3.363
X[4]	−2.210	1.838	−1.202
Delta(−1)_Income	0.161	0.183	0.877

Note first that there is now 1 "missing observation" corresponding to the initial entry that is not defined numerically for either lag[Consumption] or delta[Income]. Enter and examine these variates if you wish. Note also the automatic labeling facility in the lag[] and delta[] functions. This can be turned off selectively by using the labels -> False option within each instance of lag[] or delta[] to which it is to apply (remember to use place holders if needed in the absence of intermediate default parameters). Such labeling can also be turned off globally for both functions by entering SetOptions[lag, labels -> False] and restored by resetting this option to True. Try it if you wish.

As another example of using lag[], consider the basis for an investigation of Consumption's being an AR(3) process:

```
In[3]:= Reg[Consumption//Name,{"const",lag[Consumption,1,3]}];
Dependent variable is Consumption
RSquared = 0.993709  RBarSquared = 0.992811
R2uncentered = 0.999544   SER = 8.82361
Num of Observations = 25    Degrees of Freedom = 21
dw = 1.603 with 3 missing obs.
```

	coef.	st. err.	t
Const	1.198	6.954	0.172
Consumption(−1)	0.892	0.311	2.870
Consumption(−2)	−0.459	0.435	−1.054
Consumption(−3)	0.630	0.327	1.924

14.3.9   Testing for Serial Correlation [§8]

The consumption function we have been using has a lagged dependent variate, so the Durbin-Watson statistic dutifully posted is known to be biased toward the null hypothesis of no serial correlation. But we can readily test for quite general forms of serial correlation, even in the presence of lagged dependent variates, using an artificial-regression technique as suggested by Durbin (1970) or MacKinnon (1992). Specifically, we have only to test for the significance of appropriate lagged values of the least-squares residuals in a regression using the errors as a dependent variate.

Thus, we first run the basic equation, saving the errors (we do not need a screen display here):

```
In[1]:= {beta,err,yhat,sig2} =
          Reg[Con,{"const",Clag,dpi,r,deldpi},
            displayOutput->False];
```

And now redo the regression using `err` as the dependent variate and including `lag[err]` among the independent variates.

```
In[2]:= Reg[err@,{"Const",Clag@,dpi@,r@,deldpi@,lag[err]}];
```

```
Dependent variable is err
RSquared = 0.00480143  RBarSquared = -0.243998
R2uncentered = 0.00578165  SER = 3.6733
Num of Observations = 26    Degrees of Freedom = 20
dw = 1.91384 with 1 missing obs.
```

	coef.	st. err.	t
Const	0.991	7.551	0.131
Clag	-0.009	0.711	-0.012
dpi	0.002	0.644	0.003
r	0.303	2.249	0.135
deldpi	-0.003	0.663	-0.004
err(-1)	0.045	0.776	0.058

The estimate of the lagged error term is insignificant, so we accept the null of no first-order serial correlation. Notice that we now have one missing observation due to lagging `err`. In this instance, however, it is permissible to use a value of zero for this missing first observation. Thus, we can use the option `lagValue -> 0` to get

```
In[3]:= Reg[err@,{"Const",Clag@,dpi@,r@,deldpi@,
                    lag[err,,,lagValue->0]}];
```

```
Dependent variable is err
RSquared = 0.010537  RBarSquared = -0.225049
R2uncentered = 0.010537  SER = 3.62169
Num of Observations = 27    Degrees of Freedom = 21
dw = 1.92716 with 0 missing obs.
```

	coef.	st. err.	t
Const	2.725	6.955	0.392
Clag	-0.255	0.591	-0.431
dpi	0.230	0.530	0.434
r	-0.328	1.996	-0.164
deldpi	-0.241	0.543	-0.444
err(-1)	0.308	0.651	0.473

To test for higher orders of serial correlation, we need only include the relevant higher-ordered lags and test whether their coefficients are jointly zero. For first- and second-ordered lags, for example, we would use.

```
In[4]:= {beta,err1,yhat,sig2,se,XX} =
        Reg[err@,{"Const",Clag@,dpi@,r@,deldpi@,
        lag[err,1,2,lagValue->0]}, returnValues -> Level2];
Dependent variable is err
RSquared = 0.0158952   RBarSquared = -0.279336
R2uncentered = 0.0158952   SER = 3.70107
Num of Observations = 27    Degrees of Freedom = 20
dw = 1.87703 with 0 missing obs.
```

	coef.	st. err.	t
Const	1.153	8.555	0.135
Clag	-0.131	0.710	-0.185
dpi	0.121	0.634	0.190
r	-0.265	2.049	-0.129
deldpi	-0.138	0.637	-0.216
err(-1)	0.191	0.753	0.254
err(-2)	-0.101	0.305	-0.330

Note: The option `returnValues -> Level2` has been used here because the variance-covariance matrix will be needed for the joint test. Also, be careful about reusing symbols such as `beta`, etc. since their previous values will be overwritten. In this example, this is all right except possibly for the original values of `err`, which are still being used and which you may wish to use in further tests. For this reason, `err1` has been employed here to keep the original `err` intact.

Both `err(-1)` and `err(-2)` are individually insignificant here, but that does not guarantee that they are jointly so. The appropriate test on the joint significance of `err(-1)` and `err(-2)` is most easily done using the `Fstat[]` routine found in the package `StatUtilities.m` that accompanies `Econometrics.m`. This package is described more fully below in Section 14.5, Related Experimental Packages. For the moment, we will just read it in and use it.

```
In[5]:= <<StatUtilities.m
In[6]:= Fstat[beta,sig2*XX,{"na","na","na","na","na",0.,0.}]
Out[6]:= 0.161519
```

Here, the first two parameters are the estimated coefficients and their variance-covariance matrix. The last list gives the test values. Only numeric values count, so the `"na"`s cause this test to be marginal with respect to the last two parameters alone, as is desired. From the resulting figure we quickly accept the null of no first- and second-order serial correlation.

14.3.10   Collinearity Diagnostics and Sets of Regressions [§9]

To examine the collinearity diagnostics for the consumption function data (the scaled condition indexes and variance-decomposition proportions), one need only use the `varDCom -> True` option.

```
In[1]:= Reg[Con//Name,{"const",Clag//Name,dpi//
                Name,Call[r,Interest],
            deldpi//Name},varDCom->True];
```

```
Dependent variable is Con
RSquared = 0.999079  RBarSquared = 0.998911
R2uncentered = 0.999924  SER = 3.55721
Num of Observations = 27    Degrees of Freedom = 22
dw = 1.88922 with 0 missing obs.
```

	coef.	st. err.	t
Const	6.724	3.827	1.757
Clag	0.245	0.237	1.033
dpi	0.698	0.208	3.363
Interest	−2.210	1.838	−1.202
deldpi	0.161	0.183	0.877

```
Variance-decomposition proportions
```

Condition indexes

	375.6	39.4	7.8	4.1	1.
Const	0.421	0.264	0.310	0.004	0.001
Clag	0.995	0.005	0.000	0.000	0.000
dpi	0.995	0.005	0.000	0.000	0.000
Interest	0.001	0.984	0.013	0.001	0.000
deldpi	0.814	0.048	0.001	0.136	0.002

Now, in addition to the normal regression display, we get the pi matrix of scaled condition indexes and variance-decomposition proportions. To interpret these diagnostic values, see Belsley, Kuh, and Welsch (1980) or Belsley (1991). It is seen that there are two near dependencies among these data: one (associated with the scaled condition index of 375) is quite strong and surely involves Clag, dpi, and deldpi; the second (associated with the scaled condition index of 39) is moderately strong and surely involves r and some of the other variates whose presence here is being masked by their simultaneous involvement in the stronger near dependency.

We can examine these near dependencies in greater detail by forming a pair of "auxiliary regressions" in which two variates known to be involved in the dependencies, say, dpi and r, are regressed on the remaining variates. This is readily accomplished in Econometrics.m because of its sets or "block" regression ability. Thus, both regressions are run with the single command

```
In[2]:= Reg[{dpi//Name,Call[r,Interest]},
            {"const",Clag//Name,deldpi//Name}];
```

```
Dependent variable is dpi
RSquared = 0.999243  RBarSquared = 0.99918
R2uncentered = 0.999934  SER = 3.49913
Num of Observations = 27    Degrees of Freedom = 24
dw = 1.45209 with 0 missing obs.
```

	coef.	st. err.	t
Const	−11.547	2.345	−4.924
Clag	1.138	0.007	164.922
deldpi	0.804	0.068	11.912

```
Dependent variable is Interest
RSquared = 0.956554   RBarSquared = 0.952933
R2uncentered = 0.994532   SER = 0.395232
Num of Observations = 27   Degrees of Freedom = 24
dw = 1.01104 with 0 missing obs.
```

	coef.	st. err.	t
Const	−1.024	0.265	−3.867
Clag	0.017	0.001	22.348
deldpi	−0.014	0.008	−1.901

14.3.11   Mixed Estimation [§10]

Initially, the mixed-estimation facility was not built into `Econometrics.m`, but
it could be rigged up from the output of the regular regression facility. After
tiring of doing this a number of times, I incorporated the function into `Econo-
metrics.m`. Others can do similar things to their copies of the package. This
situation, however, offers us an opportunity for comparing how such a task
can be "hand fashioned" within the `Reg[]` facility with its being done "automatically" using the `MixedEstimation[]` function built in to this version of
`Econometrics.m`.

14.3.11.1   Background

Mixed-estimation is a procedure, devised by Theil and Goldberger (1961) and
Theil (1963, 1971), by which prior, or auxiliary, information can be introduced
into a regression analysis by adding it directly to the data matrix.

Beginning with the linear model

$$\mathbf{y} = \mathbf{X}\boldsymbol{\beta} + \boldsymbol{\epsilon} \qquad (1)$$

with $E\boldsymbol{\epsilon} = \mathbf{0}$ and $\mathbf{V}(\boldsymbol{\epsilon}) = \boldsymbol{\Sigma}$, it is assumed the investigator can construct r linear
prior restrictions on the elements of $\boldsymbol{\beta}$ in the form

$$\mathbf{c} = \mathbf{R}\boldsymbol{\beta} + \boldsymbol{\zeta} \qquad (2)$$

with $E\boldsymbol{\zeta} = \mathbf{0}$ and $\mathbf{V}(\boldsymbol{\zeta}) = \boldsymbol{\Theta}$. Here $\mathbf{R}$ is a matrix of rank r of known constants,
$\mathbf{c}$ is an r-vector of specifiable values, and $\boldsymbol{\zeta}$ is a random vector, independent
of $\boldsymbol{\epsilon}$, with mean zero and variance-covariance matrix $\boldsymbol{\Theta}$, also assumed to be
stipulated by the investigator.

In the method of mixed-estimation as suggested by Theil and Goldberger,
estimation of (1) subject to (2) proceeds by augmenting $\mathbf{y}$ and $\mathbf{X}$ with $\mathbf{c}$ and
$\mathbf{R}$, respectively, as $\mathbf{z}' = [\mathbf{y}' \ \mathbf{c}'']$ and $\mathbf{W}' = [\mathbf{X}' \ \mathbf{R}']$ (where the prime indicates

transposition) to give

$$z = W\beta + \psi, \tag{3}$$

where $V(\psi)$ is a block diagonal matrix with Σ and Θ as its diagonal blocks. If these two matrices are known, generalized least squares applied to (3) results in the unbiased mixed-estimation estimator

$$b = (X'\Sigma^{-1}X + R'\Theta^{-1}R)^{-1}(X'\Sigma^{-1}y + R'\Theta^{-1}c). \tag{4}$$

In practice, an estimate is substituted for Σ (usually in the form s^2I, where s is the standard error determined from the regression of y on X), and Θ is specified by the investigator as part of the prior information.

14.3.11.2   Mixed-estimation, "By Hand."

First we must define a function to augment one matrix with another:

```
In[1]:= Adjoin[x_,y_] := Block[{n,m},
            {n,m} = Dimensions[y];
            Map[Join[x[[#]],y[[#]]]&,Range[n]]];
```

Then do the basic regression of y on X, hanging on to the regression output:

```
In[2]:= y = Con;
        X = {Table[1.0,{Length[y]}],Clag,dpi,r,deldpi};

        {beta,err,yhat,sig2} = Reg[Con, X,
                displayOutput -> False];
```

Preserve the estimate of the regression variances s^2 for later use in the mixed-estimation weighting

```
In[3]:= sigma = Sqrt[sig2]
```

```
Out[3]:= 3.55721
```

Form the prior information matrices R, c, and Θ [See Belsley (1991, pp 304-311) for an explanation of the formation of these priors]:

```
In[4]:= R = {{0.0,0.0,1.0,0.0,0.0},{0.0,0.9,1.0,0.0,0.0},
            {0.0,0.0,0.0,0.0,1.0}};
        c = {0.7,0.9,0.25};
        S = DiagonalMatrix[0.0058,0.0003904,0.0162];
```

Create the weighted mixed-estimation data matrices

```
In[5]:= z = Join[(1.0/sigma) y, Inverse[Sqrt[S]].c];
        W = Adjoin[(1.0/sigma) X,Transpose[Inverse[Sqrt[S]].R]];
```

Now we can do the mixed-estimation regression of z on W. Here we need to use the Level2 output option so that we can get the estimated standard errors for further processing:

```
In[6]:= {beta,err,yhat,sig2,se,vcMat} =
            Reg[z@,W@,returnValues->Level2];
```

```
Dependent variable is z
RSquared = 0.999469  RBarSquared = 0.999385
R2uncentered = 0.999923  SER = 0.949539
Num of Observations = 30    Degrees of Freedom = 25
dw = 1.98472 with 0 missing obs.
```

	coef.	st. err.	t
W[1]	7.604	2.330	3.264
W[2]	0.241	0.073	3.302
W[3]	0.688	0.063	10.945
W[4]	−1.354	1.018	−1.330
W[5]	0.198	0.070	2.829

The above coefficient estimates are correct, but the st. err.'s and t's are not because they have been multiplied by this regression's SER, so . . .

. . . the proper st. err.'s are

In[7]:= **se/Sqrt[sig2]**

Out[7]:= {2.45351, 0.0769647, 0.0661976, 1.07185, 0.073881}

and the proper t's are

In[8]:= **beta/%**

Out[8]:= {3.09908, 3.13543, 10.3924, −1.26318, 2.68583}

14.3.11.3 *Mixed-estimation, Automatically*

We assume here that **c**, **R**, and **S** have been defined as above.

In[1]:= **MixedEstimation[y,X,c,R,S];**

```
Dependent variable is y[1]
RSquared = 0.999479  RBarSquared = 0.999396
R2uncentered = 0.999923  SER = 1.
Num of Observations = 30    Degrees of Freedom = 25
dw = 1.77443 with 0 missing obs.
```

	coef.	st. err.	t
X[1]	7.604	2.454	3.099
X[2]	0.241	0.077	3.135
X[3]	0.688	0.066	10.392
X[4]	−1.354	1.072	−1.263
X[5]	0.198	0.074	2.686

Ah, that's more like it!

14.3.12 Two-Stage Least Squares and IV [§11]

In the previous examples, the consumption function has been estimated by OLS. Suppose now we (quite properly) consider the income term dpi to be endogenous along with Con. We would then consider dpi as "included endogenous,"

and we would require at least two additional "excluded exogenous" variates
to estimate via (truncated) 2SLS. Although I would not normally advise this
way of proceeding, I will make life easy for this example by using `lag[dpi]`,
`lag[deldpi]` and `lag[Clag]` as "excluded exogenous" variates. This gives

```
In[1]:= TwoStage[Con,{dpi,deldpi},{"const",Clag,r},{lag[dpi],
            lag[deldpi],lag[Clag]}];
Dependent variable is y[1]
RSquared = 0.998959   RBarSquared = 0.998761
R2uncentered = 1.00003   SER = 3.73293
Num of Observations = 26    Degrees of Freedom = 21
dw = 1.92772 with 1 missing obs.


                 coef.       st. err.          t

Const           9.388        4.686          2.004
Y[1]            0.796        0.266          2.993
Y[2]            0.176        0.199          0.886
X[2]            0.111        0.312          0.355
X[3]           -1.094        2.154         -0.508

Instruments:{dpi(-1), deldpi(-1), Clag(-1)}
```

Note that the instruments that were used are listed at the end. In the case
of `TwoStage[]`, these are the excluded exogenous variates. The included
exogenous variates are automatically used as well. In the case of `IV[]`, this list
will include the full set of instrumental variates used.

We ought to get the same result using the following call to `IV[]`.

```
In[2]:= IV[Con@,{"const",dpi@,deldpi@,Clag@,r@},{"const",Clag@,r@,
            lag[dpi],lag[deldpi],lag[Clag]}];
Dependent variable is Con
RSquared = 0.998959   RBarSquared = 0.998761
R2uncentered = 1.00003   SER = 3.73293
Num of Observations = 26    Degrees of Freedom = 21
dw = 1.92772 with 1 missing obs.


                 coef.       st. err.          t

Const           9.388        4.686          2.004
dpi             0.796        0.266          2.993
deldpi          0.176        0.199          0.886
Clag            0.111        0.312          0.355
r              -1.094        2.154         -0.508

Instruments:{Const, Clag, r, dpi(-1), deldpi(-1), Clag(-1)}
```

14.4   Development Notes

14.4.1   The Package Environment

`Econometrics.m` contains a considerable amount of code using many variable
names. It has therefore been written as a package with its own context so that

its many variates will not interfere with the user's. Like any package, it can be invoked by the user at any time during the session simply by entering

```
<<Econometrics.m
```

Further, in order to remove the possibility of inadvertently redefined variables within the `Econometrics.m` context, its various modules have been written in a manner to emulate the local scoping of a truly structured language. This is accomplished by reducing global variables to an absolute minimum and by otherwise passing all relevant parameters into and out of each `Block`. In this way, a specific variable name can be altered only consciously and not inadvertently (through what has become known as a *Mathematica* "surprise"). This results in a package that can be safely expanded in the future.

Local scoping is facilitated in *Mathematica* through the use of `Blocks` or `Modules`. `Modules` are new to version 2.0 of *Mathematica* and provide lexical scoping. `Econometrics.m` was originally written before the advent of `Modules` and used `Blocks`. The latest documentation with *Mathematica*, however, appears to promote the use of `Modules` over `Blocks`. Consequently, in upgrading `Econometrics.m` to be fully compatible with version 2.0 of *Mathematica*, the necessary alterations were made so that it will work perfectly if every `Block` is changed to `Module`. I continue to use `Blocks` in `Econometrics.m`, however, because the use of `Modules` causes the package to run significantly more slowly, and there are otherwise no problems in using `Blocks`. Should future versions of *Mathematica* no longer support the `Block` statement, merely find-and-replace each occurrence of `Block` with `Module`.

Error handling in `Econometrics.m` is accomplished using a "collapse back" method; i.e., once an error is discovered, an appropriate message is displayed and the condition is fed back through each pending function to allow it to be closed out gracefully, reclaiming all temporarily allocated memory. *Mathematica*'s `Catch` and `Throw` functions could have provided similar error handling with less code, but at the cost of not being able to reclaim the memory allocated up to the point of the error, accelerating the infamous *Mathematica* "memory bar creep."

14.4.2   Configurations for Input Data

There are at least two elements of *Mathematica* that create an environment that is somewhat unusual from that normally encountered in econometrics software, such as SAS, SPSS, TROLL, TSP, etc. First, true to their mathematical heritage, vectors and $1 \times n$ (or $n \times 1$) matrices are treated as separate kinds of objects. Second, the normal mode of data entry into arrays, determined by the C-like characteristics of the *Mathematica* language, is row- rather than column-oriented. In much econometric analysis, the first distinction is rarely recognized and the second convention is typically treated oppositely (a throwback to the FORTRAN conventions of econometrics' youth).

In order to render both of these differences as transparent to the user of `Econometrics.m` as possible, a recursive routine analyzes the input data to resolve each entry into a set of vectors, which are then added, one by one, to the working data matrix. If the item is itself a vector, it is assumed to be a variate (rather than an observation), and becomes a column of the final data array. If the item is a matrix, it is assumed that the longer dimension is the number of observations, the shorter the number of variates. Thus, the input matrices may be either $n \times p$ or $p \times n$, or may even be a list of matrices of different dimensions and orientations. In every case, the p columns of n observations will be added to the working data array. The final value for n is determined by the shortest data series less any missing observations (non-numeric entries).

On the positive side, this method of data input produces one of the most easily invoked regression packages I have encountered. Weighed against this are (1) the loss in flexibility that results from requiring all data series to begin with the same observation, and (2) the difficulties that arise in finding practical means for allowing variable names to be introduced for use in the output display.

14.4.3   Choice of Algorithms

As noted at the outset, one of the shortcomings of *Mathematica*'s built-in least-squares "fitting" routines is their inability to return the information needed to compute the coefficient standard errors or, more generally, their variance-covariance matrix. This requires computing the equivalent of

```
Inverse[Transpose[X].X],
```

where X is the $n \times p$ final data array. In many circumstances, a Cholesky decomposition is quite adequate to this need and is certainly a speedy choice among the alternatives. In the event that the X matrix is quite ill-conditioned, however, a QR decomposition or a singular-value decomposition (SVD) is superior, the latter having the disadvantage only of added computational effort.

The early versions of `Econometrics.m` were based on the built-in *Mathematica* function for the singular-value decomposition. This choice was made for several reasons. First, even though the SVD is computationally slower than the alternatives in principle, the built-in SVD routine is compiled and runs considerably faster in practice than a "hand-rolled" Cholesky or QR decomposition. Second, the SVD is always a suitable way to proceed, whereas Cholesky is not if the data are ill-conditioned. And, third, the use of the SVD is mandatory if one wishes the collinearity diagnostics, for this information is not obtainable from either the Cholesky or the QR decompositions.

Happily, the QR decomposition has been added in version 2.0 of *Mathematica*, and so now it is possible to get the best of both worlds, and version 2.0 of `Econometrics.m` has been rewritten to take advantage of this situation. The faster and computationally more efficient QR decomposition is used to perform the basic regression calculations by default. When, however, the data are discovered to be so ill-conditioned that they are, for all intents and purposes, perfectly collinear (a situation that is signaled here by the failure of the QR decomposition to return an R matrix of size p), `Econometrics.m` automatically switches to the SVD with a tolerance of 10^{-30}. The user may also force the use of the SVD through the use of the option `algorithm -> SVD`.

The collinearity diagnostics, of course, require the information from the SVD. So if the QR decomposition has been used for the basic regression calculations and the collinearity diagnostics are opted for (`varDCom -> True`), the SVD is run on the R matrix. This results in the same singular values and eigenvector elements as applying the SVD to the original data matrix X, but does so much more efficiently since R is only $p \times p$, while X is $n \times p$, giving a computational savings of $2/3(n - p)p^2$.

The SVD routines in *Mathematica* return matrices of reduced rank when there are singular values that are machine zeros. This is a useful property in many contexts, but not all, and its use in `Econometrics.m` is one such. It is possible to work around this problem by setting the tolerance below machine zero, say, 10^{-30} or 10^{-40}, which is what `Econometrics.m` does by default. This, for the most part, works for the SVD routine in version 2.0, but I have found some special cases of perfect singularity where the output rank is truncated regardless of the tolerance. This is clearly an unfortunate "feature"; while a regression run under such conditions is obviously garbage, it becomes impossible to control the output, and the screen can become garbage filled as well. I suspect and hope these conditions are very special indeed. It would be nice if this feature were fixed in a future version of the SVD, thereby allowing one to control the sizes of the various matrices in the decomposition (even if not of full rank). It would also be nice if a similar tolerance option were added to the QR decomposition, which also returns truncated matrices when there is extreme ill-conditioning.

14.4.4   Extensions

14.4.4.1   *What to Incorporate*

Issues always arise as to what should be incorporated into `Econometrics.m` and what ought be left to be done through external functions. As the examples above show, it certainly seems reasonable to leave data transformations and output graphics to be done externally. These processes are already far more efficiently coded in the *Mathematica* environment. However, with other operations it is not so clear. We have also seen that mixed-estimation could readily have been implemented as an external function, having the various prior and weighting matrices as inputs, calling `Reg[]` with the appropriate arguments, and doctoring the standard errors and t's from the output. The drawbacks to this are severalfold. First, one loses the formatting and missing observation facility for the input data. Second, one must needlessly repeat the text outputting code needed for a friendly screen display. It therefore seemed reasonable to build mixed-estimation into `Econometrics.m`.

Similar considerations argued for incorporating the White (1980) heteroskedasticity-consistent variance-covariance matrix. This too could have been implemented as an external function based on the returned residual vector, `err`.

But, in addition to again losing the data input flexibility inherent in `Economet-rics.m`, it would have required that the pseudo-inverse of `X` be recalculated, an operation that is the computational heart of the regression. It clearly seems foolish to turn a single regression needlessly into two. One solution would be to add an option to `returnValues` allowing the pseudo-inverse of `X` to be returned, but this would have required storing this often large matrix throughout the entire time `Econometrics.m` was invoked. Thus, I opted to incorporate it.

I decided not to incorporate facilities for estimation of full systems of simultaneous equations. This would have produced a package unreasonably large for the purposes of simple regressions. However, the tools for constructing full-systems estimators are to be found in an accompanying package, `Block-Matrix.m`. This package, along with another called `StatUtilities.m`, is described in the final section.

14.4.4.2 Additional Output Options

The user is always free to add elements to the output and, indeed, even new output options. There is no simple step by which this can be accomplished, but the following general principles should prevail:

- Whatever variable is ultimately to be returned must, if not already there, be added to the list of "local" variables [the list of variables in the braces directly after the `Block` designation] of the four main returning functions: `Reg[]`, `TwoStage[]`, `IV[]`, and `MixedEstimation[]`.

- The variable to be returned must then be passed back to the main calling functions. If the variable is new, it must be appropriately defined during the course of the operation.

- The symbol for the variable must then be added to the appropriate output list in the `doReturn[]` function. Use the `find` command to locate this function, which is near the beginning of the package.

- If you wish to add an entirely new output level, say, `returnValues -> Level3`, simply add it to the top of the `Switch` list in `doReturn[]`, following and extending the existing syntax pattern in the obvious manner. Be sure also to add the new option name to the `$PreRead` statement at the head of the package, again following any existing pattern.

- It would also be wise to update the summary information in the options portion of the `Reg::usage` text that occurs right at the beginning of the package, just so you and anyone else using your version of the package will know what output to expect and its format.

14.5 Related Experimental Packages

In this section two accompanying packages are described that substantially augment `Econometrics.m` for conducting econometric analysis in the *Mathematica* environment. The first, `BlockMatrix.m`, gives the tools necessary

for constructing simultaneous-equations estimators. The second, StatUtil-
ities.m, gives the tools needed for constructing various random vectors and
matrices for conducting statistical or Monte Carlo experiments using Econo-
metrics.m, and for conducting various statistical tests using the output of
Econometrics.m.

14.5.1   StatUtilities.m

To facilitate testing and experimentation, this package provides the following
tools:

14.5.1.1   Generating Gaussian Variates

Gaussian[mean_:0, var_:1]
This function returns a Gaussian (normal) random variable with specified mean
and variance. The mean and variance default to values of 0 and 1, respectively.
Thus Gaussian[] returns a standard normal; Gaussian[,6] returns a normal
with mean 0 and variance 6.

SphericalStandardGaussian[size_, seriesLength_:1]
This function returns n (seriesLength) independent draws from a p (size)-
dimensional standard normal. seriesLength defaults to 1, so Spherical-
StandardGaussian[40] can also be used to produce a vector of 40 independent standard normals.

**MultivariateGaussian[size_, seriesLength_:1, mean_:Null,
variance_:Null]**
This function returns n (seriesLength) independent draws from a p (size)-
dimensional normal with mean vector (mean) and variance-covariance matrix
(variance). mean defaults to a zero vector of size p, and variance defaults
to the p-dimensional identity matrix.

14.5.1.2   Testing Hypotheses

Fstat[estBetas_, VarCovMatrix_, hypothValues_:Null]
Given estimated coefficients estBetas and their variance-covariance matrix
VarCovMatrix, this function calculates the F test of standard test of hypothesis H_0: beta = hypothValues vs. H_1: beta != hypothValues. Thus, for
example, if estBetas were the full set of regression estimates from Reg[],
VarCovMatrix would be sig2*vcMat. For conducting hypotheses on subsets of the estimated coefficients, see below.

   hypothValues is a list of the hypothesized "true" values. The dimensions
of the three arguments to Fstat[] must be p, $p \times p$, and p respectively. If an
element of hypothValues is a number, that becomes the hypothesized value
for that coefficient in the test. If an element is a non-number, such as an "na",
that coefficient is ignored in the test (i.e., the test is marginal with respect to that
coefficient). If hypothValues is omitted, Fstat[] assumes the first coefficient
is a constant term and tests that all slope coefficients are zero.

14.5.1.3 Mean and Variance

Mean[list_List]
This function returns the arithmetic mean of `list`.

Variance[list_List]
This function returns the sample variance of `list`.

14.5.1.4 Correlations

Correlation[x1_List,x2_List]
This function returns the Neyman-Pearson correlation between two lists, `x1` and `x2`. The lists must be of equal length.

CorrelationMatrix[mat_]
This function returns the matrix of correlations among the rows of the matrix `mat`.

CovarianceToCorrelationMatrix[CovMat_]
This function coverts a covariance matrix, `CovMat`, into its corresponding correlation matrix. `CovMat`, must be symmetric.

14.5.1.5 Centering and Scaling

Centered[list_,centerValue_:Infinity]
This function returns the vector `list` centered about the value `centerValue`. If `centerValue` is omitted, a mean-centered `list` is returned.

EuclideanNorm[list_]
This function returns the Euclidean length of a vector `list`.

Normalized[list_List]
This function returns the vector `list` normalized to have unit Euclidean length.

LogEscale[list_]
This function logs and e-scales `list` (i.e., normalizes it to have geometric mean e) and returns the result. This normalization is necessary for conducting the collinearity diagnostics on logged variates. See Belsley, Kuh, and Welsch (1980) or Belsley (1991).
   Note: Use `Escale[]` below to e-scale an already logged variate.

Escale[logList_]
This function returns an e-scaled `logList`, i.e., a variate that has already been logged. This normalization is necessary for conducting the collinearity diagnostics on logged variates. See Belsley, Kuh, and Welsch (1980) or Belsley (1991).
   Note: Use `LogEscale[]` above to log and e-scale an unlogged variate.

14.5.1.6 Miscellaneous

SymmetricQ[mat_]
This function returns `True` if `mat` is a symmetric matrix, otherwise `False`.

SquareQ[mat_]
This function returns True if mat is a square matrix, otherwise False.

Truncate[x_, n_]
This function returns x truncated after n digits. x can be a list here.

Grad[f_, x_]
This function returns the gradient of the function f with respect to the arguments in the list x.

Hessian[f_, x_]
This function returns the Hessian matrix of the function f with respect to the arguments in the list x.

14.5.2   BlockMatrix.m

This package provides various matrix-manipulation tools that facilitate the development of simultaneous-system and full-information estimators. At an experimental level, these estimators require means for forming block matrices and Kronecker products of matrices. The three-stage least-squares estimator, for example, is

$$\delta_{3SLS} = (\mathbf{Z}'(\mathbf{S}^{-1} \otimes \mathbf{X}(\mathbf{X}'\mathbf{X})^{-1}\mathbf{X}')\mathbf{Z})^{-1}\mathbf{Z}'(\mathbf{S}^{-1} \otimes \mathbf{X}(\mathbf{X}'\mathbf{X})^{-1}\mathbf{X}')\text{vec}(\mathbf{Y}),$$

where $\mathbf{X}$, $\mathbf{Y}$ and $\mathbf{Z}$ are data matrices, $\mathbf{S}$ is an estimated variance-covariance matrix, $\otimes$ is the Kronecker product, $\text{vec}(\mathbf{A})$ is the vector formed by stacking the columns of the matrix $\mathbf{A}$, and the prime denotes transposition. One can save considerably in both computation counts and memory storage by using an alternative formulation [in Belsley (1992)], but the types of matrix-manipulation tools required are the same. Thus, the package BlockMatrix.m provides the following tools:

14.5.2.1   Kronecker Products and Vec

KroneckerProduct[A_?MatrixQ, B_?MatrixQ]
This function forms the Kronecker Product of two matrices, A ⊗ B. The convention here goes right-to-left, that is, each element of A is multiplied by B. Although the Kronecker product is a tensor product, the form of the tensor product, Outer[Times, a, b], utilized in *Mathematica* does not produce a matrix in a form suitable for econometric applications. Such a form does, however, result from the following remapping:

```
Partition[Flatten[Map[Transpose,Outer[Times,a,b],1]],
                 Dimensions[a][[2]]*Dimensions[b][[2]]]
```

Vec[a_?MatrixQ]
This function returns a vector formed by stacking the columns of the matrix a.
    Note: the Vec[] function could be defined by convention as either stacking the rows or the columns of a given matrix. Usual econometric practice is to

stack columns, and so that has been adopted here. Some authors [Sargan (1988), for example], adopt the row-stacking convention, which would in fact be more in keeping with the *Mathematica* convention for representing matrices. Should the user desire the row-stacking definition, one need only remove the `Transpose[]` from the function definition, `Flatten[Transpose[a]]`.

14.5.2.2　Forming Block Matrices

`Adjoin[r__]`
This function, which can have any number of arguments $A, B, \ldots, G$, forms the block matrix $[A|B|\cdots|G]$ from them. Clearly, all these matrices must have the same number of rows.

`BlockDiagonalMatrix[r__]`
This function, which can have any number of arguments $A, B, \ldots, G$, forms the block diagonal matrix having $A, B, \ldots, G$ as the diagonal blocks and zeros elsewhere. There are no restrictions on the sizes of the matrix arguments, but the arguments must be matrices.

`BlockMatrix[D_]`
This function forms a block matrix from a matrix D of commensurate matrices. The i, j-th element of D becomes the i, j-block of the final matrix. Clearly all the matrices in the same row of D must have the same number of rows, and all the matrices in the same column of D must have the same number of columns.

14.6　References

Belsley, D. A. (1991), *Conditioning Diagnostics*, John Wiley & Sons: New York.

Belsley, D. A. (1992), "Paring 3SLS Calculations Down to Manageable Proportions," *Computational Science in Economics and Management*, **5**, 157–169.

Belsley, D. A., E. Kuh, and R. E. Welsch (1980), *Regression Diagnostics*, John Wiley & Sons: New York.

Durbin, J. (1970), "Testing for Serial Correlation in Least-Squares Regression when Some of the Regressors are Lagged Dependent Variables," *Econometrica*, **38**, 410–421.

Johnston, J. (1984), *Econometric Methods, 3rd Edition*, McGraw Hill: New York.

MacKinnon, J. G. "Model Specification Tests and Artificial Regressions," *Journal of Economic Literature*, **30**, 102–146.

Theil, H. (1971), *Principles of Econometrics*, John Wiley & Sons: New York.

White, H. (1980), "A Heteroskedasticity Consistent Covariance Matrix Estimator and a Direct Test of Heteroskedasticity," *Econometrica*, **48**, 817–838.

15 Bayesian Econometrics: Conjugate Analysis and Rejection Sampling

Eduardo Ley and Mark F.J. Steel

15.1   Introduction

In real-world problems we are invariably faced with making decisions in an environment of uncertainty (see also the chapter by R. Korsan in this volume). A statistical paradigm then becomes essential for extracting information from observed data and using this to improve our knowledge about the world (inference), and thus guiding us in the decision problem at hand. The underlying probability interpretation for a Bayesian is a subjective one, referring to a personal degree of belief. The rules of probability calculus are used to examine how prior beliefs are transformed to posterior beliefs by incorporating data information. The sampling model is a "window" [see Poirier (1988)] through which the researcher views the world. Here we only consider cases where such a model is parameterized by a parameter vector θ of finite dimension. A Bayesian then focuses on the inference on θ (treated as a random variable) given the observed data Y (fixed), summarized in the posterior density $p(\theta|Y)$. The observations in Y define a mapping from the prior $p(\theta)$ into $p(\theta|Y)$. This posterior distribution can also be used to integrate out the parameters when we are interested in forecasting future values, say, $\tilde{Y}$, leading to the post-sample predictive density $p(\tilde{Y}|Y) = \int p(\tilde{Y}|Y, \theta)p(\theta|Y)d\theta$ where $p(\tilde{Y}|Y, \theta)$ is obtained from the sampling model.

In Economics as in many other disciplines, the Bayesian paradigm seems ideally suited to address the questions typically arising in applied work. Whereas statisticians are often mainly attracted by the theoretical coherence and mathematical elegance of the Bayesian approach, resulting in quotes like:

"It is difficult for me to tone down the missionary zeal acquired in youth, but perhaps the good battle is justified since there are still many heathens." [I.J. Good (1976)];

"Or perhaps most statisticians now *are* Bayesians (when it matters!), but they do not want to spoil the fun by admitting it." [A.F.M. Smith (1986)];

"Every statistician would be a Bayesian if he took the trouble to read the literature thoroughly and was honest enough to admit he might have been wrong." [D.V. Lindley (1986)];

econometricians, on the other hand, have primarily stressed the practical advantages of using the Bayesian paradigm, as opposed to the classical or sampling-theoretical methodology:

"In other words, the traditional approach lacks flexibility in that it relies upon *too few* a priori restrictions that are, however, *too strict*." [J.H. Drèze (1962)];
"Necessarily, practicing economists have discarded the formal constraints of classical inference." [E.E. Leamer (1978)].

In particular, the Bayesian approach provides a formal way of incorporating any information we may have prior to observing the data, it fits perfectly with sequential learning and decision theory, and directly leads to exact small sample results. In addition, it naturally gives rise to predictive densities, where all parameters are integrated out, making it a perfect tool for missing data or forecasting. Of course, all this comes at a cost, which is typically of a computational nature. An analytical solution to the computational problem is provided by restricting ourselves to natural-conjugate prior densities to summarize the prior information [see Raiffa and Schlaifer (1961) or Zellner (1971)]. A natural-conjugate prior shares the functional form of the likelihood and in exponential families this leads to posterior densities of the same form. The first part of this essay will consider this analysis in a Normal linear regression model for health expenditure in OECD countries [see Newhouse (1977)].

A much more flexible tool is the rejection sampling method discussed in Smith and Gelfand (1992), which only requires that the maximum value of the sampling density

$$M = \max_{\theta} p(Y|\theta)$$

is finite. If we can then draw from the prior $p(\theta)$, we can generate drawings from the posterior $p(\theta|Y)$ simply by rejection. The second part of this chapter will treat this method in some detail and illustrate it with an application to demand analysis.

15.2 Conjugate Analysis

The sampling model that we will focus on here is the linear regression model

$$y = X\beta + \varepsilon$$

where the observations $y' = (y_1, y_2, \ldots, y_T)$ are related to the k explanatory variables in $X = (x_1, x_2, \ldots, x_k)$, which are assumed to be strongly exogenous in the sense of Engle *et al.* (1983)—for a Bayesian treatment of exogeneity see Florens and Mouchart (1985) and Osiewalski and Steel (1990). The error vector ε is assumed to have a Normal distribution with mean zero and covariance matrix $\sigma^2 I_T$ ($\sigma^2 > 0$).

In this application we are interested in the elasticity of the per capita health expenditure with respect to income (GDP) [Newhouse (1977)]. We use cross-country data on 24 OECD countries (the data that we use appeared in the *Health Care Financing Review* 1989 Annual Supplement). We explain per capita health expenditure, y, by GDP per capita, x_2, and the share of the public sector in total health expenses, x_3. Purchasing power parities are used to convert all magnitudes to common units. All variables are in natural logs and a constant, x_1 is included. Sample size is $T = 24$, and $k = 3$.

15.2.1   Read in Data and Define Variables

We read the data corresponding to 1986 using standard *Mathematica* procedures. We use the **SetDelayed** (':=') function instead of the **Set** ('=') function so that all the variables are automatically updated to their 1987 values when we later read the 1987 data into **data**.

```
In[1]:= data = ReadList[ "health86.dat", Table[Number, {5}] ];
        tothealthexp := Column[data, 1];
        pubhealthexp := Column[data, 2];
        population   := Column[data, 3];
        GDP          := Column[data, 4];
        PPP          := Column[data, 5];
```

Transformations are easily achieved using standard *Mathematica* functions,

```
In[2]:= y  := Log[tothealthexp/(population*PPP)];
        x2 := Log[GDP/(population*PPP)];
        x3 := Log[(pubhealthexp/tothealthexp)*100];
        X  := Table[{1, x2[[i]], x3[[i]]}, {i, 1, Length[data]}];
```

15.2.2   Bayesian Regression Analysis: Diffuse Prior

The parameter set in this problem is $\beta = (\beta_1, \beta_2, \beta_3)'$ and σ. We shall first assume that we possess no prior information at all which is translated into the improper prior density

$$p(\beta, \sigma) = p(\beta)p(\sigma) \propto \sigma^{-1}$$

The latter prior density is obtained by applying Jeffreys' rule [see Jeffreys (1961) and Zellner (1971)] under prior independence of β and σ. Calling **BayesRegression**[*ydata, Xdata*] will return the posterior densities for σ and β into the *Mathematica* variables **postdistsigma** and **postdistbeta**.

```
In[1]:= BayesRegression[y, X]
```

15.2.2.1 Sigma

As this diffuse prior can, in fact, be considered as a limiting case of a natural-conjugate prior, the posterior analysis becomes quite straightforward; in particular, the posterior density of σ will be of the inverted gamma form (see Appendix):

$$p(\sigma|y, X) = f_{i\gamma}(\sigma|T - k, s),$$

where $s^2 = y'M_x y/(T - k)$ and $M_x = I_T - X(X'X)^{-1}X'$. Typing **postdist-sigma** we obtain σ's posterior density:[1]

In[1]:= **postdistsigma**

Out[1]:= IGammaDistribution[21, 0.152788]

Moments of this density are known analytically and can be readily computed:

In[2]:= **Mean[postdistsigma]**

Out[2]:= 0.15853

In[3]:= **Variance[postdistsigma]**

Out[3]:= 0.000669825

A plot shows clearly how the prior information (with arbitrary scaling), the dashed curve, is modified substantially through the observations.

In[4]:= **Plot[{PDF[postdistsigma,s], s^{-1}}, {s, 0.01, 0.4},**
         PlotRange -> {0, 20},
         AxesLabel -> {"sigma", "density"},
         PlotStyle -> {{}, {Dashing[{0.015, 0.015}]}}]

Out[4]:= —Graphics—

15.2.2.2   Beta

For the coefficients in β, the resulting marginal posterior density is of the multivariate Student t form (see Appendix):

$$p(\beta|y, X) = f_t^k(\beta|\hat{\beta}, s^{-2}X'X, T - k),$$

[where $\hat{\beta}$ is the least-squares estimate, $\hat{\beta} = (X'X)^{-1}X'y$] which, again, has known moments, up to the order $T - k$.

---

[1] The distributions that this package adds to the existing ones in **ContinuousStatisticalDistributions** are the **IGammaDistribution**, the (non-standard) Student **UnivariateTDistribution**, the Student **MultivariateTDistribution** and the **MultivariateNormalDistribution**.

```
In[1]:= postdistbeta

Out[1]:= MultivariateTDistribution[{-3.40481, 1.45723,
            -0.077314},
           {{1028.09, 2466.91, 4423.01},
            {2466.91, 6046.67, 10644.6},
            {4423.01, 10644.6, 19077.9}}, 21]

In[2]:= Mean[postdistbeta]

Out[2]:= {-3.40481, 1.45723, -0.077314}

In[3]:= MatrixForm[Variance[postdistbeta]]

Out[3]:=   0.415384      0.00355095    -0.0982834
           0.00355095    0.0103118     -0.00657677
          -0.0982834    -0.00657677     0.0265134
```

Marginal [*list*, *MultivariateDistribution*] returns the marginal distribution of
the elements in *list*,

```
In[4]:= mar23 = Marginal[{2, 3}, postdistbeta]

Out[4]:= MultivariateTDistribution[{1.45723, -0.077314},
            {{127.328, 31.5843}, {31.5843, 49.5216}}, 21]
```

We take advantage of *Mathematica*'s powerful plotting functions to visualize
the posterior joint density of (β_2, β_3),

```
In[5]:= densityBetaDA = Plot3D[PDF[mar23, {b2, b3}],
        {b2, 1.2, 1.7}, {b3, -0.5, 0.2},
        PlotRange->All, AxesLabel -> {"b2 ", "  b3", ""}]
```

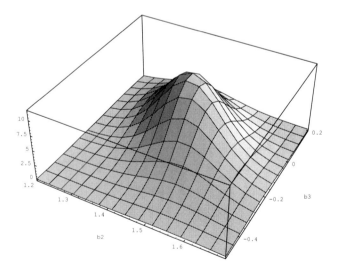

```
Out[5]:= -SurfaceGraphics-

In[6]:= contourBetaDA = ContourPlot[PDF[mar23, {b2, b3}],
        {b2, 1.2, 1.7}, {b3, -0.5, 0.2},
        PlotRange -> All, PlotPoints -> 30,
        Axes -> True, AxesLabel -> {"b2", "b3"}]
```

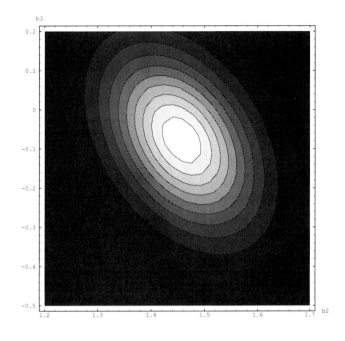

Out[6]:= —ContourGraphics—

Also, we can plot the prior (improper, therefore scaled arbitrarily) and posterior marginal densities of each of the β_i's in the same picture to graphically display the data information. For example, for β_2 we have

In[7]:= **Plot[{PDF[Marginal[{2},postdistbeta], b2], 1},**
{b2, 1.1, 1.8},
AxesLabel -> {"b2", "density"},
PlotRange -> All,
PlotStyle -> {{}, {Dashing[{0.015, 0.015}]}}]

Out[7]:= —Graphics—

15.2.2.3   Highest Posterior Density Regions

To obtain a Bayesian interval estimate for a parameter, say β_3, with a preassigned probability content q, say $q = 0.8$, we can use the *highest posterior density* (HPD) interval [see Judge *et al.* (1985)]. Since the marginal posterior density of β_3 is unimodal and symmetric, the interval will be symmetric around the posterior mean, say b_3, so we just need to find the z which solves,

$$\int_{b_3-z}^{b_3+z} p(\beta_3|y, X)d\beta_3 = 0.8$$

then,

```
In[1]:= m2 = Marginal[{2}, postdistbeta]
```

```
Out[1]:= UnivariateTDistribution[1.45723, 107.184, 21]
```

```
In[2]:= q = .80; {Mean[m2] - z, Mean[m2] + z}/.FindRoot[
            Integrate[PDF[m2, b2], {b2, Mean[m2] - z,
            Mean[m2] + z}] - q, {z, 0.10}]
```

```
Out[2]:= {1.32942, 1.58504}
```

Thus, there is a 80% posterior probability that β_3 belongs to the interval $(1.33, 1.59)$. Note that the prior probability content of that interval (as of any other bounded interval) is zero due to the improper reference prior.

15.2.2.4   Probability of Subspaces

The *Mathematica* function **NIntegrate** provides a straightforward method for computing the probabilities of certain regions in parameter space. Suppose that we are interested in the posterior probability that the elasticity of health expenditures with respect to income is greater than 1 ($\beta_2 > 1$) *and* that the elasticity with respect to the public sector participation in the health expenditures is negative ($\beta_3 < 0$). We can easily compute $Pr[\beta_2 > 1, \beta_3 < 0|y, X]$ integrating the joint density function of (β_2, β_3) over the appropiate range,

```
In[1]:= NIntegrate[PDF[mar23, {b2, b3}],
            {b2, 1, Infinity}, {b3, -Infinity, 0}]
```

```
Out[1]:= 0.688572
```

so, the desired probability is 68.86%.

15.2.2.5   Prediction

If we now wish to predict the per capita health expenses

$$\tilde{y}' = (\tilde{y}_{T+1}, \tilde{y}_{T+2}, \ldots, \tilde{y}_{T+n})$$

in other countries with explanatory variables $\tilde{X}$, we can simply use the post-sample predictive density

$$p(\tilde{y}|y, X, \tilde{X}) = f_t^n(\tilde{y}|\tilde{X}\hat{\beta}, s^{-2}(I_n + \tilde{X}(X'X)^{-1}\tilde{X}')^{-1}, T - k)$$

where all the parameters are integrated out using the posterior densities (i.e., incorporating the information on the actual observed countries).

If we take 2 unobserved countries (25, 26) with $\tilde{x}_2 = \log 20$, $\tilde{x}_3 = \log 0.5$ and $\tilde{x}_2 = \log 70$, $\tilde{x}_3 = \log 0.9$ respectively, we are led to the following post-sample predictive:

```
In[1]:= xf = {{1, Log[20.00], Log[.5]},
              {1, Log[70.00], Log[.9]}};
        BayesRegression[y, X, xf];
        preddisty
```

Out[1]:= MultivariateTDistribution[{1.01424, 2.79436},
        {{16.4694, −16.2248}, {−16.2248, 17.5988}}, 21]

which can easily be plotted using the intrinsic *Mathematica* features.

```
In[2]:= ContourPlot[PDF[preddisty, {y25, y26}],
        {y25, 0, 2.5}, {y26, 1.5, 4},
        PlotPoints -> 30,
        Axes -> True,
        AxesLabel -> {"y25", "y26"}]
```

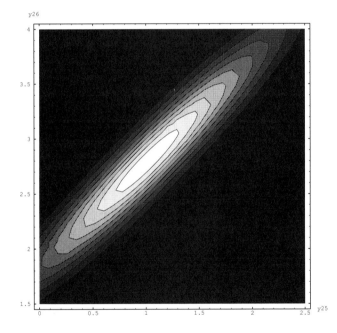

Out[2]:= −ContourGraphics−

Note from the contour plot that y_{25} and y_{26} are not uncorrelated, even though they arise from an independent sampling process. Integrating out σ makes them dependent as it changes the Normal to a multivariate Student (where the elements can never be independent even if the correlation is zero) and integrating out the common uncertainty on β introduces correlation as well.

15.2.3   Natural Conjugate Analysis

When new data become available for 1987, we can use the posterior densities from the previous analysis as prior densities to study the behavior of the model. Reading the new data into **data** automatically updates the contents of all variables.

In[1]:= **data = ReadList["health87.dat", Table[Number, {5}]];**

Given that we are in a Normal linear context, the posterior distributions obtained from the previous diffuse analysis are natural conjugate priors.[2]

In[2]:= **priordistbeta = postdistbeta;**
        priordistsigma = postdistsigma;
        BayesRegression[y, X, priordistbeta, priordistsigma]

As before, **postdistsigma** contains the posterior distribution for σ,

In[3]:= **postdistsigma**

Out[3]:= IGammaDistribution[45, 0.143222]

We can plot the prior (dashed line) and posterior densities in the same graph,

In[4]:= **Plot[{PDF[postdistsigma,s], PDF[priordistsigma,s]},**
        {s, 0.10, 0.25},
        PlotRange -> All, AxesLabel -> {"sigma", "density"},
        PlotStyle -> {{}, {Dashing[{0.025, 0.025}]}}]

Out[4]:= —Graphics—

Similarly, we obtain the posterior distribution for β,

In[5]:= **postdistbeta**

---

[2] When we want to use different prior information of a natural conjugate form, the function **BayesRegression** can alternatively be called with the hyperparameters of the prior distributions instead of the distributions themselves. Type **??BayesRegression** for details.

```
Out[5]:= MultivariateTDistribution[{-3.37346, 1.48573,
            -0.102293},
           {{2340.04, 5677.02, 10087.1}, {5677.02,
            14062.8, 24542.9}, {10087.1, 24542.9,
            43590.8}}, 45]
```

The prior and posterior densities for β_2 and β_3 can be plotted side by side in order be more easily compared,

```
In[6]:= mar23 = Marginal[{2, 3}, postdistbeta];
       densityBetaNCA = Plot3D[PDF[mar23, {b2, b3}],
         {b2, 1.2, 1.7}, {b3, -0.5, 0.2},
         PlotRange -> All, AxesLabel -> {"b2 ", "   b3", ""},
         DisplayFunction -> Identity];
       contourBetaNCA = ContourPlot[PDF[mar23, {b2, b3}],
         {b2, 1.2, 1.7}, {b3, -0.5, 0.2},
         PlotRange -> All, PlotPoints -> 30, Axes -> True,
         AxesLabel -> {"b2", "b3"},
         DisplayFunction -> Identity];
       Show[GraphicsArray[{{densityBetaDA, contourBetaDA},
         {densityBetaNCA, contourBetaNCA}}],
         DisplayFunction -> $DisplayFunction]
```

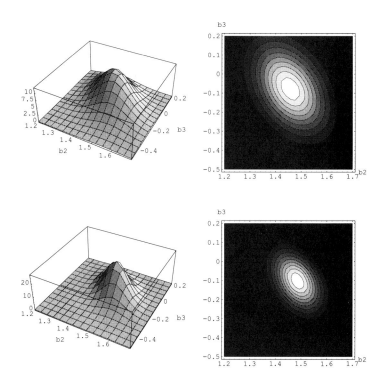

```
Out[6]:= -GraphicsArray-
```

The new data information significantly concentrates the density around its mean. There is no real conflict of information between the data in both years.

Finally, we can plot the marginal posterior densities of any of the elements in β, for example β_2,

```
In[7]:= Plot[{PDF[Marginal[{2}, postdistbeta], b2],
         PDF[Marginal[{2}, priordistbeta], b2]},
         {b2, 1.1, 1.8}, PlotStyle -> {{},
         {Dashing[{0.015, 0.015}]}},
         AxesLabel -> {"b2", "density"}, PlotRange -> All]
```

```
Out[7]:= -Graphics-
```

15.3   A Rejection Sampling Approach to Demand Analysis

15.3.1   Introduction

The sampling model applies a suggestion of Varian (1990) to a demand system. Let the utility function be completely characterized by the functional form $u(\cdot)$ and the parameter α, $u = u(x; \alpha)$. If the *actual* expenditure (for observation t), $m_t = p_t x_t$, [where $p_t = (p_{1t}, p_{2t}, \ldots, p_{nt})$ is a row vector of prices, and $x_t = (x_{1t}, x_{2t}, \ldots, x_{nt})'$ is a column vector of a bundle of n goods] is compared to the *minimum* expenditure required to yield the same utility level, say, $e(p_t, x_t; \alpha)$, Ley (1992) proposes the model

$$\log m_t - \log e(p_t, x_t; \alpha) = \varepsilon_t$$

where $\varepsilon_t > 0$ has some distribution defined over the positive real line. With only three goods, in the simple Cobb-Douglas case where the utility function is

$$u(x; \alpha) = x_1^{\alpha_1} x_2^{\alpha_2} x_3^{1-\alpha_1-\alpha_2},$$

and with exponentially distributed error terms[3] ε_t (i.i.d. for $t = 1, 2, \ldots, T$),

$$p(\varepsilon_t | \mu) = f_\gamma(\varepsilon_t | 1, \mu),$$

---

[3] Note that an exponential distribution with mean μ is just a gamma distribution with shape parameter 1; see the Appendix for the form of the gamma distribution.

we obtain for all T observations:

$$p(\log m | e(p, x; \alpha), \mu) = \exp\left\{-T \log \mu\right.$$
$$-\mu^{-1} \sum_{t=1}^{T} \left[\log m_t - \alpha_1 \log\left(\frac{p_{1t} x_{1t}}{\alpha_1}\right) - \alpha_2 \log\left(\frac{p_{2t} x_{2t}}{\alpha_2}\right)\right.$$
$$\left.\left.- (1 - \alpha_1 - \alpha_2) \log\left(\frac{p_{3t} x_{3t}}{1 - \alpha_1 - \alpha_2}\right)\right]\right\}$$

where m, $e(p, x; \alpha)$, p and x are all straightforwardly extended to the case of T observations.

Clearly, this complicated likelihood function does not allow for a natural-conjugate analysis and a numerical approach will have to be followed. Here we adopt the rejection sampling technique, which can generally be used if we need to draw from a density $f(x)$ which is too complicated to draw from directly. If we can find a density $g(x)$ such that

$$M = \max_x \frac{f(x)}{g(x)} < \infty$$

and we can generate drawings from $g(x)$, then we can use the following algorithm [see Ripley (1986), Johnson (1987)]:

[S1] Generate x_d from $g(x)$ and compute $R_d = f(x_d)/Mg(x_d)$.

[S2] Generate u_d from a uniform on $(0, 1)$.

[S3] If $u_d \leq R_d$ accept x_d; otherwise reject x_d.

The accepted drawings x_d will be distributed according to $f(x)$. As the probability of acceptance of x_d equals M^{-1}, we should attempt to make M not "too large". In practice, the function $f(x)$ will often only be the kernel of a density function, in which case the acceptance probability becomes

$$\frac{1}{M} \int f(x) dx$$

where the integral is over the support of x.

This general principle is applied to the prior-to-posterior mapping in Smith and Gelfand (1992). They observe that if we take the prior $p(\theta)$ as $g(\cdot)$, we can obtain drawings from the posterior with kernel $f(\cdot)$ provided that

$$M = \max_\theta p(Y|\theta)$$

is finite. The ratio R_d then becomes the ratio of the likelihood value at the drawn parameter vector and the maximum value of the likelihood, M.

15.3.2 Applied Demand Analysis

We use the data in Varian (1990) which consists in U.S. aggregate consumption data of three groups of goods: durables, nondurables, and services from 1947 to 1987 . We have $n = 3$ and $T = 41$. We read the data and define the variables,

```
In[1]:= data = ReadList["cons.dat", Table[Number, {6}]];
        Do[ p[i] = Column[data, i], {i, 1, 3} ];
        Do[ x[i] = Column[data, i+3], {i, 1, 3} ];
        Do[ m[i] = p[i]*x[i], {i, 1, 3} ];
        M = Sum[ m[i], {i, 1, 3} ];
```

15.3.2.1   ML Estimates via Calculus

Ley (1992) shows how in this case the MLE have simple closed-form analytical solutions (otherwise, we could use the **FindMinimum** function). In particular, the first-order conditions imply that

$$\frac{\hat{\alpha}_i}{\hat{\alpha}_j} = \left(\prod_{t=1}^{T} \frac{p_{it}x_{it}}{p_{jt}x_{jt}} \right)^{1/T}$$

for $i, j = 1, 2, 3$. We can use *Mathematica* to find the expressions for the MLE's,

```
In[1]:= eq1 = a1/(1-a1-a2) - pr[1]/pr[3];
        eq2 = a2/(1-a1-a2) - pr[2]/pr[3];
        mlesol = Flatten[Simplify[Solve[{eq1 == 0, eq2 == 0},
          {a1, a2}]]]
```

$$Out[1]:= \left\{ a1 \rightarrow \frac{pr[1]}{pr[1] + pr[2] + pr[3]}, \quad a2 \rightarrow \frac{pr[2]}{pr[1] + pr[2] + pr[3]} \right\}$$

We define the auxiliary variables,

```
In[2]:= Do[ pr[i] = (Product[m[i][[t]], {t, 1, 41}])^(1/41),
        {i, 1, 3} ];
```

The MLE for $(\alpha_1, \alpha_2, \alpha_3)$ are obtained by simply making the appropriate substitutions

```
In[3]:= a[1] = a1/.mlesol
```

```
Out[3]:= 0.153783
```

```
In[4]:= a[2] = a2/.mlesol
```

```
Out[4]:= 0.463645
```

```
In[5]:= a[3] = 1 - a[1] - a[2]
```

```
Out[5]:= 0.382572
```

Next, we compute the MLE of the mean error, μ, which is given by the average of the logs of the ratios of observed to minimum expenditure,

```
In[6]:= Do[e[t] = Product[(m[i][[t]]/a[i])^ a[i], {i,1,3}],
        {t,1,41}];
        mu = (1/41)Sum[Log[M[[t]]/e[t]],{t,1,41}]
```

```
Out[6]:= 0.0195704
```

We store in **mle** the value of the likelihood function evaluated at the maximum likelihood estimates,

```
In[7]:= mle = ((1/mu)^41)*Exp[-41]
Out[7]:=            70
           1.10756 10
          ─────────────
              41
               E
```

15.3.2.2   Rejection Sampling

We postulate a Dirichlet distribution (see Appendix) with parameter vector k for the prior distribution of α. We write a simple procedure to generate Dirichlet variables based on Devroye (1986), p. 594. First, independent gamma variables (with shape parameters given by the elements in k and scale parameters 1) are generated and, then, they are normalized by their sum.

```
In[1]:= RandomDirichlet[k_] := Module[{a,b},
          a = Table[Random[GammaDistribution[k[[i]],1]],
              {i, 1, Length[k]}];
          b = Apply[Plus, a];
          a/b];
```

We choose a gamma prior for μ^{-1} [see van den Broeck *et al.* (1992), who also suggest a convenient elicitation process].

The following instructions implement the rejection algorithm. The accepted drawings are sent to different files to prevent an interruption of the execution since the process can take a long time to finish (e.g., about three days in a DECstation 5000). The acceptance ratio in this example was, approximately, 1:100, so close to 200,000 drawings from the prior were needed in order to achieve the target of 2,000 samples from the posterior distribution. Of course, more efficient generators can be coded either inside or outside *Mathematica* [e.g., using the algorithms in Devroye (1986)] but we wanted to illustrate the method using standard *Mathematica* functions.

```
In[2]:= accepteddrawings = 0;
        totnumberdrawings = 0;
        While[accepteddrawings < 2000,
         u  = Random[Real, {0,1}];
         da = RandomDirichlet[{30,90,80}];
         dm = 1/Random[GammaDistribution[1, -1/Log[.98]]];
         ratio = ((1/dm)^41)*Exp[-(1/dm)*
          Sum[Log[M[[t]]/((m[1][[t]]/da[[1]])^da[[1]]*
           (m[2][[t]]/da[[2]])^da[[2]]*
           (m[3][[t]]/da[[3]])^da[[3]])],{t,1,41}]]/mle;
         If[u <= ratio,
           (da>>>palpha.dat; dm>>>pmu.dat; accepteddrawings++;)];
         totnumberdrawings++;]
```

We generate a uniform variable **u**, then we draw the vector of α's from a Dirichlet with parameters $(30, 90, 80)$ which are elicited postulating mean expenditure shares of 15%, 45%, and 40% with standard deviations of 2.5%, 3.5%, and 3.5% for x_1, x_2 and x_3 respectively. The inverse μ's are drawn from a gamma distribution with shape parameter 1 and scale parameter $-1/\log 0.98$; the latter is elicited through specifying the prior median efficiency as 0.98 [see van den Broeck *et al.* (1992)]. Then, **ratio** is evaluated and compared to **u** in order to decide whether to accept the drawing or not. The files **palpha.dat** and **pmu.dat** will contain the accepted drawings. The variable **totnumberofdrawings** was 176,040 in our run, so the acceptance percentage was 1.14%.

We read back into *Mathematica* the accepted drawings for μ and the α's,

```
In[3]:= pmu = ReadList["pmu.dat"];
        palpha  = ReadList["palpha.dat"];
        palpha1 = Column[palpha, 1];
        palpha2 = Column[palpha, 2];
        palpha3 = Column[palpha, 3];
```

15.3.2.3 Mu

We plot a histogram of the accepted drawings of μ to visualize its posterior distribution

```
In[1]:= HHistogram[pmu]
```

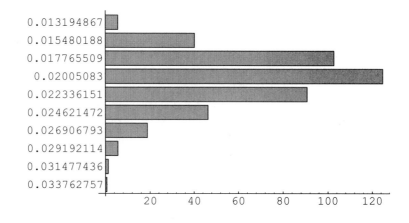

```
Out[1]:= -Graphics-
```

The **BayesE** function **HHistogram** returns a horizontal histogram with the default number of bins 10. This function was implemented because **VHistogram** doesn't allow us to display too many decimals in the bin's coordinates without lumping the numbers together. Other functions in **BayesE** that produce histograms are **VHistogram** and **SmoothedVHistogram** which are illustrated below.

We can use the procedures in the package **DescriptiveStatistics** to analyze the sampled μ's,

```
In[2]:= LocationReport[pmu]
Out[2]:= {Mean -> 0.0204403, HarmonicMean -> 0.0199447,
          Median -> 0.0202037}
```

```
In[3]:= DispersionReport[pmu]
```

```
Out[3]:= {Variance -> 0.0000104647, StandardDeviation ->
            0.00323493,
          SampleRange -> 0.0228532, MeanDeviation ->
            0.00254889,
          MedianDeviation -> 0.00207132, QuartileDeviation ->
            0.00207876}
```

We could compare the prior and posterior density function of μ by plotting the PDF that we used to draw from (dashed) and the histogram of the accepted draws,[4]

```
In[4]:= mupdf[mu_]  :=  -Log[0.98]*Exp[Log[0.98]/mu] / mu^2;
        graph1 = Plot[mupdf[mu], {mu, 0.001, 0.05},
          PlotRange -> All, PlotStyle ->
          {Dashing[{0.015, 0.015}]}],
          DisplayFunction -> Identity];
        graph2 = SmoothedVHistogram[pmu,
          DisplayFunction -> Identity];
        Show[graph1, graph2, AxesLabel -> {"mu", "density"},
          DisplayFunction -> $DisplayFunction ]
```

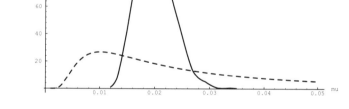

```
Out[4]:= -Graphics-
```

The previous plot clearly shows how the data information is incorporated into μ's posterior density which concentrates a lot of mass around its mean, 0.02.

15.3.2.4 Efficiency

We are probably more interested in the posterior distribution of the efficiency measure given by

$$\frac{e(p_t, x_t; \alpha)}{m_t} = e^{-\varepsilon_t} \in (0, 1]$$

---

[4] If μ^{-1} is distributed as $f_\gamma(\mu^{-1}|1, -1/\log .98)$, making a change of variable we obtain the distribution of μ (which is an inverted gamma), $p(\mu) = -\log .98 \exp\{\log .98/\mu\}/\mu^2$.

which is a parametric generalization of Afriat's efficiency index [Varian (1990)]. We can easily look at the posterior density of this efficiency measure by simply evaluating the ratio of $e(p_t, x_t; \alpha)$ and m_t for a given year t (observed) at every drawn value from the posterior of α. If we take, *e.g.*, the t associated to the median m_t (which corresponds to the year 1967, $t = 21$), we calculate

```
In[1]:= efficiency=Table[((m[1][[21]]/palpha1[[i]])^palpha1[[i]]*
        (m[2][[21]]/palpha2[[i]])^palpha2[[i]] *
        (m[3][[21]]/palpha3[[i]])^palpha3[[i]])/
        M[[21]], {i, 1, Length[palpha1]}];
        HHistogram[efficiency]
```

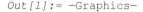

```
Out[1]:= -Graphics-
```

The corresponding prior efficiency can be found by integrating out μ from the implied joint density of (ε_t, μ) which leads to the following marginal prior density for $r_t = e^{-\varepsilon_t}$:

$$ p(r_t) = \frac{-1}{r_t \log .98} \left(1 + \frac{\log r_t}{\log .98} \right)^{-2} $$

for all years. This is the dashed line in the graph,[5]

```
In[2]:= effpdf[r_] := -1/(r*Log[0.98])(1+(Log[r]/Log[0.98]))^(-2);
        graph1 = Plot[effpdf[r], {r, 0.99, 1},
        DisplayFunction -> Identity, PlotRange -> All,
        PlotStyle -> {Dashing[{0.015, 0.015}]}];
        graph2 = SmoothedVHistogram[efficiency,
         DisplayFunction -> Identity];
        Show[graph1, graph2, AxesLabel -> {"efficiency", "density"},
         AxesOrigin -> {1, 0}, DisplayFunction -> $DisplayFunction ]
```

---

[5] The package's function **SmoothedVHistogram** uses *Mathematica*'s function **Interpolation** to fit a third-order polynomial to the histogram's heights, and then **Plot** to plot this polynomial. Any of the valid **Plot** options can be specified; as an example, we set labels for the axes and set the origin at $(1, 0)$.

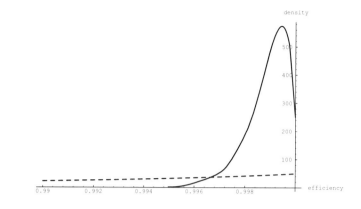

Out[2]:= —Graphics—

As before, since **efficiency** is just a **List** of numbers, we can use any of the functions in **DescriptiveStatistics** to analyze it:

In[3]:= **LocationReport[efficiency]**

Out[3]:= {Mean -> 0.998964, HarmonicMean -> 0.998963, Median -> 0.999167}

In[4]:= **DispersionReport[efficiency]**

Out[4]:=
$$-7$$
{Variance -> 6.98323 10   , StandardDeviation -> 0.000835657,
SampleRange -> 0.00502174, MeanDeviation -> 0.000651993,
MedianDeviation -> 0.000504248, QuartileDeviation -> 0.000525945}

15.3.2.5   Alphas

We use the auxiliary function **ListOfBinCounts** to get a rectangular list of the counts for each of the (default) 10×10 bins for the drawn α_1's and α_2's which we can use later to get a 3D histogram or a contour plot.[6]

In[1]:= **palpha1and2 = Transpose[ColumnJoin[**
                        {Take[palpha1, 1000]},
                        {Take[palpha2, 1000]}]];
       bc = ListOfBinCounts[palpha1and2];

The auxiliary function **ListOfBinCoordinates** will return the coordinates at which the bins are centered. These can be used in conjuction with **ListContourPlot** and **BarChart3D** whose coordinates are just the bins' numbers.

In[2]:= **ListOfBinCoordinates[palpha1and2]**

Out[2]:=

	x coord.	y coord.
1	0.1303	0.4294
2	0.1355	0.4356
3	0.1408	0.4417
4	0.146	0.4479

---

[6] Actually, only 1,000 values of the drawn α's are used (notice the '**Take**' command) since **ListOfBinCounts** might crash in some systems if more values are read.

```
Out[2](cont.)
        5     0.1512      0.454
        6     0.1564      0.4602
        7     0.1617      0.4664
        8     0.1669      0.4725
        9     0.1721      0.4787
       10     0.1774      0.4848
```

```
In[3]:= ListContourPlot[bc, Axes -> True,
         AxesLabel -> {"x: alpha1", "y: alpha2"}]
```

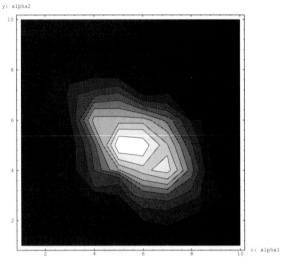

```
Out[3]:= —ContourGraphics—
```

```
In[4]:= BarChart3D[bc, AxesLabel -> {"x: alpha1 ",
         "y: alpha2   ", "counts"}]
```

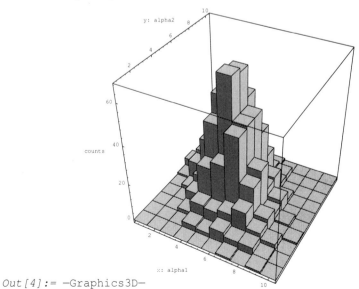

```
Out[4]:= —Graphics3D—
```

As before, we can easily get reports of the characteristics of the sampled parameters,

In[5]:= **LocationReport[palpha1]**

Out[5]:= {Mean —> 0.153261, HarmonicMean —> 0.152872,
          Median —> 0.152999}

In[6]:= **DispersionReport[palpha1]**

Out[6]:= {Variance —> 0.0000598379, StandardDeviation —>
          0.00773549,
          SampleRange —> 0.0522568, MeanDeviation —>
            0.00620629,
          MedianDeviation —> 0.00524782, QuartileDeviation —>
            0.00527508}

In[7]:= **LocationReport[palpha2]**

Out[7]:= {Mean —> 0.462792, HarmonicMean —> 0.462554, Median —>
          0.462769}

In[8]:= **DispersionReport[palpha2]**

Out[8]:= {Variance —> 0.000109767, StandardDeviation —>
          0.010477,
          SampleRange —> 0.065284, MeanDeviation —>
            0.00841525,
          MedianDeviation —> 0.00707425, QuartileDeviation —>
            0.00713225}

We can also plot histograms of any of the drawn parameters, say, α_3,

In[9]:= **HHistogram[palpha3]**

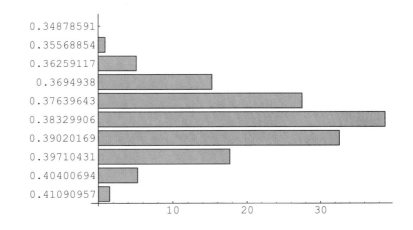

Out[9]:= —Graphics—

We can smooth the histogram and plot it in the same picture as the implied marginal prior (dashed) on α_3, which is a beta density on $(0, 1)$:

$$p(\alpha_3) = f_\beta(\alpha_3|80, 120).$$

The corresponding density function is given in the Appendix.

```
In[10]:= graph1 = Plot[PDF[BetaDistribution[80, 120], a3],
         {a3, 0.30, 0.50}, PlotRange -> All,
          PlotStyle -> {Dashing[{0.015, 0.015}]},
          DisplayFunction -> Identity];
         graph2 = SmoothedVHistogram[palpha3,
          DisplayFunction -> Identity];
         Show[graph1, graph2,
          AxesLabel -> {"alpha3", "density"},
          AxesOrigin -> {Mean[palpha3], 0},
          DisplayFunction -> $DisplayFunction ]
```

```
Out[10]:= —Graphics—
```

Finally, we can look at the posterior distribution of any transformation of the parameters. For instance, the marginal rate of substitution between x_1 and x_2, when equal amounts of both goods are consumed is given by α_1/α_2. Then,

```
In[11]:= mrs12 = palpha1/palpha2; LocationReport[mrs12]

Out[11]:= {Mean —> 0.331492, HarmonicMean —> 0.33017,
           Median —> 0.330918}
```

By saving the partition of all drawn prior values of α_1/α_2 over prespecified bins (remember that there are close to 200,000 drawings here so it would not be efficient to store all of them), we can contrast the posterior density with its prior counterpart (in a dashed line).[7] Generally, the set of *all* drawn values corresponds to the prior, whereas the subset of *accepted* drawings characterizes the posterior densities.

```
In[12]:= mrspart = ReadList["mrspart.dat"];
         graph1 = Plot[Interpolation[mrspart][x],
          {x, 0.15, 0.55},
          PlotRange->All,
          PlotStyle -> {Dashing[{0.015, 0.015}]},
          DisplayFunction -> Identity];
```

---

[7] The pairs of counts and bin coordinates were saved into the file **mrspart** which we read back into *Mathematica* now to construct the histogram.

```
In[12]:=(cont.)
        graph2 = SmoothedVHistogram[mrs12,
         DisplayFunction -> Identity];
        Show[graph1, graph2,
         AxesLabel -> {"mrs12", "density"},
         AxesOrigin -> {Mean[mrs12], 0},
         DisplayFunction -> $DisplayFunction ]
```

```
Out[12]:= -Graphics-
```

15.4   Concluding Remarks

Mathematica provides an excellent environment for doing Bayesian econometrics because of the ease with which it can be programmed and its outstanding capabilities in graphics, symbolic analysis, and data manipulation. In addition, its interactive flavor, especially in a Notebook front end, is ideally suited to the subjectivist perspective. Beliefs keep evolving while different models and representations are tried.

We have illustrated the use of *Mathematica* functions in a traditional conjugate analysis of the linear regression model. In our second example, we have shown how *Mathematica* could be used to successfully carry out the analysis of a completely nonstandard model.

We don't provide a *comprehensive* Bayesian package because that seems too ambitious a task. Different analyses and analysts will require different functions and methods that, when needed, can easily be accommodated into *Mathematica* with little programming effort. However, the method of rejection sampling seems an extremely flexible and easily understood mechanism for the application of Bayesian analysis in a very general context. Its main cost is in terms of computer time, but we feel this drawback can seriously (at least a factor of 10, and more likely a factor of 100) be reduced by performing the actual rejection sampling in a faster (compiled) computing language (such as FORTRAN) and embedding this through *MathLink* in a *Mathematica* environment to take full advantage of the graphical, symbolic, and data handling features of *Mathematica*.

15.5 Appendix

Since some of the densities used in this paper often appear in the literature with different parameterizations, we include here the forms used in the text and implemented in this package [see, *e.g.*, Zellner (1971) for more details].

The random variable $z > 0$ has a gamma distribution with parameters α and β if its density function is given by

$$f_\gamma(z|\alpha, \beta) = \frac{z^{\alpha-1} e^{-z/\beta}}{\beta^\alpha \Gamma[\alpha]},$$

with $\mathrm{E}[z] = \alpha\beta$, and $\mathrm{Var}[z] = \alpha\beta^2$. (A gamma distribution with shape parameter $\alpha = 1$ is also known as an exponential distribution.)

The random variable $\sigma > 0$ has an inverted gamma distribution if its density function is given by

$$f_{i\gamma}(\sigma|\nu, s) = \frac{2}{\Gamma(\nu/2)} \left(\frac{\nu s^2}{2}\right)^{\nu/2} \frac{1}{\sigma^{\nu+1}} \exp\left\{-\frac{\nu s^2}{2\sigma^2}\right\}$$

we have (for $\nu > 2$)

$$\mathrm{E}[\sigma] = \frac{\Gamma((\nu-1)/2)}{\Gamma(\nu/2)} \left(\frac{\nu}{2}\right)^{1/2} s, \quad \mathrm{E}[\sigma^2] = \frac{\nu}{\nu-2} s^2, \quad \mathrm{mode}[\sigma] = \left(\frac{\nu}{\nu+1}\right)^{1/2} s.$$

The k-dimensional random vector x has a multivariate-t distribution with mean μ, precision matrix H, and degrees of freedom ν, if its density is given by

$$f_t^k(x|\mu, H, \nu) = \frac{\Gamma((k+\nu)/2)}{\pi^{k/2}\Gamma(\nu/2)} \sqrt{\frac{|H|}{\nu^k}} \left[1 + \frac{1}{\nu}(x-\mu)'H(x-\mu)\right]^{-(k+\nu)/2},$$

which implies

$$\mathrm{E}[x] = \mu, \qquad \mathrm{Var}[x] = \frac{\nu}{\nu-2} H^{-1}$$

when $\nu > 2$.

The random variable $v \in (0, 1)$ is beta distributed if its density function is given by

$$f_\beta(v|a, b) = \frac{\Gamma(a+b)}{\Gamma(a)\Gamma(b)} v^{a-1}(1-v)^{b-1},$$

where $a, b > 0$. Its mean is $\mathrm{E}[v] = a/(a+b)$ and its variance $\mathrm{Var}[v] = ab(a+b)^{-2}(a+b+1)^{-1}$.

The vector $\alpha = (\alpha_1, \alpha_2, \ldots, \alpha_n)'$ with $\alpha_i > 0$, $\forall i$, and $\sum_{i=1}^n \alpha_i = 1$ has a Dirichlet distribution with parameters $\gamma = (\gamma_1, \gamma_2, \ldots, \gamma_n)'$ if its density function is given by

$$f_D^n(\alpha|\gamma) = \frac{\Gamma(g)}{\prod_{i=1}^n \Gamma(\gamma_i)} \prod_{i=1}^n \alpha_i^{\gamma_i-1},$$

where $\gamma_i > 0$, $\forall i$, and $g = \sum_{i=1}^{n} \gamma_i$. The first two moments are given by

$$\mathrm{E}[\alpha_i] = \frac{\gamma_i}{g}, \quad \text{and } \mathrm{Var}[\alpha_i] = \frac{\gamma_i(g - \gamma_i)}{g^2(g + 1)}.$$

15.6 References

Devroye, L. (1986). *Non-Uniform Random Variate Generation*, New York: Springer-Verlag.

Drèze J. H. (1962). "The Bayesian Approach to Simultaneous Equation Estimation," O.N.R. Research Memorandum no. 67, Northwestern University.

Engle, R. F., D. F. Hendry and J. F. Richard (1983). "Exogeneity," *Econometrica*, **51**, 277–304.

Florens, J,-P. and M. Mouchart (1985). "Conditioning in Dynamic Models," *Journal of Time Series Analysis*, **6**, 15–34.

Good, I. J. (1976). "The Bayesian Influence, or How to Sweep Subjectivism Under the Carpet," in *Foundations of Probability Theory, Statistical Inference, and Statistical Theories of Science*, vol. II, W. Harper and C. Hooker (eds.), Dordrecht: Reidel, 125–174.

Jeffreys, H. (1961). *Theory of Probability*, Oxford: Oxford University Press.

Judge, G. C., W. E. Griffiths, R. Carter-Hill, H. Lütkepohl, T.-C. Lee (1985). *The Theory and Practice of Econometrics*, New York: Wiley.

Johnson, M. E. (1987). *Multivariate Statistical Simulation*, New York: Wiley.

Leamer, E. E. (1978). *Specification Searches*, New York: Wiley.

Ley, E. (1992). "Applied Demand Analysis in Utility Space," mimeo.

Lindley, D. V. (1986). "Comment," *American Statistician*, **40**, 6–7.

Newhouse, J. P. (1977). "Medical Care Expenditure: A Cross-National Survey, " *Journal of Human Resources*, **12**, 115–125.

Osiewalski J. and M. F. J. Steel (1990). "A Bayesian Analysis of Exogeneity in Models Pooling Time-Series and Cross-Section Data," mimeo.

Poirier, D. J. (1988). "Frequentist and Subjectivist Perspectives on the Problems of Model Building in Economics," *Economic Perspectives*, **2**, 121–144.

Raiffa, H. A. and R. S. Schlaifer (1961). *Applied Statistical Decision Theory*, Boston: Harvard University Press.

Ripley, B. (1986). *Stochastic Simulation*, New York: Wiley.

Smith, A. F. M. (1986). "Comment," *American Statistician*, **40**, 10–11.

Smith, A. F. M. and A. E. Gelfand (1992). "Bayesian Statistics Without Tears: A Sampling-Resampling Perspective," *American Statistician*, **46**, 84–88.

van den Broeck, J., G. Koop, J. Osiewalski and M. F. J. Steel (1992). "Stochastic Frontier Models: A Bayesian Perspective," *Journal of Econometrics*, 61.

Varian, H. R. (1990). "Goodness-of-Fit in Optimizing Models," *Journal of Econometrics*, **46**, 125–140.

Zellner, A. (1971). *An Introduction to Bayesian Inference in Econometrics*, New York: Wiley.

16 Time Series Models and Mathematica

Robert A. Stine

16.1 Introduction

16.1.1 Overview of the Notebook and Package

This notebook introduces a package of *Mathematica* functions that manipulate autoregressive, integrated moving average (ARIMA) models. ARIMA models describe discrete-time stochastic processes—time series. The models are most adept at modeling stationary processes. Through differencing, however, these models accommodate certain forms of nonstationary processes as well.

Prediction is a particular strength of ARIMA models, and many of the examples chosen to illustrate the functions of the package are related to prediction. While it might be implausible to believe that an observed time series really is the realization of an ARIMA process, such a model can provide a useful approximation. Numerous studies have verified that these models give impressive short-term forecasts.

This notebook has three main sections. Following the overview of notation that follows this introduction, the first major section uses *Mathematica* in a direct, interactive fashion. For many users, this "stream-of-consciousness" mode of use is most appealing and may be all that is needed. The second section describes components of the accompanying package. Many of these functions automate expressions that are introduced and computed interactively in the first section. It is my hope that you will agree that the use of the package is more convenient and not too hard to learn. The third major section uses the programs from the package to tackle several problems in time series analysis, with the theme being the effects of estimation. The concluding section is a brief discussion and summary.

Finally, a brief disclaimer. Though I consistently refer to ARIMA models, the package routines by and large handle ARMA models that do not include differencing. In most cases, this is no real limitation since the results for the differenced (or integrated) process are easily found by understanding the underlying ARMA model. I leave extending the package to handle differencing more completely as the traditional exercise for the reader. Some hints in this direction appear as comments in the code itself.

16.1.2   ARIMA Models

This section reviews the notation of ARIMA models. Various notations appear in ARIMA modeling, and it is important to know which is being used. Here I use the polynomial sign convention of Box and Jenkins (1976) which is natural in this context, though it leads to minus signs in some alternative forms. Names of the functions and parameters included in the accompanying package correspond to those given here. Readers interested in a more complete review should consider one of the many texts on this topic, such as the classic work of Box and Jenkins (1976) or the recent, relatively applied book of Wei (1992). Brockwell and Davis (1987) provide a more elegant mathematical treatment. Bloomfield (1976) gives an excellent introduction to the less familiar frequency-domain methods and includes several wonderful examples of the power of the spectral approach.

An ARIMA model is basically a finite-parameter difference equation that describes the structure of a discrete-time stochastic process. For situations with no differencing, the general form of an ARIMA model for the process denoted y_t is

$$y_t - \phi_1 y_{t-1} - \ldots - \phi_p y_{t-p} = \epsilon_t - \theta_1 \epsilon_{t-1} - \ldots - \theta_q \epsilon_{t-q}, \qquad (1)$$

where the ϵ_t form a sequence of zero mean, finite variance σ^2, uncorrelated random variables (white noise). The mean of y_t defined by (1) is zero. To obtain a process with mean μ, replace y_t by $(y_t - \mu)$. As given, equation (1) defines an ARMA(p,q) model.

ARIMA models accommodate non-stationarity through differencing. Suppose that the process y_t is not stationary because, for example, of linear growth in the mean, $E[y_t] = \mu t$. In this case, the differences $y_t - y_{t-1}$ are stationary. ARIMA models extend the structure found in (1) by adding this feature. In this example of linear trend, we can replace y_t in (1) by $y_t - y_{t-1}$, producing an ARIMA(p,1,q) model. Other forms of nonstationarity are modeled by further differencing. Including the order of differencing d, we arrive at an ARIMA(p,d,q) model.

Under certain conditions on the $p+q$ parameters $\{\phi_1, \ldots, \phi_p\}$ and $\{\theta_1, \ldots, \theta_q\}$, ARIMA models possess alternative representations as weighted sums of either past errors or past observations. One form of these conditions is most often stated in terms of the polynomials

$$\Phi(z) = 1 - \phi_1 z - \phi_2 z^2 - \ldots - \phi_p z^p$$

and

$$\Theta(z) = 1 - \theta_1 z - \theta_2 z^2 - \ldots - \theta_q z^q.$$

Stationarity of the process implies that none of the zeros of $\Phi(z)$ have modulus 1. In order for the process to be expressed as a weighted sum of past errors, all of the zeros of $\Phi(z)$ must lie outside the unit circle in the complex plane. Similiarly, invertibility—writing the process as a weighted sum of past observations—requires that all of the zeros of $\Theta(z)$ lie outside the unit circle.

The association of polynomials with the parameters of an ARIMA model provides a very compact notation. Let B denote the operator which lags an observation so that $B^k y_t = y_{t-k}$. In this notation, the differences of the observations are $y_t - y_{t-1} = (1 - B)y_t$, or more generally $(1 - B)^d y_t$ for the dth difference. Using this convention, the most general ARIMA(p,d,q) model is

$$(1 - \phi_1 B - \ldots - \phi_p B^p)(1 - B)^d(y_t - \mu) = (1 - \theta_1 B - \ldots - \theta_q B^q)\epsilon_t$$
$$\Phi(B)(1 - B)^d(y_t - \mu) = \Theta(B)\epsilon_t. \qquad (2)$$

When the zeros of $\Phi(z)$ lie outside the unit circle, the infinite moving average form expresses the process as a weighed sum of past errors,

$$y_t = \frac{\Theta(B)}{\Phi(B)}\epsilon_t = \sum_{j=0}^{\infty} w_j \epsilon_{t-j}. \qquad (3)$$

The weights w_j in (3) are the coefficients found by polynomial division of $\Theta(z)$ by $\Phi(z)$. If the process is invertible, expansion of $\Phi(B)/\Theta(B)$ gives the coefficients needed for the infinite autoregressive form which expresses the process as a weighted sum of past observations.

The moving average representation (3) is very useful in prediction problems. Let $\hat{y}_{t+h}$ denote the minimum mean squared error predictor of y_{t+h} given observations up to time t for $h > 0$. That is, $\hat{y}_{t+h}$ is the conditional expectation of y_{t+h} given $y_t, y_{t-1}, \ldots$. The mean squared error of this predictor is

$$MSE(h) = E[(y_{t+h} - \hat{y}_{t+h})^2 | y_t, y_{t-1}, \ldots] = \sigma^2 \sum_{j=0}^{h-1} w_j^2. \qquad (4)$$

The crucial ratio $\Theta(z)/\Phi(z)$ leading to the moving average form (3) is the transfer function of the ARIMA model. The transfer function defines the spectral density function of a stationary ARIMA model,

$$f(\lambda) = \frac{\sigma^2}{2\pi} \frac{\Theta(e^{i\lambda})\Theta(e^{-i\lambda})}{\Phi(e^{i\lambda})\Phi(e^{-i\lambda})}, -\pi < \lambda < \pi. \qquad (5)$$

The covariance sequence $\gamma_j = E(y_t - \mu)(y_{t-j} - \mu)$ is the Fourier transform of the spectral density, and thus the spectral density gives a complete characterization of the second-order dependence of the process,

$$\gamma_j = \int_{-\pi}^{\pi} e^{-ij\lambda} f(\lambda)d\lambda. \qquad (6)$$

16.2 Interactive Manipulations

16.2.1 Introduction

This section illustrates the use of *Mathematica* to manipulate one representation of an ARIMA model directly, without importing the package of functions or defining many procedures. The criterion here is simplicity in both manipulation and representation. One can achieve a lot without doing much programming, all the while retaining the familiar notation of ARIMA models. The discussion begins with some basic commands, and concludes with a small program that automates several frequent instructions.

To focus the discussion, consider the following question. For what ARIMA models is the mean squared error of prediction constant for several leads? That is, for which models does the accuracy of prediction not change as the predictions are extrapolated farther into the future, giving $MSE(k) = MSE(k+1)$ for some k? In terms of the notation of the introduction, we seek models for which the moving average weight w_k from (4) is zero for some choice of prediction lead k. Clearly some such models exist, since one such model is the white noise process for which $MSE(k) = \sigma^2$ at any lead k. We are going in search of others.

The key ingredient of a general answer to this problem requires expressing the moving average weight w_k as a function of the parameters $\{\phi_1, \phi_2, \ldots, \phi_p\}$ and $\{\theta_1, \theta_2, \ldots, \theta_q\}$. The next section shows how to find these expressions interactively.

16.2.2   Back-substitution Methods Using Rules

The first issue to resolve in this problem is very important, yet perhaps one of the hardest to do in advance of solving the problem. Namely, how should ARIMA models be represented in *Mathematica*? We naturally think of these models as a combination of a difference equation and some side conditions on the errors, but equations expressed in the usual mathematical notation are ambiguous and confusing to *Mathematica*. Since our problem requires the moving average form of the model (3), we need a representation that gives this form easily and naturally.

An obvious *Mathematica* representation of an ARIMA model translates the standard difference equation into a function. For example, the AR(1) model

$$y_t = \phi_1 y_{t-1} + \epsilon_t$$

might be translated into the one-line definition

```
In[1]:=  y[t_] := p1 y[t-1]+e[t]
```

where $p1$ stands for ϕ_1. Although appealing, this definition produces an infinite recursion whenever we try to use it. For example, if we try to see the form of y_{t-2} we get a collection of error messages.

```
In[2]:= y[t-2]
```

```
$RecursionLimit::reclim: Recursion depth of 256 exceeded.
```

```
$RecursionLimit::reclim: Recursion depth of 256 exceeded.
```

```
$RecursionLimit::reclim: Recursion depth of 256 exceeded.
```

```
General::stop:
```

```
Further output of $RecursionLimit::reclim
   will be suppressed during this calculation.
```

Mathematica applies the definition to any expression of the form y[anything], recursively moving farther and farther back in time. The system halts the recursion when the depth of recursion exceeds a predetermined constant built into the software, here a depth of 256 calls.

Rules offer an alternative means for representing ARIMA models that dodge this problem yet allow an intuitive form of symbolic manipulation. Rules, unlike the simple procedural definition, offer greater control over the use of substitution. Before starting this new course, clear the previous definition that would otherwise linger and interfere with the new commands.

In[3]:= **Clear[y]**

Now enter the definition as a rule. The only change from before is that the symbol := has been replaced by ->.

In[4]:= **arRule = y[t_] -> p1 y[t-1] + e[t]**

Out[4]:= y[t_] —> e[t] + p1 y[−1 + t]

The rule gives the expected response without the problem of recursion.

In[5]:= **y[t-2] /. arRule**

Out[5]:= e[−2 + t] + p1 y[−3 + t]

Mathematica applies this rule once to the expression, giving the sought replacement. However, it appears as though we have lost the ability to do further substitutions. We could always resort to expressions like y[t] /. arRule /. arRule, but this sort of manual iteration becomes tedious very quickly. The built-in operator //. applies rules repeatedly until the result no longer changes, but that leads back to the infinite recursion.

Fortunately, there is an alternative. **ReplaceRepeated** provides the most flexible use of rule-based substitution. This function allows a rule to be applied a specified number of times. With 5 iterations of back-substitution and some simplification, the moving average associated with the original AR(1) model starts to appear.

In[6]:= **ReplaceRepeated[y[t], arRule, MaxIterations->5]**

ReplaceRepeated::rrlim: Exiting after y[t] scanned 5 times.

Out[6]:= e[t] + p1 (e[−1 + t] + p1 (e[−2 + t] +

         p1 (e[−3 + t] + p1 (e[−4 + t] + p1 y[−5 + t])))))

Since % denotes the result of the previous statement, we can expand this expression without having to re-compute it.

In[7]:= **Expand[%]**

$Out[7] :=$ $p1^4$ $e[-4 + t]$ $+$ $p1^3$ $e[-3 + t]$ $+$ $p1^2$ $e[-2 + t]$ $+$

$p1$ $e[-1 + t]$ $+$ $e[t]$ $+$ $p1^5$ $y[-5 + t]$

The geometric form of the moving average weights $w_j = \phi^j$ is clear in this expression. Unfortunately, *Mathematica*'s normal order for printing expressions differs from the usual convention (for example, constants precede symbols as in $[t-2]$ rather than $[t-2]$).

The moving average form (3) is pretty simple for first-order autoregressions, so let's move to a more complex ARMA(2,1) model $y_t = \phi_1 y_{t-1} + \phi_2 y_{t-2} + \epsilon_t - \theta_1 \epsilon_{t-1}$. We begin this example by forming the defining rule, where the symbols $p1$, $p2$, and $t1$ stand for ϕ_1, ϕ_2, and θ_1, respectively.

$In[8] :=$ **armaRule = y[t_]->p1 y[t-1] + p2 y[t-2] + e[t] - t1 e[t-1]**

$Out[8] :=$ $y[t\_]$ $\rightarrow$ $-(t1$ $e[-1 + t]) + e[t] + p2$ $y[-2 + t] + p1$ $y[-1 + t]$

The expression **back** holds four iterations of back-substitution.

$In[9] :=$ **back = Expand[ReplaceRepeated[y[t],**
armaRule,MaxIterations->4]]

ReplaceRepeated::rrlim: Exiting after $y[t]$ scanned 4 times.

$Out[9] :=$

$-(p2^3$ $t1$ $e[-7 + t]) + p2^3$ $e[-6 + t] - 3$ $p1$ $p2^2$ $t1$ $e[-6 + t] +$

3 $p1$ $p2^2$ $e[-5 + t] - 3$ $p1^2$ $p2$ $t1$ $e[-5 + t] - p2^2$ $t1$ $e[-5 + t] +$

3 $p1^2$ $p2$ $e[-4 + t] + p2^2$ $e[-4 + t] - p1^3$ $t1$ $e[-4 + t] -$

2 $p1$ $p2$ $t1$ $e[-4 + t] + p1^3$ $e[-3 + t] + 2$ $p1$ $p2$ $e[-3 + t] -$

$p1^2$ $t1$ $e[-3 + t] - p2$ $t1$ $e[-3 + t] + p1^2$ $e[-2 + t] +$

$p2$ $e[-2 + t] - p1$ $t1$ $e[-2 + t] + p1$ $e[-1 + t] - t1$ $e[-1 + t] +$

$e[t] + p2^4$ $y[-8 + t] + 4$ $p1$ $p2^3$ $y[-7 + t] + 6$ $p1^2$ $p2^2$ $y[-6 + t]$

$+ 4$ $p1^3$ $p2$ $y[-5 + t] + p1^4$ $y[-4 + t]$

The moving average coefficient w_j is the coefficient of ϵ_{t-j} in (3), but the corresponding terms are not grouped together in this result. The built-in function **Coefficient** does the trick, though, and collects the desired terms, showing for example that $w_2 = \phi_1^2 + \phi_2 - \phi_1\theta_1$.

```
In[10]:= w[2] = Coefficient[back, e[t-2]]
Out[10]:=    2
          p1  + p2 - p1 t1
```

Returning to the problem originally posed, we can now easily find the set of ARMA(2,1) models for which $MSE(3) = MSE(4)$, the models for which $w_3 = 0$. First, we extract w_3 from the previously computed expression.

```
In[11]:= w[3] = Coefficient[back, e[t-3]]
Out[11]:=    3                2
          p1  + 2 p1 p2 - p1  t1 - p2 t1
```

Now solve for the values of ϕ_1, ϕ_2 and θ_1 that imply $w_3 = 0$.

```
In[12]:= soln = Solve[0==w[3],{p1,p2,t1}]
Out[12]:=           2          p1
           {{p2 -> p1  (-1 + ---------)}, {t1 -> 0, p1 -> 0},
                             2 p1 - t1

             {t1 -> 0, p1 -> 0}, {t1 -> 0, p1 -> 0}}
```

Of the several solutions which are given as rules, the last three are identical and set ϕ_1 and θ_1 to zero. The first solution is more interesting and sets ϕ_2 to be a function of ϕ_1 and θ_1. We can easily verify the result although *Mathematica* does not recognize zero at first.

```
In[13]:= w[3] /. soln[[1]]
Out[13]:=
   3       3         p1           2      2         p1
 p1  + 2 p1  (-1 + ---------) - p1  t1 - p1  (-1 + ---------) t1
                   2 p1 - t1                       2 p1 - t1
```

The verification requires an extra simplification.

```
In[14]:= Simplify[%]

Out[14]:= 0
```

16.2.3 Building a Reusable Tool that Finds the Moving Average Weights

Building on the success in the previous section, we can explore generalizations of this problem. So far, we know how to find ARMA(2,1) models whose prediction MSE does not change from lead 3 to lead 4. Now let's solve this problem more generally. We could always continue interactively, but a little programming makes repetitive tasks more easy. Most *Mathematica* programming occurs once we have discovered interactively a set of useful manipulations and want to bind them into a re-usable tool.

The tool that we are going to build computes the moving average representation as a sequence of weights. The input to this function is a rule that defines an ARIMA model. The problem requires us to find each of the lag coefficients of the model and identify conditions which imply that the coefficient of interest is zero. The first task, then, is to find the list of coefficients.

The most obvious approach to users of *Mathematica* raised on C or Fortran is a loop. However, the built-in function **Table** does just what is needed without explicit iteration.

```
In[1]:= Table[Coefficient[back,e[t-j]],{j,0,3}]
Out[1]:=                    2                   3              2
          {1, p1 - t1, p1  + p2 - p1 t1, p1  + 2 p1 p2 - p1
            t1 - p2 t1}
```

With the symbolic list defining the moving average weights available, rules reveal the value of the weights for a specific model, here one with $\phi_1 = 1, \phi_2 = 0.5$, and $\theta_1 = 0.5$.

```
In[2]:= % /. {p1->1, p2->.5, t1->.5}

Out[2]:= {1, 0.5, 1., 1.25}
```

Now consider building a function to automate this process. Rather than starting from the back-substitution expression, the arguments of the function ought to be the defining rule and the number of sought moving average coefficients. Converting the simple interactive commands we have been using into a function, however, is not so straightforward as it first might seem. First of all, how does the function determine from a rule which symbol denotes the process and which the error? For example, suppose that the defining rule for the process uses s for the time index rather than t, and denotes the process by z rather than y, as in $z_s = \phi_1 z_{s-1} + \phi_2 z_{s-2} + \epsilon_s - \theta_1 \epsilon_{s-1}$. This process has the same statistical structure as that defined by **armaRule**, but uses different symbols.

We could always require (or dangerously assume) that the symbol y denotes the process and t denotes time, but that choice seems rather restrictive. Here is a short program that does what we need. It takes advantage of the fact that all *Mathematica* expressions resemble lists, having a labelled head followed by a list of items, each of which can be more lists.

```
In[3]:= MAWeightList[theRule_Rule, f_Integer]  :=
          Module[ {y,t, lhs, back, j, coefList},
            lhs = First[theRule];
            y = Head[lhs]; t = First[lhs];
            back = Expand[
              ReplaceRepeated[y[t],theRule,MaxIterations->f]];
            coefList = Table[Coefficient[back,e[t-j]],{j,0,f-1}];
            coefList];
```

Following the local variable declarations list, the next line of this program extracts the left hand side of the defining rule. The identifier of the series is the head of this expression, and the time symbol is the only remaining term. Even with this bit of subtlety, this function still assumes that the error term of interest is e[t]. This definition does avoid, though, knowing in advance the symbols for the series and time index. Here is an example of its use.

```
In[4]:= MAWeightList[armaRule, 3]
```

ReplaceRepeated::rrlim: Exiting after y[t_] scanned 3 times.

Out[4]:=
$$\{1,\ p1 - t1,\ p1^2 + p2 - p1\ t1\}$$

```
In[5]:= MAWeightList[z[s_]->p1 z[s-1]+p2 z[s-2]+e[s]-t1 e[s-1],
        3]
```

ReplaceRepeated::rrlim: Exiting after z[s_] scanned 3 times.

Out[5]:=
$$\{1,\ p1 - t1,\ p1^2 + p2 - p1\ t1\}$$

Now back to the problem of finding the special models for which $w_3 = 0$. The use of this function quickly reproduces the result achieved with interactive commands, as long as we remember that indexing in *Mathematica* is one-based so that w_3 is the fourth element.

```
In[6]:= wts = MAWeightList[armaRule, 4];
        soln = Solve[ wts[[4]] == 0, {p1,p2,t1}]
```

ReplaceRepeated::rrlim: Exiting after y[t_] scanned 4 times.

Out[6]:=
$$\{\{p2 \rightarrow p1^2\ (-1 + \frac{p1}{2\ p1 - t1})\},\ \{t1 \rightarrow 0,\ p1 \rightarrow 0\},$$

$$\{t1 \rightarrow 0,\ p1 \rightarrow 0\},\ \{t1 \rightarrow 0,\ p1 \rightarrow 0\}\}$$

Finally we can graph the MSE of one of these models, squaring and accumulating the moving average weights to determine the sum $\sigma^2 \sum w_j^2$. The values of the parameters ϕ_1 and θ_1 are arbitrary in this example, with ϕ_2 set by the associated solution rule. First, we find the sequence $w_0, w_1, \ldots, w_9$ and use the trailing semicolon to suppress the rather long output. Because of the large subexpressions generated in the moving average weights, this command takes a while unless the program is running on a workstation.

```
In[7]:= w2 = MAWeightList[armaRule, 10]^2;
```

ReplaceRepeated::rrlim: Exiting after y[t_] scanned 10 times.

Now simplify the result of substituting the first of the rules found above. Notice that we need a double subscript to extract the rule since it is embedded as the first element of the first list found in the solution.

```
In[8]:= w2 = Simplify[ w2 //. soln[[1,1]] ];
```

Indeed, the fourth term in this list is zero.

```
In[9]:= w2[[{1,2,3,4,5}]]
```

Out[9]:=
$$\{1,\ (p1 - t1)^2,\ (\frac{p1^3}{2\ p1 - t1} - p1\ t1)^2,\ 0,\ \frac{p1^6\ (-p1 + t1)^6}{(-2\ p1 + t1)^4}\}$$

Plots make the results even more conspicuous. First form the cumulative sums of the squared moving average weights needed in (4). So that we can plot the result, consider the sequence of weights for the specific model with $\phi_1 = 0.95$ and $\theta_1 = -0.6$.

In[10]:= **partial = FoldList[Plus,0, w2 /. {p1->.95, t1->-.6}]**

Out[10]:= {0, 1, 3.4025, 4.23598, 4.23598, 4.49694, 4.73245,
4.76314, 4.77419, 4.81335, 4.83004}

Since the function **FoldList** requires a starting value for the partial sums (here set to zero), we have to drop the first value from the list.

In[11]:= **partial = Drop[partial, 1]**

Out[11]:= {1, 3.4025, 4.23598, 4.23598, 4.49694, 4.73245,
4.76314, 4.77419, 4.81335, 4.83004}

Now we can plot the mean squared prediction error; indeed the MSE does not grow between leads 3 and 4.

In[12]:= **ListPlot[partial, PlotJoined->True,**
AxesLabel->{"Lead", "MSE"}]

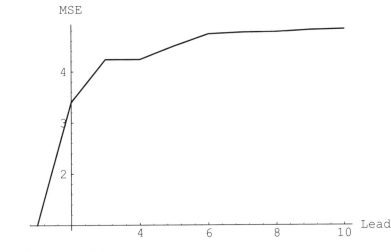

Out[12]:= —Graphics—

16.3   Using the Arima Package

16.3.1   Introduction

This section gives an overview of the tools provided in the package supplied with this notebook. Whereas the preceding section describes direct manipulations that require no external commands other than those native to *Mathematica,* this section focusses on the programs of the package. Short illustrations describe how to use various tools provided in the accompanying software. More details appear in comments within the code itself. The reader who is comfortable with *Mathematica* might prefer to skip the examples shown here and move on to the applications that follow in Section 16.4, returning to this section or the code itself as questions arise.

The accompanying package represents ARIMA models in a manner that by and large avoids rules. Whereas rules provide a natural representation for interactive manipulations, rules are not particularly efficient for many calculations that we frequently want, such as simulations. Instead of rules, a collection of six items headed with the symbol ARIMA identifies each model. (See Section 2.1.2 of Wolfram (1991) for discussion and examples of this type of data structure.) The key element of this collection is the transfer function of the process, with the order of differencing held separately. Additional items identify the mean, scale, and symbolic identifiers. Keep in mind, though, that the internal format of the data structure is not important. Rather, think of each model as a conceptual whole rather than an ordered collection of special components.

In addition to the description found here, usage messages document each of the functions of the package, just as for the built-in *Mathematica* functions. Since most of the functions begin with the identifier "Arima," the **Names** function makes it easy to list the package functions. The only exceptions to this naming convention are a set of functions for defining various special cases of ARIMA models. Alternatively, use the automatic name completion feature of the *Mathematica* front end. Before doing anything, though, import the package with the following command. The associated file "ARIMA.m" that holds the package should be in a location which is either easily found or automatically searched.

In[1]:= **<<ARIMA`**

With the functions loaded, we can list most of the defined function names with the following command.

In[2]:= **Names["Arima*"]**

```
Out[2]:=
{Arima, ArimaBiasMatrix, ArimaCoefBias, ArimaCoefficientBias,
ArimaConst, ArimaConstant, ArimaCorrelation, ArimaCovariance,
ArimaCovarianceMatrix, ArimaCreate, ArimaD, ArimaDifference,
ArimaError, ArimaErrorLabel, ArimaIsArmaQ, ArimaIsArQ,
ArimaIsInvertibleQ, ArimaIsMAQ, ArimaIsStationaryQ,
ArimaIsWhiteNoiseQ, ArimaLabel, ArimaMAWeights, ArimaMean,
ArimaMSE, ArimaNRealize, ArimaOrder, ArimaP, ArimaPhi,
ArimaPhiPolynomial, ArimaPlotPoles, ArimaPlotSDF, ArimaPlotZeros,
ArimaPoles, ArimaPrint, ArimaPrintSymbolList, ArimaQ,
ArimaResetSymbolList, ArimaRule, ArimaScale, ArimaSDF,
ArimaSymbolList, ArimaTheta, ArimaThetaPolynomial,
ArimaTransferFunction, ArimaZeros}
```

The rest of this section of the chapter describes many (but not all) of these tools. Moving from basic, essential manipulations in Section 16.3.1, Section 16.3.2

describes routines that duplicate the results of Section 16.2 without recourse to rules. The programs tend to be much more efficient than those based on rules. The remaining sections consider programs for investigating stationarity and invertibility, the spectral density (5), and the covariance function (6). All of these routines again appear in the applications of Section 16.4.

16.3.2   Basic Operations for Defining Models

16.3.2.1   Defining ARIMA Models

A set of five procedures whose names begin with "Define" create ARIMA models. To see a list of these commands, use the Names function.

In[1]:= **Names["Define*"]**

Out[1]:= {DefineAr, DefineArima, DefineArma, DefineExternal,
         DefineMA, DefineWhiteNoise}

The function **DefineExternal** is a part of *Mathematica*, not the package. Each of these procedures from the package builds an ARIMA model, with the specialization to make it easier to build particular types of ARIMA models. For example, **DefineAr** builds just finite-order autoregressions without requiring superfluous input. As an additional benefit, these functions maintain an internal table of ARIMA models that makes it easier to keep track of the models that have been formed. The procedures also do several preliminary simplifications, such as identifying and cancelling common zeros in $\Phi(z)$ and $\Theta(z)$ found in equation (2). An example of this behavior appears later.

The syntax of these defining functions is similiar, and on-line help is available in the form of brief summaries. For example, to see the syntax of the procedure that defines an AR model, use the standard *Mathematica* request for information about a symbol. That is, precede the name of the function with a question mark.

In[2]:= **?DefineAr**

DefineAr[sym_Symbol, input_ARIMA, phi_List, mean_:0] builds an
   autoregression with input parameters. Note that the scale is
   taken from that of the input white noise.

The first argument of each of the defining functions is a symbol used to identify the model. The second argument of each is the input white-noise process (denoted ϵ_t in the introduction). The procedure **DefineWhiteNoise** builds these basic processes. All of these defining procedures are silent—no news is good news. Entering the name of the process reveals the constructed object.

Here are some examples that we hope will clarify these methods. In order to build an ARIMA model, we need its white noise process, so let's begin there. The next commands build two independent white noise processes, the first with variance $\sigma^2 = 5$, the second with variance 1.

In[3]:= **DefineWhiteNoise[e,5]**
        DefineWhiteNoise[a,1]

To see the underlying data structure, enter the name of the model.

```
In[4]:= e
```

```
Out[4]:= ARIMA[1, 0, 0, 5, e, WN]
```

Building upon these white-noise processes, we can now construct various ARIMA models. The first example creates the specific AR(3) model

$$(ar_t - 7) = -.5(ar_{t-1} - 7) - .25(ar_{t-2} - 7) - .5(ar_{t-3} - 7) + a_t.$$

```
In[5]:= DefineAr[ar,a,{-.5,-.25,-.5},7]
```

Here is the internal data structure for this model.

```
In[6]:= ar
Out[6]:=
                              1
       ARIMA[─────────────────────────────────, 0, 7, 1, ar, a]
                            2         3
             1 + 0.5 z + 0.25 z  + 0.5 z
```

The defined model can also possess symbolic coefficients, as the following definition of the AR(2) model

$$symAr_t = \phi_1 symAr_{t-1} + \phi_2 symAr_{t-2} + a_t$$

shows. If the mean is not supplied as an argument, it defaults to zero.

```
In[7]:= DefineAr[symAr, a, {phi1,phi2}]
        symAr
```

```
Out[7]:=
                        1
       ARIMA[──────────────────────, 0, 0, 1, symAr, a]
                              2
             1 - phi1 z - phi2 z
```

Other routines create moving average and ARMA models. For moving average models the signs of the coefficients of ϵ_{t-j} in (1) are reversed from those of the input list of coefficients. For the ARMA (1,1) model, notice that the coefficients must be entered as a list, even if only one coefficient is to be given.

```
In[8]:= DefineMA[ma,e,{-.5,-.25}]
        DefineArma[arma,a,{.5},{-.5}]
```

It is important to recognize that the first argument of the defining routines must be a symbol, not some previously defined term. This cautious behaviour avoids over-writing previously defined expressions. The procedures echo the input command if the first argument is not a symbol. For example, e denotes white noise. If it is given as the first argument, **DefineAr** does not work and the system responds with an expanded version of the command.

```
In[9]:= DefineAr[e,a, {phi1,phi2}]
```

```
Out[9]:= DefineAr[ARIMA[1, 0, 0, 5, e, WN],
         ARIMA[1, 0, 0, 1, a, WN], {phi1, phi2}]
```

For users more accustomed to standard notation, it is often more desirable to see a model printed in a more familiar notation. The function **ArimaPrint** prints a model with subscripts and lags. White noise processes have a special format.

In[10]:= **ArimaPrint[e]**

e[t] ~ WN[5]

In[11]:= **ArimaPrint[arma]**

Out[11]:= arma   =   + 0.5 a   + a + 0.5 arma
            t   −1 + t   t   −1 + t

Though conventional, ARIMA models need not have white noise input. For example, we can think of a moving average whose input is not white noise, but instead is the AR(3) model **ar**. Such models are of interest when investigating the effects of smoothing or filtering upon observed time series. The **DefineMA** function, though, checks that the input is indeed white noise.

In[12]:= **DefineMA[comp,ar,-{.5,.25,.5}]**

Arima::noise:

$$
\text{Symbol ARIMA}\left[\frac{1}{1 + 0.5\ z + <<1>> + 0.5\ z^3},\ 0,\ 7,\ 1,\ \text{ar, a}\right]
$$

is not white noise.

The more general function, **ArimaCreate** does not require white-noise inputs and produces the desired ARMA model. The empty list { } indicates there are no autoregressive parameters in this model.

In[13]:= **ArimaCreate[comp,ar,{},0,-{.5,.25,.5}]**

In this case the composite model reduces to white noise since the polynomials $\Phi(z)$ and $\Theta(z)$ cancel.

In[14]:= **comp**

Out[14]:= ARIMA[1, 0, 0, 1, comp, a]

In[15]:= **ArimaIsWhiteNoiseQ[comp]**

Out[15]:= True

Finally, it is useful on occasion to keep track of just what models have been created. The name **ArimaSymbolList** is associated with a list of symbols which identify ARIMA models. Printing this list with **ArimaPrintSymbol-List** summarizes the symbols and the orders (p, d, q) for each.

In[16]:= **ArimaPrintSymbolList[]**

Out[16]:= {comp{0, 0, 0}, a{0, 0, 0}, e{0, 0, 0}, arma{1, 0, 1},
            ma{0, 0, 2}, symAr{2, 0, 0}, ar{3, 0, 0}}

16.3.2.2   Accessing the Components of Models

In order to maintain the abstract notion of an ARIMA model, special accessor
functions extract features from ARIMA models. Using these routines avoids
dependence on the internal representation of ARIMA models, such as remem-
bering where the autoregressive coefficient vector falls in the model data structure. This abstraction also yields an added benefit. As long as components are
extracted using the accessor functions, programs built upon this package will
work even if (when) the internal representation changes.

The functions **ArimaPhi** and **ArimaTheta** extract the lists of coefficients
from the models. These functions return a list of the coefficients of the associated
polynomials $\Phi(z)$ and $\Theta(z)$, *not* the coefficients found in the usual form of the
model as in equation (1).

In[1]:= **ArimaPhi[arma]**

Out[1]:= {1., −0.5}

In[2]:= **ArimaTheta[arma]**

Out[2]:= {1., 0.5}

ArimaOrder returns the list $\{p, d, q\}$ of the order of the autoregression, differencing, and moving average, respectively.

In[3]:= **ArimaOrder[arma]**

Out[3]:= {1, 0, 1}

Other functions extract more features of the constructed model, such as its mean
and scale. The scale returned by **ArimaScale** is that of the error process, not
the standard deviation of the observations $\gamma_0^{1/2}$. (See Section 16.3.5 for details
on the covariances.)

In[4]:= **ArimaMean[arma]**

Out[4]:= 0

In[5]:= **ArimaScale[arma]**

Out[5]:= 1

16.3.3   Moving Average Form and Prediction MSE

The package includes functions that perform all of operations described in
Section 16.2 on interactive manipulations. In particular, it includes functions
to compute and manipulate the moving average representation of the model.
Rather than using back-substitution, these functions rely upon polynomial manipulations.

For the ARMA(1,1) model **arma**, the moving average coefficients are coefficients in the expansion of the transfer function as a power series. Recall that the
transfer function is the ratio of the two polynomials $\Theta(z)/\Phi(z)$.

In[1]:= **tf[z] = ArimaTransferFunction[arma]**

Out[1]:= 1. + 0.5 z

‾‾‾‾‾‾‾‾‾‾‾

1. − 0.5 z

The **Series** function expands this rational polynomial into a power series in z.

In[2]:= **Series[tf[z],{z,0,5}]**

$$Out[2]:= 1. + 1.\ z + 0.5\ z^2 + 0.25\ z^3 + 0.125\ z^4 + 0.0625\ z^5$$

$$+ O[z]^6$$

Given this form, it is easy to read off the moving average coefficients of the model. For example, the moving average weights $w_1 = 1$ and $w_2 = 0.5$. The package function **ArimaMAWeights** automates these steps and returns a list of coefficients. By default, a list of 10 weights $w_0, w_1, \ldots, w_9$ is returned.

In[3]:= **ArimaMAWeights[arma]**

Out[3]:= {1., 1., 0.5, 0.25, 0.125, 0.0625, 0.03125, 0.015625,

0.0078125, 0.00390625}

The prediction mean squared error is proportional to partial sums of this sequence. **ArimaMSE** does this accumulation, including scaling by the factor σ^2 from the white-noise input. The output generated by this program makes it easy to plot the prediction MSE versus the degree of extrapolation.

In[4]:= **mse = ArimaMSE[arma]**

Out[4]:= {1, 2., 2.25, 2.3125, 2.32813, 2.33203, 2.33301,

2.33325, 2.33331, 2.33333}

In[5]:= **ListPlot[mse, PlotJoined->True,**

AxesLabel->{"Lead", "MSE"}]

Out[5]:= —Graphics—

16.3.4   Stationarity and Invertibility

As noted in the introduction, the zeros of $\Phi(z)$ and $\Theta(z)$ determine the stationarity and invertibility of an ARIMA model. If the moduli of all of the zeros of $\Phi(z)$, which are also known as the poles of the process, are larger than one, then the process can be written as a weighted sum of past errors and is stationary. If the zeros of $\Theta(z)$ have moduli greater than one, the process is invertible.

Some interactive calculations suggest the approach taken in the package. Begin by extracting $\Phi(z)$ from the AR(3) process **ar**.

```
In[1]:= Phi[z] = ArimaPhiPolynomial[ar]
Out[1]:=
                                2            3
           1 + 0.5 z + 0.25 z  + 0.5 z
```

The poles of the process are the zeros of this polynomial, and **Solve** gives these as a list of rules. Note that the complex zeros always come in conjugate pairs for models with real-valued coefficients.

```
In[2]:= Solve[Phi[z]==0, z]
Out[2]:= {{z -> -1.14747}, {z -> 0.323737 - 1.2799 I},

           {z -> 0.323737 + 1.2799 I}}
```

The package function **ArimaPoles** combines these operations and returns a list of the poles.

```
In[3]:= ArimaPoles[ar]

Out[3]:= {-1.14747, 0.323737 - 1.2799 I, 0.323737 + 1.2799 I}
```

Since all of the poles of this AR(3) process have modulus greater than one, the process is stationary and has an infinite moving average representation. The boolean function **ArimaIsStationaryQ** uses this approach to test for stationarity, though strictly speaking the process can be stationary when some poles are inside the unit circle. The notion of stationarity here is really a convention that also provides the basis for the infinite moving average representation (3).

```
In[4]:= ArimaIsStationaryQ[ar]

Out[4]:= True
```

It is often helpful and informative to see plots of these poles. Building such a plot by hand, though, is tedious, especially if we want to see the unit circle at the same time. First, save the list of poles.

```
In[5]:= poles = ArimaPoles[ar]

Out[5]:= {-1.14747, 0.323737 - 1.2799 I, 0.323737 + 1.2799 I}
```

Now find the real and imaginary parts of each pole.

```
In[6]:= re = Re[poles]; im = Im[poles];
```

Finally, plot the points in the plane. The transposition is needed since the plotting function expects a list of pairs, not a pair of lists.

In[7]:= **lp = ListPlot[Transpose[{re,im}]]**

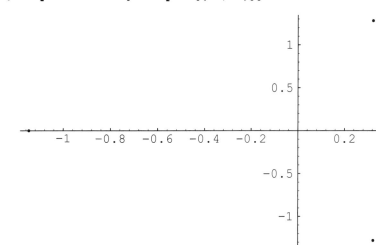

Out[7]:= −Graphics−

Adding the unit circle is a nice feature, except the scaling of the picture is usually wrong.

In[8]:= **Show[lp,Graphics[Circle[{0,0},1]]]**

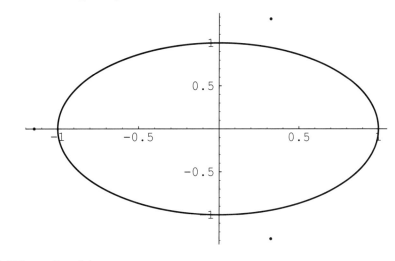

Out[8]:= −Graphics−

The package function **ArimaPlotPoles** combines these operations and forces the desired perspective so that the circle indeed looks like a circle. To yield a nicer plot, this function plots the locations of the reciprocals of the poles

since these lie inside the circle under stationarity. An analogous function plots
the zeros associated with $\Theta(z)$.

In[9]:= **ArimaPlotPoles[ar]**

{−0.87148, 0.18574 + 0.734328 I, 0.18574 − 0.734328 I}

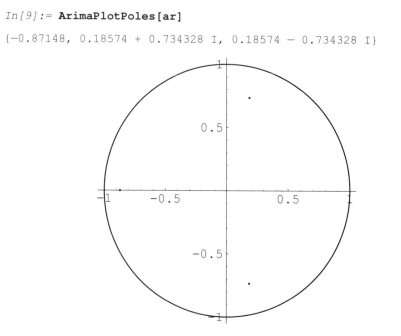

Out[9]:= −Graphics−

16.3.5 Spectral Density Function

16.3.5.1 Extracting and Plotting the Spectral Density

The spectral density function summarizes the dependence properties of an
ARIMA model, particularly the tendency of some of these models to produce
periodic time series. The function **ArimaSDF** returns a *function* that evaluates
to the spectral density of the process. Like any other function, it can be mapped
over lists and plotted. The manipulations are fairly straightforward. First we
extract the spectral density.

In[1]:= **sdf = ArimaSDF[ar]**

Out[1]:= Function[theta$, 1 /
          (2 Pi (1.5625 + 1.5 Cos[theta$] + 1. Cos[2 theta$] +
              1. Cos[3 theta$]))]

This function can be mapped over lists; here are $f(0)$, $f(\pi/2)$, and $f(\pi)$.

In[2]:= **sdf /@ {0,Pi/2,Pi}**

Out[2]:= 0.0987654   0.888889   8.
         {─────────, ─────────, ──}
            Pi   Pi   Pi

A plot of the spectral density shows the effects of the three poles associated with this model. The reciprocals of the poles of this model lie inside, though close to, the unit circle.

In[3]:= **poles = 1/ArimaPoles[ar]**

Out[3]:= {−0.87148, 0.18574 + 0.734328 I, 0.18574 − 0.734328 I}

The pole at −1/.87148 on the real axis produces a peak in the spectral density at π, indicating substantial variation at high frequency. To understand the effects of the complex poles, we need to see the polar form of these values.

In[4]:= **{Abs[#],Arg[#]}& /@ poles**

Out[4]:= {{0.87148, Pi}, {0.757454, 1.32305}, {0.757454, −1.32305}}

This calculation suggests that the complex pair produces a peak near frequency ±1.32. A plot confirms these impressions, with the added vertical lines at the frequencies suggested by the arguments of the complex poles.

In[5]:= **Plot[sdf[x],{x,-Pi,Pi},**
    Epilog->Line/@{ {{-1.323,0},{-1.323,4}},
    {{1.323,0},{1.323,4}}}]

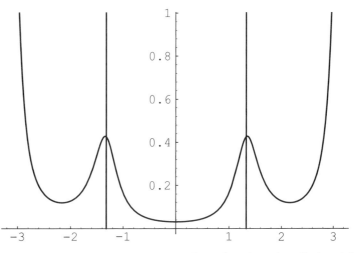

The function **ArimaPlotSDF** generates this plot directly, albeit without the vertical lines at the complex pole arguments.

The argument λ of the complex pole does not give the precise location of the local maximum of the spectral density. The added lines in the preceding figure miss the peaks which are farther from zero than this approximation would suggest. Differentiating the spectral density and solving $f'(x) = 0$ does lead to the exact zeros.

In[6]:= **d[x_] = D[sdf[x],x]**

Out[6]:= $$\frac{-(-1.5\ Sin[x]\ -\ 2.\ Sin[2\ x]\ -\ 3.\ Sin[3\ x])}{2\ Pi\ (1.5625\ +\ 1.5\ Cos[x]\ +\ 1.\ Cos[2\ x]\ +\ 1.\ Cos[3\ x])^2}$$

Solve (and the related **NSolve**) fails to find an expression for the location of any of the extrema (such as the minimum at zero).

```
In[7]:= Solve[d[x] == 0, x]
```

Solve::ifun: Warning: Inverse functions are being used by Solve,
    so some solutions may not be found.

Solve::tdep: The equations appear to involve transcendental
    functions of the variables in an essentially non-algebraic
    way.

```
Out[7]:=
```

$$\text{Solve}\left[\frac{-(-1.5\ \text{Sin}[x] - 2.\ \text{Sin}[2\ x] - 3.\ \text{Sin}[3\ x])}{2\ \text{Pi}\ (1.5625 + 1.5\ \text{Cos}[x] + 1.\ \text{Cos}[2\ x] + 1.\ \text{Cos}[3\ x])^2}\ ==\ 0,\ x\right]$$

FindRoot, however, gives a precise numerical value near the starting guess given by argument of the pole.

```
In[8]:= FindRoot[d[x] == 0, {x,1.32}]

Out[8]:= {x -> 1.34467}
```

As we might have guessed with a little hindsight, the maximum is farther from zero than λ, suggesting that the real pole at π has pulled the maximum away from the origin. The best way to visualize this effect is to move into a higher dimension.

16.3.5.2 3-D spectral plots

The spectral density of an ARIMA model is the squared modulus of the transfer function $T(z) = \Theta(z)/\Phi(z)$ for $|z| = 1$. If we think of the transfer function as a complex-valued function defined over the whole complex plane rather than just along the unit circle, we can generate some interesting images. To visualize this complex function, we are going to plot $|T(z)|$ over the complex plane with shading determined by the argument of $T(z)$. The spectral density is proportional to the squared height of this surface along the unit circle, as though we sliced through the surface with a circular cookie cutter and measured the depth of the dough.

To produce a clear example of this type of plot, consider an an AR(3) model **y** which has a specific set of poles. Since the poles of the autoregression are the zeros of $\Phi(z)$, we can build a model by setting its coefficients to be those of a polynomial that has the desired structure. Again, it is useful to consider plots of the reciprocals of the poles since these lie inside the unit circle. For example, the process with poles at $1/(-.1 \pm i.8)$ and $1/.8$ has the following coefficients:

```
In[1]:= phi=CoefficientList[(1-z(-.1 + .8I))(1-z(-.1 - .8I))(1-
        z.8),z]

Out[1]:= {1, -0.6, 0.49, -0.52}
```

The values of ϕ_1, ϕ_2, and ϕ_3 are the last three items in this list with the signs changed, so we drop the first and negate the signs when we define the model.

In[2]:= **DefineAr[y,a,-Drop[phi,1]]**

A quick check verifies our calculation.

In[3]:= **1 / ArimaPoles[y]**

Out[3]:= {−0.1 + 0.8 I, −0.1 − 0.8 I, 0.8}

Before we plot the "spectral surface," it is useful to acclimate ourselves to how the surface will be colored. The coloring of the surface encodes the phase information from the transfer function. As a point of reference, the following is a three-dimensional plot of the function $h(z) = h(re^{i\lambda}) = e^{i\lambda}$. The surface is flat since $\mid h(z) \mid = 1$. The coloring is constant on rays from the origin. When the argument λ is near zero, the color is a shade of red. When the argument is near π, the color is blue-green. Thus low frequencies are red and high frequencies are blue. These colors appear as shades of grey in the output figure. Users who are more interested in black and white displays should replace **Hue[z]** in the following command with **GrayLevel[Abs[z]]**.

In[4]:= **Plot3D [{1,Hue[.5 * Arg[x+I y]/Pi]},**
                {x,-1,1}, {y,-1,1}, ViewPoint->{0, -2, 2}]

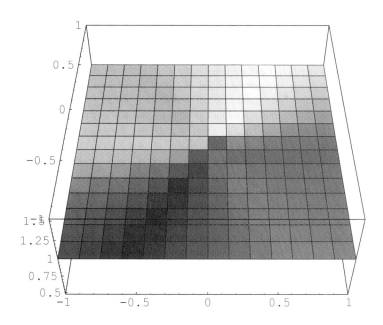

Now consider the transfer function of the AR(3) model. The color again denotes the phase, but now the magnitude of the transfer function is the height of the surface. First extract the transfer function to gain a little efficiency.

In[5]:= **tf[z_] = ArimaTransferFunction[y]**

Out[5]:=

$$\frac{1}{1 - 0.6\ z + 0.49\ z^2 - 0.52\ z^3}$$

The norm of the transfer function for $|z| < 1$ suggests the shape of the full surface. The spectral density (which is proportional to the squared norm of the transfer function for $|z| = 1$) shows the expected three peaks. Since the real pole is positive, the associated peak is at zero rather than π as in the model shown in the previous section.

In[6]:= **Plot[Abs[tf[E^(I th)]], {th,-Pi,Pi}]**

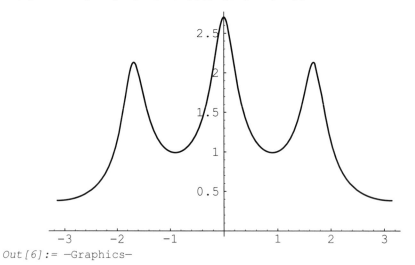

Out[6]:= —Graphics—

The shape changes quite a bit if we consider the norm of the transfer function along the circle with radius 0.5.

In[7]:= **Plot[Abs[tf[0.5 E^(I th)]],{th,-Pi,Pi}]**

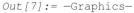

Out[7]:= —Graphics—

The surface plot joins these images and extends the plot to the complex plane, with full phase information.

```
In[8]:= Plot3D [{Abs[tf[x+I y]],Hue[1/2 Arg[ tf[x+I y]/Pi ]]},
          {x,-1.5,1.5},{y,-1.5,1.5},
          ViewPoint->{0, -2, 2},
          PlotPoints->20 ]
```

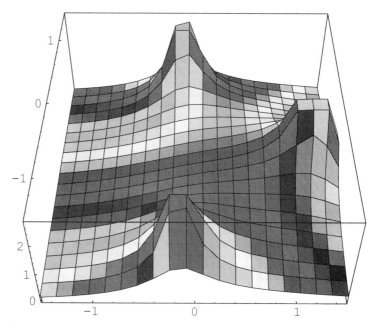

The peaks in the plot indicate the reciprocals of the poles of this model. Notice how the phase of the function changes near the poles. Since the poles for this model are well-separated, the peaks of the associated spectral density are near the arguments of the poles. As the poles of a model move closer to each other, however, the poles interfere and the locations of the maxima of the spectral density are not so easily found.

16.3.6   Covariance Structure of ARIMA Models

The spectral density suggests an elegant scheme for determining the covariances of an ARIMA model. Recall that the covariances $\gamma_j = \mathrm{Cov}(y_t, y_{t-j})$ of a second-order stationary process y_t are the Fourier coefficients of the spectral density function $f(\lambda)$,

$$\gamma_j = \int_{-\pi}^{\pi} e^{-ij\lambda} f(\lambda) d\lambda = \int_{-\pi}^{\pi} \cos j(\lambda) f(\lambda) d\lambda.$$

The second equality follows because the spectral density is an even function of λ. The simplicity of this relationship suggests it as a means for finding the covariances of an arbitrary ARIMA model, even one with symbolic coefficients.

As an example, consider an arbitrary second-order moving average, say $y_t = u_t - \theta_1 u_{t-1} - \theta_2 u_{t-2}$ with the white noise process u_t having $\text{Var}(u_t) = \sigma^2$ given as s^2.

```
In[1]:= DefineWhiteNoise[u,s]
        DefineMA[ma2, u, {theta1,theta2}]

In[2]:= ArimaPrint[ma2]

Out[2]:= ma2  =  - theta2 u        - theta1 u        + u
            t              -2 + t            -1 + t     t
```

The covariance sequence for this process is

$$\gamma_0 = \sigma^2(1 + \theta_1^2 + \theta_2^2), \gamma_1 = \sigma^2(-\theta_1 + \theta_1\theta_2), \gamma_2 = -\sigma^2\theta_2,$$

with the remaining covariances $\gamma_j = 0, j > 2$. Direct integration of the spectral density does indeed find the covariances for this symbolic moving average process.

```
In[3]:= sdf = ArimaSDF[ma2];
        Integrate[Cos[lambda]sdf[lambda],{lambda,-Pi,Pi}]

Out[3]:=   2
         s  theta1 (-1 + theta2)

In[4]:= Integrate[Cos[2 lambda]sdf[lambda],{lambda,-Pi,Pi}]

Out[4]:=    2
         -(s  theta2)

In[5]:= Integrate[Cos[3 lambda]sdf[lambda],{lambda,-Pi,Pi}]

Out[5]:= 0
```

For autoregressions, this direct approach is not as useful since the integrand for such models is a rational polynomial with a non-trivial denominator. This example also suggests some of the hazards of using symbolic algebra programs; what often seems obvious to us really is not. To keep the answer recognizable, consider a stationary first-order model $y_t = \phi_1 y_{t-1} + u_t$ with $|\phi_1| < 1$ and the same white noise u_t. The covariance function of this process is

$$\gamma_j = \frac{\sigma^2 \phi_1^j}{1 - \phi_1^2},$$

```
In[6]:= DefineAr[ar1, u, {phi1}]
        ArimaPrint[ar1]

Out[6]:= ar1  =  + u  + phi1 ar1
            t        t            -1 + t
```

Mathematica evaluates the Fourier integral, but the solution given for γ_1 does not resemble the simple form that was expected.

```
In[7]:= sdf = ArimaSDF[ar1];
        int = Integrate[Cos[theta]sdf[theta],{theta,-Pi,Pi}]
```

```
Out[7]:=              2                     2 2   2
             (1 + phi1  − Sqrt[(−1 + phi1 ) ]) s
             ────────────────────────────────────
                                      2 2
                   2 phi1 Sqrt[(−1 + phi1 ) ]
```

Mathematica has not simplified this expression as much as we would like, leaving $((\phi_1^2 - 1)^2)^{1/2}$ unreduced. What happened? *Mathematica* does not assume that the coefficient ϕ_1 is real-valued, nor have we made it aware of our assumption that $|\phi_1| < 1$. In general, the rule `Sqrt[x_^2] -> -x` is not correct since `x` might be complex or positive. Since neither of these cases occur here, we can use this rule to simplify the integral.

```
In[8]:= int //. Sqrt[x_^2] -> -x
Out[8]:=              2
                 phi1 s
             ───────────────────
                         2 2
             Sqrt[(−1 + phi1 ) ]
```

The numerator has the proper form, but the undesired term remains in the denominator. This rule does not match the term in the denominator because of the way *Mathematica* stores rational polynomials. The built-in function **FullForm** reveals the internal form of the last expression.

```
In[9]:= FullForm[%]
Out[9]:= Times[−1, Power[phi1, −1], Power[Power[Plus[−1,
         Power[phi1, 2]], 2], Rational[−1, 2]],
         Power[s, 2]]
```

The square root in the denominator is expressed in terms of a power, with the exponent $-1/2$. Consequently, the simple substitution rule is unsuccessful for the denominator. A more general rule achieves the desired simplification.

```
In[10]:= int //. Power[Power[x_,2],Rational[k_,2]]->x^k
Out[10]:=             2
                  phi1 s
             − (───────────)
                       2
                 −1 + phi1
```

Although the Fourier transform of the spectral density offers an elegant method for finding the covariances of an ARIMA model, direct manipulations of the covariances are much faster. The functions **ArimaCovariance** and **ArimaCorrelation** determine the covariances using algorithms that are based on the structure of the process. For example, if the process is an autoregression, the programs use the well-known Yule-Walker equations. For example, the first 5 covariances $\gamma_j, j = 0, 1, \ldots, 4$, of the AR(1) model **ar1** are:

```
In[11]:= ArimaCovariance[ar1,5]
```

Out[11]:=

$$\{-\left(\frac{s^2}{-1+\text{phi1}^2}\right), \ -\left(\frac{\text{phi1}\ s^2}{-1+\text{phi1}^2}\right), \ -\left(\frac{\text{phi1}^2\ s^2}{-1+\text{phi1}^2}\right), \ -\left(\frac{\text{phi1}^3\ s^2}{-1+\text{phi1}^2}\right),$$

$$-\left(\frac{\text{phi1}^4\ s^2}{-1+\text{phi1}^2}\right)\}$$

The correlation function $\rho_j = \frac{\gamma_j}{\gamma_0}$ is:

In[12]:= **ArimaCorrelation[ar1, 5]**

Out[12]:=
$$\{1, \ \text{phi1}, \ \text{phi1}^2, \ \text{phi1}^3, \ \text{phi1}^4\}$$

These functions work if the input process has either numerical or symbolic coefficients (or a mixture of the two). For the ARMA(1,1) model introduced in Section 16.3.1, the first five covariances are:

In[13]:= **ArimaCovariance[arma, 5]**

Out[13]:= {2.33333, 1.66667, 0.833333, 0.416667, 0.208333}

16.4   Numerical Methods and Estimation

16.4.1   Introduction

The applications of this section use the tools provided in the accompanying package to investigate the effects of model estimation. Using simulated realizations generated with the procedures of Section 16.4.1, the examples in Section 16.4.2 compare estimates of the spectral density and covariance functions to their theoretic counterparts. The tools in Section 16.4.3 are more theoretical and consider the bias of estimated coefficients and the effects of estimation on the accuracy of prediction.

16.4.2   Generating Time Series From ARIMA Models

Simulation provides the raw data for experimentation with ARIMA models. This section shows how to generate numerical realizations which form the input to estimation routines. The most obvious application is the comparison of estimated statistics to theoretical properties of models. In order to anticipate how an estimator performs with real data, it helps to understand its behavior with data generated from known models.

The function **ArimaNRealize** uses the obvious recursion to build a Gaussian time series realization, starting from an optional list of initial values. If these initial values are not given, the program constructs a random starting sequence drawn from the appropriate joint distribution. As an example, consider simulating a short realization from the AR(3) model **ar**.

```
In[1]:= ArimaPrint[ar]

Out[1]:=
ar  =  + a   - 0.5 ar        - 0.25 ar        - 0.5 ar
   t       t          -3 + t           -2 + t          -1 + t
```

To get a reasonable starting value, notice that the mean of the series is 7.

```
In[2]:= ArimaMean[ar]

Out[2]:= 7
```

The initial values are defined via an optional argument to this function. Using a list of 2 values is not enough to start this process since this is an AR(3) model and needs three lags.

```
In[3]:= ArimaNRealize[ar,10,initial->{7,7}]

ArimaNRealize::initial: Too few in {7, 7}; need 3

Out[3]:= {}
```

It is fine, though, to have more than the three necessary starting values.

```
In[4]:= ArimaNRealize[ar,10,initial->{7,7,7,7,7}]

Out[4]:= {7, 7, 7, 7, 7, -6.66904, -0.454985, -1.48785, 7.38296,
          0.24585, 0.176663, -1.25449, 3.31705, -0.18812,
          2.19883}
```

If the starting values are far from the mean relative to the scale of the process, the observations after such initialization appear non-stationary since the data trend to the mean of the process.

```
In[5]:= ArimaNRealize[ar,12,initial->{70,70,70}]

Out[5]:= {70, 70, 70, -82.6692, -9.00677, -6.59104, 49.6839,
          -15.3547, 0.898375, -17.1958, 19.663, -3.12448,
          7.52172, -9.95941, 7.92839}
```

Long realizations of ARIMA models provide interesting inputs to the audio features of *Mathematica*. In addition to the typical descriptive plots, *Mathematica* adds the ability to listen to data. To play an ARIMA model, first generate a fairly long realization. Make sure to use the trailing semicolon to avoid having to wait for a listing of the data. Since no initial values are supplied in this example, the first three items in the sequence of 2000 are a random draw from the trivariate normal distribution with mean vector $\mu = (7, 7, 7)'$ and the covariances of this model.

```
In[6]:= arSeries = ArimaNRealize[ar,2000];
```

To generate the audio tones, make this list the input to the function **List-Play**. As a side benefit, **ListPlay** also produces a highly compressed point-plot of the realization. The page formatting system used to produce this book is currently unable to handle the detailed image associated with sounds, and obviously books still lack an audio capability. Nonetheless, we can still show you how to generate a sound:

```
In[7]:= ListPlay[arSeries]
```

A useful reference point for learning what it means to listen to a time series is to start with some familiar signals, such as a sine wave. A good demonstration of the fact that AR models can approximate sinusoidal signals is to listen to a realization of a model that is highly periodic. The following model has a pair of complex zeros near the unit circle and is thus rather periodic. The symbol y is first cleared to avoid name conflicts with previous examples.

```
In[8]:= Clear[y];
        phi = Re /@ CoefficientList[
            (1-z/(0.9+.45I))(1-z/(0.9-.45I)),z
        ];
        DefineAr[y,a, - Drop[phi,1] ]
```

The poles are rather close to the unit circle, and hence the process is close to the bounds of stationarity.

```
In[9]:= Abs /@ ArimaPoles[y]
```

```
Out[9]:= {1.00623, 1.00623}
```

Again, generate a long realization of 2000 values.

```
In[10]:= arSeries = ArimaNRealize[y,2000];
```

A plot of the first 50 values of this series shows the strong periodicity.

```
In[11]:= ListPlot[Take[arSeries,50]]
```

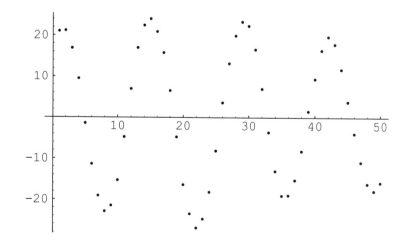

```
Out[11]:= -Graphics-
```

The sound of this process has less hiss than that of the previous model, and the summary plot (were we able to display it) shows the transient random modulation of this model.

16.4.3   Estimation and Models

16.4.3.1   Estimating Correlations

The simulation tools in Section 16.4.1 make it easy to compare features of simulated realizations to the comparable properties of the generating model. As an example, we begin by computing the first 15 correlations of the AR(3) model **ar**.

In[1]:= **arCorr = ArimaCorrelation[ar, 15]**

Out[1]:= {1., −0.5, 0.25, −0.5, 0.4375, −0.21875, 0.25,
       −0.289063, 0.191406, −0.148438, 0.170898, −0.144043,
       0.103516, −0.101196, 0.0967407}

To see how close estimates come to these correlations, we can simulate a sequence of say 50 observations from this model and make this partial realization the argument to **EstimateCorrelation**. The function **EstimateCorrelation** takes as its input a sequence and returns the standard estimate of the autocorrelations,

$$\hat{\rho}_j = \frac{\sum_{t=j+1}^{n}(y_t - \bar{y})(y_{t-j} - \bar{y})}{\sum_{t=1}^{n}(y_t - \bar{y})^2},$$

where $y_1, y_2, \ldots, y_n$ denote the observed realization. Again, it is useful in these operations to suppress the lengthy output using either the trailing semicolon or the summarizing function **Short** illustrated next.

In[2]:= **yt = ArimaNRealize[ar,50] // Short**

Out[2]:= {3.28169, 1.40333, 0.599466, <<45>>, 0.631919, 2.63362}

The estimated correlations are close to those of the process.

In[3]:= **estCorr = EstimateCorrelation[yt,15]**

Out[3]:= {1., −0.63672, 0.488421, −0.469317, 0.438543,
       −0.266399, 0.235207, −0.219708, 0.190242, −0.142283,
       0.181205, −0.19368, 0.150341, −0.0805495, −0.0390053}

Obviously a plot provides a more useful comparison of these sequences. The small utility function **DoubleListPlot** which is included in the package plots the first input list in black and the second in gray. Evidently, the estimates from this sequence approximate the correlation function of the process quite well.

In[4]:= **DoubleListPlot[arCorr,estCorr]**

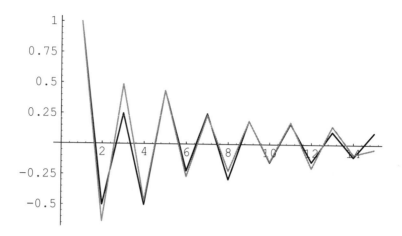

Out[4]:= —Graphics—

The results for a realization of the MA(2) model are similiar, but show more estimation error. As is well-known, the correlation sequence for a moving average cuts off after q terms. That is, $\gamma_j = 0, j = q+1, q+2, \ldots$. Here is the model and its correlations.

In[5]:= **ArimaPrint[ma]**

Out[5]:= ma   =   + 0.25 e   + 0.5 e   + e
*   t   -2 + t   -1 + t   t*

In[6]:= **maCorr = ArimaCorrelation[ma, 15]**

Out[6]:= {1., 0.47619, 0.190476, 0, 0, 0, 0, 0, 0, 0, 0, 0, 0,
*   0, 0, 0, 0}*

In contrast, estimated correlations seldom cut off to zero as sharply as those of the model. This type of estimation error makes it quite hard to use informal graphical tools based on correlation functions to identify models. The deviations of the estimated correlations from the model correlations are themselves correlated so that the estimates frequently drift above or below the actual sequence.

To illustrate the sampling variation of these estimators, we are going to use the function **MultipleListPlot**. This function is included in the supplemental graphics package supplied with *Mathematica*. Its purpose is to plot several lists at once, making it ideal to show the sample-to-sample variation. To use this additional program, first import the needed package,

In[7]:= **<<Graphics `MultipleListPlot `**

and then construct several input realizations. In this case, we simulate three series from the moving average model and find the estimated correlations.

In[8]:= **y1 = ArimaNRealize[ma, 50];**
          y2 = ArimaNRealize[ma, 50];
          y3 = ArimaNRealize[ma, 50];

```
In[8]:=(cont.)
        estCorr1 = EstimateCorrelation[ y1, 15 ];
        estCorr2 = EstimateCorrelation[ y2, 15 ];
        estCorr3 = EstimateCorrelation[ y3, 15 ];
```

Plotting these three estimates with the process correlations makes the effects of sampling variation rather clear. In this plot, gray lines join the sample estimates and black lines join the model correlations.

```
In[9]:= MultipleListPlot[maCorr, estCorr1, estCorr2, estCorr3,
            PlotJoined->True,
            LineStyles->{{GrayLevel[0.0]},
                {GrayLevel[0.75]},
                {GrayLevel[0.75]},
                {GrayLevel[0.75]}} ]
```

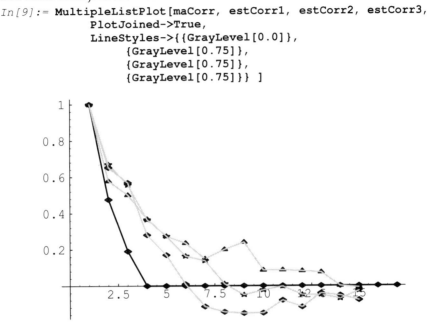

```
Out[9]:= -Graphics-
```

16.4.3.2 Estimating the Spectral Density

Estimates of the spectral density are simple to compute since *Mathematica* includes routines to find the discrete Fourier transform. As with the correlation examples, we are going to use simulated data as the raw material for the comparisons. The process is again the AR(3) model studied in Section 16.3.4. We begin this example by generating a long enough realization to permit spectral estimation. Since spectral estimation is a nonparametric method, it requires more data than estimating the few parameters of a specific model. Here the length is $n = 256$.

```
In[1]:= yt = ArimaNRealize[ar, 256];
```

The simplest spectral estimation technique smooths the periodogram. The periodogram is proportional to the squared norm of the discrete Fourier transform of the data,

$$I(\lambda) = \frac{1}{2\pi n} \mid \sum_{t=1}^{n} y_t e^{-i\lambda t} \mid^2 .$$

The following command computes the periodogram of our partial realization at the grid of equally spaced frequencies $\lambda_j = (2\pi j/n)$ for $j = 0, 1, \ldots, n-1$.

```
In[2]:= pGram = Abs[ Fourier[yt] ]^2 / (2 Pi);
```

Now we can plot the periodogram with the actual spectral density on the interval 0 to 2π. The display function option postpones the separate plotting of each graph until the two are combined and shown by the last command.

```
In[3]:= sdf = ArimaSDF[ ar ];
        sdfPlot = Plot[ sdf[x], {x,0, 2 Pi},
            DisplayFunction->Identity];
        estPlot = ListPlot[Table[{2 Pi i/256,pGram[[i]]},{i,256}],
            DisplayFunction->Identity ];
        Show[sdfPlot, estPlot, DisplayFunction->$DisplayFunction]
```

```
Out[3]:= -Graphics-
```

   This plot makes it clear that the periodogram $I(\lambda)$ is not such a good estimator of the spectral density function. As the time series grows in length, the periodogram has higher resolution with more approximately *independent* ordinates. Consequently, the periodogram is not a consistent estimator of the spectral density. What is needed is a little smoothing, such as with a simple moving average. Assuming that the length of the input weights list is odd, the function **MovingAverage** defined next computes a simple moving average.

```
In[4]:= MovingAverage[ data_, wts_] :=
            Module[       {result, nWts, sumWts},
                sumWts = Plus @@ wts;
                result = data;   (* ignore end effects *)
                half = Floor[Length[wts]/2];
                Do[result[[i]] = (wts . Take[data,
                {i-half, i+half}])/sumWts,
                {i,1+half, Length[data]-half}];
                result]
```

If we apply this smoothing to the raw periodogram, we obtain a more useful estimator of the form $\bar{I}(\lambda_j) = \sum_{k=-m}^{m} I(\lambda_{k+j})/(2m+1)$. For example, the smoothed estimator $\bar{I}$ for this example with $m = 2$ is

```
In[5]:= spGram = MovingAverage[pGram,{1,1,1,1,1}];
```

A plot of the smoothed estimator suggests the underlying spectral density, and also shows the bias induced by smoothing.

```
In[6]:= estPlot = ListPlot[Transpose[
          {Table[2 Pi i/256,{i,256}], spGram}],
          DisplayFunction->Identity ];
        Show[ sdfPlot, estPlot,
          DisplayFunction->$DisplayFunction ]
```

```
Out[6]:= -Graphics-
```

Many other examples of spectral estimation applied to well-known data series appear in Bloomfield (1976).

16.4.4   Understanding the Effects of Estimation

16.4.4.1   Overview

The properties of estimated autoregressions are better understood than those of other ARIMA models. As the simulated comparisons illustrate, estimated parameters can be quite far from corresponding model parameters. Recent results provide expressions for the bias due to estimation and the effect of estimation errors on prediction mean squared error. This section illustrates several functions that evaluate the associated expressions.

16.4.4.2   Coefficient Bias

The bias of least-squares estimators of autoregressive coefficients has been known for a long time in special cases [e.g., Kendall (1954) and Marriott and

Pope (1954)]. More recently, Shaman and Stine (1988) gave expressions for the bias and discovered the nature of its effect upon the fitted model. As it turns out, estimation bias pulls the fitted model toward a special model where the bias is zero. Some examples make the ideas more clear.

The examples of this section use two AR models, of orders 4 and 5. The function **Array** is useful for building repetitive lists like those needed for the coefficients of these models. Again, we begin by clearing the needed symbols.

In[1]:= **Clear[ar4,ar5,phi]**

Coefficient lists built using **Array** have a different appearance, though the meaning seems clear.

In[2]:= **Array[phi,4]**

Out[2]:= {phi[1], phi[2], phi[3], phi[4]}

In[3]:= **DefineAr[ar4, a, Array[phi,4]]**
         DefineAr[ar5, a, Array[phi,5]]

The function **ArimaCoefficientBias** computes the $O(1/n)$ bias associated with the least squares estimator of the coefficients of an autoregression based on a realization of length n. For the AR(4) model, the bias is seen to be a linear combination of the model coefficients.

In[4]:= **bias4 = ArimaCoefficientBias[ar4, 0]**

Out[4]:= {-phi[1], -1 - 2 phi[2] - phi[4], phi[1] - 4 phi[3], -1
         - 5 phi[4]}

Thus, for example, $E[\hat\phi_1] = \phi_1 - (\phi_1/n)$. The linear form of the bias implies that a unique AR(4) models exists for which the least squares estimators are unbiased to this order of approximation. The coefficients of this model are rational numbers which we can find using the **Solve** function and the bias expression.

In[5]:= **s4 = Solve[bias4==0, Array[phi,4]]**

Out[5]:=
{{phi[1] -> 0, phi[2] -> -($\frac{2}{5}$), phi[3] -> 0, phi[4] -> -($\frac{1}{5}$)}}

Hence, if the time series was generated by the model with coefficients $\phi_1 = 0, \phi_2 = -2/5, \phi_3 = 0$, and $\phi_4 = -1/5$, the least squares estimators are unbiased to this order.

The results for the AR(5) model show a similiar pattern. The bias terms differ, but the coefficients of the model for which the bias is zero are identical, with the addition of a trailing zero for ϕ_5.

In[6]:= **bias5 = ArimaCoefficientBias[ar5,0]**

Out[6]:= {-phi[1] - phi[5], -1 - 2 phi[2] - phi[4],
         phi[1] - 4 phi[3] - phi[5], -1 - 5 phi[4], -6 phi[5]}

In[7]:= **s5 = Solve[bias5==0, Array[phi,5]]**

Out[7]:=

$$\{\{phi[1] \;-\!\!>\; 0, \; phi[2] \;-\!\!>\; -(\frac{2}{5}), \; phi[3] \;-\!\!>\; 0, \; phi[4] \;-\!\!>\; -(\frac{1}{5}),$$

$$phi[5] \;-\!\!>\; 0\}\}$$

The poles of the models associated with no bias are particularly interesting since, for example, these determine the stationarity of the process. For the AR(4) and AR(5) models, the reciprocals of the poles of the models with no bias are symmetrically distributed within the unit circle. To plot the poles, first build a model with the special set of coefficients by replacing the symbolic coeffients in the AR(5) model by those associated with no bias.

In[8]:= **fp = First[ar5 /. s5];**
       ArimaPrint [fp]

Out[8]:=

$$ar5_t = + a_t - \frac{ar5_{-4+t}}{5} - \frac{2\,ar5_{-2+t}}{5}$$

A plot of the poles shows the symmetry of the pole positions and confirms the stationarity of this process.

In[9]:= **ArimaPlotPoles[fp]**

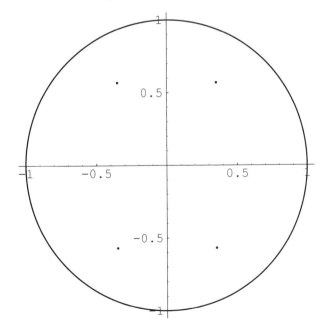

Out[9]:= —Graphics—

Elegant results about estimation bias in autoregression follow from the observation that the bias is a linear function of the vector of model coefficients. The details appear in Stine and Shaman (1989).

16.4.4.3 Inflation of the MSE of Prediction

Parameter estimation increases the mean squared error of prediction. Often the increase in mean squared error is so large that one should avoid using these models even for short-term forecasting. Consider the AR(3) model we have been using, **ar**. We have already studied and plotted its mean square error.

```
In[1]:= mse = ArimaMSE[ar,10]
```

```
Out[1]:= {1, 1.25, 1.25, 1.39063, 1.58203, 1.59766, 1.61743,
          1.6839, 1.70831, 1.71537}
```

Recall that the optimal prediction mean squared error monotonically grows to the variance of the process. This limiting value γ_0 is most easily found as the first autocovariance.

```
In[2]:= var = First[ArimaCovariance[ar,1]]
```

```
Out[2]:= 1.77778
```

In addition to finding the optimal prediction MSE, **ArimaMSE** includes a term for the effect of estimation if given a third argument. This last argument is the length n of the time series upon which estimation is to be based. The adjustment to the mean squared error is of order $1/n$. By leaving the symbol n undefined in the next command, we can see these adjustments.

```
In[3]:= estmse = ArimaMSE[ar,10,n]
```

Out[3]:=

$$\{1 + \frac{3.}{n}, \quad 1.25 + \frac{3.5}{n}, \quad 1.25 + \frac{2.5625}{n}, \quad 1.39063 + \frac{3.03125}{n},$$

$$1.58203 + \frac{4.23437}{n}, \quad 1.59766 + \frac{3.53516}{n}, \quad 1.61743 + \frac{2.93823}{n},$$

$$1.6839 + \frac{3.1554}{n}, \quad 1.70831 + \frac{2.94337}{n}, \quad 1.71537 + \frac{2.44521}{n}\}$$

How large is the effect of estimation in this model? A plot gives the most useful summary. One can either use the function **MultipleListPlot** included in the additional graphics package, or use the more simple procedure **DoubleListPlot**. Here **DoubleListPlot** shows the two mean squared error sequences for $n = 20$ with a horizontal line at the variance of the process.

```
In[4]:= DoubleListPlot[ mse, estmse/.n->20,
           Line[{{0,var}, {10,var}}]]
```

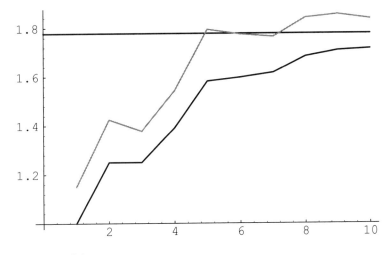

Out[4]:= —Graphics—

In contrast to the mean squared error of optimal prediction, the mean squared error of the estimated predictor does not increase monotonically, and rises above the variance of the process. One can show that this must happen for some prediction lead for every autoregressive model. The mean of the process is a more accurate predictor than the estimated autoregression at leads for which the prediction mean squared error is larger than the series variance. See Fuller and Hasza (1981) for further discussion and the details of the calculations.

16.5 Discussion

The examples chosen to illustrate the use of *Mathematica* only begin to suggest the many ways in which symbolic computing will impact time series analysis. Freed from the bounds of tedious algebra, one often finds structure once hidden by computational detail. In fact, the linear bias structure discussed in Section 16.4.3 was discovered accidentally while viewing plots of similar calculations.

Given this potential, one can approach symbolic computing from two directions. The more immediately rewarding is to make use of the features built into software like *Mathematica*, as suggested in Section 16.2. As those examples show, this strategy is very useful at first, but often becomes more tedious as the complexity of the problem increases. The representation of ARIMA models as rules gives some results easily, but does not easily extend to other problems in an efficient way. For well-specified, direct manipulations however, this is clearly the way to go.

The second approach is to learn more about symbolic computing and try to develop some programs. The area is new and full of promise. Hopefully the programs in this package will provide a useful starting point for those interested in pursuing this direction.

Other tools written in *Mathematica* might also be of interest. In particular, Evans, McClelland, and McClure (1990) describe a notebook for signal processing. Although the emphasis differs, the methods are closely related to those shown here and offer a different perspective on time series analysis. For a sense of the evolution of the programs given here, see Stine (1990) for an earlier version of the package. While the package includes some facility for estimation, keep in mind that many programs for estimating ARIMA models exist, such as those written in S Chambers and Hastie (1992). Rather than duplicate the work that has gone into those algorithms, it makes more sense to access them via Mathematica, and Cabrara and Wilks (1991) describe such a connection.

16.6   References

Box, G. E. P. and G. Jenkins (1976). *Time Series Analysis: Forecasting and Control*. New York, Holden-Day.

Brockwell, P. J. and R. A. Davis (1987). *Time Series: Theory and Methods*. New York, Springer-Verlag.

Bloomfield, P. (1976). *Introduction to Spectral Analysis*. New York, Wiley.

Cabrara, J. F. and A. R. Wilks (1992). "An interface from S to *Mathematica*". *The Mathematica Journal*, **2**, 66–74.

Chambers, J. H. and T. J. Hastie (1992). *Statistical Models in S*. Pacific Grove, Wadsworth.

Evans, B. L., J. H. McClelland, and W. B. McClure (1990). "Symbolic transforms with applications to signmal processing." *The Mathematica Journal*, **1**, 70–80.

Fuller, W. A. and D. P. Hasza (1981). "Properties of predictors for autoregressive time series." *J. of the American Statistical Association*, **76**, 155–161.

Kendall, M. G. (1954). "Note on bias in the estimation of autocorrelation." *Biometrika*, **41**, 403–404.

Marriott, F. H. C. and J. A. Pope (1954). "Bias in the estimation of autocorrelations." *Biometrika*, **41**, 390–402.

Stine, R. A. (1990). "*Mathematica* in time series analysis." *Proceedings of the Statistical Computing Section of the American Statistical Association*, Washington, D.C., 37–45.

Shaman, P. and R. A. Stine (1988). "The bias of autoregressive coefficient estimators." *J. of the American Statistical Association*, **83**, 842–848.

Stine, R. A. and Shaman, P. (1989). "A fixed point characterization for bias of autoregressive estimators." *Annals of Statistics*, **17**, 1275–1284.

Wolfram, S. (1991). *Mathematica: A System for Doing Mathematics by Computer*. Redwood City, Addison-Wesley.

17 Decision Analytica: An Example of Bayesian Inference and Decision Theory Using Mathematica

Robert J. Korsan

"There are very few things which we know; which are not capable of being reducd to a Mathematical Reasoning; and when they cannot, it's a sign our Knowledge of them is very small and confus'd," **John Arbuthnot, 1692**

"When you can measure what you are speaking about, and express it in numbers, you know something about it; but when you cannot measure it, when you cannot express it in numbers, your knowledge is of a meagre and unsatisfactory kind," **William Thompson, Lord Kelvin**

17.1 Summary

Decision analysis is a blending of four ingredients. First, subjective probability theory is used to describe a decision maker's "a priori" uncertainty (degree of belief) about the outcomes of some event(s). Second, Bayesian inference is used to determine the appropriate "a posteriori" uncertainty given the revelation of some evidence. Third, utility theory is used to describe the decision maker's values in a consistent, mathematically manipulable fashion. Fourth and finally, decision theory is used to determine the "optimal" strategy, i.e. the sequence of event-contingent actions which lead to the highest valued outcomes given the decision maker's values.

Decision analysis is an inductive, as opposed to deductive, way of learning from experience and making the most profitable decisions consistent with our expressed beliefs in the face of uncertainty.

The mathematical manipulation of probability distributions, mathematical modeling of events and their values, and optimization or strategy selection are all processes at which *Mathematica* excels. This article describes decision analysis and uses a prototypical problem to show *Mathematica*'s power in solving decision problems.

17.2   A Touch of History

Probability theory developed from the analysis of games of chance. By the end of the seventeenth century, the mathematics of many simple and complex games of chance were well understood and widely known by educated people. Fermat, Pascal, Huygens, Leibniz, Jacob Bernoulli, and Arbuthnot had delved into the enumeration and counting of permutations and combinations. These efforts were applied to understanding just what a person could say about the outcome of a game based on these properties.

These early giants never asked an important question for decision making: How, from the outcome of a game or repeated outcomes of a game, can one learn about the properties of the game? These early giants were only concerned about what could be learned before you sat down to play. The key paradigm shift came as a result of the work of the Reverend Dr. Thomas Bayes, and the Bernoulli family. They asked the question: Starting with my current knowledge, what can I learn from the sequence of outcomes that occur as I play the game?

Thomas Bayes was a Presbyterian minister, who lived in England in the early 1700s. He was greatly interested in probability theory and wrote a paper on 'inverse probability' using the binomial distribution. The article was published posthumously in the *Philosophical Transactions of the Royal Society* in 1763. The generalization of his theorem is known as Bayes' theorem. This theorem gives the only consistent relationship among three sets of beliefs:

1. Your probability of an event based only on your past experience. This probability is usually called your "prior distribution" because it is the belief held prior to seeing any evidence.

2. Your probability of obtaining evidence of the event, and

3. Your probability of the event after you have had evidence of the event revealed to you. This probability is usually called your "posterior distribution" because it is the belief you should hold **after** seeing the evidence.

Many members of the Bernoulli family contributed to the development of probability and the foundations of decision analysis. Jacob Bernoulli saw that enumerating possible cases and counting the ratio of favorable outcomes to the total number of outcomes was futile when causes are hidden and equally likely cases impossible to describe. Instead, Bernoulli proposed *"For it should be presumed that a particular thing will occur or not occur in the future as many times as it has been observed, in similar circumstances, to have occurred or not occurred in the past."* Combined with Bayes theorem his work is the key to understanding how to update our beliefs in the face of new evidence. Another member of the Bernoulli family came up with the idea of risk avoidance and the use of what would now be called a logarithmic utility function.

These great advances flowered and were applied with great skill by Gauss and most especially by Laplace in the eighteenth century. Then the aspects of this work which focused on the subjective nature of probabilities and decision making languished as the assessment of statistical evidence of data (a posteriori statements) became the focus of most work. The Gaussian or normal distribution, used as a prior, allowed the experimenter to forget the effects of the prior as long as there was sufficient data.

In the nineteenth century, Francis Galton, Francis Y. Edgeworth, and Karl Pearson helped spread probability and statistics to anthropology, economics, and the philosophy of science. By the concept of statistical design or statistical control, they were able to extend the ideas of controlled experiments so fruitful to physicists to those intellectual disciplines where controlled experimentation was totally impossible. This work, although valuable, further eroded the role of the experimenter and the experimenter's beliefs in statistics. The desire to arrive at objective truth led great minds to believe in 'objective probabilities.'

Finally, in the twentieth century, R. A. Fisher dominated probabilistic and statistical thought in the first half of this century. Jerzy Neyman and Egon Pearson (Karl Pearson's son) opposed Fisher but supported 'objective' probabilities. Bayesian thinking was relegated to obscurity.

A small group of mathematicians including Ramsey, De Finetti, and Savage opposed Fisher and created a set of axioms for probability theory based on subjective probabilities, i.e. a person's betting odds. Finally, it was shown that any work based on 'objective probabilities' would lead to contradictions. This finding slowly changed the nature of probability theory and statistics. Like turning an ocean liner, changing probabilistic research to include the decision maker's beliefs has been slow and painful. Certainly, the successes of John Von Neumann's theory of risk, utility theory, and his game theory and mathematical economics in general, have helped establish decision theory and probability theory as the proper paradigm of scientific research.

Decision analysis is simply a game played by the decision maker against nature. It is the practical application of this rich body of research to everyday decision making. Professor Howard Raiffa of Harvard and Professor Ronald Howard of Stanford have been greatly responsible for the warm embrace this decision-making technology has been given by the business community in particular.

There is a tremendous amount of research currently ongoing, aimed at insuring coherence in subjective probability assessments. The subject of "biases" in probabilistic assessment is vast and controversial. Uncertainty about uncertainty (i.e., probabilities of probabilities) is another active area. Similarly, methods for value assessment which provide consistency over time are starting to develop beyond simple multi-attribute utility methods. Finally, another important area of research is influence diagrams. A brief introduction to this area will be given in this article. The interested reader can start with the bibliography to explore the vast literature of all these topics.

17.3   An Overview of Decision Analysis

In this section, I will review the underpinnings of decision analysis. I start with a bit of philosophizing about analysis in general.

17.3.1   A Touch of Philosophy—The Dangerous Quest for Certainty

In decision making, analysis is like water in Chinese thought. Lao-tzu was a sixth century BC Chinese philosopher who said:

"Nothing is so gentle, so adaptable as water. Yet it can wear away that which is hardest and strongest."

So, I perform analysis to wear away confusion and fear of failure. I must also remember what the 3000-year-old *Book of Changes* says:

"When a thing reaches its limit, it turns around."

So it is with analysis. I perform analysis not for its own sake, but to gain clarity about the best course of action. I must never strive for certainty. If I should ever achieve certainty, the opportunity I possessed will have evaporated as the morning fog retreats before the rising sun. I must delicately balance the cost of analysis against the ability to improve my strategy.

17.3.2   Raison d'Etre—A Strategy

What is a strategy? Webster defines it as:

"The science and art of employing the armed strength of a belligerent to secure the objects of a war, especially the large scale planning and directing of operations in adjustment to combat area, possible enemy actions, political alignment, etc."

I change this, only slightly, to define a personal or corporate strategy.

"The science and art of employing limited resources (money, time, skilled labor, etc.) by a person or corporation to secure their objectives, especially the large scale planning (decision analysis) and directing of operations in adjustment to the behavior of others, the market, government, etc."

What are the desiderata of a good strategy? Certainly, they should include:

- A clear and complete *understanding of your values*.
- A choice of *objectives* consistent with your values.
- A *wide range* of flexible alternative courses of action.
- A plan detailing the *implementation* of actions over time to achieve objectives.
- *Knowledge* and *use* of relevant information when resources are committed.

- An *accurate appraisal* of the objectives or values *attained (and not attained)* by each choice.

Decision analysis is the formal planning procedure consistent with these desiderata.

17.3.3   Be Lazy, Just Analyze Enough to ACT: The Paradigm for Decision Analysis

If you are confused and worried about taking a particular course of action, you are a candidate for decision analysis. The paradigm of decision analysis is given in the following figure. Start at the center with "framing".

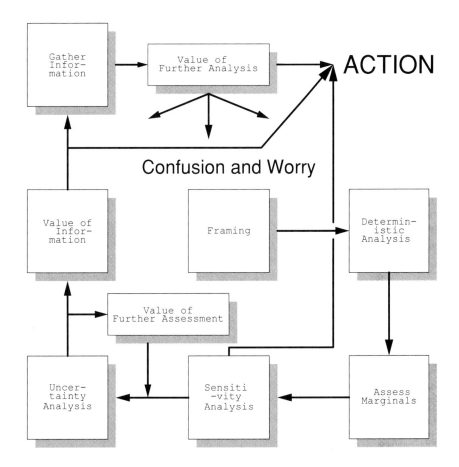

This figure represents a road map of analytic procedures leading to deeper and deeper understanding of the critical issues bearing on the decision to be taken. The map starts with "framing" and spirals outward towards final action. As each part of the analysis proceeds, the analyst must decide if enough insight has been gained to act. If so, then commit resources and turn to overseeing the implementation. Further analysis may be satisfying, however, it will waste resources that could be placed elsewhere.

Analysis starts, in the center of the figure, with a decision maker who is confused and worried. The first and most critical step is to "frame" the problem. The frame is created by understanding the values of the decision maker and choosing the objectives to be achieved. Understanding values and objectives will determine if there are actions that can be taken to narrow the range of possible outcomes to ones more favorable to the decision maker. *If this is not true*, then the decision maker has a worry and not a decision problem. Place his and your energies elsewhere and let this situation turn out the way it will.

To understand the relationship of values, information revealed over time and (possibly event-contingent) decision alternatives, influence diagrams are particularly useful and will be described in the next section.

Next the analysis focuses on the value of outcome when all uncertainties have been revealed. I call this **deterministic analysis** or, more simply, mathematical modeling. The model will have a set of uncertain variables whose values will be revealed over time. The purpose of this step and the next two steps are to determine which variables are important uncertainties, i.e. which uncertainties have a large enough impact on the value of any scenario that they must use the full power of probability theory. Those uncertainties which have a small impact on the value of scenarios can be safely set at their expected values for the remainder of the analysis.

For each set of possible outcomes of the uncertain variables, and for each setting of the decision variables, the mathematical model will compute an overall value for the decision maker. In order to understand the relevant ranges of uncertain variables, I must **assess the marginal distributions** of these variables. By looking at the domain of outcome values for these distributions that occur when we have made our choices, we can look for dominant strategies. A *dominant strategy* is one whose worst value is better than the best value of a competing strategy. This step is called **sensitivity analysis**. Many of the tools developed in the chapter "Symbolic Optimization" by Dr H. Varian can be used in this part of the process. If I am lucky, the strategy with the best outcome value will dominate, the analysis process stops, and the decision maker acts.

If there are no dominant strategies, I can still use sensitivity analysis to create an ordering of the strategies using their expected values and range of outcomes. Using this ordering I can select the subset of strategies whose range of outcomes overlap the range of outcomes of the highest valued strategy. This usually prunes the set of possible strategies.

If more than one strategy contend, I turn to **uncertainty analysis**. Using the information at hand, I can find the strategies which provide the best return ignoring the covariance of the uncertain quantities. I can also develop bounds for the gain or loss in return when this covariance is taken into account. This is the **value of further assessment**. Assessment of joint distributions is done as appropriate. Once again the analysis is performed to determine an event contingent optimal policy.

The **value of information** for each uncertainty is computed. It may be that the cost of gathering information and the concomitant delay is not worth the value gained. In this case the decision maker acts. Otherwise, more information is gained and the cycle of analysis is repeated.

The key concept is laziness. Analysis is performed only when that analysis leads to different actions which improve the return to the decision maker.

17.4 The Mathematica Packages—`InfluenceDiagram.m` and `JohnsonDistributions.m`

Two packages are distributed with this article. The package `DecisionAnalytica`InfluenceDiagram`` is used to construct graphical representations of an inference problem or decision problem. The discussion of how to use this package follows the introductory material in the next section.

The package `DecisionAnalytica`JohnsonDistributions`` is used in the same manner as the standard distributed *Mathematica* package `Statistics`ContinuousDistributions``. The reader is referred to the *Guide to Standard Mathematica Packages* for a description of this package. The usage statements for the extensions provided by `JohnsonDistributions.m` should be sufficient if you are familiar with the Johnson system of probability distributions. If you are not, see the short introduction provided in Appendix II of this article.

17.5 Influence Diagrams

17.5.1 Mapping Your Knowledge—Introducing Influence Diagrams

Influence diagrams (IDs) were created in the mid 1970s by Dr. Allen C. Miller. He was faced with the task of assessing a huge number of probabilities in a project with a limited time and dollar budget. He hit upon the simple but brilliant idea of separating the process into two parts. First, determine the structure of (in)dependencies among the uncertainties and then assess the probabilities. Decisions, values, and time were incorporated. He, Dr. Ronald A. Howard, and many others at SRI International and elsewhere, took this idea, expanded it and created a new 'tool of thought' for decision analysis [Howard and Matheson, (1983)]. I will briefly review the concepts in this section.

17.5.2 Influence Diagrams, A Precise Pictorial Language

An influence diagram is, at its most abstract level, an acyclic directed graph. The components of an influence diagram are either nodes or arrows. Usually, an analyst will deal with one of two types of influence diagrams. The **relevance diagram** consists only of chance nodes, consistency nodes, and their conditioning variables. A **decision diagram** will have only one value node and at least one decision node in addition to chance nodes and possibly consistency nodes. The term *knowledge map* is also gaining usage in addition to "influence diagram."

Accompanying this article is a *Mathematica* package called `InfluenceDiagram.m`. I will use this package to illustrate the basic concepts in influence diagrams.

17.5.2.1 Node Types

The following nodes may be present in an influence diagram:

- A **decision node** represented by a square or rectangle. The mathematical representation of a decision node (a choice available to the decision maker) may be continuous or a collection of discrete alternatives.

Decision

- A **chance node** represented by an shaded circle or ellipse. A chance node is an event not under the control of the decision maker. The mathematical representation of a chance node is a probability distribution over a continuous or discrete domain.

Chance

- A **consistency node** represented by a double-bordered circle or ellipse. Consistency nodes represent fixed or logical relationships such as "the area of a circle is a function of its radius" or "the marginal distribution of a quantity is the integral of the joint distribution with other quantities".

Consistency

- The **value node** represented a shaded octagon (stop sign). There is only one value node in an ID. This is the quantity which ultimately measures the value to the decision maker of any set of decisions, i.e. the quantity which the decision maker would like to optimize. There is only one 'value node', i.e. the node reached by following arrows starting from any node in the diagram. "All paths lead us back to our values."

Value

17.5.2.2 Influence Diagram Arrows

Arrows connect various pairs of nodes. Arrows represent different things, depending upon the nodes they connect. Here I use "connect A to B" to mean the arrow points from node A toward node B.

- Arrows cannot connect the value node to any other node.

- An arrow connecting two decision nodes, represents the chronological order in which the decisions are made. It also signifies that the decision maker remembers the alternative chosen in the previous decision.

2nd Decision   1st Decision

- An arrow connecting a chance node to a decision node represents the fact that the uncertainty will be known by the decision maker before that decision's alternative is chosen. Event-contingent actions may be taken.

1st Decision   1st Event

- An arrow connecting any node (except the value node) to a deterministic node indicates that the quantity is needed for the computation.

- When an arrow connects a consistency node to a decision node, it has an indirect interpretation. Sometimes, a consistency node represents a quantity which is computed from other quantities. In this case, logic requires that the arrow conditioning the consistency node also condition the decision conditioned by the consistency node, i.e. the quantities used for the computation are known to the decision maker before making the decision. The following example of an R&D investment decision shows such a case.

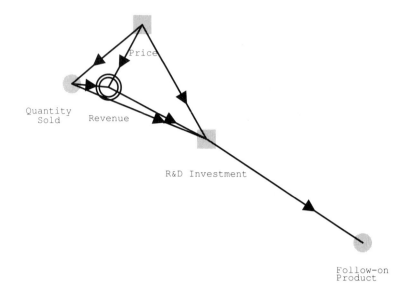

When the consistency node represents a logical requirement among various uncertainties or decisions, the decision may or may not be made with the knowledge of all those quantities. Consider an example in failure analysis. Two events A and B may lead to the same failure indicator. However, the action taken will only know of the indicator and not the event(s) actuating the indicator. The influence diagram would be:

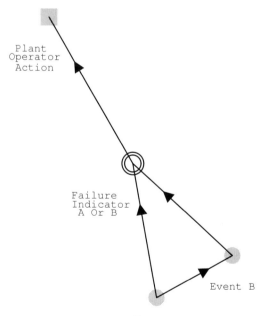

- *An arrow connecting a decision node to a chance node represents a subtle situation.* In many cases, the value the decision maker attaches to an outcome (not the uncertainty about the outcome) is what is affected by the decision. If this is so, no arrow should be drawn from the decision to the uncertainty. As a simple example, consider a party which could be given inside a house or outside in the yard. The weather (sunny or rainy) is really independent of where we hold the party. Hence, there should be no arrow connecting the decision to the uncertainty about whether or not it rains. The value of the party to the decision maker is what is affected by the choice of location and the weather.

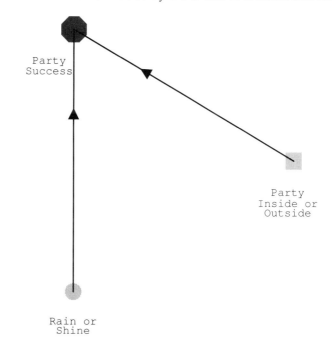

However, there are cases where this is not true. For example, if I choose to toss one die or I choose to toss two die, the domain of the outcome and the probabilities attached are dependent upon my choice. I cannot compute a value of information about an uncertainty which is dependent upon the decision maker's action. A more realistic example is an R&D investment decision where the decision maker's uncertainty about technical success is dependent upon the amount of R&D budget expended.

- An arrow connecting two chance nodes represents relevance for probability assessment. The uncertainties may not be treated as independent. The two nodes and the arrow describe a joint probability distribution on both quantities.

In a collection of n chance nodes, there are `Factorial[n]` possible representations of a joint distribution over n quantities in the form of products of conditional probabilities. Thus, there are `Factorial[n]` possible assessment

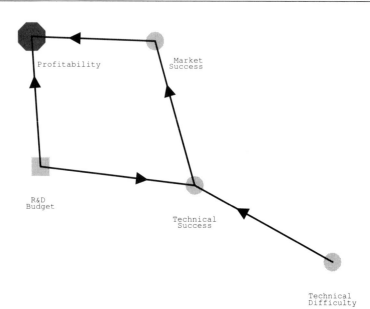

orders, one corresponding to each representation. The arrows between various nodes show which assessment order is relevant to the decision maker. When arrows are missing, it means that the possible probabilistic dependence represented by the arrow is asserted not to be present by the author of the diagram (the decision maker).

The following figure shows an example of the six possible assessment orders for three uncertainties x, y, and z which are all dependent upon one another.

- An arrow connecting any node to the value node states that the quantity represented by the first node is used in the computation of the value node.

Logical consistency requires that an influence diagram be acyclic, i.e. there are no loops in the diagram.

An influence diagram which contains only chance nodes is called a *relevance diagram*. The term relevance is chosen to emphasize that the relationships are about information necessary for prediction. Relationships among uncertainties shown in an influence diagram do not imply causality in any way. However, when an arrow connects a *decision node* to a *chance node*, causality is very likely implied.

Although the term *"influence"* is generally used to describe the relationships denoted by arrows in an ID, there is good reason to avoid this term. Many people reason that some unknown at the time of a decision may be a very important consideration when making the decision. Thus, they conclude that it "influences" the decision even when it may not be known when the decision is made. They attempt to add an arrow from the uncertainty to the decision. This confuses the analysis.

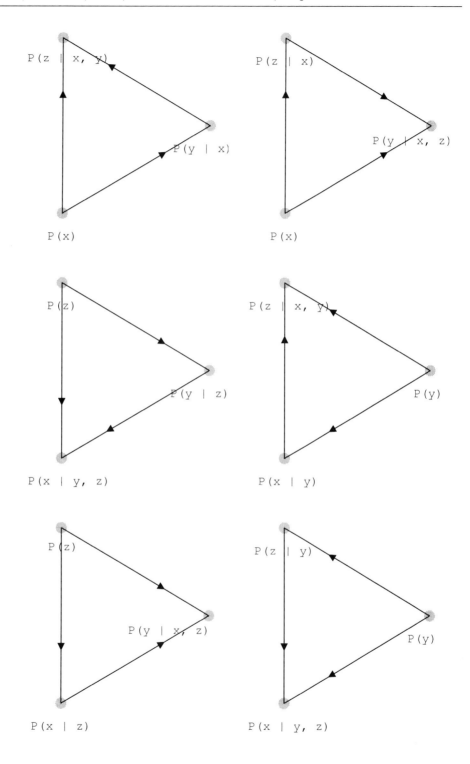

Instead, the following terms are used here and in `InfluenceDiagram.m`.
1) Decision B is "informed by" uncertainty A.

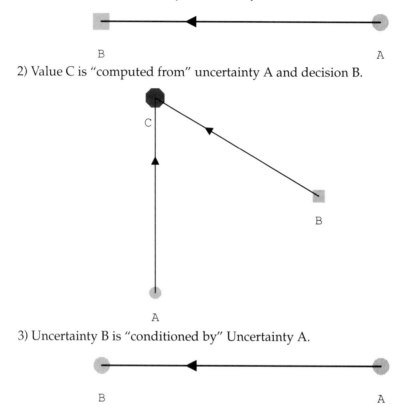

B   A

2) Value C is "computed from" uncertainty A and decision B.

C

B

A

3) Uncertainty B is "conditioned by" Uncertainty A.

B   A

4) Because there is a logical relationship R(A, B, C), *consistent* uncertainty about C is computed from the uncertainty A, the uncertainty B, and R(A, B, C).

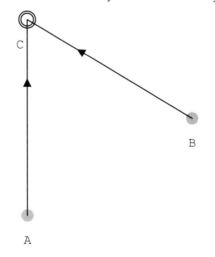

C

B

A

17.5.3   Constructing an Influence Diagram

Constructing an influence diagram sounds simple. Collect all the nodes and connect them with arrows. Unfortunately, this is not a simple task to do meaningfully. Just consider a relevance diagram consisting of only chance nodes. Probability distributions have such a rich conditioning structure that no graphical representation which completely describes an arbitrary joint distribution can be stored in polynomial memory. It has been shown [Verma, 1987] that an exponential number of directed acyclic graphs are necessary to completely describe the independence properties of an arbitrary joint probability distribution.

Any relevance diagram is a single graph and, as such, cannot fully describe the joint distribution of chance nodes under consideration. However, each relevance diagram for this collection of chance nodes will accurately describe a particular decomposition of the joint distribution into a product of conditional distributions. For such a partial description I require that no independence relationship which is true for the joint be undisplayed. I will describe an algorithm for constructing a relevance diagram which minimizes the number of un-displayed independencies for the particular decomposition chosen. This algorithm is given in [Pearl & Verma, 1987]. I recommend following a similar algorithm for decision diagrams as well.

1. Call the collection of all chance nodes X.

2. Order the chance nodes chronologically, i.e. in the order in which they will be revealed by nature over time. If there are ties, use an arbitrary ordering among that subset. Symbolically, the ordering is $x_0, x_1, \ldots, x_T$.

3. Start with x_T and work backwards through the list. For any node, x_i, determine the minimal set of predecessors of x_i which provides all the information necessary to predict x_i. Call this set of predecessors $Conditioners(x_i)$. Place arrows connecting each of the $Conditioners(x_i)$ to x_i.

In the case of a decision diagram, the value node is always taken as the last node to be revealed chronologically.

The resulting knowledge map is minimal in the following sense. Suppose I am given a joint distribution for the chance nodes X. Further, suppose I decompose the distribution into its equivalent product of conditional distributions following the chronological order stated above. Then no edge of the influence diagram can be deleted without declaring an independence among the conditional distributions which is not in the original joint distribution.

17.5.4   Using the InfluenceDiagram.m Package

Load the package in the usual fashion.

In[1]:= **<<DecisionAnalytica`InfluenceDiagram`**

Following is an example of constructing a simple relevance diagram using this package. Given:

1. There are four chance nodes, x, y, z, and w which will be revealed in this order.

2. The only chance nodes relevant to predicting w are x and y.

3. The only chance node relevant to predicting z is x.

4. The only chance node relevant to predicting y is x.

Then I would like to capture this information in a relevance diagram. I start by creating a "trivial" relevance diagram consisting of only the chance node w.

In[2]:= **?TrivialRelevanceDiagram**

```
TrivialRelevanceDiagram[n] creates a KnowledgeMap object
containing just one node n where n is a ChanceNode object.
```

In[3]:= **?Chance**

```
Chance[label] is a function which creates a ChanceNode object where
    label is a string used when displaying an Influence Diagram
    containing this node. (In the future a ChanceNode object will
    contain other quantities such as the probability distribution
    describing the decision maker's uncertainty.)
```

In[4]:= **w = Chance["w"];**
            kmap = TrivialRelevanceDiagram[w];

Now add the conditioning information about w using the ChanceConditionedBy relation as an argument of the **AddConditioningTo** function.

In[5]:= **?ChanceConditionedBy**

```
ChanceConditionedBy is a head used to indicate the conditioning
    information for a ChanceNode object.
```

In[6]:= **?AddConditioningTo**

```
AddConditioningTo[id, e] is a function to add conditioning
    information to the influence diagram object id. e is the
    conditioning information. NB: A ValueNode object may be
    conditioned by any other node object, but a ValueNode object may
    not condition any other node object. Also, the node being
    conditioned must already be present in the influence diagram
    object id.  The conditioning information, e, is given in one of
    the following forms:  (1) ValueComputedFrom[v, n]. v is a
    ValueNode object and n is a node or list of nodes. (2)
    ChanceConditionedBy[c, n]. c is a ChanceNode object and n is a
    node or list of nodes. (3) DecisionInformedBy[d, n]. d is a
    DecisionNode object and n is a node or list of nodes. (4)
    ConsistencyRequiredBy[c, n].  c is a ConsistencyNode object and
    n is a node or list of nodes of any other type.
```

From 2 above, this gives

In[7]:= **x=Chance["x"];**
            y=Chance["y"];
            AddConditioningTo[kmap, ChanceConditionedBy[w, {x, y}]];

Next, from 3 above, add the information about "z".

```
In[8]:= z=Chance["z"];
        AddConditioningTo[kmap, ChanceConditionedBy[z, x]];
InfluenceDiagram::notmember:
   Warning: InfluenceDiagram`private`ChanceNode[z] is not a node
   in kmap.
```

This warning message is provided to prevent building diagrams with spelling or other minor errors. Next, from 4 above, add the conditioning information which is relevant to "y".

```
In[9]:= AddConditioningTo[kmap, ChanceConditionedBy[y, x]];
```

Finally, I display the diagram using the **ShowID** command.

```
In[10]:= ?ShowID

ShowID[id] is a function which displays a graphical representation
    of id. id must be a KnowledgeMap object.

In[11]:= ShowID[kmap];
```

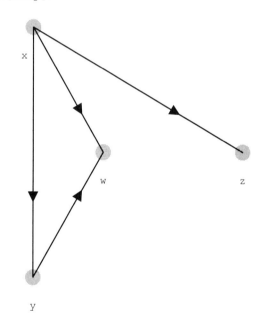

A complete list of all the functionality of InfluenceDiagram.m is given in Appendix I.

17.6   The Wildcatter's Problem, A Prototypical Decision Problem

An oil wildcatter must decide whether or not to drill at a given site before his option expires. The wildcatter is uncertain about many things: the cost of drilling, the extent of the oil or gas deposits at the site, the cost of raising the oil, and so forth. This person (the decision maker) has available, however, the records of similar and not-so-similar drillings in this geographic area. The wildcatter has discussed the peculiar features of this particular deal with a geologist and geophysicist in the wildcatter's employ. Similarly, the wildcatter consults his or her land agent.

Although perfect information is never available, geologic testing, such as seismic sounding can be undertaken to provide better understanding (reduced uncertainty) about the underlying geophysical structure. As usual, the **TANSTAAFL** principle applies. **TANSTAAFL** stands for: There Ain't No Such Thing As A Free Lunch. Collecting this information is costly. Trying to gain information in order to reduce uncertainty before making the primary decision of whether or not to drill simply introduces another decision prior to the original one, namely whether or not to spend the money to perform the tests.

The **TANSTAAFL** principle implies that the wildcatter must spend some resources to develop a strategy, i.e. an event-contingent set of actions, which leads to the greatest returns (on average). The starting point is always the wildcatter's current state of knowledge and experience. This becomes the context for analyzing the current decisions faced by the wildcatter. Once the analysis is performed (usually analysis takes the minimal expenditure of resources), insight is gained (a new state of knowledge) and further resources may be committed (actions taken) leading to further analysis or further action.

For most of the rest of this chapter, I will describe an analysis of this prototypical problem. I will adopt the viewpoint of an analyst assisting the wildcatter.

17.6.1 The Back of the Envelope, Please. (A Mini-Analysis)

Following the precept of doing as little analysis as possible, start with a very crude analysis. The purpose of this "back of the envelope" analysis is to see whether or not there is any reason to believe that further analysis will be justified. So, I start with some background.

The wildcatter currently owns a lease holding of eight potential wells in this geographic area. The past experience of oil wildcatters for this particular area of Texas can be summed up as follows:

If you drill 8 wells in a lease holding,

• 70% of the time, all wells drilled will break even or be profitable.

• 20% of the time, one well drilled will be "dry", i.e. lose money.

• 10% of the time, two wells drilled will be "dry".

• Almost never, will three or more wells be "dry".

In order for the wildcatter to break even in the long run, at least six of the eight wells will have to be profitable. In order for the wildcatter to make money, seven wells of the eight will have to be profitable. So far, the wildcatter has drilled three wells and one *has been unprofitable*. So the a question is, "What is the probability that six wells will not lose money?" (That is, two will turn out to be unprofitable.)

The first step in answering the key question is to ask "How can I describe the wildcatters' state of uncertainty?"

17.6.1.1   The Basic Approach

This simplest approach to the wildcatter's problem captures most of the relevant ideas that will be used in this article. First, the wildcatter's (prior) information is captured by the statements about the various frequencies of money-losing wells and by his/her current experience of having had one out of three wells lose money.

A person's values will be complex. In many cases, conflicting values will introduce complexity into the process of creating a mathematical model. However, multi-attribute utility theory can be used to capture just such tradeoffs. In most corporations, life and analysis are somewhat simpler. The 'bottom-line' profit can be used as a single measurable outcome, capturing all of the corporation's value to its shareholders. For this article, I simplify my task and only consider such monetary values.

The wildcatter's values are described by the term profitability. To begin the analysis at the simplest possible level, consider only two possible outcomes. Either the lease holding will be profitable, or it won't. The event in question is, "if the wildcatter continues to drill in the lease holding, will a second well be unprofitable?" If so, the whole lease will be only marginally profitable and he or she may as well stop now.

The influence diagram for this version of the wildcatter's drill decision is a bit complicated. Let me introduce a bit of notation.

Let the symbol F stand for the historical frequency of dry wells for a lease. The probability of any particular frequency is given by $G(F)$.

Let $d_1, d_2, \ldots$ denote the event of drilling a hole which could be "dry" or "wet". Each of these events is considered to be independent. If I know the frequency of "dry" holes for the lease, the probability of any particular well being "dry" is $P(d_i|F)$. (So far the wildcatter has had one "dry" and two "wet" wells.) This particular lease could have any of the frequencies of dry wells noted previously.

For any particular frequency, the probability of observing this combination of wells is $J(d_1, d_2, d_3|F) = P(d_1|F) \times P(d_2|f) \times P(d_3|F)$. In order to answer the profitability question for the wildcatter, there is a consistency relationship for the information at our disposal. The consistency relationship is known as Bayes' theorem.

The quantity of interest is the probability of each possible frequency of "dry" holes given the observed pattern. This is denoted $H(F|d_1, d_2, d_3)$. The probability of the observed pattern is denoted $Q(d_1, d_2, d_3)$. The consistency relationship imposed is that the joint distribution of frequency of "dry" holes and the observed pattern is the same regardless of how I compute it. That is $J(d_1, d_2, d_3|F)G(F) == H(F|d_1, d_2, d_3)Q(d_1, d_2, d_3)$.

The following figure shows the influence diagram. The diagram has been deliberately broken into three parts showing the relationships among the various computations.

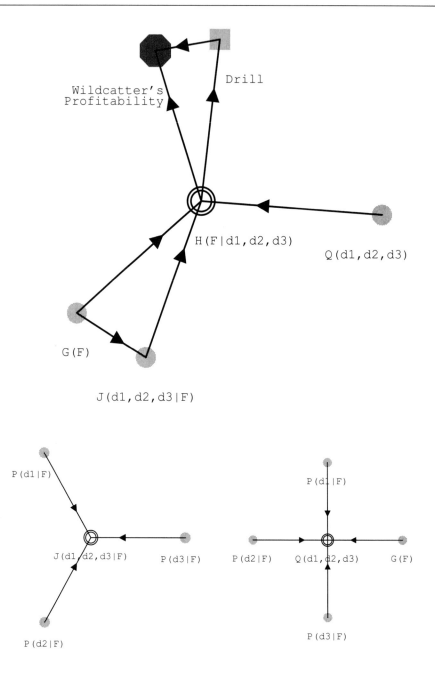

The consistency relationships are themselves chance nodes. The equality of joint distributions, i.e. $J(d1, d2, d3|F)G(F) == H(F|d1, d2, d3)Q(d1, d2, d3)$, can be shown graphically as an equality of the two influence diagrams below. Note that all we are doing is changing the direction of the arrow connecting the uncertain quantities (frequency of "dry" wells, F, and sequence of wells observed so far, d_1, d_2, d_3). The details of the computations shown in these diagrams are carried out in the sub subsections which follow this one.

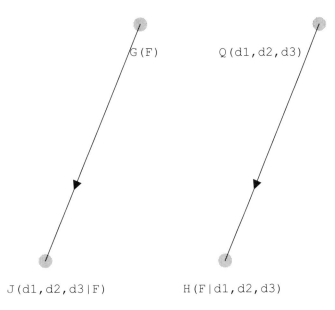

I now use *Mathematica* to perform these computations.

17.6.1.2 Uncertainty About a Frequency

There are a finite number of lease sites, M, with D of them "dry", i.e. unprofitable. The frequency of "dry" wells is D/M. I must estimate the probability that this frequency is 2/8. To be precise, I should use the hypergeometric distribution. However, if M is large, the hypergeometric distribution is closely approximated by the binomial distribution. I assert that eight is large compared to two and I use that approximation.

First, load *Mathematica's* `DiscreteDistributions.m` package.

In[1]:= `<<DiscreteDistributions.m`

The usage message describes the basic parameters of the **BinomialDistribution**.

In[2]:= `?BinomialDistribution`

```
BinomialDistribution[n, p] represents the Binomial distribution for
   n trials with probability p.
```

So, the parameter p represents the underlying frequency of unprofitable wells in this part of Texas. Instead of using *Mathematica's* symbol p, I will use the symbol f, since this represents a frequency of occurrence. The probability of any frequency being observed is given by the binomial distribution with n=8 (the number of potential wells).

The historical experience of drilling limited the possible frequencies of "dry" wells to Range[0,2]/8. Similarly, historical experience said that the probabilities of occurrence of these frequencies is given by {7/10,2/10,1/10} respectively. So, the wildcatter's prior knowledge about the probability of unprofitable wells is:

```
In[3]:= FrequencyDryWells={0,1,2}/8;
        ProbDensFreqDryWells={7,2,1}/10;
        TableForm[Transpose[N[{FrequencyDryWells,
                     ProbDensFreqDryWells}]],
           TableHeadings->{None,{ColumnForm[{
                                  "Frequency of",
                                  "Dry Wells"}],
                               ColumnForm[{
                                  "Wildcatter's",
                                  "Uncertainty"}]}}]
```

```
Out[3]:=        Frequency of    Wildcatter's
                Dry Wells       Uncertainty
                0               0.7

                0.125           0.2

                0.25            0.1
```

Suppose I could ask a clairvoyant what frequency of "dry" wells would ultimately be observed. Call the answer f. I know that the wildcatter has drilled 3 wells and one was "dry". Thus, the probability of observing these events (using our approximation above) is:

```
In[4]:= PDF[BinomialDistribution[3,f],1]
Out[4]:=            2
            3 (1 - f)  f
```

Since this is true, I can create a table which shows the wildcatter's probability of observing one "dry" well conditioned upon the possible frequency of dry wells.

```
In[5]:= TableForm[Transpose[N[{FrequencyDryWells,
                     Map[PDF[BinomialDistribution[3,#],1]&,
                          FrequencyDryWells]}]],
           TableHeadings->{None,{ColumnForm[{
                                  "Frequency of",
                                  "Dry Wells"}],
                               ColumnForm[{
                                  "Wildcatter's",
                                  "Uncertainty",
                                  "of 1 Dry Well"}]}}]
```

```
Out[5]:=        Frequency of    Wildcatter's
                Dry Wells       Uncertainty
                                of 1 Dry Well
                0               0

                0.125           0.287109

                0.25            0.421875
```

I can almost calculate the information I need to answer the key question about overall profitability of the lease holding. What is needed is the probability that f==2/8; i.e., the actual frequency of dry wells in my patch is twenty five percent (0.25). If this frequency of "dry" wells is observed, the lease holding will be unprofitable. Conversely, if the probability of observing this frequency is less than 0.5, the lease holding will be profitable. To find this probability from the information I have calculated so far, I must use Bayes' rule. I explain Bayes' rule in the next section.

17.6.1.3 Bayes' Rule (Discrete Form)

Let $x_1, x_2, \ldots$ be independent observations of events from a process whose uncertainty is described by a probability density function $g(x|\theta)$ if I am given the value θ with certainty. My uncertainty about the value of θ is described by the probability density function $h(\theta)$. θ itself may or may not be directly observable. I will assume that θ can take on only a finite number of values $\theta_1, \theta_2, \ldots$

The probability of the events $x_1, x_2, \ldots$ is given by the product of the individual probabilities, i.e.:

$$G(x_1, x_2, \ldots |\theta) = \prod_i g(x_i|\theta)$$

The joint distribution of $x_1, x_2, \ldots$ and θ is given by the product:

$$G(x_1, x_2, \ldots |\theta)h(\theta).$$

Bayes' Theorem arises from the fact that there are two distinct ways to write the joint distribution. The way shown above is the probability of the outcomes given a particular value of θ times the probability of θ. But I could also write this as the probability of a particular θ given the observations $x_1, x_2, \ldots|$, say $J(\theta|x_1, x_2, \ldots)$, times the probability of the observations. The probability of the observations is just the sum of the probabilities of these observations over all possible θ, i.e.:

$$\sum_j G(x_1, x_2, \ldots |\theta_j)h(\theta_j).$$

Setting the two quantities equal to each other and solving for $J(\theta|x_1, x_2, \ldots)$ gives:

$$J(\theta|x_1, x_2, \ldots) = \frac{G(x_1, x_2, \ldots |\theta)h(\theta)}{\sum_j G(x_1, x_2, \ldots |\theta_j)h(\theta_j)}.$$

The above is Bayes' Theorem. I will now apply this to the back of the envelope calculation I am doing for the wildcatter.

17.6.1.4 Back of the Envelope (Continued)

The parameter θ used in Bayes' theorem that is of interest for the wildcatter is the frequency of "dry" wells which I have called f. The first quantity I calculate is the probability of observing one dry hole, i.e. the sum over all possible values of f. This is the denominator in Bayes' theorem.

```
In[1]:= ProbOneDry=ProbDensFreqDryWells.
               Map[PDF[BinomialDistribution[3,#],1]&,
                   FrequencyDryWells]
```

```
Out[1]:=  51
          ───
          512
```

The frequency of "dry" wells that the wildcatter does not want to observe is f==0.25. So the numerator of Bayes' theorem is the probability that the wildcatter would observe one dry well if the frequency is f==0.25 times the probability that the frequency is 0.25. This is:

```
In[2]:= ProbOneDryAndFreq25Pct=
            PDF[BinomialDistribution[3,1/4],1]*
            ProbDensFreqDryWells[[3]]
```

```
Out[2]:=  27
          ───
          640
```

Finally, the probability that I will drill a second dry well is given by the ratio

```
In[3]:= ProbFreq25Pct=N[ProbOneDryAndFreq25Pct/ProbOneDry]
```

```
Out[3]:= 0.423529
```

Thus, the wildcatter computes that the probability of a second "dry" well in the lease holding is less than 50-50. This crude analysis indicates that the probability of the lease holding being profitable is better than 50-50. Thus, it is a good idea to devote some resources to a more complete analysis of drilling the next well. I will turn to this analysis after describing the decision analysis in more detail.

17.7 A Full Decision Analysis

The wildcatter believes that there is no better use of his/her time or resources than to pursue the next well on the lease. Similarly, for the purposes of this analysis, the wildcatter has stated that maximizing the net present value of the stream of profits from this well (i.e., increased wealth) is the proper objective of this decision. Since the wildcatter has a "take or pay" contract for oil produced from this field at a fixed price, this is further simplified since the discounted total oil production is then proportional to the increased wealth minus any costs expressed in barrels of oil.

The influence diagram capturing the wildcatter's beliefs about the structure of the decision problem is shown in the next subsection.

17.7.1   Step 1: Framing The Wildcatter's Influence Diagram

The decisions faced by the wildcatter are (1) seismic testing, and (2) drilling. The uncertainties are (1) the results of the seismic testing, and (2) the discounted total oil production over the life of the well. There is a relationship between the discounted total oil production given seismic testing and given no seismic testing. Using the `InfluenceDiagram.m` package I create a decision diagram using the algorithm outlined earlier.

```
In[1]:= d1=Decision[ColumnForm[{"Seismic","  Test","Decision"}]];
        d2=Decision[ColumnForm[{" Drill","Decision"}]];
        c1=Chance[ColumnForm[{"Seismic","Results"}]];
        k1=Consistency[ColumnForm[{"Well Revenue Given",
                                "  Seismic Results"}]];
        c2=Chance[ColumnForm[{" Well Profit      ",
                              "    Given No      ",
                              "Seismic Results   "}]];
        v=Value[ColumnForm[{" Wildcatter's","Profitability"}]];
```

Following the algorithm noted above, I put the list of nodes in chronological order. This list is: d1, c1 (depending upon d1), d2, c2 or k1 and v. Thus,
    Pick the last node in time.

```
In[2]:= wid=TrivialInfluenceDiagram[v];
```

Virtually everything must be known to compute the value.

```
In[3]:= AddConditioningTo[wid,
            ValueComputedFrom[v, {d1, d2, c1, k1, c2}]];
```

In order to compute the consistency relation, I need the seismic results and the well revenue.

```
In[4]:= AddConditioningTo[wid,
            ConsistencyRequiredBy[k1, {c1, c2}]];
```

If I have done seismic tests, the drill decision will be informed by those results and my prior decision.

```
In[5]:= AddConditioningTo[wid,
            DecisionInformedBy[d2, {d1, c1}]];
```

In the joint distribution of c1, c2 and k1, the conditioning between c1 and c2 can go either way.

```
In[6]:= AddConditioningTo[wid,
            ChanceConditionedBy[c2, c1]];

In[7]:= ShowID[wid];
```

In the next subsection, I will deal only with the problem of uncertainty in discounted total oil production.

17.7.2   Step 2: Deterministic Analysis Oil Well Economics

17.7.2.1   Introduction

If oil is present at a site, the geology of the location looks like the following diagram. Under the ground will be a dome shaped reservoir of oil, possibly with a cone of rock under it and/or water.

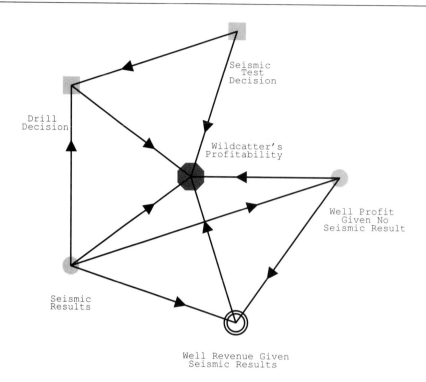

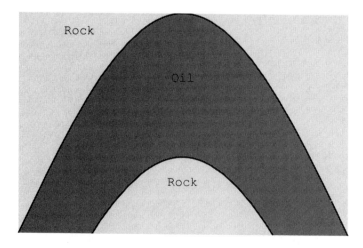

A key fact about oil wells is that the extraction rate is not under the control of the wildcatter. The mechanisms for oil flow and its decline over time are varied and well understood. Physically, they result from material balances, pressure balances, and dome geometry as well as the presence or absence of water and dissolved natural gas. The description of such rate-time analysis is known as "Decline Curve Analysis" and has been used since 1933 to predict future behavior of a producing well based on its production history.

I will use decline curves to determine the uncertainty in the value of a new well based on the wildcatter's experience with wells in this part of Texas.

17.7.2.2 The Flow of Oil Over Time

Usually, dissolved natural gas in the oil pushes it out of the ground as it expands. Many other mechanisms may be responsible for the flow rate of an oil well. However, in all cases, the flow of oil between time t and t+dt can be described as

$$F(t) = \frac{F_0}{(1 + bdt)^{\frac{1}{b}}}$$

where F_0 is the initial flow rate typically in unit of Bbl/day or Bbl/month. b is a dimensionless parameter (usually between 0 and 0.9). b is linked to the physical mechanism for oil production, i.e. $b = 0$ represents "gravity drainage with no free surface", $b = 0.3$ represents "a solution gas drive reservoir" and $b = 0.5$ represents "gravity drainage with a free surface" and so forth. "d" is the initial decline rate and its units must correspond to those of F_0. The decline rate is the derivative of the flow rate, thus:

```
In[1]:= D[(1+b d t)^(-1/b),t]
```

```
Out[1]:=               -1 - 1/b
        -(d (1 + b d t)        )
```

```
In[2]:= %/.t->0
```

```
Out[2]:= -d
```

Interestingly, the flow becomes an exponential decline as b approaches 0. Thus,

```
In[3]:= Limit[(1+b d t)^(-1/b),b->0]
```

```
Out[3]:=  -(d t)
         E
```

17.7.2.3 Discounted Total Oil Production

The wildcatter has reduced his risk by obtaining a take or pay contract at a fixed price indexed to inflation for the life of the well. This means he can run the well without having to worry about the price (shutting it off or turning it on to control his profitability).

Oil production becomes marginally profitable for the wildcatter when a west Texas well reaches a level of about 1 Bbl/day (30 Bbl/month). The wildcatter wants to do better than putting his money in the stock market and has a time value of money or discount rate of 10%/year or 10/12%/month; i.e., $r = 1/120$. Typical values for the various uncertainties are that there is an initial flow rate of $F0 = 9,000$ Bbl/month, b is 3/10 and d is 1/10. The operating period for the well can be obtained by

```
In[1]:= TmaxRule=First[Solve[FT==F0(1+b d T)^(-1/b),T]]
```

```
Solve::ifun: Warning: Inverse functions are being used by Solve,
    so some solutions may not be found.
```
$Out[1]:=$

$$\{T \;-> \; \frac{-1 + (\frac{F0}{FT})^b}{b\; d}\}$$

$In[2]:=$ `TestCaseRule={r->1/120,b->3/10,d->1/10,F0->9000,FT->30};`
`N[T/.TmaxRule/.TestCaseRule]/12.`
`(* divide by 12 for years *)`

$Out[2]:=$ `12.5979`

As can be seen, an oil well can be expected to produce for a decade and more.

The profitability will be proportional to the total oil produced. A key fact is that the rate of extraction is not under the control of the wildcatter. The present value of the production is obtained by discounting the total production.

Using the above rule, the discounted total oil production would be computed by integrating over the time period indicated. However, since the period is so long, simply integrate from zero to infinity. The discounted total oil produced is:

$In[3]:=$ `DiscTotalOil=F0*`
`Integrate[Exp[-r t]/(1+b d t)^(1/b),`
`{t,0,Infinity}]`

```
General::intinit: Loading integration packages.
```
$Out[3]:=$

$$\frac{F0 \; HypergeometricU[1, \; 2 - \frac{1}{b}, \; \frac{r}{b\; d}]}{b\; d}$$

To determine the uncertainty in discounted total oil describe:

1. the wildcatter's uncertainty about the type of production (b),

2. the initial flow rate (F0), and

3. the initial decline rate (d).

Next, do a sensitivity analysis to determine which of these uncertainties can be safely ignored.

17.7.3   Describing the Uncertainty Relevant to Sensitivity Analysis

It is critical to use the "proper" domains for each uncertain variable during sensitivity analysis. The discounted total oil production is, itself, dependent upon quantities not shown in the original influence diagram obtained from the wildcatter. It is, in a sense, a sub-problem which may be solved separately and the results used in the solution of the original problem. For this reason, the relevance diagram for this restricted problem is shown in the next sub-subsection.

17.7.3.1   The Relevance Diagram for Discounted Total Oil Production

The relevance diagram for this computation is straightforward. Since all uncertainties are independent, the algorithm for constructing a relevance diagram gives:

```
In[1]:= c1=Chance[ColumnForm[{" Initial",
                    "Flow Rate"}]];
        c2=Chance[ColumnForm[{"   Initial",
                    "Decline Rate"}]];
        c3=Chance[ColumnForm[{"Oil Production     ",
                    "   Mechanism      "}]];
        k1=Consistency[ColumnForm[{"Discounted",
                    " Total Oil"}]];
        id=TrivialKnowledgeMap[k1];
        AddConditioningTo[id,
          ConsistencyRequiredBy[k1,{c1,c2,c3}]];

        ShowID[id];
```

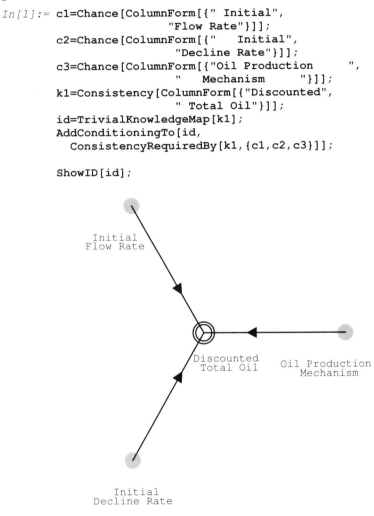

17.7.4   Step 3: Assessing the Marginals

For the purposes of sensitivity analysis, the marginal distributions are relevant because they determine the changes in each variable that are relevant to the analysis. Typically, the medians or the means of the distributions form a base case for analysis. Use the means. Next, the range of values in the discounted total oil production as each uncertainty is varied over its domain will measure the impact of each variable. Usually, increasing the value to approximately the

0.95 quantile location and decreasing the value to the 0.05 quantile location is sufficient. This procedure then measures the sensitivity to 90% of the cases likely to be encountered.

As mentioned in Section 17.7.3.1, on the wildcatter's relevance diagram, all of the uncertainties are independent. Each is described in a separate sub-subsection.

17.7.4.1 Uncertainty About "b"

In this part of Texas, the parameter b falls between zero and 0.9. The wildcatter's uncertainty in b is well represented by a beta distribution with parameters {3, 6}. The density looks like

In[1]:= **<<Statistics`ContinuousDistributions`**

In[2]:= **Plot[PDF[BetaDistribution[3, 6],10 b/9],{b,0,.9}];**

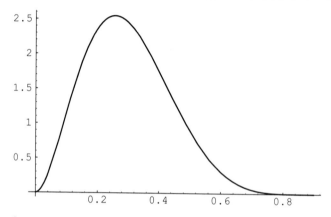

The cumulative probability is

In[3]:= **Plot[CDF[BetaDistribution[3, 6],10 b/9],{b,0,0.9}];**

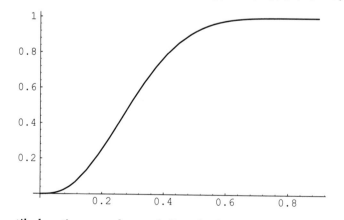

The quantile locations can be read directly from the plots, or you can use the functions provided in the Statistics`ContinuousDistributions`

package. The 0.05 quantile is located at $b=0.1$ and the 0.95 quantile is located at $b=0.54$. The expected value is $b=0.3$. The changes for sensitivity analysis are -0.2 and $+0.24$. These are the values and changes used for sensitivity analysis in a later section.

17.7.4.2   Uncertainty About "F_0"

The wildcatter's uncertainty about F_0 (the initial production rate) is well described by a power law cumulative density distribution with a mean of 4210 Bbl/month. The cumulative is given by:

`In[1]:= Plot[0.021 F0^(2/5),{F0,0,15000}];`

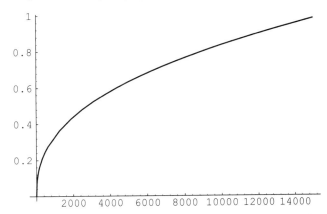

So, for F_0, the 0.05 quantile is located at 9 and the 0.95 quantile is located at 13800. Therefore, increase F_0 by 9590 and decrease it by 4201 during sensitivity analysis.

17.7.4.3   Uncertainty About "d"

The uncertainty about the initial decline rate is given by a beta distribution with parameters $\{3, 6\}$. However, for this part of Texas, d is between 0.08 and 0.20. Thus, for the cumulative distribution function, I have:

`In[1]:= Plot[CDF[BetaDistribution[3, 6],(z-0.08)/0.12],`
`         {z,0.08,0.2}];`

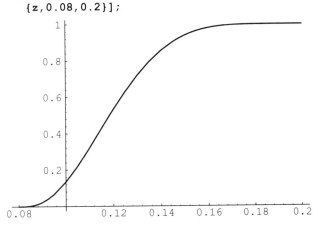

The mean is 0.12. The 0.05 quantile is located at d=0.0933 and the 0.95 quantile is located at d=0.152. For sensitivity analysis, increase d by 0.032 and decrease it by 0.0267.

17.7.4.4   Automation

The process of extracting the information needed for sensitivity analysis is easily automated using *Mathematica*. The steps in the process are:

• Obtain the linear transformation which rescales any standardized

```
Domain[DistributionName[parameters]]
```

• Give a List of pairs:

```
{variable_Symbol, DistributionName[parameters]}
```

• Return the List:

```
Quantile[DistributionName[parmeters],0.05],
    Mean[DistributionName[parameters]],
    Quantile[DistributionName[parameters],0.95]
```

17.7.5   Step 4: Sensitivity Analysis

Using the basic principle of laziness, let's determine which uncertainties make important contributions to the variation of discounted total oil production (DTOP). Compare the variation of DTOP as each of the uncertain parameters is varied over its domain as determined in the previous subsection. Any parameters which do not significantly contribute to the variation of DTOP will be set at their expected value and their probabilistic dependency ignored.

17.7.5.1   Variation About the Base Case

In a previous subsection, the discounted total oil production was computed. The wildcatter has said that the time value of money is 10% (1/10)/year or (1/120) per month. All variables which are time related will be expressed in per month or monthly units.

```
In[1]:= DiscTotalOil=
        (F0*HypergeometricU[1, 2 - b^(-1), r/(b*d)])/(b*d)/.
        r->1/120
```

```
Out[1]:=                                1      1
            F0 HypergeometricU[1, 2 - -,  -------]
                                      b   120 b d
        -------------------------------------------
                          b d
```

Because the Hypergeometric functions are notoriously sensitive to numerical evaluation, some standard transformations can be used to obtain a more useful form. This is beyond the scope of this chapter and the interested reader is referred to Jeffreys and Jeffreys or Erdelyi, et al. for a discussion of these functions. In the interim, take my word. If you are not familiar with these functions, and they arise during computations in *Mathematica*, I recommend that you check your computations by doubling the precision and verifying that the results are essentially unchanged.

First, apply Kummer's transformation.

```
In[2]:= DiscTotalOil=DiscTotalOil/.
          HypergeometricU[a_,b_,z_]->
              z^(1-b)HypergeometricU[1+a-b,2-b,z]
```

```
Out[2]:=
   1  -1 + 1/b   1  -1 + 1/b                            1  1      1
  (—)          (—)              F0 HypergeometricU[-, -, ————]
  120           b d                                     b  b   120 b d
  ———————————————————————————————————————————————————————————————————
                                  b d
```

Notice that this is a special case related to the **Gamma** and **Exp** functions. Thus,

```
In[3]:= DiscTotalOil=DiscTotalOil/.
          HypergeometricU[k_,k_,x_]->Exp[x] Gamma[1-k,x]
```

```
Out[3]:=     1  -1 + 1/b   1  -1 + 1/b   1/(120 b d)
        (((—)          (—)            E               F0
           120           b d
```
$$
        Gamma[1 - \frac{1}{b}, \frac{1}{120\ b\ d}]) / (b\ d)
$$

Now that **DiscTotalOil** is in a more usable form, calculate the base case using the following rule:

```
In[4]:= BaseCaseRule = {b->3/10,d->3/25,F0->4210};
        BestGuess = N[DiscTotalOil /. BaseCaseRule]
```

```
Out[4]:= 43544.3
```

Now to determine the relative impact on the discounted total oil production of changes from my base case, use methods analogous to the sensitivity analysis described in Dr. Hal Varian's chapter, i.e. use *Mathematica*'s total derivative function **Dt[]** to compute the various sensitivities to the uncertain variables.

First, compute the total derivative, create variables for the changes, substitute the base case parameters and apply **N[]**, or

```
In[5]:= Variation=Dt[DiscTotalOil]/.
          {Literal[Dt[b]]->Deltab,
           Literal[Dt[F0]]->DeltaF0,
           Literal[Dt[d]]->Deltad};
        BaseVariation=ExpandAll[N[Variation/.BaseCaseRule]]
```

```
Out[5]:= 580351. Deltab - 319024. Deltad + 10.3431 DeltaF0 +

                                  (1,0)
        53885.6 Deltab Gamma      [-2.33333, 0.231481]
```

Once again, there is a slight diversion, since *Mathematica* does not know about the derivative of the **Gamma** function with respect to the first parameter. The next section deals with this issue. It is not difficult, but it may be skipped if you like.

17.7.5.2   Evaluating the Derivative of the Gamma Function (skip on first reading)

As you have probably noticed, *Mathematica* does not know how to evaluate the derivative of the **Gamma** function with respect to its first parameter. This is another example of how familiarity with other disciplines is useful when using *Mathematica*. In particular, look at the integral definition of the **Gamma** function, namely

$$\Gamma(a, x) = \int_x^\infty e^{-t} t^{a-1} dt$$

Now use *Mathematica* to take the derivative with respect to a. Hence,

```
In[1]:= D[t^(a-1),a]
Out[1]:=  -1 + a
         t          Log[t]
```

So, the integral is identical except for the presence of the **Log[t]** term. Thus, evaluate

$$\frac{\partial \Gamma(a, x)}{\partial a} = \int_x^\infty e^{-t} t^{a-1} \ln t \, dt$$

Mathematica's graphics give the opportunity to examine the integrand and understand its behavior. The integrand is negative for $t < 1$ and positive for $t > 1$. Let's deal with each interval separately.

```
In[2]:= Plot[Exp[-t] t^(-7/3) Log[t],{t,0.231481,1}];
```

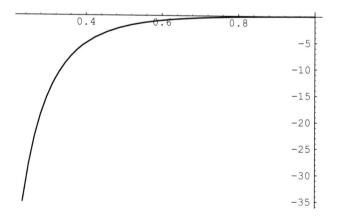

```
In[3]:= Plot[Exp[-t] t^(-7/3) Log[t],{t,1,5},PlotRange->All];
```

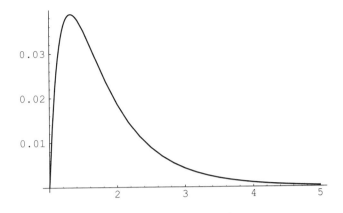

It seems that `Infinity` can be replaced by 5. Thus,

```
In[4]:= GammaDerivative=
            NIntegrate[Exp[-t] t^(-7/3) Log[t],{t,0.231481,1}]+
            NIntegrate[Exp[-t] t^(-7/3) Log[t],{t,1,5}]
```

```
Out[4]:= -3.04296
```

So, the derivative of the **Gamma** function in **BaseVariation** can be reliably replaced by -3.04296. Now return to our sensitivity analysis.

17.7.5.3   The BaseVariation, Finally

Now, using the result of the previous sub-subsection compute the total derivative for sensitivity analysis. Thus,

```
In[1]:= FinalVariation=BaseVariation/.
            Derivative[1, 0][Gamma][-2.333333333333333333,
            0.2314814814814814815]->GammaDerivative
```

```
Out[1]:= 416379. Deltab - 319024. Deltad + 10.3431 DeltaF0
```

Now this will only be useful if the discounted total oil production is approximately linear for the region in question. In order to quickly investigate this, produce an animation of **DiscTotalOil** as each quantity varies over its appropriate domain. The figure below is a **GraphicsArray** of four cells representative of an animation.

```
In[2]:= ga=Table[0,{2},{2}];
            Do[ plotarg=DiscTotalOil/.d->(8+2.5*(j+2*(i-1)))/100;
            ga[[i,j]] = Plot3D[ plotarg, {b,0.05,0.8},
                                {F0,100,14600},
                                PlotPoints->10,
                                PlotRange->{0, 350000},
                                DisplayFunction->Identity],
            {i,2},{j,2}];
            Show[GraphicsArray[ga],
                DisplayFunction->$DisplayFunction];
```

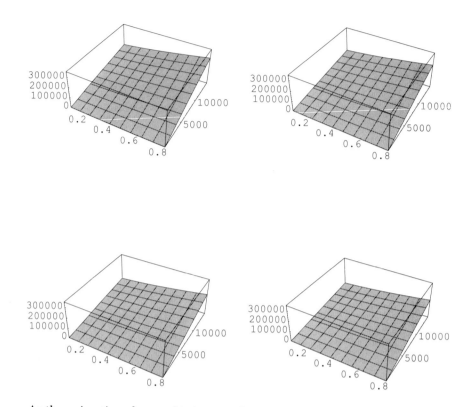

As the animation shows, this is a good approximation indeed.

Next measure the impact of each uncertain variable on the discounted total oil production.

17.7.5.4 Measuring the Impact of One Uncertain Variable at a Time

The single sensitivities are gotten by setting each appropriate chance variable to the changes obtained in Section 17.7.4, "Step 3: Assessing the Marginals". Thus, the following function will create a list of rules for all the single sensitivities.

```
In[1]:=
OneSensRules[DelVars__List,changes__List] :=
Block[{number=Length[DelVars],rules,tch=Transpose[changes]},
  rules=Partition[Map[Thread,Join[
      Thread[Table[DelVars,{number}]->DiagonalMatrix[First[tch]]],
      Thread[Table[DelVars,{number}]->DiagonalMatrix[Last[tch]]]]],
    number]//Transpose//Flatten[#,1]&]/;
    ((Length[DelVars]==Length[changes]) &&
    (2==Last[Dimensions[changes]]) &&
    Apply[And,Map[NumberQ,Flatten[changes]]] &&
    Apply[And,Map[MatchQ[Head[#],Symbol]&,Flatten[DelVars]]])
```

Using this function and the sensitivity domains gives the following rules:

```
In[2]:= SingleRules = OneSensRules[{Deltab,DeltaF0,Deltad},
          {{-0.2, 0.24},{-4201, 9590},{-0.0267, 0.032}}]
```

```
Out[2]:= {{Deltab -> -0.2, DeltaF0 -> 0, Deltad -> 0},
          {Deltab -> 0.24, DeltaF0 -> 0, Deltad -> 0},
          {Deltab -> 0, DeltaF0 -> -4201, Deltad -> 0},
          {Deltab -> 0, DeltaF0 -> 9590, Deltad -> 0},
          {Deltab -> 0, DeltaF0 -> 0, Deltad -> -0.0267},
          {Deltab -> 0, DeltaF0 -> 0, Deltad -> 0.032}}
```

The corresponding changes in discounted total oil production are computed by the following:

```
In[3]:= PairedChanges = Partition[
          Map[FinalVariation/.#&,SingleRules], 2]
Out[3]:= {{-83275.8, 99931.}, {-43451.2, 99189.9}, {8517.93,
          -10208.8}}
```

Next, let's visualize the results.

17.7.5.5 Visualizing the Sensitivity Analysis

The results of these calculations can be seen in the following plot.

```
In[1]:= names={"b","F0","d"}; BGC=BestGuess+PairedChanges;
        data=Map[{{#,BestGuess},
                  {{#,BGC[[#]][[1]]},{#,BGC[[#]][[2]]}},
                  {names[[#]]}}&,Range[Length[names]]];

In[2]:= Show[Graphics[{{GrayLevel[1],
            Point[{1.1*Length[data],BestGuess}]},
            {PointSize[0.015],
             {Point[#[[1]]], Line[#[[2]]],
              Text[Last[#],
              Scaled[{0.015, 0}, #[[1]]], {-1, 0}]}} & /@
             data },
            Axes->{False,True}, AxesOrigin->{0.9,0}]];
```

The initial decline "d" causes the smallest change while the initial flow rate "F0" is next and the type parameter "b" causes the largest change. The initial flow rate and type parameter dominates the variation. The range of discounted total oil produced, in response to changes in the type parameter, is about nine times larger than the range of values produced by changes in the initial decline rate. I can restrict my attention to the initial flow rate and type parameter and the initial decline rate "d" its expected value.

This process can be easily automated and can take into account joint sensitivities of k out of N variates by use of **ConstrainedMax** and **ConstrainedMin**. Since the response surface is approximately linear, the joint sensitivities will be additive and there is no need to compute them.

17.7.6 Needed for the Strategy Analysis: The Discounted Total Oil Production Uncertainty

In order to compute the uncertainty which is consistent with our model of discounted total oil production (DTOP), use the distribution of initial flow rate, F_0 and the distribution of type parameter, b. From these distributions, a change of variables could be performed to introduce the DTOP and then integrate to remove the unneeded variables.

Instead, compute the first four moments of the DTOP and use the package DecisionAnalytica`JohnsonDistributions` to approximate the DTOP distribution from its moments. The task is simplified since the initial decline rate can be fixed at its mean value as shown in the sensitivity analysis. The remaining uncertainties are independent and appear only as a product in the calculation of DTOP.

The discounted total oil production is given by

$$DTOP = F0 * g(b).$$

The density of the initial flow rate, F_0, is given by a power law distribution:

$$\{F_0\} = \frac{21\, F_o^{\frac{-3}{5}}}{2500}.$$

where the domain of F_0 is zero to 15000 Bbl/month.

Since the moments of a product of functions of independent chance variables is the product of the moments, calculate the moments of F_0 first. The first four moments of F_0 are:

```
In[1]:= 21 Map[Integrate[# F0^(-3/5),{F0,0,15000}]&,F0^{1,2,3,4}]/2500
Out[1]:=
          11/5    12/5   13/5        16/5   12/5   33/5
        {2       3      5     , 7 2       3      5      ,


            41/5   22/5  53/5
         7 2      3     5
        ---------------------- ,
              17


            51/5   27/5  73/5
         7 2      3     5
        ----------------------}
              11
```

```
In[2]:= F0Moments=N[%]
```

$$
Out[2]:= \{4213.85, \; 3.68712 \; 10^{7}, \; 3.90401 \; 10^{11}, \; 4.5251 \; 10^{15} \}
$$

The discounted total oil production is given by

$$DTOP = F0 * g(b)$$

where

$$
g(b) = \frac{25 \; \frac{1}{120}^{-1+\frac{1}{b}} \; \frac{25}{3}^{-1+\frac{1}{b}} \; \frac{1}{b}^{-1+\frac{1}{b}} \; e^{\frac{5}{72\,b}} \; \text{Gamma}(1-\frac{1}{b}, \frac{5}{72\,b})}{3\,b}
$$

and the initial decline rate d has been replaced by its expected value. Thus I need the first four moments of $g(b)$. Since the distribution of the well type, b, is a beta distribution,

```
In[3]:= g[b_]:=(25*(1/120)^(-1 + b^(-1))*(25/3)^(-1 + b^(-1))*
           (b^(-1))^(-1 + b^(-1))*E^(5/(72*b))*
           Gamma[1 - b^(-1), 5/(72*b)])/(3*b)

In[4]:= bExpectationOp[g_] :=
           NIntegrate[g PDF[BetaDistribution[3, 6],10 b/9],
                {b,0,9/10}];
        gMoments=10*Map[bExpectationOp, g[b]^{1,2,3,4}]/9

Out[4]:= {10.439, 110.947, 1201.38, 13261.1}
```

and the first four moments of DTOP are:

```
In[5]:= DTOPMoments=F0Moments*gMoments
```

$$
Out[5]:= \{43988.5, \; 4.09076 \; 10^{9}, \; 4.6902 \; 10^{14}, \; 6.00079 \; 10^{19} \}
$$

Thus, at $14 per barrel, the wildcatter can expect revenues of a little over $615,000 for this next well. Of course there are always those pesky drilling expenses. The overall shape of the distribution will determine the role that risk will play in the decision.

Now to complete my analysis of oil well economics, I can use the JohnsonDistributions.m package described in Appendix II to determine an approximation to the DTOP probability distribution.

```
In[6]:= <<DecisionAnalytica`JohnsonDistibutions`

In[7]:= DTOPDist=MomentsToJohnsonDistibution[Sequence@@DTOPMoments]

Out[7]:= JohnsonBoundedDistribution[0.8563, 0.571669, 0, 162500]
```

The domain of this distribution is

```
In[8]:= Domain[DTOPDist]

Out[8]:= {0, 162500}
```

The probability density of this distribution is shown in the following plot.

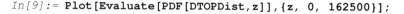

```
In[9]:= Plot[Evaluate[PDF[DTOPDist,z]],{z, 0, 162500}];
```

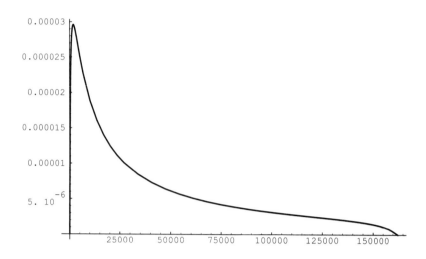

The most likely outcome, the mode, is at the peak of the distribution. As is plainly visible, this is why wildcatting is a risky business. The wildcatter will have very poor outcomes most of the time, however, the long tail extending to the right gives a giant payoff every once in a while.

With this distribution, let's complete the analysis for our wildcatter.

17.7.7   Step 5: Strategy Analysis and Dynamic Programming

17.7.7.1   Oh yes, there is a 50-50 chance of not hitting oil at all!

The analysis of the DTOP of a well was conditioned on striking oil. What the wildcatter knows (remember our back of the envelope analysis) is that there is a 42% chance of a "dry well". This will have to be taken into account as well.

17.7.7.2   Modelling the Seismic Testing Results

With our strong belief in the power of science, it is surprising to find out that seismic testing actually gives very little information about a potential well. Fundamentally, it says that either nothing is there (dry), a normal size dome (wet) or a very large dome (very wet) is under the site. The test is also not very accurate. It may say a dome is present when one is not, and vice-versa. I will ignore this second source of uncertainty and treat the test as accurate.

If a dome is not present, the wildcatter must pack up and move on to the next site. If a normal size dome is present, the high lower lobe of the distribution for DTOP which was obtained in the previous section is appropriate. Finally, if a very large dome is present, the long tail of the distribution of DTOP is appropriate. The prior probabilities of these three outcomes are 0.42 (dry) and

0.58 for the wet and very wet outcomes combined. Given that either the wet or very wet outcome occurs, the conditional probability distribution of DTOP will be the distribution that was computed previously.

Given that the wet and very wet outcomes split the DTOP distribution 50-50, the conditional distribution is:

(a) When the seismic test indicates a dry well, a value of zero has probability 1.0.

(b) When the seismic tests indicate a normal size dome, the DTOP outcomes have a domain from the 0.0-th quantile to the 0.5-th quantile.

(c) When the seismic test indicates a large dome, the DTOP outcomes have a domain from the 0.5-th quantile to the 1.0-th quantile.

This simplifying set of assumptions is followed for the remainder of the chapter.

In the case of a normal size distribution, the probability density of DTOP would be:

```
In[1]:= Domain[DTOPDist]
```

```
Out[1]:= {0, 162500}
```

```
In[2]:= Quantile[DTOPDist,0.5]
```

```
Out[2]:= 29695.2
```

```
In[3]:= Plot[Evaluate[PDF[DTOPDist,z]/0.5],
         {z, 0, 29695.2}];
```

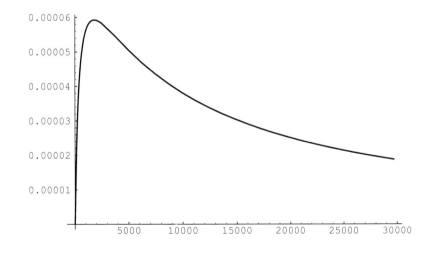

Similarly, for the large dome distribution, the distribution is:

```
In[4]:= Plot[Evaluate[PDF[DTOPDist,z]/0.5],
         {z, 29695.2, 162500}];
```

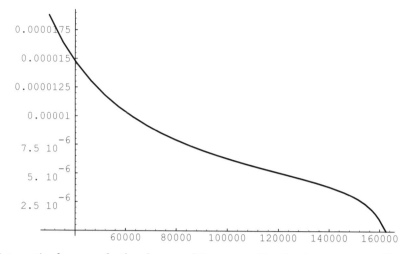

Interestingly enough, the shapes of these two distributions are actually quite similar. So this is a reasonable approximation. The wildcatter's uncertainty in the two cases is very nearly the same except for a shift in the expected value.

17.7.7.3   Reviewing the Wildcatter's Influence Diagram

Previously, we developed the influence diagram for the wildcatter. It was:

```
In[1]:= ShowID[wid];
```

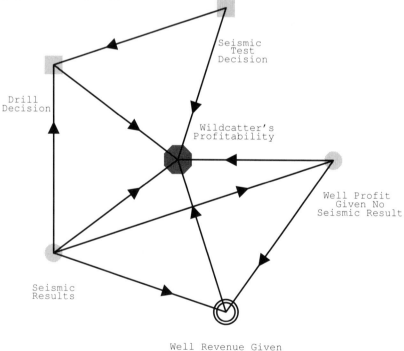

This diagram represents a two-period dynamic programming problem. The periods of time in question are (1) the time between decisions, and (2) the time between drilling and the measurement of the value of the well. In period one, the wildcatter makes the Seismic Test Decision which either costs nothing if he/she doesn't test or costs the equivalent of 5,000 barrels of oil. If the wildcatter chooses to test, the seismic test results are revealed. In period two, the wildcatter makes the drill or not to drill decision. He/she may have the seismic test results to guide their action. The cost of drilling an oil well is the equivalent of 20,000 barrels of oil.

Before analyzing the decisions further, a few more simple tools will be useful.

17.7.7.4   A Few 'Utility' Functions (Pun Intended)

To take into account risk aversion on the part of the wildcatter, he/she needs a personal utility function representing the risk aversive behavior. For simplicity, choose the exponential utility function. Similarly, the certain equivalent function is easily defined.

```
In[1]:= Utility[v_, RiskTolerance_?NumberQ] :=
                E(1-Exp[-v/RiskTolerance])/(E-1)//N;
        Utility[v_, Infinity] = v;
        CertainEquivalent[u_, Infinity] = u;
        CertainEquivalent[u_, RiskTolerance_?NumberQ] :=
                -RiskTolerance*Log[1-u(1-1/E)]//N;
```

The risk tolerance will have to be expressed in equivalent barrels of oil.

The evaluation of strategy requires taking expectations. The following *Mathematica* functions extend the capabilities of the packages used so far.

```
In[2]:= DistributionQ[f_] :=
        StringMatchQ[ToString[Head[f]], "*Distribution"];


        Expectation[expr_, f_?DistributionQ, var_Symbol] :=
         Module[{domain = Domain[f]},
          PrependTo[domain, var];
          NIntegrate[ Evaluate[expr PDF[f, var]], Evaluate[domain]]]
```

To verify that these functions are all working properly, I can compute the expected value of the DTOP distribution as:

```
In[3]:= Mean[ DTOPDist ] ==
        CertainEquivalent[
            Expectation[ Utility[z, Infinity], DTOPDist, z],
            Infinity]

Out[3]:= True
```

17.7.7.5   Step 6: The Value of Information

From the previous "back of the envelope" analysis, the wildcatter knows that there is a 0.42 probability that the next well will be "dry" and a 0.58 probability of a "wet" well. This is a Bernoulli distribution. In *Mathematica* I can use the package `Statistics`DicreteDistributions` to represent these possiblities.

```
In[1]:= <<Statistics`DiscreteDistributions`

In[2]:= ?BernoulliDistribution
BernoulliDistribution[p] represents the Bernoulli distribution
    with mean p.

In[3]:= DrillingOutcomes = {dry = 0, wet = 1};
        DrillingDistribution = BernoulliDistribution[0.58];
```

Now, ignoring seismic testing, the following *Mathematica* functions compute the certain equivalent of drilling or not drilling a well.

```
In[4]:= NumberOrInfinityQ[a_] :=
            NumberQ[a] || MatchQ[a, Infinity];

        (* The cost of drilling a well and
           the cost of seismic testing *)
        DrillingCost = 20000;
        SeismicTestCost = 5000;

        (* The utility of the venture
           if the well is dry *)
        WildUtility[dry, RiskTolerance_] :=
          Utility[-DrillingCost, RiskTolerance];

        (* The utility of the venture
           if the well is wet, ignoring
           normal or large dome *)
        WildUtility[wet, RiskTolerance_] := Module[{z},
          Expectation[
                Utility[z - DrillingCost, RiskTolerance],
                DTOPDist, z]//N ];

        (* The certain equivalent in Bbl
           of oil if we don't drill *)
        WildcattersCE[DontDrill, RiskTolerance_] := 0;

        (* The expected equivalent
           in Bbl of oil if we drill *)
        WildcattersCE[
          Drill, RiskTolerance_?NumberOrInfinityQ] :=
          CertainEquivalent[
            PDF[DrillingDistribution, wet] *
            WildUtility[wet, RiskTolerance] +
            PDF[DrillingDistribution, dry] *
            WildUtility[dry, RiskTolerance],
          RiskTolerance]//N
```

Using a risk tolerance of a million barrels of oil, the value of the drill alternative is:

```
In[5]:= WildcattersCE[Drill, 10^6]

Out[5]:= 4779.93
```

This value of almost 5,000 Bbl of oil is greater than the value of the "don't drill" alternative. Thus, the wildcatter would, on this basis, drill.

A basic principle of decision analysis states: *Information has no value if it does not change a decision.* If the wildcatter could buy information about whether or not the well would be "dry", he/she could change the decision to drill.

Think of seismic testing as a clairvoyant willing to sell this information so the wildcatter can avoid paying the drilling costs when a well will be "dry". There is a cost to this information, of course, the cost of the seismic testing. If the cost of testing is sufficiently low, the value with testing will be greater than the value without testing.

Adding this to our previous calculations will reflect all of the structure captured in the wildcatter's influence diagram. Because of the simplicity of our scenarios, I avoid the dynamic programming aspects and simply exhaustively describe all possible actions and consequences. The possibilities are:

(1) I choose not to do seismic testing, then I choose the drill alternative from the drill/don't drill decision and the wildcatter's certain equivalent is 4,780 Bbls of oil. This value is obtained from the analysis performed above.

(2) I choose to do seismic testing and

(2-a) the seismic test says *"dry"*, then the wildcatter's utility is `Utility[-SeismicTestCost, 10^6]`. The wildcatter chooses not to drill.

(2-b) the seismic test says *"wet and normal dome"*, then the wildcatter's utility is `WilcatterUtility[ wet, normalsize, 10^6]`

(2-c) the seismic test says *"wet and large dome"*, then the wildcatter's utility is: `WilcatterUtility[ wet, largesize, 10^6]`

These functions are defined as follows. Note that in each case, the drill decision is made using an **If** statement.

```
In[6]:= The utility of the venture if the well is wet,
            and normal dome *)
        WildUtility[wet, normalsize, RiskTolerance_] :=
        Module[{z, DrillDist, DontDrillDist,
            DrillEU, DontDrillEU, DrillEV, DontDrillEV,
            DrillCE, DontDrillCE},
          (* Case 1: get certain equiv for drill decision,
                 ignore sunk cost *)
          DrillDist = DTOPDist;
          DrillDist[[4]] = Quantile[DTOPDist, 0.5];
          (* Note must renormalize first half of distribution,
             i.e.  divide by 0.5 to get actual probability
             distribution *)
          DrillEU = Expectation[ Utility[z - DrillingCost,
                  RiskTolerance], DrillDist, z]/ 0.5;
          DrillEV = Expectation[ z, DrillDist, z]/
                  0.5 - DrillingCost;
          DrillCE = CertainEquivalent[DrillEU, RiskTolerance]//N;

          (* Case 2: get certain equiv for don't drill decision,
```

```
                       ignore sunk cost *)
       DontDrillEV = 0;
       DontDrillCE = 0; (* do nothing, incur no cost *)

       If[ DontDrillCE >= DrillCE,
           Print["If normal size, don't drill."];
           Utility[DontDrillEV - SeismicTestCost,
                   RiskTolerance],
       (* else *)
           Print["If normal size, drill."];
           Utility[DrillEV - SeismicTestCost,
                   RiskTolerance] ]
       ]

   The utility of the venture if the well is wet,
      and a large dome *)
   WildUtility[wet, largesize, RiskTolerance_] :=
   Module[{z, DrillDist, DontDrillDist,
           DrillEU, DontDrillEU, DrillEV, DontDrillEV,
           DrillCE, DontDrillCE},
   (* Case 1: get certain equiv for drill decision,
               ignore sunk cost *)
   DrillDist = DTOPDist;
   DrillDist[[3]] = Quantile[DTOPDist, 0.5];
   (* Note must renormalize first half of distribution,
      i.e.  divide by 0.5 to get actual probability
      distribution *)
   DrillEU = Expectation[ Utility[z - DrillingCost,
               RiskTolerance], DrillDist, z]/ 0.5;
   DrillEV = Expectation[ z, DrillDist, z]/
               0.5 - DrillingCost;
   DrillCE = CertainEquivalent[DrillEU, RiskTolerance]//N;

   (* Case 2: get certain equiv for don't drill decision,
               ignore sunk cost *)
   DontDrillEV = 0;
   DontDrillCE = 0; (* do nothing, incur no cost *)

   If[ DontDrillCE >= DrillCE,
       Print["If large size, don't drill."];
       Utility[DontDrillEV - SeismicTestCost,
               RiskTolerance],
   (* else *)
       Print["If large size, drill."];
       Utility[DrillEV - SeismicTestCost,
               RiskTolerance] ]
   ]
```

The dome distribution is also a Bernoulli distribution with parameter 0.5. Thus,

```
In[7]:= DomeDist = BernoulliDistribution[0.5];
        DomeOutcomes = {normal = 0, large = 1};
```

Finally, the certain equivalent of performing seismic testing is:

```
In[8]:= CertainEquivalent[
          PDF[DrillingDistribution, dry] * Utility[-
             SeismicTestCost, 10^6] +
          PDF[DrillingDistribution, wet] * (
            PDF[DomeDist, normal]* WildUtility[wet, normalsize,
               10^6] +
            PDF[DomeDist, large]* WildUtility[wet, largesize,
               10^6] ), 10^6]
```

```
If normal size, don't drill.
```

```
If large size, drill.
```

Out[8]:= 30269.5

Thus, delaying the drill decision and paying for seismic testing increases the certain equivalent by about a factor of six. Clearly, a bargain. The surprising information gained is "knowing the well output will be below the median value implies that the wildcatter should not drill a well." The wildcatter's opportunity to avoid these additional losing scenarios creates a tremendous increase in the certain equivalent. By leaving **SeismicTestCost** a symbolic variable, and setting the above equation equal to 4,780 Bbls of oil (the value without information), *Mathematica*'s **Solve** function can be used to determine the upper bound on the value of information.

17.8   What Hath Mathematica Wrought?

I could go on with this example, making the drilling cost uncertain, making the control over the "dry well" outcome imperfect, etc. But, it should be clear that *Mathematica* provides us with a rich set of tools to deal with real world problems.

As with any set of tools, tools help only so far as you provide an accurate description of the decision situation. *Mathematica* enhances our ability to deal with complexity and lets us build more realistic models. This added richness can provide more insight. But, the models are put together by people. We as analysts must take great care to think clearly about the problems we face. Tools such as influence diagrams help this process.

In the end, Albert Einstein's dictum is most appropriate.

"Man tries to make for himself in the fashion that suits him best a simplified picture of the world; he then tries to some extent to substitute this cosmos of his for the world of experience, and thus to overcome it [control the cosmos]. *This is what the painter, the poet, the speculative philosopher, and the natural scientist do, each in his own fashion."*

[And so does the decision analyst. So what is the payoff for this effort?]

"Supreme purity, clarity, and certainty at the cost of completeness."

[And how does one go about creating this simplified picture of the world?]

> ". . . we are seeking for the simplest possible system of thought which will bind together the observed facts. By the 'simplest' system we do not mean the one which the student will have the least trouble in assimilating, but the one which contains the fewest possible mutually independent [assumptions]."

17.9   Acknowledgment

I wish to thank Dr. Steven Kaye of the Chevron Oil Field Research Company, La Habra, CA 90631 for his kind contributions to my understanding of the economics of oil extraction.

17.10   Appendix I: `DecisionAnalytica`InfluenceDiagram``

17.10.1   `AddConditioningTo`

`AddConditioningTo[id, e]` is a function to add conditioning information to the influence diagram object `id`. `e` is the conditioning information. NB: A `ValueNode` object may be conditioned by any other node object, but a `ValueNode` object may not condition any other node object. Also, the node being conditioned must already be present in the influence diagram object `id` or a warning message will be generated.

The conditioning information, `e`, is given in one of the following forms:

(1) `ValueComputedFrom[v, n]`. `v` is a `ValueNode` object and `n` is a node or list of nodes.

(2) `ChanceConditionedBy[c, n]`. `c` is a `ChanceNode` object and `n` is a node or list of nodes.

(3) `DecisionInformedBy[d, n]`. `d` is a `DecisionNode` object and `n` is a node or list of nodes.

(4) `ConsistencyRequiredBy[c, n]`. `c` is a `ConsistencyNode` object and `n` is a node or list of nodes of any other type.

17.10.2   `Chance`

`Chance[label]` is a function which creates a `ChanceNode` object where *label* is a string used when displaying an Influence Diagram containing this node. (In future versions of this package a `ChanceNode` object will contain other quatities such as the probabililty distribution describing the decision maker's uncertainty.)

17.10.3   `ChanceConditionedBy`

`ChanceConditionedBy` is a head used to indicate the conditioning information for a `ChanceNode` object.

17.10.4 `Consistency`

`Consistency[label]` is a function which creates a `ConsistencyNode` object where label is a string used when displaying an Influence Diagram containing this node. (In future versions of this package a `ConsistencyNode` object will contain other quantities such as a input-output constraint for the quantities entering and leaving the node.)

17.10.5 `ConsistencyRequiredBy`

`ConsistencyRequiredBy` is a head used to indicate the conditioning information for a `ConsitencyNode` object.

17.10.6 `Decision`

`Decision[label]` is a function which creates a `DecisionNode` object where label is a string used when displaying an Influence Diagram containing this node. (In future versions of this package a `DecisionNode` object will contain other quantities such as the range of alternatives, whether optimization means to minimize or maximize, etc.)

17.10.7 `DecisionInformedBy`

`DecisionInformedBy` is a head used to indicate the conditioning information for a `DecisionNode` object.

17.10.8 `KnowledgeMap`

`KnowledgeMap` is a header for an Influence Diagram object. An Influence Diagram object is of the form **`KnowledgeMap[g,n]`** where g is a Graph object corresponding to the Influence Diagram, and n is a list of the nodes in the Influence Diagram.

17.10.9 `ShakeID`

`ShakeID[id]` models the graph of id as a system of springs. A minimum energy configuration is found and a **`KnowledgeMap`** object with the transformed graph is returned. This function is useful for "cleaning up" an influence diagram which has many arrow crossings. This function will not planarize the graph object.

17.10.10 `ShowID`

`ShowID[id]` is a function which displays a graphical representation of id. id must be a **`KnowledgeMap`** object.

17.10.11 **TrivialInfluenceDiagram**

TrivialInfluenceDiagram[n] creates a **KnowledgeMap** object containing just one node n where n is a ValueNode object.

17.10.12 **TrivialRelevanceDiagram**

TrivialRelevanceDiagram[n] creates a **KnowledgeMap** object containing just one node n where n is a ChanceNode object.

17.10.13 **TrivialKnowledgeMap**

TrivialKnowledgeMap[n] creates a **KnowledgeMap** object containing just one node n where n is a ChanceNode object, a DecisionNode object, a ConsistencyNode object, or a ValueNode object.

17.10.14 **Value**

Value[label] is a function which creates a ValueNode object where label is a string used when displaying an Influence Diagram containing this node. There may be only one ValueNode object in an Influence Diagram and it may condition no other object. (In the future a ValueNode object will contain other quantities such as a function to compute the value of a state of nature given the quantities entering the node.)

17.10.15 **ValueComputedFrom**

ValueComputedFrom is a head used to indicate the conditioning information for a ValueNode object.

17.11 Appendix II:
DecisionAnalytica`JohnsonDistributions`

This package give you acces to a very useful system of distributions developed by Norman L. Johnson. You can compute their densities, means, variances and other related properties. The distributions themselves are represented in the symbolic form *name[param1, param2, ...]*. Functions such as **Mean**, which give properties of statistical distributions, take the symbolic representation of the distribution as an argument.

These distributions are extremely useful because there is a unique distribution which corresponds to any skewness and kurtosis pair which can be computed from any probability distribution. Thus, all probability distributions with the same first four moments become an equivalence class and the Johnson distribution can be thought of as the representative of that equivalence class.

The bounded Johnson distributions are given in *Mathematica* as **Johnson-BoundedDistribution[gamma, delta, xi, lambda]**. As an example of the flexibility of these distributions, a few densities are plotted below.

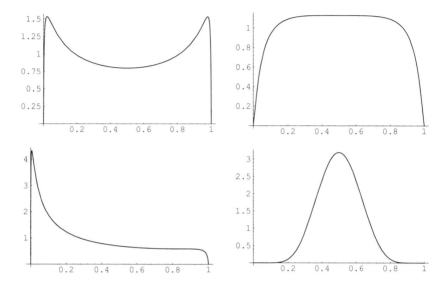

The semi-bounded Johnson distributions are given in *Mathematica* as **JohnsonLogNormalDistribution[gamma, delta, xi]**. They are simple translations of the **LogNormalDistribution** given in Statistics `Normal-Distribution`.

The unbounded Johnson distributions are given in *Mathematica* as **JohnsonUnboundedDistribution[gamma, delta, xi, lambda]**. These distributions are always unimodal.

The functions associated with each distribution are listed in the table below.

```
PDF[dist, x]                    probability density function at x
CDF[dist, x]                    cumulative distribution function at x
Quantile[dist, q]               q-th quantile
Domain[dist]                    range of values of the variable
Mean[dist]                      mean
Variance[dist]                  variance
StandardDeviation[dist]         standard deviation
Skewness[dist]                  coefficient of skewness
Kurtosis[dist]                  coeffcient of kurtosis
Random[dist]                    pseudorandom number with
                                specified distribution
```

17.12 References

Bayes, T., "An Essay Towards Solving a Problem in the Doctrine of Chances". 1989. *Phil. Trans.* **3**: 370–418. Reproduced in *Bayesian Statistics: Principles, Models, and Applications* by S. James Press, New York, John Wiley & Sons.

de Finetti, Bruno, 1962 "Does it Make Sense to Speak of 'Good Probability Appraisers?' " in *The Scientist Speculates An Anthology of Partly-Baked Ideas*, I. J. Good, Ed., pp. 357–364 London, England, Heinemann.

Erdelyi, A. et al., 1953, *Higher Transcendental Functions*, New York, McGraw-Hill Book Company.

Fetkovich,M. J., 1980, *Decline Curve Analysis Using Type Curves*, SPE Paper 9086, Society of Petroleum Engineers Book Department.

Howard, Ronald A., 1988, "The Evolution of Decision Analysis", in Howard, R. A. and Matheson, J. E., *Readings on the Principles and Applications of Decision Analysis*, Vol. I, Strategic Decisions Group, Menlo Park, Ca.

Janis, I. L. and Mann, L., 1977, *Decision Making*, New York, Macmillan Publishing Co., Inc.

Jeffreys, H. and Jeffreys, B. S., 1950. *Methods of Mathematical Physics*, England, Cambridge University Press.

Johnson, N. L. and Kotz, S., 1970. *Distributions in Statistics: Continuous Univariate Distributions 1*, New York, John Wiley & Sons.

Kahneman, D., Slovic, P., and Tversky, A., eds., 1982. *Judgement under Uncertainty: Heuristics and Biases*. England, Cambridge University Press.

Korsan, Robert J., "The Probability Wheel is Guaranteed to Work!" in *The Proceedings of 1990 IEEE International Conference on Systems, Man, and Cybernetics*, pp. 158–160. IEEE, Los Angeles, CA.

Lindley, D. V., 1972. *Bayesian Statistics, A Review*. CBMS 2, SIAM, Philadelphia.

Oliver, Robert M. and Smith, James Q., 1990. *Influence Diagrams, Belief Nets and Decision Analysis*, Chichester, England, John Wiley & Sons.

Raiffa, Howard, 1970. *Decision Analysis*, Reading, Massachusetts, Addison-Wesley Publishing Company.

Howson, Colin and Urbach, Peter, 1989. *Scientific Reasoning, The Bayesian Approach*, LaSalle, Illinois, Open Court Publishing Company.

Savage, L. J., "The Elicitation of Personal Probabilities and Expectations", *Journal of the American Statistical Association*, December 1971, Vol. 66, No. 336.

Shafer, Glen and Judea Pearl, 1990. *Readings in Uncertain Reasoning*, San Mateo, California, Morgan Kaufmann Publishers, Inc.

Skiena, Steven, 1990. *Implementing Discrete Mathematics*, Reading, Massachusetts, Addison-Wesley Publishing Company.

Smith, James Q., 1988. *Decision Analysis A Bayesian Approach*, London, England, Chapman and Hall, Ltd.,

Stigler, Steven M., 1986. *The History of Statistics*, Cambridge, Massachusetts, The Belknap Press of Harvard University Press.

Verma, T. S. and Judea Pearl, 1987. "The Logic of Representing Dependencies by Directed Graphs". *Proceedings of the Sixth National Conference on AI*, AAAI, Seattle.

Webster's New Collegiate Dictionary, 1960. Massachusetts, G.&C. Merriam Company.

Wolfram, Stephen, 1991. *Mathematica*, Reading, Massachusetts, Addison-Wesley Publishing Company.

Economic and Financial Modeling with Mathematica®

Registration Card

Since this field is fast-moving, we expect updates and changes to occur that might necessitate sending you the most current pertinent information by paper, electronic media, or both, regarding *Economic and Financial Modeling with Mathematica.* Therefore, in order to not miss out on receiving your important update information, please fill out this card and return it to us promptly. Thank you.

Name: _____

Title: _____

Company: _____

Address: _____

City: _____ State: _____ Zip: _____

Country: _____ Phone: (_____) _____

Area of Interest/Technical Expertise: _____

Comments on this Publication: _____

_____

_____

Purchased from: _____ Date: _____

☐ Please add me to your mailing list to receive updated information on *Economic and Financial Modeling with Mathematica* and other TELOS publications.

☐ I have a _____ computer system.
Describe: _____

TELOS

THE ELECTRONIC LIBRARY OF SCIENCE

Return your postage-paid registration card today!

PLEASE TAPE HERE

FOLD HERE

‖‖‖‖

NO POSTAGE
NECESSARY
IF MAILED
IN THE
UNITED STATES

BUSINESS REPLY MAIL

FIRST CLASS MAIL PERMIT NO. 1314 SANTA CLARA, CA

POSTAGE WILL BE PAID BY ADDRESSEE

THE
ELECTRONIC
LIBRARY
OF
SCIENCE

3600 PRUNERIDGE AVE STE 200
SANTA CLARA CA 95051-9835

‖‖‖‖‖‖‖‖‖‖‖‖‖‖‖‖‖‖‖‖‖‖‖‖‖‖